THE BIRDWATCH
an
DIARY

Designed and published by
Hilary Cromack

Edited by
David Cromack

BUCKINGHAM PRESS

in association with

Published in 2004 by:
Buckingham Press
55 Thorpe Park Road, Peterborough
Cambridgeshire PE3 6LJ
United Kingdom

01733 561739
e-mail: admin@buckinghampress.com

ISBN 0 9533840 8X
ISSN 0144-364 X

Cover image: Firecrests by Stephen Message.
Stephen is a freelance artist painting a wide variety of wildlife subjects including birds. He works mainly in watercolour and gouache. He has many originals, prints and limited editions for sale on his website (www.message-wildlife-art.co.uk) and accepts commissions.
Address: The Hall, Village Green, Benenden, Nr Cranbrook, Kent TN17 4DD; e-mail: smessage@willow.fsworld.co.uk

Printed and bound in Great Britain by:
Biddles Ltd Book Manufacturers, King's Lynn, Norfolk

CONTENTS

CONTENTS

PREFACE

WELCOME to the 2005 edition of *The Birdwatcher's Yearbook & Diary*. During the course of its 25-year history the publication has evolved to meet the needs of active birdwatchers, professional ornithologists and all those engaged in the wider commercial world, serving the needs of birders.

This year is no different. Feedback from some regular purchasers suggested that the presentation of the entire BOU-approved British List in log chart form made record-keeping too time-consuming, as so many of the 567 species are not regularly seen in the UK. Responding to this, I have selected 375 species - residents, annual migrants, regular passage birds and a sprinkling of the commoner vagrants - to form the basic Log Chart in this edition.

However, because *The Yearbook* is the only publication to carry the full British List, updated each year by the British Ornithologists' Union, we will continue to do so, but in a more concise format. Do let me know how you like this change and feel free to offer suggestions on other ways we might improve the usefulness of this part of *The Yearbook*.

The provision of tide-table information has always been a key feature since the first edition. The information enables birdwatchers all around the country to plan birding trips to coastal sites when tides are high and birds will be driven closer to shore. This year we have extended coverage to a 15-month period as we appreciate that many bird clubs and RSPB local groups use the tables to plan their field trip calendar far in advance.

One of the greatest strengths of *The Yearbook* is that it provides a wealth of information in a portable form, this means readers can take a copy with them on field trips to the many reserves featured each year. As always, we have tried to add new sites to this section and it is our belief that no other source can provide so much up-to-date information on UK bird and nature reserves. Editions of 'Where to watch...' guides are updated periodically, but the process can often be long-winded and information is sometimes out of date by publication time.

Regular purchasers will notice that this year a number of sites do not have the full details listed. Generally, this is because the management body for the reserve in question has indicated that information previously published in *The*

Yearbook is still current or subject to only minimal changes. People buying *The Yearbook* for the first time may be interested to know that a small stock of back issues are still available by contacting Buckingham Press (details on page 4).

We are pleased that many reserves have responded to our request for information about coach parking - knowledge that will be a boon for group field trip organisers.

Another innovation in this edition is the inclusion of club meeting nights in the County Directory section. It is our fervent hope that this small change, along with the publishing of club website addresses, will help groups recruit new members. In my role as Editor of *Bird Watching* magazine, I have pledged to do all I can to promote birding organisations and I'm pleased that *The Yearbook* can contribute to this goal too.

At this point I'd like to pay tribute to Swarovski Optik, the sponsors of *The Birdwatcher's Yearbook & Diary since 2002*. Not only does this company produce optical products of the highest quality, but it actively seeks out ways in which it can foster a vibrant birdwatching community. The company has recognised the important role provided by *The Yearbook* in this regard and their financial support enables us to use colour printing to enhance the presentation of the Nature Reserves & Observatories section of the book. We are grateful for the personal support of managing director John Brinkley and his commitment to sponsor the book in the future.

Finally, a big thank you to the army of correspondents who provide the updated information each year and help promote the publication to bird clubs and at bird reserves and retail outlets. Buckingham Press is committed to keeping the price of *The Yearbook* as low as possible and this will be the third year in a row we've been able to peg the full sale price to £15. We believe it offers amazing value for money. If you agree, we would appreciate you recommending to your family and friends - more sales means future price rises can be held at bay.

David Cromack
EDITOR

Key contributors in this Edition

DAWN BALMER works in the Demography Unit at the BTO and is the organiser for BirdTrack which follows on from Migration Watch and is also responsible for the day-to-day running of the Constant Effort Sites ringing scheme. Dawn is a keen birder with a special interest in gull identification. Other interests include photography and more recently, digi-scoping.

RICHARD FACEY is a keen birder and photographer and is a regular contributor to Buckingham Press' quarterly magazine *Birds Illustrated*. He has a degree in zoology, with his main interests being bird behaviour and evolution. Richard currently works as a Community Project Officer with RSPB Cymru.

GORDON HAMLETT, a freelance writer, is a regular contributor to *Bird Watching* magazine, both as a reviewer of books, DVDs and computer software and also as sub-editor of the UK Bird Sightings section. Gordon is the author of the forthcoming *Best Birdwatching Sites in the Highlands of Scotland* book (Buckingham Press) and in his spare time is a dedicated internet browser.

STEPHEN MESSAGE has been a freelance artist since graduating from Bournemeouth & Poole College of Art and Design. In addition to producing paintings for exhibition, his illustration work appears in many ornithological books, including *The Birds of Greece*, Bill Oddie's *Birds of Britain & Ireland* and *A Fieldguide to the Birds of SE Asia*. Currently he is working as the sole illustrator on *Waders of Europe, North America and Asia* for Helm.

STEVE HOLLOWAY has worked for the BTO for the last 13 years, principally on wetland and coastal issues, and currently coordinates the volunteer counter network for the Wetland Bird Survey. He is a keen birder and all round naturalist, has travelled widely throughout the world and has participated in several expeditions.

OUR SPECIAL THANKS go to Chris Hamlett, Cherry Hadley, Derek Toomer and Keith Offord for their help with putting this edition of the *Yearbook* together. We would also like to thank all of our contacts in the various bird groups and clubs, bird reserves and national organisations as it would be impossible to produce this book without their continued support and assistance.

FEATURES

Meadow Pipit by Keith Offord

SCIENTIFIC DISCOVERIES IN 2004

(A REVIEW OF THE YEAR'S LITERATURE)

Keeping abreast of the world's ornithological publications is an almost impossible task. To ensure you don't miss anything interesting, we are pleased to present this digest of reports compiled by Richard Facey with illustrations by Simon Patient.

The crime of the Ancient Mariner

ALBATROSSES, those well known drifters of the seas, were once held in high esteem by the ancient seafarers and it was considered bad luck to kill one of these magnificent birds. Sadly modern day trawlermen do not give much credence to such superstitions. Every year, sailors in the business of longline fishing capture approximately 300,000 seabirds, among them albatross.

Longline fishing involves paying out up to 80 miles of fishing line with as many as 10,000 squid-baited hooks, behind a large vessel. Target fish species are southern blue-finned tuna and Patagonian tooth fish; two species than turn a lucrative profit in the US and Japan.

Because the bated lines do not always sink fast enough to go undetected by birds such as albatrosses, the birds trying to get an easy meal are snared on the hooks, dragged under and die a slow watery death. The result is an annual bycatch of 100,000 albatross, a loss that has a huge impact on overall populations.

Albatross breed slowly. They do not reach sexual maturity for 15 years and it takes an arduous year or more rearing junior to independence. Losing a parent to the long-liners means the future is bleak for a dependent youngster and he is likely to starve to death before he has chance to get airborne.

As a result of longline fishing 19 out of 21 species of albatross are in serious decline and threatened with extinction. To combat this threat a number of nations, with waters important to albatross species have taken a stance. On 1 February 1, 2004 the Agreement on the Conservation of Albatrosses and Petrels (ACAP) came into force. Six countries signed up to this legally binding accord, including the UK, which was initially reluctant to ratify.

The Amsterdam Albatross could easily become extinct as a result of long-line fishing abuses.

The agreement requires vessels operating long lines in the waters of the six ACAP nations (South Africa, Australia, New Zealand, Ecuador, Spain and the UK) to take steps to reduce seabird bycatch.

These steps include:

- Installing a tube at the back of the ship to ensure the baited lines are unravelled below the waterline, immediately out of the reach of hungry birds.
- Using thawed rather that frozen bait, so the hooks sink faster.
- Dying the bait blue.
- Setting up bird scarers to frighten birds away from lines.
- Setting the lines at night when albatross are not foraging.

Together, these steps will reduce bycatch to a mere few hundred birds a year. It is felt that most fisherman see a hooked seabird as a fish lost, and are happy to adopt one or some of these measures to reduce the impact of their industry on these beautiful birds. ACAP gives a legal imperative to adopt these measures and will help in the battle against pirate fisherman, often registered in Panama, Belize and Uruguay, who poach the lucrative fish with no regard for the future of the birds they hook.

Birds such as the Amsterdam Albatross, a species with an average of 20 breeding pairs, will continue to grace our oceans only if more nations sign up to the ACAP.

New species discovered

DISCOVERING a species new to an area you regularly visit is an uplifting experience for most birdwatchers, but imagine the excitement in finding a species previously unknown to science. In the last year this has happened to a number of individuals around the world.

Researchers surveying the River Caroni, in the Orinoco Basin in Venezuela came across an entirely new species on one of the rivers islets, Carrizal. The area has been well covered by previous surveys, so it was a big surprise to find three members of the new species, which has been dubbed the Carrizal Seedeater (*Amaurospiza carrizalensis)* in honour of its island home.

The small finch, in which the males are dark grey with blue flecks and the female a yellow-brown, remained undiscovered since it inhabits Guadua bamboo, a habitat visually and physically impenetrable to even the most hardened ornithologist. Regretably, no sooner had the species been found than its only known island habitat was cleared to make way for a hydroelectric project by the Venezuelan electricity company EDELCA. The company has now offered logistical support for an expedition to seek out the new species in nearby areas of Guadua bamboo.

Surveys in the high Andes of south-west Colombia were also exciting as they revealed another unknown species; this time a wren. The bird was discovered during surveys on Cerro Munchique, one of the mountains in the Andean range.

Attention was first drawn to the new wood-wren when calls from birds resembling the Grey-breasted Wood-wren (*Henicorhina leucophyrs*) were heard. But closer views showed that the songster was a different species, which has been named the Munchique Wood-wren (*Henicorhina negreti).*

The new species is only found higher than 2,250m above sea level on Munchique's western slopes. The bird's dependence on high altitude, wet stunted cloud forest habitat means the species is potentially facing extinction. The demons of global warming and illegal logging threaten the fragile home of Colombia's newest wood-wren.

Being new to the scientific scene is not the only accolade the Munchique Wood-wren holds; it is also the first bird to be described electronically in the online journal *Ornitologia Colombiana* (www.ornitologiacolombiana.org).

Of course, a species does not have to be new to science to get ornithologists popping champagne corks; rediscovering a long lost species can be equally as exciting. Researchers from BirdLife International were one year into a survey of the Fijian island of Viti Levu when they heard a song unlike any other of the island' birds. When it was seen the culprit turned out to be the Long-legged Warbler (*Trichocichla rufa)*, a species that was presumed extinct since there had been no confirmed reports of the bird since 1894.

In a two kilometre stretch of stream a total of nine pairs, two with newly-fledged young, were seen at altitudes above 800m. Government and community officials are restricting logging in the Long-legged Warbler's thicket home and have set a side an area for conservation.

Plucky Peregrines on the up

THE FLEXIBILITY of the Peregrine to adopt novel structures as breeding sites was an interesting development revealed by the British Trust for Ornithology's (BTO) fifth national survey of the raptor.

The results were published in 2004. The survey is usually conducted every ten years, with the last one in 1991. However, with the country gripped by foot and mouth in 2001, Peregrine lovers among the BTO volunteers had to wait for the 2002 season to get out and survey.

They discovered Peregrines nesting on castles, bridges, pylons, cathedrals and power stations, along with tree-nesting pairs – a rare occurrence in the UK. One pair with a lust for danger nested in a chemical works, 4m from a conveyor belt carrying more than 1,000 tonnes of limestone a day!

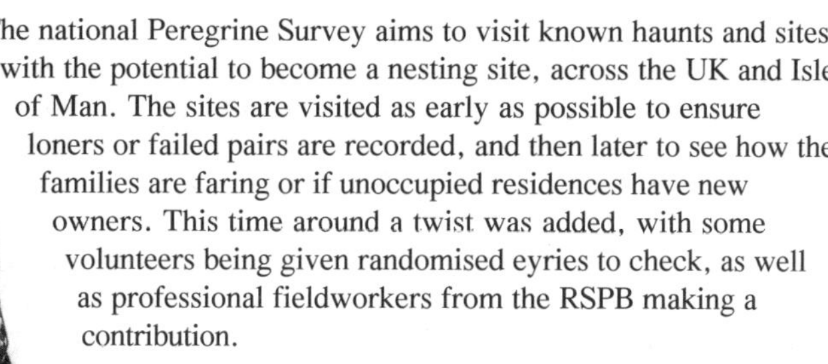

The national Peregrine Survey aims to visit known haunts and sites with the potential to become a nesting site, across the UK and Isle of Man. The sites are visited as early as possible to ensure loners or failed pairs are recorded, and then later to see how the families are faring or if unoccupied residences have new owners. This time around a twist was added, with some volunteers being given randomised eyries to check, as well as professional fieldworkers from the RSPB making a contribution.

Across the UK and Isle of Man the Peregrine appears to be on the up. The number of occupied territories was up by 13% (from 1,316 in 1991 to 1,492 in 2002). The number of breeding pairs also increased to 1,402 - 10% more than 1991 and 61% more than the 1930s when the population crashed.

Peregrines have proved highly adaptable when choosing new nest sites.

A spoonful of medicine helps the vultures decline

THE 2004 EDITION of *The Yearbook* reported on the alarming and rapid decline of India's three Gyps vulture species. In the early 1990s the populations of Slender-billed (*G. tenuirostris*), Indian (*G. indicus)*, and White-rumped Vultures (*G. bengalensis)* had been subjected to a 95% decline in just three years.

In former strongholds dead and dying birds all seemed to show the same symptoms; a drooping head and dangly neck. Autopsies revealed white crystals covering the internal organs and determined that the birds had died from visceral gout caused by renal failure. If the cause of the decline was a disease or infection the one certainty was that the victim would never recover.

The situation deteriorated as symptoms of the 'disease' began to be witnessed in Pakistan by 2000. However in 2003 at a meeting of raptor biologists, it was suggested that an anti-inflammatory drug, Diclofenac, may be the cause of the problem.

Though the search for a mystery disease continued, work got underway to find if Diclofenac was behind the decline. In January 2004 a team of researchers published in the journal *Nature* results of a three year study that firmly points the finger of blame at the drug. Of 265 birds examined, 85% had died of visceral gout and residue testing revealed traces of the drug in these birds.

Diclofenac, an anti-inflammatory drug, was originally used in human medicine, but entered the veterinary world in the early 1990s; the same time the declines of Gyps vultures started. The vultures become contaminated scavenging from carcases of livestock treated with Diclofenac, which is lethal to the birds at 10% of the recommended dose for mammals.

Even though the cause has been accurately identified, the extinction of the three species of vulture remains a real, if not imminent, possibility within the sub-continent. A ban in the use of Diclofenac is needed, but this will take a long time to implement and with vulture populations at an all-time low it could come too late.

Extinction of the Gyps vulture in the subcontinent could have huge cultural and health impacts. With vultures absent from many areas, feral dog populations have boomed, and with them the rabies virus. Until recently some religious groups such as the Parsees used Gyps vultures to dispose of their dead – with so few vultures about, this is no longer feasible.

Elsewhere in Asia the situation looks brighter. In Cambodia 120 Slender-billed and White-rumped Vultures were recorded in Siem Pang District. This is the single largest gathering of Gyps in Indochina in the last 15 years. Diclofenac is rarely used in Cambodia, where the greatest threat to vultures is persecution and food shortages, so Cambodia could prove an important conservation stronghold for these species.

State of the worlds birds

ONE IN EIGHT of the world's birds are threatened with global extinction. That translates as 1,211 species, of which 179 are labelled as critically endangered.

These grim statistics are contained in BirdLife International's sobering 70-page report, *State of the World's Birds 2004*. It brings together for the first time what is known about the current distribution, status and conservation priorities of the globe's birds, as well as what our avifauna tells us about the state of the environment and biodiversity in general. It is not the most cheerful of reads.

Though extinction is a normal course for any species, human actions have managed to push rates from between 1,000 and 10,000 times higher than the natural rate – and these could be under-estimates.

In the last 500 years the world has lost around 150 species of bird; in the last quarter of the 20th Century 75 species became a zoological footnote. Two species have become extinct since 2000. Spix's Macaw (*Cyanopsitta spixii)* became the incarnation of Monty Python's Norwegian Blue when the last wild individual died in 2000 – truly the species is now 'an ex parrot'. In June 2002 the two remaining Hawaiian Crows (*Melamprosops phaeosoma)* vanished.

Habitat destruction is one of the biggest bird killers – some Brazilian species have disappeared from 99% of their former range. And our knack for introducing alien species has impacted on 67% of globally threatened species inhabiting islands.

On a more cheerful note, the report demonstrates how the BirdLife Partnership is taking direct steps to implement action for 42% of the world's globally threatened species. For example, Birdlife representatives spoke to local people on the island of Vantau about their over-harvesting of the eggs of the Vanuatu Megapode. As a result local chiefs imposed a suspension of egg collecting during certain times of year, and a five year total ban in the south east of the island.

If you want to get your hands on the *State of the World's Birds 2004* you can download it from BirdLife International's website (www.birdlife.org) or buy it from The Natural History Bookshop (www.nhbs.co.uk).

Waders in retreat

DURING the spring and summer wet meadows in the UK can be packed with breeding waders, but a report published this year shows that all is not well for certain species.

Though still found on nearly half the sites, making it Britain's most far-flung wader, the Lapwing (*Vanellus vanellus)* has showed declines across the board; England has lost 35% of its Lapwings, while across the border in Wales the story is even worse with the Celtic nation losing 69% since 1982.

The same sorry tale of decline holds true for the second most widespread wader - the Redshank (*Tringa tetanus)*. Away from its eastern and south-eastern English strongholds, the Redshank showed declines. In Wales only 19 breeding pairs were found - and they were only in Gwent.

The Curlew *(Numenius arquata),* normally associated with upland habitats, declined by 33% across its lowland range in England and Wales. However the most alarming and rapid decline was seen in the Snipe (*Gallinago gallinago)*. In 1982 the Snipe was Britain's third most numerous wader species, but after a 61% decline the species is now outnumbered by Avocet and Oystercatcher. So steep has been the decline that 90% of the population was found on only three of the sites surveyed.

Though spread widely across the UK, Lapwing populations are in steep decline.

For one species, the hyperactive squeaky toy known as the Oystercatcher (*Haematopus ostralegus)*, things are going superbly. With a total of 973 pairs being found in 2002, their population has increased by 52% since 1982, though the species remains rare in Wales.

The 2002 Breeding Waders of Wet Meadows survey, organised by BTO, English Nature, RSPB and MAFF, covered all of the sites covered in 1982, as well as some new ones. More than 1,000 sites, averaging 150 hectares/ 1.5km^2, were visited by volunteer counters three times from mid-April to mid-June, and were concentrated in areas where the habitat is widespread such as the Somerset Levels.

Twenty-five years of the big one

IN ITS 25-year history, the RSPB's Big Garden Birdwatch had developed into the world's biggest mass participation single day bird count. When it started in 1979, Big Garden Birdwatch attracted a mere 30,000 participants, but 2004 saw a record-obliterating 409,000 people recording 8.6 million birds in 247,000 gardens.

Though each volunteer spends only one hour counting birds in his or her garden, the huge amount of data generated across the nation, has the capacity to show trends that may have conservation value.

For instance, take the case of House Sparrow *(Passer passer).* Though it retains its status as Britain's number one garden species, numbers have halved in the last 25 years. The situation is worse for the Starling *(Sturnus vulgaris)*, which claimed the number two spot. In 1979 the average garden contained 15 Starlings, but in 2004 this had dropped to less than five - a decline of 71%.

Old favourites - the Blackbird *(Turdus merula),* and Robin *(Erithacus rubecula)*, have both suffered declines of 31.8% since the start of Big Garden Birdwatch, even though the Blackbird was seen in 94% of participating gardens. The Song Thrush *(Turdus philomelos),* which held the number seven spot in 1979, miserably failed to make the top ten, ranking a disappointing 19th in 2004 after a decline of nearly 34%.

On the plus side, there are some species booming in gardens. First recorded breeding in the UK in 1955, the Collared Dove *(Streptopelia decaocto)* has increased by a staggering 525%, but has been outdone by its larger cousin, the Woodpigeon *(Columba palumbus),* which has increased by 594%. At the other end of the size scale, the Coal Tit *(Parus ater)* has increased by almost 300% and the Wren *(Troglodytes troglodytes)* rose by 170% since the start of Big Garden Birdwatch 25 years ago.

Increased levels of garden feeding have boosted Coal Tit appearances.

It wasn't just the familiar garden birds that were recorded, as more than 100 species made it into the 2004 survey, including 2,134 Ring-necked Parakeets in gardens of the south east of England. Some people recorded Snow Bunting, Ringed Plover, Lesser Spotted Woodpecker and Redshank. One garden on Anglesey was blessed with a Chough, while a flock of 45 Waxwings dropped into a garden in Nottingham. In Devon Yellow-browed and Pallas's Warblers were seen. Perhaps its time to move?

AN UPDATED GUIDE TO WEBSITES OF INTEREST TO BIRDWATCHERS

The Internet is a dynamic environment with a multitude of new sites catering for the needs of birdwatchers appearing each year. Sometimes the scale of the search can seem too daunting, so take advantage of the research conducted annually for *The Yearbook* by Gordon Hamlett.

MY ANNUAL SURVEY of websites of interest to birdwatchers was introduced in the 2002 edition of *The Yearbook* and was planned to operate on a three-yearly cycle. The first year concentrated on general ornithology and what can loosely be termed 'miscellaneous'. The second year dealt with British websites, local clubs and the like and the third year covered foreign birding.

This edition sees us back at the start of the cycle and it is interesting to see how things have developed. The obvious difference is that sites set up by individuals have taken a severe battering. After an initial bout of enthusiasm, people have either given up or left university etc. A lot of my bookmarked sites from those days are now either totally dead or have not been updated for a long time.

What has replaced them on many educational sites are large searchable databases that are ideal tools for researchers, but not necessarily great for the casual browser. These sites excel in providing bird record and movement data with an increasing number of records leading to a better appreciation of what is going on. I'm sure many web browsers enjoy looking at the moving maps plotting migration data against time and satellite tracking of key species on sites such as Migration Watch (see feature elsewhere in this edition).

The larger organisations are still finding it difficult to strike a happy medium between the needs and interests of the casual browser and the research scientist. Look at the sites of the Royal Society for the Protection of Birds or Scottish Natural Heritage and you might agree with me that they need dividing into two sites. For ordinary birdwatchers the ideal will be a sort of lite-version which details the reserves, the birds found there, what's on and a bit of news, leaving the other site to present main research papers and so on.

One final change that is noteworthy is the demise of the newsgroup. Four years ago, these were the main discussion groups on the net, but the presence of a few sad individuals whose sole aim was to upset and annoy people with their misguided rantings turned people away in droves.

The need to communicate with fellow enthusiasts is still there, but is now being serviced by local e-mail discussion groups and the international Bird Forum site on the net. All messages being posted to Bird Forum are monitored for content before being broadcast and subscribers know that they will not have to suffer a torrent of abuse.

ANNUAL WEBSITE SURVEY

HOW TO USE THIS GUIDE

To help you navigate through this survey, I have divided the entries into the following categories (listed alphabetically):

- Bird art and artists
- Bird books
- Bird species and families
- Birds on stamps
- Bird photography and digiscoping
- Discussion groups
- Escaped raptors
- Folklore
- Garden birds
- Links to birding sites
- Magazines
- Miscellaneous
- Online services
- Optics
- Organisations
- Ornithology
- Ringing
- Taxonomy, rarities and lists
- Trip reports
- Weather

BIRD ART AND ARTISTS

http://www.birdingart.com/index.htm
Six artists exhibit here, the best known of whom is probably Jan Wilczur. Clicking on a thumbnail brings up a large format version together with details of how much it costs etc. There is a good selection of links to other bird art pages.

http://www.ian-lewington.co.uk/index.htm
The illustration work of Ian Lewington is very distinctive and desired by a great many birdwatchers. This site features a large selection of Ian's work in both colour and black and white to view online or to buy.

http://www.jamesmccallum.co.uk/index.htm
James McCallum is a Norfolk artist, specialising in the local wildlife. His two most recent books concentrate on winter geese and Norfolk in summer. There are many sample plates to enjoy. Website design is excellent and a perfect example of how less is often an awful lot more.

http://myweb.tiscali.co.uk/akroyd/
Another of my favourite artists, Carry Akroyd produces work in a variety of media from aquatints and linocuts to oils. She has just embarked on a set of prints, which feature some of the birds and animals beloved by poet John Clare and are coupled with appropriate quotations. It's just a pity that the pages take so long to load.

BIRD BOOKS

http://www.acblack.com
The biggest publisher of bird books in Britain, A&C Black's web pages are something of a curate's egg. You never quite feel that they are up to date, but you do get to read extracts from some of their titles (sample plates would be good) and there are often special offers available. You can't help but feel that they are underselling themselves though.

http://www.abebooks.co.uk/
If you are looking for a specific secondhand, or out-of-print title, then this is by far the best place on the web. One giant database has stock details from some 12,000 secondhand bookshops around the world. The results of your search are sorted according to price and you can even search for first editions or signed copies.

http://www.birdjournals.com/
Looking for that obscure bird report? Or that one missing copy of a bird magazine that the dog chewed and which stops you from having a complete set? Then look no further. Bird Journals seems to have copies of most reports and journals for sale. A very simple site, it does exactly what it sets out to do.

http://www.hbw.com/
The world is divided into two groups – those who already own the magnificent *Handbook of the Birds of the World* and those who lust after it. The site gives detail of the status of forthcoming volumes, together with sample plates, text, species accounts and photos.

http://www.wildsounds.co.uk/
This is my favourite among the sites specialising in bird books, not just for its thoughtful design and ease of use, but also because it has a useful section on what is coming out in the near future. Excellent for other bird and wildlife-related media such as CDs, DVDs etc.

BIRD SPECIES AND FAMILIES

http://www.birdcare.com/birdon/birdcare/items/sonb.html
The entire text of the late Chris Meads' *State of the Nations' Birds* can be found here. Every breeding bird is discussed with its fortunes over the past century – good or bad - monitored. Future prospects are also considered. Despite all the doom and gloom you hear about, there is more good news than bad.

ANNUAL WEBSITE SURVEY

http://www.blackgrouse.info/
Whether you are a birder, a landowner or, mention it quietly, a shooter, this site tells you everything you want to know about that fast-declining species, the Black Grouse. There are details of current research projects as well as a biodiversity action plan. Don't expect any 'where-to watch' sites though.

http://www.blackredstarts.org.uk/index.html
This is an unusual site because it is aimed more towards town planners and developers than active birdwatchers, but it does detail the history of Black Redstarts in Britain, and their ecology. There is plenty of discussion as to how to work with the birds, rather than against them, overcoming the conflict between development and conservation.

http://www.bsc-eoc.org/avibase/avibase.jsp
A truly amazing site. Listing every species in the world in one giant database. Type in the name you want – in any major language – and you get a summary of the species, map showing the countries it is recorded, searches in Google for text and images and, if appropriate, BirdLife International. The number one site for researchers.

http://cyberbirding.uib.no/gull/index.php
There are no bigger fanatics than gull lovers and the Norwegian Gull pages should suit them well with plenty of illustrations covering all the species likely to be seen in the UK. There is discussion (in English) of unusual birds and plumages and a comprehensive set of links to other gull sites.

http://digilander.libero.it/avifauna/w_palearctic/cover.html
This site has distribution maps for every species in the Western Palearctic. There are also checklists. There is plenty of useful information here, but only if you persevere. The problem is finding it. Site navigation is an absolute nightmare. Even clicking on the home page logo doesn't always take you back to where you think that you ought to be.

http://www.goldeneagle.ie/
Investigate another relocation project – this time taking Scottish Golden Eagles to Donegal in Ireland. As well as latest details of the project, there is a page devoted to the status of all birds of prey in Ireland. A monthly diary, albeit a couple of months out date, discusses all the recent sightings.

http://www.hummingbirds.net
Here you will find anything you want to know about hummingbirds so long as they are the species that turn up in North America. Pictures, biology, research, migration maps, feeding tips abound, but the design of the site is somewhat messy. You may or may not like the trail of hummingbirds that follow the route of your mouse pointer.

http://montereybay.com/creagrus/index.html
Though the design is fairly basic, there is an excellent overview of the various bird families together with a good personal selection of information, hints and tips about birding round the world. The author hails from Monterey in California so anyone interested in pelagic trips from the town will also find extra sections to interest them.

http://www.oceanwanderers.com
Though this is primarily a site devoted to pelagic birding, there is plenty of other interesting material here too, with sections on waders/shorebirds and whale watching. One page takes an in-depth look at the different races of Canada Geese, important now that the Americans have decided to split them.

http://www.ospreys.org.uk/AWOP/Home.htm
Here's the full story of the Osprey reintroduction programme at Rutland Water, now updated to include one of the Rutland birds which bred in Wales in 2004. There are full maps of the satellite tracking of migrating birds (1999-2001) and a good series of links to other satellite tracking sites.

http://owlpages.com/
Birds of ill omen or something far more lovable? Mankind has always had a huge fascination with owls and this site will tell you everything you ever wanted to know, ranging from biology through mythology to owl antiques.

http://www.roydennis.org/honeybuzzard.htm
Honey Buzzard is one of our most secretive birds of prey, but this site gives a potted biology of the species as well as a few facts and figures. What is of most interest though is satellite tracking of ringed birds so that you can follow their migration routes.

http://www.savingcranes.org
The pages of the International Crane Foundation have details on every species of crane in the world, together with news on various research projects. There are assorted scientific papers and dissertations to download. The overall feel is scholarly rather than a general appeal to the casual browser.

BIRDS ON STAMPS

http://www.bird-stamps.org/index.htm
An excellent site illustrating every known bird stamp, searchable by either species or country, so there is no problem if you want to look at eg Willow Warbler on stamps (four examples). There is discussion of tricky identification problems (of which there are plenty).

http://www.birdtheme.org/
Not as user-friendly as the site above, the unique selling point of this one is that is has details of all the various bird stamps currently being auctioned on eBay, sorted by the items with least remaining bidding time. So, if you are looking for a bargain, try this site.

BIRD PHOTOGRAPHY AND DIGISCOPING

http://www.digiscoped.com/
With the ever-increasing numbers of birders trying out digiscoping, this is a good first place to start with plenty of practical advice including such commonly asked questions as 'Which of the thousands of settings on my camera do I actually use?' There are plenty of links to other sites including the appropriate discussion pages on Bird Forum.

http://www.fatbirder.com/links/images_and_sound/photos.html
This is another subsection of Fatbirder, giving links to dozen of bird photography sites. Bo Beolen's regular features in *Birds Illustrated* magazine give you a taster of some of the outstanding work available to view via this site.

http://www.hbw.com/ibc/
This offshoot of the *Handbook of Birds of the World* features more than 1,000 species for you to view. Quality is variable, though images can usually be downloaded in both high and low-resolution quality. Can be quite time-consuming if you don't have broadband.

http://www.laurencepoh.com/
Laurence Poh pioneered the technique of digiscoping. His site contains a few articles on the basics as well as galleries of Malaysian and Australian birds.

http://www.md.ucl.ac.be/peca/test/a.html
Digiscoping and digital birding is the theme of this site with the less-than-catchy address. There are plenty of technical articles though not as many pictures as I might have expected. A section gives details of all the digiscoping discussion groups.

http://members.lycos.co.uk/nigelblake/
Nigel combines his time making models for Hollywood blockbusters and taking bird photographs, a pretty stunning combination. Diary entries are sporadic due to film commitments, but there are plenty of inspiring images here.

http://www.nature-photography.co.uk.
An excellent site from photographer Mike Lane, whose work is published widely and who has written a UK site guide for fellow bird snappers. As well as hundreds of fantastic shots, there are several trip reports, written from a bird photographer's point of view.

http://www.oiseaux.ca/anglais.html
A good selection of North American birds, albeit on a slightly fussy and slow-loading site.

http://www.surfbirds.co.uk/
This is the best place to find photos of recent rarities with pictures appearing online, often within hours of the bird being found. The rest of the site is a birding magazine with trip reports, news, artwork, discussion group etc. Site organisation is somewhat chaotic.

DISCUSSION GROUPS

http://www.birdforum.net/
More than 14,000 members can't be wrong. This is currently the best general discussion site on the net by a considerable distance. Monitoring means that there are no abusive posts. Very well designed, totally free to use and with the added bonuses of massive picture galleries, site guides and species database, this is one site that you must see.

http://www.fatbirder.com/links/signpost_and_discussion/mailing_lists.html
There are huge numbers of discussion groups around the world, covering everything from birds in a specific area to individual species or groups of birds. This page lists many of them and allows an easy way to sign up to the ones you feel may relevant to your interests.

http://dir.groups.yahoo.com/dir/Recreation___Sports/Outdoors/Birding
Similar to the Fatbirder site, this lists all the groups currently run by Yahoo! There were 476 birding groups listed at the time of writing and if nothing there takes your fancy, you can always start one of your own.

ESCAPED RAPTORS

http://www.ibr.org.uk/index.htm
Just when you think that you have seen a rare bird of prey, you see the jesses dangling down from its legs. You would be amazed at the number of escaped owls, hawks and falcons there are. The Independent Bird Register lists missing birds and tries to reunite found birds with their owner. Report any sightings here.

FOLKLORE

http://www.geocities.com/Paris/LeftBank/9314/stevewren.html#Wren
The Wren is known as the King of the Birds in folk tales. Though it is considered bad luck to kill one, nevertheless, the bird was traditionally hunted on December 26 in Celtic countries. This site examines the various myths, songs and folklore associated with Wren hunting.

http://www.nzbirds.com/Maorimyths.html
This site looks at a dozen or so tales from Maori mythology. The rest of the site is devoted to birds and birding in New Zealand. There is also a page listing national birds from around the world – the UK's national bird is a Robin in case you wondered.

http://www.royal.gov.uk/output/Page384.asp
Love them or loathe them, the fascination with the Royal Family continues unabated. This official website is massive and contains all sorts of trivia. This page is devoted to Swan Upping, which is the origin of the pub name the Swan with Two Necks, being a corruption of 'two nicks'.

GARDEN BIRDS

http://www.biggonline.co.uk/
This site follows the fluctuating fortunes of the page-owners' Blue Tits. Cameras have been installed inside and outside a nest box for the past three years and there are plenty of pictures, all archived, letting you see how the chicks develop from hatching to fledging.

http://www.birdcare.com/birdon/encyclopedia
A huge amount of information on everything to do with garden birds – nest boxes, food, predators, squirrels and salmonella are just a few of the topics covered. Presentation is fairly basic and a few photographs wouldn't have gone amiss.

http://www.garden-birds.co.uk/
This is a fantastic site covering everything that you might want to know about garden birding. Based on a Sheffield garden, it just goes to show what an enthusiastic individual can produce. Practical hints, photos, charts, sounds, quizzes etc. Anyone interested in garden birds should look here.

LINKS TO BIRDING SITES

http://www.fatbirder.com/
http://www.camacdonald.com/birding/birding.htm
http://birdingonthe.net/
http://www.bsc-eoc.org/links/links.jsp
http://www.eurobirding.com/links/links.php

All these pages consist of huge numbers of links to other birding websites around the world. Different sites have their strengths and weaknesses and I recommend that you bookmark all of them. Because of the fickle nature of the Internet, it is inevitable that you will come across a few broken links as pages close down. The better the site, and the more regularly it is maintained, the fewer the broken links.

Of the sites mentioned here, Fatbirder is perhaps the best known, and is now expanding to include articles on all the world's bird families. My other favourite site is 'Where do you want go Birding Today' (second on the list) which is an excellent starting point for birding abroad.

MAGAZINES

http://www.birdingworld.freeserve.co.uk/
A fairly simple site for monthly journal *Birding World* includes a few sample articles and an index of all their other articles. There is also an online bookshop and a few photographs.

http://www.birdsofbritain.co.uk/index.htm
There are some interesting articles, details on some reserves and features on 100 or so species. The overall impression is one of a project initially set up with great passion but which has recently run out of steam.

http://www.britishbirds.co.uk/index.htm
British Birds has a much changed and improved site. Contents of all recent issues are listed with a couple of abstracts included. There is a full index from 1945-2003 and you can order a sample copy for free to see if you like the UK's longest-established journal.

MISCELLANEOUS

http://www.bavarianbirds.de/indexe.html
I dread to think how many hours have been wasted on the quizzes here when the boss isn't looking. Different pictures every time, it starts off very easy, but soon brings in tricky camera angles or unusual plumages (gull chicks anyone?). The rest of the site is devoted to Bavarian birds and there is a useful bird name translator.

http://bible.christiansunite.com/Torreys_Topical_Textbook/ttt056.shtml
This is a concordance of all the birds mentioned in the Bible. As well as all the references, you can also get translations from seven different bibles, mostly American but including the King James version.

http://www.freewebs.com/richbonser/birdingtwitching.htm
Why do people go twitching? This is one student's university dissertation exploring various aspects of the hobby, including the wonderfully named 'A place for twitching in cultural geography'. And you thought you were just going to see a rare bird. The rest of the site has various trip reports.

http://www.kami.demon.co.uk/gesithas/birdlore/fugsrc.html
Just to show that even the most obscure research can be fascinating, this site looks at birds in Anglo-Saxon England, the evidence for them and the

origin of their names. Delightfully illustrated with contemporary images.

http://www.kami.demon.co.uk/gesithas/birdlore/listsrc.html
In combination with the site above, this details, and gives references for old names for birds. We are not looking at folk names here, but citations from Beowulf or Chaucer.

http://www.ladbrokes.com/bigbirdrace/
Ladbrokes and birds? The connection centres on sponsored radio-tagged albatrosses with customers betting on which birds would do best. That side of things was a bit of fun, but there is plenty of information here about the birds' plight. At the time of writing, most of the birds had disappeared, presumed victims of illegal fishing activities.

http://www.pbs.org/lifeofbirds/index.html
There is plenty of information here about David Attenborough's television series *The Life of Birds*. Interestingly, this isn't from the BBC's site, but the American Public Broadcasting Service.

http://www.usd.edu/~tgannon/bird.html
This site has an extensive collection of bird poetry. Despite the garish colour scheme there is some interesting stuff, ranging from folk ballads (the twa corbies) through a parody of Poe's *Raven* to a detailed annotated version of Shelley's *Skylark*.

ONLINE SERVICES

http://www.birdcallonline.com
This is a sort of hybrid site, a mixture of the free bird news offered by BirdGuides and the discussion forums offered by Bird Forum, though without anywhere near the same numbers of users. One advantage is that sightings are arranged by county rather than just listed as records are received. Onsite navigation has been much improved recently.

http://www.birdguides.com
You can get the latest bird news for free here, but only in headline form. If you want full details plus access to a whole host of other features, messages sent to your mobile phone etc, then there are a number of packages to which you can subscribe.

http://www.rarebirdalert.co.uk
One of the best-looking sites of this type. Subscribers can filter the sightings to get just the information they need. As with all these companies, take the free guided tour and trial subscription first to see what suits you best.

http://www.swarovskibirding.com
As well as the latest rare bird news, there are articles, an online encyclopaedia based on the *Collins Bird Guide*, computerised birding lists, space for your photos and much more besides. Prices range from £19 to £89 per annum depending on the level of service you want. A 90-day free trial is available.

OPTICS

http://www.betterviewdesired.com/
Historically, this American site has the reputation for having the most objective optical product reviews on the net. You will be surprised by some of the conclusions here.

http://www.optics4birding.com
Though it is an American site, and some of the brand names may be unfamiliar to European viewers, this is a good site to get the basic specifications on binocular and telescope models that may interest you. There are some online user comments, but these seemed well out of date. However, there are plenty of links to other review sites.

http://www.bushnell.com/
http://www.kowascope.com/
http://www.leica.com/
http://www.nikon.co.uk/
http://www.opticron.co.uk/
http://www.swarovskioptik.at/
http://www.zeiss.com/

The sites above are the home pages of the main optical manufacturers selling into the UK. Here you can get full specifications, latest details of new models, and, in many case, a full glossary of terms you might come across when reading about telescopes and binoculars. Don't expect the text to be entirely objective though.

Some of the sites (e.g. Swarovski) are excellent, and others (e.g. Zeiss) less than intuitive. Nikon cunningly fools you by listing all binoculars and scopes under the heading 'sport.'

ORGANISATIONS

http://www.birdingpal.org/
This is an excellent idea. If you are travelling abroad, the site aims to put you in touch with a local birder who will either pass on local knowledge, or even offer to show you round. The flip side is that some day, someone might get in touch with you asking for the same sort of advice.

http://www.bto.org/index.htm
The British Trust for Ornithology has an excellent site. Members of the public are invited to join in the Migration Watch and you can see the results plotted on animated maps, a service which will surely improve as more data is obtained. Other surveys include a Garden Watch and there is plenty of information about the organisation as well.

ANNUAL WEBSITE SURVEY

http://www.disabledbirdersassociation.org.uk
The Disabled Birders' Association seeks to improve access for people with disabilities to reserves, facilities and services for birding. Online details include access information for assorted reserves and hotels. The club organises a foreign birding trip each year and there are reports from previous trips.

http://www.gbc-online.org.uk/
The Gay Birders' Club aims to bring gay and lesbian birdwatchers together. More than 300 members enjoy a full calendar of outdoor field trips and events – about 100 a year – and there is a quarterly newsletter. Full details of how to join are online.

http://www.proact-campaigns.net/
Proact is concerned with organising environmental campaigns, primarily concerned with saving birds and their habitats. Current campaigns are in countries as widespread as Norway, Ukraine, Korea, Malta, Italy and Germany. Most of the action is usually geared to getting you to sign online petitions or send e-mails to assorted interested parties. Proact aims to be non-political independent and voluntary.

http://www.rspb.org.uk/
The RSPB's website has undergone a massive redesign since it last featured in this book and has managed to drag itself up from truly awful to so-so. The overall tone is earnest when you are crying out for more passion. Little things still annoy. There is no entry for Loch Garten under reserves – it is now called Abernethy Forest. How can anyone afford to ditch such a fantastic brand name? It was the one bird reserve known by everyone in the country.

http://www.the-soc.fsnet.co.uk/
The best description that can be applied to the Scottish Ornithological Club site is 'bland'. It looks exactly the same as it did three years ago and items that were being developed then, such as some of the 'where to watch' sites, are still awaiting completion.

http://www.uk400clubonline.co.uk/
The pages for the UK 400 Club – a club devoted to listing and the pursuit of rare birds is a perfect example of how not to do things. There is nothing on the site to say what membership benefits you get for your hard-earned cash, sample pages to entice you in or anything even remotely welcoming. Very disappointing.

ORNITHOLOGY

http://www.birrding.freeserve.co.uk/
This is not a collection of birdsongs on the web, but rather a reference as to where to find recordings from commercial sources. The author claims to have tracked down recordings of nearly 75% of the world's birds and these are all fully indexed here, together with a useful collection of links. NB: note the spelling of 'birrding' is correct when typing this address.

http://www.jncc.gov.uk/species/Birds/default.htm
The Joint Nature Conservation Committee acts as the government's nature advisor. It also plays a major part in nature conservation and there are many pages here devoted to anything and everything affecting bird life in Britain, including individual species and protected sites.

http://www.ornithology.com/
There is a little bit of everything on this site – science, checklists, lecture notes, garden birding, tips on how to get a career in birding, etc. All of this has a noticeable American bias, but there is still plenty of interest. Site layout, if not exactly confusing, is somewhat daunting and it is not always obvious how to get to where you want to be.

http://www.pacifier.com/~mpatters/details/details.html
When you are confronted with something unusual in the field, you need to take a detailed set of field notes. These pages suggest a series of steps that will produce good records. There are also basic diagrams showing you how to make a field sketch.

http://www.rbbp.org.uk/index.html
The aim of the Rare Birds Breeding Panel is to act as a secure depository of sensitive information on the breeding of rare birds in Britain. There is a species list showing which records the panel is interested in, and you can submit any records you have. For obvious reasons, no data appears online though there are annual summaries in *British Birds* magazine.

http://www.saltspring.com/capewest/pron.htm
Do you struggle with all those scientific names? Are you afraid of embarrassing yourself when you use a soft 'c' when all around you use a hard 'c'. Well help is at hand with this guide to pronunciation of biological Latin. Working along similar lines **http://ic.ucsc.edu/~ggilbert/envs122/ConventionsScienceWriting.html** has details of some of the conventions in scientific writing.

RINGING

http://www.euring.org/
Everything connected with bird ringing has been collated on this site. Many results have been included so there are maps and statistics to study. And if you should chance upon a colour marked bird, you should be able to find out details here and pass your sighting on to the appropriate source.

TAXONOMY, RARITIES AND LISTS

http://www.bbrc.org.uk/
The pages for the British Birds Rarities Committee are still being developed, but the intention is to put all the reports online with the 2001 report already available. Statistical summaries of all scarce bird records from 1958 are included.

http://www.birdlist.org/
If you can get past the hideous colour schemes and an ever-increasing array of menus, you eventually end up with list of birds, mammals, fish etc, for every country in the world. They are all arranged in order according to Sibley and Monroe and use the names adopted by these authors, so expect some big differences if your fieldguide still uses the traditional Voous order.

http://www.bou.org.uk/index.htm
The British Ornithologists' Union is the official guardian of the British list and there is plenty of information online, explaining various taxonomic decisions and keeping the list up to date. You can subscribe to read articles online though several are available for free. Content is dry and scientific, but it does exactly what it sets out to do and does it well.

http://www.dvz.be/Portal/links_tax.htm
This is basically a links page, but one entirely concerned with systematic lists. Again, it is not just for birds but covers anything and everything in the natural kingdom. The page is delightfully uncluttered and easy to use and the included links tend towards the obscure – I quickly found a checklist for Isosaari, an island off Finland.

http://www.ornitaxa.com/SM/New/NewSpecies.html
New species are still being discovered and this site details the most recent (78 species detailed at the time of writing). The home page discusses changes in bird taxonomy since 1993.

http://species.enviroweb.org/obird.html
A strange site. With no design whatsoever, this is a sort of list of lists, offering a whole collection of links to other websites that offer lists of one sort or another. There are taxonomic list and checklists for countries, while some of the more obscure and transitory lists include endangered birds on stamps and items for sale.

http://www.surfnet.fi/ecosyd/bird/download.phtml
This is another world checklist, available to download, but following the Howard and Moore sequence this time.

http://www.wpbirds.com/Index.htm
This site is currently undergoing a major revamp. The ultimate aim is to give a country-by-country breakdown of every species to have occurred in the Western Palearctic, listing every incidence of vagrancy. The site was some way off completion at the time of writing, but should be a worthwhile reference if everything goes according to plan.

TRIP REPORTS

http://www.eurobirding.com/tripreports/
This is currently the best place on the net to search for a foreign trip report, with more than 4,400 listed. You can refine your search further by specifying which period interests you. For example, a query for Bulgaria in April, May and June returned 11 hits. There is also an index to articles in birding magazines.

WEATHER

http://www.bbc.co.uk/weather/
The BBC's weather pages have been totally revamped and now offer an excellent service for anywhere in the world. Maps are updated regularly and a click of the mouse now shows those all-important wind directions. Type in your postcode or that of your local nature reserve and you get a personalised five-day forecast. First class.

WHY WeBS IS GOOD FOR YOU!

BTO Steve Holloway explains the appeal of going out to count wildfowl and waders across the UK as part of the Wetland Bird Survey.

WHAT IS THE FIRST image that comes into your head when hearing the word 'webs'? As likely as not it will be a scene of sticky, spider-infested orbs, glistening with autumn dew. On the other hand, to hundreds of other folk, 'WeBS' means participating in the largest waterbird recording scheme of its kind in the world.

The acronym 'WeBS' stands for 'The Wetland Bird Survey', a scheme in which volunteers take part in monthly synchronised counts of divers, grebes, cormorants, wildfowl, waders, gulls and terns on the UK's estuaries, coastline and inland waters. The huge amounts of data collected by the WeBS Core Count scheme over the years is used by both the government and conservation organisations to monitor the health of our wetlands, many of which hold internationally important populations of waterbirds during the winter months. In addition to the high tide Core Counts, some tidal sites are counted at low tide every few years, whilst there are other occasional surveys to target particular species. There is something for everyone!

WeBS volunteer counters join the scheme for many reasons. For some, it is the perfect excuse to get out of the house for an hour or two each month. Many of the counted sites are situated in attractive countryside, while others are of a more urban nature. Combine this with the fact that they are usefully contributing to scientific knowledge, both at a local and national level, and it is easy to understand why some counters have remained loyal to WeBS for more than a decade!

Noting the numbers of common species such as Pochard is as valuable as spotting rarities.

Many counters develop quite an attachment to 'their' site(s), so it is quite fitting that WeBS data is often presented by conservation organisations and government advisers at public enquiries in order to protect valuable wetland sites. The ongoing saga of a possible third London Airport at Cliffe Marshes provides an excellent example of the conservation importance of WeBS data. Another recent conservation 'battle' was over the plans for a new container port at Dibden Bay in Southampton Water. Once again, WeBS data was vital in influencing the final outcome, which was to reject the scheme on the grounds that it would irrevocably damage important intertidal mudflats.

WeBS data also provides the basis for understanding changes in waterbird numbers. Recent work has suggested that the numbers of waders wintering on English east coast estuaries is increasing, while numbers using estuaries in south west England and Wales have declined during the winter months. The east coast of England is generally colder than the south west in the winter, and previously was apparently less preferred as a wintering area. However, as our winter climate has become generally milder over the last 10 to 15 years, more waders have chosen to settle on the eastern side of the country. This is just one example of the usefulness of long-term datasets such as WeBS.

Monitoring any site on a regular basis is a good way of learning more about the wildlife using it and there must be few, if any, WeBS counters who cannot admit to finding out something new and interesting about their local 'patch'. Most of the larger WeBS sites are counted by teams of volunteers, co-ordinated by a Local Organiser. Many Local Organisers arrange informal 'get-togethers', which are a good way of meeting other waterbird enthusiasts in your area.

I think that it would be true to say that many of us dream of finding something unusual while out birdwatching, and if it is on our local 'patch', then so much the better! Regularly counting a site for WeBS provides ample opportunities for turning up that rare duck or wader, and though it could be argued that these displaced individuals are of little scientific interest, chancing upon one can make a good morning an excellent one!

A glance through the 'Wildfowl and Wader Counts' (the annual WeBS report sent free to all participating WeBS counters) shows that many weird and wonderful species are out there. Some of these are obviously escapees from private collections (the Ringed Teal and Rosybill from South America and the Chestnut Teal from Australia - all recorded during recent WeBS counts). However, some of the American species recorded such as Lesser Scaup and American Wigeon are probably genuine trans-Atlantic migrants. Similarly, several species of American wader are also regularly recorded by WeBS.

However, perhaps the most dramatic addition to the WeBS counter's list of regularly encountered species is the Little Egret. This species was formally a write-in 'extra species' on the WeBS recording forms, such was its rarity. Now, we will need to redesign the forms as it is so frequently recorded!

So if you feel that WeBS would help your health and you would like to find out more about becoming involved, please contact the WeBS Office at the BTO (See contact details under National Organisations section).

WeBS is a partnership of the BTO, WWT, RSPB and JNCC.

CONTRIBUTING TO A DEEPER UNDERSTANDING OF BIRD MIGRATION

Dawn Balmer, organiser of Migration Watch, explains how the network of volunteer birdwatchers contributing records on-line to the scheme over the last three years have helped ornithologists develop a more complete picture of the spread of migrant species throughout the UK.

MOST SERIOUS birders in Britain look at the weather maps as autumn weekends approach, hoping for systems over Europe that will bring in rare vagrants from the east. Migration Watchers involved in the on-line survey developed by the British Trust for Ornithology have learned to do the same in spring, when weather systems over North Africa and Iberia help to explain the patterns of arrivals from the south.

Migration Watch was set up by the British Trust for Ornithology (BTO) and BirdWatch Ireland in spring 2002 to track the arrival of spring migrants over three years. A special website (www.bto.org/migwatch) was designed and birdwatchers across Britain and Ireland have submitted their records using the Internet in spring 2002-2004.

Thanks to the efforts of this amateur network of observers, some interesting new information about migrant species has emerged in the last three years. For instance, a Migration Watch recorder in Cambridgeshire discovered wintering Turtle Doves in February 2004.

Unusual birds found in gardens and reported to Migration Watch include Hoopoe, Common Rosefinch (a first for Warwickshire!) and Rose-coloured Starling. The county bird recorders were informed in each case.

Bird observatories recorded their daily counts in Migration Watch and counts at Spurn (East Riding of Yorkshire) and Gibraltar Point (Lincolnshire) revealed an amazing passage of Swifts on June 18, 2003 with 7,500 recorded at Spurn and 6,800 at Gibraltar Point. This is almost certainly the same massive feeding flock following a high-pressure system. In 2002 there were 4,000 Swifts at Spurn and 4,700 at Gibraltar Point on June 22.

Why Migration Watch?

Migration is surely one of the most fascinating aspects of bird ecology and the study of migration has interested birdwatchers and scientists for hundreds of years. Ringing has obviously contributed enormously to our understanding, but there are still areas to be explored, and it is exciting that birdwatchers across Britain and Ireland can make a contribution to improving knowledge.

In Britain and Ireland much of our detailed knowledge of migration comes from the excellent work of the bird observatories dotted around our coastline. The BTO Guide *Seasonal Movements of Summer Migrants* by Nick Riddiford and Peter Findlay, published in 1981, summarised the movements of migrants through observatories in spring and autumn. The bird observatory records tell us what's going on at 15-20 sites around the coastline - but what happens in the gaps in between?

By encouraging large numbers of birdwatchers to take part in Migration Watch and enter lists of birds on to the website, we can start to look more closely at the way birds enter Britain and Ireland and flow through these countries.

There has been great interest in the timing of migration and the excellent UK Phenology Network (www.phenology.org.uk) has gathered information on first arrival dates. Migration Watch differs in that it is interested in when the majority of migrants have arrived, and not just the first birds. Knowing about the timing of arrival of spring migrants is important, especially if we want to think about the possible effects of climate change and changing weather patterns on migratory journeys and breeding success.

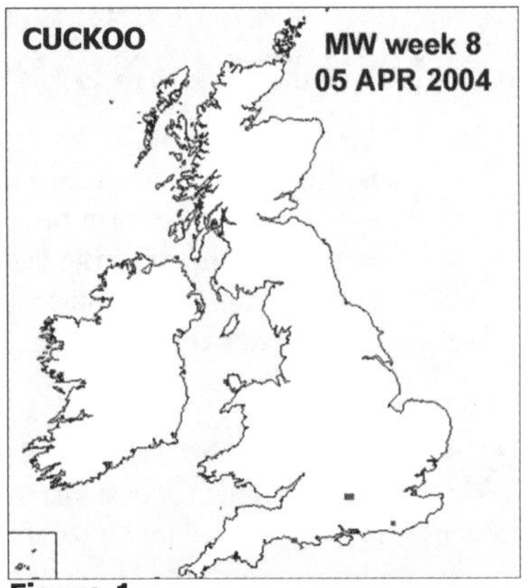

Figure 1

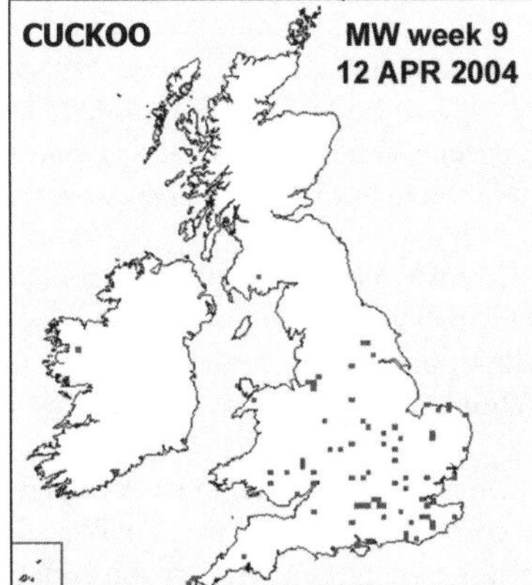

Figure 2

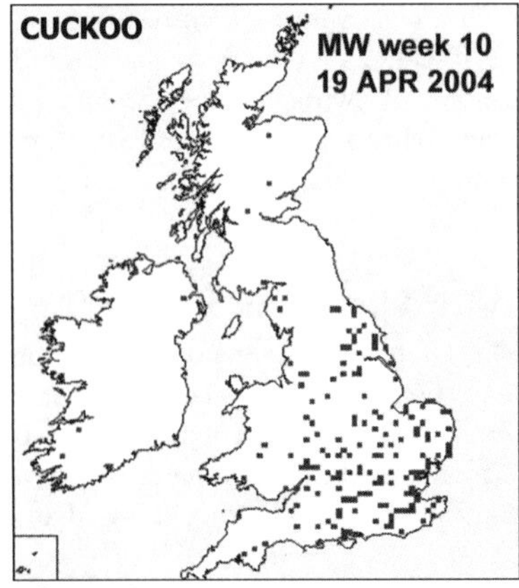

Figure 3

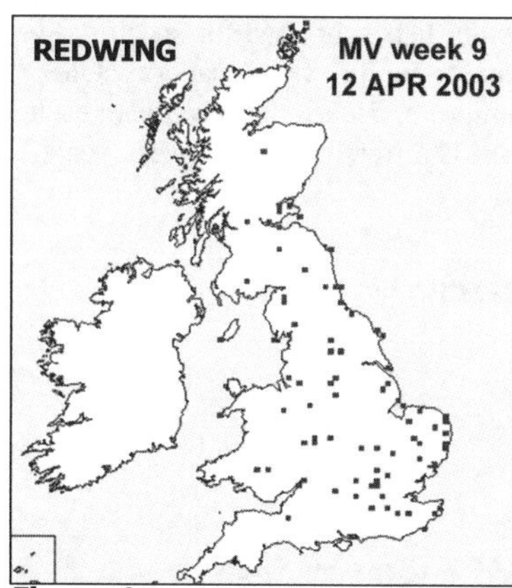

Figure 4

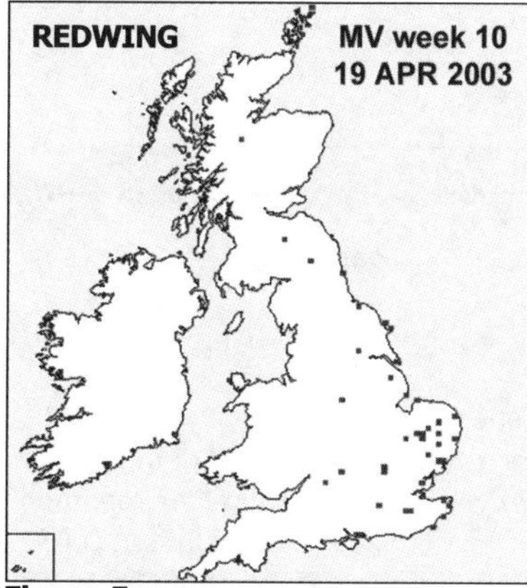

Figure 5

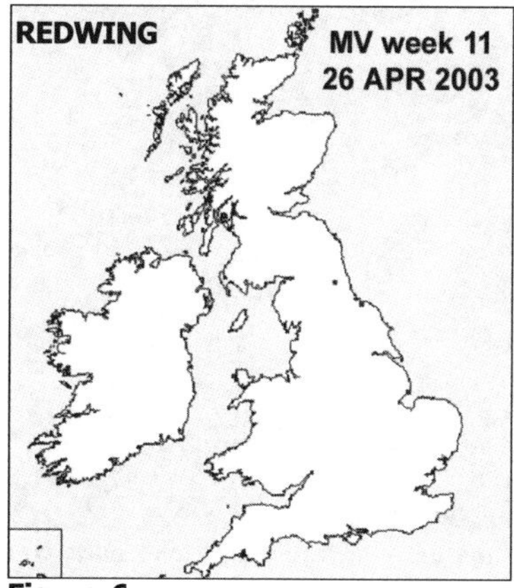

Figure 6

Novel outputs, interesting results

Contributors to Migration Watch submit lists of birds they have seen while out birdwatching, whether it's a visit to a local park, nature reserve or simply watching from the garden. Graphs and maps of coverage throughout the spring are easily produced and updated daily.

Perhaps the most interesting output from Migration Watch are the animated maps which show the week-by-week arrival of migrants. The arrival of Cuckoos in spring 2004 is shown in Figure 1 (left); the first few Cuckoos arrive in week 8 of Migration Watch (April 6-11) but then birds arrive in good numbers from the south east in week 9 (Figure 2) and spread north and west through week 10 (Figure 3) and subsequent weeks.

As well as recording the arrival of spring migrants, Migration Watch has also been able to monitor the departure of Redwing, Fieldfare and Brambling. The animated maps clearly show birds moving eastwards and northwards as the spring progresses. An example of the departure of Redwing in spring 2003 is shown in Figure 4 (left), with a rapid disappearance between mid (Figure 5) and late April (Figure 6).

By using lists of birds we can look at the proportion of lists submitted for specific species and by showing this graphically we can pick out some interesting patterns. One of the most amazing features of the graphs is how similar the pattern of arrival is in each of the three years, though the start of the migration period differs slightly between years.

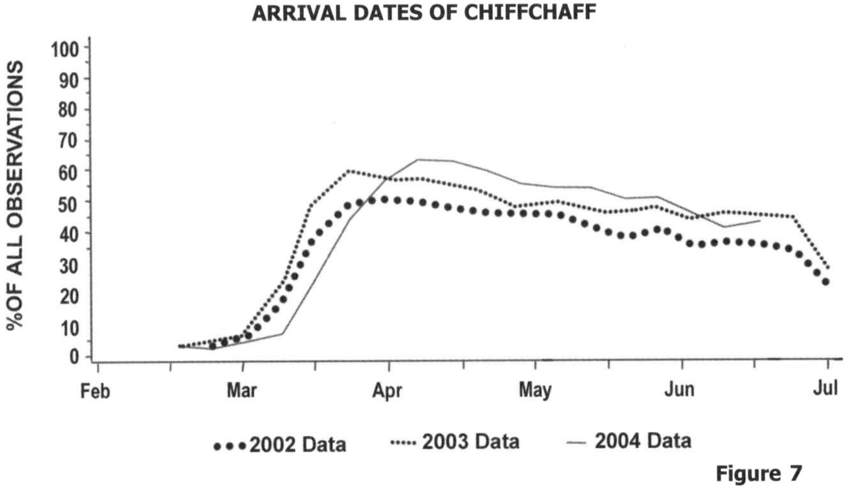

Figure 7

A good example of this is Chiffchaff. When Migration Watch starts each year in mid February, small numbers of wintering Chiffchaffs are recorded. The arrival of migrant Chiffchaffs is clearly shown on the graph (Figure 7) by an upward leap in the proportion of people recording this species. Arrival in 2004 was latest in 2002 and earliest in 2003.

The graph for Wheatear (Fig 8) is interesting too. It clearly shows two peaks in the submission of records. The peak in late March and early April records those Wheatears that breed in Britain and Ireland; they arrive on our shores and head quickly towards their breeding grounds. In late April and early May we see another peak as larger Greenland birds pass through Britain and Ireland on their way to their breeding grounds in Greenland and Iceland. They move through

Wheatear by Keith Offord

Wheatear sightings peak in late March and early April.

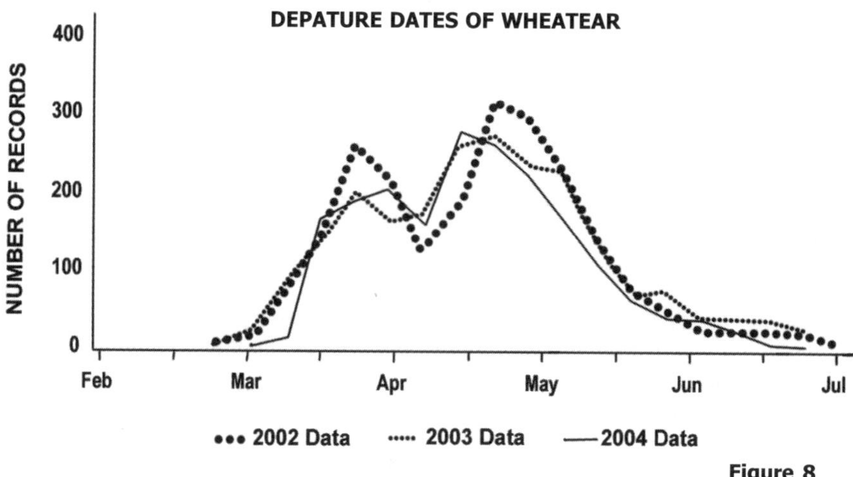

Figure 8

later than our own breeding birds because their breeding grounds would still be inhospitable in early April.

The future

Following the success of Migration Watch, the BTO is keen to develop online bird recording throughout the year. A new website, BirdTrack, will be set up as a year-round recording project so that movement and migration can be followed during the whole year.

Tracking the arrival of winter visitors and the departure of our summer visitors is particularly exciting. The website will also be able to collect data on the distribution of scarce species such as Hawfinch, Lesser Spotted Woodpecker and Willow Tit throughout the year, providing an important resource for conservation. BirdTrack is organised by BTO on behalf of BTO, RSPB and BirdWatch Ireland. For further information visit the website www.birdtrack.net or e-mail birdtrack@bto.org

Migration Watch was generously sponsored by Northumbrian Water Limited and Essex & Suffolk Water with support from the BTO's Swallow Appeal. *Bird Watching* magazine helped throughout with promoting the project. Special thanks to the several thousand birdwatchers who contributed records.

Further reading

The BTO's *Migration Atlas* (Wernham *et al*) is a fantastic source of information on the migrations and movements of birds in Britain and Ireland based on ringing. A more general book on migration called *Time to Fly* by Jim Flegg is available through the BTO or any good bookshop. This new book explores bird migration with easy-to-read text and colourful maps.

An added personal bonus – View your own data

As well as contributing records to the national picture, Migration Watch recorders can also view their own records. One of the most interesting reports on offer is the 'View 1st observations' which presents your first dates for a wide range of summer migrants in each year 2002-2004.

It also shows the first date for each species in your geographical region, so you can see how your own first dates compare with others in the same part of the country (Fig 5). Other reports allow you to look at and compare the species you have recorded at each site visited and on each occasion.

Your first arrival dates for East of England
DAWN BALMER

Please note: The data are for migrant species only

Species	Detail	2002	2003	2004
Garganey	My 1st date	-	Sat, 22 Mar, 2003	-
	My Location	-	Titchwell (TF7544)	-
	Region 1st date	-	Thu, 13 Mar, 2003	-
Hobby	My 1st date	Sun, 28 Apr, 2002	Sun, 11 May, 2003	Sun, 9 May, 2004
	My Location	Lakenheath (TL7186)	Lakenheath (TL7186)	Lakenheath (TL7186)
	Region 1st date	Tue, 26 Mar, 2002	Sun, 23 Mar, 2003	Mon, 29 Mar, 2004
Quail	My 1st date	-	-	Sun, 23 May, 2004
	My Location	-	-	Stiffkey (TF9643)
	Region 1st date	-	-	Mon, 10 May, 2004
Stone-curlew	My 1st date	**Thu, 7 Mar, 2002**	**Mon, 3 Mar, 2003**	Mon, 5 Apr, 2004
	My Location	Elveden (TL87)	Cavenham (TL77)	Cavenham (TL77)
	Region 1st date	**Thu, 7 Mar, 2002**	**Mon, 3 Mar, 2003**	Sat, 28 Feb, 2004
Little Ringed Plover	My 1st date	Sat, 30 Mar, 2002	Sat, 22 Mar, 2003	Tue, 23 Mar, 2004
	My Location	Lackford (TL7970)	Pentney Lakes (TF7113)	Nunnery Lakes (TL8781)
	Region 1st date	Sat, 9 Mar, 2002	Thu, 6 Mar, 2003	Sun, 14 Mar, 2004

NATIONAL PROJECTS

NOTICE TO BIRDWATCHERS

National ornithological projects depend for their success on the active participation of amateur birdwatchers. In return they provide birdwatchers with an excellent opportunity to contribute in a positive and worthwhile way to the scientific study of birds and their habitats, which is the vital basis of all conservation programmes. The following entries provide a description of each particular project and a note of whom to contact for further information (full address details are in the previous section).

BARN OWL MONITORING PROGRAMME

A BTO project

Volunteers monitor nest sites to record site occupancy, clutch size, brood size and breeding success. Qualified ringers may catch and ring adults and chicks and record measurements. Volunteers must be qualified bird ringers or nest recorders with a Schedule 1 licence for Barn Owl. Contact Peter Beaven, e-mail: barnowls@bto.org

BirdTrack

Organised by BTO on behalf of BTO, RSPB and BirdWatch Ireland.

BirdTrack is a major new scheme, which developed out of Migration Watch, an Internet project to study spring migration. This year-round bird recording scheme is designed to collect large numbers of lists of birds. The idea is simple - you make a note of the birds seen at each site you visit and enter your daily observations on a simple-to-use web page. Birdwatchers can also send in other types of records including counts and casual observations. The focus of the website (www.birdtrack.net) will be spring and autumn migration, seasonal movements and the distribution of scarce species. Contact: Dawn Balmer, BTO

BREEDING BIRD SURVEY

Supported by the BTO, JNCC and the RSPB.

Begun in 1994, the BBS is designed to keep track of the changes in populations of our common breeding birds. It is dependent on volunteer birdwatchers throughout the country who can spare about five hours a year to cover a 1x1km survey square. There are just two morning visits to survey the breeding birds each year.

Survey squares are picked at random by computer to ensure that all habitats and regions are covered. Since its inception it has been a tremendous success, with more than 2,200 squares covered and more than 200 species recorded each year. Contact: Mike Raven, BTO, or your local BTO Regional Representative (see County Directory).

CORE MONITORING CENSUS (formerly COMMON BIRDS CENSUS)

This survey has officially finished. This was the main source of population monitoring in the wider countryside from 1962-2000, but has now been superseded by the Breeding Bird Survey. Nevertheless, CBC is still the best method to use at a local scale, producing maps showing the locations of bird's territories for a defined area. This is especially useful to study the relationship of breeding birds with their habitats. Although new participants are not needed currently, the method is still valuable and will be available on the BTO website.

CONCERN FOR SWIFTS

A Concern for Swifts Group project.

Endorsed by the BTO and the RSPB, the Group monitors Swift breeding colonies, especially where building restoration and maintenance are likely to cause disturbance. Practical information can be provided to owners, architects, builders and others. The help of interested birdwatchers is always welcome. Contact: Jake Allsop, 01353 740540; e-mail: jakeallsop@aol.com

CONSTANT EFFORT SITES SCHEME

A BTO project for bird ringers, funded by a partnership of the BTO, the JNCC, The Environment and Heritage Service in Northern Ireland - National Parks & Wildlife Service (Ireland) and the ringers themselves.

Participants in the scheme monitor common songbird populations by mist-netting and ringing birds throughout the summer at more than 130 sites across Britain and Ireland. Changes in numbers of adults captured provide an index of population changes between years, while the ratio of juveniles to adults gives a measure of productivity. Between-year recaptures of birds are used to study variations in adult survival rates. Information from CES complements that from other long-term BTO surveys. Contact: Dawn Balmer, BTO.

CORMORANT ROOST SITE INVENTORY AND BREEDING COLONY REGISTER

R. Sellers and WWT.

Daytime counts carried out under the Wetland Bird Survey provide an index of the number of Cormorants wintering in Great Britain, but many birds are known to go uncounted on riverine and coastal habitats.

Dr Robin Sellers, in association with WWT, therefore established the Christmas Week Cormorant Survey which, through a network of volunteer counters, sought to monitor the numbers of Cormorants at about 70 of the most important night roosts in GB. In 1997, this project was extended to produce a comprehensive Cormorant Roost Site Inventory for Great Britain. Over 100 county bird recorders and local bird experts helped compile the inventory, which currently lists 291 night roosts, mostly in England.

In 1990, Robin Sellers also established the Cormorant Breeding Colony Survey to monitor numbers and breeding success of Cormorants in the UK at both coastal and inland colonies. Some 1,500 pairs of Cormorants, representing perhaps 15% of the local UK population, now breed inland. New colonies are forming every year as the population inland increases annually by 19%. The first European-wide Cormorant survey was undertaken in January 2003, organised in the UK by WWT. Anyone wishng to take part in either roost or breeding surveys should contact Colette Hall at WWT.

GARDEN BIRD FEEDING SURVEY

A BTO project.

The 2003/04 season completed 34 years of the GBFS. Each year 250 observers record the numbers and variety of garden birds fed by man in the 26 weeks between October and March. It is the longest running survey of its type in the world. Gardens are selected by region and type, from city flats, suburban semis and rural houses to outlying farms. Contact: David Glue, BTO.

BTO/CJ GARDEN BIRDWATCH

A BTO project, supported by C J WildBird Foods.

Started in January 1995, this project is a year-round survey that monitors the use that birds make of gardens. Approximately 17,000 participants from all over the UK and Ireland keep a weekly log of species using their gardens. The data collected are used to monitor regional, seasonal and year-to-year changes in the garden populations of our commoner birds. To cover costs there is an annual fee of £12. There is a quarterly colour magazine and all new joiners receive a full-colour, garden bird handbook. Results and more information are available online: www.bto.org/gbww. E-mail: gbw@bto.org Contact: Jacky Prior/Carol Povey, BTO.

GOLDEN ORIOLE CENSUS

A Golden Oriole Group project.

With support from the RSPB, the Golden Oriole Group has undertaken a systematic annual census of breeding Golden Orioles in the Fenland Basin since 1987. In recent years national censuses have been made, funded by English Nature and the RSPB, in which some 60 volunteer recorders have participated. The Group is always interested to hear of sightings of Orioles and to receive offers of help with its census work. Studies of breeding biology, habitat and food requirements are also carried out.

Contact: Jake Allsop, Golden Oriole Group.

GOOSE CENSUSES

A WWT project

Britain and Ireland support internationally important goose populations. During the day, many of these feed away from wetlands and are therefore not adequately censused by the Wetland Bird Survey. Additional surveys are therefore undertaken to provide estimates of population size. These primarily involve roost counts, supplemented by further counts of feeding birds.

Most populations are censused up to three times a year, typically during the autumn, midwinter, and spring. In addition, counts of the proportion of juveniles in goose flocks are undertaken to provide estimates of annual productivity. Further volunteers are always needed. In particular, counters in Scotland, Lancashire and Norfolk are sought. For more information contact: Richard Hearn, WWT, e-mail richard.hearn@wwt.org.uk.

HERONRIES CENSUS
A BTO project.
This survey started in 1928 and has been carried out under the auspices of the BTO since 1934. It represents the longest continuous series of population data for any European breeding bird. Counts are made at a sample of heronries each year, chiefly in England and Wales, to provide an index of the current population level; data from Scotland and Northern Ireland are scant and more contributions from these countries would be especially welcomed.
Herons may be hit hard during periods of severe weather but benefit by increased survival over mild winters. Their position at the top of a food chain makes them particularly vulnerable to pesticides and pollution. Contact: John Marchant, BTO.

IRISH WETLAND BIRD SURVEY (I-WeBS)
A joint project of BirdWatch Ireland, the National Parks & Wildlife Service of the Dept of Arts, Culture & the Gaeltacht, and WWT, and supported by the Heritage Council and WWF-UK.
Established in 1994, I-WeBS aims to monitor the numbers and distribution of waterfowl populations wintering in Ireland in the long term, enabling the population size and spatial and temporal trends in numbers to be identified and described for each species. Methods are compatible with existing schemes in the UK and Europe, and I-WeBS collaborates closely with the Wetland Bird Survey (WeBS) in the UK. Synchronised monthly counts are undertaken at wetland sites of all habitats during the winter.

Counts are straightforward and counters receive a newsletter and full report annually. Additional help is always welcome, especially during these initial years as the scheme continues to grow. Contact: Olivia Crowe, BirdWatch Ireland.

LITTLE OWLS - PROJECT *ATHENE*
Little Owl Study Group
The Little Owl is declining at an alarming rate across Europe and is endangered in at least three Western European countries. To combat this, a European Species Action Plan is being developed, to put in place the necessary monitors, conservation, and education measures for its long term survival. Project *Athene* is the British leg of this plan.
It is a two-tier monitoring programme that is open to anybody. To monitor numbers of Little Owls a playback method is employed using standardised protocol. Nest site recording provides a more in-depth information on the population dynamics of the owls. You can join the LOSG and dependant on your time and expertise, carry out Little Owl surveys in your own patch. Contact Roy Leigh: Little Owl Study Group, c/o Biota, 71-73 Ascot Court, Middlewish Road, Northwich, Cheshire CW9 7BP. 01606 333296;
e-mail: RSL@biota.co.uk for further information

LOW TIDE COUNTS SCHEME
see Wetland Bird Survey

MANX CHOUGH PROJECT
A Manx registered charitable trust.
Established in 1990 to help the conservation of the Chough in the Isle of Man, leading to its protection and population increase. The main considerations are the maintenance of present nest sites, provision of suitable conditions for the reoccupation of abandoned sites and the expansion of the range of the species into new areas of the Island. Surveys and censuses are carried out. Raising public awareness of and interest in the Chough are further objects. Contact: Allen S Moore, Lyndale, Derby Road, Peel, Isle of Man IM5 1HH. 01624 843798.

MIGRATION WATCH Replaced by BirdTrack (see above)

NEST RECORD SCHEME
A BTO Project forming part of the BTO's Integrated Population Monitoring programme carried out under contract with the JNCC.
All birdwatchers can contribute to this scheme by sending information about nesting attempts they observe into the BTO on standard Nest Record Cards or electronically via the IPMR

computer package. The NRS monitors changes in the nesting success and the timing of breeding of Britain's bird species. Guidance on on how to record and visit nests safely, without disturbing breeding birds, is available in a free starter pack from the Nest Records Unit. Contact: Peter Beaven at e-mail: nest.records@bto.org

RAPTOR AND OWL RESEARCH REGISTER

A BTO project

The Register has helped considerably over the past 28 years in encouraging and guiding research, and in the co-ordination of projects. There are currently almost 500 projects in the card index file through which the Register operates.

The owl species currently receiving most attention are Barn and Tawny. As to raptors, the most popular subjects are Kestrel, Buzzard, Sparrowhawk, Hobby and Peregrine, with researchers showing increasing interest in Red Kite, and fewer large in-depth studies of Goshawk, Osprey and harriers. Contributing is a simple process and involves all raptor enthusiasts, whether it is to describe an amateur activity or professional study. The nature of research on record varies widely – from local pellet analyses to captive breeding and rehabilitation programmes to national surveys of Peregrine, Buzzard and Golden Eagle. Birdwatchers in both Britain and abroad are encouraged to write for photocopies of cards relevant to the species or nature of their work. The effectiveness of the Register depends upon those running projects (however big or small) ensuring that their work is included. Contact: David Glue, BTO.

RED KITE RE-INTRODUCTION PROJECT

An English Nature/SNH/RSPB project supported by Forest Enterprise, Yorkshire Water and authorities in Germany and Spain

The project involves the translocation of birds from Spain, Germany and the expanding Chilterns population for release at sites in England and Scotland.

Records of any wing-tagged Red Kites in England should be reported to Ian Carter at English Nature, Northminster House, Peterborough, PEI IUA (tel 01733 455281). Scottish records should be sent to Brian Etheridge at RSPB's North Scotland Regional Office, Etive House, Beechwood Park, Inverness, IV2 3BW (tel 01463 715000).

Sightings are of particular value if the letter/number code (or colour) of wing tags can be seen or if the bird is seen flying low over (or into) woodland. Records should include an exact location, preferably with a six figure grid reference.

RETRAPPING ADULTS FOR SURVIVAL PROJECT

A BTO project for bird ringers, funded by a partnership of the BTO, the JNCC, The Environment and Heritage Service in Northern Ireland - National Parks & Wildlife Service (Ireland) and the ringers themselves.

This project started in 1998 and is an initiative of the BTO Ringing Scheme. It aims to gather re-trap information for a wide range of species, especially those of conservation concern, in a variety of breeding habitats, allowing the monitoring of survival rates.

Detailed information about survival rates from the RAS Project will help in the understanding of changing population trends. Ringers choose a target species, decide on a study area and develop suitable catching techniques. The aim then is to catch all the breeding adults of the chosen species within the study area. This is repeated each breeding season for a minimum of five years. The results will be relayed to conservation organisations who can use the information to design effective conservation action plans. Contact: John Marchant, BTO.

RINGING SCHEME

A BTO project for bird ringers, funded by a partnership of the BTO, the JNCC, -The National Parks & Wildlife Service (Ireland) and the ringers themselves.

The purpose of the Ringing Scheme is to study survival productivity and movements by marking birds with individually numbered metal rings which carry a return address. About 2,000 trained and licensed ringers operate in Britain and Ireland, and together they mark around 750,000 birds each year. All birdwatchers can contribute to the scheme by reporting any ringed birds they find either via the BTO website or by letter. Anyone finding a ringed bird should note the ring number, species (if known), when and where the bird was found, and what happened to it.

If the bird is dead, please remove the ring, flatten it out and tape it to your letter and send it to us. If details are phoned in, please keep the ring in case there is a query. Finders who send their name and address will be given details of where and when the bird was ringed. About 12,000 ringed birds are reported each year and an annual report is published. Contact: Jacquie Clark, BTO.

SCARCE WOODLAND BIRD AND HABITAT SURVEY 2005 / 06

A BTO volunteer-based project, funded by the JNCC.

This project aims to assess variations in the abundance of a range of scarce and declining woodland bird species with respect to habitat and geographical region. Volunteers will be asked to map the presence of a range of species along woodland routes and to record details of the habitat. Contact: Chris Hewson (chris.hewson@bto.org).

SWIFTS see Concern for Swifts

WATERWAYS BIRD SURVEY

A BTO project

From March to July each year participants survey linear waterways (rivers and canals) to map the position and activity of riparian birds. Results show both numbers and distribution of breeding territories for each waterside species at each site. An annual report on population change is published in *BTO News*. Since 1998, WBS has run parallel with the Waterways Breeding Bird Survey, which uses a transect method.

WBS maps show the habitat requirements of the birds and can be used to assess the effects of waterway management. Coverage of new plots is always required, especially in poorly covered areas such as Northern Ireland, Scotland, Wales, SW England and the North East. Contact: John Marchant, BTO.

WATERWAYS BREEDING BIRD SURVEY

A BTO project, supported by the Environment Agency

WBBS uses transect methods like those of the Breeding Bird Survey to record bird populations along randomly chosen stretches of river and canal throughout the UK. Just two survey visits are needed during April-June. WBBS began in 1998 and is currently in a development phase, in which its performance is being assessed against the long-established Waterways Bird Survey. Coverage of random sites requires a further boost in 2004-05. Contact BTO Regional Representative (see County Directory) to enquire if any local stretches require coverage, otherwise John Marchant at BTO HQ.

WETLAND BIRD SURVEY

A joint scheme of BTO, WWT, RSPB & JNCC

The Wetland Bird Survey (WeBS) is the monitoring scheme for non-breeding waterbirds in the UK. The principal aims are:

1. to determine the population sizes of waterbirds
2. to determine trends in numbers and distribution
3. to identify important sites for waterbirds
4. to conduct research which underpins waterbird conservation.

WeBS data are used to designate important waterbird sites and protect them against adverse development, for research into the causes of declines, for establishing conservation priorities and strategies and to formulate management plans for wetland sites and waterbirds.

Once monthly, synchronised Core Counts are made at as many wetland sites as possible. Low Tide Counts are made on about 20 estuaries each winter to identify important feeding areas. Counts take just a few hours and are relatively straightforward. The 3,000 participants receive regular newsletters and a comprehensive annual report. New counters are always welcome. Contacts: WeBS Office, BTO (Core Counts - Sarah Jackson, Low Tide Counts - Alex Banks and general enquiries - Andy Musgrove/Steve Holloway, at BTO HQ, E-mail WeBS@bto.org

WeBS WINTER RIVER BIRD SURVEY

A Wetland Bird Survey project (qv)

While the Wetland Bird Survey (WeBS) achieves excellent coverage of estuaries and inland still waters, rivers are poorly monitored by comparison. Consequently, WeBS undoubtedly misses a significant proportion of the UK populations of several species which use rivers, eg. Little Grebe, Mallard, Tufted Duck, Goldeneye and Goosander. A pilot survey undertaken in 2000 and 2001 indicated that the full national survey should cover at least 8,000 river sections of 500 metres length to allow an accurate estimation of population sizes for waterbirds wintering on rivers. The 2004 survey was unfortunately cancelled, as problems were encountered regarding the process of random selection of river sections for the survey. It is hoped that the January 2005 survey will be run. Many counters in addition to those involved in the pilot will be required. WWT aims to provide a dedicated Winter River Bird Survey Web site with on-line functions for registering to take part in the survey, for downloading instructions and count forms, and also for web-based data submission once the survey is completed. Contact: WWT, 01453 891900, or e-mail: research@wwt.org.uk

WHOOPER SWAN RESEARCH

A WWT/Icelandic Museum of Nature History project

WNW's long-term study of Whooper Swans commenced in 1979 with the completion of swan pipes at Caerlaverock (Dumfries & Galloway) and Welney (Norfolk) and the subsequent development of a ringing programme for this species. Whooper Swans have been ringed at Martin Mere (Lancashire) from 1990 onwards. Since 1988, staff have made regular expeditions to Iceland where they collaborate with Icelandic ornithologists in monitoring clutch and brood sizes, and in catching the families and non-breeding flocks. The study aims to determine factors affecting the reproductive success of the Icelandic-breeding Whooper Swan population which winters mainly in Britain and Ireland. Relocating the families in winter is important for assessing the number of cygnets that survive autumn migration. Efforts made by birdwatchers to read Whooper Swan rings and to report the number of juveniles associated with ringed birds, are therefore particularly useful. The first and last dates on which ringed birds are seen at a site are also valuable for monitoring the movements of the swans in winter. Contact: Eileen Rees, WWT.

WILDFOWL COLOUR RINGING

A WWT project

The Wildfowl & Wetlands Trust co-ordinates all colour ringing of swans, geese and ducks on behalf of the BTO. The use of unique coloured leg-rings enables the movements and behaviour of known individuals to be observed without recapture. The rings are usually in bright colours with engraved letters and/or digits showing as black or white, and can be read with a telescope at up to 200m. Colour-marked neck collars, and plumage dyes, have also been used on geese and swans. Any records of observations should include species, location, date, ring colour and mark, and which leg the ring was on (most rings read from the foot upwards). The main study species are Mute Swan, Bewick's Swan, Whooper Swan, Pink-footed Goose, Greylag Goose, Greenland and European White-fronted Geese, Barnacle Goose, Brent Goose, Shelduck and Wigeon. Records will be forwarded to the relevant study, and when birds are traced ringing details will be sent back to the observer. All sightings should be sent to: Research Dept (Colour-ringed Wildfowl), WWT.

WINTER GULL ROOST SURVEY (WinGS) 2003/04-2005/06

A BTO project, funded by JNCC, EN, SNH, CCW EHSNI, Northumbrian Water.

The seventh Winter Gull Roost Survey will monitor all known major sites, as well as surveying other areas using a sampling approach. The survey aims to produce total population estimates and to identify the most important gull roost sites. Contact: Alex Banks.

EVENTS DIARY 2005

JANUARY

29-30 – Big Garden Birdwatch
Contact RSPB on 01767 680551; www.rspb.org.uk

30-31 – World Wetlands Day 2005
Free entry to all nine WWT centres to mark the event. www.wwt.org.uk

FEBRUARY

12 -13 – Great West Bird Fair
WWT Slimbridge, Glos, 01453 890333; www.wwt.org.uk

19-20 – Lea Valley Bird Fair
Lea Valley Park Farms, Nr Fishers Green, Essex. 01992 702200. www.leavalleypark.org.uk

26 – Southwest Ringers' Conference
Cotswold Water Park. Contact Robin Ward, e-mail: robin.ward@wwt.org.uk

MARCH

25-April 3 – National Wildlife Carving and Sculpture Exhibition
Pensthorpe, Fakenham, Norfolk. 01328 851465; www.pensthorpe.com

APRIL

1-3 – Wind, Fire and Water – Renewable Energy and Birds
BOU conference at University of Leicester, 01 865 281 842; www.bou.org.uk

2–4 – BTO Bird Survey Techniques Workshop
Nettlecombe Court Field Centre, Exmoor.

8-10 – RSPB Members Weekend in York
Contact RSPB on 01767 680551; www.rspb.org.uk

23-24 – Minsmere Bird Fair
Minsmere RSPB Reserve, 01728 648281; www.rspb.org.uk

MAY

8 – BTO Bird Survey Techniques Workshop
Caerlaverock WWT Centre

7-8 Leighton Moss Bird Fair
Contact Leighton Moss RSPB reserve, 01524 701601.

7- June 11 – Wildlife Photographer of the Year Exhibition
Pensthorpe, Fakenham, Norfolk. 01328 851465; www.pensthorpe.com

14 – BTO Bird Survey Techniques Workshop
Catterick Garrison, North Yorkshire.

JUNE

1-3 – BTO Bird Survey Techniques Workshop
Flatford Mill Field Centre, East Bergholt, Suffolk

3-5 – BTO Bird Survey Techniques Workshop
Kindrogan Field Centre, Blairgowrie, Scotland.

4-5 – Birdwatchers' Summer Fair 2005 and Wildlife Digital Photo Show
Brandon Marsh Nature Reserve, Coventry. 01527 852357; e-mail: interbirdnet@birder.co.uk

AUGUST

19-21 – The British Birdwatching Fair
Rutland Water www.birdfair.org.uk

SEPTEMBER

17-18 – British Birdcarving Championship
Exhibition and annual competition for members of the BWDCA. Agricultural Business Centre, Bakewell, Derbyshire. 01625 877988.

The Wildlife Art Society International Annual Exhibition,
Bristol Zoo Gardens
Date to be confirmed, please contact + 44 (0) 1843 291170; www.twasi.com

28-October 9 – SWLA Annual Exhibition
Mall Galleries, London. Contact SWLA.

OCTOBER

8 – RSPB AGM
Queen Elizabeth II Conference Centre, London
Contact RSPB on 01767 680551; www.rspb.org.uk

NOVEMBER

10-December 7 – The Wildlife Art Society International Exhibition,
Milan Touring Club, Milan. Contact + 44 (0) 1843 291170; www.twasi.com

12-13 – North West Bird Fair
WWT Martin Mere, 01704 895181; www.wwt.org.uk

DECEMBER

2-4 – BTO Annual Conference.
Hayes Conference Centre, Swanwick, Derbyshire. Contact Sue Starling, BTO.

Contact details for the organisations listed here can be found under their entries in the National Directory. For BTO workshops please contact the following: Two-and-a-half-day courses, Rebecca Cranston, BTO Scotland, e-mail: rebecca.cranston@bto.org; One-day courses, Su Gough, BTO Thetford HQ, e-mail: su.gough@bto.org

DIARY - JANUARY 2005

1	Sat	*New Year's Day*
2	Sun	*Holiday (Scotland)*
3	Mon	
4	Tue	
5	Wed	
6	Thu	
7	Fri	
8	Sat	
9	Sun	
10	Mon	
11	Tue	
12	Wed	
13	Thu	
14	Fri	
15	Sat	
16	Sun	
17	Mon	
18	Tue	
19	Wed	
20	Thu	
21	Fri	
22	Sat	
23	Sun	
24	Mon	
25	Tue	
26	Wed	
27	Thu	
28	Fri	
29	Sat	
30	Sun	
31	Mon	

BIRD NOTES - JANUARY 2005

DIARY - FEBRUARY 2005

1	Tue
2	Wed
3	Thu
4	Fri
5	Sat
6	Sun
7	Mon
8	Tue
9	Wed
10	Thu
11	Fri
12	Sat
13	Sun
14	Mon
15	Tue
16	Wed
17	Thu
18	Fri
19	Sat
20	Sun
21	Mon
22	Tue
23	Wed
24	Thu
25	Fri
26	Sat
27	Sun
28	Mon

DIARY - MARCH 2005

1	Tue	
2	Wed	
3	Thu	
4	Fri	
5	Sat	
6	Sun	*Mothering Sunday*
7	Mon	
8	Tue	
9	Wed	
10	Thu	
11	Fri	
12	Sat	
13	Sun	
14	Mon	
15	Tue	
16	Wed	
17	Thu	
18	Fri	
19	Sat	
20	Sun	
21	Mon	
22	Tue	
23	Wed	
24	Thu	
25	Fri	*Good Friday*
26	Sat	
27	Sun	*British Summertime begins* *Easter Day*
28	Mon	*Easter Monday*
29	Tue	
30	Wed	
31	Thu	

DIARY - APRIL 2005

1	Fri
2	Sat
3	Sun
4	Mon
5	Tue
6	Wed
7	Thu
8	Fri
9	Sat
10	Sun
11	Mon
12	Tue
13	Wed
14	Thu
15	Fri
16	Sat
17	Sun
18	Mon
19	Tue
20	Wed
21	Thu
22	Fri
23	Sat
24	Sun
25	Mon
26	Tue
27	Wed
28	Thu
29	Fri
30	Sat

BIRD NOTES - APRIL 2005

DIARY - MAY 2005

1	Sun	
2	Mon	*May Day*
3	Tue	
4	Wed	
5	Thu	
6	Fri	
7	Sat	
8	Sun	
9	Mon	
10	Tue	
11	Wed	
12	Thu	
13	Fri	
14	Sat	
15	Sun	
16	Mon	
17	Tue	
18	Wed	
19	Thu	
20	Fri	
21	Sat	
22	Sun	
23	Mon	
24	Tue	
25	Wed	
26	Thu	
27	Fri	
28	Sat	
29	Sun	
30	Mon	*Spring Bank Holiday*
31	Tue	

DIARY - JUNE 2005

1	Wed
2	Thu
3	Fri
4	Sat
5	Sun
6	Mon
7	Tue
8	Wed
9	Thu
10	Fri
11	Sat
12	Sun
13	Mon
14	Tue
15	Wed
16	Thu
17	Fri
18	Sat
19	Sun
20	Mon
21	Tue
22	Wed
23	Thu
24	Fri
25	Sat
26	Sun
27	Mon
28	Tue
29	Wed
30	Thu

BIRD NOTES - JUNE 2005

DIARY - JULY 2005

1	Fri
2	Sat
3	Sun
4	Mon
5	Tue
6	Wed
7	Thu
8	Fri
9	Sat
10	Sun
11	Mon
12	Tue
13	Wed
14	Thu
15	Fri
16	Sat
17	Sun
18	Mon
19	Tue
20	Wed
21	Thu
22	Fri
23	Sat
24	Sun
25	Mon
26	Tue
27	Wed
28	Thu
29	Fri
30	Sat
31	Sun

DIARY - AUGUST 2005

1	Mon	*Bank Holiday (Scotland)*
2	Tue	
3	Wed	
4	Thu	
5	Fri	
6	Sat	
7	Sun	
8	Mon	
9	Tue	
10	Wed	
11	Thu	
12	Fri	
13	Sat	
14	Sun	
15	Mon	
16	Tue	
17	Wed	
18	Thu	
19	Fri	
20	Sat	
21	Sun	
22	Mon	
23	Tue	
24	Wed	
25	Thu	
26	Fri	
27	Sat	
28	Sun	
29	Mon	*Late Summer Holiday (not Scotland)*
30	Tue	
31	Wed	

BIRD NOTES AUGUST 2005

DIARY - SEPTEMBER 2005

1	Thu	
2	Fri	
3	Sat	
4	Sun	
5	Mon	
6	Tue	
7	Wed	
8	Thu	
9	Fri	
10	Sat	
11	Sun	
12	Mon	
13	Tue	
14	Wed	
15	Thu	
16	Fri	
17	Sat	
18	Sun	
19	Mon	
20	Tue	
21	Wed	
22	Thu	
23	Fri	
24	Sat	
25	Sun	
26	Mon	
27	Tue	
28	Wed	
29	Thu	
30	Fri	

BIRD NOTES -SEPTEMBER 2005

DIARY - OCTOBER 2005

1	Sat	
2	Sun	
3	Mon	
4	Tue	
5	Wed	
6	Thu	
7	Fri	
8	Sat	
9	Sun	
10	Mon	
11	Tue	
12	Wed	
13	Thu	
14	Fri	
15	Sat	
16	Sun	
17	Mon	
18	Tue	
19	Wed	
20	Thu	
21	Fri	
22	Sat	
23	Sun	
24	Mon	
25	Tue	
26	Wed	
27	Thu	
28	Fri	
29	Sat	*British Summertime ends*
30	Sun	
31	Mon	

DIARY - NOVEMBER 2005

1	Tue	
2	Wed	
3	Thu	
4	Fri	
5	Sat	
6	Sun	
7	Mon	
8	Tue	
9	Wed	
10	Thu	
11	Fri	
12	Sat	
13	Sun	*Remembrance Sunday*
14	Mon	
15	Tue	
16	Wed	
17	Thu	
18	Fri	
19	Sat	
20	Sun	
21	Mon	
22	Tue	
23	Wed	
24	Thu	
25	Fri	
26	Sat	
27	Sun	
28	Mon	
29	Tue	
30	Wed	

DIARY - DECEMBER 2005

1	Thu	
2	Fri	
3	Sat	
4	Sun	
5	Mon	
6	Tue	
7	Wed	
8	Thu	
9	Fri	
10	Sat	
11	Sun	
12	Mon	
13	Tue	
14	Wed	
15	Thu	
16	Fri	
17	Sat	
18	Sun	
19	Mon	
20	Tue	
21	Wed	
22	Thu	
23	Fri	
24	Sat	
25	Sun	*Christmas Day*
26	Mon	*Boxing Day*
27	Tue	*Bank Holiday*
28	Wed	
29	Thu	
30	Fri	
31	Sat	

BIRD NOTES -DECEMBER 2005

YEAR PLANNER 2006

January
February
March
April
May
June
July
August
September
October
November
December

LOG CHARTS

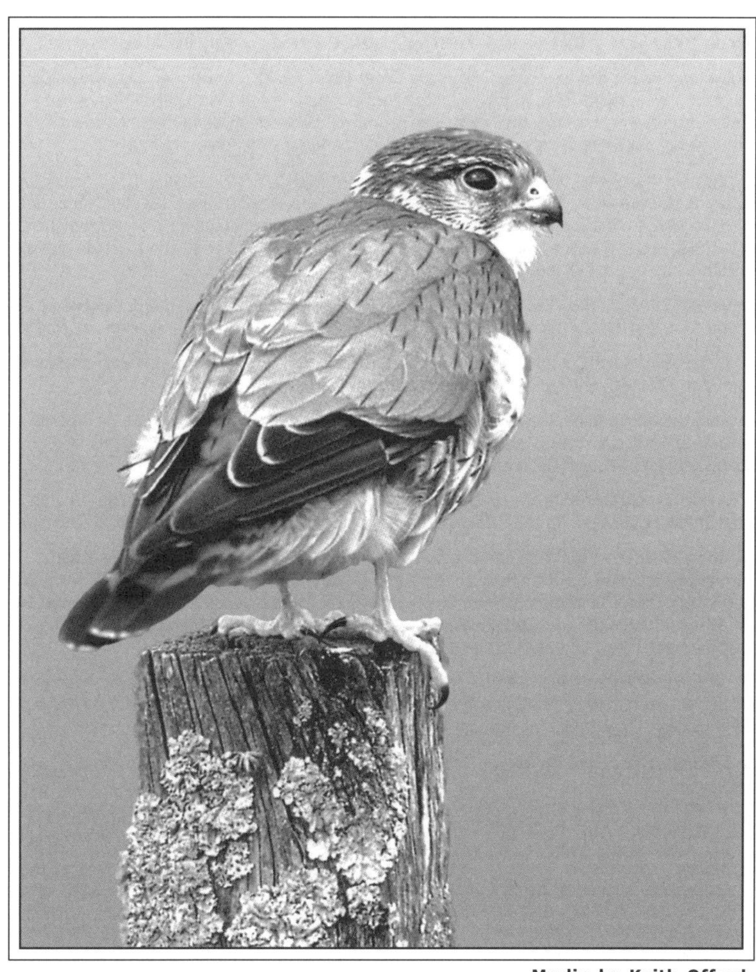

Merlin by Keith Offord

NEW ORDER OF THE BRITISH LIST
an explanation

NEWCOMERS to birdwatching are sometimes baffled when they examine their first fieldguide as it is not immediately clear why the birds are arranged the way they are. The simple answer is the order is meant to reflect the evolution of the included species. If one were to draw an evolutionary tree of birds, those families that branch off earliest (i.e are the most ancient) should be listed first.

Previously the British List was based on Voous Order (BOU 1977), the work of an eminent Dutch taxonomist. However, more than 26 phylogenetic studies, many using DNA analysis, have been published in recent years that together form a large body of evidence showing that the order of birds in the British List did not properly reflect their evolution. A change in order was required.

The British Ornithologists' Union's Records Committee (BOURC) is responsible for maintaining the British List and it relies on its Taxonomic Sub-Committee (BOURC-TSC) to advise on taxonomic issues relating to the species that form the British List. This advice usually takes the form of recommendations relating to the status of a species or sub-species which sometimes results in 'splitting' (creating two or more species from a single species) and 'lumping' (creating a single species from two or more).

At the end of 2002, BOURC-TSC recommended that the order of species on the British List be changed as it accepted the most likely hypotheses for bird evolution stemmed from the following key characters:

1. That the deepest branch point in the evolutionary tree of birds splits them into the Palaeognathae (tinamous and 'ratites') and the Neognathae (all other birds).
2. That within the Neognathae, the deepest branch-point splits them into Galloanserae (composed of two 'sister' groups – Anseriformes (waterfowl) and Galliformes (turkeys, guineafowl, megapodes, grouse, pheasants etc) and Neoaves (all remaining birds).
3. The World list would therefore start with Palaeognathae, but because only Neognathae occur in Britain, the new British List starts with the Galloanserae, as the deepest split from all other birds (Neoaves).

Within the Galloanserae there are fewer species of Anseriformes than Galliformes, therefore Anseriformes are listed first in accordance with normal custom. The orders of families within these groups remains unchanged, so the British List now starts with Anatidae (swans, ducks, geese), followed by Tetraonidae and Phasianidae (grouse, pheasants, quail and partridges), followed by all remaining families as in the old order (divers, grebes etc).

These recommendations have been accepted by the British Ornithologists' Union who have advised all book, magazine and bird report editors and publishers to begin using the new order as soon as possible and preferably no later than the publication of reports covering the year 2003.

Martin Collinson & Steve Dudley - British Ornithologists' Union

SPECIES, CATEGORIES, CODES AND GUIDE TO USE

Species list
The charts include all species on the British List and is based on the 1992 *BOU Checklist of Birds of Britain and Ireland* and the various BOURC reports published up to September 2002, when a major revision of taxonomic order was announced by the BOU.

The current list is augmented by birds which breed or occur regularly in Europe - almost 600 species altogether. Vagrants which are not on the British List, but which may have occurred in other parts of the British Isles, are not included. Readers who wish to record such species may use the extra rows provided on the last page. In this connection it should be noted that separate lists exist for Northern Ireland (kept by the Northern Ireland Birdwatchers' Association) and the Isle of Man (kept by the Manx Ornithological Society), and that Irish records are assessed by the Irish Rare Birds Committee.

Taxonomic changes introduced last year mean there is a new order of species (as outlined on the previous page). The species names are those most widely used in the current field guides (with some proposed changes shown in parentheses); each is followed by its scientific name, printed in italics.

Species categories
The following categories are those assigned by the British Ornithologists' Union.

A Species which have been recorded in an apparently natural state at least once since January 1, 1950.

B Species which would otherwise be in Category A but have not been recorded since December 31, 1949.

C Species that, although originally introduced by man, either deliberately or accidentally, have established breeding populations derived from introduced stock that maintain themselves without necessary recourse to further introduction. (This category has been subdivided to differentiate between various groups of naturalised species, but these subdivisions are outside the purpose of the log charts).

D Species that would otherwise appear in Categories A or B except that there is reasonable doubt that they have ever occurred in a natural state. (Species in this category are included in the log charts, though they do not qualify for inclusion in the British List, which comprises species in Categories A, B and C only. One of the objects of Category D is to note records of species which are not yet full additions, so that they are not overlooked if acceptable records subsequently occur. Bird report editors are encouraged to include records of species in Category D as appendices to their systematic lists).

E Species that have been recorded as introductions, transportees or escapees from captivity, and whose populations (if any) are thought not to be self-sustaining. They do not form part of the British List and are not included in the log charts.

EU Species not on the British List, or in Category D, but which either breed or occur regularly elsewhere in Europe.

Life list
Ticks made in the 'Life List' column suffice for keeping a running personal total of species. However, added benefit can be obtained by replacing ticks with a note of the year of first occurrence. To take an example: one's first-ever Marsh Sandpiper, seen on April 14, 2004, would be logged with '04' in the Life List and '14' in the April column (as well as a tick in the 2004 column). As Life List entries are carried forward annually, in years to come it would be a simple matter to relocate this record.

First and last dates of migrants
Arrivals of migrants can be recorded by inserting dates instead of ticks in the relevant month columns. For example, a Common Sandpiper on March 11 would be recorded by inserting '11' against Common Sandpiper in the March column. The same applies to departures, though dates of last sightings can only be entered at the end of the year after checking one's field notebook.

Unheaded columns
The three unheaded columns at the right hand end of each chart are for special (personal) use. This may be, for example, a, second holiday, a particular county or a 'local patch'. Another use could be to indicate species on, for example, the Northern Ireland List or the Isle of Man List.

BTO species codes
British Trust for Ornithology two-letter species codes are shown in brackets in the fourth column from the right. They exist for many species, races and hybrids recorded in recent surveys. Readers should refer to the BTO if more codes are needed. In addition to those given in the charts, the following are available for some well-marked races or forms - Whistling Swan (WZ), European White-fronted Goose (EW), Greenland White-fronted Goose (NW), dark-bellied Brent Goose (DB), pale-bellied Brent Goose (PB), Black Brant (BB), domestic goose (ZL), Green-winged Teal (TA), domestic duck (ZF), Yellow-legged Gull (YG), Kumlien's Gull (KG), Feral Pigeon (FP), White Wagtail (WB), Black-bellied Dipper (DJ), Hooded Crow (HC), intermediate crow (HB).

Rarities
Rarities are indicated by a capital letter 'R' immediately preceding the 'Euring No.' column.

EURING species numbers
EURING species numbers are given in the last column. As they are taken from the full Holarctic bird list there are many apparent gaps. It is important that these are not filled arbitrarily by observers wishing to record species not listed in the charts, as this would compromise the integrity of the scheme. Similarly, the addition of a further digit to indicate sub-species is to be avoided, since EURING has already assigned numbers for this purpose. The numbering follows the Voous order of species.

Rare breeding birds
Species monitored by the Rare Breeding Birds Panel (see National Directory) comprise all those on Schedule 1 of the Wildlife and Countryside Act 1981 (see Quick Reference) together with all escaped or introduced species breeding in small numbers. The following annotations in the charts (third column from the right) reflect the RBBP's categories:

- (b)^A Rare species. All breeding details requested.
- (b)^B Less scarce species. Totals requested from counties with more than 10 pairs or localities; elsewhere all details requested.
- (b)^C Less scarce species (specifically Barn Owl, Kingfisher, Crossbill). County summaries requested.
- (b)^D Escaped or introduced species. Treated as less scarce species.

LOG CHART FOR THE MOST COMMONLY-OCCURRING SPECIES IN THE UK

	SWANS, GEESE, DUCKS		Life list	2004 list	24 hr	Garden	Holiday	Jan	Feb	Mar	Apr	May	Jun	Jul	Aug	Sep	Oct	Nov	Dec				BTO	RBBP	Bou	EU No
A C	**Mute Swan**	*Cygnus olor*																					M S			0152
A	**Bewick's (Tundra) Swan**	*C. columbianus*																					B S			0153
A	**Whooper Swan**	*C. cygnus*																					W S	b^{AD}		0154
A	**Bean Goose**	*Anser fabalis*																					B E	b^{D}		0157
A	**Pink-footed Goose**	*A. brachyrhynchus*																					P G	b^{AD}		0158
A	**White-fronted Goose**	*A. albifrons*																					W G	b^{D}		0159
A	**Lesser White-fr Goose**	*A. erythropus*																					L C	b^{B}	R	0160
A C	**Greylag Goose**	*A. anser*																					G J			0161
A	**Snow Goose**	*A. caerulescens*																					S J	b^{D}		0163
A C	**Canada Goose**	*Branta canadensis*																					C G			0166
A	**Barnacle Goose**	*B. leucopsis*																					B Y	b^{D}		0167
A	**Brent Goose**	*B. bernicla*																					B G	b^{D}		0168
C	**Egyptian Goose**	*Alopochen aegyptiacus*																					E G	b^{D}		0170
B	**Ruddy Shelduck**	*Tadorna ferruginea*																					U D	b^{D}		0171
A	**Shelduck**	*T. tadorna*																					S U			0173
C	**Mandarin Duck**	*Aix galericulata*																					M N			0178
A	**Wigeon**	*Anas penelope*																					W N	b^{B}		0179
A C	**Gadwall**	*A. strepera*																					G A	b^{B}		0182
A	**Eurasian Teal**	*A. crecca*																					T			0184
A C	**Mallard**	*A. platyrhynchos*																					M A			0186
	Sub-total																									

	DUCKS, GAMEBIRDS		Life list	2005 list	24 hr	Garden	Holiday	Jan	Feb	Mar	Apr	May	Jun	Jul	Aug	Sep	Oct	Nov	Dec				BTO	RBBP	Bou	EU No
A	**Pintail**	*A. acuta*																					P T	b^A		0189
A	**Garganey**	*A. querquedula*																					G Y	b^A		0191
A	**Shoveler**	*A. clypeata*																					S V			0194
A	**Red-crested Pochard**	*Netta rufina*																					R Q	b^D		0196
A	**Pochard**	*A. ferina*																					P O	b^B		0198
A	**Tufted Duck**	*A. fuligula*																					T U			0203
A	**Scaup**	*A. marila*																					S P	b^A		0204
A	**Lesser Scaup**	*A. affinis*																					A Y		R	0205
A	**Eider**	*Somateria mollissima*																					E			0206
A	**King Eider**	*S. spectabilis*																					K E		R	0207
A	**Long-tailed Duck**	*Clangula hyemalis*																					LN	b^A		0212
A	**Common Scoter**	*Melanitta nigra*																					CX	b^A		0213
A	**Velvet Scoter**	*M. fusca*																					V S			0215
A	**Goldeneye**	*B. clangula*																					G N	b^{AD}		0218
A	**Smew**	*Mergellus albellus*																					S Y			0220
A	**Red-breasted Merganser**	*Mergus serrator*																					R M			0221
A	**Goosander**	*M. merganser*																					G D			0223
c	**Ruddy Duck**	*Oxyura jamaicensis*																					B Y			0225
A	**Red (Willow) Grouse**	*Lagopus lagopus*																					R G			0329
A	**Ptarmigan**	*L. mutus*																					P M			0330
A	**Black Grouse**	*Tetrao tetrix*																					B K			0332
B C	**Capercaillie**	*T. urogallus*																					C P			0335
C	**Red-legged Partridge**	*A. rufa*																					RL			0358
A C	**Grey Partridge**	*Perdix perdix*																					P			0367
	Sub-total																									

	GAMEBIRDS, DIVERS, GREBES, FULMAR, PETRELS, SHEARWATERS, HERONS		Life list	2004 list	24 hr	Garden	Holiday	Jan	Feb	Mar	Apr	May	Jun	Jul	Aug	Sep	Oct	Nov	Dec				BTO	RBBP	Bou	EU No
A	**Quail**	*Coturnix coturnix*																					Q	b^B		0370
C	**Pheasant**	*Phasianus colchicus*																					P H			0394
C	**Golden Pheasant**	*Chrysolophus pictus*																					G F	b^D		0396
C	**Lady Amherst's Pheasant**	*C. amherstiae*																					LM	b^D		0397
A	**Red-throated Diver**	*Gavia stellata*																					R H	b^B		0002
A	**Black-throated Diver**	*G. arctica*																					B V	b^A		0003
A	**Great Northern Diver**	*G. immer*																					N D			0004
A	**Little Grebe**	*Tachybaptus ruficollis*																					LG			0007
A	**Great Crested Grebe**	*Podiceps cristatus*																					G G			0009
A	**Red-necked Grebe**	*P. grisegena*																					RX	b^A		0010
A	**Slavonian Grebe**	*P. auritus*																					SZ	b^A		0011
A	**Black-necked Grebe**	*P. nigricollis*																					B N	b^A		0012
A	**Fulmar**	*Fulmarus glacialis*																					F			0020
A	***'Soft-plumaged Petrel**	*Pterodroma mollis/madeira/feae*																							R	0026
A	**Sooty Shearwater**	*P. griseus*																					O T			0043
A	**Manx Shearwater**	*P. Puffinus*																					MX			0046
A	**Wilson's Petrel**	*Oceanites oceanicus*																							R	0050
A	**Storm Petrel**	*Hydrobates pelagicus*																					T M			0052
A	**Leach's Petrel**	*Oceanodroma leucorhoa*																					TL	b^B		0055
A	**Gannet**	*Morus bassanus*																					GX			0071
A	**Cormorant**	*Phalacrocorax carbo*																					C A			0072
A	**Shag**	*P. aristotelis*																					S A			0080
A	**Bittern**	*Botaurus stellaris*																					BI	b^A		0095
A	**Little Egret**	*Egretta garzetta*																					E T	b^A		0119
	Sub-total																									

*Alternative sub-species

	HERON, SPOONBILL, RAPTORS, RAILS		Life list	2005 list	24 hr	Garden	Holiday	Jan	Feb	Mar	Apr	May	Jun	Jul	Aug	Sep	Oct	Nov	Dec				BTO	RBBP	Bou	EU No
A	**Grey Heron**	*A. cinerea*																					H			0122
A	**Spoonbill**	*Platalea leucorodia*																					N B	b^{A}		0144
A	**Honey Buzzard**	*Pernis apivorus*																					H Z	b^{A}		0231
A C	**Red Kite**	*M. milvus*																					K T	b^{A}		0239
A	**White-tailed Eagle**	*Haliaeetus albicilla*																					W E	b^{A}		0243
A	**Marsh Harrier**	*Circus aeruginosus*																					M R	b^{A}		0260
A	**Hen Harrier**	*C. cyaneus*																					H H	b^{B}		0261
A	**Montagu's Harrier**	*C. pygargus*																					M O	b^{A}		0263
A C	**Goshawk**	*Accipiter gentilis*																					G I	b^{B}		0267
A	**Sparrowhawk**	*A. nisus*																					S H			0269
A	**Buzzard**	*Buteo buteo*																					B Z			0287
A	**Rough-legged Buzzard**	*B. lagopus*																					R F			0290
A	**Golden Eagle**	*A. chrysaetos*																					E A	b^{B}		0296
A	**Osprey**	*Pandion haliaetus*																					O P	b^{A}		0301
A	**Kestrel**	*F. tinnunculus*																					K			0304
A	**Red-footed Falcon**	*F. vespertinus*																					F V		R	0307
A	**Merlin**	*F. columbarius*																					M L	b^{B}		0309
A	**Hobby**	*F. subbuteo*																					H Y	b^{B}		0310
A	**Gyrfalcon**	*F. rusticolus*																					Y F		R	0318
A	**Peregrine**	*F. peregrinus*																					P E	b^{B}		0320
A	**Water Rail**	*Rallus aquaticus*																					W A			0407
A	**Spotted Crake**	*Porzana porzana*																					A K	b^{A}		0408
A	**Corncrake**	*Crex crex*																					C E	b^{A}		0421
A	**Moorhen**	*Gallinula chloropus*																					M H			0424
	Sub-total																									

	RAIL, CRANE, WADERS		Life list	2004 list	24 hr	Garden	Holiday	Jan	Feb	Mar	Apr	May	Jun	Jul	Aug	Sep	Oct	Nov	Dec				BTO	RBBP	Bou	EU No
A	**Coot**	*Fulica atra*																					C O			0429
A	**Crane**	*Grus grus*																					A N	b^A		0433
A	**Oystercatcher**	*Haematopus ostralegus*																					O C			0450
A	**Black-winged Stilt**	*Himantopus himantopus*																					I T		R	0455
A	**Avocet**	*Recurvirostra avosetta*																					A V	b^A		0456
A	**Stone Curlew**	*Burhinus oedicnemus*																					T N	b^A		0459
A	**Little Ringed Plover**	*Charadrius dubius*																					LP	b^B		0469
A	**Ringed Plover**	*C. hiaticula*																					R P			0470
A	**Dotterel**	*C. morinellus*																					D O	b^B		0482
A	**Golden Plover**	*P. apricaria*																					G P			0485
A	**Grey Plover**	*P. squatarola*																					G V			0486
A	**Lapwing**	*V. vanellus*																					L			0493
A	**Knot**	*C. canutus*																					K N			0496
A	**Sanderling**	*C. alba*																					S S			0497
A	**Little Stint**	*C. minuta*																					LX			0501
A	**Temminck's Stint**	*C. temminckii*																					T K	b^A		0502
A	**Curlew Sandpiper**	*C. ferruginea*																					C V			0509
A	**Purple Sandpiper**	*C. maritima*																					P S	b^A		0510
A	**Dunlin**	*C. alpina*																					D N			0512
A	**Ruff**	*Philomachus pugnax*																					R U	b^A		0517
A	**Jack Snipe**	*Lymnocryptes minimus*																					J S			0518
A	**Snipe**	*Gallinago gallinago*																					S N			0519
A	**Woodcock**	*Scolopax rusticola*																					W K			0529
A	**Black-tailed Godwit**	*Limosa limosa*																					B W	b^A		0532
	Sub-total																									

WADERS (cont), PHALAROPES, SKUAS, GULLS			Life list	2005 list	24 hr	Garden	Holiday	Jan	Feb	Mar	Apr	May	Jun	Jul	Aug	Sep	Oct	Nov	Dec				BTO	RBBP	Bou	EU No
A	**Bar-tailed Godwit**	*L. lapponica*																					B A			0534
A	**Whimbrel**	*N. phaeopus*																					W M	b[A]		0538
A	**Curlew**	*N. arquata*																					C U			0541
A	**Spotted Redshank**	*T. erythropus*																					D R			0545
A	**Redshank**	*T. totanus*																					R K			0546
A	**Marsh Sandpiper**	*T. stagnatilis*																					M D		R	0547
A	**Greenshank**	*T. nebularia*																					G K	b[B]		0548
A	**Green Sandpiper**	*T. ochropus*																					G E			0553
A	**Wood Sandpiper**	*T. glareola*																					O D	b[A]		0554
A	**Common Sandpiper**	*Actitis hypoleucos*																					C S			0556
A	**Turnstone**	*Arenaria interpres*																					T T			0561
A	**Red-necked Phalarope**	*P. lobatus*																					N K	b[A]		0564
A	**Grey Phalarope**	*P. fulicarius*																					PL			0565
A	**Pomarine Skua**	*Stercorarius pomarinus*																					P K			0566
A	**Arctic Skua**	*S. parasiticus*																					A C			0567
A	**Long-tailed Skua**	*S. longicaudus*																					O G			0568
A	**Great Skua**	*Catharacta skua*																					NX			0569
A	**Mediterranean Gull**	*L. melanocephalus*																					M U	b[A]		0575
A	**Laughing Gull**	*L. atricilla*																					LF		R	0576
A	**Little Gull**	*L. minutus*																					LU			0578
A	**Sabine's Gull**	*L. sabini*																					A B			0579
A	**Black-headed Gull**	*L. ridibundus*																					B H			0582
A	**Ring-billed Gull**	*L. delawarensis*																					I N			0589
A	**Common (Mew) Gull**	*L. canus*																					C M			0590
	Sub-total																									

	GULLS (cont), TERNS, AUKS, DOVES/PIGEONS		Life list	2004 list	24 hr	Garden	Holiday	Jan	Feb	Mar	Apr	May	Jun	Jul	Aug	Sep	Oct	Nov	Dec				BTO	RBBP	Bou	EU No
A	**Lesser Black-backed Gull**	*L. fuscus*																					LB			0591
A	**Herring Gull**	*L. argentatus*																					H G			0592
A	**Iceland Gull**	*L. glaucoides*																					I G			0598
A	**Glaucous Gull**	*L. hyperboreus*																					GZ			0599
A	**Great Black-backed Gull**	*L. marinus*																					G B			0600
A	**Kittiwake**	*Rissa tridactyla*																					KI			0602
A	**Sandwich Tern**	*S.sandvicensis*																					T E			0611
A	**Roseate Tern**	*S.dougallii*																					R S	b[A]		0614
A	**Common Tern**	*S.hirundo*																					C N			0615
A	**Arctic Tern**	*S.paradisaea*																					A E			0616
A	**Little Tern**	*S.albifrons*																					A F	b[B]		0624
A	**Whiskered Tern**	*Chlidonias hybrida*																					WD		R	0626
A	**Black Tern**	*C. niger*																					BJ			0627
A	**White-winged Black Tern**	*C. leucopterus*																					WJ		R	0628
A	**Guillemot**	*Uria aalge*																					G U			0634
A	**Razorbill**	*Alca torda*																					R A			0636
A	**Black Guillemot**	*Cepphus grylle*																					T Y			0638
A	**Little Auk**	*Alle alle*																					LK			0647
A	**Puffin**	*Fratercula arctica*																					P U			0654
A C	**Rock Dove**	*Columba livia*																					D V			0665
A	**Stock Dove**	*C. oenas*																					S D			0668
A	**Woodpigeon**	*C. palumbus*																					W P			0670
A	**Collared Dove**	*Streptopelia decaocto*																					C D			0684
A	**Turtle Dove**	*S. turtur*																					T D			0687
	Sub-total																									

CUCKOO, OWLS, KINGFISHER, HOOPOO, WOODPECKERS, MARTINS, SWALLOW			Life list	2005 list	24 hr	Garden	Holiday	Jan	Feb	Mar	Apr	May	Jun	Jul	Aug	Sep	Oct	Nov	Dec				BTO	RBBP	Bou	EU No
C	**Rose-ringed Parakeet**	*Psittacula krameri*																					RI	b^D		0712
A	**Cuckoo**	*Cuculus canorus*																					CK			0724
A	**Barn Owl**	*Tyto alba*																					BO	b^C		0735
A	**Snowy Owl**	*Nyctea scandiaca*																					SO	b^A	R	0749
c	**Little Owl**	*Athene noctua*																					LO			0757
A	**Tawny Owl**	*Strix aluco*																					TO			0761
A	**Long-eared Owl**	*Asio otus*																					LE			0767
A	**Short-eared Owl**	*A. flammeus*																					SE			0768
A	**Nightjar**	*Caprimulgus europaeus*																					NJ			0778
A	**Swift**	*Apus apus*																					SI			0795
A	**Kingfisher**	*Alcedo atthis*																					KF	b^C		0831
A	**Bee-eater**	*M. apiaster*																					MZ			0840
A	**Hoopoe**	*Upupa epops*																					HP			0846
A	**Wryneck**	*Jynx torquilla*																					WY	b^A		0848
A	**Green Woodpecker**	*P. viridis*																					G			0856
A	**Great Spotted Woodpecker**	*Dendrocopos major*																					GS			0876
A	**Lesser Spotted Woodpecker**	*D. minor*																					LS			0887
A	**Wood Lark**	*Lullula arborea*																					WL	b^B		0974
A	**Sky Lark**	*Alauda arvensis*																					S			0976
A	**Shore (Horned) Lark**	*Eremophila alpestris*																					SX			0978
A	**Sand Martin**	*Riparia riparia*																					SM			0981
A	**Swallow**	*Hirundo rustica*																					SL			0992
A	**House Martin**	*Delichon urbica*																					HM			1001
A	**Tree Pipit**	*A. trivialis*																					TP			1009
	Sub-total																									

PIPITS, WAGTAILS, WAXWING, DIPPER, WREN, CHATS, THRUSHES, WARBLERS			Life list	2004 list	24 hr	Garden	Holiday	Jan	Feb	Mar	Apr	May	Jun	Jul	Aug	Sep	Oct	Nov	Dec				BTO	RBBP	Bou	EU No
A	**Meadow Pipit**	*A. pratensis*																					M P			1011
A	**Rock Pipit**	*A. petrosus*																					R C			1014
A	**Water Pipit**	*A. spinoletta*																					WI			1014
A	**Yellow Wagtail**	*Motacilla flava*																					YW			1017
A	**Grey Wagtail**	*M. cinerea*																					GL			1019
A	**Pied (White) Wagtail**	*M. alba*																					P W			1020
A	**(Bohemian) Waxwing**	*Bombycilla garrulus*																					WX			1048
A	**Dipper**	*Cinclus cinclus*																					D I			1050
A	**Wren**	*Troglodytes troglodytes*																					WR			1066
A	**Dunnock**	*Prunella modularis*																					D			1084
A	**Robin**	*Erithacus rubecula*																					R			1099
A	**Nightingale**	*L. megarhynchos*																					N			1104
A	**Black Redstart**	*Phoenicurus ochruros*																					BX	b^A		1121
A	**Redstart**	*P. phoenicurus*																					R T			1122
A	**Whinchat**	*Saxicola rubetra*																					W C			1137
A	**Stonechat**	*S. torquata*																					S C			1139
A	**Wheatear**	*O. O.*																					W			1146
A	**Ring Ouzel**	*Turdus torquatus*																					RZ			1186
A	**Blackbird**	*T. merula*																					B			1187
A	**Fieldfare**	*T. pilaris*																					F F	b^A		1198
A	**Song Thrush**	*T. philomelos*																					S T			1200
A	**Redwing**	*T. iliacus*																					R E	b^A		1201
A	**Mistle Thrush**	*T. viscivorus*																					M			1202
A	**Cetti's Warbler**	*Cettia cetti*																					C W	b^A		1220
	Sub-total																									

	WARBLERS (cont), 'CRESTS', FLYCATCHERS, TITS		Life list	2005 list	24 hr	Garden	Holiday	Jan	Feb	Mar	Apr	May	Jun	Jul	Aug	Sep	Oct	Nov	Dec				BTO	RBBP	Bou	EU No
A	**Grasshopper Warbler**	*L.naevia*																					G H			1236
A	**Sedge Warbler**	*A. schoenobaenus*																					S W			1243
A	**Marsh Warbler**	*A. palustris*																					M W	b[A]		1250
A	**Reed Warbler**	*A. scirpaceus*																					R W			1251
A	**Icterine Warbler**	*H. icterina*																					I C			1259
A	**Melodious Warbler**	*H. polyglotta*																					M E			1260
A	**Dartford Warbler**	*S. undata*																					D W	b[B]		1262
A	**Lesser Whitethroat**	*S. curruca*																					LW			1274
A	**Whitethroat**	*S. communis*																					W H			1275
A	**Garden Warbler**	*S. borin*																					G W			1276
A	**Blackcap**	*S. atricapilla*																					B C			1277
A	**Yellow-browed Warbler**	*P. inornatus*																					Y B			1300
A	**Wood Warbler**	*P. sibilatrix*																					W O			1308
A	**Common Chiffchaff**	*P. collybita*																					C C			1311
A	**Willow Warbler**	*P. trochilus*																					WW			1312
A	**Goldcrest**	*Regulus regulus*																					G C			1314
A	**Firecrest**	*R. ignicapilla*																					F C	b[A]		1315
A	**Spotted Flycatcher**	*Muscicapa striata*																								1335
A	**Red-breasted Flycatcher**	*Ficedula parva*																					F Y			1343
A	**Pied Flycatcher**	*F. hypoleuca*																					P F			1349
A	**Bearded Tit**	*Panurus biarmicus*																					BR	b[B]		1364
A	**Long-tailed Tit**	*Aegithalos caudatus*																					LT			1437
A	**Marsh Tit**	*Parus palustris*																					M T			1440
A	**Willow Tit**	*P. montanus*																					WT			1442
	Sub-total																									

	TITS (cont), NUTHATCH, ORIOLE, SHRIKES, CORVIDS, STARLING, SPARROWS, FINCHES		Life list	2004 list	24 hr	Garden	Holiday	Jan	Feb	Mar	Apr	May	Jun	Jul	Aug	Sep	Oct	Nov	Dec				BTO	RBBP	Bou	EU No
A	**Crested Tit**	*P.cristatus*																					C I	b[B]		1454
A	**Coal Tit**	*P. ater*																					C T			1461
A	**Blue Tit**	*P. caeruleus*																					B T			1462
A	**Great Tit**	*P. major*																					G T			1464
A	**Nuthatch**	*S. europaea*																					N H			1479
A	**Treecreeper**	*Certhia familiaris*																					T C			1486
A	**Golden Oriole**	*Oriolus oriolus*																					O L	b[A]		1508
A	**Red-backed Shrike**	*L. collurio*																					E D	b[A]		1515
A	**Lesser Grey Shrike**	*L. minor*																							R	1519
A	**Great Grey Shrike**	*L. excubitor*																					S R			1520
A	**Jay**	*Garrulus glandarius*																					J			1539
A	**Magpie**	*Pica pica*																					M G			1549
A	**Chough**	*P. pyrrhocorax*																					C F	b[B]		1559
A	**Jackdaw**	*Corvus monedula*																					J D			1560
A	**Rook**	*C. frugilegus*																					R O			1563
A	**Carrion (Hooded) Crow**	*C. corone*																					C			1567
A	**Hooded Crow**	*C. cornix*																								
A	**Raven**	*C. corax*																					R N			1572
A	**Starling**	*S. vulgaris*																					S G			1582
A	**House Sparrow**	*Passer domesticus*																					H S			1591
A	**Tree Sparrow**	*P.r montanus*																					T S			1598
A	**Chaffinch**	*Fringilla coelebs*																					C H			1636
A	**Brambling**	*F. montifringilla*																					BL	b[A]		1638
A	**Serin**	*Serinus serinus*																					N S	b[A]		1640
	Sub-total																									

	FINCHES (cont), BUNTINGS		Life list	2005 list	24 hr	Garden	Holiday	Jan	Feb	Mar	Apr	May	Jun	Jul	Aug	Sep	Oct	Nov	Dec				BTO	RBBP	Bou	EU No
A	**Greenfinch**	*Carduelis chloris*																					G R			1649
A	**Goldfinch**	*C carduelis*																					G O			1653
A	**Siskin**	*C. spinus*																					S K			1654
A	**Linnet**	*C. cannabina*																					LI			1660
A	**Twite**	*C. flavirostris*																					T W			1662
	Lesser Redpoll	*C. cabaret*																								
A	**Mealy Redpoll**	*C. flammea*																					LR			1663
A	**Two-barred Crossbill**	*Loxia leucoptera*																					P D		R	1665
A	**Crossbill**	*L. curvirostra*																					C R	b^{C}		1666
A	**Scottish Crossbill**	*L. scotica*																					C Y	b^{B}		1667
A	**Parrot Crossbill**	*L. pytyopsittacus*																					P C	b^{A}	R	1668
A	**Common Rosefinch**	*Carpodacus erythrinus*																					S Q	b^{A}		1679
A	**Bullfinch**	*Pyrrhula pyrrhula*																					B F			1710
A	**Hawfinch**	*Coccothraustes coccothraustes*																					H F			1717
A	**Snow Bunting**	*Plectrophenax nivalis*																					S B	b^{A}		1850
A	**Yellowhammer**	*E. citrinella*																					Y			1857
A	**Cirl Bunting**	*E. cirlus*																					C L	b^{A}		1958
A	**Reed Bunting**	*E. schoeniclus*																					R B			1877
A	**Corn Bunting**	*Miliaria calandra*																					C B			1882
	Sub-total																									

BOU-APPROVED BRITISH LIST

SWANS, GEESE, DUCKS			Life list	2005 list			BTO	RBBP	BOU	EU No
AC	**Mute Swan**	*Cygnus olor*					MS			0152
A	**Bewick's (Tundra) Swan**	*C. columbianus*					BS			0153
A	**Whooper Swan**	*C. cygnus*					WS	b^{AD}		0154
A	**Bean Goose**	*Anser fabalis*					BE	b^{D}		0157
A	**Pink-footed Goose**	*A. brachyrhynchus*					PG	b^{AD}		0158
A	**White-fronted Goose**	*A. albifrons*					WG	b^{D}		0159
A	**Lesser White-fr Goose**	*A. erythropus*					LC	b^{B}	R	0160
AC	**Greylag Goose**	*A. anser*					GJ			0161
A	**Snow Goose**	*A. caerulescens*					SJ	b^{D}		0163
AC	**Canada Goose**	*Branta canadensis*					CG			0166
A	**Barnacle Goose**	*B. leucopsis*					BY	b^{D}		0167
A	**Brent Goose**	*B. bernicla*					BG	b^{D}		0168
A	**Red-breasted Goose**	*B. ruficollis*					EB	b^{B}	R	0169
C	**Egyptian Goose**	*Alopochen aegyptiacus*					EG	b^{D}		0170
B	**Ruddy Shelduck**	*Tadorna ferruginea*					UD	b^{D}		0171
A	**Shelduck**	*T. tadorna*					SU			0173
C	**Mandarin Duck**	*Aix galericulata*					MN			0178
A	**Wigeon**	*Anas penelope*					WN	b^{B}		0179
A	**American Wigeon**	*A. americana*					AW		R	0180
D	**Falcated Duck**	*A. falcata*					FT		R	0181
AC	**Gadwall**	*A. strepera*					GA	b^{B}		0182
D	**Baikal Teal**	*A. formosa*					IK		R	0183
A	**Eurasian Teal**	*A. crecca*					T			0184
A	**Green-winged Teal**	*A. carolinensis*								
AC	**Mallard**	*A. platyrhynchos*					MA			0186
A	**American Black Duck**	*A. rubripes*					BD		R	0187
A	**Pintail**	*A. acuta*					PT	b^{A}		0189
A	**Garganey**	*A. querquedula*					GY	b^{A}		0191
A	**Blue-winged Teal**	*A. discors*					TB	b^{B}	R	0192
A	**Shoveler**	*A. clypeata*					SV			0194
D	**Marbled Duck**	*Marmaronetta angustirostris*							R	0195
A	**Red-crested Pochard**	*Netta rufina*					RQ	b^{D}		0196
A	**Canvasback**	*Aythya valisineria*							R	0197
A	**Pochard**	*A. ferina*					PO	b^{B}		0198
A	**Redhead**	*A. americana*					AZ		R	0199
A	**Ring-necked Duck**	*A. collaris*					NG			0200
A	**Ferruginous Duck**	*A. nyroca*					FD			0202
A	**Tufted Duck**	*A. fuligula*					TU			0203
A	**Scaup**	*A. marila*					SP	b^{A}		0204
A	**Lesser Scaup**	*A. affinis*					AY		R	0205
A	**Eider**	*Somateria mollissima*					E			0206
A	**King Eider**	*S. spectabilis*					KE		R	0207
A	**Steller's Eider**	*Polysticta stelleri*					ES		R	0209
A	**Harlequin**	*Histrionicus histrionicus*					HQ		R	0211
A	**Long-tailed Duck**	*Clangula hyemalis*					LN	b^{A}		0212
A	**Common Scoter**	*Melanitta nigra*					CX	b^{A}		0213
A	**Surf Scoter**	*M. perspicillata*					FS			0214
A	**Velvet Scoter**	*M. fusca*					VS			0215
A	**Bufflehead**	*Bucephala albeola*					VH		R	0216
A	**Barrow's Goldeneye**	*B. islandica*							R	0217
A	**Goldeneye**	*B. clangula*					GN	b^{AD}		0218
A	**Smew**	*Mergellus albellus*					SY			0220
A	**Red-breasted Merganser**	*Mergus serrator*					RM			0221
A	**Goosander**	*M. merganser*					GD			0223
Sub total										

	DUCKS, GAMEBIRDS, DIVERS, GREBES, PETRELS, SHEARWATERS, HERONS		**Life list**	**2005 list**			**BTO**	**RBBP**	**BOU**	**EU No**
C	**Ruddy Duck**	*Oxyura jamaicensis*					BY			0225
EU	**White-headed Duck**	*O. Leucocephala*					WQ			0226
EU	**Hazel Grouse**	*Bonasa bonasia*								0326
A	**Red (Willow) Grouse**	*Lagopus lagopus*					RG			0329
A	**Ptarmigan**	*L. mutus*					PM			0330
A	**Black Grouse**	*Tetrao tetrix*					BK			0332
BC	**Capercaillie**	*T. urogallus*					CP			0335
EU	**Rock Partridge**	*Alectoris graeca*								0357
C	**Red-legged Partridge**	*A. rufa*					RL			0358
EU	**Barbary Partridge**	*A. barbara*								0359
AC	**Grey Partridge**	*Perdix perdix*					P			0367
A	**Quail**	*Coturnix coturnix*					Q	b^{B}		0370
C	**Pheasant**	*Phasianus colchicus*					PH			0394
C	**Golden Pheasant**	*Chrysolophus pictus*					GF	b^{D}		0396
C	**Lady Amherst's Pheasant**	*C. amherstiae*					LM	b^{D}		0397
A	**Red-throated Diver**	*Gavia stellata*					RH	b^{B}		0002
A	**Black-throated Diver**	*G. arctica*					BV	b^{A}		0003
A	**Great Northern Diver**	*G. immer*					ND			0004
A	**White-(Yellow)billed Diver**	*G. adamsii*					IW		R	0005
A	**Pied-billed Grebe**	*Podilymbus podiceps*					PJ		R	0006
A	**Little Grebe**	*Tachybaptus ruficollis*					LG			0007
A	**Great Crested Grebe**	*Podiceps cristatus*					GG			0009
A	**Red-necked Grebe**	*P. grisegena*					RX	b^{A}		0010
A	**Slavonian Grebe**	*P. auritus*					SZ	b^{A}		0011
A	**Black-necked Grebe**	*P. nigricollis*					BN	b^{A}		0012
A	**Black-browed Albatross**	*Thalassarche melanophris*					AA		R	0014
A	**Fulmar**	*Fulmarus glacialis*					F			0020
A	***'Soft-plumaged Petrel'**	*Pterodroma mollis/madeira/feae*							R	0026
B	**Capped Petrel**	*Pterodroma hasitata*							R	0029
B	**Bulwer's Petrel**	*Bulweria bulwerii*							R	0034
A	**Cory's Shearwater**	*Calonectris diomedea*					CQ			0036
A	**Great Shearwater**	*Puffinus gravis*					GQ			0040
A	**Sooty Shearwater**	*P. griseus*					OT			0043
A	**Manx Shearwater**	*P. Puffinus*					MX			0046
A	**Mediterranean Shearwater**	*P. mauretanicus*								0046
A	**Little Shearwater**	*P. assimilis*							R	0048
A	**Wilson's Petrel**	*Oceanites oceanicus*							R	0050
B	**White-faced Petrel**	*Pelagodroma marina*							R	0051
A	**Storm Petrel**	*Hydrobates pelagicus*					TM			0052
A	**Leach's Petrel**	*Oceanodroma leucorhoa*					TL	b^{B}		0055
A	**Swinhoe's Petrel**	*O. monorhis*							R	0056
B	**Madeiran Petrel**	*O. castro*							R	0058
A	**Red-billed Tropicbird**	*Phaethon aethereus*								
A	**Gannet**	*Morus bassanus*					GX			0071
A	**Cormorant**	*Phalacrocorax carbo*					CA			0072
A	**Double-crested Cormorant**	*P. auritus*							R	0078
A	**Shag**	*P. aristotelis*					SA			0080
EU	**Pygmy Cormorant**	*P. pygmeus*								0082
D	**Great White Pelican**	*Pelecanus onocrotalus*					YP		R	0088
EU	**Dalmatian Pelican**	*P. crispus*								0089
A	**Ascension Frigatebird**	*Fregata aquila*							R	
A	**Bittern**	*Botaurus stellaris*					BI	b^{A}		0095
A	**American Bittern**	*B. lentiginosus*					AM		R	0096
A	**Little Bittern**	*Ixobrychus minutus*					LL		R	0098
A	**Night Heron**	*Nycticorax nycticorax*					NT	b^{AD}	R	0104
A	**Green Heron**	*Butorides virescens*					HR		R	0107
A	**Squacco Heron**	*Ardeola ralloides*					QH		R	0108
A	**Cattle Egret**	*Bubulcus ibis*					EC		R	0111
A	**Little Egret**	*Egretta garzetta*					ET	b^{A}		0119
	Sub total									

HERONS, RAPTORS, RAILS, CRAKES, GALLINULES, COOTS, CRANES

			Life list	2005 list			BTO	RBBP	BOU	EU No
A	**Great White Egret**	*Ardea alba*					HW		R	0121
A	**Grey Heron**	*A. cinerea*					H			0122
A	**Purple Heron**	*A. purpurea*					UR			0124
A	**Black Stork**	*Ciconia nigra*					OS		R	0131
A	**White Stork**	*C. ciconia*					OR			0134
A	**Glossy Ibis**	*Plegadis falcinellus*					IB			0136
A	**Spoonbill**	*Platalea leucorodia*					NB	b^A		0144
D	**Greater Flamingo**	*Phoenicopterus roseus*					FL		R	0147
A	**Honey Buzzard**	*Pernis apivorus*					HZ	b^A		0231
EU	**Black-winged Kite**	*Elanus caeruleus*								0235
A	**Black Kite**	*Milvus migrans*					KB		R	0238
AC	**Red Kite**	*M. milvus*					KT	b^A		0239
A	**White-tailed Eagle**	*Haliaeetus albicilla*					WE	b^A		0243
D	**Bald Eagle**	*H. leucocephalus*							R	0244
EU	**Lammergeier**	*Gypaetus barbatus*								0246
BD	**Egyptian Vulture**	*Neophron percnopterus*							R	0247
D	**Black (Monk) Vulture**	*Aegypius monachus*							R	0255
A	**Short-toed Eagle**	*Circaetus gallicus*								0256
A	**Marsh Harrier**	*Circus aeruginosus*					MR	b^A		0260
A	**Hen Harrier**	*C. cyaneus*					HH	b^B		0261
A	**Pallid Harrier**	*C. macrourus*							R	0262
A	**Montagu's Harrier**	*C. pygargus*					MO	b^A		0263
AC	**Goshawk**	*Accipiter gentilis*					GI	b^B		0267
A	**Sparrowhawk**	*A. nisus*					SH			0269
EU	**Levant Sparrowhawk**	*A. brevipes*								0273
A	**Buzzard**	*Buteo buteo*					BZ			0287
EU	**Long-legged Buzzard**	*B. rufinus*								0288
A	**Rough-legged Buzzard**	*B. lagopus*					RF			0290
EU	**Lesser Spotted Eagle**	*Aquila pomarina*								0292
B	**Greater Spotted Eagle**	*A. clanga*							R	0293
EU	**Imperial Eagle**	*A. heliaca*								0295
A	**Golden Eagle**	*A. chrysaetos*					EA	b^B		0296
EU	**Booted Eagle**	*Hieraaetus pennatus*								0298
EU	**Bonelli's Eagle**	*H. fasciatus*								0299
A	**Osprey**	*Pandion haliaetus*					OP	b^A		0301
A	**Lesser Kestrel**	*Falco naumanni*							R	0303
A	**Kestrel**	*F. tinnunculus*					K			0304
A	**American Kestrel**	*F. sparverius*							R	0305
A	**Red-footed Falcon**	*F. vespertinus*					FV		R	0307
A	**Merlin**	*F. columbarius*					ML	b^B		0309
A	**Hobby**	*F. subbuteo*					HY	b^B		0310
A	**Eleonora's Falcon**	*F. eleonorae*							R	0311
EU	**Lanner**	*F. biarmicus*					FB			0314
D	**Saker**	*F. cherrug*					JF		R	0316
A	**Gyrfalcon**	*F. rusticolus*					YF		R	0318
A	**Peregrine**	*F. peregrinus*					PE	b^B		0320
EU	**Andalusian Hemipode**	*Turnix sylvatica*								0400
A	**Water Rail**	*Rallus aquaticus*					WA			0407
A	**Spotted Crake**	*Porzana porzana*					AK	b^A		0408
A	**Sora**	*P. carolina*							R	0409
A	**Little Crake**	*P. parva*					JC		R	0410
A	**Baillon's Crake**	*P. pusilla*					VC		R	0411
A	**Corncrake**	*Crex crex*					CE	b^A		0421
A	**Moorhen**	*Gallinula chloropus*					MH			0424
B	**Allen's Gallinule**	*Porphyrula alleni*							R	0425
A	**American Purple Gallinule**	*P. martinica*							R	0426
EU	**Purple (Swamp-hen) Gallinule**	*Porphyrio porphyrio*								0427
A	**Coot**	*Fulica atra*					CO			0429
A	**American Coot**	*F. americana*							R	0430
	Sub total									

BUSTARDS, WADERS			Life list	2005 list			BTO	RBBP	BOU	EU No
EL	**Crested Coot**	*F. cristata*								0431
A	**Crane**	*Grus grus*					AN	b^A		0433
A	**Sandhill Crane**	*G. canadensis*							R	0436
A	**Little Bustard**	*Tetrax tetrax*							R	0442
C	**Houbara Bustard**	*Chlamydotis undulata*							R	0441
B	**Macqueen's Bustard**	*Chlamydotis macqueenii*							R	0442
A	**Great Bustard**	*Otis tarda*					OC		R	0446
A	**Oystercatcher**	*Haematopus ostralegus*					OC			0450
A	**Black-winged Stilt**	*Himantopus himantopus*					IT		R	0455
A	**Avocet**	*Recurvirostra avosetta*					AV	b^A		0456
A	**Stone Curlew**	*Burhinus oedicnemus*					TN	b^A		0459
A	**Cream-coloured Courser**	*Cursorius cursor*					R			0464
A	**Collared Pratincole**	*Glareola pratincola*							R	0465
A	**Oriental Pratincole**	*G. maldivarum*					GM		R	0466
A	**Black-winged Pratincole**	*G. nordmanni*					KW		R	0467
A	**Little Ringed Plover**	*Charadrius dubius*					LP	b^B		0469
A	**Ringed Plover**	*C. hiaticula*					RP			0470
A	**Semipalmated Plover**	*C. semipalmatus*					TV		R	0471
A	**Killdeer**	*C. vociferus*					KL		R	0474
A	**Kentish Plover**	*C. alexandrinus*					KP			0477
A	**Lesser Sand Plover**	*C. mongolus*							R	0478
FA	**Greater Sand Plover**	*C. leschenaultii*					DP		R	0479
A	**Caspian Plover**	*C. asiaticus*							R	0480
A	**Dotterel**	*C. morinellus*					DO	b^B		0482
A	**American Golden Plover**	*Pluvialis dominica*					ID		R	0484
A	**Pacific Golden Plover**	*P. fulva*					IF		R	0484
A	**Golden Plover**	*P. apricaria*					GP			0485
A	**Grey Plover**	*P. squatarola*					GV			0486
EU	**Spur-winged Plover**	*Hoplopterus spinosus*					UW			0487
A	**Sociable Lapwing**	*Vanellus gregarius*					IP		R	0491
A	**White-tailed Lapwing**	*V. leucurus*							R	0492
A	**Lapwing**	*V. vanellus*					L			0493
A	**Great Knot**	*Calidris tenuirostris*					KO		R	0495
A	**Knot**	*C. canutus*					KN			0496
A	**Sanderling**	*C. alba*					SS			0497
A	**Semipalmated Sandpiper**	*C. pusilla*					PZ		R	0498
A	**Western Sandpiper**	*C. mauri*					ER		R	0499
A	**Red-necked Stint**	*C. ruficollis*							R	0500
A	**Little Stint**	*C. minuta*					LX			0501
A	**Temminck's Stint**	*C. temminckii*					TK	b^A		0502
A	**Long-toed Stint**	*C. subminuta*							R	0503
A	**Least Sandpiper**	*C. minutilla*					EP		R	0504
A	**White-rumped Sandpiper**	*C. fuscicollis*					WU		R	0505
A	**Baird's Sandpiper**	*C. bairdii*					BP		R	0506
A	**Pectoral Sandpiper**	*C. melanotos*					PP			0507
A	**Sharp-tailed Sandpiper**	*C. acuminata*					VV		R	0508
A	**Curlew Sandpiper**	*C. ferruginea*					CV			0509
A	**Purple Sandpiper**	*C. maritima*					PS	b^A		0510
A	**Dunlin**	*C. alpina*					DN			0512
A	**Broad-billed Sandpiper**	*Limicola falcinellus*					OA		R	0514
A	**Stilt Sandpiper**	*Micropalama himantopus*					MI		R	0515
A	**Buff-breasted Sandpiper**	*Tryngites subruficollis*					BQ			0516
A	**Ruff**	*Philomachus pugnax*					RU	b^A		0517
A	**Jack Snipe**	*Lymnocryptes minimus*					JS			0518
A	**Snipe**	*Gallinago gallinago*					SN			0519
A	**Great Snipe**	*G. media*					DS		R	0520
A	**Short-billed Dowitcher**	*Limnodromus griseus*							R	0526
A	**Long-billed Dowitcher**	*L. scolopaceus*					LD		R	0527
A	**Woodcock**	*Scolopax rusticola*					WK			0529
Sub total										

	WADERS, GULLS, PHALAROPES, SKUAS, GULLS, TERNS		Life list	2005 list			BTO	RBBP	BOU	EU No
A	**Black-tailed Godwit**	*Limosa limosa*					BW	b^{A}		0532
A	**Hudsonian Godwit**	*L. haemastica*					HU		R	0533
A	**Bar-tailed Godwit**	*L. lapponica*					BA			0534
A	**Little Whimbrel (Curlew)**	*N. minutus*							R	0536
B	**Eskimo Curlew**	*N. borealis*							R	0537
A	**Whimbrel**	*N. phaeopus*					WM	b^{A}		0538
A	**Curlew**	*N. arquata*					CU			0541
A	**Upland Sandpiper**	*Bartramia longicauda*					UP		R	0544
A	**Spotted Redshank**	*T. erythropus*					DR			0545
A	**Redshank**	*T. totanus*					RK			0546
A	**Marsh Sandpiper**	*T. stagnatilis*					MD		R	0547
A	**Greenshank**	*T. nebularia*					GK	b^{B}		0548
A	**Greater Yellowlegs**	*T. melanoleuca*					LZ		R	0550
A	**Lesser Yellowlegs**	*T. flavipes*					LY		R	0551
A	**Solitary Sandpiper**	*T. solitaria*					I		R	0552
A	**Green Sandpiper**	*T. ochropus*					GE			0553
A	**Wood Sandpiper**	*T. glareola*					OD	b^{A}		0554
A	**Terek Sandpiper**	*Xenus cinereus*					TR		R	0555
A	**Common Sandpiper**	*Actitis hypoleucos*					CS			0556
A	**Spotted Sandpiper**	*A. macularia*					PQ		R	0557
A	**Grey-tailed Tattler**	*Heteroscelus brevipes*					YT		R	0558
A	**Turnstone**	*Arenaria interpres*					TT			0561
A	**Wilson's Phalarope**	*Phalaropus tricolor*					WF		R	0563
A	**Red-necked Phalarope**	*P. lobatus*					NK	b^{A}		0564
A	**Grey Phalarope**	*P. fulicarius*					PL			0565
A	**Pomarine Skua**	*Stercorarius pomarinus*					PK			0566
A	**Arctic Skua**	*S. parasiticus*					AC			0567
A	**Long-tailed Skua**	*S. longicaudus*					OG			0568
A	**Great Skua**	*Catharacta skua*					NX			0569
B	**Great Black-headed (Pallas's) Gull**	*L. ichthyaetus*							R	0573
A	**Mediterranean Gull**	*L. melanocephalus*					MU	b^{A}		0575
A	**Laughing Gull**	*L. atricilla*					LF		R	0576
A	**Franklin's Gull**	*L. pipixcan*					FG		R	0577
A	**Little Gull**	*L. minutus*					LU			0578
A	**Sabine's Gull**	*L. sabini*					AB			0579
A	**Bonaparte's Gull**	*L. philadelphia*					ON		R	0581
A	**Black-headed Gull**	*L. ridibundus*					BH			0582
A	**Slender-billed Gull**	*L. genei*					EI			0585
FU	**Audouin's Gull**	*L. audouinii*								0588
A	**Ring-billed Gull**	*L. delawarensis*					IN			0589
A	**Common (Mew) Gull**	*L. canus*					CM			0590
A	**Lesser Black-backed Gull**	*L. fuscus*					LB			0591
A	**Herring Gull**	*L. argentatus*					HG			0592
A	**Iceland Gull**	*L. glaucoides*					IG			0598
A	**Glaucous Gull**	*L. hyperboreus*					GZ			0599
A	**Great Black-backed Gull**	*L. marinus*					GB			0600
A	**Ross's Gull**	*Rhodostethia rosea*					QG		R	0601
A	**Kittiwake**	*Rissa tridactyla*					KI			0602
A	**Ivory Gull**	*Pagophila eburnea*					IV		R	0604
A	**Gull-billed Tern**	*S.nilotica*					TG		R	0605
A	**Caspian Tern**	*S.caspia*					CJ		R	0606
A	**Royal Tern**	*S.maxima*					QT		R	0607
A	**Lesser Crested Tern**	*S.bengalensis*					TF	b^{A}	R	0609
A	**Sandwich Tern**	*S.sandvicensis*					TE			0611
A	**Roseate Tern**	*S.dougallii*					RS	b^{A}		0614
A	**Common Tern**	*S.hirundo*					CN			0615
A	**Arctic Tern**	*S.paradisaea*					AE			0616
A	**Aleutian Tern**	*S.aleutica*							R	0617
A	**Forster's Tern**	*S.forsteri*					FO		R	0618
	Sub total									

TERNS, AUKS, SANDGROUSE, DOVES, CUCKOOS, OWLS, NIGHTJARS, SWIFTS, WOODPECKERS			Life list	2005 list			BTO	RBBP	BOU	EU No
A	**Bridled Tern**	*S.anaethetus*							R	0622
A	**Sooty Tern**	*S.fuscata*							R	0623
A	**Little Tern**	*S.albifrons*					AF	b^{B}		0624
A	**Whiskered Tern**	*Chlidonias hybrida*					WD		R	0626
A	**Black Tern**	*C. niger*					BJ			0627
A	**White-winged Black Tern**	*C. leucopterus*					WJ		R	0628
A	**Guillemot**	*Uria aalge*					GU			0634
A	**Brünnich's Guillemot**	*U. lomvia*					TZ		R	0635
A	**Razorbill**	*Alca torda*					RA			0636
A	**Black Guillemot**	*Cepphus grylle*					TY			0638
A	**Ancient Murrelet**	*Synthliboramphus antiquus*							R	0645
A	**Little Auk**	*Alle alle*					LK			0647
A	**Puffin**	*Fratercula arctica*					PU			0654
EU	**Black-bellied Sandgrouse**	*Pterocles orientalis*								0661
EU	**Pin-tailed Sandgrouse**	*P. alchata*								0662
A	**Pallas's Sandgrouse**	*Syrrhaptes paradoxus*							R	0663
AC	**Rock Dove**	*Columba livia*					DV			0665
A	**Stock Dove**	*C. oenas*					SD			0668
A	**Woodpigeon**	*C. palumbus*					WP			0670
A	**Collared Dove**	*Streptopelia decaocto*					CD			0684
A	**Turtle Dove**	*S. turtur*					TD			0687
A	**Rufous (Oriental) Turtle Dove**	*S. orientalis*							R	0689
A	**Mourning Dove**	*Zenaida macroura*							R	0695
C	**Rose-ringed Parakeet**	*Psittacula krameri*					RI	b^{D}		0712
A	**Great Spotted Cuckoo**	*Clamator glandarius*					UK		R	0716
A	**Cuckoo**	*Cuculus canorus*					CK			0724
A	**Black-billed Cuckoo**	*Coccyzus erythrophthalmus*							R	0727
A	**Yellow-billed Cuckoo**	*C. americanus*							R	0728
A	**Barn Owl**	*Tyto alba*					BO	b^{C}		0735
A	**Scops Owl**	*Otus scops*							R	0739
EU	**Eagle Owl**	*Bubo bubo*					EO	b^{D}		0744
A	**Snowy Owl**	*Nyctea scandiaca*					SO	b^{A}	R	0749
A	**Hawk Owl**	*Surnia ulula*							R	0750
EU	**Pygmy Owl**	*Glaucidium passerinum*								0751
C	**Little Owl**	*Athene noctua*					LO			0757
A	**Tawny Owl**	*Strix aluco*					TO			0761
EU	**Ural Owl**	*S. uralensis*								0765
EU	**Great Grey Owl**	*S. nebulosa*								0766
A	**Long-eared Owl**	*Asio otus*					LE			0767
A	**Short-eared Owl**	*A. flammeus*					SE			0768
A	**Tengmalm's Owl**	*Aegolius funereus*							R	0770
A	**Nightjar**	*Caprimulgus europaeus*					NJ			0778
B	**Red-necked Nightjar**	*C. ruficollis*							R	0779
A	**Egyptian Nightjar**	*C. aegyptius*							R	0781
A	**Common Nighthawk**	*Chordeiles minor*							R	0786
A	**Chimney Swift**	*Chaetura pelagica*							R	0790
A	**White-throated Needletail**	*Hirundapus caudacutus*					NI		R	0792
A	**Swift**	*Apus apus*					SI			0795
A	**Pallid Swift**	*A. pallidus*							R	0796
A	**Pacific Swift**	*A. pallidus*							R	0797
A	**Alpine Swift**	*A. pacificus*					AI		R	0798
EL	**White-rumped Swift**	*A. melba*								0799
A	**Little Swift**	*A. affinis*							R	0800
A	**Kingfisher**	*Alcedo atthis*					KF	b^{C}		0831
A	**Belted Kingfisher**	*Ceryle alcyon*							R	0834
A	**Blue-checked Bee-eater**	*Merops superciliosus*							R	0839
A	**Bee-eater**	*M. apiaster*					MZ			0840
A	**Roller**	*Coracias garrulus*							R	0841
A	**Hoopoe**	*Upupa epops*					HP			0846
Sub total										

WOODPECKERS, LARKS, PIPITS, WAGTAILS, CHATS			Life list	2005 list			BTO	RBBP	BOU	EU No
A	**Wryneck**	*Jynx torquilla*					WY	b[A]		0848
EU	**Grey-headed Woodpecker**	*Picus canus*								0855
A	**Green Woodpecker**	*P. viridis*					G			0856
EU	**Black Woodpecker**	*Dryocopus martius*								0863
A	**Yellow-bellied Sapsucker**	*Sphyrapicus varius*							R	0872
A	**Great Spotted Woodpecker**	*Dendrocopos major*					GS			0876
EU	**Syrian Woodpecker**	*D. syriacus*								0878
EU	**Middle Spotted Woodpecker**	*D. medius*								0883
EU	**White-backed Woodpecker**	*D. leucotos*								0884
A	**Lesser Spotted Woodpecker**	*D. minor*					LS			0887
EU	**Three-toed Woodpecker**	*Picoides tridactylus*								0898
A	**Eastern Phoebe**	*Sayornis phoebe*							R	0909
EU	**Dupont's Lark**	*Chersophilus duponti*								0959
A	**Calandra Lark**	*Melanocorypha calandra*							R	0961
A	**Bimaculated Lark**	*M. bimaculata*							R	0962
A	**White-winged Lark**	*M. leucoptera*							R	0965
A	**Short-toed Lark**	*Calandrella brachydactyla*					VL			0968
A	**Lesser Short-toed Lark**	*C. rufescens*							R	0970
A	**Crested Lark**	*Galerida cristata*							R	0972
EU	**Thekla Lark**	*G. theklae*								0973
A	**Wood Lark**	*Lullula arborea*					WL	b[B]		0974
A	**Sky Lark**	*Alauda arvensis*					S			0976
A	**Shore (Horned) Lark**	*Eremophila alpestris*					SX			0978
A	**Sand Martin**	*Riparia riparia*					SM			0981
A	**Tree Swallow**	*Tachycineta bicolor*							R	0983
A	**Crag Martin**	*Ptyonoprogne rupestris*							R	0991
A	**Swallow**	*Hirundo rustica*					SL			0992
A	**Red-rumped Swallow**	*H. daurica*					VR		R	0995
A	**Cliff Swallow**	*H. pyrrhonota*							R	0998
A	**House Martin**	*Delichon urbica*					HM			1001
A	**Richard's Pipit**	*Anthus novaeseelandiae*					PR			1002
A	**Blyth's Pipit**	*A. godlewskii*							R	1004
A	**Tawny Pipit**	*A. campestris*					TI			1005
A	**Olive-backed Pipit**	*A. hodgsoni*					OV		R	1008
A	**Tree Pipit**	*A. trivialis*					TP			1009
A	**Pechora Pipit**	*A. gustavi*							R	1010
A	**Meadow Pipit**	*A. pratensis*					MP			1011
A	**Red-throated Pipit**	*A. cervinus*					VP		R	1012
A	**Rock Pipit**	*A. petrosus*					RC			1014
A	**Water Pipit**	*A. spinoletta*					WI			1014
A	**Buff-bellied Pipit**	*A. rubescens*							R	1014
A	**Yellow Wagtail**	*Motacilla flava*					YW			1017
A	**Citrine Wagtail**	*M. citreola*							R	1018
A	**Grey Wagtail**	*M. cinerea*					GL			1019
A	**Pied (White) Wagtail**	*M. alba*					PW			1020
A	**Cedar Waxing**	*Bombycilla cedrorum*							R	1046
A	**(Bohemian) Waxwing**	*Bombycilla garrulus*					WX			1048
A	**Dipper**	*Cinclus cinclus*					DI			1050
A	**Wren**	*Troglodytes troglodytes*					WR			1066
A	**Northern Mockingbird**	*Mimus polyglottos*							R	1067
A	**Brown Thrasher**	*Toxostoma rufum*							R	1069
A	**Gray Catbird**	*Dumetella carolinensis*								1080
A	**Dunnock**	*Prunella modularis*					D			1084
A	**Alpine Accentor**	*P. collaris*							R	1094
A	**Rufous-tailed Scrub Robin**	*Cercotrichas galactotes*							R	1095
A	**Robin**	*Erithacus rubecula*							R	1099
A	**Thrush Nightingale**	*Luscinia luscinia*					FN		R	1103
A	**Nightingale**	*L. megarhynchos*					N			1104
A	**Siberian Rubythroat**	*L. calliope*							R	1105
Sub total										

	CHATS, WHEATEAR, THRUSHES, WARBLERS		Life list	2005 list			BTO	RBBP	BOU	EU No
A	**Bluethroat**	*L. svecica*					BU			1106
A	**Siberian Blue Robin**	*L. cyane*								1112
A	**Red-flanked Bluetail**	*Tarsiger cyanurus*							R	1113
A	**White-throated Robin**	*Irania gutturalis*							R	1117
A	**Black Redstart**	*Phoenicurus ochruros*					BX	b^A		1121
A	**Redstart**	*P. phoenicurus*					RT			1122
A	**Moussier's Redstart**	*P. moussieri*							R	1127
A	**Whinchat**	*Saxicola rubetra*					WC			1137
A	**Stonechat**	*S. torquata*					SC			1139
A	**Isabelline Wheatear**	*Oenanthe isabellina*							R	1144
A	**Wheatear**	*O. O.*					W			1146
A	**Pied Wheatear**	*O. pleschanka*					PI		R	1147
A	**Black-eared Wheatear**	*O. hispanica*							R	1148
A	**Desert Wheatear**	*O. deserti*							R	1149
A	**White-crowned(-tailed) Black Wheatear**									
		O. leucopyga								1157
EU	**Black Wheatear**	*O. Leucura*							R	1158
A	**Rock Thrush**	*Monticola saxatilis*					OH		R	1162
A	**Blue Rock Thrush**	*M. solitarius*							R	1166
A	**White's Thrush**	*Zoothera dauma*							R	1170
A	**Siberian Thrush**	*Z. sibirica*							R	1171
A	**Varied Thrush**	*Z. naevia*					VT		R	1172
A	**Wood Thrush**	*Hylocichla mustelina*							R	1175
A	**Hermit Thrush**	*Catharus guttatus*							R	1176
A	**Swainson's Thrush**	*C. ustulatus*							R	1177
A	**Grey-cheeked Thrush**	*C. minimus*							R	1178
A	**Veery**	*C. fuscescens*							R	1179
A	**Ring Ouzel**	*Turdus torquatus*					RZ			1186
A	**Blackbird**	*T. merula*					B			1187
IA	**Eyebrowed Thrush**	*T. obscurus*							R	1195
A	**Dusky Thrush**	*T. naumanni*							R	1196
A	**Dark-throated Thrush**	*T. ruficollis*					XC		R	1197
A	**Fieldfare**	*T. pilaris*					FF	b^A		1198
A	**Song Thrush**	*T. philomelos*					ST			1200
A	**Redwing**	*T. iliacus*					RE	b^A		1201
A	**Mistle Thrush**	*T. viscivorus*					M			1202
A	**American Robin**	*T. migratorius*					AR		R	1203
A	**Cetti's Warbler**	*Cettia cetti*					CW	b^A		1220
A	**Zitting Cisticola (Fan-tailed Warbler)**									
		Cisticola juncidis							R	1226
A	**Pallas's Grasshopper Warbler**	*Locustella certhiola*							R	1233
A	**Lanceolated Warbler**	*L.lanceolata*							R	1235
A	**Grasshopper Warbler**	*L.naevia*					GH			1236
A	**River Warbler**	*L.fluviatilis*					VW		R	1237
A	**Savi's Warbler**	*L.luscinioides*					VI	b^A	R	1238
A	**Moustached Warbler**	*Acrocephalus melanopogon*							R	1241
A	**Aquatic Warbler**	*A. paludicola*					AQ			1242
A	**Sedge Warbler**	*A. schoenobaenus*					SW			1243
A	**Paddyfield Warbler**	*A. agricola*					PY		R	1247
A	**Blyth's Reed Warbler**	*A. dumetorum*							R	1248
A	**Marsh Warbler**	*A. palustris*					MW	b^A		1250
A	**Reed Warbler**	*A. scirpaceus*					RW			1251
A	**Great Reed Warbler**	*A. arundinaceus*					QW		R	1253
A	**Thick-billed Warbler**	*A. aedon*							R	1254
A	**Eastern Olivaceous Warbler**	*Hippolais pallida*							R	1255
A	**Western Olivaceous Warbler**	*Hippolais opaca*							R	
A	**Booted Warbler**	*H. caligata*								1256
A	**Syke's Warbler**	*H. rama*								
EU	**Olive-tree Warbler**	*H. olivetorum*								1258
	Sub total									

	WARBLERS, 'CRESTS', FLYCATCHERS, TITS, NUTHATCHES, SHRIKES, CORVIDS		Life list	2005 list			BTO	RBBP	BOU	EU No
A	**Icterine Warbler**	*H. icterina*					IC			1259
A	**Melodious Warbler**	*H. polyglotta*					ME			1260
A	**Marmora's Warbler**	*Sylvia sarda*					MM			1261
A	**Dartford Warbler**	*S. undata*					DW	b^B		1262
A	**Spectacled Warbler**	*S. conspicillata*								1264
A	**Subalpine Warbler**	*S. cantillans*								1265
A	**Sardinian Warbler**	*S. melanocephala*								1267
EU	**Cyprus Warbler**	*S. melanothorax*								1268
A	**Rüppell's Warbler**	*S. rueppelli*								1269
A	**Desert Warbler**	*S. nana*								1270
A	**Orphean Warbler**	*S. hortensis*								1272
A	**Barred Warbler**	*S. nisoria*					RR			1273
A	**Lesser Whitethroat**	*S. curruca*					LW			1274
A	**Whitethroat**	*S. communis*					WH			1275
A	**Garden Warbler**	*S. borin*					GW			1276
A	**Blackcap**	*S. atricapilla*					BC			1277
A	**Greenish Warbler**	*Phylloscopus trochiloides*					NP			1293
A	**Arctic Warbler**	*P. borealis*					AP			1295
A	**Pallas's Warbler**	*P. proregulus*					PA			1298
A	**Yellow-browed Warbler**	*P. inornatus*					YB			1300
A	**Hume's Leaf Warbler**	*P. humei*								1300
A	**Radde's Warbler**	*P. schwarzi*								1301
A	**Dusky Warbler,**	*P. fuscatus*					UY		R	1303
A	**Western Bonelli's Warbler**	*P. bonelli*					IW		R	1307
A	**Eastern Bonelli's Warbler**	*P. orientalis*							R	1307
A	**Wood Warbler**	*P. sibilatrix*					WO			1308
A	**Common Chiffchaff**	*P. collybita*					CC			1311
A	**Iberian Chiffchaff**	*P. ibericus*							R	1311
A	**Willow Warbler**	*P. trochilus*					WW			1312
A	**Goldcrest**	*Regulus regulus*					GC			1314
A	**Firecrest**	*R. ignicapilla*					FC	b^A		1315
D	**Asian Brown Flycatcher**	*Muscicapa dauurica*								1335
A	**Spotted Flycatcher**	*Muscicapa striata*								1335
A	**Red-breasted Flycatcher**	*Ficedula parva*					FY			1343
D	**Mugimaki Flycatcher**	*F. mugimaki*							R	1344
EU	**Semi-collared Flycatcher**	*F. semitorquata*								1347
A	**Collared Flycatcher**	*F. albicollis*							R	1348
A	**Pied Flycatcher**	*F. hypoleuca*					PF			1349
A	**Bearded Tit**	*Panurus biarmicus*					BR	b^B		1364
A	**Long-tailed Tit**	*Aegithalos caudatus*					LT			1437
A	**Marsh Tit**	*Parus palustris*					MT			1440
EU	**Sombre Tit**	*P. lugubris*								1441
A	**Willow Tit**	*P. montanus*					WT			1442
EU	**Siberian Tit**	*P. cinctus*								1448
A	**Crested Tit**	*P.cristatus*					CI	b^B		1454
A	**Coal Tit**	*P. ater*					CT			1461
A	**Blue Tit**	*P. caeruleus*					BT			1462
A	**Great Tit**	*P. major*					GT			1464
EU	**Krüper's Nuthatch**	*Sitta krueperi*								1469
EU	**Corsican Nuthatch**	*S. whiteheadi*								1470
A	**Red-breasted Nuthatch**	*S. canadensis*							R	1472
A	**Nuthatch**	*S. europaea*					NH			1479
EU	**Rock Nuthatch**	*S. neumayer*								1481
A	**Wallcreeper**	*Tichodroma muraria*							R	1482
A	**Treecreeper**	*Certhia familiaris*					TC			1486
A	**Short-toed Treecreeper**	*C. brachydactyla*					TH		R	1487
A	**Penduline Tit**	*Remiz pendulinus*					DT		R	1490
A	**Golden Oriole**	*Oriolus oriolus*					OL	b^A		1508
A	**Brown Shrike**	*Lanius cristatus*							R	1513
	Sub total									

	CORVIDS, STARLINGS, SPARROWS, FINCHES		Life list	2005 list			BTO	RBBP	BOU	EU No
A	**Isabelline Shrike**	*L. isabellinus*					IL		R	1514
A	**Red-backed Shrike**	*L. collurio*					ED	b[A]		1515
A	**Lesser Grey Shrike**	*L. minor*							R	1519
A	**Great Grey Shrike**	*L. excubitor*					SR			1520
A	**Southern Grey Shrike**	*L. meridionalis*							R	1520
A	**Woodchat Shrike**	*L. senator*					OO			1523
EU	**Masked Shrike**	*L. nubicus*								1524
A	**Jay**	*Garrulus glandarius*					J			1539
EU	**Siberian Jay**	*Perisoreus infaustus*								1543
EU	**Azure-winged Magpie**	*Cyanopica cyana*								1547
A	**Magpie**	*Pica pica*					MG			1549
A	**Nutcracker**	*Nucifraga caryocatactes*					NC		R	1557
EU	**Alpine Chough**	*Pyrrhocorax graculus*								1558
A	**Chough**	*P. pyrrhocorax*					CF	b[B]		1559
A	**Jackdaw**	*Corvus monedula*					JD			1560
A	**Rook**	*C. frugilegus*					RO			1563
A	**Carrion (Hooded) Crow**	*C. corone*					C			1567
A	**Hooded Crow**	*C. cornix*								
A	**Raven**	*C. corax*					RN			1572
D	**Daurian Starling**	*Sturnus sturninus*							R	1579
A	**Starling**	*S. vulgaris*					SG			1582
EU	**Spotless Starling**	*S. unicolor*								1583
A	**Rose-coloured (Rosy) Starling**									
		Sturnus roseus					OE		R	1594
A	**House Sparrow**	*Passer domesticus*					HS			1591
A	**Spanish Sparrow**	*P. hispaniolensis*							R	1592
A	**Tree Sparrow**	*P.r montanus*					TS			1598
A	**Rock Sparrow**	*Petronia petronia*							R	1604
D	**Snow Finch**	*Montifringilla nivalis*							R	1611
A	**Yellow-throated Vireo**	*Vireo flavifrons*							R	1628
A	**Philadelphia Vireo**	*V. philadelphicus*							R	1631
A	**Red-eyed Vireo**	*V.olivaceus*					EV		R	1633
A	**Chaffinch**	*Fringilla coelebs*					CH			1636
A	**Brambling**	*F. montifringilla*					BL	b[A]		1638
A	**Serin**	*Serinus serinus*					NS	b[A]		1640
A	**Greenfinch**	*Carduelis chloris*					GR			1649
A	**Goldfinch**	*C carduelis*					GO			1653
A	**Siskin**	*C. spinus*					SK			1654
A	**Linnet**	*C. cannabina*					LI			1660
A	**Twite**	*C. flavirostris*					TW			1662
	Lesser Redpoll	*C. cabaret*								1663
A	**Mealy Redpoll**	*C. flammea*					LR			1663
A	**Arctic Redpoll**	*C. hornemanni*					AL		R	1664
A	**Two-barred Crossbill**	*Loxia leucoptera*					PD		R	1665
A	**Crossbill**	*L. curvirostra*					CR	b[C]		1666
A	**Scottish Crossbill**	*L. scotica*					CY	b[B]		1667
A	**Parrot Crossbill**	*L. pytyopsittacus*					PC	b[A]	R	1668
A	**Trumpeter Finch**	*Bucanetes githagineus*							R	1676
A	**Common Rosefinch**	*Carpodacus erythrinus*					SQ	b[A]		1679
A	**Pine Grosbeak**	*Pinicola enucleator*							R	1699
A	**Bullfinch**	*Pyrrhula pyrrhula*					BF			1710
A	**Hawfinch**	*Coccothraustes coccothraustes*					HF			1717
A	**Evening Grosbeak**	*Hesperiphona vespertina*							R	1718
A	**Black-and-white Warbler**	*Mniotilta varia*							R	1720
A	**Golden-winged Warbler**	*Vermivora chrysoptera*							R	1722
A	**Tennessee Warbler**	*V. peregrina*							R	1724
A	**Northern Parula**	*Parula americana*							R	1732
A	**Yellow Warbler**	*Dendroica petechia*							R	1733
A	**Chestnut-sided Warbler**	*D. pensylvanica*							R	1734
	Sub total									

NORTH AMERICAN WARBLERS, NEW WORLD SPARROWS, BUNTINGS			Life list	2005 list			BTO	RBBP	BOU	EU No
A	**Blackburnian Warbler**	*D. fusca*							R	1747
A	**Cape May Warbler**	*D. tigrina*							R	1749
A	**Magnolia Warbler**	*D. magnolia*							R	1750
A	**Yellow-rumped Warbler**	*D. coronata*							R	1751
D	**Palm Warbler**	*D. palmarum*							R	1752
A	**Blackpoll Warbler**	*D. striata*							R	1753
A	**Bay-breasted Warbler**	*D. castanea*							R	1754
A	**American Redstart**	*Setophaga ruticilla*					AD		R	1755
A	**Ovenbird**	*Seiurus aurocapilla*							R	1756
A	**Northern Waterthrush**	*S. noveboracensis*							R	1757
A	**Yellowthroat**	*Geothlypis trichas*							R	1762
A	**Hooded Warbler**	*Wilsonia citrina*							R	1771
A	**Wilson's Warbler**	*Wilsonia pusilla*							R	1772
A	**Summer Tanager**	*Piranga rubra*							R	1786
A	**Scarlet Tanager**	*P. olivacea*							R	1788
A	**Eastern Towhee**	*Pipilo erythrophthalmus*							R	1798
A	**Lark Sparrow**	*Chondestes grammacus*							R	1824
A	**Savannah Sparrow**	*Passerculus sandwichensis*							R	1826
A	**Song Sparrow**	*Melospiza melodia*							R	1835
A	**White-crowned Sparrow**	*Zonotrichia leucophrys*							R	1839
A	**White-throated Sparrow**	*Z. albicollis*							R	1840
A	**Dark-eyed Junco**	*Junco hyemalis*					JU		R	1842
A	**Lapland Bunting**	*Calcarius lapponicus*					LA			1847
A	**Snow Bunting**	*Plectrophenax nivalis*					SB	b^{A}		1850
A	**Black-faced Bunting**	*Emberiza spodocephala*							R	1853
A	**Pine Bunting**	*E. leucocephalos*					EL		R	1856
A	**Yellowhammer**	*E. citrinella*					Y			1857
A	**Cirl Bunting**	*E. cirlus*					CL	b^{A}		1958
A	**Rock Bunting**	*E. cia*							R	1860
EU	**Cinereous Bunting**	*E. cineracea*								1865
A	**Ortolan Bunting**	*E. hortulana*					OB			1866
A	**Cretzschmar's Bunting**	*E. caesia*							R	1868
A	**Yellow-browed Bunting**	*E. chrysophrys*							R	1871
A	**Rustic Bunting**	*E. rustica*							R	1873
A	**Little Bunting**	*E. pusilla*					LJ			1874
D	**Chestnut Bunting**	*E. rutila*							R	1875
A	**Yellow-breasted Bunting**	*E. aureola*							R	1876
A	**Reed Bunting**	*E. schoeniclus*					RB			1877
A	**Pallas's Bunting**	*E. pallasi*							R	1878
D	**Red-headed Bunting**	*E. bruniceps*								1880
A	**Black-headed Bunting**	*E. melanocephala*							R	1881
A	**Corn Bunting**	*Miliaria calandra*					CB			1882
A	**Rose-breasted Grosbeak**	*Pheucticus ludovicianus*							R	1887
D	**Blue Grosbeak**	*Guiraca caerulea*							R	1891
A	**Indigo Bunting**	*Passerina cyanea*							R	1892
A	**Bobolink**	*Dolichonyx oryzivorus*							R	1897
A	**Brown-headed Cowbird**	*Molothrus ater*							R	1899
A	**Baltimore Oriole**	*Icterus galbula*							R	1918
Sub total										

DIRECTORY OF ART, PHOTOGRAPHY AND LECTURERS

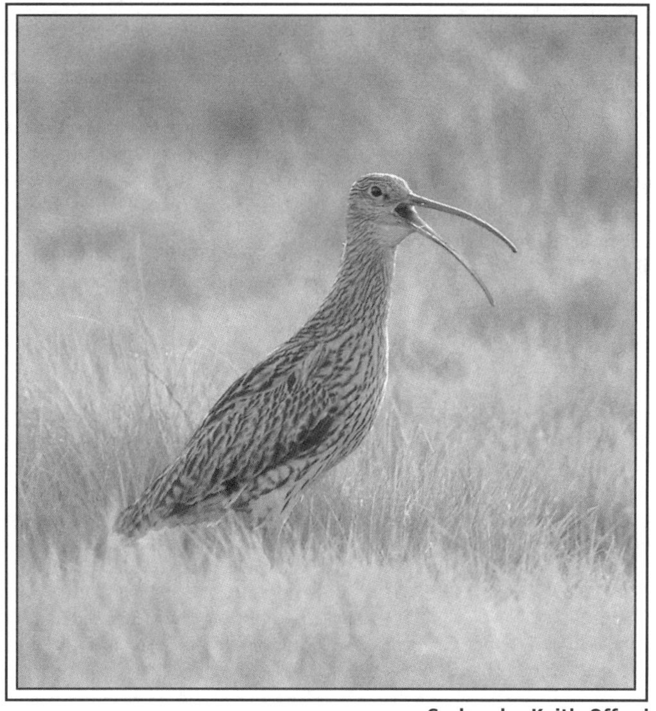

Curlew by Keith Offord

DIRECTORY OF WILDLIFE ART GALLERIES

NATURE IN ART MUSEUM AND ART GALLERY

World's first museum dedicated to art inspired by nature. Picasso to David Shepherd, Flemish Masters to contemporary crafts. Permanent collection plus regular special exhibitions and 70 artists in residence each year. See website for details.
Opening times: Tues-Sun (10am-5pm) and Bank holidays. Closed Dec 24-26.
Address: Wallsworth Hall, A38, Twigworth, Gloucester, GL2 9PA; 01452 731422; (Fax)01452 730937.
e-mail: ninart@globalnet.co.uk
www.nature-in-art.org.uk

OLD BREWERY STUDIOS

Changing exhibitions of work the whole year through. Various painting and drawing courses available.
Opening times: Variable, best to telephone first.
Address; The Manor House, Kings Cliffe, Peterborough, PE8 6XB; 01780 470247; (Fax)01780 470334.
www.oldbrewerystudios.co.uk

THE WILDLIFE ART GALLERY

Opened in 1988 as a specialist in 20th Century and contemporary wildlife art. It exhibits work by many of the leading European wildlife artists, both painters and sculptors, and has published several wildlife books.
Opening times: Mon-Sat (10am-4.30pm) and Sun (2pm-4.30pm).
Address: 97 High Street, Lavenham, Suffolk CO10 9PZ; (Tel)+44 (0) 1787 248562; (Fax)+44 (0) 1787 247356.
E-mail: wildlifeartgallery@btinternet.com
www.wildlifeartgallery.com

DIRECTORY OF WILDLIFE ARTISTS

BURTON, Philip

Acrylics on canvas; current enthusiasm seabirds. Many book illustrations e.g. in recent *Raptors of the World*. Founder member of Society of Wildlife Artists.
Exhibitions for 2005: Some at SWLA, London, annually.
Address: High Kelton, Doctors Commons Road, Berkhamsted, Herts, HP4 3DW; 01442 865020. e-mail: pjkburton@aol.com

CALE, Steve

Steve is a keen naturalist and specialises in painting in acrylics. His paintings have gone as far afield as Hong Kong and New Zealand. Undertaking work for The Mareeba Wetland Foundation in Australia and for Pensthorpe. His mural for the RSPB at Titchwell shows the birds of the reserve.
Address: Bramble Cottage, Westwood Lane, Gt Rysburgh, Fakenham, Norfolk, NR21 7AP; 01328 829589.

COOK, David

Sponsor of PJC Drawing Award via SWLA. Original paintings, drawings, paper cuts and paper sculptures of wildlife, especially waterfowl. Book, videos, WWT greetings cards, open & limited edition prints available through www.wwt.org.uk/shop. Annual residency each September, Nature in Art, Gloucestershire.
Exhibitions for 2005: SWLA exhibition, Mall Galleries, London.
Address: Holly House, 3 Lynn Road, South Runcton, King's Lynn, Norfolk, PE33 0EW; 01553 811980.

JONES, Chris

Painter of all wildlife subjects, especially birds and poultry. International Young Artist of the Year 1998. the Wildlife Art Society 2000 Gold Award Winner.
Exhibitions for 2005: Peter Hedley Gallery, Wareham, Dorset, Bradford-on-Avon

Library, Wiltshire, Falconry Fair, Shropshire, Marwell Zoo, Hants, Crossing Gates Gallery, Hants.
Products for sale: Original paintings and drawings, prints, cards (by Medici) and postcards. Commission and illustration work undertaken. See website for examples.
Address: 47 Church Lane, North Bradley, Trowbridge, Wilts, BA14 0TE; 01225 769717; e-mail: chrisjonesart@yahoo.co.uk www.chrisjoneswildlifeart.com

KOSTER, David

Original prints - etchings, woodcuts, linocuts, lithographs - of birds, fish, flowers, insects etc. Watercolours, oils. Commissions accepted. Published work includes wood engravings for *Down to Earth* by John Stewart Collis, ink drawings for *Fellow mortals*, anthology of animal poetry.
Exhibitions for 2005: SWLA London, September, Nature in Art, one-man show in September (to coincide with the launch of a book about the artist).
Address: 5 East Cliff Gardens, Folkestone, Kent, CT19 6AR; 01303 240544.

MACKAY, Andrew

Colour and line artwork of birds and insects. Illustrations in *Concise BWP, RSPB Birds of Britain and Europe, Birds of South-east Asia* etc. Commissions for paintings and illustrations welcome.
Address: 68 Leicester Road, Markfield, Leicester, LE67 9RE:01530 243770.
e-mail: andy@ajm-wildlife-art.co.uk
www.ajm-wildlife-art.co.uk

MESSAGE, Stephen

Freelance artist painting a wide variety of wildlife subjects including birds. He works mainly in watercolour and gouache. He has illustrated several books including *The Birds of Greece*, Bill Oddie's *Birds of Britain & Ireland* and *A Fieldguide to the Birds of SE Asia*. Currently he is working as the sole illustrator on *Waders of Europe, North America and Asia* for Helm.
Products for sale: Originals, prints and limited editions for sale. Commissions welcome. Please see website for range of paintings available.
Address: The Hall, Village Green, Benenden, Nr Cranbrook, Kent TN17 4DD; e-mail: smessage@willow.fsworld.co.uk
www.message-wildlife-art.co.uk

PARTINGTON, Peter NDD, ATC, SWLA

Beloved medium is watercolour followed by oils and sculpture. Happiest in the field with sketchbook - favourite habitat: Shoreline plus marsh. Travels widely. Many one man shows, work widely collected. Books; HarperCollins *Learn to Draw* series, *Farm Animals, Wildlife* and *Birds,* A&C Black's *Secret Lives of Garden Birds* (2004).
Exhibitions for 2005: Represented by Wildlife Art Gallery, Lavenham, Suffolk, HC Dickins, Bloxham, Nr Banbury, SWLA, London, September.
Address: The Hall, Kettlebaston, Suffolk, IP7 7QA; 01449 741538.
e-mail: peter.partington@kettlebaston.co.uk
www.peter-partington.fsnet.co.uk

POMROY, Jonathan

Works in watercolour and oils, always from sketches, made on trips across the British Isles, most recently to North West Scotland, North Yorkshire Moors and coast and Slimbridge as well as around home in Wiltshire. Recent exhibitions at WWT Slimbridge and Barnes, annually at The Gallery, Cirencester.
Exhibitions for 2005: Great West bird fair, Slimbridge, West Barn at Bradford on Avon, Wiltshire in July, Cirencester in November. See website for latest details.
Products for sale: Chiefly selling original watercolours and oils at one man exhibitions and from website. Commissions accepted only for subjects the artist has observed and sketched.
Address: 10, Bobbin Lane, Westwood, Bradford on Avon, Wiltshire BA15 2DL; 01225 864726. www.jonathanpomroy
e-mail: jonathanpomroy@supanet.com

ROSE, Chris
Originals in oils and acrylics of birds and animals in landscapes. Particularly interested in painting water and its myriad effects. Limited edition prints available. Illustrated many books including *Grebes of the World* (publ. end 2002), *Handbook to The Birds of The World* and *Robins and Chats of the World* (in progress), *In a Natural Light - the Wildlife Art of Chris Rose* (in progress)
Exhibitions for 2005: SWLA, London, September, British Birdwatching Fair, Rutland, August.
Products for sale: Original drawings and paintings, illustrations, limited edition reproductions, postcards.
Address: Maple Cottage, Holydean, Bowden, Melrose, Scotland TD6 9HT; (Tel/Fax)01835 822547.
e-mail: chrisroseswla@onetel.com
www.chrisrose-artist.co.uk

SNOW, Philip
Original & atmospheric paintings, sketches, reproductions, illustrations & writings on wildlife, mainly birds in landscape. Has illustrated or contributed to/written, over 50 books (& in many magazines etc), including *The Real Life of Birds,* 2005, DayOne publishers; *Collins Guide: Birds by Behaviour* 2003; *Tall Tales from an Estuary, & A Hebridean Wildlife and Landscape Sketchbook*, publication delayed.
Exhibitions for 2005: Biennial: September 11 - 25, Tegfryn Gallery, Menai Bridge, Anglesey, tel:01248 715128, open daily. Pensychnant Conservation Centre, Conwy, N Wales, summer, or by appointment, Tel: 01492 592595.
Products for sale: A wide selection of limited edition reproduction prints, sketches & originals, from many countries. Website: http://artofcreation.org.uk.
Address: 2 Beach Cottages, Malltraeth, Anglesey, North Wales, LL62 5AT; (Tel/Fax)01407 840512.
e-mail: philip@snow4083.freeserve.co.uk
http://artofcreation.org.uk

SYKES, Thelma K SWLA
Artist printmaker: (haunts coastal marsh and estuaries). Original linocuts, woodcuts of British birds. Published work includes BTO Atlases, *Birdwatcher's Yearbooks* to 1996, RSPB and Medici Society greetings cards. Exhibits SWLA, Society of Wood Engravers. Artist in residence with Nature in Art, Gloucester.
Exhibitions for 2005: English Nature, London Wetland Centre Jan 15 - Mar 1, SWLA London, September, SWE UK touring exhibition, NEWA, Cheshire.
Address: Blue Neb Studios, 18 Newcroft, Saughall, Chester, CH1 6EL; 01244 880209. e-mail: thelmasykes@tiscali.co.uk

WALLACE, D.Ian.M.
Gouache paintings, pencil and ink drawings; "paints birds like birdwatchers see them".
Exhibitions for 2005: SWLA London (Sept).
Products for sale: Supplies roughs free for commissions. Some illustrations from *Beguiled by Birds* published in 2004, by Christopher Helm, available.
Address: Mount Pleasant Farm, Main Road, Anslow, Burton-on-Trent, Staffs, DE13 9QE; 01283 812364.

WARREN, Michael
Original watercolour paintings of birds, all based on field observations. Books, calendars, cards and commissions.
Exhibitions for 2005: One-man shows at London Wetland Centre Mar 5 - Apr 19 and Slimbridge Nov 14 - Jan 2006. British Birdwatching Fair, Rutland, August, SWLA, London, September.
Address: The Laurels, The Green, Winthorpe, Nottinghamshire, NG24 2NR; 01636 673554; (Fax)01636 611569.
e-mail: mike.warren.birdart@care4free.net
www.mikewarren.co.uk

WOODHEAD, Darren MA (RCA), SWLA
Original watercolours and woodcuts of birds, butterflies, mammals and other wildlife subjects, as well as landscapes and cloudscapes. All subjects painted direct in the field. Commissions undertaken.

Exhibitions for 2005: SWLA, London, Sept 2005.
Address: 44F(2F3), Millhill, Musselburgh, East Lothian, EH21 7RN; 0131 665 6802.
e-mail: darren.woodhead@virgin.net

WOOLF, Colin

Beautiful original watercolour paintings. The atmosphere of a landscape and the character of his subject are his hallmark, also the pure watercolour technique that imparts a softness to the natural subjects he paints. Owls, birds of prey and ducks are specialities. Wide range of limited edition prints and greetings cards, special commissions also accepted.
Exhibitions for 2005: British Birdwatching Fair and other shows around the country. Ring for details.
Products for sale: Original paintings, limited edition prints and greetings cards.
Address: Tremallt, Penmachno, Betws y Coed, Conwy, LL24 0YL; +44 (0) 1690 760 308. e-mail: colin@wildart.co.uk
www.wildart.co.uk

DIRECTORY OF WILDLIFE PHOTOGRAPHERS

BASTON, Bill

Photographer
Subjects: East Anglian rarities and common birds, Mediterranean birds and landscapes, UK wildlife and landscapes, Florida birds and landscapes.
Products for sale: Prints, slides, digital, mounted/unmounted.
Address: 86 George Street, Hadleigh, Ipswich, IP7 5BU; 01473 827062.
e-mail: bill.baston@bt.com
www.billbaston.com

BATES,Tony

Photographer and lecturer.
Subjects: Mainly British wildlife, landscapes and astro landscapes.
Products for sale: 35mm, prints (loose, mounted or framed), original handmade photo greetings cards.
Address: 22 Fir Avenue, Bourne, Lincs, PE10 9RY; 01778 425137.
e-mail: mtr@masher.f9.co.uk

BEJARANO, Santiago

Wildlife photographer and tour leader.
Subjects: Wildlife and scenery of the Galapagos Islands and Andes.
Address: 25 Trinity Lane, Beverley, East Yorkshire HU17 0DY; 01482 872716.
e-mail:
santiago@thinkgalapagos.karoo.co.uk
www.thinkgalapagos.com

BORG, Les

Photographer, course leader.
Subjects: Mostly British wildlife, with some from Florida, Jamaica, Europe and elsewhere.
Products for sale: Formats, 6x6 and 35mm scans and CDs. Mounted, unmounted or framed, inkjet prints or Ilfochromes if required. Table mats and coasters, greetings cards.
Address: 17 Harwood Close, Tewin, Welwyn, Herts, AL6 0LF; 01438 717841, (Fax)01438 840459.
e-mail: les@les-borg-photography.co.uk
www.les-borg-photography.co.uk

BROADBENT, David

Professional photographer.
Subjects: UK birds and wild places.
Products for sale: Top quality photographic prints.
Address: Rose Cottage, Bream Road, Whitepool, St Briavels, Lydney, GL15 6TL;01594 531381; (M)07771 664973.
e-mail: info@davidbroadbent.com
www.davidbroadbent.com

BROOKS, Richard
Wildlife photographer, writer, lecturer.
Subjects: Owls (Barn especially), raptors, Kingfisher and a variety of European birds (Lesvos especially) and landscapes.
Products for sale: Mounted and unmounted computer prints (6x4 - A3+ size), framed pictures, A5 greetings cards, surplus slides for sale.
Address: 24 Croxton Hamlet, Fulmodeston, Fakenham, Norfolk, NR21 0NP; 01328 878632. www.richard-brooks.co.uk
e-mail: email@richard-brooks.co.uk

CANIS, Robert
Professional photographer, tour leader.
Subjects: British flora and fauna, landscapes and environment of southern England, also Finland and Poland.
Products for sale: 35mm transparencies. Digital and conventional mounted/ unmounted prints available.
Address: 26 Park Avenue, Sittingbourne, Kent, ME10 1QY; 07939 117570.
www.robertcanis.com
e-mail: rmcanis@msn.com

CONWAY, Wendy PSA4. AFIAP
Award-winning wildlife photographer.
Subjects: Birds, mammals, landscapes: UK, USA, Lesvos and Africa.
Products for sale: 35mm and medium format. Prints matted and unmatted, greetings cards.
Address: The Oaks, Parkend Walk, Coalway, Coleford, Glos GL16 7JR; 01594 832956. e-mail: wendy@terry-wall.com

DENNING, Paul
Wildlife photographer, lecturer.
Subjects: Birds, mammals, reptiles, butterflies and plants from UK, Europe, Canaries, North and Central America.
Products for sale: 35mm transparencies and prints.
Address: 17 Maes Maelwg, Beddau, Pontypridd, CF38 2LD; (H)01443 202607; (W)02920 673243.
e-mail: pgdenning.naturepics@virgin.net

DOODY, Dee
Professional wildlife cameraman, TV presenter, film-maker, writer and artist. (Also voice-overs).
Subjects: All UK wildlife (plus Gambia, Iceland and Europe.
Products for sale: Stunning wildlife film available on broadcast quality digital video. Dee supplies wildlife footage for the making of TV documentaries and promotional films i.e. water authorities, Wildlife Trusts, reserves etc.
Address: 2 Fan Terrace, Fan, Llanidloes, Powys, SY18 6NW: 01686 413819.

FEATHERBE, David
Wildlife and landscape photographer.
Subjects: General selection of wildlife and landscape photography, the majority of which are of UK subjects.
Products for sale: Mounted and framed images can be purchased from an extensive website.
Address: 16 East Cliff Gardens, Folkestone, Kent CT19 6AP. 01303 244489;
e-mail: david.featherbe@mac.com
http://homepage.mac.com/david.featherbe

HARROP, Hugh
Professional wildlife guide, photographer and author.
Subjects: European birds, cetaceans, wild flowers, butterflies and dragonflies. I specialise in all Shetland subjects.
Products for sale: 35mm transparency. Digital images on CD or via modem. Commercial enquiries only please.
Address: Longhill, Maywick, Shetland, ZE2 9JF; 01950 422483; (Fax) 01950422430.
e-mail: hugh@hughharrop.com
www.hughharrop.com

LANE, Mike
Wildlife photographer, workshops, photo shoots.
Subjects: Birds and wildlife from around the world also landscapes and the environment.
Products for sale: 35mm, medium format and digital.
Address: 36 Berkeley Road, Shirley, Solihull, West Midlands, B90 2HS; 0121

744 7988. e-mail: mikelane@nature-photography.co.uk
www.nature-photography.co.uk

LANGSBURY, Gordon FRPS
Professional wildlife photographer, lecturer, author and tour leader.
Subjects: Birds and mammals from UK, Europe, Scandinavia, N America, Gambia, Kenya, Tanzania, Morocco and Falklands.
Products for sale: 35mm transparencies for publication, lectures and prints.
Address: Sanderlings, 80 Shepherds Close, Hurley, Maidenhead, Berkshire, SL6 5LZ; (Tel/fax)01628 824252.
e-mail: gordonlangsbury@birdphoto.org.uk

McKAVETT, Mike
Wildlife photographer and lecturer.
Subjects: Birds and mammals from India, Kenya, The Gambia, Lesvos, N.America and UK.
Products for sale: 35mm transparencies for publication and commercial use, prints and lectures.
Address: 34 Rectory Road, Churchtown, Southport, PR9 7PU; 01704 231358.

MOCKLER, Mike
Safari guide, tour leader, writer and photographer.
Subjects: Birds and wildlife of Britain, Europe, Central and South America, India and several African countries.
Products for sale: 35mm transparencies.
Address: Gulliver's Cottage, Chapel Rise, Avon Castle, Ringwood, Hampshire, BH24 2BL; 01425 478103.
e-mail: mikemockler@lineone.net

OFFORD, Keith
Photographer, writer, tour leader, conservationist.
Subjects: Raptors, UK wildlife and scenery, birds and other wildlife of USA, Africa, Spain, Australia, India.
Products for sale: Conventional prints, greetings cards, framed pictures.
Address: Yew Tree Farmhouse, Craignant, Selattyn, Nr Oswestry, Shropshire, SY10 7NP; 01691 718740.
e-mail: keith-offord@virgin.net
www.keithofford.co.uk

PARKER, Susan and Allan ARPS
Professional photographers (ASPphoto - Images of Nature) lecturers and tutors.
Subjects: Birds, plus other flora and fauna from the UK, Spain, Lesvos, Cyprus, Florida and Texas.
Products for sale: 35mm 645 medium format, slides, mounted digital prints, greetings cards and digital images on CD for reproduction (high quality scans up to A3+).
Address: Ashtree House, 51 Kiveton Lane, Todwick, Sheffield, South Yorkshire, S26 1HJ; 01909 770238.
e-mail: aspaspphoto@clara.co.uk

PIKE, David
Photographer, presenter and writer.
Subjects: Wildlife, including birds from Japan, N America and Africa.
Products for sale: 35mm mounted slides. Conventional prints and digital.
Address: Uffington Manor, Main Road, Uffington, Lincs, PE9 4SN; 01780 751944;(W) 01780 767711; (Fax) 01780 489218.
e-mail: david.pike@ukphotographics.co.uk
www.ukphotographics.co.uk.com

READ, Mike
Photographer (wildlife and landscapes), tour leader, writer.
Subjects: Birds, mammals, plants, landscapes, and some insects. UK, France, USA, Ecuador (including Galapagos).
Products for sale: Prints, greetings cards, books.
Address: Claremont, Redwood Close, Ringwood, Hampshire, BH24 1PR; 01425 475008, (Fax) 01425 473160.
e-mail: mike@mikeread.co.uk
www.mikeread.co.uk

SIMPSON, Geoff
Professional natural history and landscape photographer.
Subjects: Specialises in evocative images of Britain's wildlife and landscape.

Products for sale: 35mm and panoramic. Slides and CD.
Address: Camberwell, 1 Buxton Road, New Mills, High Peak, Derbyshire, SK22 3JS; 01633 743089.
e-mail: info@geoffsimpson.co.uk
www.wildphoto.demon.co.uk

SWASH, Andy
Photographer, author, tour leader.
Subjects: Birds, habitats/landscapes and general wildlife from all continents; photographic library currently 1,700 bird species.
Products for sale: Slides for publication and duplicates for lectures. High resolution scans on CD-Rom. Conventional and digital prints, unmounted, mounted or framed.
Address: Stretton Lodge, 9 Birch Grove, West Hill, Ottery St Mary, Devon, EX11 1XP; (H&fax) 01404 815383, (W) 01392 822901. www.wildguides.co.uk
e-mail: andy_swash@wildguides.co.uk

TIPLING, David
Wildlife and landscape photographer, photographic tour leader, author, with a passion for birds.
Subjects: Worldwide wildlife and landscapes, with an emphasis on birds.
Products for sale: Greetings cards, book and limited edition prints for sale. Prints are truly archival, using the finest printing techniques and finest papers.
Address: 99 Noah's Ark, Kemsing, Sevenoaks, Kent, TN15 6PD; 01732 763486. www.davidtipling.com
e-mail: dt@windrushphotos.demon.co.uk

WALL, Terry ARPS EFIAP PPSA
Wildlife photographer.
Subjects: Birds, mammals, landscapes from UK, USA, Lesvos, Africa and Galapagos.
Products for sale: 35mm/medium. Prints matted/unmatted, greetings cards. 35mm scanning service and restoration and retouching service. Quality printing service. *One-to-One Photoshop Tuition* book and individual lessons.
Address: The Oaks, Parkend Walk, Coalway, Coleford, Glos GL16 7JR; 01594 832956. e-mail: wildimages@terry-wall.com
www.terry-wall.com

WARD, Chris
Photographer.
Subjects: Birds and landscapes, plus some other wildlife. UK (mostly commoner species, some rarities), W.Palearctic, S.Africa, Florida, California, Venezuela, Argentina, Australia.
Products for sale: Prints and framed pictures, slide copies for lectures.
Address: 276 Bideford Green, Linslade, Leighton Buzzard, Beds, LU7 2TU; 01525 375528.
e-mail: chris@chriswardphotography.co.uk

WILKES, Mike FRPS
Professional wildlife photographer, tour leader.
Subjects: African, European and British birds.
Address: 43 Feckenham Road, Headless Cross, Redditch, Worcestershire, B97 5AS; 01527 550686.
e-mail: wilkes@photoshot.com

WILLIAMS, Nick
Photographer, lecturer, author, tour leader.
Subjects: W.Palearctic including Cape Verde Islands and Falkland Islands.
Products for sale: Duplicate slides, some originals, prints also available.
Address: Owl Cottage, Station Road, Rippingale, Lincs, PE10 0TA; (Tel/Fax) 01778 440500.
e-mail: birdmanandbird@hotmail.com

WILMSHURST, Roger
Wildlife photographer, particularly birds.
Subjects: All aspects of wildlife, particularly British and European birds, butterflies, plants, mammals etc.
Products for sale: 35mm, 6x6, 6x7, 645. Digital, mounted and framed pictures. Gallery in 'The Granary'.
Address: Sandhill Farmhouse, Sandhill Lane, Washington, Pulborough, West Sussex, RH20 4TD; 01903 892210, (Fax) 01903 893376.
e-mail: roger@nature-pics.co.uk
www.nature-pictures.co.uk

DIRECTORY OF LECTURERS

Lecturers who have indicated that they are willing to travel to all parts of Britain are listed first. For the remainder we have grouped them geographically in the following regions: England, Eastern; North-eastern; North-western; South-eastern; South-western; West Midlands and Wales; Scotland.

To ensure this valuable section continues strongly in the future, we would be grateful if you would mention the *Yearbook* when contacting any of the listed lecturers.

If your group has enjoyed a talk from anyone not listed here, we would appreciate receiving contact details so they might be included in the 2006 edition.

NO LIMITS

BATES, Tony

Photographer and lecturer.
Subjects: Mainly British wildlife, landscapes and astro landscapes.
Fees: £70 plus travel. **Limits:** None. **Times:** To suit.
Address: 22 Fir Avenue, Bourne, Lincs, PE10 9RY; 01778 425137.
e-mail: mtr@masher.f9.co.uk

BEJARANO, Santiago

Galapagos guide, tour leader and wildlife photographer.
Subjects: Natural history of the Galapagos Islands and an account of his life as a naturalist and photographer in the islands for over a decade.
Fees: £45 plus petrol. **Limits:** None. **Times:** Not May or November.
Address: 25 Trinity Lane, Beverley, East Yorkshire HU17 0DY; 01482 872716.
e-mail:
santiago@thinkgalapagos.karoo.co.uk
www.thinkgalapagos.com

BELL, Graham

Cruise lecturer worldwide, photographer, author.
Subjects: Arctic, Antarctic, America, Siberia, Australia, Canada, Iceland, Seychelles, UK - identification, behaviour, seabirds, garden birds, entertaining bird sound imitations etc.
Fees: £35 plus travel. **Limits:** None. **Times:** Any.
Address: Ros View, South Yearle, Wooler, Northumberland, NE71 6RB; (Tel/Fax) 01668 281310.
e-mail: seabirdsdgb@hotmail.com

BROOKS, Richard

Wildlife photographer, writer, lecturer.
Subjects: 12 talks (including Lesvos, Evros Delta, Israel, Canaries, E.Anglia, Scotland, Wales, Oman).
Fees: £75 plus petrol. **Limits:** None if accom provided. **Times:** Any.
Address: 24 Croxton Hamlet, Fulmodeston, Fakenham, Norfolk, NR21 0NP; 01328 878632.
e-mail: email@richard-brooks.co.uk
www.richard-brooks.co.uk

BOND, Terry

International consultant, ex-bank director, photographer, group field leader, conference speaker worldwide.
Subjects: 8 talks (including Scilly Isles, Southern Europe, USA - shorebirds and inland birds, Birdwatching Identification - a new approach).
Fees: By arrangement (usually only expenses). **Limits:** Most of UK. **Times:** Evenings.
Address: 3 Lapwing Crescent, Chippenham, Wiltshire, SN14 6YF; 01249 462674.
e-mail: terryebond@btopenworld.com

BUCKINGHAM, John

Lecturer, photographer, tour leader.
Subjects: 60+ titles covering birds, wildlife, botany, ecology and habitats in UK, Europe, Africa, Australia, India and the Americas.
Fees: £58 plus expenses. **Limits:** None. **Times:** Any.
Address: 3 Cardinal Close, Tonbridge, Kent, TN9 2EN; (Tel/Fax) 01732 354970.

BURROWS, Ian

Tour leader.
Subjects: Papua New Guinea, Cape Clear Island and 'Food from the Wild'.
Fees: £70 plus mileage over 100. **Limits:** Anything considered. **Times:** Evenings preferable, but other times considered.
Address: Well Cottage, 38 Creake Road, Sculthorpe, Fakenham, Norfolk, NR21 9NQ; 01328 856925; (Fax) 01328 862014.
e-mail: Ian@sicklebill.demon.co.uk
www.sicklebill.com

CANIS, Robert

Professional photographer, tour leader.
Subjects: Illustrated talks (including British and Finnish wildlife).
Fees: £45 plus petrol. **Limits:** None. **Times:** Oct-Mar.
Address: 26 Park Avenue, Sittingbourne, Kent, ME10 1QY; 07939 117570.
e-mail: rmcanis@msn.com
www.robertcanis.com

CARRIER, Michael

Lifelong interest in natural history.
Subjects: 1) 'Birds in Cumbria', 2) 'The Solway and its Birds' and 3) 'The Isle of May', 4) 'A look at Bird Migration'.
Fees: £20. **Limits:** None but rail connection essential. **Times:** Sept-March inclusive, afternoons or evenings.
Address: Lismore Cottage, 1 Front Street, Armathwaite, Carlisle, Cumbria, CA4 9PB; 01697 472218.

CHARTERS, Roger

Experienced wildlife sound recordist and one-time professional photographer.
Subjects: 'Sound recordings, a new dimension to identification', 'Scandinavia with emphasis on the Arctic', 'Ukraine - a birdwatcher's paradise' 'Spain', including the Cota Danãna, 'The Australian Outback'. Each talk lasts about one hour with extensive use of sound recordings and visual sequences.
Fees: £30 made payable to Warwickshire Wildlife Trust, plus 25p per mile.
Limits: None.
Address: 11 Eastnor Grove, Leamington Spa, Warwickshire CV31 1LD: 01926 882583.
e-mail: Roger.Charters@btinternet.com

CROUCHER, Roy

Wildlife tour leader, former local authority ecologist.
Subjects: Four talks (Northern France, Montenegro, Managing Britain's Habitats, Bird Song).
Fees: £50 plus petrol from Birmingham.
Limits: Mainland Britain. **Times:** November and December.
Address: Place de L'Eglise, 53700, Averton, Mayenne, France; 0033 2430 06969.
e-mail: roy_croucher@lineone.net

DOODY, Dee

Ornithologist, wildlife cameraman, wildlife artist, television presenter (wildlife) and voice-overs.
Subjects: Dee can offer an evening of wildife films taken from his recent TV series.

Subjects are; The Coast, Rivers, Moorland, Woodland, Estuaries, Urban, Lakes and Reservoirs, Farmland, Welsh Bird Reserves, plus The Red Kite, The Goshawk. All are 23mins long, any combination available plus talk, art display and questions.
Fees: £190 plus travel and accom. **Limits:** None. **Times:** Any (birdwatching fairs), Autumn and Winter preferred (groups).
Address: 2 Fan Terrace, Fan, Llanidloes, Powys, SY18 6NW: (Day) 01686 413819; (Eve) 01686 412163.

DUGGAN, Glenn
Ex-Commander Royal Navy, tour leader, researcher.
Subjects: Ten talks including, birds of paradise and bower birds, history of bird art (caveman to present day), modern day bird art, famous Victorian bird artists (John Gould, the Birdman and John James Andubohon.
Fees: £50 plus expenses. **Limits:** none with o.n accom. **Times:** Any.
Address: 25 Hampton Grove, Fareham, Hampshire, PO15 5NL; 01329 845976, (M) 07771 605320. http:// homepage.ntlworld.com/glenn.m.duggan/ e-mail: glenn.m.duggan@ntlworld.com

EYRE, John
Author, photographer, conservationist and chairman Hampshire Ornithological Society.
Subjects: World birding (Europe, Africa, Australasia and the Americas), plus special Hampshire subjects (eg. Gilbert White's birds and heathland birds).
Fees: £60 plus travel. **Limits:** Any location negotiable. **Times:** Any.
Address: 3 Dunmow Hill, Fleet, Hampshire, GU51 3AN; 01252 677850.
e-mail: John.Eyre@ntlworld.com

GALLOP, Brian
Speaker, photographer, tour leader.
Subjects: 30 talks covering UK, Africa, India, Galapagos and Europe - all natural history subjects.
Fees: £45 plus 20p per ml. **Limits:** None - o.n acc. if over 100 mls. **Times:** Any.
Address: 13 Orchard Drive, Tonbridge, Kent, TN10 4LT; 01732 361892.

GARNER, David
Wildlife photographer.
Subjects: 17 live talks and audio-visual shows on all aspects of wildlife in UK and some parts of Europe - list available.
Fees: £35 plus 20p per ml. **Limits:** None. **Times:** Any.
Address: 73 Needingworth Road, St Ives, Cambridgeshire, PE27 5JY; (H) 01480 463194; (W) 01480 463194. e-mail: davidgarner@hushwing.freeserve.co.uk http//hushwing.mysite.wanadoo-members.co.uk

GUNTON, Trevor
Ex.RSPB staff, recruitment advisor, lecturer and consultant.
Subjects: 'An Empire in the Atlantic' (Norse culture and wildlife), 'I Know an Island' (UK Bird Islands), 'A Norwegian Coastal Adventure', 'Birds and Pits', 'Birds of The Broadacres' (Yorkshire), 'Nature in Trust' (NT), 'Look Again at Birds', 'Shetland - Isles of the Simmer Dim' also membership recruitment workshops for wildlife organisations.
Fees: Variable (basic £60 plus expenses). **Limits:** None. **Times:** Anytime, anywhere.
Address: 15 St James Road, Little Paxton, St Neots, Cambs, PE19 6QW; (tel/Fax) 01480 473562. e-mail: trevor.gunton@tesco.net

HARROP, Hugh
Professional wildlife guide, photographer and author.
Subjects: 15 talks including Shetland wildlife, Shetland birds, polar bears, whales and dolphins, Galapagos, seals and sea lions, Alaska, Iceland, general wildlife photography.
Fees: £125 plus accom at cost and return flight from Shetland. **Limits:** UK only. **Times:** November to March.
Address: Longhill, Maywick, Shetland, ZE2 9JF; 01950 422483; (Fax) 01950422430.
e-mail: hugh@hughharrop.com
www.hughharrop.com

HASSELL, David

Birdwatcher and photographer.
Subjects: Six talks (including British seabirds, Shetland birds, British birds, USA birds, including Texas, California, Florida etc.).
Fees: £45 plus petrol. **Limits:** None.
Times: Any.
Address: 15 Grafton Road, Enfield, Middlesex, EN2 7EY; 020 8367 0308.
e-mail: david@hassell99.freeserve.co.uk
www.davidhassell.co.uk

KNYSTAUTAS, Algirdas

Ornithologist, photographer, writer, tour leader.
Subjects: Birds and natural history of Russia, Baltic States, S America, Indonesia, Birding the Great Silk Route (seven talks).
Fees: £1 per person. £70 minimum plus £25 travelling. **Limits:** None - in UK, o.n accom needed. **Times:** Oct and Nov.
Address: 7 Holders Hill Gardens, London, NW4 1NP; 020 8203 4317.
e-mail ibisbill@talk21.com

LANE, Mike

Wildlife photographer.
Subjects: Seven talks from the UK and worldwide, mostly on birds.
Fees: Varies. **Limits:** None. **Times:** None.
Address: 36 Berkeley Road, Shirley, Solihull, West Midlands, B90 2HS; 0121 744 7988,.e-mail: mikelane@nature-photography.co.uk
www.nature-photography.co.uk

LANGSBURY, Gordon FRPS

Professional wildlife photographer, lecturer, author and tour leader.
Subjects: 20 talks - Africa, Europe, USA, Falklands and UK. Full list provided.
Fees: £80 plus travel expenses. **Limits:** None. **Times:** Any.
Address: Sanderlings, 80 Shepherds Close, Hurley, Maidenhead, Berkshire, SL6 5LZ; (Tel/Fax) 01628 824252.
e-mail: gordonlangsbury@birdphoto.org.uk

McKAVETT, Mike

Photographer.
Subjects: Five talks; Birds and Wildlife of India, North and Western Kenya and the Gambia, Bird Migration in North America.
Fees: £40 plus expenses. **Limits:** None.
Times: Any.
Address: 34 Rectory Road, Churchtown, Southport, PR9 7PU; 01704 231358.

MOCKLER, Mike

Safari guide, tour leader, writer and photographer.
Subjects: Birds and other wildlife of: Botswana, Kenya, Tanzania, Zambia, Spain, Finland and Norway, Costa Rica, Antarctica and South Georgia, India and Brazil.
Fees: negotiable. **Limits:** None. **Times:** evenings.
Address: Gulliver's Cottage, Chapel Rise, Avon Castle, Ringwood, Hampshire, BH24 2BL; 01425 478103.
e-mail: mikemockler@lineone.net

MOIR, Geoffrey DFC, FRGS, FRPSL

Ret. Schoolmaster, lecturer, writer, philatelist, lived in Falkland Islands.
Subjects: Fully illustrated talks on subjects including: 'Falklands 2000', 'The Island of South Georgia and its Wildlife', 'The Flora of the Falkland Islands', 'Falkland's Wildlife'.
Fees: £20. **Limits:** None. **Times:** Any.
Address: 37 Kingscote Road, Croydon, Surrey, CR0 7DP; Tel/Fax 020 8654 9463.

MORRIS, Rosemary and YATES, Bas

Both members of Cookhill and Studley Camera Club (Wildlife photographers / Travel)
Subjects: England Naturally, Ecuador-Rainforests and Galapagos Islands, Savage Beasts and Noble Savages (Tanzania), Tanzania up Close, Southern Ireland to the Highlands, other talks in the pipeline.
Fees: Worcs/Warwicks £35 + mileage if over 40 miles. Distant talks negotiable.
Limits: Please ask, Will travel from Feb 2005. **Times:** Any.

Address: Wrens Nest, Droitwich Rd, New End, Astwoodbank, Redditch Worcs B96 6NE. e-mail: gilbert.morris1@btopenworld,com.uk

OFFORD, Keith

Photographer, writer, tour leader, conservationist.
Subjects: 14 talks covering raptors, uplands, gardens, migration, woodland wildlife, Australia, Southern USA, Tanzania, Gambia, Spain, SW.Africa.
Fees: £90 plus travel costs. **Limits:** none.
Times: Sept - April.
Address: Yew Tree Farmhouse, Craignant, Selattyn, Nr Oswestry, Shropshire, SY10 7NP; 01691 718740.
e-mail: keith-offord@virgin.net
www.keithofford.co.uk

PICKFORD, Terry

Co-ordinator NW Raptor Protection Group, advisory member to the government's raptor forum committee. Advisory member of the Lancashire Access Forum.
Subjects: 1) Raptor conservation/persecution NW England; 2) Home Life of the Golden Eagle in Scotland; 3) Wildlife of the Czech Republic.
Fees: £70 plus 15p per ml. **Limits:** None.
Times: Any.
Contact: 07977 890116.
e-mail: terry.pickford@fsmail.net

ROBINSON, Peter

Consultant ornithologist and former Scilly resident, author of *Birds of the Isles of Scilly.*
Subjects: Various talks on sea and landbirds of Scilly and life in an island environment; Song Thrushes, Storm Petrels and Kittiwakes.
Fees: £45 plus petrol. **Limits:** None.
Times: Any.
Address: 19 Pine Park Road, Honiton, Devon, EX14 2HR; 01404 549873.
e-mail: pjrobinson2@compuserve.com

RUMLEY-DAWSON, Ian

Photographer, course leader, cruise lecturer.
Subjects: 96 talks using twin dissolving projectors. Birds, mammals, insects, plants, habitats, ethology. Arctic, Antarctic, Falklands, N and S America, N.Z, Seychelles, North Pacific islands. Albatrosses, penguins, Snowy Owls, polar bears etc.
Fees: £50 plus expenses. **Limits:** None.
Times: Any.
Address: Oakhurst, Whatlington Road, Battle, East Sussex, TN33 0JN; 01424 772673.

SCOTT, Ann and Bob

Ex-RSPB staff, tour leaders, writers, lecturers, tutors, trainers.
Subjects: 16+ talks (including nature reserves, RSPB, tours, gardening, Europe, Africa, S America, after-dinner talks etc).
Fees: £60 plus travel over 50 mls. **Limits:** None (by arrangement). **Times:** Any.
Address: 8 Woodlands, St Neots, Cambridgeshire, PE19 1UE; 01480 214904; (Fax) 01480 473009.
e-mail: abscott@tiscali.co.uk

SWASH, Andy

Photographer, author, tour leader.
Subjects: Birds, general wildlife, scenery and tales from travels in: Antarctica, Argentina, Australia, Brazil, Chile, China, Costa Rica, Cuba, Galápagos, Kenya, Namibia, South Africa, USA or Venezuela.
Fees: £85 plus petrol. **Limits:** None. **Times:** Evenings.
Address: Stretton Lodge, 9 Birch Grove, West Hill, Ottery St Mary, Devon, EX11 1XP; (H&Fax) 01404 815383, (W) 01392 822901.
e-mail: andy_swash@wildguides.co.uk
www.wildguides.co.uk

TODD, Ralph

Tour leader.
Subjects: Nine talks incl. 'Galapagos Wildlife', 'On the Trail of the Crane', 'Polar Odyssey', 'Osprey Wardening at Loch Garten', Pyrenees, Iceland and Antarctica.
Fees: £60 plus expenses. **Limits:** None, neg over 120 mls. **Times:** Any - also short notice.

Address: 9 Horsham Road, Bexleyheath, Kent, DA6 7HU; (Tel/Fax) 01322 528335.
e-mail: rbtodd@todds9.fsnet.co.uk

WATTS, Nicholas

Farmer, conservationist, ornithologist, photographer.
Subjects: Farming and Wildlife', 'Birds on my Farm'.
Fees: £40 within 40 miles. Over 40 miles, larger fee. **Limits:** None. **Times:** Evenings, not Jun-Sep.
Address: Vine House Farm, Deeping St Nicholas, Spalding, PE11 3DG; 01775 630208.
e-mail: p.n.watts@farming.co.uk

WILKES, Mike FRPS

Professional wildlife photographer, tour leader.
Subjects: 13 talks on natural history in Africa, America, South America, Europe, Gt Britain.
Fees: According to distance, on request.
Limits: None. **Times:** Any.
Address: 43 Feckenham Road, Headless Cross, Redditch, Worcestershire, B97 5AS; 01527 550686.
e-mail: wilkes@photoshot.com

WILLIAMS, Nick

Photographer, lecturer, author, tour leader.
Subjects: Several audio visual shows (including Spain, Camargue, Turkey, Canaries and Cape Verde Islands, Falklands) and birds of prey.
Fee: £90-£110, depending on group size and distance. **Limits:** None. **Times:** Any.
Address: Owl Cottage, Station Road, Rippingale, Lincs, PE10 0TA; (Tel/Fax) 01778 440500.
e-mail: birdmanandbird@hotmail.com

WREN, Graham ARPS

Wildlife photographer, lecturer, tour guide.
Subjects: 22 talks: Birds - UK and Scandinavia, the environment - recent habitat changes and effect on bird populations; wildlife - Ohio and Kenya. Detailed information package supplied on request.
Fees: £50-70 plus petrol. **Limits:** None.
Times: Any.
Address: The Kiln House, Great Doward, Whitchurch, Ross-on-Wye, Herefordshire, HR9 6DU; 01600 890488, (Fax) 01600 890294.
e-mail: grahamjwren@aol.com

WYATT, John

Tour leader, photographer, writer, co-author of first *Teach Yourself Bird Sounds* cassette series.
Subjects: Over 40 talks (including birds and other wildlife of Africa, Central America, Europe and of specific habitats within these areas, bird identification by sight and sound, general natural history topics).
Fees: £60 plus travel. **Limits:** England and Wales only. **Times:** Any.
Address: Little Okeford, Christchurch Road, Tring, Hertfordshire, HP23 4EF; 01442 823356.
e-mail: wyatt@waxwing.u-net.com

EASTERN ENGLAND

BROOKS, David

Freelance naturalist.
Subjects: Various talks on wildlife, principally birds, in UK and overseas.
Fees: £50 plus petrol. **Limits:** 50 mls without o.n. accom. **Times:** Any.
Address: 2 Malthouse Court, Green Lane, Thornham, Norfolk, PE36 6NW; 01485 512548.
e-mail: david.g.brooks@tesco.net

COOK, Tony MBE

35 years employed by WWT. Travelled in Europe, Africa and N. America.
Subjects: 22 talks from Birds of The Wash, garden birds to travelogues of Kenya, E and W North America, Europe (Med to North Cape).
Fees: £35 plus 20p per ml. **Limits:** 100 mls.
Times: Any.

Address: 11 Carnoustie Court, Sutton Bridge, Spalding, Lincs, PE12; 01406 350069.

COURT, John

Enthusiastic amateur naturalist and photographer.
Subjects: Seven talks (including general wildlife, butterflies, dragonflies and birdwatching).
Fees: £35 plus 20p per mile. **Limits:** 100 mls. **Times:** All months apart from July and August, also short notice.
Address: Cedars, Hulletts Lane, Pilgrims Hatch, Brentwood, Essex, CM15 9RX; 01277 372217.

CROMACK, David

Editor of *Bird Watching* and *Birds Illustrated* magazines, bird tour leader.
Subjects: 1) 'Bird Magazines and the Art of Bird Photography', 2) 'World Class Bird Images (International Wildbird Photographer competition) and 3) 'Birds of Arizona and California'.
Fees: 1 and 2) No fee - expenses only, 3) £50 plus expenses. **Limits:** 175 mls. **Times:** Dec-Feb.
Address: c/o *Bird Watching* Magazine, Bretton Court, Peterborough, PE3 8DZ.
e-mail: david.cromack@emap.com

PIKE, David

Photographer, presenter and writer
Subjects: 'Winter Birds of Japan', 'Wildlife Photography'.
Fees: £100.
Address: Uffington Manor, Main Road, Uffington, Lincs, PE9 4SN; 01780 751944; (W) 01780 767711; (Fax) 01780 489218.
e-mail: david.pike@ukphotographics.co.uk
www.ukphotographics.co.uk.com

NORTH EASTERN ENGLAND

DOHERTY, Paul

Video maker/photographer.
Subjects: Five talks (Bids of Prey, Waders, Wetlands, Israel and California).
Fees: £60 plus petrol. **Limits:** 100 mls.
Times: Any.
Address: 28 Carousel Walk, Sherburn in Elmet, North Yorkshire, LS25 6LP; (Tel/Fax) 01977 684666.
e-mail: paul@birdvideodvd.com

MATHER, John Robert

Ornithologist, writer, tour guide, lecturer.
Subjects: Birds and wildlife of: Kenya, Tanzania, Uganda, South Africa, Costa Rica, Romania/Bulgaria, India, Nepal, Algonquin to Niagara. 'Bird on the Bench'.
Fees: £65 plus 20p per ml. **Limits:** 100 mls.
Times: Evenings.
Address: Eagle Lodge, 44 Aspin Lane, Knaresborough, North Yorkshire, HG5 8EP; 01423 862775.

PARKER, Susan and Allan ARPS

Professional photographers, (ASPphoto - Images of Nature), lecturers and tutors.
Subjects: Talks on birds and natural history, natural history photography - countries include UK, USA (Texas, Florida), Spain, Greece, Cyprus.
Fees: On application. **Limits:** Up to 120 mls without o.n accom. **Times:** Any.
Address: Ashtree House, 51 Kiveton Lane, Todwick, Sheffield, South Yorkshire, S26 1HJ; 01909 770238.
e-mail: aspaspphoto@clara.co.uk

SOUTH EASTERN ENGLAND

BEVAN, David

Conservation officer, photographer, writer.
Subjects: Nature conservation, natural history of the garden, butterflies, wild flowers. SAE for full details.
Fees: £70 plus petrol. **Limits:** 50 miles without o.n. accom, 150 mls otherwise.
Times: Evenings, days poss.
Address: 3 Queens Road, Bounds Green, London, N11 2QJ; (H) 020 8889 6375, (W) 020 8348 6005, (Fax) 020 8342 8754.
e-mail: conserving.bevan@virgin.net

BORG, Les

Photographer, course leader.
Subjects: Florida (mostly birds), nature photography (parts I, II and III), cetaceans of the Azores, 'A Year of Nature Photography', 'A Hint of Finland and Norway'.
Fees: Negotiable. **Limits:** 150 mls without o.n accom. **Times:** Any.
Address: 17 Harwood Close, Tewin, Welwyn, Herts, AL6 0LF; 01438 717841.
e-mail: les@les-borg-photography.co.uk
www.les-borg-photography.co.uk

BRITTEN, John

Former leader of local RSPB group.
Subjects: Birding trips to Antarctica, Caribbean, Galapagos, Australia, New Zealand, Baltics, former Soviet Union etc (full list available).
Fees: No fee (donation to RSPB requested), petrol costs. **Limits:** About an hour or two from Watford. **Times:** Any.
Address: Harlestone, 98 Sheepcot Lane, Garston, Hertfordshire, WD25 0EB; 01923 673205.
e-mail; john.britten@btinternet.com

CLEAVE, Andrew MBE

Head of environmental education centre, author, tour leader.
Subjects: 30 talks (including Galapagos, Arctic, Mediterranean and Indian birds, dormice, woodlands). List available.
Fees: £60 plus petrol. **Limits:** 60 mls without o.n accom. **Times:** Evenings, not school holidays.
Address: 31 Petersfield Close, Chineham, Basingstoke, Hampshire, RG24 8WP; (H) 01256 320050, (W) 01256 882094, (Fax) 01256 880174.
e-mail: andrew@bramleyfirth.co.uk

COOMBER, Richard

Tour leader, photographer, writer.
Subjects: Alaska, Australia, Botswana, Namibia, Seychelles, Falklands, Galapagos, S America, USA, seabirds.
Fees: £65 plus petrol. **Limits:** 50 mls without o.n. accom 150 mls otherwise. **Times:** Afternoons or evenings.
Address: 1 Haglane Copse, Lymington, Hampshire, SO41 8DT; 01590 674471.
e-mail: richard@coomber1.fsbusiness.co.uk

FEATHERBE, David

Wildlife and landscape photographer.
Subjects: Wildlife of the Dover Straits, Kalahari Gemsbok and South West Cape Province, Zimbabwe, Western Matabeleland.
Fees: £60. **Limits:** Primarily S.E England, further a field by negotiation. **Times:** 7.30 to 8.00 start.
Address: 16 East Cliff Gardens, Folkestone, Kent CT19 6AP. 01303 244489;
e-mail: david.featherbe@mac.com
http://homepage.mac.com/david.featherbe

FURNELL, Dennis

Natural history writer, radio and television broadcaster, artist and wildlife sound recordist.
Subjects: British and European wildlife, France, (*The Nature of France*). Wildlife sound recording, wildlife and disability access issues.
Fees: £100. **Limits:** 50 miles, further with o.n. accom. **Times:** Afternoons or evenings according to commitments.
Address: 19 Manscroft Road, Gadebridge, Hemel Hempstead, Hertfordshire, HP1 3HU; 01442 242915, (Fax) 01442 242032.
e-mail; dennis.furnell@btinternet.com
www.natureman.co.uk

NOBBS, Brian

Amateur birdwatcher and photographer.
Subjects: Wildlife of the Wild West, Israel, Mediterranean, Florida, Wildlife Gardening, Reserved for Birds.
Fees: £30 plus 25p per ml. **Limits:** Kent, Surrey, Sussex. **Times:** Evenings.
Address: The Grebes, 36 Main Road, Sundridge, Sevenoaks, Kent, TN14 6EP; 01959 563530.
e-mail: Brian.nobbs@tiscali.co.uk

READ, Mike

Photographer, tour leader, writer.
Subjects: 12 talks featuring British and

foreign subjects (list available on receipt of sae).
Fees: £70 plus travel. **Limits:** 175 mls. **Times:** Any.
Address: Claremont, Redwood Close, Ringwood, Hampshire, BH24 1PR; 01425 475008, (Fax) 01425 473160.
e-mail: mike@mikeread.co.uk
www.mikeread.co.uk

TREVIS, Barry

Nature reserve warden, bird-ringer, widely travelled birdwatcher.
Subjects: Birding in Peru; Birds of Churchill, Manitoba; Tanzania - birds, parks and Kilimanjaro; Birding 'Down-under'; Lemford Springs Nature Reserve.
Fees: £75. **Limits:** Up to 20mls, travel costs otherwise. **Times:** Any.
Address: 11 Lemsford Village, Welwyn Garden City, Hertfordshire, AL8 7TN; (H) 01707 335517.
e-mail: trevis@unisonfree.net

WARD, Chris

Photographer.
Subjects: 16 talks on UK and worldwide topics (W.Palearctic, Americas, Africa, Australia) – primarily birds, some other wildlife.
Fees: £35 plus petrol. **Limits:** 100 mls. **Times:** Evenings, afternoons poss.
Address: 276 Bideford Green, Leighton Buzzard, Bedfordshire, LU7 2TU; 01525 375528;
e-mail: chris@chriswardphotography.co.uk

WRIGHT, Barry

Biomedical scientist, widely travelled abroad.
Subjects: Various South American countries and West Indies. 'A Year Abroad!', 'Journey across South America', 'Travels in Tibet', 'Travels in Uganda' - all talks based on birding trips. Also 'Highs and Lows of Global Birding'.
Fees: £50 plus petrol. **Limits:** 60 mls without o.n accom. **Times:** Evenings.
Address: 6 Hatton Close, Northfleet, Kent DA11 8SD; (H) 01474 320918, (W) 01322 428100 (4895).
e-mail: barry@birding98.fsnet.co.uk

SOUTH WESTERN ENGLAND

COOMBER, Richard

Tour leader, photographer, writer.
Subjects: Alaska, Australia, Botswana, Namibia, Seychelles, Falklands, Galapagos, S America, USA, seabirds.
Fees: £65 plus petrol. **Limits:** 50 mls without o.n. accom 150 mls otherwise. **Times:** Afternoons or evenings.
Address: 1 Haglane Copse, Lymington, Hampshire, SO41 8DT; 01590 674471.
e-mail: richard@coomber1.fsbusiness.co.uk

COUZENS, Dominic

Full-time birdwatcher, tour leader (UK and overseas), writer and lecturer.
Subjects: The Secret Habits of Garden Birds', 'Birds Behaving Badly - the trials and tribulations of birds through the year', 'Bird Sounds - As You've Never Heard Them Before'.
Fees: £50 plus travel. **Limits:** London and south. **Times:** Any.
Address: 3 Clifton Gardens, Ferndown, Dorset, BH22 9BE; (Tel/Fax) 01202 874330. e-mail: Dominic@birdwords.co.uk
www.birdwords.co.uk

WEST MIDLANDS AND WALES

BROADBENT, David

Photographer.
Subjects: UK birds and wild places. In praise of natural places.
Fees: £70 plus travel. **Limits:** 50mls without o.n accom. Anywhere otherwise. **Times:** Any.
Address: Rose Cottage, Bream Road, Whitepool, St Briavels, Lydney, GL15 6TL.
e-mail: info@davidbroadbent.com
www.davidbroadbent.com

CONWAY, Wendy PSA4. AFIAP

Award-winning wildlife photographer.
Subjects: Several talks, birds, mammals, landscapes from UK, USA, Lesvos and Africa.

Fees: £45 plus petrol. **Limits:** Over 50mls please contact. **Times:** Any.
Address: The Oaks, Parkend Walk, Coalway, Coleford, Glos GL16 7JR; 01594 832956. e-mail: wendy@terry-wall.com

DENNING, Paul
Wildlife photographer, lecturer.
Subjects: 15 talks (birds, mammals, reptiles, butterflies etc, UK, western and eastern Europe, north and central America, Canaries).
Fees: £40 plus petrol. **Limits:** 100 mls.
Times: Evenings, weekends.
Address: 17 Maes Maelwg, Beddau, Pontypridd, CF38 2LD; (H) 01443 202607; (W) 02920 673243.
e-mail: pgdenning.naturepics@virgin.net

SHERWIN, Andrew
Interests in natural history and photography.
Subjects: Ten talks including Kenya, Gambia, Israel, California, Canada, India, Lesvos, Pyrenees.
Fees: £45. **Limits:** 50 mls. **Times:** Evenings only.
Address: 26 Rockingham Close, Ashgate, Chesterfield, Derbyshire, S40 1JE; 01246 221070.
e-mail: andrew.sherwin@btinternet.com

TAYLOR, Mick
Co-ordinator South Peak Raptor Group, photographer, ornithologist, writer.
Subjects: Several talks including Merlins, Peak District birds, Peak District raptors, Alaskan wildlife.
Fees: £50 plus petrol. **Limits:** Negotiable.
Times: Evenings preferred.
Address: 76 Hawksley Avenue, Chesterfield, Derbyshire, S40 4TL; 01246 277749.

WALL, Terry ARPS EFIAP PPSA
Wildlife photographer.
Subjects: Several (birds, mammals, landscapes - USA, UK, Lesvos, Africa and Galapagos).
Fees: £45 plus petrol. **Limits:** Over 50 mls please contact. **Times:** Any.
Address: The Oaks, Parkend Walk, Coalway, Coleford, Glos GL16 7JR; 01594 832956. e-mail: wildimages@terry-wall.com
www.terry-wall.com

Directory of BTO Speakers

This directory has been compiled to assist bird clubs and similar organisations in locating speakers for their indoor meetings.
Each entry within the directory consists of a named individual along with their e-mail address, a list of talks/lectures undertaken and details of fees, expenses and travelling distances.
If you wish to contact anyone listed in this directory, you may do so directly by letter or telephone or by e-mail as indicated by the individual speaker's entry.
Clubs that are part of the BTO/Bird Clubs Partnership, and are more than 120 miles from Thetford should contact Derek Toomer about special rates.

APPLETON, Graham
Head of Fundraising and Publicity.
Subjects: The Work of the BTO, The BTO Migration Atlas, Time to Fly - Bird Migration. **Fee:** BTO fee £35–£40. **Expenses:** Negotiable. **Distance:** Dependant on expenses.
E-mail: graham.appleton@bto.org

BAILLIE, Dr Stephen
Director of Populations Research.
Subjects: Migration Watch, Population Monitoring.
Fee: BTO fee £35–£40.
Expenses: Travel. **Distance:** By agreement. E-mail: stephen.baillie@bto.org

BAKER, Jeff
Head of Membership
Subjects: The work of the BTO, 'Little brown jobs' - Warblers and how to identify them. **Fee:** £40. **Expenses:** Travel expenses. **Distance:** Dependent on expenses.
E-mail: jeff.baker@bto.org

BALMER, Dawn
Demography Unit Population Biologist.
Subjects: Bird Ringing,

Ringing in Lesbos , BTO Work in General, Golden Pheasants.
Fee: BTO fee £35–£40.
Expenses: Travel. **Distance:** Anywhere. E-mail: dawn.balmer@bto.org

BEAVEN, Peter
Nest Records Officer.
Subjects: Barn Owls in Britain, Nests and Nest Recording , In Search of British Sand Martins - Ringing in West Africa, The Wonders of Bird Migration, The Work of the BTO. **Fee:** BTO fee £35–£40, £50 for private talks. **Expenses:** Travel. **Distance:** Anywhere. E-mail: peter.beaven@bto.org

BLACKBURN, Jez
Ringing Unit Recoveries and Licencing Team Leader.
Subjects: Bird Moult (suitable for ringers), Sule Skerry.
Fee: BTO fee £35–£40, £50 for private talks. **Expenses:** Travel. **Distance:** East Anglia. E-mail: jez.blackburn@bto.org

CHAMBERLAIN, Dr Dan
Senior Research Ecologist, BTO Scotland.
Subjects: Garden BirdWatch, Breeding Bird Survey.
Fee: BTO fee £35–£40.
Expenses: Travel. **Distance:** By agreement. E-mail: dan.chamberlain@bto.org

CLARK, Jacquie
Head of Ringing Unit.
Subjects: Waders and Severe Weather, Why Ring Birds? Ringing for Conservation , Birds and Weather, The Migration Atlas. **Fee:** BTO fee £35–40. **Expenses:** Petrol. **Distance:** 100 mile radius of Thetford. E-mail: jacquie.clark@bto.org

CLARK, Dr Nigel
Head of Projects Development Unit.
Subjects: Waders, Man and Estuaries, Horseshoe Crabs and Waders, Migration through Delaware in Spring.
Fee: BTO fee £35–40.
Expenses: Petrol. **Distance:** 100 mile radius of Thetford. E-mail: nigel.clark@bto.org

Crick, Dr Humphrey
Head of Demography Unit.
Subjects: Climate Change and Birds, One Million Nests.
Fee: BTO fee £35–£40 £50 for private. **Expenses:** Mileage @ 25p per mile.
Distance: Willing to travel prefer less than 100 miles from Cambridge. E-mail: humphrey.crick@bto.org

FULLER, Dr Rob
Director of Habitats Research.
Subjects: Monitoring Woods for Biodiversity, Woodland Management and Birds, The Importance of BTO Surveys to Bird Conservation. **Fee:** BTO fee £35–£40. **Expenses:** Travel. **Distance:** Anywhere. E-mail: rob.fuller@bto.org

GILLINGS, Dr Simon
Terrestrial Ecology Unit Research Ecologist.
Subjects: Winter Golden Plovers and Lapwings, Winter Farmland Birds. **Fee:** BTO fee £35–£40. **Expenses:** Travel. **Distance:** Anywhere. E-mail: simon.gillings@bto.org

GOUGH, Su
Terrestrial Ecology Unit Research Ecologist.
Subjects: Bird Biology, London Bird Project, Wildlife of Canada non-BTO talk, Wildlife of European Mountains non-BTO talk.
Fee: BTO fee £35–£40, expenses for private talks.
Expenses: Travel. **Distance:** Negotiable.
E-mail: su.gough@bto.org

GRANTHAM, Mark
Ringing Unit Recoveries Officer.
Subjects: A range of general talks on ringing, migration and Bird Observatories, Oiled sea-birds. **Fee:** BTO fee £35–£40. **Expenses:** Travel. **Distance:** 100 miles. E-mail: mark.grantham@bto.org

GREENWOOD, Professor J J D
BTO Director.
Subjects: How to Change Government Policy by Counting Birds, Why Ring Birds? The Future for Birds .. and People, GM and Birds: What's the Problem?
Fee: BTO fee £35–£40. £50 for private talks. **Expenses:** Public transport or 35p/mile. **Distance:** 100 miles from Thetford - further by arrangement. E-mail: jeremy.greenwood@bto.org

HENDERSON, Dr Ian
Terrestrial Ecology Unit Research Manager.
Subjects: Arable Farming and Birds.
Fee: BTO fee £35–£40.
Expenses: Travel. **Distance:** By agreement. E-mail: ian.henderson@bto.org

HOLLOWAY, Steve
Wetland & Coastal Ecology Unit Research Ecologist.
Subjects: Wetland Bird Survey. **Fee:** BTO fee £35–£40. **Expenses:** Travel. **Distance:** By agreement. E-mail: steve.holloway@bto.org

LACK, Dr Peter
Head of Information Systems Unit.
Subjects: Bird Atlassing, Palearctic Migrants in Africa, On Foot in Rwanda and Zambia, Bird Ecology in East African Savannahs, General Natural History of Eastern Africa. All are given as non-BTO talks **Fee:** Negotiable. **Expenses:** Travel. **Distance:** 60 miles from Bury St Edmunds.
E-mail: peter.lack@bto.org

MARCHANT, John
Census Unit Team Leader.
Subjects: Heronries, Waterways Bird Survey/ Waterways Breeding Bird Survey, Breeding Bird Trends in the UK. **Fee:** BTO fee £35–£40. **Expenses:** Travel. **Distance:** By agreement. E-mail: john.marchant@bto.org

MUSGROVE, Dr Andy
Wetland & Coastal Ecology Unit Research Manager.
Subjects: The Wetland Bird Survey, Little Egrets in the UK, Recording Moths in Your Garden non-BTO.
Fee: BTO fee £35–£40, £30 for private talk. **Expenses:** Travel. **Distance:** By agreement. E-mail: andy.musgrove@bto.org

NOBLE, Dr David
Head of Census Unit.
Subjects: The Farmland Bird Indicator, Population Trends. **Fee:** BTO fee £35–£40. **Expenses:** Travel. **Distance:** By agreement. E-mail: david.noble@bto.org

RAVEN, Mike
Breeding Bird Survey Organiser.
Subjects: Latest Findings from the Breeding Bird Survey. **Fee:** BTO fee £35–£40. **Expenses:** Travel. **Distance:** By agreement.
E-mail: mike.raven@bto.org

REHFISCH, Dr Mark
Head of Wetland & Coastal Ecology Unit.
Subjects: Introduced Species Waterbird Alerts, Golden Pheasants Wetland Work at the BTO, Climate Change, Water Quality and Waterbirds, Monitoring Waterbirds, Sea Level Rise and Climate Change.
Fee: BTO fee £35–£40 up to £40 for private talk.
Expenses: Travel. **Distance:** By agreement. E-mail: mark.rehfisch@bto.org

ROBINSON, Dr Rob
Demography Unit Senior Population Biologist.
Subjects: Farming and Birds, House Sparrows, Starling Population Declines.
Fee: BTO fee £35–£40.
Expenses: Travel. **Distance:** By agreement. E-mail: rob.robinson@bto.org

SIRIWARDENA, Dr Gavin
Terrestrial Ecology Unit Research Manager.
Subjects: Marsh and Willow Tits - Analysis of BTO Data, Evidence of Impacts of Nest Predation and Competition, Quantifying Migratory Strategies. Currently all short talks. **Fee:** BTO fee £35–£40. **Expenses:** Travel. **Distance:** 50 miles further with accommodation. E-mail: gavin.siriwardena@bto.org

TOMS, Mike
Garden BirdWatch Organiser.
Subjects: The BTO Garden BirdWatch. **Fee:** £40.00. **Expenses:** Petrol. **Distance:** 50 miles, further by Arrangement. E-mail: michael.toms@bto.org

TOOMER, Dr Derek
Membership Development Officer.
Subjects: Making Your Birding Count - the Work of the BTO. **Fee:** BTO fee £35–£40. **Expenses:** Travel. **Distance:** Negotiable. E-mail: derek.toomer@bto.org

VICKERY, Dr Juliet
Head of Terrestrial Ecology Unit.
Subjects: Farmland Birds.
Fee: BTO fee £35–£40.
Expenses: Travel. **Distance:** 100 miles. E-mail: juliet.vickery@bto.org

WERNHAM, Dr Chris
Senior Research Ecologist, BTO Scotland.
Subjects: The BTO's Migration Research including the Migration Atlas and later developments, The work of BTO Scotland.
Fee: £40. **Expenses:** Petrol. **Distance:** Scotland and northeast England. E-mail: chris.wernham@bto.org

TRADE DIRECTORY

Goldfinch by Keith Offord

BIRD GARDEN SUPPLIERS

BAMFORDS TOP FLIGHT

Company ethos: Family-owned manufacturing company providing good quality bird foods via a network of UK stockists or mail order. RSPB Corporate Member, BTO Business Ally, Petcare Trust Member.
Key product lines: A range of wild bird mixtures containing the revolutionary new 'Pro-tec Health Aid', developed by Bamfords, to protect and promote the welfare of wild birds. Vast array of other foods and seeds for birds.
Other services: Trade suppliers of bulk and pre-packed bird and petfoods. Custom packing/own label if required.
Opening times: Mon-Fri (8am-5.30pm); Sat (8am–12 noon); Sunday (10am–12.00 noon, Mill Shop only).
Address; Globe Mill, Midge Hall, Leyland, Lancashire, PR26 6TN. 01772 456300;(Fax) 01772 456302;
e-mail: sales@bamfords.co.uk
www.bamfords.co.uk

CJ WILDBIRD FOODS LTD

Company ethos: High quality products, no-quibble guarantee, friendly, professional service.
Key product lines: Complete range of RSPB Birdcare feeders, food, nest boxes, bird tables and accessories alongside a collection of other wildlife-related products.
Other services: Mail order company, online ordering, 24hr delivery service. Free handbook.
Opening times: Mon-Fri (9am-5pm).
Address; The Rea, Upton Magna, Shrewsbury, Shropshire, SY4 4UR; 0800 731 2820; Fax; 01743 709504.
e-mail: enquiries@birdfood.co.uk
www.birdfood.co.uk

ERNEST CHARLES

Company ethos: Member of Birdcare Standards Assoc. ISO 9001 registered. Offering quality bird foods/wildlife products through a friendly mail-order service.
Key product lines: Bird foods, feeders, nest boxes and other wildlife products.
Other services: Own label work for other companies considered and trade enquiries.
Opening times: Mon to Fri (8am-5pm).
Contact: Stuart Christophers, Copplestone Mills, Crediton, Devon EX17 5NF; 01363 84842; (Fax) 01363 84147.
e-mail: stuart@ernest-charles.com
www.ernest-charles.com

foodforbirds.co.uk

Company ethos: Specialist mail order company supplying high quality wild bird foods via a fast and friendly next day service. Supporter of RSPB and BTO through parent company.
Key product lines: A great range of tried and tested, freshly made wild bird mixtures, together with a whole host of straight foods – peanuts, sunflowers, niger seed, fat foods etc.
Other services: Vast array of bird feeders from peanuts and seed, plus other wildlife foods, all of which can be ordered via a secure on-line website. Send for free catalogue.
Opening times: Telesales (freephone) 8am-5.30pm (order before midday for next day delivery). Answer phone outside these hours. On-line ordering and fax, 24 hours.
Contact: Foodforbirds, PO Box 247, Leyland, Lancashire PR26 6TN; (Freephone) 0800 043 9022; (Fax) 01772 456 302. e-mail: sales@foodforbirds.co.uk
www.foodforbirds.co.uk

JACOBI JAYNE & CO.

Company ethos: Supplying market-leading products of highest quality and proven conservation worth for almost 20 years. Offering expertise and special prices to wildlife groups, schools and colleges.
Key product lines: Birdfeeders, birdfoods, nest boxes & accessories. UK distributor of Schwegler woodcrete nest boxes, Droll Yankees feeders and Jacobi Jayne wildlife foods.
Other services: *Wild Bird News* mail-order catalogue.
Opening times: 24hrs (use websites or

answering service when office is closed). **Contact:** Graham Evans/Sally Haynes, Jacobi Jayne & Co, Wealden Forest Park, Canterbury, Kent, CT6 7LQ; 0800 072 0130; (Fax) 01227 719235.
e-mail: enquiries@jacobijayne.com
www.jacobijayne.com www.birdon.com
www.wildbirdnews.com

JAMIE WOOD LTD

Company ethos: Quality hand-made products at competitive prices as supplied to the RSPB, universities, film units, householders. Thirty years' experience.
Key products: Hides, photographic electronics, nest boxes, feeders, bird tables, patio stands, bird food.
Other services: Mail order, delivery ex-stock, within seven days.
Opening times: Telesales, Mon to Fri (9am-9pm), Sat to Sun (10am-4pm).
Contact: Keith, Karen or Ron, Jamie Wood Ltd, Dept BYD, 1 Green Street, Old Town, Eastbourne, Sussex, BN21 1QN; Tel/Fax; 01323 727291. www.birdtables.com
e-mail: Jamiewood@birdtables.com

VINE HOUSE FARM BIRD FOODS

Company ethos: Growing and selling black sunflowers, red and white millet, canary seed, naked oats and now niger direct from the farm to the public.
Key product lines: Full range of bird food plus feeders and other accessories.
Other services: Open days in the winter (January 16 and February 20) to view all the finches and buntings feeding at our farm. Farm walks in the summer.
Opening times: Mon to Sat (8am-5pm).
Contact: Nicholas Watts, Vine House Farm, Deeping St Nicholas, Spalding, PE11 3DG;01775 630208; (Fax) 01775 630244.
e-mail p.n.watts@farming.co.uk
www.vinehousefarmbirdfoods.co.uk

BOOK PUBLISHERS

BRITISH ORNITHOLOGISTS' UNION

Expected during 2005: *The Birds of Uganda; The Birds of São Tome, Principé and Annobon; The Birds of Borneo.*
Address: BOU, Dept of Zoology, University of Oxford,South Parks Road, Oxford OX1 3PS. (Tel/fax) 01865 281842.
e-mail: sales@bou.org.uk
www.bou.org.uk

CHRISTOPHER HELM PUBLISHERS

Imprints: An imprint of A & C Black Publishers Ltd, incorporating Pica Press (acquired Oct 2000) and T&AD Poyser (acquired June 2002).
New for 2005: *The Good Bird Guide; RSPB Childen's Book of Birdwatching; Orchids of Britain and Ireland; Lapland: A Natural History; Where to Watch Mammals in Britain and Ireland; Everything You Always Wanted to Know About Birds.. But Were Afraid to Ask.*
Address: 37 Soho Square, London, W1D 3QZ; 020 7758 0200; (Fax) 020 7758 0222.
e-mail: ornithology@acblack.com

HARPER COLLINS PUBLISHERS

Imprints: Collins Natural History — the leading publisher of fieldguides to the natural world.
Collins New Naturalist Series — the encyclopaedic reference for all areas of British natural history.
HarperCollins — publisher of the best illustrated books.
New for 2005: Bill Oddie's *How to Watch Wildlife; Field Guide to Sharks of the World*, L Compagno, S Fowler & M Dando; *Field Guide Birds of South America, Non-passerines*, F Erize & J R Mata; *Collins Encyclopedia of Birds*, Dominic Couzens.
Address: 77-85 Fulham Palace Rd, Hammersmith, London, W6 8JB; 020 8307 4998; (Fax) 020 8307 4037. e-mail: myles.Archibald@harpercollins.co.uk
www.fireandwater.com
www.collins.co.uk

NEW HOLLAND PUBLISHERS (UK) LTD

Imprints; New Holland, illustrated bird books, general wildlife and personality-led natural history.
New for 2005: *Garden Bird Behaviour;*

Wildlife Trusts Birdwatcher's Guide: Fieldcraft and Identification; The Ultimate Bird Feeder Handbook; Wildlife Trusts Birdwatcher's Guide: Bird Migration; Complete Back Garden Bird Watcher; Concise Guide to Birds of South East Asia; Photographic Field Guide to Birds of Costa Rica.
Address: Garfield House, 86-88 Edgware Road, London, W2 2EA; 020 7724 7773; (Fax) 020 7258 1293.
e-mail: postmaster@nhpub.co.uk
www.newhollandpublishers.com

WILD*Guides* LTD

Imprints; WILD*Guides* — definitive natural history fieldguides. Hardback and flexicover.
OCEAN*Guides* — definitive identification guides to marine wildlife. Hardback and flexicover.
WILD eARTh — lavishly illustrated celebrations of wildlife and natural places. Hardback.
Your Countryside Guides — regional heritage guides for walkers. Hardback. Sales of all books benefit conservation.
New for 2005: *A Photographic Guide to the Nightjars of the World, Wildlife of the Seychelles, Whales and Dolphins of the North American Pacific, Britain's Mammals, Wildlife Walks in the Thames Valley.*
Address: Parr House, 63 Hatch Lane, Old Basing, Hants, RG24 7EB; 01256 478309; (Fax) 01256 818039.
e-mail: info@wildguides.co.uk
www.wildguides.co.uk

BOOK SELLERS

NHBS MAIL ORDER BOOKSTORE

Company ethos: A unique natural history, conservation and environmental bookstore.
Key subjects: Natural history, conservation, environmental science, zoology, habitats and ecosystems, botany, marine biology.
Other services: NHBS.com offers a searchable and browseable web catalogue with more than 95,000 titles.
Opening times: Mon-Fri (9am-5pm). for mail-order service.
Address; 2-3 Wills Road, Totnes, Devon, TQ9 5XN; 01803 865913; (Fax) 01803 865280. e-mail: nhbs@nhbs.co.uk
www.nhbs.com

PICTURE BOOK

Company ethos: Knowledgeable staff, natural history books new and secondhand available during shop hours to browse, or post free.
Key subjects: Birdwatching, natural history, travel guides.
Other services: Mail order, catalogue available.
Opening times: Mon-Sat (9.15am-5pm).
Address; Picture Book, 6 Stanley Street, Leek ST13 5HG; 01538 384337; (Fax) 01538 399696.
e-mail: sally@thebookshopleek
www.leekbooks.co.uk

PORTLAND OBSERVATORY BOOK SHOP

Company ethos: To meet the needs of amateur and professional naturalists.
Key subjects: Ornithology, general natural history, topography, art and local history. New and secondhand.
Other services: Mail order, discount on new books, increased discount for observatory members.
Opening times: Wed, Sat and Sunday; (10am to 4pm). Other times on request.
Address; Bird Observatory, Old Lower Light, Portland Bill, Dorset, DT5 2JT; 01305 820553, (shop) 01305 826625, (home) 01225 700728.
e-mail: petermowday@tiscali.co.uk
www.portlandbirdobs.btinternet.co.uk

SECOND NATURE

Company ethos: Buying and selling out-of-print/secondhand/antiquarian books on natural history, topography and travel.
Key subjects: Birds, mammals and travel with a natural history interest. Very large specialist stock.
Other services; Occasional catalogues issued. Often exhibiting at bird/natural history fairs.

Opening times: Mail order only.
Address; Knapton Book Barn, Back Lane, Knapton, York, YO26 6QJ; (Tel/fax) 01904 339493.
e-mail: SecondnatureYork@aol.com

ORNITHOLIDAYS *BOOK STOP*

Company ethos: Friendly and helpful staff on hand to assist in the purchase of ornithological and natural history books.
Key subjects: Ornithology and natural history books by mail order.
Other services; We are primarily a tour operator sending birdwatching and natural history tours worldwide, including cruises to Antarctica, the Amazon, Sea of Cortez and Galapagos. Since 2000 we have complemented our business by successfully supplying a wide range of books published by the leading companies at a 10% discount with free postage and packing within the UK.
Opening times: Mail order only. Mon-Fri (9am-5pm).
Address: 29 Straight Mile, Romsey, Hampshire SO51 9BB; 01794 523500; (Fax) 01794 523544.
e-mail: info@ornitholidays.co.uk
www.ornitholidays.co.uk and www.cruisesfornature.co.uk

SUBBUTEO BOOKS

Company ethos: Specialist knowledge on all aspects of natural history, friendly service.
Key subjects: Wildlife, natural history and travel books.
Other services: Source any natural history book from around the world. Online ordering, free catalogue.
Opening times: Mon-Fri (9am-5pm).
Address: The Rea, Upton Magna, Shrewsbury, Shropshire, SY4 4UR; 0870 010 9700; (Fax) 0870 010 9699.
e-mail: info@wildlifebooks.com
www.wildlifebooks.com

CLOTHING SUPPLIERS

COUNTRY INNOVATION

Company ethos: Friendly advice by well-trained staff.
Key product lines: Full range of outdoor wear: Jackets, smocks, fleeces, trousers, walking boots, poles, lightweight clothing, hats, gloves, bags and pouches. Ladies fit available.
Other services: Mail order.
Opening times; Mon-Fri (9am-5pm).
Address: 1 Broad Street, Congresbury, North Somerset, BS49 5DG; 01934 877 333; (Fax) 01934 877999.
e-mail: sales@countryinnovation.com
www.countryinnovation.com

EQUIPMENT AND SERVICES

ALWICH BOOKS

Company ethos: Serving the practical needs of the active birdwatcher.
Key product lines: The Bird Watcher's All-weather Flexible Pocket Book, notebooks that can be used in all weather conditions.
Address: Grace, JR Reid Print and Media Group, 79-109 Glasgow Road, Blantyre, Glasgow G72 0LY;01698 307415.
www.alwych.co.uk

BIRDGUIDES LTD

Company ethos: Top quality products and services, especially using new technologies such as CD-ROM, DVD, websites, plus one-stop on-line shop for books, bird food etc.
Key product lines: DVD-ROM, CD-ROM, DVD, video guides to British, European and American birds. Rare bird news services via e-mail, website and SMS.
New for 2005: *BWPi (Birds of the Western Palearctic)* DVD-ROM
Address: Dave Gosney, Jack House, Ewden, Sheffield, S36 4ZA; 0114 2831002; order line (freephone) 0800 919391.
e-mail: birdguides@birdfood.co.uk
www.birdguides.com

BIRD IMAGES

Company ethos: High quality products at affordable prices.
Key product lines: Bird videos and DVDs.
New for 2005: *The DVD Guide to British Birds.*

Opening times: Telephone first.
Address: 28 Carousel Walk, Sherburn in Elmet, North Yorkshire LS25 6LP; 01977 684666. www.birdvideodvd.com

EagleEye OpticZooms

Company ethos: Innovative design, quality manufacturing, custom products, comprehensive and expert advice on all aspects of digital photography and digiscoping.
Key product lines: Telephoto lenses for fixed lens digital cameras/camcorders, digiscoping adapters and accessories, custom digital camera accessories.
New for 2005: Open days every Saturday (see website for details).
Opening times: Mon-Fri (9am-5.30pm).
Address: Carlo Bonacci, Wentshaw Lodge, Fairseat, Sevenoaks, Kent, TN15 7LR, UK; Tel/(Fax) 01474 871219.
e-mail: info@eagleeyeuk.com
www.eagleeyeuk.com

EVERETT ASSOCIATES LTD

Company ethos: Friendly support for all customers, especially for those new to computing.
Key product lines: CDs of Western Palearctic, world birds, butterflies and moths databases.
New for 2005: Fishing and house contents databases.
Address: Peter Everett, Longnor House, Gunthorpe, Norfolk NR24 2NS; Tel/fax 01263 860035.
e-mail: everett:birdsoftware.co.uk
www.birdsoftware.co.uk

GOLDEN VALLEY INSURANCE SERVICES

Company ethos: Knowledgeable, friendly insurance services. Free information pack on request. Freephone telephone number for all enquiries.
Key product lines: Insurance for optical/photographic/video/computer equipment for birdwatchers. Also, public liability for ornithological clubs and societies.
Opening times: Mon-Fri (9am-5pm), answering machine at other times
Address: Sharron or Marion, Golden Valley Insurance Services, The Olde Shoppe, Ewyas Harold, Herefordshire HR2 0ES;0800 015 4484; (Fax) 01981 240451.
e-mail: gvinsurance@aol.com

WILDSOUNDS

Company ethos: Donates a significant portion of profit to bird conservation, committed to sound environmental practices, official bookseller to African Bird Club (ABC) and Ornithological Society of the Middle East (OSME). Operates a Commission for Conservation Programme.
Key product lines: Mail order, post-free books and multi-media guides i.e.
the award winning *Bird Sounds of Europe and North-west Africa* on 10 CDS.
Field recording equipment.
New for 2005: eGuides for PDAs - mobile versions of popular field guides complete with bird sounds and listing software.
Opening times: Weekdays (9.30am-5pm).
Address: Cross Street, Salthouse, Norfolk, NR25 7XH; (Tel/fax) +44(UK) (0) 1263 741100. e-mail: duncan@wildsounds.com
www.wildsounds.com

WILDLIFE WATCHING SUPPLIES

Company ethos: To bring together a comprehensive range of materials, clothing and equipment to make it easier and more comfortable for you to blend in with the environment. Quick and friendly service.
Key product lines: Hides, camouflage, bean bags, lens and camera covers, clothing etc.
New for 2005: New on-line shop, see new products page on website.
Opening times: Mon to Fri (9am-5pm), Mail order. Visitors by appointment.
Address: Town Living Farmhouse, Puddington, Tiverton, Devon, EX16 8LW; 01884 860692(24hr); (Fax) 01884 860994.
e-mail:
enquiries@wildlifewatchingsupplies.co.uk
www.wildlifewatchingsupplies.co.uk

HOLIDAY COMPANIES

ATLAS TRAVEL CLUB LTD

Company ethos: ATC's aim is to provide a quality service with flexible products at affordable prices.
Types of tours: Tailor made tours for bird watching enthusiasts at low cost.
Destinations: PO Delta, Italy
New for 2005: Po Delta, Italy including camping holidays.
Brochure from: 200 Earls Court Road, London SW5 9QF; 0207 598 2124; (Fax) 0207 598 2156. www.atlastc.co.uk
e-mail: info@atlastc.co.uk

AVIAN ADVENTURES

Company ethos: Top quality, value for money tours, escorted by friendly, experienced leaders at a fairly relaxed pace. ATOL 3367.
Types of tours: Birdwatching, birds and wildlife photography and wildlife safaris, all suitable for both the first-time and the more experienced traveller.
Destinations: More than 70 tours worldwide.
Brochure from: 49 Sandy Road, Norton, Stourbridge, DY8 3AJ; 01384 372013; (Fax) 01384 441340.
e-mail: aviantours@argonet.co.uk
www.avianadventures.co.uk

BRITISH-BALKAN FRIENDSHIP SOCIETY

Company ethos: To introduce people to the beauty of Bulgarian wildlife at exceptional value prices with expert leaders.
Types of tours: Birdwatching tours in all seasons, also butterfly, wild flower and natural history tours. Small groups of 12-14 persons.
Destinations: Specialists to Bulgaria.
New for 2005: Additional winter, spring and autumn tours.
Brochure from: 106 Globe Wharf, 205 Rotherhithe Street, London SE16 5XX; (Tel/fax) 020 7237 7616.
e-mail: dranniekay@aol.com
www.bbfs.org.uk

BIRDFINDERS

Company ethos: Top-value birding tours to see all specialities/endemics of a country/area, using top UK and local guides. ATOL 5406.
Types of tours: Birdwatching tours for all abilities.
Destinations: 47 tours in UK, Europe, Africa, Asia, Australasia, North and South America and Antarctica.
New for 2005: Alaska, Cuba, Jamaica, Oman, South Africa, UAE.
Brochure from: Vaughan Ashby, Westbank, Cheselbourne, Dorset, DT2 7NW. 01258 839066; (Fax) 01258 837449. Our office is open seven days a week.
e-mail: birdfinders@compuserve.com
www.birdfinders.co.uk

BIRD HOLIDAYS

Company ethos: Relaxed pace, professional leaders, small groups, exciting itineraries.
Types of tours: Birdwatching for all levels, beginners to advanced.
Destinations: Worldwide (40 tours, 5 continents).
New for 2005: Oman, Uganda, Ecuador, Corsica and Sardinia.
Brochure from: 10 Ivegate, Yeadon, Leeds, LS19 7RE; (Tel/fax) 0113 3910 510.
e-mail: info@birdholidays.co.uk
www.birdholidays.co.uk

CAMBRIAN BIRD HOLIDAYS

Company ethos: Friendly and personal attention. We don't twitch, our aim is to enjoy good views of those birds and other wildlife that we find.
Types of tours: Birdwatching and general natural history. Some themed holidays: Birds and Flowers, Birds and Butterflies, Birds and Geology, Birding for Beginners etc.
Destinations: West Wales and Southern Ireland.
New for 2005: A continuation of our recent and evolving programme.
Brochure from: Rhydlewis, Llandysul, Ceredigian, SA44 5SP; 01239 851758.
www.cambihols.co.uk

CARPATHIAN WILDLIFE SOCIETY

Company ethos: A non-profit organisation bringing together people with a shared interest in conservation of large mammals and birds.
Types of tours: Wildlife tours for everyone contributing to research. Tracking of wolves, bears and lynx. Enjoyable birdwatching holidays.
Destinations: Slovakia. National parks, primeval forests and wetlands.
New for 2005: Top birding site, Senne wetland and Polana Wildlife Reserve.
Brochure from: Driftwood, The Marrams, Sea Palling, Norfolk NR12 0UN; 01692 598135; (Fax) 01692 598141.
e-mail: cws@szm.sk
www.cws.szm.sk

CLASSIC JOURNEYS

Company ethos: Professional and friendly company, providing well organised and enjoyable birdwatching holidays.
Types of tours: General birdwatching and wildlife holidays on the Indian sub-continent.
Destinations: Nepal, India, Bhutan, Sri Lanka.
New for 2005: South India.
Brochure from: 33 High Street, Tibshelf, Alfreton, Derbyshire, DE55 5NX; 01773 873497; (Fax) 01773 590243.
e-mail: birds@classicjourneys.co.uk
www.classicjourneys.co.uk

GULLIVERS NATURAL HISTORY HOLIDAYS

Company ethos: The small company that takes care of you, while fulfilling your holiday dreams. ATOL 4256.
Types of tours: Friendly, expertly guided tours enjoying birds, flowers and wildlife in an informal, considerate atmosphere.
Destinations: Worldwide.
New for 2005: Bulgaria, Galapagos, Ghana, Hungary, Romania, S Africa, Zambia.
Brochure from: Bob Gulliver, 11 Market Square (H), Aylesbury, HP20 1TJ; 01296 334230; (Fax) 01296 429932.

HEATHERLEA

Company ethos: Exciting holidays to see all the birds of Scotland and selected overseas destinations. Experienced guides and comfortable award-winning hotel to give great customer service.
Types of tours: Birdwatching and other wildlife watching tours.
Destinations: Scottish Highlands, including holidays from our base in Nethybridge, plus Outer Hebrides, Orkney, Shetlands and more. Selected destinations include Pyrenees, Lesvos, Mallorca and Trinidad.
New for 2005: Two-centre birding and culture breaks, choose Po Delta/Venice and Czech owls and woodpeckers/Prague.
Brochure from: The Mountview Hotel, Nethybridge, Inverness-shire, PH25 3EB; 01479 821248; (Fax) 01479 821515.
e-mail: hleabirds@aol.com
www.heatherlea.co.uk

HONEYGUIDE WILDLIFE HOLIDAYS

Company ethos: Relaxed natural history holidays with wildlife close to home. Quality accommodation, expert leaders, beginners welcome.
Types of tours: Birds, flowers and butterflies, with a varied mix depending on the location.
Destinations: Europe, including Extremadura, Spanish Pyrenees, Crete, Lesvos, Menorca, Camargue, French Pyrenees, Dordogne and Danube Delta.
New for 2005: Algarve, Hungary, South Africa's Western Cape.
Brochure from: 36 Thunder Lane, Thorpe St Andrew, Norwich, Norfolk, NR7 0PX; 01603 300552 (Evenings).
e-mail: honeyguide@tesco.net
www.honeyguide.co.uk

HOSKING TOURS LTD

Company ethos: The best in wildlife photographic holidays.
Types of tours: Wildlife photography for all levels of experience.
Destinations: Africa, America, Europe.
New for 2005: Australia, Galapagos.
Brochure from: Pages Green House,

Wetheringsett, Stowmarket, Suffolk, IP14 5QA; 01728 861113; (Fax) 01728 860222. www.hosking-tours.co.uk

ISLAND HOLIDAYS

Company ethos: Relaxed holidays with conservation and responsibility to the environment paramount.
Types of tours: Relaxed birding and natural history tours. We like to enjoy all aspects of the islands we visit, not just the birds.
Destinations: More than 30 island destinations in the UK and worldwide.
New for 2005: North Cyprus, Baja California (Mexico), Tysfjord (Arctic Norway), Cayan Islands, Isle of Skye.
Brochure from: Drummond Street, Comrie, Perthshire, PH6 2DS; 01764 670107; (Fax) 01764 670958. www.islandholidays.net e-mail: enquiries@islandholidays.net

LIMOSA HOLIDAYS

Company ethos: The very best in birdwatching and wildlife holidays - expertly led, fun, friendly and packed with great birding and wildlife. ATOL 2950. AITO member. AITO Trust 1049.
Types of tours: Birdwatching and wildlife tours - everything from birds, mammals and butterflies to plants, volcanoes and wildlife cruises.
Destinations: Our 'new look' 2005 brochure includes more than 100 departures - from Norfolk to New Zealand, Suffolk to South Africa, Alaska to Antarctica.
New for 2005: Antarctic cruise, Estonia, Kos, Lesbos autumn, Outer Hebrides, Oregon spring, Poland winter, Spitsbergen cruise, Uganda (Shoebills and gorillas).
Brochure from: Limosa Holidays, Suffield House, Northrepps, Norfolk, NR27 0LZ; 01263 578143; (Fax) 01263 579251. e-mail: info@limosaholidays.co.uk www.limosaholidays.co.uk

NATURETREK

Company ethos: Friendly, gentle-paced, birdwatching holidays with broad-brush approach. Sympathetic to other wildlife interests, history and local culture. ATOL no 2962.
Types of tours: Escorted birdwatching, botanical and natural history holidays worldwide.
Destinations: Worldwide - see brochure.
New for 2005: Antarctica, Austria, Czech Republic, Jamaica, Guyana, Rwanda, St Lucia.
Brochure from: Cheriton Mill, Cheriton, Alresford, Hampshire, SO24 0NG; 01962 733051; (Fax) 01962 736426. e-mail: info@naturetrek.co.uk www.naturetrek.co.uk

NORTHERN FRANCE WILDLIFE TOURS

Company ethos: Friendly personal attention. Normally a maximum of five in a group. Totally flexible.
Types of tours: Mini-bus trips catering for all from beginners to experienced birders. Local birds include Bluethroat, Black Woodpecker, Melodious Warbler.
Destinations: Brittany, Normandy and Pays de la Loire.
Brochure from: Place de L'Eglise, 53700, Averton, Mayenne, France; 0033 243 006 969. e-mail: nfwt@online.fr www.northernfrancewildlifetours.com

NORTH WEST BIRDS

Company ethos: Friendly, relaxed and unhurried, but targetted to scarce local birds.
Types of tours: Very small groups (up to four) based on large family home in South Lakes with good home cooking. Short breaks with birding in local area. Butterflies in season.
Destinations: Local to Northwest England. Lancashire, Morecambe Bay and Lake District.
Brochure from: Mike Robinson, Barn Close, Beetham, Cumbria, LA7 7AL; (Tel/fax) 015395 63191. www.nwbirds.co.uk e-mail: mike@nwbirds.co.uk

ORIOLE ADVENTURES

Company ethos: Enhancing your ID skills and enjoyment of birding.
Types of tours: Norfolk-based birding tours year round, covering all the best sites and species, plus a selection of Britain's best destinations.

Destinations: Norfolk (seven tours), Suffolk, Cornwall and Northumberland.
New for 2005: Fair Isle, North-east Grand Tour, Suffolk coast.
Brochure from: 28 Scarborough Road, Great Walsingham, Norfolk NR22 6AB; 01328 820751.
e-mail: subalpine19@whsmithnet.co.uk
www.orioleadventures.co.uk

ORNITHOLIDAYS AND CRUISES FOR NATURE

Company ethos: Full-time tour leaders and a company with 40 years' experience. ABTA member. ATOL no 0743.
Types of tours: Birdwatching and natural history tours as well as cruises to Antarctica, the Amazon, Sea of Cortez and Galapagos.
Destinations: 80 tours to all seven continents.
New for 2005: Jamaica and Cayman Islands, South Africa, Ecuador, Spitzbergen, Russia and Finland, Menorca and Kos.
Brochure from: 29 Straight Mile, Romsey, Hampshire, SO51 9BB; 01794 519445; (Fax) 01794 523544.
e-mail: info@ornitholidays.co.uk
www.ornitholidays.co.uk and www.cruisesfornature.co.uk

SHETLAND WILDLIFE

Company ethos: Award-winning small group travel with the very best naturalist guides.
Types of tours: A unique blend of itineraries to bring you the very best of Shetland. Week-long or three-day holidays dedicated to wildlife, photography, walking and archaeology.
Destinations: All corners of Shetland including Fair Isle.
Brochure from: Longhill, Maywick, Shetland, ZE2 9JF; 01950 422483; (Fax) 01950 422430.
e-mail; info@shetlandwildlife.co.uk
www.shetlandwildlife.co.uk

SICKLEBILL SAFARIS LTD

Company ethos: Qualified and very experienced, genial leader, to show you the real natural world. Under ATOL 4002.
Types of tours: Birdwatching and general natural history tours including mammals, insects, higher plants and macrofungi.
Destinations: East Anglia, Ireland, Papua New Guinea and other South Pacific countries we have lived in.
New for 2005: Irian Jaya and Burma.
Brochure from: Well Cottage, 38 Creake Road, Sculthorpe, Fakenham, Norfolk, NR21 9NQ;01328 856925; (Fax) 01328 862014. www.sicklebill.com
e-mail: Ian@sicklebill.demon.co.uk

SPEYSIDE WILDLIFE

Company ethos: Expert leaders, personal attention and a sense of fun - it's your holiday. ATOL no 4259.
Types of tours: Experts in Scotland and leaders worldwide - birdwatching, mammals and whale watching.
Destinations: Speyside and the Scottish Islands, Scandinavia, the Arctic, Europe, Middle East, N America.
New for 2005: India, Arizona and Grand Canyon, Botswana.
Brochure from: Garden Office, Inverdruie House, Inverdruie, Aviemore, Inverness-shire, PH22 1QH; (Tel/fax) 01479 812498.
e-mail: enquiries@speysidewildlife.co.uk
www.speysidewildlife.co.uk

SUNBIRD

Company ethos: Enjoyable birdwatching tours led by full-time professional leaders. ATOL no 3003
Types of tours: Birdwatching, Birds & Music, Birds & History, Birds & Butterflies, Sunbirder events.
Destinations: Worldwide.
New for 2005: Sicuan; China - Crested Ibis and terracotta warriors; Northern China; Taiwan; Karelia (NE Finland & NW Russia); N Spain - Birds and Butterflies; Transylvania; New England; Zambia.
Brochure from: PO Box 76, Sandy, Bedfordshire, SG19 1DF; 01767 682969; (Fax) 01767 692481.
e-mail: sunbird@sunbirdtours.co.uk
www.sunbirdtours.co.uk

THE BIRD ID COMPANY

Company ethos: Expert tour guides teaching birdwatchers of all levels bird identification and fieldcraft skills.
Types of tours: Daily guided tours £30. Weekend breaks, five-day migration tours, rare breeding bird tours to see Golden Oriole, Montagu's Harrier and Honey Buzzard. Personalised and customised tours UK and abroad.
Destinations: Norfolk, Britain, Europe, America, Middle East.
New for 2005: Northern France, Dorset, Kent.
Brochure from: Paul Laurie, 9B Chapel Yard, Albert Street, Holt, Norfolk, NR25 6HG; 1263 710203. www.birdtour.co.uk e-mail: paul.seethebird@fsmail.net

THE TRAVELLING NATURALIST

Company ethos: Friendly, easy-going, expertly-led birdwatching and wildlife tours. ATOL no.3435. AITO 1124.
Types of tours: Tours include birds and history, birds and bears, whale-watching, birds and flowers.
Destinations: Worldwide.
New for 2005: Antarctica, Baja California, Loire Valley, Peru, Western Australia.
Brochure from: PO Box 3141, Dorchester, Dorset, DT1 2XD; 01305 267994; (Fax) 01305 265506. www.naturalist.co.uk e-mail: jamie@naturalist.co.uk

THE ULTIMATE TRAVEL COMPANY

Company ethos: Quality wildlife experiences and shared enjoyment of the natural world.
Types of tours: Relaxed wildlife and birdwatching holidays with friendly groups and Britain's most experienced leaders.
Destinations: Various locations in Africa, Antarctica, Central and South America, India, Indian Ocean, South-east Asia and Europe
Brochure from: The Ultimate Travel Company, 27 Vanston Place, London, SW6 1AZ; 020 7386 4676; (Fax) 020 7381 0836. email: enquiry@theultimatetravelcompany.co.uk

THINKGALAPAGOS

Company ethos: Specialists in the Galapagos Islands, with expert guides and personal attention to ensure a once-in-a-lifetime adventure travel experience.
Types of tours: Friendly and relaxing holidays that are educationally orientated for people with a keen interest in wildlife and photography. Suitable for both the first-time and more experienced traveller.
Destinations: Galapagos and mainland Ecuador.
Brochure from: Rachel Dex, 25 Trinity Lane, Beverley, East Yorkshire HU17 0DY; 01482 872716. www.thinkgalapagos.com e-mail: info@thinkgalapagos.karoo.co.uk

WILD INSIGHTS

Company ethos: Our goal is to enable clients to savour, understand and enjoy birds and wildlife fully, rather than simply build large tick lists. ATOL no 5429 (in association with Wildwings)
Types of tour: Relaxed UK workshops, Reader Breaks for *Bird Watching* magazine and skills-building UK courses, plus selected overseas tours.
Destinations: Various UK locations, plus USA, Africa, Northern India and Europe.
New for 2005: Gambia, South Africa (Western Cape), Holland.
Calender brochure from: Yew Tree Farmhouse, Craignant, Selattyn, Oswestry, Salop SY10 7NP. (Tel/fax) 01691 718 7401; e-mail: keith.offord@virgin.net www.wildinsights.co.uk

WILDWINGS

Company ethos: Superb value holidays led by expert guides.
Types of tours: Birdwatching holidays, whale and dolphin watching holidays, wildlife cruises, ecovolunteers.
Destinations: Europe, Arctic, Asia, the Americas, Antarctica, Africa, Trinidad and Tobago, Jamaica.
New for 2005: Surinam, Christmas Island, Tom Gullicks' Spain.
Brochure from: 577-579 Fishponds Road, Fishponds, Bristol, BS16 3AF. 0117 965 8333. e-mail: wildinfo@wildwings.co.uk

OPTICAL MANUFACTURERS AND IMPORTERS

ACE OPTICS

Company ethos: To be the best - service, price and stock.
Product lines: Importers of Optolyth, Ace Avian, Questar and other products. All the best tripods and an array of optical related accessories.
Address: 16 Green Street, Bath, BA1 2JZ; 01225 466364; (fax) 01225 469761.
e-mail: aceoptics@ba12jz.freeserve.co.uk
www.acecameras.co.uk

CARL ZEISS LTD

Company ethos: World renowned, high quality performance and innovative optical products.
Product lines: Product ranges of stabilised, Victory, Dialyt, compacts and binoculars, now enhanced by the introduction of the FL family of binoculars, and Diascope telescopes.
Address: PO Box 78, Woodfield Road, Welwyn Garden City, Hertfordshire, AL7 1LU; 01707 871350; (Fax) 01707 871287.
e-mail: binos@zeiss.co.uk
www.zeiss.co.uk

INTRO 2020 LTD

Company ethos: Experienced importer of photo and optical products.
Product lines: Summit (binoculars and scopes), Velbon (tripods), Kenko (range of scopes), Slik (tripods), Hoya and Cokin (filters), Oyster and Crumpler (bags).
Address: Unit 1, Priors Way, Maidenhead, Berkshire, SL6 2HR; 01628 674411; (Fax) 01628 771055.
e-mail: sales@intro2020.co.uk
www.intro2020.co.uk

LEICA CAMERA LTD

Company ethos: Professional advice from Leica factory-trained staff.
Product lines: Duovid the world's first dual magnification binocular. Trinovid and new Ultravid full-size binoculars, Trinovid compacts. Televid 62 and 77 spotting scopes with angled or straight view with a choice of five eyepieces, a photo-adapter and a digiscope adaptor for the Leica Digilux 1 digital camera.
Address: Leica Camera Limited, Davy Avenue, Knowlhill, Milton Keynes, MK5 8LB; 01908 256400; (Fax) 01908 671316.
e-mail: info@leica-camera.co.uk
www.leica-camera.com

MARCHWOOD

Company ethos: Quality European optics offering outstanding value for money.
Product lines: Kahles binoculars from Austria, Meopta telescopes from the Czech Republic and Eschenbach Optik binoculars from Germany. Dowling and Rowe optics for the discerning observer.
Address: Unit 308, Cannock Chase Enterprise Park, Hednesford, Staffordshire, WS15 5QU; 01543 424255; (Fax) 01543 422082.
e-mail: john@lancashirej.freeserve.co.uk

MINOX UK LIMITED

Company ethos: A very old brand name with new company technology and attitude.
Product lines: Minox binoculars, telescopes and cameras.
Address: Old Sawmills Road, Faringdon, Oxon SN7 7DS; 01367 243535; (Fax) 01367 241124.
e-mail: sales@minoxuk.co.uk
www.minox.com

OPTICRON

Company ethos: To provide the highest quality, value-for-money optics for today's birdwatcher.
Product lines: Official importers of Opticron binoculars and telescopes, plus mounting systems and accessories.
Address: PO Box 370, Unit 21, Titan Court, Laporte Way, Luton, LU4 8YR; 01582 726522: (Fax) 01582 273559.
e-mail: info@opticron.co.uk

SWAROVSKI UK

Company ethos: Constantly improving on what is good in terms of products and

committed to conservation world-wide.
Product lines: ATS/STS 80 spotting scope and EL 8x32 and 10x32 binoculars, the latest additions to a market-leading range of telescopes and binoculars. Swarovski tripods also available, plus a range of branded rucksacks and other travel bags.
Address: Perrywood Business Park, Salfords, Surrey, RH1 5JQ; 01737 856812: (Fax) 01737 856885.
e-mail: christine.percy@swarovski.com

VICKERS SPORTS OPTICS

Company ethos: Importers of world renowned products from American-based company Bushnell.
Product lines: High performance binoculars (including compacts) and telescopes, includes market-leading Natureview range and Legacy compacts.
Address: Unit 9, 35 Revenge Road, Lordswood, Kent, ME5 8DW; 01634 201284: (Fax) 01634 201286.
e-mail: info@jjvickers.co.uk
www.jjvickers.co.uk

OPTICAL DEALERS

EAST MIDLANDS AND EAST ANGLIA

BIRDNET OPTICS LTD

Company ethos: To provide the birdwatcher with the best value for money on optics, books and outdoor clothing.
Viewing facilities: Clear views to distant hills for comparison of optics at long range and wide variety of textures and edges for clarity and resolution comparison.
Optical stock: Most leading binocular and telescope ranges stocked. If we do not have it in stock we will endeavour to get it for you.
Non-optical stock: Books incl. New Naturalist Series and Poysers, videos, CDs, audio tapes, tripods, hide clamps, accessories and clothing.
Opening times: Mon-Sat (9:30am-5:30pm). Sundays by appointment only.
Address: 5 London Road, Buxton, Derbyshire, SK17 9PA; 01298 71844; (Fax) 01298 73052.
e-mail: paulflint@birdnet.co.uk
www.birdnet.co.uk

In focus

Company ethos: The binocular and telescope specialists, offering customers informed advice at birdwatching venues throughout the country. Main sponsor of the British Birdwatchng Fair.
Viewing facilities: Available at all shops (contact your local outlet), or at field events (10am-4pm) at bird reserves (see *Bird Watching* magazine or website www.at-infocus.co.uk for calendar)
Optical stock: Many leading makes of binoculars and telescopes, plus own-brand Delta range of binoculars and tripods.
Non-optical stock: Wide range of tripods, clamps and other accessories. Repair service available.
Opening times: Vary - please contact local shop or website before travelling.
NORFOLK; Main Street, Titchwell, Nr King's Lynn, Norfolk, PE31 8BB; 01485 210101.
RUTLAND; Anglian Water Birdwatching Centre, Egleton Reserve, Rutland Water, Rutland, LE15 8BT; 01572 770656.

LONDON CAMERA EXCHANGE

Company ethos: To supply good quality optical equipment at a competitive price, helped by knowlegeable staff.
Viewing facilities: In shop and at local shows. Contact local branch.
Optical stock: All leading makes of binoculars and scopes.
Non-optical stock: All main brands of photo, digital and video equipment.
Opening times: Mon-Sat (9am-5.30pm).
CHESTERFIELD: 1A South Street, Chesterfield, Derbyshire, S40 1QZ; 01246 211891; (Fax) 01246 211563;
e-mail: chesterfield@lcegroup.co.uk

DERBY: 17 Sadler Gate, Derby, Derbyshire, DE1 3NH; 01332 348644; (Fax) 01332 369136; e-mail: derby@lcegroup.co.uk
LINCOLN; 6 Silver Street, Lincoln, LN2 1DY; 01522 514131; (Fax) 01522 537480; e-mail: lincoln@lcegroup.co.uk
NOTTINGHAM: 7 Pelham Street, Nottingham, NG1 2EH; 0115 941 7486; (Fax) 0115 952 0547;
e-mail: nottingham@lcegroup.co.uk

WAREHOUSE EXPRESS

Company ethos: Mail order and website.
Viewing facilities: By appointment only.
Optical stock: All major brands including, Leica, Swarvoski, Opticron, Kowa, Zeiss, Nikon, Bushnell, Canon, Minolta etc.
Non-optical stock: All related accessories including hides, tripods and window mounts etc.
Opening times: Mon-Fri (9am-5.30pm).
Address: PO Box 659, Norwich, Norfolk, NR2 1UJ; 01603 626222; (Fax) 01603 626446. www.warehouseexpress.com

NORTHERN ENGLAND

FOCALPOINT

Company ethos: Friendly advice by well-trained staff. Competitive prices, no 'grey imports'.
Viewing facilities: Fantastic open country-side for superb viewing from the shop, plenty of wildlife. Parking for up to 20 cars.
Optical stock: All leading brands of binoculars and telescopes from stock, plus many pre-owned binoculars and telescopes available.
Non-optical stock: Bird books, outdoor clothing, boots, tripods plus full range of Skua products etc. available from stock.
Opening times: Mon-Sat (9:30am-5pm).
Address: Marbury House Farm, Bentleys Farm Lane, Higher Whitley, Warrington, Cheshire, WA4 4QW; 01925 730399; (Fax) 01925 730368.
e-mail: focalpoint@dial.pipex.com
www.fpoint.co.uk

In focus

(see entry in Eastern England).
LANCASHIRE: WWT Martin Mere, Burscough, Ormskirk, Lancs, L40 0TA: 01704 897020.
WEST YORKSHIRE: Westleigh House Office Est. Wakefield Road, Denby Dale, West Yorks, HD8 8QJ: 01484 864729.

LONDON CAMERA EXCHANGE

(See entry in Eastern England).
CHESTER: 9 Bridge Street Row, CH1 1NW; 01244 326531.
MANCHESTER: 37 Parker Street, Picadilly, M1 4AJ; 0161 236 5819.

PHOTO EXPRESS (LAKELAND) LTD

Company ethos: Friendly and independent advice, UK dealers for all top brands, comptitive prices.
Viewing facilities: Dedicated optical viewing room with full showroom facilities at Ulverston branch.
Optical stock: Leica, Swarovski, Zeiss, Opticron, Kowa and selection of other brands.
Non-optical stock: Digital cameras, camcorders and accessories, tripods,m clamps and cases.
Opening times: Mon-Sat (9am-6pm).
Address: 39 Market Street, Ulverston, Cumbria LA12 7LR; 01229 583050; (Fax) 01229 480135.
e-mail: dave@photo-express.net

SOUTH EAST ENGLAND

BINOCULARS-ONLINE LTD

Company ethos: Small retail and mail order binocular specialist. Friendly advice.
Viewing facilities: Shop has views across the Thames Estuary.
Optical stock: Wide range of binoculars including Swarovski, Leica, Zeiss, Opticron, Nikon and Steiner.
Non-optical stock: Manfrotto and Velbon tripods.
Opening times: Tue-Sat (10am-4pm).

Address: 144 Eastern Esplanade (seafront), Southend-on-Sea, Essex SS1 2YH; 01702 601603. www.binoculars-online.co.uk

FORESIGHT OPTICAL

Company ethos: Personal service is our pleasure. Quality optical products - no 'grey imports'.
Viewing facilities: Showroom with viewing facilities.
Optical stock: Wide range of binoculars and telescopes, most popular brands stocked. New, secondhand and ex-demonstration stock for sale. Part exchange undertaken. Mail order available, credit cards accepted and credit facilities.
Non-optical stock: Night vision equipment, magnifiers, microscopes, tripods and accessories.
Opening times: Mon-Fri (8:30am-5:30pm).
Address: 13 New Road, Banbury, Oxon, OX16 9PN; 01295 264365.

In focus

(see entry in Eastern England).
ST ALBANS; Bowmans Farm, London Colney, St Albans, Herts, AL2 1BB: 01727 827799: (Fax) 01727 827766.
SOUTH WEST LONDON: WWT The Wetland Centre, Queen Elizabeth Walk, Barnes, London, SW13 9WT: 020 8409 4433.

KAY OPTICAL (1962)

Company ethos: Unrivalled expertise, experience and service, since 1962.
Viewing facilities: At Morden. Also field-days every weekend at reserves in South.
Optical stock: All leading makes of binoculars and telescopes stocked. Also giant binoculars and astronomical.
Non-optical stock: Tripods, clamps etc.
Opening times: Mon-Sat (9am-5pm) closed (1-2pm).
Address: 89(B) London Road, Morden, Surrey, SM4 5HP: 020 8648 8822; (Fax) 020 8687 2021.www.kayoptical.co.uk
e-mail: info@kayoptical.co.uk
www.bigbinoculars.co.uk

LONDON CAMERA EXCHANGE

(See entry in Eastern England).
FAREHAM: 135 West Street, Fareham, Hampshire, PO16 0DU; 01329 236441; (Fax) 01329 823294;
e-mail: fareham@lcegroup.co.uk
PORTSMOUTH: 40 Kingswell Path, Cascados, Portsmouth, PO1 4RR; 023 9283 9933; (Fax) 023 9283 9955;
e-mail: portsmouth@lcegroup.co.uk
GUILDFORD: 8/9 Tunsgate, Guildford, Surrey, GU1 2DH; 01483 504040; (Fax) 01483 538216;
e-mail: guildford@lcegroup.co.uk
READING: 7 Station Road, Reading, Berkshire, RG1 1LG; 0118 959 2149; (Fax) 0118 959 2197;
e-mail: reading@lcegroup.co.uk
SOUTHAMPTON: 10 High Street, Southampton, Hampshire, SO14 2DH; 023 8022 1597; (Fax) 023 8023 3838;
e-mail: southampton@lcegroup.co.uk
STRAND, LONDON: 98 The Strand, London, WC2R 0AG; 020 7379 0200; (Fax) 020 7379 6991;
e-mail: strand@lcegroup.co.uk
WINCHESTER: 15 The Square, Winchester, Hampshire, SO23 9ES; 01962 866203; (Fax) 01962 840978;
e-mail: winchester@lcegroup.co.uk

SOUTH WEST ENGLAND

ACE OPTICS

Company ethos: To be the best for service, price and stock.
Viewing facilities: Bird of prey at 100 yds, Leica test card to check quality.
Optical stock: All the top brands, including Questar. Official importer for Optolyth products.
Non-optical stock: All the best tripods and an array of optical related accessories.
Opening times: Mon-Sat (8:45am-6pm).
Address: 16 Green Street, Bath, BA1 2JZ; 01225 466364; (fax) 01225 469761.
e-mail: aceoptics@balzjz.freeserve.co.uk

LONDON CAMERA EXCHANGE

(See entry in Eastern England).
BATH: 13 Cheap Street, Bath, Avon, BA1 1NB; 01225 462234; (Fax) 01225 480334. e-mail: bath@lcegroup,co.uk
BOURNEMOUTH: 95 Old Christchurch Road, Bournemouth, Dorset, BH1 1EP; 01202 556549; (Fax) 01202 293288; e-mail: bournemouth@lcegroup.co.uk
BRISTOL: 53 The Horsefair, Bristol, BS1 3JP; 0117 927 6185; (Fax) 0117 925 8716; e-mail: bristol.horsefair@lcegroup.co.uk
EXETER: 174 Fore Street, Exeter, Devon, EX4 3AX;01392 279024/438167; (Fax) 01392 426988.
e-mail: exeter@lcegroup.co.uk
PAIGNTON: 71 Hyde Road, Paignton, Devon, TQ4 5BP;01803 553077; (Fax) 01803664081.
e-mail: paignton@lcegroup.co.uk
PLYMOUTH: 10 Frankfort Gate, Plymouth, Devon, PL1 1QD; 01752 668894; (Fax) 01752 604248.
e-mail: plymouth@lcegroup.co.uk
SALISBURY: 6 Queen Street, Salisbury, Wiltshire, SP1 1EY; 01722 335436; (Fax) 01722 411670;
e-mail: salisbury@lcegroup.co.uk
TAUNTON: 6 North Street, Taunton, Somerset, TA1 1LH; 01823 259955; (Fax) 01823 338001.
e-mail: taunton@lcegroup.co.uk

WESTERN ENGLAND

FOCUS OPTICS

Company ethos: Friendly, expert service. Top quality instruments. No 'grey imports'.
Viewing facilities: Our own pool and nature reserve with feeding stations.
Optical stock: Full range of leading makes of binoculars and telescopes.
Non-optical stock: Waterproof clothing, fleeces, walking boots and shoes, bird food and feeders. Books, videos, walking poles.
Opening times: Mon-Sat (9am-5pm). Some bank holidays.
Address: Church Lane, Corley, Coventry, CV7 8BA; 01676 540501/542476; (Fax) 01676 540930. e-mail: focopt1@aol.com www.focusoptics.co.uk

In focus

(see entry in Eastern England).
GLOUCESTERSHIRE:
WWT Slimbridge, Gloucestershire, GL2 7BT: 01453 890978.

LONDON CAMERA EXCHANGE

(see entry in Eastern England).
CHELTENHAM: 10-12 The Promenade, Cheltenham, Gloucestershire, GL50 1LR; 01242 519851; (Fax) 01242 576771;
e-mail: cheltenham@lcegroup.co.uk
GLOUCESTER: 12 Southgate Street, Gloucester, GL1 2DH; 01452 304513; (Fax) 01452 387309;
e-mail: gloucester@lcegroup.co.uk
LEAMINGTON: Clarendon Avenue, Leamington, Warwickshire, CV32 5PP; 01926 886166; (Fax) 01926 887611;
e-mail: leamington@lcegroup.co.uk
WORCESTER: 8 Pump Street, Worcester, WR1 2QT; 01905 22314; (Fax) 01905 724585; e-mail: worcester@lcegroup.co.uk

BIRD RESERVES AND OBSERVATORIES

Osprey by Keith Offord

PLEASE NOTE:
It is our intention to update this section annually, adding new reserves where we can. This means that space becomes limited and some reserves that have not changed for some time are now shown merely with contact details and a location point on the county map. These sites have been shown in full in previous editions of *The Yearbook* and will so again in future ones. However, if you require more information on a particular site that is not shown in full, please contact Buckingham Press and we will do our best to provide you with more complete information.

Bedfordshire

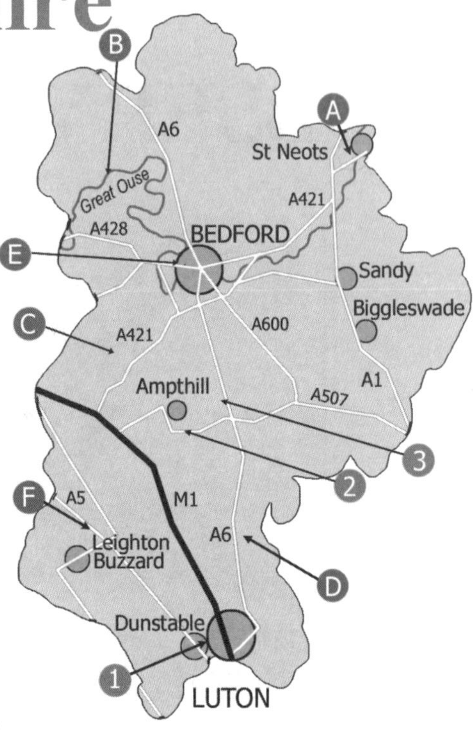

1. BLOW'S DOWNS

The Wildlife Trust for Beds, Cambs, Northants and Peterborough.

Location: TL 033 216. On the outskirts of Dunstable, W of Luton. Parking is at Skimpot roundabout, off Hatters Way on A505, and in Half Moon Lane, Dunstable.

Access: Open all year.

Facilities: None.

Public transport: None.

Habitat: Chalk downland, scrub and grassland, that is a traditional resting place for incoming spring migrants.

Key birds: *Spring/summer*: Hobby, Turtle Dove, Grasshopper Warbler, Lesser Whitethroat, Cuckoo, Spotted Flycatcher, Golden Plover. *Winter*: Buzzard, winter thrushes, possible Brambling. *Passage*: Ring Ouzel, Wheatear, Redstart. *All year*: Marsh and Willow Tits, Bullfinch, Sparrowhawk.

Contact: Wildlife Trust HQ, The Manor House, Broad Street, Great Cambourne, Cambridgeshire CB3 6DH, 01954 713500; fax 01954 710051. e-mail: cambridgeshire@wildlifebcnp.org www.wildlifebcnp.org

2. FLITWICK MOOR

The Wildlife Trust for Beds, Cambs, Northants and Peterborough.

Location: TL 046 354. SE of Ampthill. From Flitwick town centre, take the road towards Greenfield. After approx 0.8km turn L into Maulden Road. Head N to Folly Farm (approx 0.8km), opposite an industrial estate. Turn R at the farm and follow road to car park.

Access: Open all year.

Facilities: Car park. Please stick to public paths.

Public transport: None.

Habitat: SSSI, valley fen, woodland, sedge, reed.

Key birds: *Spring/summer*: Turtle Dove, possible Grasshopper Warbler, Chiffchaff, Cuckoo, warblers. *Winter*: Teal, Lapwing, Woodcock, Siskin. *All year*: Water Rail, Little Owl, Great Spotted and Lesser Spotted Woodpeckers, possible Willow and Marsh Tits, Jay.

Contact: Wildlife Trust HQ, The Manor House, Broad Street, Great Cambourne, Cambridgeshire CB3 6DH01954 713500; fax 01954 710051. e-mail:cambridgeshire@wildlifebcnp.org www.wildlifebcnp.org

3. MAULDEN WOODS

Forestry Commission.

Location: TL 070 390. E of Ampthill. 1.5km N of Clophill, W of A6. Car parking is in a lay-by.

Access: Open all year.

Facilities: Nature trail.

Public transport: None.

Habitat: Plantation.

Key birds: *Spring/summer*: Cuckoo, Turtle Dove, Tree Pipit, Nightingale, Grasshopper Warbler, Garden Warbler, Spotted Flycatcher, Whitethroat. *Winter:* Crossbill. *All year*: Woodcock, all three woodpeckers, possible Willow Tit, Marsh Tit.

Contact: Forestry Commission, Upper Icknield Way, Aston Clinton, Aylesbury, HP22 5NF.

OTHER SITES

(full details in previous editions)

A. Begwary Brook
Contact: Wildlife Trust HQ, 01954 713500.

B. Harrold Odell Country Park
Contact: 01234 720016.

C. Marston Vale Millenium Country Park
Contact: Forest Centre, 01234 767037.

D. Pegsden Hill Reserve
Contact: Wildlife Trust HQ, 01954 713500.

E. Priory Marina Country Park
Contact: Visitor Centre, 01234 211182.

F. Stockgrove Country Park
Contact: 01525 237760.

Berkshire

1. DINTON PASTURES

Wokingham District Council.
Location: SU 784 718. Country Park, E of Reading off B3030 between Hurst and Winnersh.
Access: Open all year, dawn to dusk.
Facilities: Hides, information centre, car park, café, toilets. Suitable for wheelchairs.
Public transport: Information not available.
Habitat: Mature gravel pits and banks of River Loddon.
Key birds: Kingfisher, Water Rail, Little Ringed Plover, Common Tern, Nightingale. *Winter*: Wildfowl (inc. Goldeneye, Wigeon, Teal, Gadwall).
Contact: Dave Webster, Ranger, Dinton Pastures Country Park, Davis Street, Hurst, Berks. 0118 934 2016.

2. MOOR GREEN LAKES

Blackwater Valley Countryside Partnership.
Location: SU 805 628. Main access and parking off Lower Sandhurst Road, Finchampstead. Alternatively, Rambler's car park, Mill Lane, Sandhurst (SU 820 619).
Access: Car parks open dawn-dusk. Two bird hides open to members of the Moor Green Lakes Group (contact BVCP for details). Dogs on leads. Site can be used by people in wheelchairs, though surface not particularly suitable.
Facilities: Two bird hides, footpaths around site, Blackwater Valley Long Distance Path passes through site.
Public transport: Nearest bus stop, Finchampstead (approx 1.5 miles from main entrance). Local bus companies - Stagecoach Hants & Surrey, tel 01256 464501, First Beeline & Londonlink, tel 01344 424938.
Habitat: Thirty-six hectares (90 acres) in total. Three lakes with gravel islands, beaches and scrapes. River Blackwater, grassland, surrounded by willow, ash, hazel and thorn hedgerows.
Key birds: *Spring/summer*: Redshank, Little Ringed Plover, Sand Martin, Willow Warbler, and of particular interest, a flock of Goosander. Also Whitethroat, Sedge Warbler, Common Sandpiper, Common Tern, Dunlin and Black Tern. Lapwings

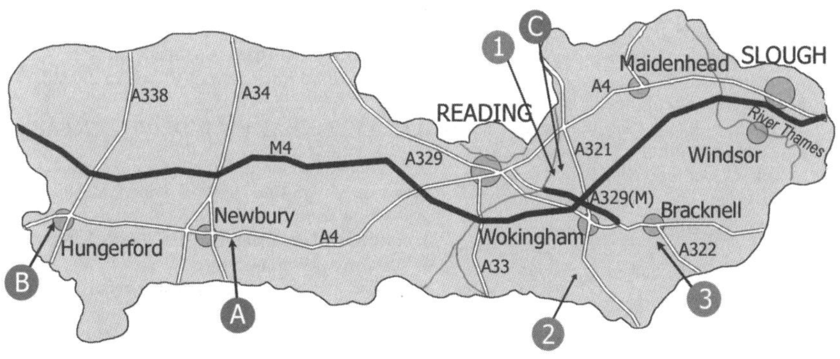

breed on site and several sightings of Red Kite. *Winter*: Ruddy Duck, Wigeon, Teal, Gadwall.
Contact: Blackwater VCP, Ash Lock Cottage, Government Road, Aldershot, Hants GU11 2PS. 01252 331353. www.blackwater-valley.org.uk e-mail: blackwater.valley@hants.gov.uk

3. WILDMOOR HEATH

Berks, Bucks & Oxon Wildlife Trust.
Location: SU 842 627. Between Bracknell and Sandhurst. From Sandhurst shopping area, take A321 NW towards Wokingham. Turn E at mini-roundabout on to Crowthorne Road. Continue for about one mile through one set of traffic lights. Car park is on R at bottom of hill.
Access: Open all year. No access to woodland N of Rackstraw Road at Broadmoor Bottom. Please keep dogs on a lead.
Facilities: Car park.
Public transport: None.
Habitat: Wet and dry lowland heath, bog, mixed woodland and mature Scots pine plantation.
Key birds: *Spring/summer*: Wood Lark, Nightjar, Dartford Warbler, Stonechat. Good for dragonflies.
Contact: Wildlife Trust HQ, 01865 775476.

OTHER SITES
(full details in previous editions)

A. Baynes and Bowdown Reserve
Contact: Wildlife Trust HQ, 01865 775476.
B. Hungerford Marsh
Contact: Wildlife Trust HQ, 01865 775476.
C. Lavell's Lake
Contact: Dinton Pastures,0118 934 2016.

Buckinghamshire

1. BURNHAM BEECHES NNR

Corporation of London.
Location: SU 950 850. N of Slough and on W side of A355, running between J2 of the M40 and J6 of the M4. There are several entrances from A355. Also entrances from Hawthorn Lane and Pumpkin Hill to S and Park Lane to W. Small network of metalled roads, several meet at Victory Cross.
Access: Open all year. Main Lord Mayor's Drive open from 8am-dusk.
Facilities: Car parks, toilets, café, seasonal refreshment book.
Public transport: Train: nearest station Slough on the main line from Paddington.
Habitat: Ancient woodland, streams, pools, heathland, grassland, scrub.
Key birds: *Spring/summer*: Whitethroat, Cuckoo, possible Turtle Dove. *Winter*: Siskin, Redpoll, Crossbill, regular large flocks c100 Brambling. Possible Woodcock. *All year*: Mandarin (good population), all three woodpeckers, Sparrowhawk, Marsh Tit, possible Willow Tit.
Contact: Corporation of London, Open Spaces Department, PO Box 270, Guildhall, London EC2P 2EJ. 020 7332 3514.

2. CHURCH WOOD RSPB RESERVE

RSPB Central England Office
Location: SU 972 872. Reserve lies three miles from J2 of M40 in Hedgerley. Park in village, walk down small track beside pond for approx 200m. Reserve entrance is on L.
Access: Open all year.
Facilities: Two marked paths.
Public transport: None.
Habitat: Mixed woodland.
Key birds: *Spring/summer*: Blackcap, Garden Warbler, Spotted Flycatcher, Swallow. *Winter*: Redpoll, Siskin. *All year*: Marsh Tit, Willow Tit, Nuthatch, all three woodpeckers.
Contact: RSPB, 46 The Green, South Bar, Banbury, Oxfordshire, OX16 9AB. 01295 253330.

3. COLLEGE LAKE WILDLIFE CENTRE

Berks, Bucks & Oxon Wildlife Trust.
Location: SP 935 139. On B488 Tring/Ivinghoe road at Bulbourne.
Access: Open daily 10am-5pm. Permits available on site or from Wildlife Trust HQ.
Facilities: Hides, nature trails, visitor centre, toilets.

Public transport: None.
Habitat: Marsh area, lake, islands, shingle.
Key birds: *Spring/summer*: Breeding Lapwing, Redshank, Little Ringed Plover. Hobby. Passage waders inc. Green Sandpiper.
Contact: Graham Atkins, College Lake Wildlife Centre, Upper Icknield Way, Bulbourne, Tring, Herts HP23 5QG. H: 01296 662890.

4. LITTLE MARLOW GRAVEL PITS

Lefarge Redland Aggregates.
Location: SU 880 880. NE of Marlow from J4 of M40. Use permissive path from Coldmoorholm Lane to Little Marlow village. Follow path over a wooden bridge to N end of lake. Permissive path ends just past the cottages where it joins a concrete road to sewage treatment works.
Access: Open all year. Please do not enter the gravel works.
Facilities: Paths.
Public transport: None.
Habitat: Gravel pit, lake, scrub.
Key birds: *Spring*: Passage migrants, Sand Martin, Garganey, Hobby. *Summer*: Reed warblers, Kingfisher, wildfowl. *Autumn*: Passage migrants. *Winter*: Wildfowl, possible Smew, Goldeneye, Yellow-legged Gull, Lapwing, Snipe.

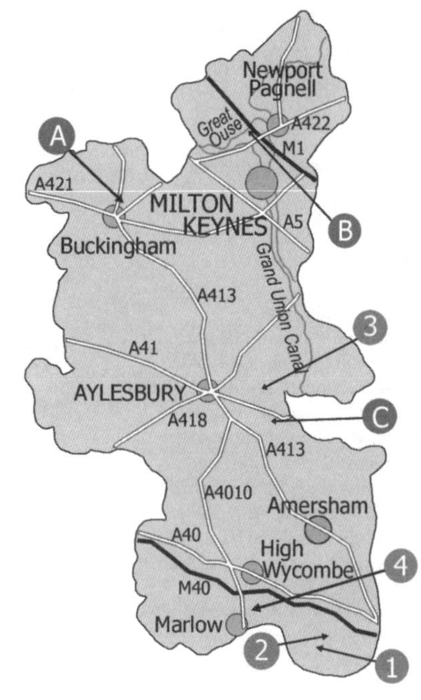

OTHER SITES
(full details in previous editions)

A. Foxcote and Hydelane Waters
Contact: Wildlife Trust HQ, 01865 775476.

B. Hanson Environmental Study Centre
Contact: 01908 604810.

C. Weston Turville
Contact: Wildlife Trust HQ, 01865 775476.

Cambridgeshire

1. BRAMPTON WOOD

The Wildlife Trust for Beds, Cambs, Northants and Peterborough.
Location: TL 185 698. Two miles E of Grafham village on N side of road to Brampton. From A14 take main road S from Ellington.
Access: Open daily. Coaches able to drop passengers off, but insufficient space available to park.
Facilities: Car park, interpretative shelter.
Public transport: None.
Habitat: SSSI. Primarily ash and field maple with hazel coppice.
Key birds: *Summer*: Breeding Grasshopper Warbler, Nightingale, Spotted Flycatcher, Woodcock; all three woodpeckers. *Winter*: thrushes.
Contact: Wildlife Trust HQ, The Manor House, Broad Street, Great Cambourne, Cambridgeshire CB3 6DH. 01954 713500; fax 01954 710051.
e-mail:cambridgeshire@wildlifebcnp.org
www.wildlifebcnp.org

Cambridgeshire

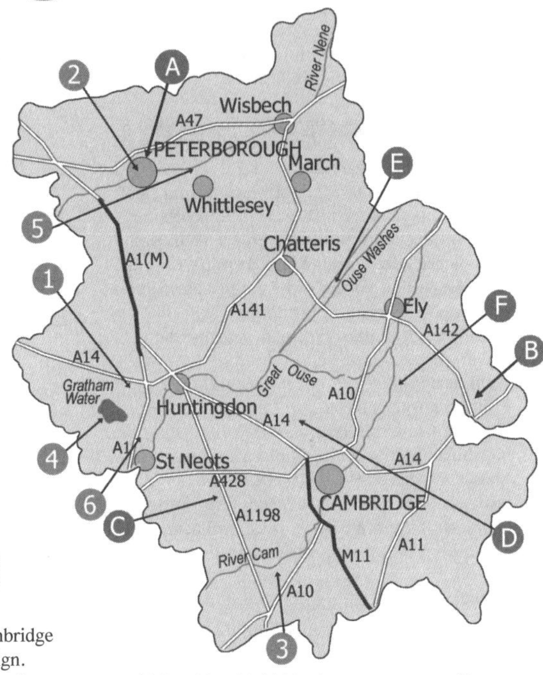

2. FERRY MEADOWS CP

Nene Park Trust.
Location: TL 145 975. Three miles W of Peterborough town centre, signed off A605.
Access: Open all year.
Facilities: Car park (fee at weekends), visitor centre, toilets, café, hide.
Public transport: Tel. 01733 453540.
Habitat: Lakes, meadows, scrub, woodland and small nature reserve.
Key birds: *Spring*: Grey Heron, Common and Arctic Terns, waders, Yellow Wagtail. *Winter*: Siskin, Redpoll, Water Rail, occasional Hawfinch. *All year*: Good selection of woodland and water birds, Kingfisher.
Contact: Nene Park Trust, Ham Farm House, Orton, Peterborough, PE2 5UU. 01733 234443.

3. FOWLMERE

RSPB (East Anglia Office).
Location: TL 407 461. Turn off A10 Cambridge to Royston road by Shepreth and follow sign.
Access: Access at all times along marked trail.
Facilities: Three hides, portable toilets. Space for one coach, prior booking essential.
Public transport: Shepreth railway station 3km.
Habitat: Reedbeds, meres, woodland, scrub.
Key birds: *Summer*: Nine breeding warblers. *All year:* Water Rail, Kingfisher. *Winter*: Snipe, raptors. Corn Bunting roost.
Contact: Doug Radford, RSPB, Manor Farm, High Street, Fowlmere, Royston, Herts SG8 7SH. Tel/fax 01763 208978.

4. GRAFHAM WATER

The Wildlife Trust for Beds, Cambs, Northants and Peterborough.
Location: TL 143 671. Follow signs for Grafham Water from A1 at Buckden or A14 at Ellington. Nature Reserve entrance is from Mander car park, W of Perry village.
Access: Open all year. Dogs barred in wildlife garden only, on leads elsewhere.
Facilities: Five bird hides in nature reserve. Two in wildlife garden accessible to wheelchairs. Cycle track through reserve also accessible to wheelchairs. Visitor centre with restaurant, shop and toilets. Disabled parking.
Public transport: None.
Habitat: Open water, ancient and plantation woodland, grassland.
Key birds: *Winter*: Wildfowl, gulls. *Spring/summer*: Breeding Nightingale, Reed, Willow and Sedge Warblers, Common and Black Terns. *Autumn*: Passage waders.
Contact: The Warden, Grafham Water Nature Reserve, c/o The Lodge, West Perry, Huntingdon, Cambs PE28 0BX. 01480 811075.
e-mail: grafham@cix.co.uk

5. NENE WASHES

RSPB (East of England Office).
Location: TL 300 995. N of Whittlesey and six miles E of Peterborough.

Access: Open at all times along South Barrier Bank, accessed at Eldernell, one mile NE of Coates, off A605. Group visits by arrangement. No access to fields.
Facilities: Small car park.
Public transport: Bus and trains to Whittlesey, bus to Coates.
Habitat: Wet grassland with ditches. Frequently flooded.
Key birds: *Spring/early summer*: Breeding waders, including Black-tailed Godwit, duck, including Garganey, Marsh Harrier and Hobby. *Winter*: Waterfowl including Bewick's Swan and Pintail, Barn Owl, Hen Harrier.
Contact: Charlie Kitchin, RSPB Nene Washes, 21a East Delph, Whittlesey, Cambs PE7 1RH. 01733 205140.

6. PAXTON PITS

Huntingdonshire District Council.
Location: TL 197 629. Access from A1 at Little Paxton, two miles N of St Neots.
Access: Free entry. Open 24 hours. Visitor centre manned at weekends. Dogs allowed under control. Heron trail suitable for wheelchairs during summer.
Facilities: Toilets available most days 9am-5pm (including disabled), two bird hides (always open), marked nature trails.
Public transport: 565/566 run between Huntingdon and St Neots Mon-Sat. Tel: 0870 608 2608.
Habitat: Grassland, scrub, lakes.
Key birds: *Spring/summer*: Nightingale, Kingfisher, Common Tern, Sparrowhawk, Hobby, Grasshopper, Sedge and Reed Warblers, Lesser Whitethroat. *Winter*: Smew, Goldeneye, Goosander, Gadwall, Pochard.
Contact: Jim Stevenson, Ranger, The Visitor Centre, High Street, Little Paxton, St Neots, Cambs PE19 6ET. 01480 406795.
e-mail: mail@paxtonpits.uklinux.net
www.paxton-pits.org.uk

OTHER SITES

(full details in previous editions)

A. Dogsthorpe Star Pit SSSI
Contact: Wildlife Trust HQ, 01954 713500.
B. Fordham Woods SSSI
Contact: English Nature, 01733 405850.
C. Hayley Wood
Contact: Wildlife Trust HQ, 01954 713500.
D. Mare Fen
Contact: English Nature, 01733 405850.
E. Ouse Washes
Contact: Site Manager, 01354 680212.
F. Wicken Fen
Contact: Visitor Centre, 01353 720274.

Cheshire

1. FIDDLERS FERRY

AEP (American Electric Power)
Location: SJ 552 853. Off A562 between Warrington and Widnes.
Access: Parking at main gate of power station. Summer (8am-8pm); winter (8am-5pm). For free permit apply in advance with sae to Manager, Fiddlers Ferry Power Station, Warrington WA5 2UT.
Facilities: Hide, nature trail.
Public transport: Arriva bus 110 every 20 minutes.
Habitat: Ash and water lagoons, tidal and non-tidal marshes with phragmites and great reedmace, meadow grassland with small woods.
Key birds: *Summer*: Breeding Gadwall, Pochard, Buzzard, Peregrine and Raven. *Winter:* Glaucous and Iceland Gulls, Short-eared Owl, Peregrine, Jack Snipe and Twite. *Recent rarities*: Little Egret, Marsh Harrier, Hobby, Caspian, Mediterranean and Kumlien's Gull and Chiffchaff.
Contact: Keith Massey, 4 Hall Terrace, Great Sankey, Warrington WA5 3EZ. 01925 721382.

2. GAYTON SANDS

RSPB Dee Estuary Office.
Location: SJ 275 785. On W side of Wirral, S of Birkenhead. View high tide activity from Old Baths car park near Boathouse pub, Parkgate.
Access: Open at all times. Viewing from public footpaths and car parks. Please do not walk on the saltmarsh, the tides are dangerous.

Cheshire

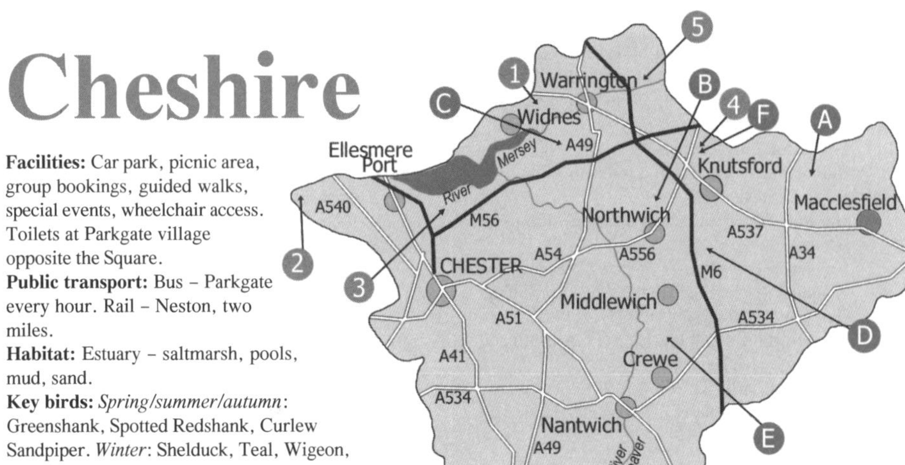

Facilities: Car park, picnic area, group bookings, guided walks, special events, wheelchair access. Toilets at Parkgate village opposite the Square.
Public transport: Bus - Parkgate every hour. Rail - Neston, two miles.
Habitat: Estuary - saltmarsh, pools, mud, sand.
Key birds: *Spring/summer/autumn*: Greenshank, Spotted Redshank, Curlew Sandpiper. *Winter*: Shelduck, Teal, Wigeon, Pintail, Oystercatcher, Black-tailed Godwit, Curlew, Redshank, Merlin, Peregrine, Water Rail, Short-eared Owl.
Contact: Colin E Wells, Burton Point Farm, Station Road, Burton, Nr Neston, Cheshire CH64 5SB. 0151 3367681.

3. GOWY MEADOWS

Cheshire Wildlife Trust.
Location: SJ 435 740. N of Chester and E of Ellesmere Port. Take A5117 E from J10 of M53 turn L to Thornton-le-Moors. Park next to church, footpath is opposite.
Access: Through public footpath gate on Thornton Green Lane. Open all year, please keep to footpath.
Facilities: None.
Public transport: The Arriva bus service stops on the Thornton Green Lane opposite the church.
Habitat: Lowland grazing marsh.
Key birds: *Spring/summer*: Wildfowl, warblers, Whinchat, Green Sandpiper, Lapwing, Jack Snipe, Snipe. *Winter*: Reed Bunting. *Passage*: Stonechat, Wheatear.
Contact: Wildlife Trust HQ, Grebe House,Reaseheath, Nantwich, Cheshire CW5 6DG. 01270 610180; e-mail: cheshirewt@cix.co.uk www.wildlifetrust.org.uk/cheshire/

4. ROSTHERNE MERE

English Nature (Cheshire to Lancashire team).
Location: SJ 744 843. Lies N of Knutsford and S of M56 (junction 8).
Access: View from Rostherne churchyard and lanes; no public access, except to A W Boyd Observatory (permits from D A Clarke, 1 Hart Avenue, Sale M33 2JY, tel 0161 973 7122). Not suitable for coach parties, but can accommodate smaller group visits by prior arrangement.
Facilities: None. **Public transport:** None.
Habitat: Deep lake, woodland, willow bed, pasture.
Key birds: *Winter*: Good range of duck (inc Ruddy Duck and Pintail), gull roost (inc. occasional Iceland and Glaucous). Passage Black Terns.
Contact: Tim Coleshaw, Site Manager, English Nature, Attingham Park, Shrewsbury SY4 4TW. 01743 282000; fax 01743 709303; e-mail: tim.coleshaw@english-nature.org.uk.

5. WOOLSTON EYES

Woolston Eyes Conservation Group.
Location: SJ 654 888. E of Warrington between the River Mersey and Manchester Ship Canal. Off Manchester Road down Weir Lane or from Latchford to end of Thelwall Lane.
Access: Open all year. Permits required from Chairman, £6 each, £12 per family (see address below).
Facilities: No toilets or visitor centre. Good hides, some elevated.
Public transport: Buses along A57 nearest stop to Weir Lane.
Habitat: Wetland, marsh, scrubland, wildflower meadow areas.
Key birds: Breeding Black-necked Grebe, warblers, all raptors (Merlin, Peregrine, Marsh

Harrier). SSSI for wintering wildfowl, many duck species breed.
Contact: B R Ankers, 9 Lynton Gardens, Appleton, Cheshhire WA4 5ED. 01925 267355.

OTHER SITES

(full details in previous editions)

A. Alderley Woods
Contact: National Trust, 0161 928 0075.
B. Marbury Reedbed Nature Reserve
Contact: Wildlife Trust HQ, 01270 610180.
C. Moore Nature Reserve
Contact: Paul Cassidy, c/o Arpley Landfill Site, 01925 444 689.
D. Rudheath Woods Nature Reserve
Contact: Wildlife Trust HQ, 01270 610180.
E. Sandbach Flashes
Contact: Patrick Whalley, 01270 624420.
F. Tatton Park
Contact: Wildlife Trust HQ, 01270 610180.

Cornwall

1. BRENEY COMMON

Cornwall Wildlife Trust.
Location: SX 054 610. Three miles S of Bodmin. Take minor road off A390 one mile W of Lostwithiel to Lowertown.
Access: Open at all times but please keep to paths. Disabled access.
Facilities: Wilderness trail.
Public transport: None.
Habitat: Wetland, heath and scrub.
Key birds: Willow Tit, Nightjar, Tree Pipit, Sparrowhawk, Lesser Whitethroat, Curlew.
Contact: Gavin Henderson, 5 Acres, Allet, Cornwall TR4 9DJ. 01872 273939.
e-mail: cornwt@cix.co.uk
www.cornwallwildlifetrust.org.uk

2. DRIFT RESERVOIR

South West Lakes Trust/Cornwall BWPS.
Location: Two miles W of Penzance on A30 (signposted).
Access: CBWPS members only (not suitable for disabled). Non-members welcome to try the site, but please take out membership if wishing to visit frequently. Membership forms available in the hide.
Facilities: Walk round W side of reserve to the unlocked hide for CBWPS members only.
Public transport: Bus service passes through Drift on route to Lands End.
Habitat: Reservoir, fresh water with muddy margins.
Key birds: *Autumn*: Gulls, ducks, waders plus regular rarities.
Contact: Graham Hobin, Lower Drift Farmhouse, Buryas Bridge, Drift, Penzance, 01736 362206.

3. GOLITHA NNR

English Nature (Cornwall & Isles of Scilly Team).
Location: SX 227 690. Golitha is three miles NW of Liskeard in E Cornwall. Take minor roads N for 2.5 miles from Dobwalls on A38.
Access: Various paths from 0.5 mile to four miles. Can be muddy after rain. Limited disabled access.
Facilities: Toilets.
Public transport: None.
Habitat: Ancient woodland, deep granite gorge.
Key birds: *All year*: Sparrowhawk, Buzzard, Kingfisher, all three woodpeckers, Jay, Grey Wagtail, Dipper, Marsh Tit, Treecreeper, Nuthatch. *Summer:* Redstart, Wood Warbler, Pied Flycatcher.
Contact: English Nature, Trevint House, Strangways Villas, Truro, Cornwall TR1 2PA. 01872 265710.
e-mail: cornwall@english-nature.org.uk

4. HAYLE ESTUARY

RSPB (South West England Office).
Location: SW 550 370. In town of Hayle. Follow signs to Hayle from A30.
Access: Open at all times. No permits required. No admission charges. Dogs on leads please. Sorry - no coaches.
Facilities: Eric Grace Memorial Hide at Ryan's Field has disabled parking and viewing. Nearest disabled toilets at Wyevale Garden centre, Lelant, 600 yards W just off the roundabout. No visitor

Cornwall

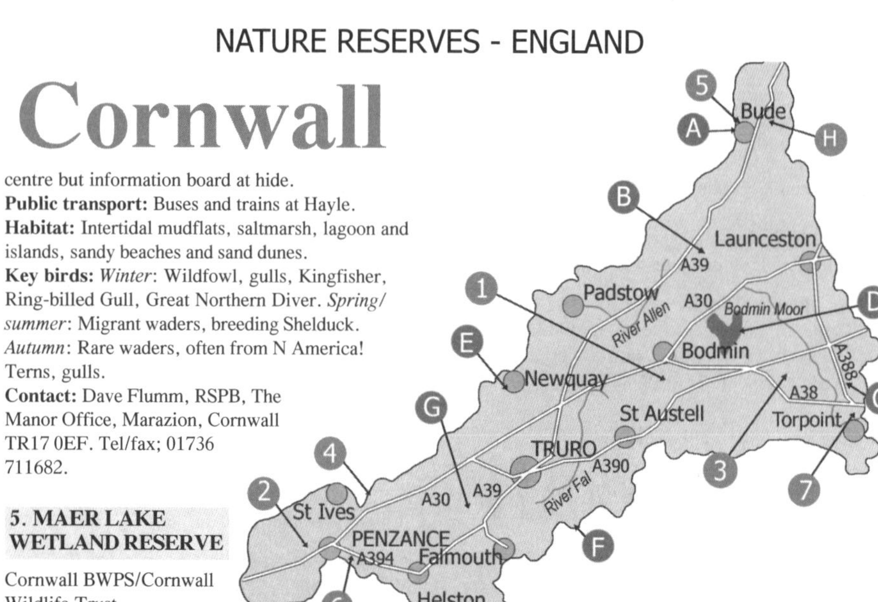

centre but information board at hide.
Public transport: Buses and trains at Hayle.
Habitat: Intertidal mudflats, saltmarsh, lagoon and islands, sandy beaches and sand dunes.
Key birds: *Winter*: Wildfowl, gulls, Kingfisher, Ring-billed Gull, Great Northern Diver. *Spring/ summer*: Migrant waders, breeding Shelduck. *Autumn*: Rare waders, often from N America! Terns, gulls.
Contact: Dave Flumm, RSPB, The Manor Office, Marazion, Cornwall TR17 0EF. Tel/fax; 01736 711682.

5. MAER LAKE WETLAND RESERVE

Cornwall BWPS/Cornwall Wildlife Trust.
Location: SS 208 075. N of Bude town centre, close to see. View from private road next to Maer Lodge Hotel, heading N.
Access: View from private road above the reserve. Please park in nearest public road.
Facilities: None.
Habitat: Wetland meadow (22 acres) and lake.
Key birds: Wildfowl and waders (inc. rarities eg. Temminck's Stint, Wilson's Phalarope).
Contact: Cornwall Wildlife Trust, 01872 273939.

6. MARAZION MARSH

RSPB (South West England Office).
Location: SW 510 315. Reserve is one mile E of Penzance, 500 yards W of Marazion. Entrance off seafront road near Marazion.
Access: Open at all times. No permits required. No admission charges. Dogs on leads please. Sorry - no coaches.
Facilities: One hide. No toilets. No visitor centre. Nearest toilets in Marazion and seafront car park.
Public transport: Bus from Penzance.
Habitat: Wet reedbed, willow carr.
Key birds: *Winter*: Wildfowl, Snipe, occasional Bittern. *Spring/summer*: Breeding Reed, Sedge and Cetti's Warblers, herons, swans. *Autumn*: Occasional Aquatic Warbler, Spotted Crake. Large roost of swallows and martins in reedbeds, migrant warblers and waders.
Contact: Dave Flumm, RSPB, The Manor Office, Marazion, Cornwall TR17 0EF. Tel/fax; 01736 711682.

7. TAMAR ESTUARY

Cornwall Wildlife Trust.
Location: SX 434 631. (Northern Boundary). SX 421 604 (Southern Boundary). From Plymouth head W on A38. Access parking at Cargreen and Landulph from minor roads off A388.
Access: Open at all times.
Facilities: Information boards at Cargreen and Landulph.
Public transport: None.
Habitat: Tidal mudflat with some saltmarsh.
Key birds: *Winter*: Avocet, Snipe, Black-tailed Godwit, Redshank, Dunlin, Curlew, Whimbrel, Spotted Redshank, Green Sandpiper, Golden Plover, Kingfisher.
Contact: Stuart Hutchings, 5 Acres, Allet, Cornwall TR4 9DJ. 01872 273939.
e-mail: cornwt@cix.co.uk

OTHER SITES

(full details in previous editions)

A. Bude Marshes

Contact: North Cornwall District Council, 01208 893333.

B. Crowdy Reservoir

Contact: Leisure Services Dept, South West Water, 01837 871565.

C. Kit Hill Country Park
Contact: Kit Hill CP, Cornwall, 01579 370030.
D Loveny Reserve - Colliford Reservoir
Contact: Cornwall Wildlife Trust, 01872 273939.
E. Nansmellyn Marsh
Contact: Cornwall Wildlife Trust, 01872 273939.
F. Nare Head
Contact: National Trust, 01208 432691.
G. Stithians Reservoir
Contact: Cornwall BPS.
H. Tamar Lakes
Contact: Visitor Centre, 01288 321262.

Cumbria

1. CAMPFIELD MARSH

RSPB (North of England Office).
Location: NY 207 620. On S shore of Solway estuary, W of Bowness-on-Solway. Follow signs from B5307 from Carlisle.
Access: Open at all times, no charge. View high-tide roosts from roadside (suitable for disabled).
Facilities: Viewing screens overlooking wetland areas, along nature trail (1.5 miles). No toilets or visitor centre.
Public transport: Nearest railway station – Carlisle (13 miles). Infrequent bus service to reserve.
Habitat: Saltmarsh/intertidal areas, open water, peat bog, wet grassland.
Key birds: *Winter*: Waders and wildfowl include Barnacle Goose, Shoveler, Scaup, Grey Plover. *Spring/summer*: Breeding Lapwing, Redshank, Snipe, Tree Sparrow and warblers. *Autumn*: Passage waders.
Contact: Norman Holton, North Plain Farm, Bowness-on-Solway, Wigton, Cumbria CA7 5AG. e-mail: norman.holton@rspb.org.uk

2. FOULNEY ISLAND

Cumbria Wildlife Trust.
Location: SD 246 640. Three miles SE of Barrow town centre on the A5087 from Barrow or Ulverston. At a roundabout 2.5 miles S of Barrow take a minor road through Rampside to Roa Island. Turn L into reserve car park. Walk to main island along stone causeway.
Access: Open all year. Access restricted to designated paths during bird breeding season. Slitch Ridge is closed at this time. No dogs allowed during bird breeding season.
Facilities: None.
Public transport: Bus: regular service from Barrow to Roa Island.
Habitat: Shingle, sand, grassland.
Key birds: *Summer*: Arctic and Little Terns, Oystercatcher, Ringed Plover, Eider Duck. *Winter*: Brent Goose, Redshank, Dunlin, Sanderling.
Contact: Wildlife Trust HQ, Plumgarths, Crook Road, Kendal LA8 8LX. 01539 816300; (fax)01539 816301.
www.cumbriawildlifetrust.org.uk
e-mail: mail@cumbriawildlifetrust.org.uk

3. HODBARROW

RSPB (North of England Office).
Location: SD 174 791. Lying beside Duddon Estuary on the outskirts of Millom. Follow signs via Mainsgate Road.
Access: Open at all times, no charge.
Facilities: One hide overlooking island. Public toilets in Millom (two miles). Nature trail around the lagoon.
Public transport: Nearest trains at Millom (two miles).
Habitat: Brackish coastal lagoon bordered by limestone scrub and grassland.
Key birds: *Winter*: Waders and wildfowl includes Redshank, Dunlin, Goldeneye, Red-breasted Merganser. *Spring/summer*: Breeding gulls and terns, Eider, grebes, Lapwing. *Autumn*: Passage waders.
Contact: Dave Blackledge, Warden, North Plain Farm, Bowness-on-Solway, Wigton, Cumbria CA7 5AG. e-mail: dave.blackledge@rspb.org.uk

4. ST BEES HEAD

RSPB (North of England Office).
Location: NX 962 118. S of Whitehaven via the B5345 road to St Bees village.
Access: Open at all times, no charge. Access via coast-to-coast footpath. The walk to the viewpoints is long and steep in parts.

Cumbria

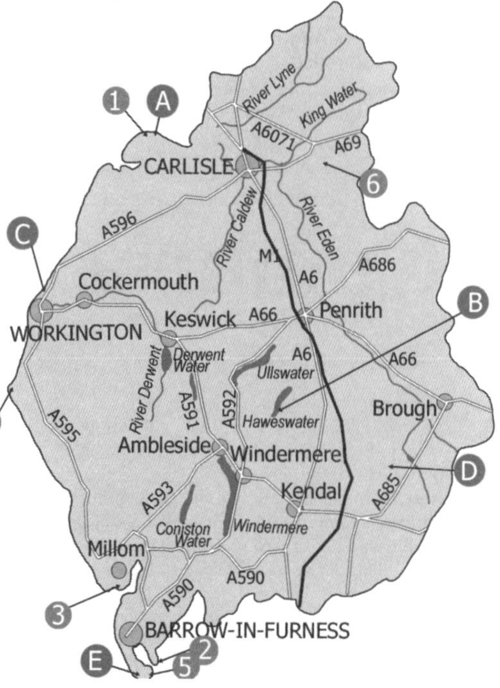

Facilities: Three viewpoints overlooking seabird colony. Public toilets in St Bees beach car park at entrance to reserve.
Public transport: Nearest trains at St Bees (0.5 mile).
Habitat: Three miles of sandstone cliffs up to 300 ft high.
Key birds: *Summer*: Largest seabird colony on W coast of England: Guillemot, Razorbill, Puffin, Kittiwake, Fulmar and England's only breeding Black Guillemot.
Contact: Dave Blackledge, Warden, North Plain Farm, Bowness-on-Solway, Wigton, Cumbria CA7 5AG.
e-mail: dave.blackledge@rspb.org.uk

5. SOUTH WALNEY

Cumbria Wildlife Trust.
Location: SD 215 620. Six miles S of Barrow-in-Furness. From Barrow, cross Jubilee Bridge onto Walney Island, turn L at lights. Continue through Biggar village to South End Caravan Park. Follow unsurfaced road for 1 mile to reserve.
Access: Open daily (10am-5pm) plus Bank Holidays. No dogs except assistance dogs. Day permits £2 adults, 80p children. Cumbria Wildlife Trust members free.
Facilities: Toilets, nature trails, eight hides (two with wheelchair accessible), 200m boardwalk, cottage available to rent.
Public transport: Bus service as far as Biggar.
Habitat: Shingle, lagoon, sand dune, saltmarsh.
Key birds: *Spring/autumn*: Passage migrants. *Summer*: Breeding Eider, Herring, Greater and Lesser Black-backed Gulls, Shelduck. *Winter*: Teal, Wigeon, Goldeneye, Redshank, Greenshank, Curlew, Oystercatcher, Knot, Dunlin, Twite.
Contact: The Warden, No 1 Coastguard Cottages, South Walney Nature Reserve, Walney Island, Barrow-in-Furness, Cumbria LA14 3YQ. 01229 471066. e-mail: mail@cumbriawildlifetrust.org.uk www.cumbriawildlifetrust.org.uk

6. TALKIN TARN COUNTRY PARK

Cumbria County Council.
Location: NY544 591. Twelve miles E of Carlisle. From A69 E at Brampton, head S on B6413 for two miles. Talkin Tarn is on E just after level crossing.
Access: All year. Wheelchair access restricted by ten kissing gates. Coaches welcome.
Facilities: Toilets and restaurant open all year (11am-4pm Easter-Oct, limited opening times in winter). Dogs allowed around Tarn.
Public transport: Bus: infrequent. Tel: 0870 608 2608. Train: nearest station is Brampton Junction. Tel: 0845 748 4950. Footpath from Brampton.
Habitat: Natural tarn, mature woodland.
Key birds: *Spring/summer*: Pied Flycatcher, Spotted Flycatcher, Redstart, Chiffchaff, Wood Warbler. *Winter*: Grebes, Smew, Long-tailed Duck, Goosander, Gadwall.
Contact: Talkin Tarn Country Park, CA8 1HN. 01697 741050. e-mail: philg@carlisle.gov.uk

OTHER SITES

(full details in previous editions)

A. Drumburgh Moss NNR
Contact: Wildlife Trust HQ, 01539 816300.
B. Haweswater
Contact: RSPB, 01931 713376.

C. Siddick Pond
Contact: Leisure Services, Parks Development Officer, Allerdale BC, 01900 326324.

D. Smardale Gill NNR
Contact: Wildlife Trust HQ, 01539 816300.

E. Walney Bird Observatory
Contact: As South Walney.

Derbyshire

1. CARR VALE NATURE RESERVE

Derbyshire Wildlife Trust.
Location: SK 45 70. Approach Bolsover on A632 from Chesterfield. Continue over roundabout, take 1st R on to Villas Road at crossroads. At very sharp L bend, carry straight on to rough track. Follow to R. Small parking area next to old railway embankment. Alternatively, turn R at roundabout. Car park at end of road. Reserve is reached via footpath over reclaimed colliery tip.
Access: Open all year.
Facilities: Car park, good disabled access, paths, viewing platform. Coach parking on approach to car park.
Public transport: Various Stagecoach services from Chesterfield (Stephenson Place) all pass close to the reserve: Mon to Sat - 83 serves Villas Road, 81, 82, 82A and 83 serve the roundabout on the A632. Sun - 81A, 82A serve the roundabout on the A632.
Habitat: Lakes, wader flashes, reed bed, sewage farm, scrub, arable fields.
Key birds: *Spring/summer*: Warblers, waders, farmland birds, wildfowl. *Winter*: Wildfowl.
Contact: Wildlife Trust HQ, East Mill, Bridgefoot, Belper, Derbyshire DE56 1XH. 01773 881188. www.derbyshirewildlifetrust.org.uk
e-mail: enquiries@derbyshirewt.co.uk

2. CARSINGTON RESERVOIR

Severn Trent Water.
Location: SK 24 51. Follow B5035 from either Ashbourne or B5036, then B5035 from Cromford.
Access: Open all year except Dec 25,(7am to sunset). There are various access points. Track is very steep in places and can be slippery in winter.
Facilities: Car parks (charge made) visitor centre, toilets, restaurant, hides.
Public transport: D&G Coach & Bus 111 (Sun and BH Mon) from Derby. D&G Coach & Bus (daily) Matlock-Ashbourne via Wirksworth. D&G Coach & Bus (Wed only) from Derby. Some D&G Coach & Bus 109 journeys from Derby are extended to Carsington Water Sun & BH Mon.
Habitat: Reservoir, woodland.
Key birds: *Spring/summer*: Gulls, winter thrushes and wildfowl species. *Winter*: Usual woodland and farmland species, gulls. 200-plus species recorded and planned reedbeds and scrapes should increase biodiversity.
Contact: Severn Trent Water, Sherbourne House, 87 St Martin's Road, Finham, Coventry CV3 6SD.
e-mail: customer.relations@severntrent.co.uk

3. DRAKELOW WILDFOWL RESERVE

Powergen PLC.
Location: SK 22 72 07. Drakelow Power Station, one mile NE of Walton-on-Trent.
Access: Permit holders only for time being. Reserve is subject to closure at short notice during demolition of power station. Scheduled to last to end of 2005. Any problems, please ring warden during evenings.
Facilities: Seven hides, no other facilities.
Public transport: None.
Habitat: Disused flooded gravel pits with wooded islands and reedbeds.
Key birds: *Summer*: Breeding Reed and Sedge Warblers. Water Rail, Hobby. *Winter*: Wildfowl (Goldeneye, Gadwall, Smew), Merlin. Regular sightings of Peregrine in station area. Recent rarities include Great White and Little Egret, Cetti's Warbler and Golden Oriole, Bittern and Spotted Crake. Excellent for dragonflies and butterflies.
Contact: Tom Cockburn, Hon, Warden, 1 Dickens Drive, Swadlincote, Derbys DE11 0DX. 01283 217146.

Derbyshire

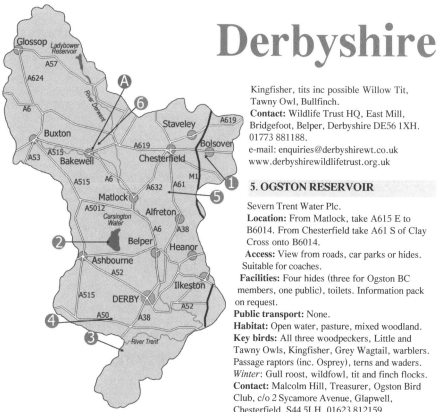

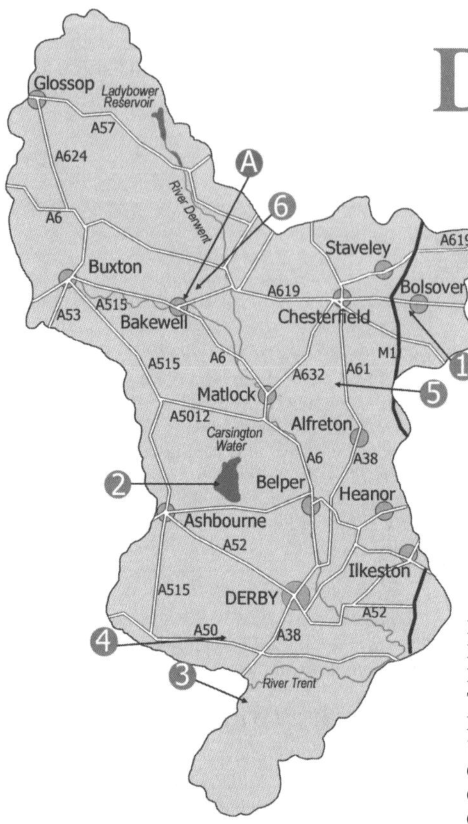

4. HILTON GRAVEL PITS

Derbyshire Wildlife Trust.
Location: SK 24 31. From Derby, take A516 from Mickleover W past Etwall. Follow this to A50 junction at Hilton. Turn R at first island onto Willow Pit Lane. Turn L onto old road next to a large white house. Park next to gate. Follow track along the S side of pools. Alternatively, take A516 into Hilton. Take first R at crossroads opposite pub. Follow road to Sutton-on-the-Hill over A50. Take first R onto old road and park at end.
Access: Open all year.
Facilities: Tracks. Please observe the footpath restrictions along the side of the lakes.
Public transport: Local bus services from Derby.
Habitat: Ponds, scrub, wood, fen.
Key birds: *Spring/summer*: Canada Goose, possible Common Tern, warblers. *Winter*: Siskin, Goldcrest. *All year*: All three woodpeckers, Kingfisher, tits inc possible Willow Tit, Tawny Owl, Bullfinch.
Contact: Wildlife Trust HQ, East Mill, Bridgefoot, Belper, Derbyshire DE56 1XH. 01773 881188.
e-mail: enquiries@derbyshirewt.co.uk
www.derbyshirewildlifetrust.org.uk

5. OGSTON RESERVOIR

Severn Trent Water Plc.
Location: From Matlock, take A615 E to B6014. From Chesterfield take A61 S of Clay Cross onto B6014.
Access: View from roads, car parks or hides. Suitable for coaches.
Facilities: Four hides (three for Ogston BC members, one public), toilets. Information pack on request.
Public transport: None.
Habitat: Open water, pasture, mixed woodland.
Key birds: All three woodpeckers, Little and Tawny Owls, Kingfisher, Grey Wagtail, warblers. Passage raptors (inc. Osprey), terns and waders. *Winter*: Gull roost, wildfowl, tit and finch flocks.
Contact: Malcolm Hill, Treasurer, Ogston Bird Club, c/o 2 Sycamore Avenue, Glapwell, Chesterfield, S44 5LH. 01623 812159.
www.ogstonbirdclub.co.uk

6. PADLEY GORGE

The National Trust (East Midlands).
Location: From Sheffield, take A625. After eight miles, turn L on B6521 to Nether Padley. Grindleford Station is just off B6521 (NW of Nether Padley) and one mile NE of Grindleford village.
Access: All year. Not suitable for disabled people or those unused to steep climbs. Some of the paths are rocky. No dogs allowed.
Facilities: Café and toilets at Grindleford Station.
Public transport: Bus: from Sheffield to Bakewell stops at Grindleford/Nether Padley. Tel: 01709 566 000. Train: from Sheffield to Manchester Piccadilly stops at Grindleford Station. Tel: 0161 228 2141.
Habitat: Steep-sided valley containing largest area of sessile oak woodland in south Pennines.

Key birds: *Summer*: Pied Flycatcher, Spotted Flycatcher, Redstart, Wheatear, Whinchat, Wood Warbler, Tree Pipit.
Contact: High Peak Estate Office, Edale End, Edale Road, Hope S33 2RF. 01433 670368. www.nationaltrust.org.uk

OTHER SITES
(full details in previous editions)

A. Great Longstone Country Park
Contact: Peak District National Park, 01629 813227.

Devon

1. AYLESBEARE COMMON

RSPB
Location: SY 058 897. Five miles E of J30 of M5 at Exeter, 0.5 miles past Halfway Inn on B3052. Turn R to Hawkerland, car park is on L. The reserve is on the opposite side of main road.
Access: Open all year. One track suitable for wheelchairs and pushchairs.
Facilities: Car park, picnic area, group bookings, guided walks and special events. Disabled access via metalled track to private farm
Public transport: Buses (Exeter to Sidmouth, 53, 52a, 52b). Request stop at Joynes Grass (reserve entrance).
Habitat: Heathland, wood fringes, streams and ponds.
Key birds: *Spring/summer*: Nightjar, Stonechat. *All year*: Dartford Warbler, Buzzard. *Winter*: Possible Hen Harrier.
Contact: Toby Taylor, Hawkerland Brake Barn, Exmouth Road, Aylesbeare, Nr Exeter, Devon, Nr Exeter, Devon EX5 2JS. 01395 233655.

2. BOWLING GREEN MARSH

RSPB (South West England Office).
Location: SX 972 876. On the E side of River Exe, four miles SE of Exeter, 0.5 miles SE of Topsham.
Access: Open at all times. Please park at the public car parks in Topsham, not in the lane by the reserve.
Facilities: One hide suitable for wheelchair access. Viewing platform overlooking estuary reached by steps from track. No toilets or visitor centre.
Public transport: Exeter to Exmouth railway has regular (every 30 mins) service to Topsham station (half a mile from reserve). Stagecoach Devon – 57 bus has frequent service (Mon-Sat every 12 mins, Sun every half-hour) from Exeter to Topsham.
Habitat: Coastal grassland, open water/marsh, hedgerows.
Key birds: *Winter*: Wigeon, Shoveler, Teal, Black-tailed Godwit, Curlew, Golden Plover. *Spring*: Shelduck, passage waders, Whimbrel, passage Garganey and Yellow Wagtail. *Summer*: Gull/tern roosts, high tide wader roosts contain many passage birds. *Autumn*: Wildfowl, Peregrine, wader roosts.
Contact: RSPB, Unit 3, Lions Rest Estate, Station Road, Exminster, Exeter EX6 8DZ. 01392 824614. www.rspb.org.uk

3. DAWLISH WARREN

Teignbridge District Council.
Location: SX 983 788. At Dawlish Warren on S side of Exe estuary mouth. Turn off A379 at sign to Warren Golf Club, between Cockwood and Dawlish. Turn into car park adjacent to Lea Cliff Holiday Park. Pass under tunnel and turn left away from amusements. Park at far end of car park and pass through two pedestrian gates.
Access: Open public access, but avoid mudflats. Also avoid beach beyond groyne nine around high tide due to roosting birds. Parking charges apply. Restricted access for dogs, so please contact the wardens for more information.
Facilities: Visitor centre (tel 01626 863980) open most weekends all year (10.30am-1pm and 2pm-5pm). Summer also open most weekdays as before, can be closed if warden on site. Toilets at entrance tunnel and in resort area only. Hide open at all times – best around high tide.
Public transport: Train station at site, also regular bus service operated by Stagecoach.
Habitat: High tide roost site for wildfowl and waders of Exe estuary on mudflats and shore. Dunes, dune grassland, woodland, scrub, ponds.
Key birds: *Winter*: Waders and wildfowl – large numbers. Also good for divers and Slavonian Grebe offshore. *Summer*: Particularly good for terns. Excellent variety of birds all year, especially on migration.

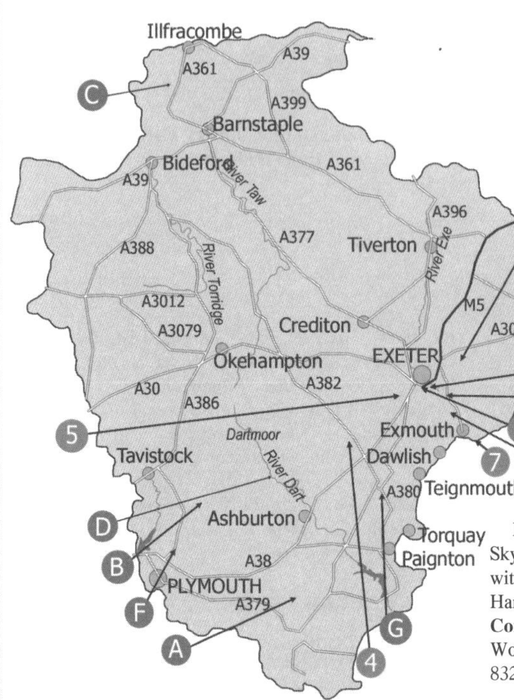

Devon

Contact: Andrea Buckley/Philip Chambers, Countryside Management Section, Forde House, Brunel Road, Newton Abbot, Devon TQ12 4XX. Visitor centre: 01626 863980. Teignbridge District Council: 01626 361101 (Ext 5754).

4. EAST DARTMOOR WOODS & HEATHS NNR

English Nature (Devon team).
Location: SX 778 787. Yarner Wood is two miles from Bovey Tracey on road to Becky Falls and Manaton. Road continues across Trendlebere Down where there are roadside car parks and adjacent paths.
Access: Yarner wood car park open from 8.30am-7pm or dusk if earlier. Outside these hours, access on foot from Trendlebere Downs. Dogs must be on leads.
Facilities: Information/interpretation display and self-guided trails available in Yarner Wood car park also hide with feeding station (Nov-Mar).
Public transport: Nearest bus stops are in Bovey Tracey. Buses from here to Exeter/ Plymouth (every two hours off-peak, one hour peak) and Newton Abbot (hourly).
Habitat: The reserve consists of three adjacent sites (Yarner Wood, Trendlebere Down and Bovey Valley Woodlands) totalling 365 hectares of upland oakwood and heathland.
Key birds: *All year*: Raven, Buzzard, Goshawk, Sparrowhawk, Lesser Spotted, Great Spotted and Green Woodpeckers, Grey Wagtail and Dartford Warbler (on Trendlebere Down). *Spring/summer*: Pied Flycatcher, Wood Warbler, Redstart, Tree Pipit, Linnet, Stonechat, Cuckoo, Whitethroat, Sky Lark. *Autumn/winter*: Good range of birds with feeding at hide – Siskin, Redpoll, plus Hen Harrier on Trendlebere Down.
Contact: Site Manager, English Nature, Yarner Wood, Bovey Tracey, Devon TW13 9LJ. 01626 832330. www.english-nature.org.uk

5. HALDON WOODS/DARTMOOR VIEW/ BIRD OF PREY VIEWPOINT

Forest Enterprise.
Location: Five miles W of Exeter. Follow signs for the racecourse. At A38 junction signed for Haldon Racecourse, take the off-slip road NW towards Dunchideock. Continue NW for nearly two miles until you reach the Bird of Prey Viewpoint threshold sign on the L. Turn L into car park, leave vehicle and follow all-ability trail to the viewpoint.
Access: Open Easter to end October.
Facilities: Viewing point with benches. Path suitable for wheelchair access.
Public transport: None.
Habitat: Plantations, clearings.
Key birds: *Spring/summer*: Wood, Grasshopper and other warblers, Redstart, Whinchat, possible Honey Buzzard, Cuckoo, Hobby, Nightjar, Turtle Dove, Tree Pipit, Woodcock. *All year*: Goshawk, Sparrowhawk, Great and Lesser Spotted Woodpecker, Stonechat, Willow Tit, Crossbill, Siskin, Redpoll.
Contact: Bullers Hill, Kennford, Exeter, Devon, EX6 7XR. 01392 832262. www.forestry.gov.uk/england

6. OLD SLUDGE BEDS

Devon Wildlife Trust.
Location: SX 952 888. Located on S edge of Exeter. Park at University boathouse car park at entrance to SWW sewage treatment works off A379 towards Dawlish. Walk along canal past sewage works to reach reserve.
Access: Open at all times. Please keep dogs on short lead and keep to paths. Not suitable for coaches.
Facilities: Path with boardwalks runs through reserve. There are steps and ramps to negotiate and the path can be waterlogged at times.
Public transport: Stagecoach, tel 01392 427711. Buses run from Exeter city centre to Countess Wear roundabout (services 57, K and T).
Habitat: Freshwater reedbed, open water and willow carr.
Key birds: *Summer*: Reed and Sedge Warblers. *All year*: Cetti's Warbler and Water Rail.
Contact: Shirehampton House, 35-37, St David's Hill, Exeter EX4 4DA. 01392 279244.
e-mail: devonwt@cix.co.uk
www.devonwildlifetrust.org

7. OTTER ESTUARY

Devon Wildlife Trust.
Location: SY 075 824. Lies on E edge of Budleigh Salterton. Park at Lime Kiln car park at eastern end of seafront. Public footpath runs alongside reserve from here.
Access: Open at all times. Access is along public footpaths (which run both sides of estuary) only. Path on western side is suitable for wheelchairs. Not suitable for coaches.
Facilities: Viewing platforms on western side; a hide (maintained by DBWPS) is on eastern side.
Public transport: Stagecoach, tel 01392 427711. Service 57 runs from Exeter Bus Station to Budleigh Salterton approx every 20 minutes.
Habitat: Estuary, saltmarsh and reedbed.
Key birds: Wintering and passage waders and wildfowl - Curlew, Redshank, Lapwing, Snipe, Wigeon, Teal, Little Egret, Water Rail and Kingfisher.
Contact: Shirehampton House, 35-37, St David's Hill, Exeter EX4 4DA. 01392 279244.
e-mail: devonwt@cix.co.uk

OTHER SITES

(full details in previous editions)

A. Andrew's Wood
Contact: Devon Wildlife Trust, 01392 279244.
B. Burrator Reservoir
Contact: South West Lakes Trust, 01837 871565.
C. Chapel Wood.
Contact: RSPB, 01392 824614.
D. Dart Valley
Contact: Devon Wildlife Trust, 01392 279244.
E. Exminster Marshes
Contact: RSPB, 01392 824614.
F. Plymbridge Wood
Contact: National Trust, 01208 432691.
G. Stover Lake and Woods Country Park.
Contact: Rangers Office, Devon County Council, 01626 835236.

Dorset

1. ARNE

RSPB (South West England Office).
Location: SY 973 882. Four miles SE of Wareham, turn off A351 at Stoborough.
Access: Shipstal Point and Coombe Birdwatchers' trails open all year. Bird hides available on both trails. Accessed from car park. Coaches and escorted parties by prior arrangement.
Facilities: Toilets in car park. Bird hide at Shipstal. Various footpaths. Reception hut (open end-May-early Sept).
Public transport: None.
Habitat: Lowland heath, woodland, reedbed and saltmarsh, extensive mudflats of Poole Harbour.
Key birds: *All year*: Dartford Warbler, Little Egret, Stonechat. *Winter*: Hen Harrier, Red-breasted Merganser, Black-tailed Godwit. *Summer*: Nightjar, warblers. *Passage*: Spotted Redshank, Whimbrel, Greenshank, Osprey.
Contact: Neil Gartshore, (Senior Warden), Syldata, Arne, Wareham, Dorset BH20 5BJ. 01929 553360.
e-mail: neil.gartshore@rspb.org.uk

Dorset

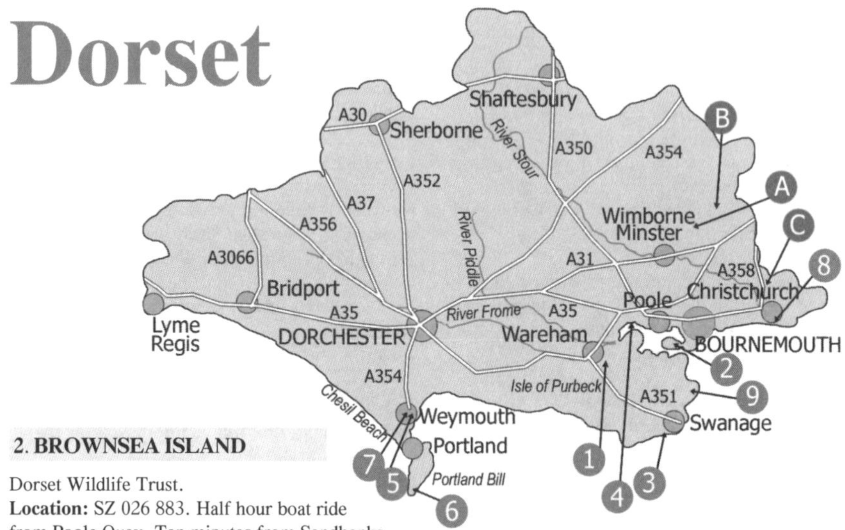

2. BROWNSEA ISLAND

Dorset Wildlife Trust.
Location: SZ 026 883. Half hour boat ride from Poole Quay. Ten minutes from Sandbanks Quay (next to Studland chain-ferry).
Access: Apr, May, Jun, Sept and Oct. Access by self-guided nature trail. Costs £2 adults, £1 children. Jul, Aug access by afternoon guided tour (2pm daily, duration 105 minutes). Costs £2 adults, £1 children.
Facilities: Toilets, information centre, five hides, nature trail.
Public transport: Poole Rail/bus station for access to Poole Quay and boats.
Habitat: Saline lagoon, reedbed, lakes, coniferous and mixed woodland.
Key birds: *Spring*: Avocet, Black-tailed Godwit, waders, gulls and wildfowl. *Summer*: Common and Sandwich Terns, Yellow-legged Gull, Little Egret, Little Grebe, Golden Pheasant. *Autumn*: Curlew Sandpiper, Little Stint.
Contact: Chris Thain, The Villa, Brownsea Island, Poole, Dorset BH13 7EE. 01202 709445. e-mail: dorsetwtisland@cix.co.uk www.wildlifetrust.org.uk/dorset

3. DURLSTON COUNTRY PARK

Dorset County Council.
Location: SZ 032 774. One mile S of Swanage (signposted).
Access: Visitor centre in car park open weekends and holidays during winter and daily in other seasons (phone for times).
Facilities: Guided walks, toilets, bookshop.
Public transport: Two buses per day except Sundays and Bank Holidays.
Habitat: Grassland, hedges, cliff, meadows, downland.
Key birds: Cliff-nesting seabird colonies; good variety of scrub and woodland breeding species; spring and autumn migrants; seawatching esp. Apr/May & Aug/Nov.
Contact: The Ranger, Durlston Country Park, Swanage, Dorset BH19 2JL. 01929 424443. www.durlston.co.uk

4. HAM COMMON LNR

Poole Borough Council.
Location: SY 99. W of Poole. In Hamworthy, take the Blandford Road S along Lake Road, W along Lake Drive and Napier Road, leading to Rockley Park. Park in beach car park by Hamworthy Pier or Rockley Viewpoint car park, off Napier Road, opposite the entrance to Gorse Hill Central Park.
Access: Open all year. Not suitable for coaches.
Facilities: None.
Public transport: None.
Habitat: Heathland, scrub, reedbeds, lake. Views over Wareham Channel and Poole Harbour.
Key birds: *Spring/summer:* Stonechat, Dartford Warbler. *Winter*: Brent Goose, Red-breasted Merganser, occasional divers, rarer grebes, Scaup. Waders inc Whimbrel, Greenshank and Common Sandpiper. *All year*: Little Egret.
Contact: Civic Centre, Poole BH15 2RU. 01202 633633. e-mail: information@poole.gov.uk

5. LODMOOR

RSPB (South West England Office).
Location: SY 686 807. Adjacent Lodmoor Country Park, in Weymouth, off A353 to Wareham.
Access: Open all times.
Facilities: One viewing shelter, network of paths.
Public transport: Local bus service.
Habitat: Marsh, shallow pools, reeds and scrub, remnant saltmarsh.
Key birds: *Spring/summer*: Breeding Common Tern, warblers (including Reed, Sedge, Grasshopper and Cetti's), Bearded Tit. *Winter*: Wildfowl, waders. *Passage*: Waders and other migrants.
Contact: Keith Ballard, RSPB Visitor Centre, Swannery Car Park, Weymouth DT4 7TZ. 01305 778313. www.rspb.org.uk

6. PORTLAND BIRD OBSERVATORY

Portland Bird Observatory (registered charity).
Location: SY 681 690. Six miles S of Weymouth beside the road to Portland Bill.
Access: Open at all times. Parking only for members of Portland Bird Observatory. Self-catering accommodation for up to 20. Take own towels, sheets, sleeping bags.
Facilities: Displays and information, toilets, natural history bookshop, equipped kitchen, laboratory.
Public transport: Bus service from Weymouth (First Dorset Transit Route 1).
Habitat: Scrub and ponds.
Key birds: *Spring/autumn*: Migrants including many rarities. *Summer*: Breeding auks, Fulmar, Kittiwake.
Contact: Martin Cade, Old Lower Light, Portland Bill, Dorset DT5 2JT. e-mail: obs@btinternet.com www.portlandbirdobs.btinternet.co.uk

7. RADIPOLE LAKE

RSPB (South West England Office).
Location: SY 677 796. In Weymouth. Enter from Swannery car park on footpaths.
Access: Visitor centre and nature trail open every day, summer (9am-5pm), winter (9am-4pm). Hide open (8.30am-4.30pm). Permit available from visitor centre required by non-RSPB members.
Facilities: Network of paths, one hide, one viewing shelter.
Public transport: Close to train station serving London and Bristol.
Habitat: Lake, reedbeds.
Key birds: *Winter*: Wildfowl. *Summer*: Breeding reedbed warblers (including Cetti's), Bearded Tit, passage waders and other migrants. Garganey regular in Spring. Good for rarer gulls.
Contact: Keith Ballard, RSPB Visitor Centre, Swannery Car Park, Weymouth DT4 7TZ. 01305 778313. www.rspb.org.uk

8. STANPIT MARSH SSSI, LNR

Christchurch Borough Council/Stanpit Marsh Advisory Panel, Community Services.
Location: SZ 167 924. In Christchurch.
Access: Public open space.
Facilities: Information centre.
Public transport: Wilts & Dorset bus no 123 (tel 01202 673555) Stanpit recreation ground stop. Bournemouth Yellow Buses no 20 (tel 01202 636000) Purewell Cross roundabout stop.
Habitat: Salt, fresh, brackish marsh, sand dune and scrub.
Key birds: *Estuarine*: Waders, winter wildfowl, migrants. *Reedbed*: Bearded Tit, Cetti's Warbler. Scrub: Sedge Warbler, Reed Warbler. *River/streams/bankside*: Kingfisher. Feeding and roosting site.
Contact: Peter Holloway, Christchurch Countryside Service, Steamer Point Nature Reserve, Highcliffe, Christchurch, Dorset BH23 4XX. 01425 272479.
e-mail: countrysideservice@christchurch.gov.uk

9. STUDLAND & GODLINGSTON HEATHS

National Trust.
Location: SZ 030 846. N of Swanage. From Ferry Road, N of Studland village.
Access: Open all year.
Facilities: Hides, nature trails.
Public transport: None.
Habitat: Woodland, heath, dunes, inter-tidal mudflats, saltings, freshwater lake, reedbeds, carr.
Key birds: Water Rail, Reed and Dartford Warblers, Nightjar, Stonechat. *Winter*: Wildfowl. Studland Bay, outside the reserve, has winter Black-necked and Slavonian Grebes, Scoter, Eider.
Contact: The National Trust, Countryside Office, Middle Beach Car Park, Studland, Swanage BH19 3AX.

OTHER SITES

(full details in previous editions)

A. Holt Heath
Contact: Ian Nicol, (Site Manager), English Nature 01202 841026.

B. Moors Valley Country Park and Ringwood Forest
Contact: Moors Valley CP, 01425 470721.

C. Sopley Common
Contact: Dorset Wildlife Trust, 01305 264620.

Durham

1. CASTLE EDEN DENE

English Nature (Northumbria Team).
Location: NZ 435 397. Adjacent to Peterlee, signposted from A19 and Peterlee town centre.
Access: Open from 8am-8pm or sunset if earlier. Car park. Dogs under tight control please. Pre-booked coach parties welcome. Parking available for one coach only.
Facilities: Car parking with toilet block at Oakerside Dene Lodge. 12 miles of footpath, two waymarked trails.
Public transport: Bus service to Peterlee centre.
Habitat: Yew/oak/sycamore woodland, paramaritime, limestone grassland.
Key birds: More than 170 recorded, 50 regular breeding species, typical woodland species.
Contact: Rob Lamboll, Oakerside Dene Lodge, Stanhope Chase, Peterlee, Co Durham SR8 1NJ. 0191 586 0004.

2. HAMSTERLEY FOREST

Forest Enterprise.
Location: NZ 093 315. Eight miles W of Bishop Auckland. Main entrance is five miles from A68, S of Witton-le-Wear and signposted through Hamsterley village and Bedburn.
Access: Open all year. Toll charge. Vehicles should not be left unattended after dark.
Facilities: Visitor centre, toilets, shop, access for disabled. Visitors should not enter fenced farmland.
Public transport: None.
Habitat: Commercial woodland, mixed and broadleaved trees.
Key birds: *Spring/summer*: Willow Warbler, Chiffchaff, Wood Warbler, Redstart, Pied Flycatcher. *Winter*: Crossbill, Redwing, Fieldfare. *All year*: Jay, Dipper, Green Woodpecker.
Contact: Eels Burn, Bellingham, Hexham, Northumberland, NE48 2AJ. 01434 220242.

3. JOE'S POND NATURE RESERVE

Durham Wildlife Trust.
Location: NZ 32 48. Between Durham and Sunderland on A690. N from Durham, leave A690 S of Houghton-le-Spring on B21284 to Fence Houses and Hetton-le-Hole. Head W towards Fence Houses and turn L at 1st roundabout, after 800 metres, into an opencast colliery site, signed Rye Hill Site.
Access: Open all year.
Facilities: Car park, bird hide.
Public transport: None.
Habitat: Scrub, pond, grassland.
Key birds: *Spring/summer*: Ruddy Duck, hirundines, Whinchat, Lesser Whitethroat, Whitethroat, Blackcap. Possible Yellow Wagtail, Redstart, Grasshopper Warbler. *Passage*: Waders, Wheatear. *Winter*: Teal, Pochard, Water Rail, Woodcock, Short-eared Owl, Kingfisher, thrushes. Chance of Merlin, Jack Snipe.
Contact: Rainton Meadows, Chilton Moor, Houghton-le-Spring, Tyne & Wear, DH4 6PU. 01388 488 728.

4. RAINTON MEADOWS

Durham Wildlife Trust, the City of Sunderland and RJB Mining (UK) Ltd.
Location: NZ 326 486. Located W of A690 between Durham and Sunderland. Just S of Houghton-le-Spring turn onto B1284, signposted to Fence Houses and Hetton-le-Hole. Head W towards Fence Houses and turn L at the first roundabout after 0.5 miles into Rye Hill Site.
Access: Park at Visitor centre (entrance gate locked at 4.30pm) or Mallard Way. Paths generally wheelchair-accessible, but there are some muddy areas. Main circular walk.
Facilities: Visitor centre, toilets, café, log book, shop, wildlife display. Dogs on lead.
Public transport: Buses from Sunderland and

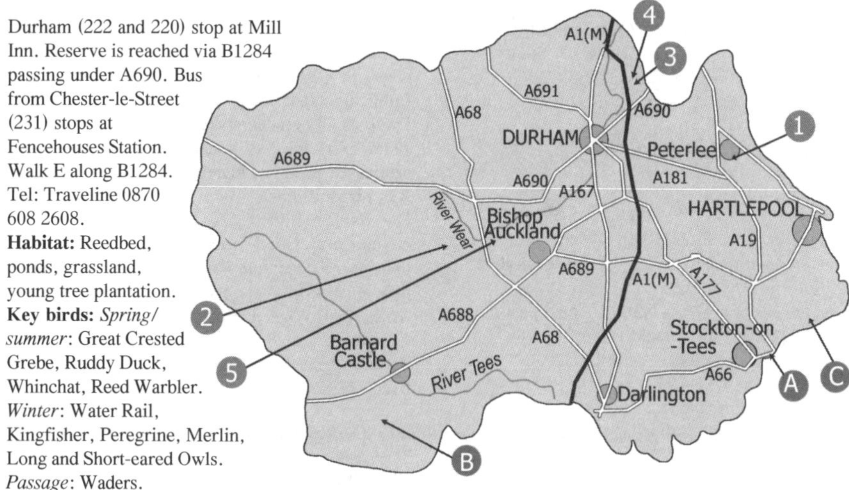

Durham (222 and 220) stop at Mill Inn. Reserve is reached via B1284 passing under A690. Bus from Chester-le-Street (231) stops at Fencehouses Station. Walk E along B1284. Tel: Traveline 0870 608 2608.
Habitat: Reedbed, ponds, grassland, young tree plantation.
Key birds: *Spring/ summer*: Great Crested Grebe, Ruddy Duck, Whinchat, Reed Warbler. *Winter*: Water Rail, Kingfisher, Peregrine, Merlin, Long and Short-eared Owls. *Passage*: Waders.
Contact: Wildlife Trust HQ, Rainton Meadows, Chilton Moor, Houghton-le-Spring, Tyne & Wear, DH4 6PU. 0191 5843112.

5. WITTON-LE-WEAR (Low Barns)

Durham Wildlife Trust.
Location: NZ 160 315. W of Bishop Auckland. Off unclassified road between Witton-le-Wear (signposted on A68) and High Grange.
Access: Open all year.
Facilities: Five hides (four with disabled access), observation tower above visitor centre (manned), nature trail, coffee shop.
Public transport: None.
Habitat: Former gravel workings, lake, ponds, riverbank and newly constructed reedbeds.
Key birds: *All year*: Greylag Goose, Kingfisher. *Summer*: Goosander, Grey Wagtail, Redpoll have bred. *Winter*: Wildfowl (inc. Goldeneye, Shoveler), Curlew, Redshank, Wheatear, Snipe.
Contact: Visitor Centre Manager, Low Barns Nature Reserve, Witton-le-Wear, Bishop Auckland, Co Durham DL14 0AG. 01388 488728.

OTHER SITES
(full details in previous editions)

A. Maze Park and Portrack Marsh
Contact: Tees Valley Wildlife Trust, 01642 759900.

B. Stang Forest and Hope Moor
Contact: Forest Enterprise, 01434 220242.

C. Teesmouth
Contact: English Nature, 01429 853325.

Essex

1. ABBERTON RESERVOIR

Essex Wildlife Trust.
Location: TL 963 185. Six miles SW of Colchester on B1026. Follow signs from Layer-de-la-Haye.
Access: Open Tue-Sun (9am-5pm) except Christmas Day and Boxing Day.
Facilities: Visitor centre, toilets, nature trail, five hides (disabled access). Also good viewing where roads cross reservoir.
Public transport: Phone Trust for advice.
Habitat: Nine acres on edge of 1200a reservoir.
Key birds: Nationally important for Mallard, Teal, Wigeon, Shoveler, Gadwall, Pochard, Tufted Duck, Goldeneye (most important inland site in Britain). Smew regular. Passage waders, terns, birds of prey. Tree-nesting Cormorants (largest colony in Britain); raft-nesting Common Tern. *Summer*: Yellow Wagtail, warblers, Nightingale, Corn Bunting; *Autumn*: Red-crested Pochard, Water Rail; *Winter*: Goosander.

Contact: Centre Manager, Abberton Reservoir Visitor Centre, Layer-de-la-Haye, Colchester CO2 0EU. 01206 738172.
e-mail: abberton@essexwt.org.uk

2. ABBOTTS HALL FARM

Essex Wildlife Trust.
Location: TL 963 145. Seven miles SW from Colchester. Turn E off B1026 (Colchester–Maldon road) towards Peldon. Entrance is about 0.5 mile on R.
Access: Weekdays (9am-5pm). No dogs please. Working farm so please take care.
Facilities: Toilets, hides, guided walks, fact-sheets.
Public transport: None.
Habitat: Saltmarsh, saline lagoons, grazing marsh, farmland.
Key birds: *Winter*: Waders and wildfowl.
Contact: Abbotts Hall Farm, Great Wigborough, Colchester, Essex CO5 7RZ. 01621 862960.
e-mail: admin@essexwt.org.uk

3. COLNE POINT

Essex Wildlife Trust.
Location: TM 108 125. W of Clacton, via B1027 to St Osyth then Lee Wick Lane. Car park before reserve (liable to flood at very high tides).
Access: Day permit for non-Trust members.
Facilities: None.
Public transport: Phone Trust for advice.
Habitat: Mudflats, shingle pools.
Key birds: On major migration route for finches and chats. *Spring/autumn*: Birds of prey. *Summer*: Breeding Little Tern, Ringed Plover, Oystercatcher, Redshank. *Winter*: Divers, grebes, ducks, and feeding ground for Brent Geese.
Contact: The Warden, Abbotts Hall Farm, Great Wigborough, Colchester, Essex CO5 7RZ.
www.essexwt.org.uk
e-mail: admin@essexwt.org.uk

4. FINGRINGHOE WICK

Essex Wildlife Trust.
Location: TM 046 197. Colchester five miles. The reserve is signposted from B1025 to Mersea Island, S of Colchester.
Access: Open six days per week (not Mon or Christmas or Boxing Day). No permits needed. Donations invited. Centre/reserve open (9am-5pm). Dogs must be on a lead.
Facilities: Visitor centre – toilets, shop, light refreshments, car park, displays. Reserve – seven bird hides, two nature trails, plus one that wheelchair users could use with assistance.
Public transport: None.
Habitat: Old gravel pit, large lake, many ponds, sallow/birch thickets, young scrub, reedbeds, saltmarsh, gorse heathland.
Key birds: *Autumn/winter*: Brent Goose, waders, Hen Harrier, Little Egret. *Spring*: 40 male Nightingales. Good variety of warblers in scrub, thickets, reedbeds and Turtle Dove, Green/Great Spotted Woodpeckers. *Winter*: Little Grebe, Mute Swan, Teal, Wigeon, Shoveler, Gadwall on lake.
Contact: Laurie Forsyth, Wick Farm, South Green Road, Fingringhoe, Colchester, Essex CO5 7DN. 01206 729678. e-mail: admin@essexwt.org.uk

5. OLD HALL MARSHES

RSPB (East Anglia Office).
Location: TL 97 51 25. Approx eight miles S of Colchester. From A12 take B1023, via Tiptree, to Tolleshunt D'Arcy. Then take Chapel Road (back road to Tollesbury), after one mile turn left into Old Hall Lane. Continue up Old Hall Lane, over speed ramp and through iron gates to cattle grid, then follow signs to car park.
Access: By permit only in advance from Warden, write to address below. Open 9am-9pm or dusk, closed Tues. No coaches.
Facilities: Two trails – one of three miles and one of 6.5 miles. Two viewing screens overlooking saline lagoon area at E end of reserve. No visitor centre or toilets.
Public transport: None.
Habitat: Coastal grazing marsh, reedbed, open water saline lagoon, saltmarsh and mudflat.
Key birds: *Summer*: Breeding Avocet, Redshank, Lapwing, Pochard, Shoveler, Gadwall, Garganey, Barn Owl. *Winter*: Brent Goose, Wigeon, Teal Shoveler, Goldeneye, Red-breasted Merganser, all the expected waders, Hen Harrier, Merlin, Short-eared Owl and Twite. *Passage*: All expected waders (particularly Spotted Redshank, Green Sandpiper and Whimbrel), Yellow Wagtail, Whinchat and Wheatear.
Contact: Paul Charlton, Site Manager, c/o 1 Old Hall Lane, Tolleshunt D'Arcy, Maldon, Essex CM9 8TP. 01621 869015.
e-mail: paul.charlton@rspb.org.uk

6. STOUR ESTUARY

RSPB (East Anglia Office).
Location: TM 191 310. Car park – by B1352

Essex

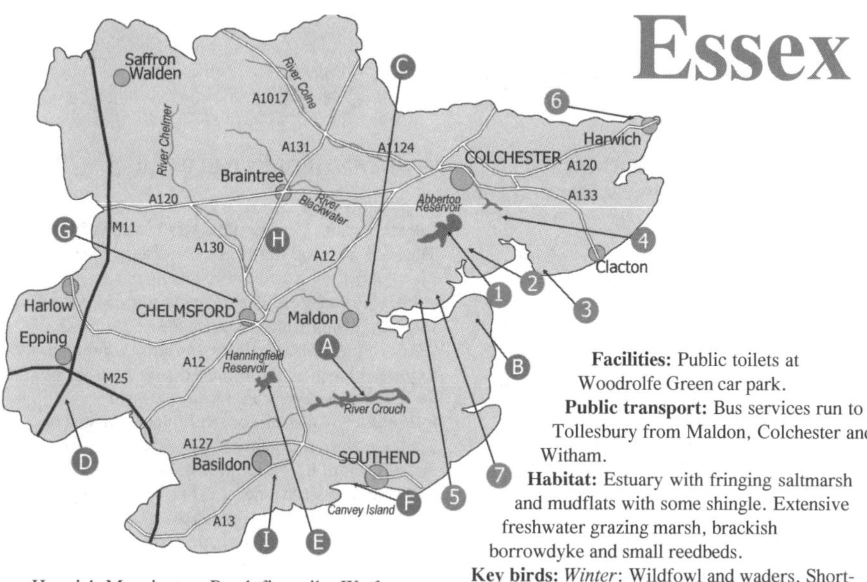

Harwich-Manningtree Road, five miles W of Harwich, 0.5 miles E of Wrabness.
Access: No charges – donation appreciated. Open at all times, except Christmas Day.
Facilities: Three hides. No visitor centre/toilets. Cycle racks in car park, height barrier to restrict overnight parking.
Public transport: Harwich/Colchester via Wrabness. Bus service passes entrance. Wrabness railway station 0.5 mile W of the reserve.
Habitat: Extensive areas of mudflats and saltmarsh with adjacent woodland and scrub.
Key birds: *Winter*: Wading birds and wildfowl, Dunlin, Grey Plover, Knot, Black-tailed Godwit, Pintail, Brent Goose. *Summer*: Nightingale, migratory warblers and all three woodpeckers.
Contact: Rick Vonk, RSPB East Anglia Office, 01255 886043. e-mail: rick.vonk@RSPB.org.uk www.RSPB.org.uk

7. TOLLESBURY WICK

Essex Wildlife Trust.
Location: GR 970 104. On Blackwater Estuary eight miles E of Maldon. Follow B1023 to Tollesbury via Tiptree, leaving A12 at Kelvedon. Then follow Woodrolfe Road S towards the marina. Use car park at Woodrolfe Green. Small public car park near reserve suitable for cars and mini-buses only.
Access: Open at all times along public footpath on top of sea wall.
Facilities: Public toilets at Woodrolfe Green car park.
Public transport: Bus services run to Tollesbury from Maldon, Colchester and Witham.
Habitat: Estuary with fringing saltmarsh and mudflats with some shingle. Extensive freshwater grazing marsh, brackish borrowdyke and small reedbeds.
Key birds: *Winter*: Wildfowl and waders, Short-eared Owl, Hen Harrier. *Summer*: Breeding Avocet, Redshank, Lapwing, occasional Little Tern, Reed and Sedge Warblers, Barn Owl. *Passage*: Whimbrel, Spotted Redshank.
Contact: Jonathan Smith, Tollesbury, Maldon, Essex CM9 8RJ. 01621 868628.
e-mail: jonathans@essexwt.org.uk

OTHER SITES
(full details in previous editions)

A. Blue House Farm
Contact: Essex Wildlife Trust, CO5 7RZ. 01621 862960.

B. Bradwell Bird Observatory
Contact: Graham Smith, 01277 354034.

C. Chigborough Lakes
Contact: Essex Wildlife Trust, 01621 862960.

D. Hainault Forest
Contact: Hainault Forest CP, 0208 500 7353.

E. Hanningfield Reservoir
Contact: Hanningfield Reservoir, 01268 711001.

F. Leigh
Contact: Essex Wildlife Trust, 01621 862960

G. Little Waltham Meadows
Contact: Essex Wildlife Trust, 01621 862960.

H. Phyllis Currie Nature Reserve
Contact: Essex Wildlife Trust, 01621 862960.

I. Wat Tyler Country Park
Contact: Wat Tyler Country Park, 01268 550088.

Gloucestershire

1. ASHLEWORTH HAM AND MEEREND THICKET

Gloucestershire Wildlife Trust.
Location: SO830265. Leave Gloucester N on A417; R at Hartpury and follow minor road through Ashleworth towards Hasfield.
Access: Access prohibited at all times, but birds may be viewed from new hide in Meerend Thicket.
Facilities: Bird viewing hide and screen, interpretation panels.
Public transport: None.
Habitat: Low-lying grassland flood plain.
Key birds: *Winter*: Wildfowl (inc. 4,000 Wigeon, 1500 Teal, Pintail, Goldeneye, Bewick's Swan); passage waders; Peregrine, Hobby.
Contact: Dulverton Building, Robinswood Hill Country Park, Reservoir Road, Gloucester GL4 6SX. 01452 383333.
www.wildlifetrust.org.uk/gloucswt/

2. COKES PIT LOCAL NATURE RESERVE (LAKE 34)

Cotswold Water Park Society.
Location: SU 026 957. Lake 34 is located adjacent to Keynes Country Park. From the A419, take B4696 towards Ashton Keynes. At staggered crossroads, go straight over, heading towards Somerford Keynes. Take next R turn to Circencester. The entrance to Keynes Country Park is second entrance on R.
Access: Open at all times. Parking charge applies.
Facilities: Paths are flat with footbridges. Some wheelchair access. Toilets, refreshments, car parking and information available from adjacent Keynes Country Park. A hide with log book is located on the E shore.
Public transport: Buses from Kemble, Cheltenham, Cirencester and Swindon. Tel: 08457 090 899. Nearest station is four miles away at Kemble. Tel: 08457 484 950.
Habitat: Small lake with wooded and reedbed margins with feeding station in winter.
Key birds: *Winter*: Common wildfowl, Red-crested Pochard. *Summer*: Breeding ducks, warblers, Nightingale, Hobby, Common Tern, Reed Bunting.
Contact: Cotswold Water Park Society, See details below.

3. COTSWOLD WATER PARK

Cotswold Water Park Society.
Location: The CWP comprises 140 lakes in Upper Thames Valley, between Cirencester and Swindon. Many of these lakes are accessible by public using public rights of way. The Cotswold Water Park Gateway Visitor Centre is place to start. SU 072 971. From A419, take B4696 towards Ashton Keynes. Visitor Centre is immediately on L after the A419. Coach parking, toilets, cafe and information available. For the Millennium Visitor Centre at Keynes Country Park SU 026 957, from the A419, take B4696 towards Ashton Keynes. At staggered crossroads, go straight over, heading towards Somerford Keynes. Take next R turn to Circencester. Entrance to Keynes Country Park is the second on R. Parking charge applies. Coach parking on request - please call ahead. Toilets, refreshments and information available. Plus bathing beach, high ropes course and other activities.
Access: Cotswold Water Park is open all year round. The visitor centres are open every day except Christmas Day.
Facilities: Paths are flat but there are stiles and footbridges. Many are wheelchair accessible. Toilets, refreshments, car parking and information available from the visitor centres. Hides available at Cleveland Lakes/Waterhay (lakes 68a and 68c), Shorncote Reed Bed (lakes 84/85), Cokes Pit (Lake 34) and Whelford Pools (Lake 111). Free copies of the CWP Leisure Guide are available from the visitor centres. These have maps showing the lake numbering. The guidebook *Wildlife in the Cotswold Water Park: Where to go and what to see* is also available from these centres.
Public transport: Bus: from Kemble, Cheltenham, Cirencester and Swindon. Tel: 08457 090899. Train: nearest station is four miles away at Kemble. Tel: 08457 484950.
Habitat: Gravel extraction has created more than 1000ha of standing open water or 140 lakes plus other associated wetland habitats, creating one of the largest man-made wetlands in Europe.
Key birds: *Winter*: Common wildfowl, Smew, Red-crested Pochard, Merlin, Peregrine. *Summer*: Breeding ducks, warblers, Nightingale, Hobby, Common Tern, Black-headed Gull colony, Reed Bunting, hirundines.

Contact: Cotswold Water Park Society, Keynes Country Park, Spratsgate Lane, Shorncote, Cirencester, Glos GL7 6DF. 01285 861459;(Fax)01285 860186.
e-mail: info@waterpark.org

4. HIGHNAM WOODS

RSPB (Central England Office).
Location: SO 778 190. Signed on A40 three miles W of Gloucester.
Access: Open at all times, no permit required. Disabled access to a hide 120 yards from car park. The nature trails can be very muddy. Dogs allowed on leads.
Facilities: One nature trail (approx 1.5 miles), one birdwatching hide with winter bird-feeding programme.
Public transport: Contact Glos. County Council public transport information line. Tel: 01452 425543.
Habitat: Ancient woodland in the Severn Vale with areas of coppice and scrub.
Key birds: *Spring/summer:* The reserve has about 12 pairs of breeding Nightingales. Resident birds include all three woodpeckers, Buzzard and Sparrowhawk. Ravens are frequently seen. *Winter*: feeding site in front of hide for woodland birds.
Contact: Ivan Proctor, The Puffins, Parkend, Lydney, Glos GL15 4JA. 01594 562852.
e-mail: ivan.proctor@rspb.org.uk

5. LOWER WOODS

Gloucestershire Wildlife Trust.
Location: Reserve is about one mile E of Wickwar. Main parking is at Lower Woods Lodge, via a track off the Wickwar-Hawkesbury road. Public footpaths and bridleways cross the reserve.
Access: Open all year.
Facilities: Footpaths and bridleways. Walk leaflet available.
Public transport: None.
Habitat: Mixed woodland, mildly acidic or slightly calcareous clay, grassland, river, springs.
Key birds: *Spring/summer*: Nightingale. *All year*: Usual woodland species.
Contact: Dulverton Building, Robinswood Hill Country Park, Reservoir Road, Gloucester GL4 6SX. 01452 383333.

6. NAGSHEAD

RSPB (Central England Office).
Location: SO 097 085. In Forest of Dean, N of Lydney. Signed immediately W of Parkend village on the road to Coleford.
Access: Open at all times, no permit required. The reserve is hilly and there are some stiles on nature trails. Dogs must be kept under close control.
Facilities: There are two nature trails (one mile and 2.25 miles). Information centre open at weekends mid-Apr to end Aug. Schools education programme available.
Public transport: Contact Glos. County Council public transport information line, 01452 425543.
Habitat: Much of the reserve is 200-year-old oak plantations, grazed in some areas by sheep. The rest of the reserve is a mixture of open areas and conifer/mixed woodland.
Key birds: *Spring*: Pied Flycatcher, Wood Warbler, Redstart, warblers. *Winter*: Siskin, Crossbill in some years. *All year*: Buzzard, Raven, all three woodpeckers.
Contact: Ivan Proctor, The Puffins, Parkend, Lydney, Glos GL15 4JA. 01594 562852.
e-mail: ivan.proctor@rspb.org.uk

7. SHORNCOTE REEDBED (LAKES 84/85)

Cotswold Water Park Society.
Location: SU 026 957. Lakes 84/85 located

adjacent to Keynes Country Park. From A419, take the B4696 towards Ashton Keynes. At staggered crossroads, go straight over, heading towards Somerford Keynes. Take the next R turn to Circencester. Entrance to Keynes Country Park is second entrance on R.
Access: Open at all times.
Facilities: Paths are uneven with footbridges. No disabled access. Toilets, refreshments, car parking and information available from adjacent Keynes Country Park. A hide with log book is located on the E shore.
Public transport: Bus: from Kemble, Cheltenham, Cirencester and Swindon. Tel: 08457 090 899. Train: nearest station is four miles away at Kemble. Tel: 08457 484 950.
Habitat: Only lakes in the Cotswold Water Park restored specifically for wildlife. Lakes with reedbed, marsh, ditches, islands and loafing areas.
Key birds: *Winter*: Common wildfowl, Smew, Peregrine, Merlin, Bittern, Stonechat. *Summer*: Breeding ducks, warblers, Hobby, Reed Bunting.
Contact: Cotswold Water Park Society, see above.

8. SLIMBRIDGE

The Wildfowl & Wetlands Trust.
Location: SO 723 048. S of Gloucester. Signposted from M5 (exit 13 or 14).
Access: Open daily except Christmas Day, (9am-5.30pm, 5pm in winter). Group visits a speciality. Contact Bookings Officer 01453 891900.
Facilities: Hides, observatory, observation tower, Hanson Discovery Centre, wildlife art gallery, tropical house, facilities for disabled, worldwide collection of wildfowl species.
Public transport: None.
Habitat: Reedbed, saltmarsh, freshwater pools, mudflats.
Key birds: Kingfisher, waders, raptors. *Winter*; Wildfowl esp. Bewick's Swans, White-fronted Geese, Wigeon, Teal.
Contact: Jane Allen, Marketing Manager, Slimbridge, Gloucester GL2 7BT. 01453 891900;(Fax) 01453 890927.
e-mail: info.slimbridge@wwt.org.uk

9. WATERHAY AND CLEVELAND LAKES RESERVE

Cotswold Water Park Society.
Location: SU 060 933. The Waterhay is located S of Ashton Keynes, accessed from Waterhay Car Park (free of charge).
Access: Cleveland Lakes are a series of lakes located adjacent to the Waterhay, which were purchased by the Cotswold Water Park Society in March 2003. While no public access exists at present, access will be created in the future. In the intervening period, hides are being installed which overlook the lakes, accessed from the Thames National Trail. Until the appropriate rights of way are created with the necessary screening, please stay on the footpath. The site is still part of an active sand and gravel quarry and thus public access is not permitted. The Thames National Trail and Waterhay Car Park are open all year round. Note that the footpath and car park flood in winter and may not be easily accessible.
Facilities: Paths are even with footbridges. Hides are located at Lakes 68a and 68c. See the *Cotswold Water Park Leisure Guide* (available from the Cotswold Water Park Society or download from www.waterpark.org).
Public transport: Bus: From Kemble, Cheltenham, Cirencester and Swindon. Tel: 08457 090 899.
Habitat: Wide variety of wetland habitats: open water, water channels, reedbeds, willow beds, silt lagoons, flooded fields in winter, open grassland. Series of restored and unrestored gravel workings.
Key birds: *Winter*: Large numbers of wildfowl, Teal, Goldeneye, Pintail, Bittern, Peregrine, Merlin, Cetti's Warbler, Hen and Marsh Harriers, Little Egret, Water Rail. Gull roost, Kumlien's Gull (occasional), Lapwing and Golden Plover flocks, Curlew. *Summer*: Breeding ducks, warblers, Hobby, Reed Bunting, Sand Martin, heron. *Passage*: Whinchat, Stonechat, Wheatear, warblers, 30 species of waders in good years, inc Spotted Redshank, Whimbrel, Little Stint, plus large numbers of hirundines.
Contact: Cotswold Water Park Society, see above.

10. WHELFORD POOLS

Gloucestershire Wildlife Trust.
Location: SU 174 995. E of Cirencester, SE of Fairford. Leave Fairford E on A417, turn towards Whelford and reserve is on left (just before Whelford sign).
Access: Open at all times.
Facilities: Two hides, one with wheelchair access. Leaflet available.
Public transport: None.
Habitat: Flooded gravel pits in eastern section of Cotswold Water Park.
Key birds: On main passage flight route (Yellow Wagtail, Black Tern, Osprey, waders). *Summer:*

Breeding Common Tern, Heron, Hobby. *Winter*: Wildfowl.
Contact: Wildlife Trust HQ, 01452 383333.

OTHER SITES
(full details in previous editions)

A. Coombe Hill Meadows
Contact: Wildlife Trust HQ, 01452 383333.

B. Littleton Brick Pits
Contact: The Wildlife Centre, 0117 917 7270.

C. Symond's Yat
Contact: The Puffins, 01594 562852.

D. Woorgreens Lake and Marsh
Contact: Wildlife Trust HQ, 01452 383333.

Hampshire

1. FARLINGTON MARSHES

Hampshire & Isle of Wight Wildlife Trust.
Location: SU 685 045. E side of Portsmouth. Entrance of roundabout at junction of A2030 (Eastern Road) and A27, or from Harts Farm Way, Broadmarsh, Havant (S side of A27).
Access: Open at all times, no charge or permits, but donations welcome. Dogs on leads only. Not suitable for disabled. Groups please book to avoid clash of dates.
Facilities: Information at entrance and in shelter area of building. No toilets.
Public transport: None.
Habitat: Coastal grazing marsh with pools and reedbed within reserve. Views over intertidal mudflats/saltmarshes of Langstone Harbour.
Key birds: *Autumn to spring*: Waders and wildfowl. *Winter*: Brent Goose, Wigeon, Pintail etc and waders (Dunlin, Grey Plover etc). On migration wide range of waders including rarities. Reedbeds with Bearded Tit, Water Rail etc, scrub areas attract small migrants (Redstart, Wryneck, warblers etc).
Contact: Bob Chapman, Beechcroft House, Vicarage Lane, Curdridge, Hants SO32 2DP. 01489 774 400. www.hwt.org.uk - go to 'Reserves' and then 'news' for sightings, etc

2. FLEET POND LNR

Hart District Council.
Location: SY 85. Located in Fleet. From the B3013, head to Fleet Station. Park in the long-stay car park at Fleet Station. Parking also available in Chestnut Grove and Westover Road.
Access: Open all year.
Facilities: None. **Public transport:** None.
Habitat: Lake, reedbed, willow scrub.
Key birds: *Spring/autumn*: Migrant waders inc Little Ringed Plover, Dunlin, Greenshank, Little Gull, occasional Kittiwake, terns, Wood Lark, Sky Lark, occasional Ring Ouzel, Firecrest, Pied Flycatcher. *Summer*: Hobby, Common Tern, Tree Pipit. *Winter*: Bittern, wildfowl, occasional Smew, Snipe, occasional Jack Snipe, Siskin, Redpoll.
Contact: Civic Office, Harlington Way, Fleet, Hampshire GU51 4AE. 01252 622122.

3. HAMBLE COMMON AND COPSE

Eastleigh Borough Council (Countryside Service)
Location: SU 48 09. Hamble Common is reached via Copse Lane from B3397 Hamble Lane, which links with A27 and M27 at Windhover roundabout near Bursledon.
Access: Open all year.
Facilities: Car parks are linked to each other and the rest of the site by a good network of footpaths. Ground conditions good in summer, but in winter/ after rain, stout waterproof footwear is advisable.
Public transport: None.
Habitat: Wet heathland, scrub, woodland, meadow, grassland.
Key birds: *Winter*: Wildfowl and waders. On the Southampton Water shore, Oystercatchers, Grey Plovers, Ringed Plovers, Dunlin, Turnstone, Curlew and Brent Goose common. In the creek wader numbers are lower, with Redshank, Lapwing and Dunlin, occasional Greenshank, Teal, Mallard, Shelduck, Grey Heron, Kingfisher most years.
Contact: Civic Office, Leigh Road, Eastleigh, Hampshire SO50 9YN. 0238 068 8000.

Hampshire

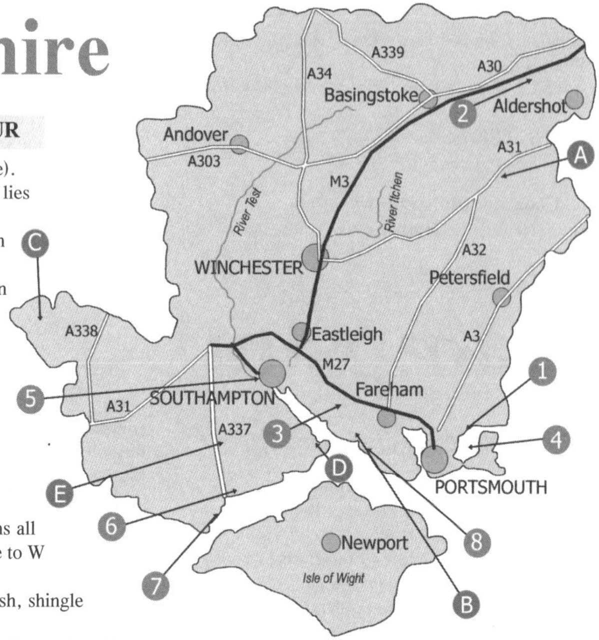

4. LANGSTONE HARBOUR

RSPB (South East England Office).
Location: SU 695 035. Harbour lies E of Portsmouth, one mile S of Havant. Car parks at Broadmarsh (SE of A27/A3(M) junction) and West Hayling LNR (first right on A2030 after Esso garage).
Access: Restricted access. Good views from West Hayling LNR, Broadmarsh and Farlington Marshes LNR (qv). Winter boat trips may be booked from the nearby Portsmouth Outdoor Centre.
Facilities: None.
Public transport: Mainline trains all stop at Havant. Local bus service to W Hayling LNR.
Habitat: Intertidal mud, saltmarsh, shingle islands.
Key birds: *Summer*: Breeding waders and seabirds inc. Mediterranean Gull and Little Tern. *Passage/ winter:* Waterfowl, inc. Black-necked Grebes, dark-bellied Brent Goose c5000, Shelduck, Shoveler, Goldeneye and Red-breasted Merganser. Waders inc. Oystercatcher, Ringed and Grey Plover, Dunlin, Black and Bar-tailed Godwit and Greenshank. Peregrine, Merlin and Short-eared Owl.
Contact: Chris Cockburn (Warden), RSPB Langstone Harbour,Unit B3, Wren Centre,Emsworth, Hants PO10 7SU. 01243 378784; e-mail: chris.cockburn@rspb.org.uk

5. LOWER TEST

Hampshire & Isle of Wight Wildlife Trust.
Location: SU 364 150. M271 S to Redbridge, three miles from Southampton city centre.
Access: Open at all times, guide dogs only.
Facilities: One hide and two screens, suitable for disabled (access by arrangement with the warden).
Public transport: Totton train station and bus stops within easy walking distance.
Habitat: Saltmarsh, brackish grassland, wet meadows, reedbed, scrapes, meres, estuary.
Key birds: *Summer*: Breeding Little, Sandwich and Common Terns, Black-headed and Mediterranean Gulls, waders. *Passage/winter*: Waders. *Autumn/ winter:* Waders (inc. Black-tailed and Bar-tailed Godwits, Oystercatcher, Ringed and Grey Plover, Dunlin). Wildfowl (inc. Shelduck, Shoveler, Goldeneye, Red-breasted Merganser and dark-bellied Brent Goose c7000). Black-necked Grebe, Short-eared Owl, Peregrine.
Contact: Clare Bishop, Trust HQ, Beechcroft House, Vicarage Lane, Curdridge, Hants SO32 2DP. 023 8042 4206. e-mail: clareb@hwt.org.uk

6. LYMINGTON REEDBEDS

Hampshire & Isle of Wight Wildlife Trust.
Location: SZ 324 965. From Lyndhurst in New Forest take A337 to Lymington. Turn L after railway bridge into Marsh Lane. Park in the lay-by next to allotments. The reserve entrance is on opposite side, to R of the house and over railway crossing. The footpath exits the reserve near the Old Ampress Works, leading to a minor road between the A337 and Boldre.
Access: Open all year. The best viewpoint over the reedbeds is from Bridge Road or from the Undershore leading from the B3054.
Facilities: None.
Public transport: Bus: at either end of the footpath through site, Marsh Lane and on the A337 (route 112). Five minutes walk from train station.
Habitat: One of largest reedbeds on S coast,

fringed by alder and willow woodland.
Key birds: One of highest concentrations of Water Rail in the country; resident but most evident in winter. *Spring/summer*: Cetti's Warbler, Bearded Tit, Yellow Wagtail, Swallows, martins, Reed Warbler. *Passage*: Snipe, ducks. Otters in the area.
Contact: Michael Boxall, Beechcroft House, Vicarage Lane, Curdridge, Hants SO32 2DP. 01489 774 400. e-mail: feedback@hwt.org.uk

7. LYMINGTON-KEYHAVEN NNR

Hampshire County Council.
Location: SZ 315 920. S of Lymington along seawall footpath; car parks at Bath Road, Lymington and at Keyhaven Harbour.
Access: Open all year
Facilities: None.
Public transport: None.
Habitat: Coastal marshland and lagoons.
Key birds: *Spring*: Passage waders (inc. Knot, Sanderling, Bar-tailed and Black-tailed Godwits, Whimbrel, Spotted Redshank), Pomarine and Great Skuas. Breeding Oystercatcher, Ringed Plover and Sandwich, Common and Little Terns. *Autumn*: Passage raptors, waders and passerines. *Winter*: Wildfowl (inc. Brent Goose, Wigeon, Pintail, Red-breasted Merganser), waders (inc. Golden Plover), Little Egret, gulls.
Contact: Hampshire County Council, Mottisfont Court, High Street, Winchester, Hants SO23 8ZF.

8. TITCHFIELD HAVEN

Hampshire County Council.
Location: SU 535 025. From A27 W of Fareham; public footpath follows derelict canal along W of reserve and road skirts S edge.
Access: Open Wed-Sun all year, plus Bank Hols, except Christmas and Boxing days.
Facilities: Centre has information desk, toilets, tea room and shop. Guided tours (book in advance). Hides.
Public transport: None.
Habitat: Reedbeds, freshwater scrapes, wet grazing meadows.
Key birds: *Spring/summer*: Bearded Tit, waders (inc. Black-tailed Godwit, Ruff), wildfowl, Common Tern, breeding Cetti's Warbler, Water Rail. *Winter*: Bittern.
Contact: Barry Duffin, Titchfield Haven Visitor Centre, Cliff Road, Hill Head, Fareham, Hants PO14 3JT. 01329 662145; fax 01329 667113.

OTHER SITES

(full details in previous editions)

A. Alice Holt Forest
Contact: Forest Enterprise, 0117 906 6000.
B. Hook-With-Warsash LNR
Contact: Titchfield Haven Visitor Centre, 01329 662145.
C. Martin Down
Contact: David Burton, Parsonage Down NNR, 01980 620485.
D. North Solent
Contact: English Nature, 023802 86428.
E. Roydon Woods
Contact: Hampshire and Isle of Wight Wildlife Trust, 01590 622708.

Hertfordshire

1. CASSIOBURY PARK

Welwyn & Hatfield Council.
Location: TL 090 970. Close to Watford town centre.
Access: Open all year.
Facilities: Car park, footpaths.
Public transport: Watford Metropolitan Underground station.
Habitat: Municipal park, wetland, river, alder/willow wood.
Key birds: *Spring/summer*: Kingfisher, Grey Wagtail. *Winter*: Snipe, Water Rail, occasional Bearded Tit.
Contact: Council Offices, The Campus, Welwyn Garden City, Herts AL8 6AE. 01707 357000. e-mail: council.services@welhat.gov.uk

2. LEMSFORD SPRINGS

Herts & Middlesex Wildlife Trust.
Location: TL 223 123. Lies 1.5 miles W of Welwyn Garden City town centre, off roundabout leading to Lemsford village on B197, W of A1(M).
Access: Access, via key, by arrangement with warden. Open at all times, unless work parties or group visits in progress. Keep to paths. No dogs. Not ideal for disabled due to steps up to hides.

Coaches welcome but limit of 30 persons.
Facilities: Two hides, chemical toilet, paths.
Public transport: Bus service to Valley Road, WGC No 366 (Sovereign Bus & Coach Co Ltd, tel 01438 726688). Nearest railway station Welwyn Garden City.
Habitat: Former water-cress beds, open shallow lagoons. Stretch of the River Lea, marsh, hedgerows. Nine acres.
Key birds: *Spring/summer*: Breeding warblers, Grey Wagtail, Kestrel. *Autumn/winter*: Green Sandpiper, Water Rail, Snipe, Siskin, occasional Jack Snipe. *All Year*: Kingfisher, Grey Heron, Sparrowhawk.
Contact: Barry Trevis, 11 Lemsford Village, Welwyn Garden City, Herts AL8 7TN. 01707 335517. e-mail: info@hmwt.org

3. RYE MEADS

RSPB (Central England Region)/Hertfordshire & Middlesex Wildlife Trust.
Location: TL 387 099. E of Hoddesdon, signed from A10, near Rye House railway station.
Access: Open every day 10am-5pm (or dusk if earlier), except Christmas Day and Boxing Day.
Facilities: Disabled access and toilets. Drinks machine, staffed reception, classrooms, picnic area, car park, bird feeding area. Nature trails, hides. RSPB reserve has close circuit TV on Kingfisher and Common Terns in summer.
Public transport: Rail (Rye House) 55 metres, bus (310) stops 600 metres from entrance.
Habitat: Marsh, willow scrub, pools, scrapes, lagoons and reedbed.
Key birds: *Summer*: Breeding Tufted Duck, Gadwall, Common Tern, Kestrel, Kingfisher, nine species of warblers. *Winter*: Bittern, Shoveler, Water Rail, Teal, Snipe, Jack Snipe, Redpoll and Siskin.
Contact: The Site Manager, RSPB Rye Meads Visitor Centre, Rye Road, Stanstead Abbotts, Herts SG12 8JS. 01992 708383; (Fax) 01992 708389.

4. STANBOROUGH REED MARSH

Herts & Middlesex Wildlife Trust.
Location: TL 230 105. Leave the A1M at J4 on A6129 Stanborough Road. At next small roundabout, turn R to Welwyn Garden City town centre. Continue past lakes to next roundabout. Take a U turn and then turn L into reserve car park. Follow path between river and lake into reserve.
Access: Open all year. No access into reedbed. Circular walk.
Facilities: None.
Public transport: Bus: stops on Stanborough Road. Train: nearest station Welwyn Garden City.
Habitat: Willow woodland, river, reed marsh.
Key birds: *Summer*: Good numbers of Reed and Sedge Warblers. *Winter*: Water Rail and Corn Bunting roost.
Contact: Wildlife Trust HQ, Grebe House, St Michael's Street, St Albans, Herts, AL3 4SN. 01727 858901. e-mail: info@hmwt.org

5. TRING RESERVOIRS

Wilstone Reservoir – Herts & Middlesex Wildlife Trust/British Waterways; other reservoirs – British Waterways/Friends of Tring Res.
Location: Wilstone Reservoir SP90 51 34. Other reservoirs SP 92 01 35. WTW Lagoon SP 92 31

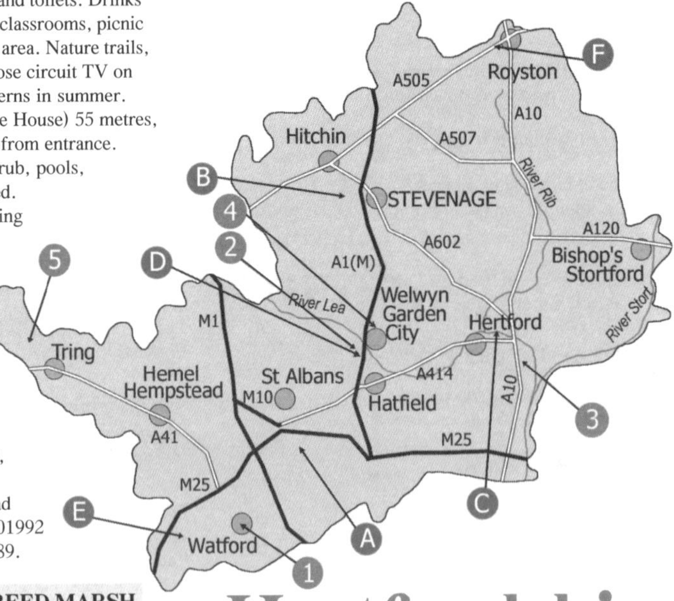

Hertfordshire

34 adjacent to Marsworth Reservoir. Reservoirs 1.5 miles due N of Tring, all accessible from B489 which leaves A41 at Aston Clinton.
Access: Reservoirs – open at all times. WTW Lagoon: open at all times by permit from FOTR. All group visits need to be cleared with British Waterways.
Facilities: Café and public house adjacent to Startops Reservoir car park, safe parking for cycles. Also disabled trail from here. Wilstone Reservoir: Public house about 0.5 mile away in village and cafe about 0.25 mile from car park at Farm Shop. Hides with disabled access at Startops/ Marsworth Reservoir & WTW Lagoon. Also other hides.
Public transport: Buses from Aylesbury & Tring including a weekend service, tel. 0870 6082608. Tring Station is 2.5 miles away via canal towpath.
Habitat: Four reservoirs with surrounding woodland, scrub and meadows. Two of the reservoirs with extensive reedbeds. WTW Lagoon with islands, surrounding hedgerows and scrub.
Key birds: *Spring/summer*: Breeding warblers, regular Hobby, occasional Black Tern, Marsh Harrier, Osprey. *Autumn*: Passage waders and wildfowl. *Winter*: Gull roost, large wildfowl flocks, bunting roosts, Bittern.
Contact: FOTR: see Peter Hearn in Bucks BTO entry. www.fotr.org.uk
British Waterways, Ground Floor, Witangate House, 500-600 Witan Gate, Milton Keynes MK9 1BW. 01908 302500.

OTHER SITES
(full details in previous editions)

A. Broad Colney Lakes
Contact: Wildlife Trust HQ, 01727 858 901.
B. Hill End Pit
Contact: Wildlife Trust HQ, 01727 858901.
C. Meads, The
Contact: Wildlife Trust HQ, 01727 858901.
D. Sherrards Park Wood
Contact: Welwyn & Hatfield Council, 01707 357000.
E. Stocker's Lake
Contact: Wildlife Trust HQ, 01727 858901.
F. Therfield Heath Local Nature Reserve
Contact: Wildlife Trust HQ, 01727 858901.

Kent

1. BLEAN WOODS NNR

RSPB (South East England Office).
Location: TR 126 592. From Rough Common (off A290, one and a half miles NW of Canterbury).
Access: Open 8am-9pm.
Facilities: Public footpaths and five waymarked trails.
Public transport: 24 and 24a buses from Canterbury to Rough Common.
Habitat: Woodland (mainly oak and sweet chestnut), relics of heath.
Key birds: Nightingale, Nightjar in summer, three species of woodpecker.
Contact: Michael Walter, 11 Garden Close, Rough Common, Canterbury, Kent CT2 9BP. 01227 455972.

2. BLEAN WOODS

English Nature (Kent Team).
Location: TR 120 609. NW of Canterbury on A290. Road opposite Chapel Lane at Blean.
Access: Keep to paths. **Facilities:** None.
Public transport: Buses every 15mins (between Canterbury and Whitstable) pass close to reserve.
Habitat: Mixed coppice with standard sessile oak, glades, rides.
Key birds: *Summer:* Some 70 breeding species, inc. Woodcock, all three woodpeckers, Tree Pipit, Redstart, Nightingale, Wood Warbler, Hawfinch.
Contact: David Maylam, Coldharbour Farm, Wye, Ashford, Kent TN25 5DB. 01233 812525.

3. DUNGENESS

RSPB (South East England Office).
Location: TR 063 196. SE of Lydd.
Access: Open daily 9am-9pm or sunset when earlier. Visitor centre open (10am-5pm, 4pm Nov-Feb). Parties over 20 by prior arrangement.
Facilities: Visitor centre, toilets (including disabled access), five hides, nature trail, wheelchair access to visitor centre and four hides.
Public transport: Service 12 from Lydd or

Folkestone (not Sun) stops at reserve entrance on request - one mile walk to visitor centre.
Habitat: Shingle, flooded gravel pits, sallow scrub, reedbed, wet grassland.
Key birds: *Resident*: Bearded Tit. *Winter*: Bittern, Wildfowl (including Wigeon, Goldeneye, Goosander, Smew), divers and grebes. Migrant waders, landfall for passerines. *Summer*: Breeding Lapwing, Redshank, wildfowl, terns and gulls.
Contact: Christine Hawkins/Bob Gomes, Boulderwall Farm, Dungeness Road, Lydd, Romney Marsh, Kent TN29 9PN. 01797 320588/ fax 01797 321962. e-mail: dungeness@rspb.org.uk

4. DUNGENESS BIRD OBSERVATORY

Dungeness Bird Observatory Trust.
Location: TR 085 173. Three miles SE of Lydd. Turn south off Dungeness Road at TR 087 185 and continue to end of road.
Access: Observatory open throughout the year.
Facilities: Accommodation available. Bring own sleeping bag/sheets and toiletries. Shared facilities including fully-equipped kitchen.
Public transport: Bus service between Rye and Folkestone, numbers 11, 12, 711, 712. Alight at the Pilot Inn, Lydd-on-Sea. Tel 01227 472082.
Habitat: Shingle promontory with scrub and gravel pits. RSPB reserve nearby.
Key birds: Breeding birds include Wheatear and Black Redstart and seabirds on RSPB Reserve. Important migration site.
Contact: David Walker, 11 RNSSS, Dungeness, Kent TN29 9NA. 01797 321309.
e-mail dungeness.obs@tinyonline.co.uk
www.dungenessbirdobs.org.uk

5. ELMLEY MARSHES

RSPB (South East England Office).
Location: TQ 93 86 80. Isle of Sheppey signposted from A249, one mile beyond Kingsferry Bridge. Reserve car park is two miles from the main road.
Access: Open every day except Tue, Christmas and Boxing days (9am-9pm or dusk if earlier). No charge to RSPB members. Dogs are not allowed on the reserve. Less able may drive closer to the hides.
Facilities: Five hides. Disabled access to Wellmarsh hide. No visitor centre. Toilets located in car park 1.25 miles from hides.
Public transport: Swale Halt, a request stop is nearest railway station on Sittingbourne to Sheerness line. From there it is a three mile walk to reserve.
Habitat: Coastal grazing marsh, ditches and pools alongside the Swale Estuary with extensive intertidal mudflats and saltmarsh
Key birds: *Spring/summer*: Breeding waders - Redshank, Lapwing, Avocet, Yellow Wagtail, passage waders, Hobby. *Autumn*: Passage waders. *Winter*: Spectacular numbers of wildfowl, especially Wigeon and White-fronted Goose. Waders. Hunting raptors - Peregrine, Merlin, Hen Harrier and Short-eared Owl.
Contact: Barry O'Dowd, Elmley RSPB Reserve, Kingshill Farm, Elmley, Sheerness, Kent ME12 3RW. 01795 665969.

6. FOOTSCRAY MEADOWS LNR

Bexley Council.
Location: TQ 475 717. From J3 of M25, head W on A20 to Sidcup. Reserve accessible from A223 (Northcray Rd) or Rectory Lane, which runs from Bexley Lane, Sidcup to Footscray High St.
Access: Open all year.
Facilities: Car parks, display boards.
Public transport: Train: Sidcup or Bexley. Bus: 492 passes along North Cray Road.
Habitat: Largest open space in Borough. Ancient woodland, River Cray wildflower margins.
Key birds: *Spring*: Warblers, possible Lesser Spotted Woodpecker, Spotted Flycatcher. *Winter*: Water Rail, Green Sandpiper, Siskin, Redpoll, thrushes. *All year*: Kingfisher, Ring-necked Parakeet, Green and Great Spotted Woodpeckers, usual woodland species.
Contact: Bexley Council, Broadway, Bexleyheath, Kent DA6 7LB. 0208 3037777 ext 5562.
e-mail: worksdirect@bexley.gov.uk
www.bexley.gov.uk

7. JEFFERY HARRISON RESERVE

Jeffery Harrison Memorial Trust.
Location: TQ 519 568. From A25 immediately N of Sevenoaks.
Access: Wed, Sat, Sun and bank holidays 10am-5pm (or dusk). Closed Xmas to New Year. Coach parking available.
Facilities: Visitor centre, nature trail, hides.
Public transport: 15 minutes walk from Bat & Ball station, 20 minutes from Sevenoaks station.
Habitat: Flooded gravel pits.
Key birds: Wintering wildfowl, waders, woodland birds.
Contact: John Tyler, Tadorna, Bradbourne Vale Road, Sevenoaks, Kent TN13 3DH. 01732 456407.
e-mail: sevenoakswildfowl@kentwildlife.org.uk

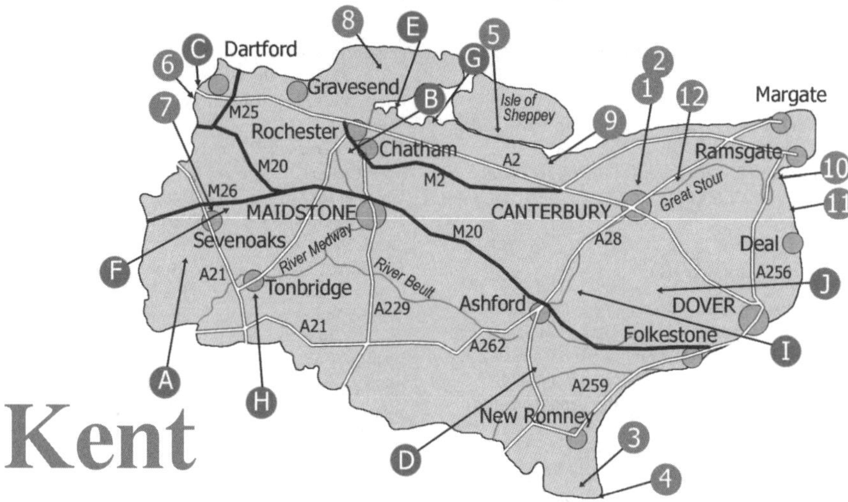

8. NORTHWARD HILL

RSPB (South East England Office).
Location: TQ 780 765. Adjacent to High Halstow, off A228, approx six miles N of Rochester.
Access: Open all year, free access, trails in public area of wood joining Saxon Shoreway link to grazing marsh. Sanctuary area accessible by permit only - write to warden. Dogs allowed in public area on leads. Trails often steep and not suitable for wheelchair users.
Facilities: Three nature trails in the wood and one joining with long distance footpath. Toilets at village hall, small car park adjacent to wood.
Public transport: Buses to village of High Halstow. Contact Arriva buses for timetable details.
Habitat: Ancient and scrub woodland (approximately 130 acres), grazing marsh (approximately 350 acres).
Key birds: *Spring/summer*: Wood holds UK's largest heronry (155 pairs in 2001), inc growing colony of Little Egrets (c32 pairs 2003), breeding Nightingale, Turtle Dove, scrub warblers and woodpeckers. Marshes - breeding Lapwing, Redshank, Avocet (most years), Marsh Harrier, Shoveler, Pochard. *Winter*: Wigeon, Teal, Shoveler. Passage waders (ie Black-tailed Godwit). Long-eared Owl roost.
Contact: Gordon Allison, Bromhey Farm, Eastborough, Cooling, Rochester, Kent ME3 8DS. 01634 222480.

9. OARE MARSHES LNR

Kent Wildlife Trust.
Location: TR 01 36 48 (car park). Two miles N of Faversham. From A2 follow signs to Oare and Harty Ferry.
Access: Open at all times. Access along marked paths only. Dogs under strict control to avoid disturbance to birds and livestock.
Facilities: Information centre, open weekends, Bank Holidays. Two hides.
Public transport: Bus to Oare Village one mile from reserve. Train: Faversham (two miles)
Habitat: Grazing marsh, mudflats/estuary.
Key birds: *All year*: Waders and wildfowl. *Winter*: Hen Harrier, Merlin, Peregrine. Divers, grebes and sea ducks on Swale. *Spring/summer*: Avocet, Garganey, Green and Wood Sandpipers, Little Stint, Black-tailed Godwit etc. Black Tern.
Contact: Tony Swandale, Kent Wildlife Trust, Tyland Barn, Sandling, Maidstone, Kent ME14 3BD. 01622 662012. www.kentwildlife.co.uk e-mail: kentwildlife@cix.co.uk

10. SANDWICH AND PEGWELL BAY

Kent Wildlife Trust.
Location: TR 34 26 35. Main car park is off A256 Sandwich - Ramsgate road at Pegwell Bay.
Access: Open 8am-8pm or dusk.
Facilities: Toilets, hide, car parking and trails
Public transport: Bus stop within 400m (Stagecoach). Sustrans National Bike Route passes along the edge of the reserve.

Habitat: Saltmarsh, mudflats, sand dunes and coastal scrub.
Key birds: Range of wetland birds all year.
Contact: Pete Forrest, Kent Wildlife Trust, Tyland Barn, Sandling, Maidstone, Kent ME14 3BD. 01622 662012. e-mail: kentwildlife@cix.co.uk www.kentwildlife.co.uk

11. SANDWICH BAY BIRD OBSERVATORY

Sandwich Bay Bird Observatory Trust.
Location: TR 355 575. 2.5 miles from Sandwich, five miles from Deal, 15 miles from Canterbury. A256 to Sandwich from Dover or Ramsgate. Follow signs to Sandwich Station and then Sandwich Bay.
Access: Open daily. Disabled access.
Facilities: New Field Study Centre. Visitor centre, toilets, refreshments, hostel-type accommodation, plus self-contained flat.
Public transport: Sandwich train station two miles from Observatory. No buses within walking distance.
Habitat: Coastal, dune land, farmland, marsh, two small scrapes.
Key birds: *Spring/autumn passage*: Good variety of migrants and waders, especially Corn Bunting. Annual Golden Oriole. *Winter*: Golden Plover.
Contact: Kevin Thornton, Guildford Road, Sandwich Bay, Sandwich, Kent CT13 9PF. 01304 617341. www.sbbo.co.uk
e-mail: sbbot@talk21.com

12. STODMARSH NNR

English Nature (Kent Team).
Location: TR 222 618. Lies alongside River Stour and A28, five miles NE of Canterbury.
Access: Open at all times. Keep to reserve paths and keep dogs under control.
Facilities: Fully accessible toilets are available at the Stodmarsh entrance car park. Four hides (one fully accessible), easy access nature trail, footpaths and information panels. Car park, picnic area and toilets adjoining the Grove Ferry entrance with easily accessible path, viewing mound and two hides.
Public transport: There is a regular bus service from Canterbury to Margate/Ramsgate. Alight at Upstreet for Grove Ferry. Hourly on Sun.
Habitat: Open water, reedbeds, wet meadows, dry meadows, woodland.
Key birds: *Spring/summer*: Breeding Bearded Tit, Cetti's Warbler, Garganey, Reed, Sedge and Willow Warblers, Nightingale. Migrant Black Tern, Hobby, Osprey, Little Egret. *Winter*: Wildfowl. Hen Harrier, Bittern.
Contact: David Feast, Coldharbour Farm, Wye, Ashford, Kent TN25 5DB. 01233 812525 or 07767 321058 (mobile).

OTHER SITES

(full details in previous editions)

A. Bough Beech Reservoir
Contact: Kent Wildlife Trust, 01622 662012.
B. Burham Marshes
Contact: Kent Wildlife Trust, 01622 662012.
C. Danson Park LNR
Contact: Bexley Council, 0208 3037777 ext 5562.
D. Hamstreet Woods
Contact: English Nature, 01233 812525.
E. Nor Marsh
Contact: RSPB, 01273 775333.
F. Oldbury Hill And Styant's Wood
Contact: The National Trust Regional Office for the South East, 01372 453401.
G. Riverside Country Park
Contact: Riverside Country Park, 01634 378987.
H. Tudeley Woods
Contact: RSPB, 01273 775333.
I. Wye
Contact: RSPB, 01233 812525.
J. Yockletts Bank SSSI.
Contact: Kent Wildlife Trust, 01622 662012.

Lancashire

1. CUERDEN VALLEY PARK

Cuerden Valley Park Trust.
Location: SD 565 238. S of Preston on the A6. Easy access from J28 and J29 of the M6 and J8 and J9 on the M62.
Access: Open all year.
Facilities: Visitor centre, toilets.
Public transport: None.
Habitat: Woodland, river, pond, agricultural grassland.
Key birds: *All year*: Kingfisher, Dipper, Great Spotted Woodpecker, Goldcrest and usual woodland birds.
Contact: Cuerden Valley Park Trust, The Barn, Berkeley Drive, Bamber, Preston PR5 6BY. 01772 317234 / 01772 324129.
e-mail: cvp@lancswt.cix.co.uk or lancswt@cix.co.uk

2. HEYSHAM NATURE RESERVE & BIRD OBSERVATORY

The Wildlife Trust for Lancashire, Manchester and North Merseyside in conjunction with British Energy Estates.
Location: Main reserve is at SD 404 596 W of Lancaster. Take A683 to Heysham port. Turn L at traffic lights by Duke of Rothesay pub, then first right after 300m.
Access: Gate to reserve car park usually open 9.30am-6pm (longer in summer and shorter in winter). Pedestrian access at all times. Dogs on lead. Limited disabled access.
Facilities: Hide overlooking Power Station outfalls. Map giving access details at the reserve car park. No manned visitor centre or toilet access, but someone usually in reserve office, next to the main car park, in the morning. Latest sightings board can be viewed through the window if office closed.
Public transport: Train services connect with nearby Isle of Man ferry. Plenty of buses to Lancaster from various Heysham sites within walking distance (ask for nearest stop to the harbour).
Habitat: Varied: wetland, acid grassland, alkaline grassland, foreshore.
Key birds: Passerine migrants in the correct conditions. Good passage of seabirds in Spring, especially Arctic Tern. Storm Petrel and Leach's Petrel during strong onshore (SW-WWNW) winds in midsummer and autumn respectively. Good variety of breeding birds (e.g. eight species of warbler on the reserve itself). Two-three scarce land-birds each year, most frequent being Yellow-browed Warbler. Notable area for dragonflies.
Contact: Rueben Neville, Reserve Warden, The Barn, Berkeley Drive, Bamber Bridge, Preston, PR5 6BY. 07979 652138. Annual report from Leighton Moss RSPB reserve shop.

3. LEIGHTON MOSS

RSPB (North West England Office).
Location: SD 478 750. Four miles NW of Carnforth. Signposted from A6 N of Carnforth.
Access: Reserve open daily 9am-dusk. Visitor centre open daily 10am-5pm (except Christmas Day). No dogs. No charge to RSPB members.
Facilities: Visitor centre, shop, tea-room and toilets. Nature trails and five hides (four have wheelchair access).
Public transport: Silverdale train station 150 metres from reserve. Tel: 08457 484950.
Habitat: Reedbed, shallow meres and woodland.
Key birds: *All year*: Bittern, Bearded Tit, Water Rail, Pochard and Shoveler. *Summer*: Marsh Harrier, Reed and Sedge Warblers.
Contact: Robin Horner, Leighton Moss RSPB Nature Reserve, Myers Farm, Silverdale, Carnforth, Lancashire LA5 0SW. 01524 701601. www.rspb.org.uk

4. MARTIN MERE

The Wildfowl & Wetlands Trust.
Location: SD 428 145. Six miles N of Ormskirk via Burscough Bridge (A59), 20 miles from Liverpool and Preston.
Access: Opening times: 9.30am-5.00pm (Nov-Feb), 9.30am-5.30pm (rest of year). Special dawn and evening events. Guide dogs only allowed. Admission charge. No charge for members. Fully accessible to disabled. Coach park available. Special rates for coach parties.
Facilities: Visitor centre with toilets, gift shop, restaurant, education centre, play area, nature reserve and nature trails, hides, waterfowl

Lancashire

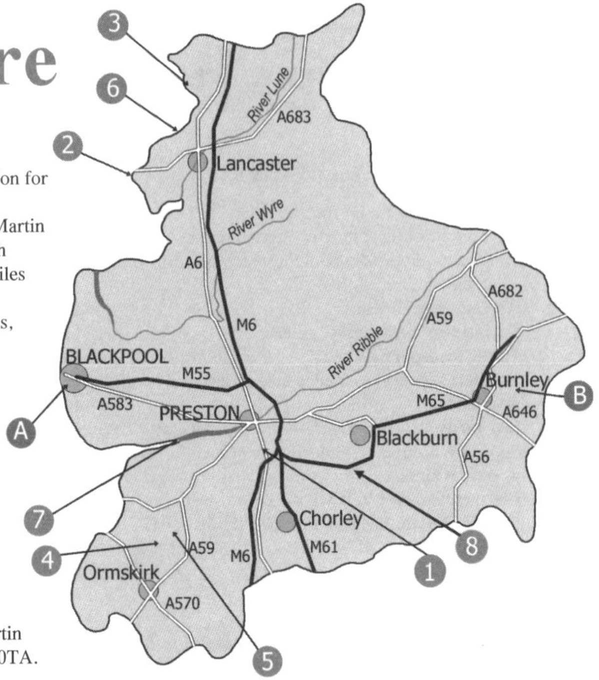

collection and sustainable garden. Provision for disabled visitors.
Public transport: Bus service to WWT Martin Mere from Ormskirk. Train to Burscough Bridge or New Lane Stations (both 1.5 miles from reserve).
Habitat: Open water, wet grassland, moss, copses, reedbed, parkland.
Key birds: *Winter*: Whooper and Bewick's Swans, Pink-footed Goose, various duck, Ruff, Black-tailed Godwit, Peregrine, Hen Harrier, Tree Sparrow. *Spring*: Ruff, Shelduck, Little Ringed and Ringed Plover, Lapwing, Redshank. *Summer*: Marsh Harrier, Garganey, hirundines, Tree Sparrow. Breeding Avocet, Lapwing, Redshank, Shelduck. *Autumn*: Pink-footed Goose, waders on passage.
Contact: Patrick Wisniewski, WWT Martin Mere, Fish Lane, Burscough, Lancs L40 0TA. 01704 895181. www.wwt.org.uk
e-mail: info.martinmere@wwt.org.uk

5. MERE SANDS WOOD

The Wildlife Trust for Lancashire, Manchester and North Merseyside.
Location: SD 44 71 57. Four miles inland of Southport, 0.5 miles off A59 Preston – Liverpool road, in Rufford along B5246 (Holmeswood Road).
Access: Visitor centre open 9am-5pm daily except Christmas Day. Car park open until 8pm in summer. Half mile of wheelchair-accessible path, leading to two hides and viewpoint.
Facilities: Visitor centre with toilets (disabled), seven hides, two trails, exhibition room, latest sightings board. Feeding stations
Public transport: Bus: Southport-Chorley 347 stops in Rufford, 0.5 mile walk. Train: Preston-Ormskirk train stops at Rufford station, one mile walk.
Habitat: Freshwater lakes, mixed woodland, sandy grassland/heath. 105h.
Key birds: *Winter*: Nationally important for Teal and Gadwall, good range of waterfowl, Kingfisher. Feeding stations attract Tree Sparrow, Bullfinch, Reed Bunting. Woodland: Treecreeper. *Summer*: Little Ringed Plover, Kingfisher, Lesser Spotted Woodpecker. *Passage*: Most years, Osprey, Crossbill, Green Sandpiper, Greenshank, Wood Warbler, Turtle Dove.
Contact: Dominic Rigby, Warden, Mere Sands Wood Nature Reserve, Holmeswood Road, Rufford, Ormskirk, Lancs L40 1TG. 01704 821809. e-mail: lancswtmsw@cix.co.uk
www.wildlifetrust.org/lancashire

6. MORECAMBE BAY

RSPB (North West England Office).
Location: SD 468 667. Two miles N of Morecambe at Hest Bank.
Access: Open at all times. Do not venture onto saltmarsh or intertidal area, there are dangerous channels and quicksands.
Facilities: Viewpoint at car park.
Public transport: No 5 bus runs between Carnforth and Morecambe. Tel: 0870 608 2608.
Habitat: Saltmarsh, estuary.
Key birds: *Winter*: Wildfowl (Pintail, Shelduck, Wigeon) and waders – important high tide roost for Oystercatcher, Curlew, Redshank, Dunlin, Bar-tailed Godwit.

Contact: Robin Horner, Myers Farm, Silverdale, Carnforth, Lancashire LA5 0SW. 01524 701601. www.rspb.org.uk

7. RIBBLE ESTUARY

English Nature (Cheshire to Lancashire team).
Location: SD 380 240.
Access: Open at all times.
Facilities: No formal visiting facilities.
Public transport: None.
Habitat: Saltmarsh, mudflats.
Key birds: High water wader roosts (of Knot, Dunlin, Black-tailed Godwit, Oystercatcher and Grey Plover) are best viewed from Southport, Marshside, Lytham and St Annes. Pink-footed Goose and wintering swans are present in large numbers from Oct-Feb on Banks Marsh and along River Douglas respectively. The large flocks of Wigeon, for which the site is renowned, can be seen on high tides from Marshside but feed on saltmarsh areas at night. Good numbers of raptors also present in winter.
Contact: Site Manager, Old Hollow, Marsh Road, Banks, Southport PR9 8EA. 01704 225624.

8. WITHNELL FOLD LNR

Lancashire County Council.
Location: SD 610 232. SW of Blackburn, near Leeds and Liverpool canal Junction 3 of M65, take A674 SW towards Chorley. Turn R on B road after Ollerton Fold.
Access: Open all year.
Facilities: Car park, hide.
Public transport: None.
Habitat: Lagoons, reed, scrub.
Key birds: *Spring/summer*: Warblers, hirundines.
Contact: Lancashire Countryside Service, Guild House, Cross Street, Preston, Lancs PR1 8RD. 01772 534709.
e-mail: countrysideservices@env.lancscc.gov.uk

OTHER SITES

(full details in previous editions)

A. Marton Mere
Contact: Blackpool Borough Council, Community & Tourism Services, 01253 830 830.

B. Upper Coldwell Reservoir
Contact: Trust HQ, 01772 324129.

Leicestershire and Rutland

1. BEACON HILL COUNTRY PARK

Leicestershire County Council.
Location: SK 522 149. From Loughborough, take A512 SW for 2.5 miles. Turn L onto Breakback Road and follow it for 2.5 miles through Nanpantan. Park in car park on left in Woodhouse Lane.
Access: Open all year from 8am-dusk. If opening times are different, these will be clearly displayed at the park. A permissive path from Deans Lane to Woodhouse Lane is occasionally closed during the year. Please check first.
Facilities: Two pay and display car parks, easy to follow, well waymarked tracks and woodland paths. Several climbs to hill tops. Rocky outcrops slippy after rain. Information boards. Toilets at lower car park, Outwoods car park and Woodhouse Eves. Wheelchair access along park paths but no access to summit. Refreshments at Bull's Head, Woodhouse Eaves.
Public transport: Bus: No 123 Leicester to Shepshed calls at Woodhouse Eaves. Tel: 0870 608 2608. Train: from Loughborough and Leicester.
Habitat: Forest, one of the oldest geological outcrops in England and the second highest point in Leicestershire.
Key birds: *All year*: Treecreeper, Nuthatch, Lesser Spotted and Green Woodpeckers, Great and Coal Tits, Little Owl, wagtails. *Summer*: Pied Flycatcher, Whitethroat, Blackcap, Whinchat, Garden Warbler, Stonechat.
Contact: Beacon Hill Estate Office, Broombriggs Farm, Beacon Road, Woodhouse Eaves, Loughborough, Leics LE12 8SR. 01509 890048.

2. EYEBROOK RESERVOIR

Corby & District Water Co.
Location: SP 853 964. Reservoir built 1940. S of Uppingham, from unclassified road W of A6003 at Stoke Dry.
Access: Access to 150 acres private grounds granted to members of Leics and Rutland Ornithological Society and Rutland Nat Hist Soc.

Organised groups with written permission (from Corby Water Co.
Facilities: SSSI since 1955. Good viewing from public roads. Trout fishery season Apr-Oct.
Public transport: None.
Habitat: Open water, plantations and pasture.
Key birds: *Summer*: Good populations of breeding birds, sightings of Ospreys and Red Kite. Passage waders and Black Tern. *Winter*: Wildfowl (inc. Goldeneye, Goosander, Bewick's Swan) and waders.
Contact: Corby Water Co. PO Box 101, Weldon Road, Corby NN17 5UA). Tel. Fishing lodge 01536 770264.
www.eyebrook.com or www.eyebrook.org.uk

3. RUTLAND WATER

Leics and Rutland Wildlife Trust.
Location: SK 866 6760 72. 1. Egleton Reserve: from Egleton village off A6003 S of Oakham. 2. Lyndon Reserve: south shore E of Manton village off A6003 S of Oakham.
Access: 1. Open daily 9am-5pm, (4pm Nov to Jan). 2. Open winter (Sat, Sun 10am-5pm), summer daily (10am-5pm). Day permits available for both.
Facilities: 1: Anglian Water Birdwatching Centre, now enlarged. Toilets and disabled access to 11 hides, electric buggies, conference facilities. 2: Interpretive centre. Marked nature trail leaflet.
Public transport: None.
Habitat: Reservoir, lagoons, scrapes, woods, meadows, plantations.
Key birds: *Spring/autumn*: Outstanding wader passage. Also harriers, owls, passerine flocks, terns (Black, Arctic, breeding Common, occasional Little and Sandwich). *Winter*: Wildfowl (inc Goldeneye, Smew, Goosander, rare grebes, all divers), Ruff. *Summer:* Breeding Osprey.
Contact: Tim Appleton, Fishponds Cottage, Stamford Road, Oakham, Rutland LE15 8AB. 01572 770651; fax 01572 755931; e-mail awbc@rutlandwater.org.uk; www.rutlandwater.org.uk www.ospreys.org.uk

4. SENCE VALLEY FOREST PARK

Forest Enterprise.
Location: SK 400 115. Ten miles NW of Leicester and two miles SW of Coalville, between Ibstock and Ravenstone. The car park is signed from the A447 N of Ibstock. Do not leave valuables in cars as there have been some break-ins.
Access: Open all year.
Facilities: Car park, information and recent sightings boards, hide, paths.
Public transport: None.
Habitat: Forest, rough grassland, pools, wader scrape.
Key birds: *Spring/summer*: Wheatear, Whinchat, Redstart, Common and Green Sandpiper, Ringed and Little Ringed Plovers, Redshank. Dunlin and Greenshank frequent, possible Wood Sandpiper. Reed Bunting, Meadow Pipit, Sky Lark, Linnet, Yellow Wagtail. Possible Quail. *Winter*: Stonechat, Redpoll, Short-eared Owl. Merlin, Peregrine, Buzzard occasionally seen. Goosander and Wigeon possible.
Contact: Forest Enterprise, 340 Bristol Business Park, Coldharbour Lane, Bristol BS16 1EJ. 0117 906 6000.

OTHER SITES

(full details in previous editions)

A. Burbage Common
Contact: Hinckley and Bosworth Borough Council, 01455 238141.

Lincolnshire

1. DONNA NOOK

Lincolnshire Wildlife Trust.
Location: TF 422 998. Near North Somercotes, off A1031 coast road, S of Grimsby.
Access: Donna Nook beach is closed on weekdays as this is an active bombing range, but dunes remain open. Dogs on leads. Some disabled access.
Facilities: No toilets or visitor centre.
Public transport: None.
Habitat: Dunes, slacks and intertidal areas, seashore, mudflats, sandflats.
Key birds: *Summer*: Little Tern, Ringed Plover, Oystercatcher. *Winter*: Brent Goose, Shelduck, Twite, Lapland Bunting, Shore Lark, Linnet.
Contact: Lincolnshire Wildlife Trust, Banavallum House, Manor House Street, Horncastle, Lincs LN9 5HF. 01507 526667.
e-mail: lincstrust@cix.co.uk
www.lincstrust.co.uk

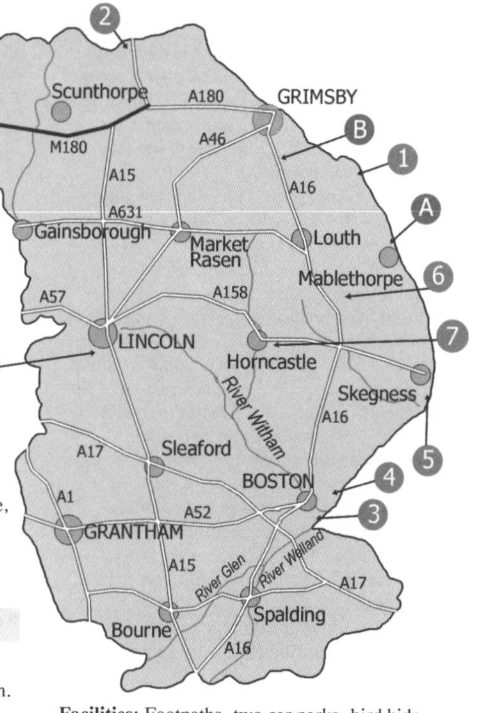

2. FAR INGS

Lincolnshire Wildlife Trust.
Location: TA 011 229 and TA 023 230. Off Far Ings Lane, W of Barton-on-Humber, the last turn off before the Humber Bridge.
Access: Open all year. No dogs. Limited disabled access.
Facilities: Toilets, visitor centre open some weekends and weekdays – not all week. Hides and paths.
Public transport: None.
Habitat: Chain of flooded clay pits and reedbeds.
Key birds: *Summer*: Marsh Harrier, Bittern, Bearded Tit, Water Rail. *Winter*: Wildfowl (Mallard, Teal, Gadwall, Pochard, Tufted and Ruddy Ducks).
Contact: Lionel Grooby, Far Ings Visitor Centre, Far Ings Road, Barton on Humber DN18 5RG. 01652 634507. e-mail: farings@lincstrust.co.uk www.lincstrust.co.uk

3. FRAMPTON MARSH

RSPB (East Anglia Office).
Location: TR 36 43 85. Four miles SE of Boston. From A16 follow signs to Frampton then Frampton Marsh.
Access: Open at all times. Free. Coaches by prior arrangement.
Facilities: Footpaths, bench, car park, bicycle rack. Free information leaflets available (please contact the office), guided walks programme.
Public transport: None.
Habitat: Saltmarsh.
Key birds: *Summer*: Breeding Redshank, passage waders (inc Greenshank, Ruff and Black-tailed Godwit) and Hobby. *Winter*: Hen Harrier, Short-eared Owl, Merlin, dark-bellied Brent Goose, Twite, Golden Plover.
Contact: John Badley, RSPB Lincolnshire Wash Office, 61a Horseshoe Lane, Kirton, Kirton, Boston, Lincs PE20 1LW. 01205 724678.
e-mail: john.badley@rspb.org.uk

4. FREISTON SHORE

RSPB (East Anglia Office).
Location: TF 39 74 24. Four miles E of Boston. From A52 at Haltoft End follow signs to Freiston Shore.
Access: Open at all times, free. Coaches by prior arrangement.
Facilities: Footpaths, two car parks, bird hide. Free information leaflets available on site, guided walks programme. Bicycle rack.
Public transport: None.
Habitat: Saltmarsh, saline lagoon, mudflats.
Key birds: *Summer:* Breeding waders including Avocets, Ringed Plovers and Oystercatchers, Corn Bunting and Tree Sparrow. *Winter:* Lapland Bunting, Twite, dark-bellied Brent Goose, wildfowl, waders, birds of prey including Short-eared Owl and Hen Harrier. *Passage:* Waders, including Curlew Sandpiper and Little Stint. *Autumn:* Occasional seabirds including Arctic and Great Skuas.
Contact: John Badley, RSPB Lincolnshire Wash Office, 61a Horseshoe Lane, Kirton, Boston, Lincs PE20 1LW. 01205 724678.
e-mail: john.badley@rspb.org.uk

5. GIBRALTAR POINT NNR & BIRD OBSERVATORY

Lincolnshire Wildlife Trust.
Location: TF 556 580. Three miles S of Skegness on the N edge of The Wash. Signposted from Skegness town centre.
Access: Reserve is open dawn-dusk all year.

Seasonal charges for car parking. Free admission to reserve, visitor centre and toilets. Some access restrictions to sensitive sites at S end, open access to N. Dogs on leads at all times – no dogs on beach during summer. Visitor centre and toilets suitable for wheelchairs, as well as network of surfaced foot paths. Bird observatory and four hides suitable for wheelchairs. Day visit groups must be booked in advance. Access for coaches. Contact Gibraltar Point Field Station for residential or day visits.
Facilities: Site also location of Wash Study Centre and Bird Observatory. Field centre is an ideal base for birdwatching/natural history groups in spring, summer and autumn. Visitor centre and gift shop open daily (May-Oct) and weekends for remainder of the year. Toilets open daily. Network of foot paths bisect all major habitats. Public hides overlook freshwater and brackish lagoons. Wash viewpoint overlooks saltmarsh and mudflats.
Public transport: Bus service from Skegness runs in occasional years but summer service only. Otherwise taxi/car from Skegness. Cycle route from Skegness.
Habitat: Sand dune grassland and scrub, saltmarshes and mudflats, freshwater marsh and lagoons.
Key birds: Large migration visible during spring and autumn passage – hirundines, chats, pipits, larks, thrushes and occasional rarities. Large numbers of waterfowl including internationally important populations of non-breeding waders. Sept-May impressive wader roosts on high tides. *Summer*: Little Tern and good assemblage of breeding warblers. *Winter*: Shore Lark, raptors, waders and wildfowl.
Contact: Kev Wilson, (Site Manager), Gibraltar Point Field Centre, Gibraltar Road, Skegness, Lincs PE24 4SU. 01754 762677.
e-mail: lincstrust@gibpoint.freeserve.co.uk

6. RIGSBY WOOD

Lincolnshire Wildlife Trust.
Location: TF 421 762. On A1104 between Ulceby Cross and Alford turn L to South Thoresby. Wood is about two miles on L. Park on the road. Entrance is down a track from the road.
Access: Open all year.
Facilities: Waymarked route.
Public transport: None.
Habitat: Ancient woodland.
Key birds: *Spring/summer*: Chiffchaff, Garden Warbler, Blackcap, Whitethroat, Cuckoo, Great-spotted Woodpecker, Treecreeper, Tawny Owl. *Autumn/winter*: Woodcock, Redpoll.
Contact: Lincolnshire Wildlife Trust, Banovallum House, Manor House Street, Horncastle, Lincs, LN9 5HF. 01507 526 667.

7. SNIPE DALES NATURE RESERVE

Lincolnshire Wildlife Trust.
Location: TF 319 683 (nature reserve) and TF 330 682 (country park) E of Horncastle. Well signposted off A158 (Skegness-Lincoln road) and from the B1195 (Horncastle-Spilsby road).
Access: Open all year. Dogs on leads allowed in country park but not in the nature reserve. Car park charge. Some disabled access.
Facilities: Toilets, interpretation boards, one small hide, footpaths.
Public transport: Restricted bus service.
Habitat: Nature reserve – steep-sided valleys fretted by streams. Unspoilt wet-valley system. Country park – attractive walks through coniferous woodland, new plantings of broad-leaved trees, plus ponds.
Key birds: *Spring/summer*: Chaffinch, Redpoll, Willow Warbler, Willow Tit, Long-tailed Tit, Siskin, Tawny Owl, Barn Owl, Grasshopper Warbler. *Winter*: Woodcock.
Contact: Peter Graves, Snipe Dales Country Park, Lusby, Spilsby PE23 4JB. 01507 588401.
www.lincstrust.co.uk

8. WHISBY NATURE PARK

Lincolnshire Wildlife Trust.
Location: SK 914 661. W of Lincoln off A46 southern end of Lincoln relief road. Brown tourist signs.
Access: Nature Park open dawn to dusk. Consult notice board at entrance. Car park closed out of hours. Free entry. Natural World Visitor Centre open (10am-5pm), free entry. Some special exhibitions will have a charge. Disabled access. Dogs on leads.
Facilities: Coach park, toilets, visitor centre, café, education centre, waymarked routes, interpretation signs, leaflets.
Public transport: No. 65 bus Mon-Sat from Lincoln to Thorpe-on-the-Hill (1/4 mile away).
Habitat: Flooded sand, gravel pits, scrub woodland and grassland.
Key birds: *Summer*: Common Tern on specially-built rafts, Nightingale, Whitethroat, Lesser Whitethroat, Tree Sparrow. *Winter*: Wigeon, Teal, Pochard, Tufted Duck, Goldeneye.

Contact: Phil Porter, Moor Lane, Thorpe-on-the-Hill, Lincoln LN6 9BW. 01522 500676. e-mail: whisby@cix.co.uk www.lincstrust.co.uk

OTHER SITES
(full details in previous editions)

A. Saltfleetby-Theddlethorpe Dunes
Contact: English Nature, 01205 311674.

B. Tetney Marshes
Contact: RSPB, 0191 281 3366.

London, Greater

1. BEDFONT LAKES COUNTRY PARK

Ecology and Countryside Parks Service.
Location: TQ 080 728. OS map sheet 176 (west London). 0.5 miles from Ashford, Middx, 0.5 miles S of A30, Clockhouse Roundabout, on B3003 (Clockhouse Lane).
Access: Open 7.30am-9pm or dusk, whichever is earlier, all days except Christmas Day. Disabled friendly. Dogs on leads. Main nature reserve area only open Sun (2pm-4pm).
Facilities: Toilets, information centre, several hides, nature trail, free parking, up-to-date information.
Public transport: Train to Feltham and Ashford. Bus - H26 and 116 from Hounslow.
Habitat: Lakes, wildflower meadows, woodland, scrub.
Key birds: *Winter*: Water Rail, Bittern, Smew and other wildfowl, Meadow Pipit. *Summer*: Common Tern, Willow, Garden, Reed and Sedge Warblers, Whitethroat, Lesser Whitethroat, hirundines, Hobby, Blackcap, Chiffchaff, Sky Lark. *Passage*: Wheatear, Wood Warbler, Spotted Flycatcher, Ring Ouzel, Redstart, Yellow Wagtail.
Contact: Paul Morgan (Ecology Ranger), BLCP, Clockhouse Lane, Bedfont, Middx TW14 8QA. 01784 423556; Fax: 423451.

2. BRAMLEY BANK

London Wildlife Trust.
Location: TQ 352 634. Entrance off Riesco Drive, or off Broadcombe, Croydon.
Access: Open all year.
Facilities: None.
Public transport: South Croydon British Rail.
Habitat: Oak/sycamore woodland, large pond, acidic grassland and heath.
Key birds: Good range of woodland and parkland birds including woodpeckers and Nuthatch.
Contact: London Wildlife Trust, Skyline House, 200 Union Street, London SE1 0LW. 0207 261 0447; e-mail: enquiries@wildlondon.org.uk

3. CAMLEY STREET NATURAL PARK

London Wildlife Trust.
Location: From Kings Cross Station drive or walk up Pancras Road between Kings Cross and St Pancras Stations. At the junction under a railway bridge turn R into Goods Way. Turn L into Camley Street and follow the telegraph pole fence to the large wrought-iron gates.
Access: Weekdays (9am-5pm), weekends (11am-5pm). Closed Fri.
Facilities: Path.
Public transport: Nearest train/tube: Kings Cross, St Pancras.
Habitat: Woodland scrub, reedbeds, meadow, pond.
Key birds: *Spring/summer*: Warblers. *All year*: Mallard, Tufted Duck, Moorhen, Grey Heron. *Winter*: Siskin, Reed Warbler. *All year*: Sparrowhawk. Good for dragonflies.
Contact: Skyline House, 200 Union Street, London SE1 0LW. 0207 261 0447.

4. CHASE (THE) LNR

London Wildlife Trust.
Location: TQ 515 860. Lies in the Dagenham Corridor, an area of green belt between the London Boroughs of Barking & Dagenham and Havering.
Access: Open throughout the year and at all times. Reserve not suitable for wheelchair access. Eastbrookend Country Park which borders The Chase LNR has surfaced footpaths for wheelchairs.

Facilities: Millennium visitor centre, toilets, ample car parking, Timberland Trail walk.
Public transport: Rail: Dagenham East (District Line) 15 minute walk. Bus: 174 from Romford five minute walk.
Habitat: Shallow wetlands, reedbeds, horse-grazed pasture, scrub and wetland. These harbour an impressive range of animals and plants including the nationally rare black poplar tree. A haven for birds, with approx 190 different species recorded.
Key birds: *Summer*: Breeding Reed Warbler, Lapwing, Water Rail, Lesser Whitethroat and Little Ringed Plover, Kingfisher, Reed Bunting. *Winter*: Significant numbers of Teal, Shoveler, Redwing, Fieldfare and Snipe dominate the scene. *Spring/autumn migration*: Yellow Wagtail, Wheatear, Ruff, Wood Sandpiper, Sand Martin, Ring Ouzel, Black Redstart and Hobby regularly seen.
Contact: Gareth Winn/Tom Clarke, Project Manager/Project Officer, The Millennium Centre, The Chase, Off Dagenham Road, Rush Green, Romford, Essex RM7 0SS. 020 8593 8096.

5. LONDON WETLAND CENTRE

The Wildfowl & Wetlands Trust.
Location: TQ 228 770. Less than 1 mile from South Circular (A205) at Roehampton. In London, Zone 2, one mile from Hammersmith.
Access: Winter (9.30am-5pm: last admission 4pm), summer (9.30am-6pm: last admission 5pm). Charge for admission.
Facilities: Visitor centre, hides, nature trails, art gallery, discovery restaurant (hot and cold food), cinema, shop, observatory centre, seven hides (one with a lift for wheelchair access), three interpretative buildings.
Public transport: Train: Barnes. Tube: Hammersmith then Duckbus 283 (comes into centre). Bus from Hammersmith – 283, 33, 72, 209. Bus from Richmond 33, 72.
Habitat: Main lake, reedbeds, wader scrape, mudflats, open water lakes, grazing marsh.
Key birds: Nationally important numbers of wintering waterfowl, including Gadwall and Shoveler. Important numbers of wetland breeding birds, including grebes, swans, a range of duck species such as Pochard, plus Lapwing, Little Ringed Plover, Redshank, warblers, Reed Bunting and Bittern.
Contact: John Arbon (Grounds and Facilities Manager), Stephanie Fudge (Manager), London Wetland Centre, Queen Elizabeth Walk, Barnes, London SW13 9WT. 0208 409 4400.

6. RIPPLE NATURE RESERVE

London Wildlife Trust/London Borough of Barking and Dagenham.
Location: TQ 467 824. About eight miles from the centre of London, next to Thamesmead Park City Farm on the Thames Road/Renwick road.
Access: Open all year.
Facilities: None
Public transport: Bus: to the end of route in Thames View Estate. Tube: Barking/District Line.
Habitat: Meadow, roughland, reeds, copse, water.
Key birds: *Spring/summer*: Warblers inc Reed Warbler, migrants. *All year*: Kingfisher, Chaffinch, woodpeckers, usual woodland species.
Contact: Trust HQ. 0207 261 0447.

7. SYDENHAM HILL WOOD

London Wildlife Trust.
Location: TQ 335 722. SE London, SE26, between Forest Hill and Crystal Palace, just off South Circular (A205).
Access: Open at all times, no permits required. Some steep slopes make disabled access limited
Facilities: Nature trail, no toilets.
Public transport: Train – Sydenham Hill, Forest Hill. Bus – 363, 202, 356, 185, 312, 176.
Habitat: Oak and hornbeam woodland, small pond, meadow and glades.
Key birds: *Resident*: Kestrel, Sparrowhawk, Tawny Owl, all three woodpeckers, Treecreeper, Nuthatch, Song Thrush. *Summer*: Chiffchaff, Blackcap. *Winter*: Redwing, Fieldfare.
Contact: The Warden, London Wildlife Trust, Horniman Museum, 100 London Road, London SE23 3PQ. 020 8699 5698.

OTHER SITES

(full details in previous editions)

A. Battersea Park

Contact: London Wildlife Trust, 0207 261 0447.

Manchester, Greater

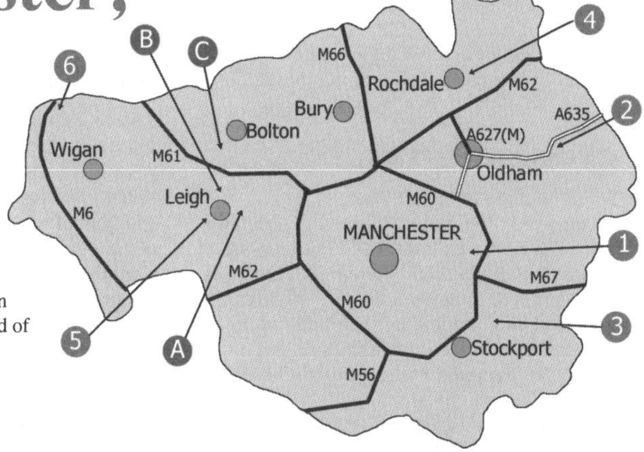

1. AUDENSHAW RESERVOIRS

United Utilities, Bottoms Office.
Location: NW Water SJ915965. Access and parking on Audenshaw Road B6390 at N end of site.
Access: No disabled access.
Facilities: Hide.
Public transport: None.
Habitat: Reservoir.
Key birds: Major migration point; *Winter*: Notable gull roost inc. regular Mediterranean Gull; large Goosander roost; many rarities.
Contact: R Travis on 0161 330 2607. Permit (free) from D Tomes, UU Bottoms Office, Woodhead Road, Tintwistle, Glossop SK13 1HS.

2. DOVESTONES RESERVOIR

Peak District National Park.
Location: Close to Saddleworth Moor, E of Oldham. From A635, look for sign on R having passed through Greenfield. Park at bottom of dam.
Access: Open all year.
Facilities: Several easy uphill paths. Toilets at Peak District NP office. Limited access for disabled.
Public transport: None.
Habitat: Reservoir, moorland.
Key birds: *Spring/summer*: Ring Ouzel, Twite, Peregrine, Raven, Stonechat, Whinchat, Wheatear, Dipper, Common Sandpiper. Possibility of Redstart and Crossbill. *All year*: Wildfowl.
Contact: Peak District National Park, 01629 816200.

3. ETHEROW COUNTRY PARK

Stockport Metropolitan Borough Council.
Location: SJ 965 908. B6104 into Compstall near Romiley, Stockport.
Access: Open at all times; permit required for conservation area. Keep to paths.
Facilities: Reserve area has SSSI status. Hide, nature trail, visitor centre, scooters for disabled.
Public transport: None.
Habitat: River Etherow, woodlands, marshy area.
Key birds: Sparrowhawk, Buzzard, Dipper, all three woodpeckers, Pied Flycatcher, warblers. *Winter*: Brambling, Siskin, Water Rail. Frequent sightings of Merlin and Raven over hills.
Contact: John Rowland, Etherow Country Park, Compstall, Stockport, Cheshire SK6 5JD. 0161 427 6937; fax 0161 427 3643.

4. HOLLINGWORTH LAKE

Hollingworth Lake Country Park - Rochdale MBC.
Location: SD 939 153 (visitor centre). Four miles NE of Rochdale, signed from A58 Halifax Road. Near J21 of M62 - B6225 to Littleborough.
Access: Access open to lake and surroundings at all times.
Facilities: Cafes, hide, trails and education service, car parks. Visitor centre open 10.30am-6pm (Mon-Sun) in summer, 11am-4pm (Mon-Fri), 10.30am-5pm (Sat & Sun) in winter.
Public transport: Bus Nos 452, 450. Train to Littleborough or Smithy Bridge.
Habitat: Lake (116 acres 47 ha includes 20 acre nature reserve), woodland, streams, marsh, willow scrub.
Key birds: *All year*: Great Crested Grebe, Kingfisher, Lapwing, Little Owl, Bullfinch, Cormorant. Occasional Peregrine Falcon, Sedge Warbler, Water Rail, Snipe. *Spring/autumn*: passage waders, wildfowl, Kittiwake. *Summer*: Reed Bunting, Dipper, Common Sandpiper, Curlew, Oystercatcher, Black Tern, 'Commic' Tern, Grey Partridge, Blackcap. *Winter*:

Goosander, Goldeneye, Siskin, Redpoll, Golden Plover.
Contact: The Ranger, Hollingworth Lake Visitor Centre, Rakewood Road, Littleborough, OL15 0AQ. 01706 373421. www.rochdale.gov.uk

5. PENNINGTON FLASH

Wigan Leisure and Culture Trust
Location: SJ 640 990. One mile from Leigh town centre. Main entrance on A572 (St Helens Road).
Access: Park is signposted from A580 (East Lancs Road) and is permanently open. Four largest hides, toilets and information point open 9am-dusk (except Christmas Day). Main paths flat and suitable for disabled. Coach parking available if booked in advance.
Facilities: Toilets including disabled toilet and information point. Total of seven bird hides. Site leaflet available and Rangers based on site. Group visits welcome, guided tours or a site introduction can be arranged subject to staff availability.
Public transport: Only 1 mile from Leigh bus station. Several services stop on St Helens Road near entrance to park. Contact GMPTE 0161 228 7811.
Habitat: Lowland lake, ponds and scrapes, fringed with reeds, rough grassland, scrub and young woodland.
Key birds: Waterfowl all year, waders mainly passage spring and autumn (14-plus species). Breeding Common Tern and Little Ringed Plover. Feeding station attracts Willow Tit and Bullfinch all year.
Contact: Peter Alker, Pennington Flash Country Park, St Helens Road, Leigh WN7 3PA. (Tel/fax)01942 605253. e-mail: pfcp@wlct.org

6. WIGAN FLASHES

Lancashire Wildlife Trust/Wigan Council.
Location: SD 580 035. One mile from J25 of M6.
Access: Free access, open at all times. Areas suitable for disabled but some motor cycle barriers with gates. Paths being upgraded. Access for coaches – contact reserve manager for details.
Facilities: Two hide screens being built 2004.
Public transport: 610 bus (Hawkley Hall Circular).
Habitat: Wetland with reedbed.
Key birds: Black Tern on migration. *Summer*: Nationally important for Reed Warbler and breeding Common Tern. Willow Tit, Grasshopper Warbler, Kingfisher. *Winter*: Wildfowl especially diving duck and Gadwall. Bittern (especially winter).
Contact: Mark Champion, 225 Poolstock Lane, Wigan, Lancs WN3 5JE. 01942 236337. e-mail: mark@championx.freeserve.co.uk

OTHER SITES
(full details in previous editions)

A. Astley Moss
Contact: Cuerden Park Wildlife Centre, 01772 324129.

B. Hope Carr
Contact: Leigh Environmental Education Centre, 01942 269027.

C. Rumworth Lodge
Contact: Wildlife Trust HQ, 01722 924729.

Merseyside

1. AINSDALE & BIRKDALE LNR
Sefton Council.
Location: SD 300 115. SD 310 138. Leave the A565 just N of Formby and car parking areas are off the unnumbered coastal road.
Access: Track from Ainsdale or Southport along the shore. Wheelchair access across boardwalks at Ainsdale Sands Lake Nature Trail and the Queen's Jubilee Nature Trail, opposite Weld Road.
Facilities: Ainsdale Visitor Centre open Summer and toilets (Easter-Oct).
Public transport: Ainsdale and Southport stations 20 minute walk. Hillside Station is a 30 minute walk across the Birkdale Sandhills to beach.
Habitat: Foreshore, dune scrub and pine woodland.
Key birds: *Spring/summer*: Grasshopper Warbler, Chiffchaff, waders. *Winter*: Blackcap, Stonechat, Redwing, Fieldfare, waders and wildfowl. *All year*: Sky Lark, Grey Partridge.
Contact: Southport Town Hall, Lord Street, Southport, PR8 1DA. www.sefton.gov.uk

2. DEE ESTUARY

Metropolitan Borough of Wirral.
Location: SJ 255 815. Leave A540 Chester to Hoylake road at Heswall and head downhill (one mile) to the free car park at the shore end of Banks Road. Heswall is 30 minutes from South Liverpool and Chester by car.
Access: Open at all times. Best viewpoint 600 yards along shore N of Banks Road. No disabled access along shore, but good birdwatching from bottom of Banks Road. Arrive 2.5 hours before high tide. Coach parking available.
Facilities: Toilets in car park and information board. Wirral Country Park Centre three miles N off A540 has toilets, hide, café, kiosk (all accessible to wheelchairs). Birdwatching events programme available from visitor centre.
Public transport: Bus service to Banks Road car park from Heswall bus station. Contact Mersey Travel (tel 0151 236 7676).
Habitat: Saltmarsh and mudflats.
Key birds: *Autumn/winter*: Large passage and winter wader roosts - Redshank, Curlew, Black-tailed Godwit, Oystercatcher, Golden Plover, Knot, Shelduck, Teal, Red-breasted Merganser, Peregrine, Merlin, Hen Harrier, Short-eared Owl. Smaller numbers of Pintail, Wigeon, Bar-tailed Godwit, Greenshank, Spotted Redshank, Grey and Ringed Plovers, Whimbrel, Curlew Sandpiper, Little Stint, occasional Scaup and Little Egret.
Contact: Martyn Jamieson, Head Ranger, Wirral Country Park Centre, Station Road, Thustaston, Wirral, Merseyside CH61 0HN. 0151 648 4371/ 3884. e-mail: wirralcountrypark@wirral.gov.uk www.wirral.gov.uk/er

3. HILBRE ISLAND

Wirral Country Park Centre (Metropolitan Borough of Wirral).
Location: SJ 184 880. Three tidal islands in the mouth of the Dee Estuary. Park in West Kirby which is on the A540 Chester-to-Hoylake road - 30 minutes from Liverpool, 45 minutes from Chester. Follow the brown Marine Lake signs to Dee Lane pay and display car park. Coach parking available at West Kirby but please apply for permit to visit island well in advance as numbers limited.
Access: Two mile walk across the sands from Dee Lane slipway. No disabled access. Do not cross either way within 3.5 hours of high water - tide times and suggested safe route on noticeboard at slipway. Prior booking and permit needed for parties of six or more - maximum of 50. Book early.
Facilities: Toilets at Marine Lake and Hilbre (primitive!). Permits, leaflets and tide times from Wirral Country Park Centre. Hilbre Bird Observatory.
Public transport: Bus and train station (from Liverpool) within 0.5 mile of Dee Lane slipway. Contact Mersey Travel, tel 0151 236 7676.
Habitat: Sandflats, rocky shore and open sea.
Key birds: *Late summer/autumn*: Seabird passage - Gannets, terns, skuas, shearwaters and after NW gales good numbers of Leach's Petrel. *Winter*: Wader roosts at high tide, Purple Sandpiper, Turnstone, sea ducks, divers, grebes. Passage migrants.
Contact: Martyn Jamieson, Head Ranger (see Dee Estuary above).

4. MARSHSIDE

RSPB (North West England Office).
Location: SD 355 202. On south shore of Ribble Estuary, one mile north of Southport centre on Marine Drive.
Access: Open 8.30am-5pm all year. No toilets. No dogs please. Coach parties please book in advance. No charges but donations welcomed.

Facilities: Two hides and trails accessible to wheelchairs.
Public transport: Bus service to Elswick Road/ Marshside Road half-hourly, bus No 44. Contact Southport Buses (01704 536137).
Habitat: Coastal grazing marsh and lagoons.
Key birds: *Winter*: Pink-footed Goose, wildfowl, waders, raptors. *Spring*: Breeding waders and wildfowl, Garganey, migrants. *Autumn*: Migrants. *All year*: Black-tailed Godwit.
Contact: Tony Baker, RSPB, 24 Hoghton Street, Southport PR9 0PA. 01704 536378.
e-mail: tony.baker@rspb.org.uk

5. RED ROCKS MARSH

Cheshire Wildlife Trust.
Location: SJ 206 880. Six miles W of Birkenhead immediately W of Hoylake and adjacent to the Dee estuary.
Access: Open all year.**Facilities:** Car park, hide.
Public transport: None.
Habitat: Sand dune, reedbed.
Key birds: *Spring/summer*: Wildfowl, warblers. *Passage*: Finches, Snow Bunting, thrushes.
Contact: Grebe House, Reaseheath, Nantwich, Cheshire CW5 6DG01270 610 180.
e-mail: cheshirewt@cix.co.uk

6. SEAFORTH NATURE RESERVE

The Wildlife Trust for Lancashire, Manchester and North Merseyside.
Location: SJ 315 970. Five miles from Liverpool city centre. From M57/M58 take A5036 to docks.
Access: Only organised groups who pre-book are now allowed access. Groups should contact the reserve office (see below) at least seven days in advance of their planned trip. Coaches welcome.
Facilities: Toilets when visitor centre open, three hides.
Public transport: Train to Waterloo or Seaforth stations from Liverpool. Buses to dock gates from Liverpool.
Habitat: Saltwater and freshwater lagoons, scrub grassland.
Key birds: Little Gull on passage (Apr) plus Roseate, Little and Black Terns. Breeding and passage Common Tern (Apr-Sept) plus Roseate, Little and Black Terns on passage. Passage and winter waders and gulls. Passage passerines, especially White Wagtail, pipits and Wheatear.
Contact: Steve White, Seaforth Nature Reserve, Port of Liverpool, L21 1JD. 0151 9203769.
e-mail: lwildlife@cix.co.uk

Norfolk

1. BERNEY MARSHES

RSPB (East Anglia Office).
Location: TG 465 055. W of Great Yarmouth. In the Halvergate Marshes.
Access: Public footpath by Berney Arms Station on the Norwich to Yarmouth railway line NE of Reedham. Boat service to reserve departs from Burgh Castle Marina first Sun of month at 10am & 2pm, returning 1pm & 4pm (phone 01493 700645 to book).
Facilities: None.
Public transport: Train to Berney Arms from Yarmouth.
Habitat: Marsh.
Key birds: *Winter*: Bewick's Swan, Wigeon, birds of prey (inc. Hen Harrier, Merlin, Peregrine, Short-eared Owl). *Spring*: Migrants can include Spoonbill, Little Egret, Ruff.
Contact: Mark Smart, Warden, Ashtree Farm, Goodchild Marine, Butt Lane, Burgh Castle, Great Yarmouth, Norfolk NR31 9PE.

2. NWT CLEY MARSHES

Norfolk Wildlife Trust.
Location: TG 054 441. NWT Cley Marshes is situated three miles N of Holt on A149 coast road, half a mile E of Cley-next-the-Sea. Visitor centre and car park on inland side of the road.
Access: Open all year. Visitor centre open Apr-Oct (10am-5pm daily), Nov-mid Dec (10am-4pm Wed-Sun). Cost: adults £3.75, children under 16 free. NWT members free.
Facilities: Visitor centre, birdwatching hides, wildlife gift shop, refreshments, toilets, coach parking, car park, disabled access to centre, boardwalk and hides and toilets, groups welcome.
Public transport: Bus service from Norwich, Fakenham and Holt Mon-Sat. The Coasthopper service stops outside daily. Connections for train and bus services at Sheringham. Special discounts to visitors arriving by bus.
Habitat: Reedbeds, salt and freshwater marshes, scrapes and shingle ridge with international

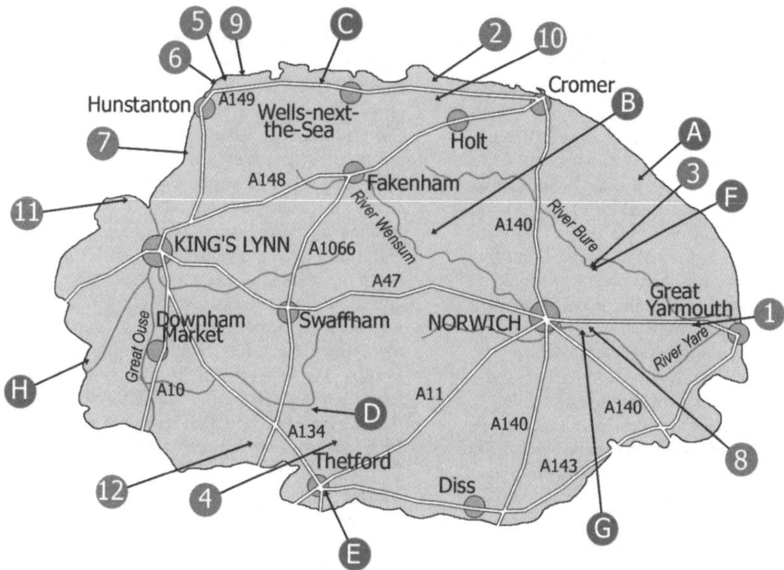

reputation as one of the finest birdwatching sites in Britain.
Key birds: *Feb:* Brent Goose, warblers, Wigeon, Teal, Shoveler, Pintail. *Spring*: Chiffchaff, Wheatear, Sandwich Tern, Reed and Sedge Warblers, Ruff, Black-tailed Godwit. *Jun*: Spoonbill, Avocet, Bittern, Bearded Tit. *Autumn*: Green and Wood Sandpiper, Greenshank, Whimbrel, Little Ringed Plover. Many rarities.
Contact: Dick Bagnall, Oakeley Centre, NWT Cley Marshes, Cley, Holt, Norfolk NR25 7RZ. 01263 740008. e-mail: BernardB@nwt.cix.co.uk

3. NWT COCKSHOOT BROAD

Norfolk Wildlife Trust.
Location: TG 344 165. Eight miles NE of Norwich. From B1140 Acle-Wroxham road, follow signs for Woodbastwick. Head E to Ranworth. On a sharp R bend, go straight down a narrow road signed 'River Only'. There is a small car park at the bottom.
Access: Open all year.
Facilities: Car park, paths.
Public transport: None.
Habitat: Part of Bure Marshes NNR. Marshes, woodland, river.
Key birds: *Spring/summer*: Reed Warbler, possible Cetti's Warbler, Blackcap, Garden Warbler, Marsh Tit, hirundines, Common Tern, Cuckoo. *All year*: Wildfowl, common woodland birds.
Contact: Bewick House, 22 Thorpe Road, Norwich NR1 1UD. 01603 625 540.
e-mail: admin@nwt.cix.co.uk
www.wildlifetrust.org.uk/norfolk

4. NWT EAST WRETHAM HEATH

Norfolk Wildlife Trust.
Location: TL 913 887. Site lies in the centre of Breckland, N of Thetford. From A11 take turning for A1075 to Watton and travel for about two miles over the level crossing and pass the lay-by to the left. Car park and entrance to reserve are by the first house on the left.
Access: Open all year dawn to dusk.
Facilities: Car park. Trail, hide.
Public transport: None.
Habitat: Breckland grass heath and meres, scrub and woodland.
Key birds: Wildfowl, wading birds, Redstart, Wood Lark.
Contact: Bev Nichols, Bewick House, 22 Thorpe Road, Norwich NR1 1RY. 01603 625540.
e-mail: BevN@norfolkwildlifetrust.co.uk

5. HOLME BIRD OBSERVATORY

Norfolk Ornithologists' Association (NOA).
Location: TF 717 450. E of Hunstanton, signposted from A149. Access from Broadwater Road.
Access: Reserve open daily to members dawn to

dusk; non-members (9am-5pm) by permit from the Observatory. Please keep dogs on leads in the reserve. Parties by prior arrangement.
Facilities: Accredited Bird Observatory operating 12 months of the year, bird ringing, MV moth trapping and other scientific monitoring. Visitor centre, car park and several hides (seawatch hide reserved for NOA members) together with access to beach and coastal path.
Public transport: Coastal bus service runs from Hunstanton to Sheringham roughly every 30 mins but is seasonal and times may vary. Phone Norfolk Green Bus, 01553 776 980.
Habitat: In ten acres of diverse habitat: sand dunes, Corsican pines, scrub and reed-fringed lagoon making this a migration hotspot.
Key birds: Species list over 320. Ringed species over 150. Recent rarities have included Red Kite, Common Crane, Red-backed Shrike, Osprey, Pallas's, Yellow-browed, Greenish and Barred Warblers.
Contact: Jed Andrews, Holme Bird Observatory, Broadwater Road, Holme, Hunstanton, Norfolk PE36 6LQ. 01485 525406. www.noa.org.uk e-mail: info@noa.org.uk

6. REDWELL MARSH

Norfolk Ornithologists' Association (NOA).
Location: TF 702 436. In Holme, off A149, E of Hunstanton. Access from Broadwater Road.
Access: View from public footpath from centre of Holme village to Broadwater Road. Open at all times.
Facilities: Member's hide, offering wheelchair access, (access from Broadwater Road).
Public transport: As for Holme Bird Observatory.
Habitat: Wet grazing marsh with ditches, pond and two large wader scrapes.
Key birds: Wildfowl and waders inc. Curlew/ Green/Wood and Pectoral Sandpipers, Greenshank, Spotted Redshank, Avocet and Black-tailed Godwit. Recent rarities have included American Wigeon, Ring Ouzel, Mediterranean Gull and Grasshopper Warbler. Also a raptor flight path.
Contact: Jed Andrews, as for Holme Bird Observatory.

7. SNETTISHAM

RSPB (East Anglia Office).
Location: TF 630 310. Car park two miles along Beach Road, signposted off A149 King's Lynn to Hunstanton, opposite Snettisham village.
Access: Open at all times. Dogs to be kept on leads. Two hides are suitable for wheelchairs. Disabled access is across a private road. Please phone office number for permission and directions. Coaches welcome, but please book in advance as a height barrier needs to be removed.
Facilities: Four birdwatching hides, connected by reserve footpath. No toilets on site.
Public transport: Nearest over two miles away.
Habitat: Intertidal mudflats, saltmarsh, shingle beach, brackish lagoons, and unimproved grassland/scrub. Best visited on a high tide.
Key birds: *Autumn/winter/spring*: Waders (particularly Knot, Bar and Black-tailed Godwits, Dunlin, Grey Plover), wildfowl (particularly Pink-footed and Brent Geese, Wigeon, Gadwall, Goldeneye), Peregrine, Hen Harrier, Merlin, owls. Migrants in season. *Summer*: Breeding Ringed Plover, Redshank, Avocet, Common Tern. Marsh Harrier regular.
Contact: Jim Scott, RSPB, 43 Lynn Road, Snettisham, King's Lynn,Norfolk PE31 7LR. 01485 542689.

8. STRUMPSHAW FEN

RSPB (East Anglia Office).
Location: TG 33 06. Seven miles ESE of Norwich. Follow signposts. Entrance across level-crossing from car park, reached by turning sharp right and right again into Low Road from Brundall, off A47 to Great Yarmouth.
Access: Open dawn-dusk. RSPB members free, adults £2.50, children 50p, family £5. Guide dogs only. Viewing platform for wheelchair users.
Facilities: Toilets, reception hide and two other hides, two walks, five miles of trails.
Public transport: Brundall train station about one mile. Bus stop half a mile - contact NORBIC (0845 300 6116).
Habitat: Reedbed and reedfen, wet grassland and woodland.
Key birds: *Summer*: Bittern, Bearded Tit, Marsh Harrier, Cetti's Warbler and other reedbed birds. *Winter*: Bittern, wildfowl, Marsh and Hen Harrier. Swallowtails butterflies in Jun.
Contact: Tim Strudwick, Staithe Cottage, Low Road, Strumpshaw, Norwich, Norfolk NR13 4HS. 01603 715191. e-mail: strumpshaw@rspb.org.uk

9. TITCHWELL MARSH

RSPB (East Anglia Office).
Location: TF 749 436. Near Hunstanton. Footpath

along sea wall from A149 between Thornham and Titchwell.
Access: Fen and meadow trails are new additions, allowing further access to the reserve. Reserve and hides open at all times.
Facilities: Visitor centre, shop with large selection of binoculars, telescopes and books, open every day 9.30am to 5pm (Nov 15 - Feb 16, 2005, 9.30 to 4pm). Our new tearoom is open from 9.30am to 4.30pm every date (Nov 15 - Feb 16, 2005, 9.30am to 4pm). Visitor centre and tearoom closed on Christmas day and Boxing day.
Public transport: Phone Norfolk Green Bus 01553 776980.
Habitat: Reedbed, brackish & freshwater pools, saltmarsh, dunes, shingle.
Key birds: *Spring/summer*: Nesting Avocet, Bearded Tit, Water Rail, Marsh Harrier, Reed and Sedge Warblers. *Autumn*: Knot. *Winter*: Brent Goose, Goldeneye, Scoter, Eider, Hen Harrier roost, Snow Bunting and Shore Lark on beach.
Contact: Centre Manager, Titchwell Marsh Reserve, King's Lynn, Norfolk PE31 8BB. Tel/fax 01485 210779.

10. WALSEY HILLS

Norfolk Ornithologists' Association (NOA).
Location: TG 062 441. Up footpath and steps from A149 at Cley.
Access: Open daily throughout year.
Facilities: Important migration watchpoint. Excellent views across adjoining reserves between Cley and Salthouse, and members' hide with superb panoramic views of the whole area. Wardened visitor centre providing up-to-date birding information. Short walk through scrub.
Public transport: Phone Norfolk Green Bus 01553 776980.
Habitat: Scrub.
Key birds: Recent rarities have included Alpine Swift, Richard's and Water Pipits, Little Bunting Cetti's, Booted, Yellow-browed and Pallas' Warblers.
Contact: Tom Fletcher, 01263 740875.

11. THE WASH NNR

English Nature East Midlands Team.
Location: Between TF 484 280 and TF 598 237. W of King's Lynn. For main entrance off A17, follow road along East bank of River Nene at Sutton Bridge.
Access: Open access W of River Ouse, though remain on public footpaths along seabank and keep dogs under control.
Facilities: Car parks at Gedney Drove End (TF 481 284), Guy's Head (TF 491 256), Peter Scott's Lighthouse (TF 493 255), Ongar Hill (TF 582 247).
Public transport: None.
Habitat: Saltmarsh and mudflats.
Key birds: *Summer*: Redshank, Oystercatcher. Marsh Harrier, Shelduck, Reed Bunting. Massive numbers of passage and wintering waterfowl including Brent Goose, Knot, Oystercatcher, Lapwing, Redshank, Dunlin, godwits, Shelduck and raptors.
Contact: Simon Cooter, English Nature, 78 High Street, Boston, Lincs PE21 8SX. 01205 311674. e-mail: simon.cooter@english-nature.org.uk

12. NWT WEETING HEATH

Norfolk Wildlife Trust.
Location: TL 756 881. Weeting Heath is signposted from the Weeting-Hockwold road, two miles W of Weeting near to Brandon in Suffolk. Nature reserve can be reached via B1112 at Hockwold or B1106 at Weeting.
Access: Open daily from Apr-Sep. Cost: adults £2.50, children free. NWT members free. Disabled access to visitor centre and hides.
Facilities: Visitor centre open daily Apr-Aug, birdwatching hides, wildlife gift shop, refreshments, toilets, coach parking, car park, groups welcome (book first).
Public transport: Train services to Brandon and bus connections (limited) from Brandon High Street.
Habitat: Breckland, grass heath.
Key birds: Stone curlew, migrant passerines, Wood Lark.
Contact: Bev Nichols, Bewick house, 22 Thorpe Road, Norwich NR1 1RY. 01603 625540.
e-mail: BevN@norfolkwildlifetrust.org.uk

OTHER SITES

(full details in previous editions)

A. NWT Hickling Broad
Contact: Norfolk Wildlife Trust, 01603 625540.
B. NWT Foxley Wood
Contact: Norfolk Wildlife Trust, 01603 625540.
C. Holkham
Contact: English Nature, 01328 711183.
D. Lynford Arboretum
Contact: Forest Enterprise, 01832 810 271.
E. Nunnery Lakes
Contact: BTO, 01842 750050.
F. NWT Ranworth Broad
Contact: Norfolk Wildlife Trust, 01603 625540.
G. Surlingham Church Marsh
Contact: The Warden, Strumpshaw Fen, 01603 715191.
H. Welney
Contact: The Warden, 01353 860711.

Northants

1. CLIFFORD HILL GRAVEL PITS

Location: SP 781 595. Take the A428 Bedford Road from Northampton town centre E to A45 roundabout. Go straight over and turn L to park by the Courtyard Hotel.
Access: Open all year. Shooting may take place Tues.
Facilities: Car park, toilets.
Public transport: None.
Habitat: Reservoir, river, grassland.
Key birds: *Spring*: Wheatear, Sand Martin, Yellow Wagtail. *Winter*: Excellent for wintering wildfowl inc Goosander, Pintail, Red-crested Pochard and Smew. Geese, Golden Plover, Green Sandpiper, Redshank, Meadow Pipit, Reed Bunting, thrushes. *All year*: Meadow Pipit, Reed Bunting, Grey Wagtail, Redpoll, Linnet, Green Woodpecker.

2. HOLLOWELL RESERVOIR

Anglian Water.
Location: SP 683 738. From Northampton, take the A5199 NW. After eight miles, turn L. The car park is on the L.
Access: Open all year. Permit required. Keep dogs on lead.
Facilities: None.
Public transport: Bus: No 60 from Northampton, first one arriving at 8.58am. Tel: 01604 676 060.
Habitat: Grass, mature, mixed and conifer plantations.
Key birds: *Autumn/winter*: Dunlin, Greenshank, Redshank, Green Sandpiper, Mediterranean Gull, ducks. Crossbill occurs in invasion years. Bearded Tit and Dartford Warbler occasional.
Contact: Anglian House, Ambury Road, Huntingdon, Cambs, PE29 3NZ. 01480 323000.

3. PITSFORD RESERVOIR

Beds, Cambs, Northants and Peterborough Wildlife Trust.
Location: SP 787 702. Five miles N of Northampton. On A43 take turn to Holcot and Brixworth. On A508 take turn to Brixworth and Holcot.
Access: Lodge open mid-Mar to mid-Nov from 8am-dusk. Winter opening times variable, check in advance. Permits for reserve available from Lodge

on daily or annual basis. Reserve open to permit holders 365 days a year. No dogs. Disabled access from Lodge to first hide.
Facilities: Toilets available in Lodge, 15 miles of paths, eight bird hides, car parking.
Public transport: None.
Habitat: Open water (up to 120 ha), marginal vegetation and reed grasses, wet woodland, grassland and mixed woodland (40 ha).
Key birds: 162 species in 2003. *Summer*: Breeding warblers, terns, Hobby, Tree Sparrow. *Autumn*: Waders only if water levels suitable. *Winter*: Wildfowl, feeding station with Tree Sparrow and Corn Bunting.
Contact: Dave Francis, Pitsford Water Lodge, Brixworth Road, Holcot, Northampton NN6 9SJ. 01604 780148.
e-mail: pitsford@cix.compulink.co.uk

4. STANFORD RESERVOIR

Severn Trent Water/Beds, Cambs, Northants and Peterborough Wildilfe Trust.
Location: SP 600 805. One mile SW of South Kilworth off Kilworth/Stanford-on-Avon road.
Access: Daytime, permits from Northants Wildlife Trust. No dogs. Limited access for disabled.
Facilities: Toilets (inc disabled). Two hides, perimeter track. Disabled parking.
Public transport: None.
Habitat: Reservoir with willow, reed and hedgerow edges.
Key birds: *Winter*: Wildfowl, especially Ruddy Duck. *Spring*: Migratory terns and warblers. *Late summer*: Terns, Hobby, waders.
Contact: Trust HQ, 01954 712500; fax 01954 710051.
e-mail: cambridgeshire@wildlifebcnp.org
www.wildlifebcnp.org

5. SUMMER LEYS LNR

Northamptonshire County Council.
Location: SP 886 634. Three miles from Wellingborough, accessible from A45 and A509, situated on Great Doddington to Wollaston Road.
Access: Open 24 hours a day, 365 days a year, no permits required. Dogs welcome but must be kept on leads at all times. 40 space car park, small tarmaced circular route suitable for wheelchairs.
Facilities: Three hides, one feeding station. No toilets, nearest are at Irchester Country Park on A509 towards Wellingborough.
Public transport: Nearest main station is Wellingborough. No direct bus service, though buses run regularly to Great Doddington and Wollaston, both about a mile away. Tel: 01604 236712 (24 hrs) for copies of timetables.
Habitat: Scrape, two ponds, lake, scrub, grassland, hedgerow.
Key birds: Hobby, Lapwing, Golden Plover, Ruff, Gadwall, Garganey, Pintail, Shelduck, Shoveler, Little Ringed Plover, Tree Sparrow, Redshank, Green Sandpiper, Oystercatcher, Black-headed Gull colony, terns.
Contact: Chris Haines, Countryside and Tourism, Northamptonshire Council, PO Box 163, County Hall, Northampton NN1 1AX. 01604 237227 - please ring for a leaflet about the reserve.
e-mail: countryside@northamptonshire.gov.uk

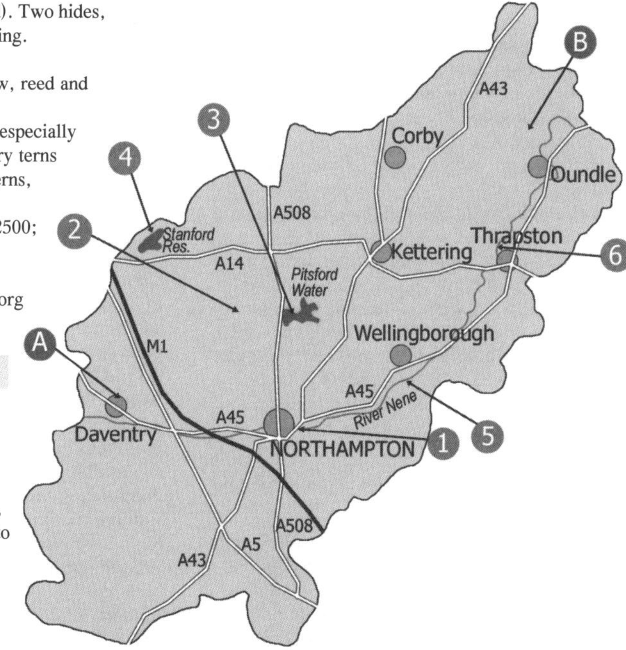

6. THRAPSTON GRAVEL PITS & TITCHMARSH LNR

Beds, Cambs, Northants and Peterborough Wildlife Trust/English Nature.
Location: TL 008 804.
Access: Public footpath from layby on A605 N of Thrapston. Car park at Aldwincle, W of A605 at Thorpe Waterville.
Facilities: Two hides.
Public transport: Bus service to Thrapston.
Habitat: Alder/birch/willow wood; old duck decoy, series of water-filled gravel pits.
Key birds: *Summer*: Breeding Grey Heron (no access to Heronry), Common Tern, Little Ringed Plover; warblers. Migrants, inc. Red-necked and Slavonian Grebes, Bittern and Marsh Harrier recorded.
Contact: Wildlife Trust HQ, 01954 713500; fax 01954 710051.
e-mail:cambridgeshire@wildlifebcnp.org
www.wildlifebcnp.org

OTHER SITES
(full details in previous editions)

A. Daventry Reservoir Country Park
Contact: Daventry Country Park, 01327 877193.
B. Short Wood
Contact: Northants Wildlife Trust, 01954 713500.

Northumberland

1. ARNOLD RESERVE, CRASTER

Northumberland Wildlife Trust.
Location: NU255197. Lies NE of Alnwick and SW of Craster village.
Access: Public footpath from car park in disused quarry.
Facilities: Interpretation boards, information centre open in Summer. Toilets (incl disabled) and picnic site in quarry car park.
Public transport: Arriva Northumberland nos. 501 and 401.
Habitat: Semi-natural woodland and scrub near coast.
Key birds: Good site for migrant passerines to rest and feed. Interesting visitors can inc. Bluethroat, Red-breasted Flycatcher, Barred and Icterine Warblers, Wryneck; moulting site for Lesser Redpoll. *Summer* : Breeding warblers.
Contact: Wildlife Wildlife Trust HQ, The Garden House, St Nicholas Park, Jubilee Road, Newcastle upon Tyne, NE3 3XT. 0191 284 6884; fax 0191 284 6794. e-mail: northwildlife@cix.co.uk
www.wildlifetrust.org.uk/northumberland

2. BOLAM LAKE COUNTRY PARK

Northumberland County Council.
Location: NZ 08 81. 4.8km N of main Jedburgh Road (A696), 27km NW of Newcastle. Signed along a minor road from Belsay.
Access: Open all year, small parking fee.
Facilities: Car parks, leaflets from warden's house in the main car park.
Public transport: None.
Habitat: Parkland, lake, carr, conifers, woodland.
Key birds: *Spring/summer*: Ruddy Duck, Woodcock, Common Sandpiper, Sand Martin, House Martin, Redstart, warblers inc Grasshopper, Garden, Wood and Willow, possible flycatchers, waders. *Winter*: Whooper Swan, Greylag and Canada Geese, Wigeon, Pintail, Goosander, Water Rail, Woodcock, thrushes, Siskin, Redpoll. *All year*: possible Grey Partridge, Green and Great Spotted Woodpeckers, Goldcrest, tits, Treecreeper, Nuthatch, Bullfinch.
Contact: County Hall, Morpeth NE61 2EF. 01670 533100.

3. BRIARWOOD BANKS

Northumberland Wildlife Trust.
Location: NY 791 620. From Haydon Bridge, take minor road from A686 to Plankey Mill, three miles away at junction of Kingswood Burn and River Allen.
Access: Footpaths open to public. One steep route may be impassable after heavy rain.
Facilities: Parking at Plankey Mill. Picnic site and toilets at NT carpark at Allenbanks.
Public transport: None.
Habitat: Ancient woodland along steep valley.
Key birds: Pied Flycatcher, Wood Warbler, Redstart, Dipper, Woodcock, Treecreeper, Nuthatch.
Contact: Wildlife Wildlife Trust HQ, The Garden House, St Nicholas Park, Jubilee Road, Newcastle

upon Tyne, NE3 3XT. 0191 284 6884; fax 0191 284 6794; e-mail: northwildlife@cixcouk wwwwildlifetrustorguk/northumberland.

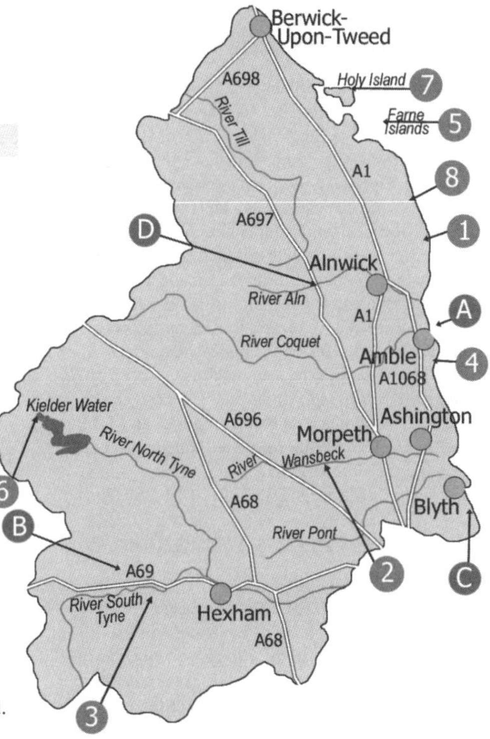

4. DRURIDGE BAY RESERVES

Northumberland Wildlife Trust.
Location: 1. NU 285 023. S of Amble. Hauxley (67a) approached by track from road midway between High and Low Hauxley. 2. Druridge Pools NZ 272 965. 3. Cresswell Pond NZ 283 945. Half mile N of Cresswell.
Access: Day permits for all three reserves.
Facilities: 1. Visitor centre, five hides (one suitable for disabled). Disabled toilet. Lake with islands behind dunes. 2. Three hides. 3. Hide.
Public transport: None.
Habitat: 2. Deep lake and wet meadows with pools behind dunes. 3. Shallow brackish lagoon behind dunes fringed by saltmarsh and reedbed, some mudflats.
Key birds: 1. *Spring and autumn*: Good for passage birds (inc. divers, skuas). *Summer*: Coastal birds, esp. terns (inc. Roseate). 2. Especially good in spring. Winter and breeding wildfowl; passage and breeding waders. 3. Good for waders, esp. on passage.
Contact: Jim Martin, Hauxley Nature Reserve, Low Hauxley, Amble, Morpeth, Northumberland. 01665 711578.

5. FARNE ISLANDS

The National Trust.
Location: NU 230 370. Access by boat from Seahouses Harbour. Access from A1.
Access: Apr, Aug-Sept: Inner Farne and Staple 10.30am-6pm (majority of boats land at Inner Farne). May-Jul: Staple Island 10.30am-1.30pm, Inner Farne: 1.30pm-5pm. Disabled access possible on Inner Farne, telephone Property Manager for details. Dogs allowed on boats - not on islands.
Facilities: Toilets on Inner Farne.
Public transport: Nearest rail stations at Alnmouth and Berwick.
Habitat: Maritime islands, 15-28 in number, depending on state of tide.
Key birds: 18 species of seabirds/waders, four species of tern (including Roseate), 34,000-plus pairs of Puffin, Rock Pipit, Pied Wagtail, Starling, 1,200 Eider etc.
Contact: John Walton, 8 St Aidans, Seahouses, Northumberland NE68 7SR. 01665 720651.

6. KIELDER FOREST

Forest Enterprise.
Location: NY 632 934. Kielder Castle is situated at N end of Kielder Water, NW of Bellingham.
Access: Forest open all year. Toll charge on 12 mile forest drive. Visitor centre has limited opening in winter.
Facilities: Visitor centre, exhibition, toilets, shop, access for disabled, licensed café. Local facilities include Youth Hostel, camp site, pub and garage.
Public transport: Bus: 814, 815, 816 from Hexham and seasonal service 714 from Newcastle.
Habitat: Commercial woodland, mixed and broadleaved trees.
Key birds: *Spring/summer*: Goshawk, Chiffchaff, Willow Warbler, Redstart, Siskin. *Winter*: Crossbill. *Resident*: Jay, Dipper, Great Spotted Woodpecker, Tawny Owl, Song Thrush, Goldcrest.
Contact: Forest Enterprise, Eels Burn, Bellingham, Hexham, Northumberland, NE48 2AJ. 01434 220242.
e-mail: pippa.kirkham@forestry.gsi.gov.uk

7. LINDISFARNE NNR

English Nature (Northumbria Team).
Location: NU 090 430. Island access lies two miles E of A1 at Beal, eight miles S of Berwick-on-Tweed.
Access: Open all hours. Some restricted access (refuges). Coach parking available on Holy Island.
Facilities: Toilets, visitor centre in village. Hide on island (new hide with disabled access at Fenham-le-Moor). Self-guided trail on island.
Public transport: Irregular bus service to Holy Island, mainly in summer. Bus route follows mainland boundary of site north-south.
Habitat: Dunes, sand and mudflats.
Key birds: *Passage and winter*: Wildfowl and waders, including pale-bellied Brent Goose, Long-tailed Duck and Whooper Swan. Rare migrants.
Contact: Phil Davey, Site Manager, Beal Station, Berwick-on-Tweed, TD15 2PB. 01289 381470.

8. NEWTON POOL NATURE RESERVE

National Trust (North East).
Location: NU 243 240. Follow signs to High Newton N of Embleton at the junction of the B1339 and B1340. In the village, follow signs to Low Newton. Just before the village is a car park which must be used as no public parking is available further on. A National Trust sign in the village square shows the way to the bird hide along the Craster footpath (about a five minute walk).
Access: Open all year. From May to mid-August parts of the beach may be cordoned off to avoid disturbing nesting birds.
Facilities: Car park, hide.
Public transport: None.
Habitat: Dunes, tidal flats, beach, freshwater pool with artificial islands, scrub.
Key birds: *Spring/summer*: Grasshopper Warbler, Water Rail, Little Grebe, Whitethroat, Yellow Wagtail, Whinchat, Stonechat, Corn Bunting, terns, gulls. *Winter*: waders, gulls.
Contact: National Trust (North East), Scots' Gap, Morpeth, Northumberland, NE61 4EG. 01670 774691.

OTHER SITES

(full details in previous editions)

A. Coquet Island
Contact: RSPB, 0191 281 3366.
B. Grindon Lough
Contact: 0191 284 6884.
C. Holywell Pond
Contact: 0191 284 6884.
D. Thrunton Wood
Contact: 01904 696300.

Nottinghamshire

1. ATTENBOROUGH GRAVEL PITS

Nottinghamshire Wildlife Trust.
Location: SK 523 343. On A6005, seven miles SW of Nottingham alongside River Trent. Signed from main road.
Access: Open at all times. Dogs on leads. Paths suitable for disabled access.
Facilities: Nature trail (leaflet from Notts WT), one hide (key £2.50 from Notts WT). Visitor centre due to open Spring 2005.
Public transport: Railway station at Attenborough, several buses pass close to reserve (Rainbow 525A from Nottingham every ten minutes).
Habitat: Disused, flooded gravel workings with associated marginal and wetland vegetation.
Key birds: *Spring/summer*: Breeding Common Tern (40-plus pairs), Reed Warbler, Black Tern regular (bred once). *Winter*: Wildfowl (Bittern has wintered for last two years), Grey Heron colony, adjacent Cormorant roost.
Contact: The Old Ragged School, Brook Street, Nottingham NG1 1EA. 0115 958 8242.
e-mail: nottswt@cix.co.uk

2. BESTWOOD COUNTRY PARK

Nottingham County Council.
Location: From Nottingham, take A611 to Hucknall. After passing Bulwell Forest Golf Course, turn R down B683 to Bestwood Village. Take first R, car park is on R after road bends L.
Access: Open all year.
Facilities: Car parks, trails.
Public transport: None.

Habitat: Parkland, wood, lakes.
Key birds: *Spring/summer*: Turtle Dove, Cuckoo, warblers, hirundines. *Winter*: Finches, tits, thrushes. *All year*: Kingfisher, tits, Treecreeper, Green Woodpecker.
Contact: County Hall, West Bridgford, Nottingham NG2 7QP. 0115 982 3823. e-mail: enquiries@nottscc.gov.uk

3. COLWICK COUNTRY PARK

Nottingham City Council.
Location: SK 610 395. Off A612 three miles E of Nottingham city centre.
Access: Open at all times, but no vehicle access after dusk or before 7am.
Facilities: Nature trails. Sightings log book in Fishing Lodge.
Public transport: Call park office for advice
Habitat: Lakes, pools, woodlands, grasslands, new plantations, River Trent.
Key birds: *Summer*: Warblers, Hobby, Common Tern (15+ pairs). *Winter*: Wildfowl and gulls. Passage migrants.
Contact: Head Ranger, The Fishing Lodge, Colwick Country Park, River Road, Colwick, Nottingham NG4 2DW. 0115 987 0785. www.colwick2000.freeserve.co.uk

4. LOUND GRAVEL PITS

Tarmac, ARC, Nottinghamshire Wildlife Trust.
Location: SK 690 856. Two miles N of Retford off A638 adjacent to Sutton and Lound villages.
Access: Open at all times. Use public rights of way only (use OS Map Sheet No 120 - 1:50,000 Landranger Series).
Facilities: Public viewing platform/screen off Chainbridge lane (overlooking Chainbridge NR Scrape).
Public transport: Buses from Bawtry (Church Street), Retford bus station and Worksop (Hardy Street) on services 27/27A/83/83A/84 to Lound Village crossroads (Chainbridge Lane).
Habitat: Working sand and gravel quarries, restored gravel workings, large areas of recently designated SSSI (Apr 2003), woodland, reedbeds, fishing ponds, river valley, in-filled and disused fly ash tanks, farmland, scrub, open water.
Key birds: Over 235 species recorded. *Summer*: Gulls, terns, wildfowl and waders. Passage waders, terns, passerines and raptors. *Winter*: Wildfowl, gulls, raptors. Rarities have inc. Ring-billed Gull, Caspian, White-winged Black and Whiskered Terns, Manx Shearwater, Lesser Scaup, Green-winged and Blue-winged Teal, Richard's Pipit, Baird's, Pectoral and Buff-breasted Sandpiper, Long-billed Dowitcher, Killdeer, Spoonbill, Bluethroat, Nightingale, Snow Bunting, Shore Lark, Great Skua.
Contact: Lound Bird Club, Gary Hobson (Secretary), 11 Sherwood Road, Harworth, Doncaster, South Yorks DN11 8HY. 01302 743654. e-mail: loundbirdclub@tiscali.co.uk

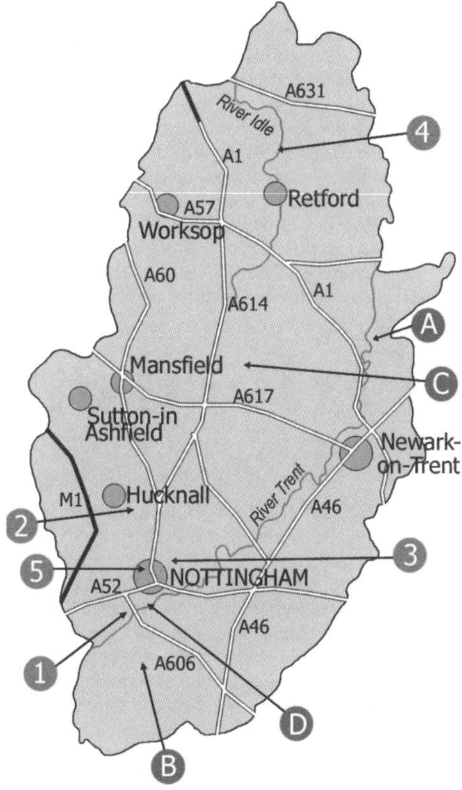

5. WOLLATON PARK

Wollaton Hall.
Location: Situated approx 5 miles W of Nottingham City Centre.
Access: Open all year from dawn-dusk.
Facilities: Pay/display car parks. Some restricted access (deer), leaflets.
Public transport: Trent Buses: no 22, and Nottingham City Transport: nos 31, and 28 running at about every 15 mins.
Habitat: Lake, small reedbed, woodland.

Key birds: *All year*: Main woodland species present, with good numbers of Nuthatch, Treecreeper and all three woodpeckers. *Summer*: Commoner warblers, incl Reed Warbler, all four hirundine species, Spotted Flycatcher. *Winter*: Pochard, Gadwall, Wigeon, Ruddy Duck, Goosander, occasional Smew and Goldeneye. Flocks of Siskin and Redpoll, often feeding by the lake, Redwing and occasional Fieldfare.
Contact: Wollaton Hall & Park, Wollaton, Nottingham NG8 2AE. 0115 915 3920. e-mail: wollaton@ncmg.demon.co.uk

OTHER SITES
(full details in previous editions)

A. Besthorpe Nature Reserve
Contact: Wildlife Trust HQ, 0115 958 8242
B. Bunny Old Woods West
Contact: Wildlife Trust HQ, 0115 958 8242
C. Duke's Wood Nature Reserve
Contact: Wildlife Trust HQ, 0115 958 8242
D. Wilwell Farm Nature Reserve
Contact: Wildlife Trust HQ, 0115 958 8242

Oxfordshire

1. ASTON ROWANT NNR

English Nature (Thames & Chiltern Team).
Location: SU 731 966. From Lewknor interchange at J6 of M40, travel NE for a short distance and turn R onto A40. After 1.5 miles at top of hill, turn R and R again into a narrow, metalled lane. Drive to end of this road to car park.
Access: Open all year. Some wheelchair access, please contact site manager for more information.
Facilities: On-site parking, easy access path to viewpoint, seats, interpretation panels.
Public transport: Bus: stops near the reserve (Stokenchurch, Lewknor and Oxford to London bus).
Habitat: Chalk grassland, chalk scrub, beech woodland.
Key birds: *Spring/summer*: Blackcap, warblers, Turtle Dove, Tree Pipit. *Winter*: Possible Short-eared Owl, Brambling, Siskin, winter thrushes. *Passage*: Whinchat, Wheatear, Ring Ouzel. *All year*: Red Kite, Buzzard, Sparrowhawk, Woodcock, Little and Tawny Owls, Green and Great Spotted Woodpeckers, Sky Lark, Meadow Pipit, Marsh Tit.
Contact: Aston Rowant Reserve Office, Aston Hill, Lewknor, Watlington OX9 5SG. 01844 351833. www.english-nature.org.uk

2. BLENHEIM PARK

Blenheim Palace.
Location: SP 440 160. 9.5km from Oxford at Woodstock on A34. Various entrances available for cars and pedestrians.
Access: Open all year (9am - 4.45pm, last entry) £2 entry fee, £1 children.
Facilities: Car parks, toilets, footpaths. Dogs on leads. Disabled toilet in Pleasure Gardens.
Public transport: None.
Habitat: Lakes, woodland, pastureland.
Key birds: *Spring/summer*: Spotted Flycatcher, Blackcap, Garden Warbler, migrating Garganey. *Winter*: Wildfowl, possible Smew, Bittern, Water Rail. *All year*: Gadwall, Barn Owl, Tawny Owl, Little Owl, Kingfisher, Great Spotted and Green Woodpeckers, Jay, other usual woodland species.
Contact: Blenheim Palace, Woodstock, Oxford. 01993 811091.

3. OTMOOR NATURE RESERVE

RSPB (Central England Office).
Location: SP 570 126. Car park seven miles NE of Oxford city centre. From B4027, take turn to Horton-cum-Studley, then first left to Beckley. After 0.67 miles at the bottom of a short hill turn R (before the Abingdon Arms public house). After 200 yards, turn left into Otmoor Lane. Reserve car park is at the end of the lane (approx one mile).
Access: Open dawn-dusk. No permits or fees. No dogs allowed on the reserve visitor trail (except public rights of way). In wet conditions, the public bridleway (which forms part of the visitor trail) can become virtually impassable and wellington boots are essential.
Facilities: Limited. Small car park with cycle racks, visitor trail (three mile round trip) and two screened viewpoints. The reserve is not accessible by coach and is unsuitable for large groups.
Public transport: None.
Habitat: Wet grassland and open water lagoons. The lagoons are in the process of being converted into a reedbed.

Key birds: *Summer*: Breeding birds include Lapwing, Redshank, Curlew, Snipe, Yellow Wagtail, Shoveler, Gadwall, Pochard, Tufted Duck, Little Grebe, Great Crested Grebe. Hobby breeds locally. *Winter*: Wigeon, Teal, Shoveler, Pintail, Gadwall, Pochard, Tufted Duck, Lapwing, Golden Plover, Hen Harrier, Peregrine, Merlin. *Autumn and spring passage*: Marsh Harrier, Short-eared Owl, Greenshank, Green Sandpiper, Common Sandpiper, Spotted Redshank and occasional Black Tern.
Contact: Neil Lambert, Site Manager, RSPB, c/o Lower Farm, Noke, Oxford OX3 9TX. 01865 848385. www.rspb.org.uk

4. SHOTOVER COUNTRY PARK

Oxford City Council.
Location: SP 565 055. Approach from Wheatley or Old Road, Headington.
Access: Open all year, best early morning or late in the evening.
Facilities: Car park, toilets, nature trails, booklets.
Public transport: None.
Habitat: Woodland, farmland, heathland, grassland, scrub.
Key birds: *Spring/summer*: Willow Warbler, Blackcap, Garden Warbler, Spotted Flycatcher, Whitethroat, Lesser Whitethroat, Pied Flycatcher, Redstart, Tree Pipit. *Autumn*: Crossbill, Redpoll, Siskin, thrushes. *All year*: Sparrowhawk, Jay, tits, finches, woodpeckers, Corn Bunting.
Contact: Oxford City Council, PO Box 10, Oxford OX1 1EN. 01865 249811.

5. WARBURG RESERVE, THE

Berks, Bucks & Oxon Wildlife Trust.
Location: SU 720 879. Leave Henley-on-Thames NW on A4130. Turn R at the end of Fair Mile onto the B480. L fork in Middle Assendon. After 1 mile, follow road round to R at grassy triangle, then on for 1 mile. Car park is on R.
Access: Open all year. Please keep dogs on a lead. In some areas, only guide dogs allowed.
Facilities: Visitor Centre, car park, hide with disabled access, nature trail, leaflets. Visitors with disabilities and groups wishing to visit should contact the warden.
Public transport: None.
Habitat: Scrub, mixed woodland, grassland, ponds.
Key birds: *Spring/summer*: Whitethroat, Lesser Whitethroat. *All year*: Sparrowhawk, Red Kite, Treecreeper, Nuthatch, Tawny Owl. *Winter*: Redpoll, Siskin, sometimes Crossbill, Woodcock. Good for orchids, butterflies and mammals.
Contact: Warburg Reserve, Bix Bottom, Henley-on-Thames, Oxfordshire, 01491 642001.
e-mail: bbowtwarburg@cix.co.uk

OTHER SITES
(full details in previous editions)

A. Chimney Meadows NNR
Contact: BBOWT, 01865 775476.
B. Foxholes Reserve
Contact: BBOWT, 01865 775476.

Shropshire

1. CHELMARSH RESERVOIR

South Staffordshire Water/Shropshire Wildlife Trust.
Location: SO 726 881.6km south of Bridgnorth, off the B4555. From Chelmarsh village head S towards Highley. Turn L at Sutton and L at the T-junction. From the car park, walk to the other end of the reservoir to the hides.
Access: Open all year.
Facilities: Car park.
Public transport: None.
Habitat: Reservoir, reedbed.
Key birds: *Winter*: wildfowl inc Pintail, Smew, geese, swans, Water Rail. *Spring/summer*: Reed and Sedge Warblers, Reed Bunting. *Passage*: Possible Osprey.
Contact: Wildlife Trust HQ, 193 Abbey Foregate, Shrewsbury SY2 6AH. 01743 284280; Fax 01743 284 281.

2. FENN'S WHIXALL AND BETTISFIELD MOSSES NNR

English Nature (North Mercia Team).
Location: The reserve is located four miles SW of

Whitchurch, ten miles SW of Wrexham. It is to S of A495 between Fenn's bank, Whixall and Bettisfield. There is roadside parking at entrances, car parks at Morris's Bridge, Roundthorn Bridge, World's End and a large car park at Manor House. Disabled access by prior arrangement along the railway line.
Access: Permit required except on Mosses trail routes.
Facilities: There are panels at all of the main entrances to the site, and leaflets are available when permits are applied for. Three interlinking Mosses trails explore the NNR and canal from Morris's and Roundthorn bridges.
Public transport: Bus passes nearby. Railway two miles away.
Habitat: Peatland meres and mosses.
Key birds: *Spring/summer*: Nightjar, Hobby, Curlew, Tree Sparrow. *All year*: Sky Lark, Linnet. Water vole, brown hare. *Winter*: Short-eared Owl.
Contact: Manor House, Mosshore, Wixhall, Shropshire SY13 2PD. 01948 880362.
e-mail: jean.daniels@english-nature.org.uk

3. LLYNCLYS HILL

Shropshire Wildlife Trust.
Location: SJ 273 237. SSW of Oswestry. Park in layby on A495 at SJ277242 and walk up Turner's Lane.
Access: Open at all times.
Facilities: None.
Public transport: None.
Habitat: Old mixed limestone sward with some woodland and scrub, small pond.
Key birds: Sparrowhawk, Green Woodpecker, Goldcrest, large warbler population. Occasional Peregrine, Buzzard. Eight species of orchid.
Contact: Wildlife Trust HQ, 193 Abbey Foregate, Shrewsbury, Shropshire SY2 6AH. 01743 284280.
e-mail: shropshirewt@cix.co.uk

4. MONKMOOR POOL

Severn Trent Water/Shropshire Wildlife Trust.
Location: SJ 524 136. Take the Whitchurch road out of Shrewsbury to the Heathgates roundabout. Follow Telford Way to the Monkmoor roundabout by the police station. Turn L into no-through road. The reserve is just before the track turns under the by-pass. Park here.
Access: Open all year. Permit required.
Facilities: Car park, hide.
Public transport: None.
Habitat: Lagoon, trees, scrub.

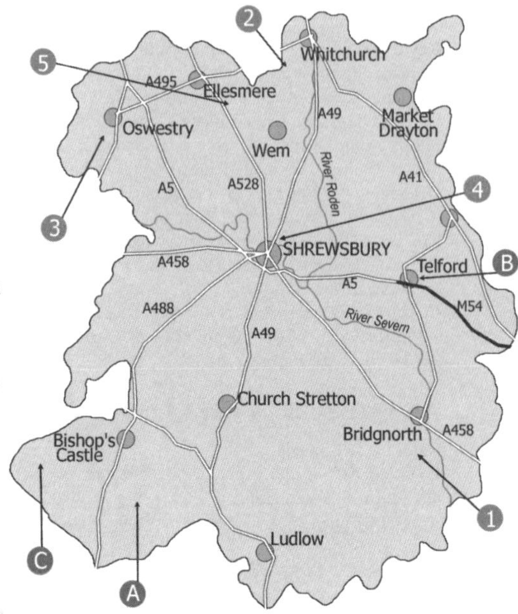

Shropshire

Key birds: *Spring/summer*: Swallow, Sand Martin, House Martin, Kingfisher. *Winter*: Snipe, Water Rail, wildfowl, geese.
Contact: Wildlife Trust HQ, 193 Abbey Foregate, Shrewsbury, Shropshire SY2 6AH. 01743 284 280 Fax 01743 284 281.

5. WOOD LANE

Shropshire Wildlife Trust.
Location: SJ 421 331. Turn off A528 at Spurnhill, 1 mile SE of Ellesmere.
Access: Open at all times.
Facilities: Car parks clearly signed. Hides (access by permit).
Public transport: None.
Habitat: Gravel pit.
Key birds: *Summer*: Breeding Sand Martins. Popular staging post for waders (inc. Redshank, Greenshank, Ruff, Dunlin, Little Stint, Green and Wood Sandpiper). *Winter*: Lapwing and Curlew.
Contact: 193 Abbey Foregate, Shrewsbury, Shropshire SY2 6AH. 01743 284280.
e-mail: shropshirewt@cix.co.uk
www.shropshirewildlifetrust.org.uk

OTHER SITES

(full details in previous editions)

A. Clunton Coppice
Contact: Wildlife Trust HQ, 01743 284280.

B. Granville Nature Reserve
Contact: Wildlife Trust HQ, 01743 284280.
C. Rhos Fiddle.
Contact: Wildlife Trust HQ, 01743 284 280.

Somerset

1. BRANDON HILL NATURE PARK

Bristol City Council/Avon Wildlife Trust.
Location: 578 728. The reserve is in centre of Bristol, in SW corner of Brandon Hill Park which overlooks Jacobs Wells Road. Metered parking in nearby roads - Great George Street, Berkeley Square, NCP car park on Jacobs Wells Road.
Access: Open all year. Wheelchair access from Great George Street and Berkeley Square only.
Facilities: Woodland walk, butterfly garden, picnic area.
Public transport: Travel line, 0870 6082608.
Habitat: Wildflower meadow, woodland.
Key birds: *Spring/summer*: Blackcap, other warblers. *All year*: Jay, Bullfinch, usual woodland species.
Contact: Wildlife Centre, 32 Jacobs Wells Road, Bristol, BS8 1DR. 0117 917 7270; fax 0117 929 7273. e-mail: mail@avonwildlifetrust.org.uk www.avonwildlifetrust.org.uk

2. BRIDGWATER BAY NNR

English Nature (Somerset & Gloucestershire Team).
Location: ST 270 470. Nine miles N of Bridgwater. Take J23 or 24 off M5. Turn N off A39 at Cannington.
Access: Hides open every day except Christmas Day. Permits needed for Steart Island (by boat only). Dogs on leads - grazing animals/nesting birds. Disabled access to hides by arrangement, other areas accessible.
Facilities: Car park at Steart. Footpath approx 0.5 miles to tower and hides.
Public transport: None.
Habitat: Estuary, intertidal mudflats, saltmarsh.
Key birds: *Winter:* Wildfowl and waders, birds of prey. *Spring/autumn:* Passage migrants.
Contact: Robin Prowse, Dowells Farm, Steart, Bridgwater, Somerset TA5 2PX. 01278 652426.

3. CHEW VALLEY LAKE

Avon Wildlife Trust, Bristol Water Plc.
Location: ST 570 600. Reservoir (partly a Trust reserve) between Chew Stoke and West Harptree, crossed by A368 and B3114, nine miles S of Bristol.
Access: Permit for access to hides (five at Chew, two at Blagdon). Best roadside viewing from causeways at Herriott's Bridge (nature reserve) and Herons Green Bay. Day, half-year and year permits from Bristol Water, Recreation Department, Woodford Lodge, Chew Stoke, Bristol BS18 8SH. Tel/fax 01275 332339.
Facilities: Hides.
Public transport: Travel line, 0870 6082608.
Habitat: Reservoir.
Key birds: *Autumn/winter*: Concentrations of wildfowl (inc. Bewick's Swan, Goldeneye, Smew, Ruddy Duck), gull roost (inc. regular Mediterranean, occasional Ring-billed). Migrant waders and terns (inc. Black). Recent rarities inc. Blue-winged Teal, Spoonbill, Alpine Swift, Citrine Wagtail, Little Bunting, Ring-necked Duck, Kumlien's Gull.
Contact: Wildlife Centre, 32 Jacobs Wells Road, Bristol, BS8 1DR. 0117 917 7270; fax 0117 929 7273. e-mail: mail@avonwildlifetrust.org.uk www.avonwildlifetrust.org.uk

4. HORNER WOOD NATURE RESERVE

Somerset Wildlife Trust.
Location: From Minehead, take A39 W to a minor road 0.8km E of Porlock signed to Horner. Park in village car park.
Access: Open all year.
Facilities: None.
Public transport: Bus: Porlock.
Habitat: Oak woodland, moorland.
Key birds: *Spring/summer*: Wood Warbler, Pied Flycatcher, Redstart, Stonechat, Whinchat, Tree

Pipit, Dartford Warbler possible. *All year*: Dipper, Grey Wagtail, woodpeckers, Buzzard, Sparrowhawk.
Contact: Somerset Wildlife Trust, Fyne Court, Broomfield, Bridgewater, Somerset TA5 2EQ. 01823 451587. e-mail: somwt@cix.co.uk

5. LEIGH WOODS

National Trust (Bristol).
Location: ST 560 736. Two miles W from centre of Bristol. Pedestrian access from North Road, Leigh Woods or via Forestry Commission car park at end of Coronation Avenue, Abbots Leigh. Access to both roads is from A369 which goes from Bristol to J19 of M5.
Access: Open all year. A good network of paths around the plateau. The paths down to the towpath are steep and uneven.
Facilities: Two waymarked trails from Forestry Commission car park: purple trail (1.75 miles) on level ground, red trail (2.5 miles) more undulating.
Public transport: Bristol-Portishead. Bus service (358/658 and 359/659) goes along A369. Leaves Bristol generally at 20 and 50 minutes past the hour. More details from First Badgerline. Tel: 0117 955 3231.
Habitat: Ancient woodland, former wood pasture, two grassland areas, calcareous grassland and scree by towpath.
Key birds: *Summer:* Peregrine, Blackcap, Chiffchaff, Spotted Flycatcher. *Winter:* Great Spotted and Green Woodpeckers, Song Thrush, Long-tailed, Marsh and common tits.
Contact: Bill Morris, Reserve Office, Valley Road, Leigh Woods, Bristol, 01936 429336. e-mail: wlwbgm@smtp.ntrust.org.uk

6. SHAPWICK HEATH NNR

English Nature (Somerset & Gloucester Team).
Location: Situated between Shapwick and Westhay, near Glastonbury. The nearest car park to site is at Willows garden centre, in Westhay.
Access: Open all year. Disabled access to displays, hides.
Facilities: Network of paths, hides. Toilets, leaflets and refreshments available at the garden centre.
Public transport: None.
Habitat: Traditionally managed herb-rich grassland, ferny wet woodland, fen, scrub, ditches, open water, reedswamp and reedbed.
Key birds: *All year*: Ducks, waders.
Contact: English Nature, Roughmoor, Bishop's Hull, Taunton, Somerset, TA1 5AA. 01823 283211. e-mail: somerset@english-nature.org.uk

7. WALBOROUGH

Avon Wildlife Trust.
Location: ST 315 579. On S edge of Weston-super-Mare at mouth of River Axe.
Access: Access from Uphill boatyard. Special access trail suitable for less able visitors.
Facilities: None.
Public transport: Travel line, 0870 6082608.
Habitat: Limestone grassland, scrub, saltmarsh, estuary.
Key birds: The Axe Estuary holds good numbers of migrant and wintering wildfowl (inc. Teal, Shelduck) and waders (inc. Black-tailed Godwit, Lapwing, Golden Plover, Dunlin, Redshank). Other migrants inc. Little Stint, Curlew Sandpiper, Ruff. Little Egret occurs each year, mostly in late summer.
Contact: Avon Wildlife Trust, Wildlife Centre, 32

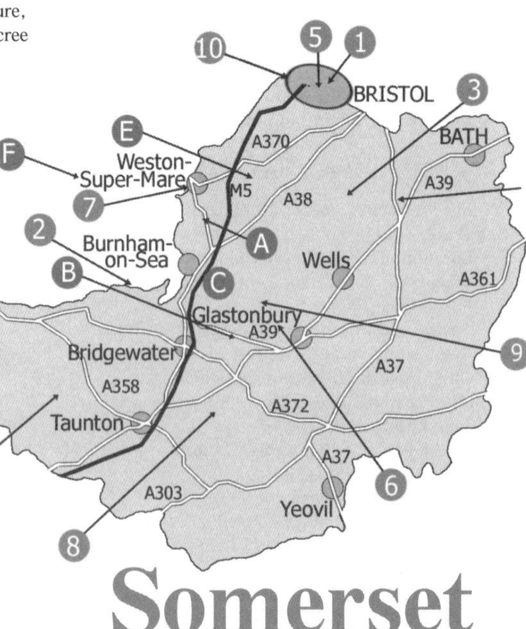

Jacobs Wells Road, Bristol, BS8 1DR. 0117 917 7270; fax 0117 929 7273.
e-mail: mail@avonwildlifetrust.org.uk

8. WEST SEDGEMOOR

RSPB (South West England Office).
Location: ST 361 238. Entrance down by-road off A378 Taunton-Langport road, one mile E of Fivehead.
Access: Access at all times to woodland car park and both hides.
Facilities: Heronry hide, two nature trails and moorland hide.
Public transport: Bus from Taunton to Fivehead.
Habitat: Semi-natural ancient oak woodland and wet grassland. Part of the Somerset Levels and Moors.
Key birds: *Spring/summer*: Breeding Grey Heron, Curlew, Lapwing, Redshank, Snipe, Buzzard, Sedge Warbler, Nightingale. Passage Whimbrel and Hobby. *Winter*: Large flocks of waders and wildfowl (including Lapwing, Golden Plover, Shoveler, Teal and Wigeon).
Contact: The Warden, Dewlands Farm, Redhill, Curry Rivel, Langport, Somerset TA10 0PH. 01458 252805, fax 01458 252184.
e-mail: sally.brown@rspb.org.uk
www.rspb.org.uk

9. WESTHAY MOOR NNR

Somerset Wildlife Trust.
Location: ST 458 438. From Glastonbury, take B3151 to site approx one mile NW of Westhay village on minor road to Godney.
Access: Open at all times.
Facilities: Hides and viewing screens, no toilets. Hides have disabled access.
Public transport: None.
Habitat: Open water and reedbeds.
Key birds: *Winter*: Bittern and wildfowl, Red-breasted Merganser, Water Rail, Goosander. *Summer*: Hobby, Reed, Sedge and Cetti's Warblers, Whitethroat.
Contact: David Reid, SWT, Fyne Court, Broomfield, Bridgwater, Somerset TA5 2EQ. 01823 451587.

10. WILLSBRIDGE MILL

Avon Wildlife Trust.
Location: ST 665 708. Turn N off A431 at Longwell Green along Long Beach Road, park after quarter mile in car park overlooking valley.
Access: Unrestricted access
Facilities: Heritage sculpture trail, owl prowls and bird ID days. Ring for details.
Public transport: 332 bus, hourly service Bristol/ Bath. 45 bus Bristol/Park Estate every 20 mins.
Habitat: Broadleaved woodland, grassland, scrub, stream, pond.
Key birds: High densities of birds of woodland and scrub. *Winter*: Kingfisher and Dipper regular.
Contact: Ruth Worsley, Avon Wildlife Trust, Willsbridge Mill, Willsbridge Hill, Bristol BS30 6EX. 0117 932 6885. www.avonwildlifetrust.co.uk
e-mail: mail@avonwildlifetrust.co.uk

OTHER SITES

(full details in previous editions)

A. Brean Down
Contact: The National Trust, 01934 844518.
B. Catcott Lows
Contact: Somerset Wildlife Trust, 01823 451587.
C. Hankridge Farm
Contact: Somerset Wildlife Trust, 01823 451587.
D. Langford Heathfield
Contact: Somerset Wildlife Trust, 01823 451587.
E. Puxton Moor. Contact
Avon Wildlife Trust, 0117 917 7270.
F. Steep Holm Island
Contact: Mrs Joan Rendell, Stonedale, 11 Fairfield Close, Milton, Weston-super-Mare BS22 8EA. 01934 632307.
G. Stephen's Vale
Contact: Avon Wildlife Trust, 0117 917 7270.

Staffordshire

1. ALLIMORE GREEN COMMON

Staffordshire Wildlife Trust.
Location: SJ 858 193. From the A518 Stafford/Newport road in Haughton take a minor road S to Church Eaton. Follow the road for about one mile to the reserve, which is on the L just before Allimore Green. Roadside parking only. Please park with care and consideration.
Access: Open all year. Access is via a stile at the N end of the Common by the road. Groups of more than eight people require a permit available from the Trust.
Facilities: Interpretation board.
Public transport: None.
Habitat: Woodland, scrub, wet pasture, ditch.
Key birds: *Spring/summer*: Whitethroat, Willow Tit, Willow Warbler. *Winter*: Siskin.
Contact: Wildlife Trust HQ, The Wolseley Centre, Wolseley Bridge, Stafford ST17 0WT. 01889 880100. e-mail: staffswt@cix.co.uk www.staffs-wildlife.org.uk

2. BLACK BROOK

Staffordshire Wildlife Trust.
Location: SK 020 645. N of Leek, W of A53. West of road from Royal Cottage to Gib Tor.
Access: Access is via public footpath from Gib Tor to Newstone Farm; this first passes through a conifer plantation which is outside the reserve.
Facilities: None.
Public transport: None.
Habitat: Heather and bilberry moorland, and upland acidic grassland.
Key birds: Merlin, Kestrel, Red Grouse, Golden Plover, Snipe, Curlew, Dipper, Wheatear, Whinchat, Twite.
Contact: Wildlife Trust HQ, The Wolseley Centre, Wolseley Bridge, Stafford ST17 0WT. 01889 880100. e-mail: staffswt@cix.co.uk

3. BRANSTON WATER PARK

East Staffordshire Borough Council.
Location: SK 217 207. Follow the brown tourist sign from the A38 N. No access from the S - head to the Barton-under-Needwood exit and return N. The park is 0.5 miles S of the A5121 Burton-upon-Trent exit.
Access: Open all year. Paths flat and generally dry.
Facilities: Toilets, picnic benches.
Public transport: None.
Habitat: Reedbed, willow carr woodland, scrub.
Key birds: *Spring/summer*: Reed Warbler, Cuckoo, Reed Bunting. Important roost for Swallow and Sand Martin. *Winter*: Waders, Little Ringed Plover occasionally, Pied Wagtail roost.
Contact: East Staffordshire Borough Council, Midland Grain Warehouse, Derby Street, Burton-on-Trent, Staffordshire DE14 2JJ. 01283 508573; (Fax) 01283 508571.

4. BROWN END QUARRY

Staffordshire Wildlife Trust/North Staffordshire Group of the Geologists' Association.
Location: SK 090 502. Reserve is at E end of Waterhouses on the A523 Leek-Ashbourne road. The Quarry is on the N side of the road just W of the Manifold Cycle Track.
Access: Open all year. Access to the parking area is over a bridge shared with a cycle hire company.
Facilities: Interpretative trail.
Public transport: None.
Habitat: Scrub, limestone.
Key birds: *Spring/summer*: warblers.
Contact: The Wolseley Centre, Wolseley Bridge, Stafford ST17 0WT. 01889 880100. e-mail: staffswt@cix.co.uk www.staffs-wildlife.org.uk

5. BURNT WOOD

Staffordshire Wildlife Trust.
Location: SJ 736 355. From Newcastle on A53 to Market Drayton. When the main road crosses B5026 turn into Kestrel Drive and then Pheasant Drive. Access also possible from B5026 Eccleshall Road 0.3 miles from A53. Parking is difficult for this reserve.
Access: Open all year.
Facilities: None.
Public transport: None.
Habitat: Ancient oak woodland, pond.
Key birds: *All year*: Goshawk, Raven, Woodcock, all three woodpeckers. Good for butterflies and moths, adder, grass snake, slow worm and common lizard
Contact: Wildlife Trust HQ, 01889 880100.

6. COOMBES VALLEY

RSPB (North West England Office).
Location: SK 005 530. Four miles from Leek along A523 between Leek and Ashbourne and 0.5 miles down unclassified road - signposted.
Access: No dogs allowed. Most of the trails are unsuitable for disabled. Open daily – no charge. Coach groups welcome by prior arrangement.
Facilities: Visitor centre, toilets, two miles of nature trail, one hide.
Public transport: None.
Habitat: Sessile oak woodland, unimproved pasture and meadow.
Key birds: *Spring:* Pied Flycatcher, Redstart, Wood Warbler. *Jan-Mar*: Displaying birds of prey.
Contact: Nick Chambers, Six Oaks Farm, Bradnop, Leek, Staffs ST13 7EU. 01538 384017. www.RSPB.org.uk

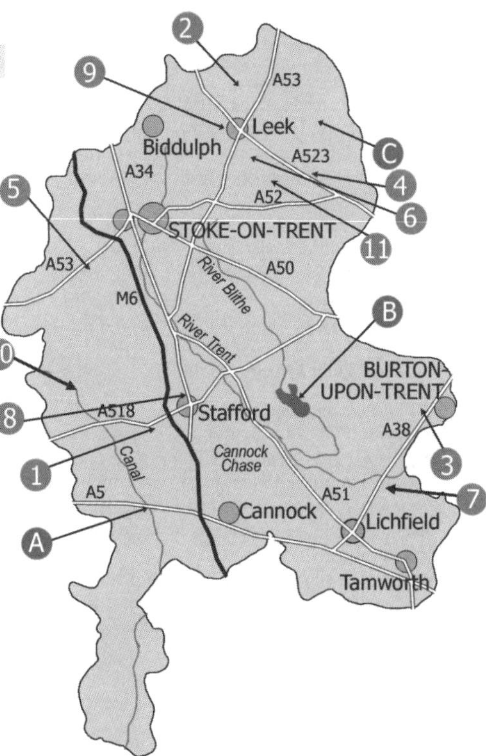

7.CROXALL LAKES

Staffordshire Wildlife Trust.
Location: SK 188 139. From Rugeley follow the A 513 passing through Kings Bromley and Alrewas. Continue along this road passing over the A38. After approx one mile, you will pass over the River Tame, which forms the W boundary of the reserve. The entrance to the reserve is the second track on the L.
Access: Open all year. Gravel track to the N of the reserve.
Facilities: Interpretation boards, two bird hides, parking and access to be improved.
Public transport: None.
Habitat: Two lakes, wader scrapes, pools, floodplain grassland.
Key birds: *Winter*: Teal, Wigeon, Smew. *Spring/ summer*: Breeding Lapwing, Redshank, Little Ringed Plover, Oystercatcher.
Contact: Wildlife Trust HQ, The Wolseley Centre, Wolseley Bridge, Stafford ST17 0WT. 01889 880100. e-mail: staffswt@cix.co.uk www.staffs-wildlife.org.uk

8. DOXEY MARSHES

Staffordshire Wildlife Trust.
Location: SJ 903 250. In Stafford. Parking 0.25 miles off M6 J14/A5013 or walk from town centre.
Access: Open at all times. Dogs on leads. Disabled access being improved. Coach parking off Wooton Drive.
Facilities: One hide, three viewing platforms, two are accessible to wheelchairs.
Public transport: Walk from town centre via Sainsbury's.
Habitat: Marsh, pools, reedbeds, hedgerows, reed sweet-grass swamp.
Key birds: *Spring/summer*: Breeding Snipe, Lapwing, Redshank, warblers, buntings, Sky Lark, Water Rail. *Winter*: Snipe, wildfowl, thrushes, Short-eared Owl. Passage waders, vagrants.
Contact: Wildlife Trust HQ, The Wolseley Centre, Wolseley Bridge, Stafford ST17 0WT. 01889 880100. e-mail: staffswt@cix.co.uk www.staffs-wildlife.org.uk

9. LONGSDON WOODS

Staffordshire Moorlands District Council
Location: SK 965 555. Part of Ladderedge Country Park. Reserve lies off A53 Leek road. Can be approached from Ladderedge near Leek; City Lane, Longsdon; or Rudyard Station.
Access: Public rights of way only.

Facilities: None.
Public transport: None.
Habitat: Woodland and wet grassland.
Key birds: Heronry, Sparrowhawk, Curlew, Snipe, Jack Snipe, Woodcock, Little and Tawny Owls, all three woodpeckers, Redstart, Blackcap, Garden Warbler.
Contact: Countryside Service, Staffordshire Moorlands District Council, Moorlands House, Stockwell Street, Leek, Staffordshire ST13 6HQ. 01538 483577.
e-mail: countryside@staffsmoorlands.gov.uk

10.LOYNTON MOSS

Staffordshire Wildlife Trust.
Location: SJ 789 243. Go through Woodseaves on the A519 towards Newport. Within a mile you will cross the Shropshire Union Canal, which forms the E boundary of the reserve. Approx 200m past the canal on the R is the entrance to the reserve into a small car park.
Access: Open all year. Bridle path and permissive paths throughout reserve. Some paths inaccessible during the winter months.
Facilities: None.
Public transport: None.
Habitat: Fen, woodland mire, willow/alder carr, secondary woodland, wet pasture.
Key birds: *Spring/summer*: Sky Lark, Lapwing, Marsh Tit, Willow Tit, Sedge Warbler, Greater and Lesser Spotted Woodpeckers, Woodcock.
Contact: Wildlife Trust HQ, 01889 880100.

11. SWINEHOLES WOOD

Staffordshire Wildlife Trust.
Location: SK 046 503. From Ipstones take the B5053 N for 0.75 miles to a crossroads. Turn R up a minor road for 1.25 miles to a radio mast where there is a small lay-by on the R opposite the reserve. Please park carefully.
Access: Open all year. Tussocky ground so walking can be difficult.
Facilities: None.
Public transport: None.
Habitat: Lowland heath, upland moorland, woodland.
Key birds: *Spring/summer*: Roding Woodcock at dawn and dusk. *All year*: Good range of woodland birds.
Contact: Wildlife Trust HQ, 01889 880100.

OTHER SITES

(full details in previous editions)

A. Belvide Reservoir
Contact: Miss M Surman, 6 Lloyd Square, 12 Niall Close, Edgbaston, Birmingham B15 3LX.
www.westmidlandbirdclub.com/belvide

B. Blithfield Reservoir
Contact: As Belvide Reservoir above.

C. Castern Wood
Contact: Wildlife Trust HQ, 01889 880100.

Suffolk

1. CARLTON MARSHES

Suffolk Wildlife Trust.
Location: TM 508 920. SW of Lowestoft, at W end of Oulton Broad. Take A146 towards Beccles and turn R after Tesco garage.
Access: Open during daylight hours. Keep to marked paths. Dogs only allowed in some areas, on leads at all times. Car park suitable for coaches.
Facilities: Information centre and shop. Snacks available.
Public transport: Bus and train in walking distance.
Habitat: 100 acres of grazing marsh, peat pools and fen.
Key birds: Wide range of wetland and Broadland birds, including Marsh Harrier.
Contact: Catriona Finlayson, Suffolk Broads Wildlife Centre, Carlton Colville, Lowestoft, Suffolk NR33 8HU. 01502 564250.
www.wildlifetrust.org.uk/suffolk

2. DINGLE MARSHES, DUNWICH

Suffolk Wildlife Trust/RSPB.
Location: TM 48 07 20. Eight miles from Saxmundham. Follow brown signs from A12 to Minsmere and continue to Dunwich. Forest carpark (hide) – TM 46 77 10. Beach carpark – TM 479 707. The reserve forms part of the Suffolk Coast NNR.
Access: Open at all times. Access via public rights

of way and permissive path along beach. Dogs on lead please. Coaches can park on beach car park.
Facilities: Toilets at beach car park, Dunwich. Hide in Dunwich Forest overlooking reedbed, accessed via Forest car park. Circular trail waymarked from carpark.
Public transport: None.
Habitat: Grazing marsh, reedbed, shingle beach and saline lagoons
Key birds: *All year*: In reedbed, Bittern, Marsh Harrier, Bearded Tit. *Winter*: Hen Harrier, White-fronted Goose, Wigeon, Snipe, Teal on grazing marsh. *Summer*: Lapwing, Avocet, Snipe, Black-tailed Godwit, Hobby. Good for passage waders.
Contact: Alan Miller, Suffolk Wildlife Trust, 9 Valley Terrace, Valley Road, Leiston, Suffolk IP16 4AP. 01728 833405.
e-mail: alanm@suffolkwildife.cix.co.uk

3. HAVERGATE ISLAND

RSPB (East Anglia Office).
Location: TM 425 496. Part of the Orfordness NNR at the mouth of the River Alde. Orford is 17km NE Woodbridge, signposted off the A12.
Access: Open Apr-Aug (1st & 3rd weekends and every Thu), Sep-Mar (1st Sat every month). Book in advance through Minsmere RSPB visitor centre, tel 01728 648281. Park in Orford at the large pay and display car park next to the quay.
Facilities: Toilets, picnic area, five birdwatching hides, viewing platform, visitor trail (approx 2km).
Public transport: Boat trips from Orford (one mile)
Habitat: Shallow brackish water, lagoons with islands, saltmarsh, shingle beaches.
Key birds: *Summer*: Breeding Arctic, Common and Sandwich Terns, migrants. Leading site for Avocet. *Winter*: Wildfowl and waders.
Contact: Ian Paradine, Manager, RSPB, c/o Friends Garage, Front Street, Orford, Suffolk IP12 2LD. 01394 450732.

4. HAZELWOOD MARSHES

Suffolk Wildlife Trust.
Location: TM 435 575. Four miles W of Aldeburgh. Small car park on A1094. Mile walk down sandy track.
Access: Open dawn to dusk.
Facilities: Hide.
Public transport: Call Trust for advice.
Habitat: Estuary, marshes.
Key birds: Marshland and estuary birds; spring and autumn migrants.
Contact: Brook House, The Green, Ashbocking, Ipswich, Suffolk IP6 9JY. 01473 890089.
e-mail: info@suffolkwildlife.cix.co.uk

5. LACKFORD LAKES

Suffolk Wildlife Trust.
Location: TL 803 708. Via track off N side of A1101 (Bury St Edmunds to Mildenhall road), between Lackford and Flempton. Five miles from Bury.
Access: New reserve centre open winter (10am-4pm), summer (10am-5pm) Wed to Sun, (closed Mon and Tues). Tea and coffee facilities, toilets.
Facilities: New visitor centre with viewing area upstairs. Tea and coffee facilities, toilets. Eight hides. Coaches should pre-book.
Public transport: None.
Habitat: Restored gravel pit with open water, lagoons, islands, willow scrub.
Key birds: *Winter*: Bittern, Water Rail, Bearded Tit. Large gull roost. Wide range of waders and

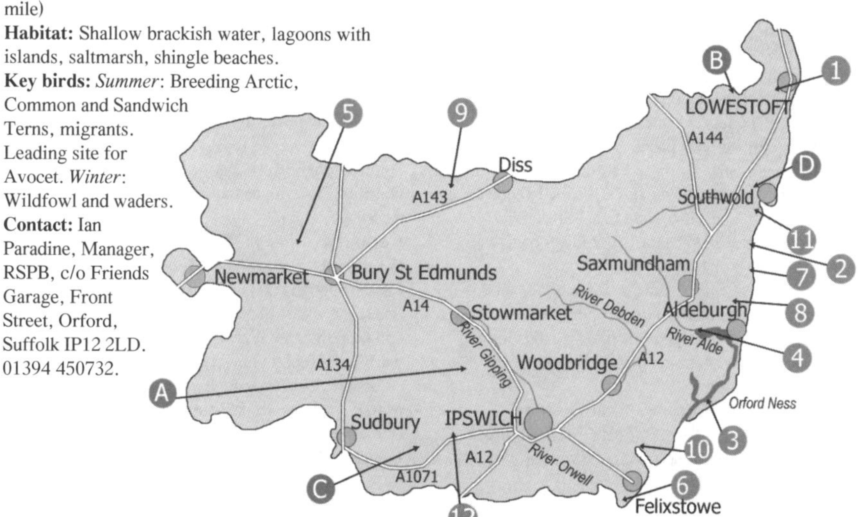

wildfowl (inc. Goosander, Pochard, Tufted Duck, Shoveler. *Spring/autumn*: Migrants, inc. raptors. Breeding Shelduck, Little Ringed Plover and reed warblers.
Contact: Joe Davis, Lackford Lakes Visitor Centre, Lackford, Bury St Edmunds, Suffolk IP28 6HX. 01284 728706.
e-mail: suffolkwildlife@cix.co.uk

6. LANDGUARD BIRD OBSERVATORY

Location: TM 283 317. Road S of Felixstowe to Landguard Nature Reserve and Fort.
Access: Visiting by appointment.
Facilities: Migration watch point and ringing station.
Public transport: Call for advice.
Habitat: Close grazed turf, raised banks with holm oak, tamarisk, etc.
Key birds: Unusual species and common migrants. Seabirds.
Contact: Paul Holmes, Landguard Bird Observatory, View Point Road, Felixstowe, Suffolk IP11 8TW. Ms J Cawston 01473 748463.

7. MINSMERE

RSPB (Eastern England Regional Office)
Location: TM 452 680. Six miles NE of Saxmundham. From A12 head for Westleton, N of Yoxford. Access from Westleton (follow the brown tourist signs).
Access: Open every day, except Tues, Christmas Day and Boxing Day (9am-9pm or dusk if earlier). Visitor centre open 9am-5pm (9am-4pm Nov-Jan). Tea-room 10.30am-4.30pm (10am-4pm Nov-Jan). Free to RSPB members, otherwise £5 adults, £1.50 children, £3 concession. Max two coaches per day (not Bank Holiday weekends).
Facilities: Toilets, visitor centre, hides, nature trails, family activity packs.
Public transport: Train to Saxmundham then taxi.
Habitat: Woodland, wetland – reedbed and grazing marsh, heathland, dunes and beach, farmland – arable conversion to heath, coastal lagoons, 'the scrape'.
Key birds: *Summer*: Avocet, Bittern, Marsh Harrier, Bearded Tit, Redstart, Nightingale, Nightjar. *Winter*: Wigeon, White-fronted Goose, Bewick's Swan. *Autumn/spring*: Passage migrants, waders etc.
Contact: RSPB Minsmere Nature Reserve, Saxmundham, Suffolk IP17 3BY. 01728 648281.
e-mail: minsmere@rspb.org.uk www.rspb.org.uk

8. NORTH WARREN & ALDRINGHAM WALKS

RSPB (East Anglia Office).
Location: TM 468 575. Directly N of Aldeburgh on Suffolk coast. Use main car park on beach.
Access: Open at all times. Please keep dogs under close control. Beach area suitable for disabled.
Facilities: Three nature trails, leaflet available from TIC Aldeburgh or Minsmere RSPB. Toilets in Aldeburgh and Thorpeness.
Public transport: Bus service to Aldeburgh. First Eastern Counties (08456 020121).
Habitat: Grazing marsh, lowland heath, reedbed, woodland.
Key birds: *Winter*: White-fronted Goose, Tundra Bean Goose, Wigeon, Shoveler, Teal, Gadwall, Pintail, Snow Bunting. *Spring/summer*: Breeding Bittern, Garganey, Marsh Harrier, Hobby, Nightjar, Wood Lark, Nightingale, Dartford Warbler.
Contact: Dave Thurlow, 1 Ness House Cottages, Sizewell, Leiston, Suffolk IP16 4UB. 01728 832719. e-mail: dave.thurlow@rspb.org.uk

9. REDGRAVE AND LOPHAM FENS

Suffolk Wildlife Trust.
Location: TM 05 07 97. Five miles from Diss, signposted and easily accessed from A1066 and A143 roads.
Access: Open all year, dogs strictly on leads only. Visitor centre open all year at weekends, call for details on 01379 688333
Facilities: Visitor centre with coffee shop, toilets, including disabled toilets, car park with coach space, disabled/wheelchair accessible boardwalk and viewing platform. Other general circular trails (not wheelchair access).
Public transport: Buses and trains to Diss town – Simonds coaches to local villages of Redgrave and South Lopham from Diss.
Habitat: Calcareous fen, wet acid heath, scrub and woodland
Key birds: *All year*: Water Rail, Snipe, Teal, Woodcock, Sparrowhawk, Kestrel, Great Spotted, Lesser Spotted and Green Woodpeckers, Tawny and Little Owls, Shelduck. *Summer*: Reed, Sedge and Grasshopper Warblers, other leaf and *Sylvia* warblers, Hobby plus large Swallow and Starling roosts. *Winter/ occasionals passage*: Bearded Tit, Marsh Harrier, Greenshank, Green Sandpiper, Gadwall, Pintail, Garganey, Jack Snipe, Bittern.
Contact: Andrew Excell, Low Common Road,

South Lopham, Diss, Norfolk IP22 2HX. 01379 687618.
e-mail: redgrave@suffolkwildlife.cix.co.uk

10. TRIMLEY MARSHES

Suffolk Wildlife Trust.
Location: TM 260 352. Main Road A14 – Felixstowe two miles – Ipswich ten miles. Parking at top of Cordy's Lane, Trimley St Mary two miles from reserve.
Access: Reserve open at all times. Visitor centre open at weekends. Dogs on lead. Best time to visit – all year.
Facilities: Visitor centre, toilets (open at weekends), five hides.
Public transport: Train station at Trimley (Station Road/Cordy's Lane).
Habitat: Wetland (84 hectares).
Key birds: *Summer:* Avocet, Marsh Harrier, Redshank, Garganey, etc. *Passage*: Curlew Sandpiper, Wood Sandpiper. *Winter:* Wildfowl, Spoonbill, Little Egret.
Contact: Mick Wright, 15 Avondale Road, Ipswich, Suffolk IP3 9JT. 01473 710032.
e-mail: micktwright@btinternet.com

11. WALBERSWICK

English Nature (Suffolk Team).
Location: TM 475 733. Good views from B1387 and from lane running W from Walberswick towards Westwood Lodge; elsewhere keep to public footpaths or shingle beach.
Access: Parties and coach parking by prior arrangement.
Facilities: Hide on S side of Blyth estuary, E of A12.
Public transport: Call for advice.
Habitat: Tidal estuary, fen, freshwater marsh and reedbeds, heath, mixed woodland, carr.
Key birds: *Spring/summer*: Marsh Harrier, Bearded Tit, Water Rail, Bittern, Nightjar. *Passage/winter*: Wildfowl, waders and raptors.
Contact: Adam Burrows, English Nature, Regent House, 110 Northgate Street, Bury St Edmunds IP33 1HP. 01502 676171.

12. WOLVES WOOD RSPB RESERVE

RSPB (East Anglia Office).
Location: Two miles E of Hadleigh on the A1071 to Ipswich.
Access: Open all year. Wellington boots advisable between Sept-May. Charge for non-members.
Facilities: Car park for fifteen cars (no coaches), group bookings, guided walks and special events, no dogs except guide dogs.
Public transport: Bus: Hadleigh (two miles). Train: nearest station Ipswich.
Habitat: Ancient woodland.
Key birds: *Spring/summer*: Nightingale, usual woodland species.
Contact: Mark Nowers, Warden, RSPB, Unit 3, Court Farm, 3 Stutton Road, Brantham, Ipswich, Suffolk C11 1PW. 01473 328006.
e-mail: mark.nowers@rspb.org.uk

OTHER SITES
(full details in previous editions)

A. Bonny Wood
Contact: Suffolk Wildlife Trust, 01473 890089.
B. Castle Marshes
Contact: Suffolk Wildlife Trust, 01473 890089.
C. Groton Wood LNR
Contact: Suffolk Wildlife Trust, 01473 890089.
D. Hen Reedbed NNR
Contact: Suffolk Wildlife Trust, 01473 890089.

Surrey

1. FRENSHAM COMMON

Waverley BC and National Trust.
Location: SU 855 405. Common lies on either side of A287 between Farnham and Hindhead.
Access: Open at all times. Car park (locked 9pm-9am). Keep to paths.
Facilities: Information rooms, toilets and refreshment kiosk at Great Pond.
Public transport: Call Trust for advice.
Habitat: Dry and humid heath, woodland, two large ponds, reedbeds.
Key birds: *Summer*: Dartford Warbler, Wood Lark, Hobby, Nightjar, Stonechat. *Winter*: Wildfowl (inc. occasional Smew), Bittern, Great Grey Shrike.
Contact: Mike Coates, Rangers Office, Bacon Lane, Churt, Surrey GU10 2QB. 01252 792416.

2. LIGHTWATER COUNTRY PARK

Surrey County Council.
Location: SU 921 622. From J3 of M3, take the A322 and follow brown Country Park signs. From the Guildford Road in Lightwater, turn into The Avenue. Entrance to the park is at the bottom of the road.
Access: Open all year dawn-dusk.
Facilities: Car park, visitor centre open most days during summer, toilets, leaflets.
Public transport: Train: Bagshot two miles. Tel 08457 484950. Bus: No 34 from Woking, Guildford and Camberley. Tel: 08706 082608.
Habitat: Reclaimed gravel quarries. Heath, woodland, bog.
Key birds: *Summer*: Dartford Warbler, Stonechat, Wood Lark, Tree Pipit, Hobby, Nightjar, all three woodpeckers. *Autumn*: Ring Ouzel, Crossbill, Siskin, Fieldfare, Redwing, possible Woodcock.
Contact: County Hall, Penrhyn Road, Kingston-upon-Thames, Surrey KT1 2DN. 08456 009 009. www.surreycc.gov.uk

3. RIVERSIDE PARK, GUILDFORD

Guildford Borough Council.
Location: TQ 005515 (Guildford BC). From car park at Bowers Lane, Burpham (TQ 011 527). Three miles from town centre.
Access: Open at all times. Follow marked paths. Access to far side of lake and marshland area via boardwalk.
Facilities: Boardwalk.
Public transport: Guildford town centre to Burpham (Sainsburys) No 36 Bus (Arriva timetable information. Tel 0870 608 2608).
Habitat: Wetland, lake, meadow, woodland.
Key birds: *Summer*: Sedge, Reed and Garden Warblers, Common Tern, Lesser Whitethroat, Hobby. *Winter*: Jack Snipe, Chiffchaff, Water Rail. *Passage*: Common Sandpiper, Whinchat, Water Pipit (up to 12 most years).
Contact: Parks Helpdesk, Millmead House, Millmead, Guildford, Surrey GO2 5BB. 01483 444715. e-mail: parks@guildford.gov.uk www.guildfordborough.co.uk

4. ROWHILL COPSE LNR

Rushmoor Borough Council/Rowhill Nature Reserve Society.
Location: SU 853 497. In either direction from Farnham or Farnborough along the A325 towards Aldershot, until you come to a mini-roundabout which will be the junction with Cranmore Lane. Turn down Cranmore Lane and take the 1st R after the central bollards. Park in the car park.
Access: Open all year.
Facilities: Footpaths around the site, visitor centre open Sunday afternoons, Blackwater Valley long-distance path runs through site.
Public transport: None.
Habitat: Heathland, alder carr, ponds.
Key birds: *All year*: All three woodpeckers, Grey Heron, Kingfisher.
Contact: Blackwater Valley Countryside Partnership, Ash Lock Cottage, Government Road, Aldershot, Hampshire GU11 2PS. 01252 331353 . e-mail: blackwater-valley@hants.gov.uk

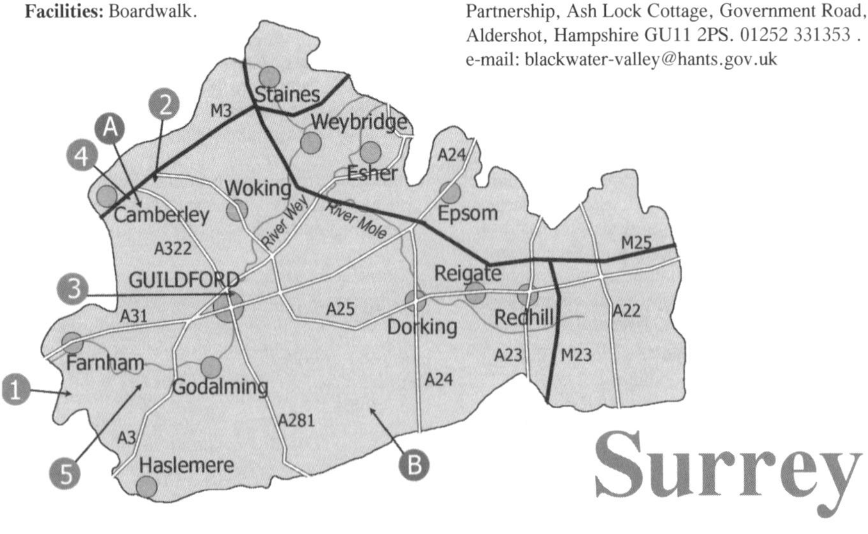

Surrey

5. THURSLEY COMMON

English Nature (Sussex & Surrey Team).
Location: SU 900 417. From Guildford, take A3 SW to B3001 (Elstead/Churt road). Use the Moat car park.
Access: Open access. Parties must obtain prior permission.
Facilities: Boardwalk in wetter areas.
Public transport: None.
Habitat: Wet and dry heathland, woodland, bog.
Key birds: *Winter*: Hen Harrier and Great Grey Shrike. *Summer*: Hobby, Wood Lark, Dartford Warbler, Stonechat, Curlew, Snipe, Nightjar.
Contact: Simon Nobes, Uplands Stud, Brook, Godalming, Surrey GU8 5LA. 01428 685878.

OTHER SITES

(full details in previous editions)

A. Brentmoor Heath LNR
Contact: Surrey Wildlife Trust, 01483 795440.
B. Wallis Wood LNR
Contact: Surrey Wildlife Trust, 01483 795440.

Sussex, East

1. BEWL WATER

Sussex Wildlife Trust/Southern Water.
Location: TQ 674 320. On B2099 coming from Tilehurst to Wadhurst.
Access: Open all year.
Facilities: Car park, hide. Footpath round reservoir. Southern Water have a Visitor Centre on the N side but the reserve cannot be viewed from there. Call 01892 890661.
Public transport: None.
Habitat: Reservoir, woodland, plantation.
Key birds: *Spring/summer*: Chiffchaff, warblers, terns. *Passage*: Osprey, Common Sandpiper, Green Sandpiper, Greenshank, stints. *All year*: Pochard, Wigeon, Teal, Gadwall.
Contact: Sussex Wildlife Trust, Woods Mill, Shoreham Road, Henfield, West Sussex, BN5 9SD. 01273 492630. e-mail: enquiries@sussexwt.co.uk

2. LULLINGTON HEATH

English Nature (Sussex & Surrey Team).
Location: TQ 525 026. W of Eastbourne, after six miles on A259 turn N on minor road to Lullington Court for parking, then one mile up hill (bridleway).
Access: Permit only off rights of way
Facilities: None. **Public transport:** None.
Habitat: Chalk downland and heath, dense woodland scrub and areas of gorse.
Key birds: *Summer*: Breeding Nightingale, Nightjar and Grasshopper Warbler, Turtle Dove. *Winter*: Raptors (inc. Hen Harrier), Woodcock.
Contact: Malcolm Emery, English Nature, Phoenix House, 33 North Street, Lewes, E Sussex BN7 2PH. 01273 476595; fax 01273 483063; e-mail: sussexsurrey@english-natureorguk

3. OLD LODGE RESERVE

Sussex Wildlife Trust.
Location: Near Crowborough. Part of Ashdown Forest.
Access: Open all year.
Facilities: Car park, public footpaths, nature trails. No dogs.
Public transport: None.
Habitat: Heather, pine woodland.
Key birds: *Spring/summer*: Nightjar, Redstart, Woodcock, Tree Pipit, Stonechat.
Contact: Woods Mill, Shoreham Road, Henfield, West Sussex BN5 9SD. 01273 492630.
e-mail: enquiries@sussexwt.org.uk

4. PEVENSEY LEVELS

English Nature (Sussex & Surrey Team).
Location: TQ 665 054. NE of Eastbourne. S of A259, one mile along minor road from Pevensey E to Norman's Bay.
Access: Good views from road.
Facilities: None.
Public transport: Call for advice.
Habitat: Freshwater grazing marsh, subject to light flooding after rains.
Key birds: *Summer*: Breeding Reed and Sedge Warblers, Yellow Wagtail, Snipe, Redshank, Lapwing. *Winter*: Large numbers of wildfowl (inc. some Bewick's and Whooper Swans) and waders (inc. Golden Plover). Birds of prey (inc. Merlin, Peregrine, Hobby, Short-eared Owl).

Sussex, East

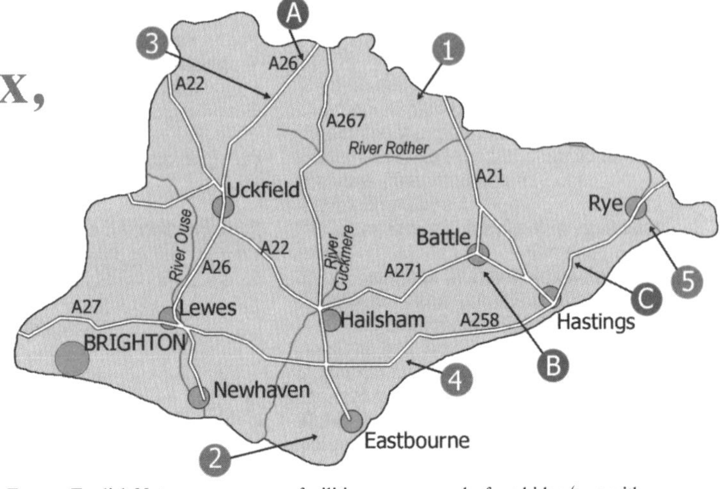

Contact: Malcolm Emery, English Nature, Phoenix House, 33 North Street, Lewes, E Sussex BN7 2PH. 01273 476595; fax 01273 483063; e-mail sussexsurrey@english-natureorguk; www.english-natureorguk.

5. RYE HARBOUR

Rye Harbour Local Nature Reserve Management Committee.

Location: TQ 941 188. One mile from Rye off A259 signed Rye Harbour. From J10 of M20 take A2070 until it joins A259.

Access: Open at all times by footpaths. Organised groups please book.

Facilities: Car park in Rye Harbour village. Information kiosk in car park. Toilets and disabled facilities near car park, four hides (two with wheelchair access, one with induction sound loop fitted), information centre open most days (10am-4pm) by volunteers.

Public transport: Train (tel: 08457 484950), bus (tel: 0870 608 2608), Rye tourist information (tel: 01797 226696).

Habitat: Sea, sand, shingle, pits and grassland.

Key birds: *Spring*: Passage waders, especially roosting Whimbrel. *Summer*: Breeding terns, waders, Wheatear, Yellow Wagtail. *Winter*: Wildfowl, Water Rail, Bittern.

Contact: Barry Yates, (Manager), 2 Watch Cottages, Winchelsea, East Sussex TN36 4LU. 01797 223862. e-mail: yates@clara.net www.naturereserve.ryeharbour.org

OTHER SITES

(full details in previous editions)

A. Eridge Rocks Reserve
Contact: Sussex Wildlife Trust, 01273 492630.

B. Fore Wood
Contact: RSPB, 01273 775333.

C. Pett Pools
Contact: Sussex Wildlife Trust, 01273 492630.

Sussex, West

1. ARUNDEL

The Wildfowl & Wetlands Trust.
Location: TQ 020 081. Clearly signposted from Arundel, just N of A27.
Access: Summer (9.30am-5.30pm) winter (9.30am-4.30pm). Closed Christmas Day. Approx 1.5 miles of level footpaths, suitable for wheelchairs. No dogs except guide dogs.
Facilities: Visitor centre, restaurant, shop, hides, picnic area, seasonal nature trails. Eye of The Wind Wildlife Gallery. Corporate hire facilities.
Public transport: Arundel station, 15-20 minute walk. Tel: 01903 882131.
Habitat: Lakes, wader scrapes, reedbed.
Key birds: *Summer*: Nesting Redshank, Lapwing, Oystercatcher, Common Tern, Sedge, Reed and Cetti's Warblers, Peregrine, Hobby. *Winter*: Teal, Wigeon, Reed Bunting, Water Rail, Cetti's Warbler and occasionally roosting Bewick's Swan.
Contact: James Sharpe, Mill Road, Arundel, West Sussex BN18 9PB. 01903 883355.
e-mail: info.arundel@wwt.org.uk

2. IPING AND STEDHAM COMMONS

Sussex Wildlife Trust/Sussex Downs Conservation Board.
Location: 2.5 miles W of Midhurst on the A272. The car park is 0.5 miles down the road to Elsted on the R. There is a height barrier to prevent tall vehicles entering.
Access: Open all year.
Facilities: Car park, paths.
Public transport: None.
Habitat: Heathland, coniferous plantations, woodland.
Key birds: *Spring/summer*: Willow Warbler, Tree Pipit Whitethroat, Yellowhammer, Turtle Dove, Nightjar, Woodcock. *Winter*: Stonechat, possible Hen Harrier, finches, Siskin, Redpoll. *All year*: Sparrowhawk, Green and Great Spotted Woodpeckers, Goldcrest, Marsh Tit.
Contact: Woods Mill, Shoreham Road, Henfield, West Sussex, BN5 9SD. 01273 492630.
e-mail: sussexwt@cix.co.uk
www.wildlifetrust.org.uk/sussex

3. PAGHAM HARBOUR

West Sussex County Council.
Location: SZ 857 966. Five miles S of Chichester on B2145 towards Selsey.
Access: Open at all times, dogs must be on leads, disabled trail with accessible hide. All groups and coach parties must book in advance.
Facilities: Visitor centre open at weekends (10am-4pm), toilets (including disabled), three hides, one nature trail.
Public transport: Bus stop by visitor centre.
Habitat: Intertidal saltmarsh, shingle beaches, lagoons and farmland.
Key birds: *Spring*: Passage migrants. *Autumn*: Passage waders, other migrants. *Winter*: Brent Goose, Slavonian Grebe, wildfowl. *All year*: Little Egret.
Contact: Sarah Patton, Pagham Harbour LNR, Selsey Road, Sidlesham, Chichester, West Sussex PO20 7NE. 01243 641508.
e-mail: pagham.nr@westsussex.gov.uk

4. PULBOROUGH BROOKS

RSPB (South East England Office).
Location: TQ 054 170. Signposted on A283 between Pulborough (via A29) and Storrington (via A24). Two miles SE of Pulborough.
Access: Open daily. Visitor centre 10am-5pm (Tea-room 4.45pm, 4pm Mon-Fri in winter), closed Christmas Day and Boxing Day. Nature trail and hides (9am-9pm or sunset), closed Christmas Day. Admission fee for nature trail (free to RSPB members). No dogs. All four hides accessible to wheelchair users, though a strong helper is needed.
Facilities: Visitor centre (incl RSPB shop, tea room with terrace, displays, toilets). Nature trail and four hides and two viewpoints. Large car park.

Play and picnic areas. A mobility buggy is available for free hire.
Public transport: Two miles from Pulborough train station. Connecting bus service regularly passes reserve entrance (not Suns). Compass Travel (01903 233767). Cycle stands.
Habitat: Lowland wet grassland (wet meadows and ditches). Hedgerows and woodland.
Key birds: *Winter*: Wintering waterbirds, Bewick's Swan. *Spring*: Breeding wading birds and songbirds (incl Lapwing and Nightingale). *Summer*: Butterflies and dragonflies, warblers. *Autumn*: Passage wading birds, Redstart, Whinchat.
Contact: Tim Callaway, Site Manager, Upperton's Barn, Wiggonholt, Pulborough, West Sussex RH20 2EL. 01798 875851.
e-mail: pulborough.brooks@rspb.org.uk

5. WARNHAM NATURE RESERVE

Horsham District Council.
Location: TQ 167 324. One mile from Horsham Town Centre. Reserve is located just off the A24 'Robin Hood' roundabout, on the B2237.
Access: Open every day throughout the year and Bank Hols (10am-6pm or dusk). Free access over part of the Reserve, small charge (day/annual permits) for some areas. No dogs allowed. Good disabled access over most of the Reserve.
Facilities: Visitor centre and café open Sat and Sun in summer, Sun only in winter. Public car park with access for coaches at request. Toilets (including disabled), two hides, reserve leaflets, a new nature trail, new bird feeding station, boardwalks, benches and hardstanding paths.
Public transport: From Horsham Railway Station it is a mile walk along Hurst Road, with a R turn onto Warnham Road. A bus from the 'Carfax' in Horsham Centre can take you to within 150 yards of the reserve. Travel line, 0870 608 2608.
Habitat: 17 acre millpond, reedbeds, marsh, meadow and woodland (deciduous and coniferous).
Key birds: Heronry, Kingfisher, Cetti's Warbler, three woodpeckers, Willow Tit, Goldcrest. *Summer*: Hirundines, Hobby, Cuckoo, Spotted Flycatcher, warblers. *Winter*: Cormorant, gulls, Little Grebe, Water Rail, Siskin, Lesser Redpoll, thrushes, waders. *Passage:* Waders, Wheatear, Whinchat, Meadow Pipit, terns.
Contact: Sam Bayley, Countryside Warden, Leisure Services, Park House Lodge, North Street, Horsham, W Sussex RH12 1RL. 01403 256890.
e-mail: sam.bayley@horsham.gov.uk

OTHER SITES

(full details in previous editions)

A. Adur Estuary
Contact: RSPB office, 01273 775333.

B. Kingley Vale
Contact: English Nature, 01243 575353.

C. Waltham Brooks
Contact: Sussex Wildlife Trust, 01273 492630.

D. Woods Mill
Contact: Sussex Wildlife Trust, 01273 492630.

Sussex, West

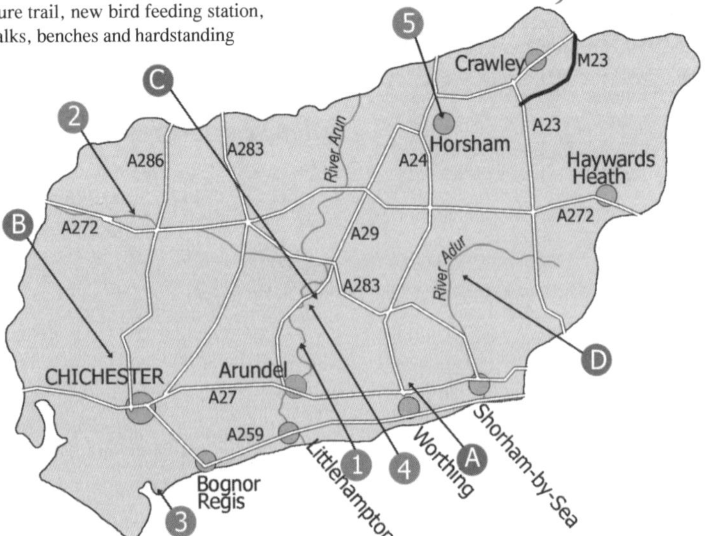

Tyne & Wear

1. BOLDON FLATS

South Tyneside Metropolitan Council.
Location: NZ 377 614. Take A184 N from Sunderland to Boldon.
Access: View from Moor Lane on minor road NE of East Boldon station towards Whitburn.
Facilities: None.
Public transport: East Boldon Metro Station is 10 minutes walk, regular bus service along Station Road (nos 30 and 34).
Habitat: Meadows, part SSSI, managed flood in winter, pond, ditches.
Key birds: *Passage/winter*: Wildfowl and waders. Gull roost may inc. Mediterranean, Glaucous, Iceland; Merlin fairly regular.
Contact: Countryside Officer, South Tyneside Metropolitan Council, Town Hall, Westoe Road, South Shields, NE33 2RL. 0191 427 1717; (Fax) 0191 455 0208. www.southtyneside.info

2. DERWENT WALK COUNTRY PARK

Gateshead Council.
Location: NZ 178 604. Along River Derwent, four miles SW of Newcastle and Gateshead. Several car parks along A694.
Access: Site open all times. Thornley visitor centre open weekends and Bank Holidays (12-5pm). Keys for hides available from Thornley Woodlands Centre (£2).
Facilities: Toilets at Thornley visitor centre. Toilets at Swalwell visitor centre. Hides at Far Pasture Ponds and Thornley feeding station.
Public transport: 45, 46, 46A, M20 and 611 buses from Newcastle/Gateshead to Swalwell/ Rowlands Gill. Bus stop Thornley Woodlands Centre. (Regular bus service from Newcastle). Information from News Travel Line. Tel: 0191 2325325.
Habitat: Mixed woodland, river, ponds, meadows.
Key birds: *Summer*: Wood Warbler, Pied Flycatcher, Green Sandpiper, Kingfisher, Dipper, Great Spotted and Green Woodpeckers, Blackcap, Garden Warbler, Nuthatch. *Winter*: Brambling, Marsh Tit, Bullfinch, Great Spotted Woodpecker, Nuthatch, Goosander, Kingfisher.
Contact: Stephen Westerberg, Thornley Woodlands Centre, Rowlands Gill, Tyne & Wear NE39 1AU. 01207 545212.
e-mail: countryside@gateshead.gov.uk
www.gatesheadbirders.co.uk

3. MARSDEN BAY/ROCK

National Trust.
Location: NZ 404 648. Off A183 Sunderland - South Shields road.
Facilities: Popular Grotto pub built into foot of mainland cliffs opposite Marsden Rock. Also cafe and shop at Souter Lighthouse.
Habitat: Cliffs and rocks.
Key birds: Significant seabird colony with nesting Fulmars, Cormorants, Herring Gulls and Kittiwakes the most numerous. Also 25-30 pairs of Razorbills.
Contact: National Trust, Souter Lighthouse Information Centre, 0191 529 3161.

4. RYTON WILLOWS

Gateshead Council.
Location: NZ 155 650. Five miles W of Newcastle. Access along several tracks running N from Ryton.
Access: Open at all times.
Facilities: Nature trail and free leaflet.
Public transport: Regular service to Ryton from Newcastle/Gateshead. Information from Nexus Travelline on 0191 232 5325.
Habitat: Deciduous woodland, scrub, riverside, tidal river.
Key birds: *Winter*: Goldeneye, Goosander, Green Woodpecker, Nuthatch, Treecreeper. *Autumn*: Greenshank. *Summer*: Lesser Whitethroat, Sedge Warbler, Yellowhammer, Linnet, Reed Bunting, Common Sandpiper.
Contact: Andrew McLay, Thornley Woodlands Centre, Rowlands Gill, Tyne & Wear NE39 1AU. 1208 545212.
e-mail: countryside@gateshead.gov.uk
www.gatesheadbirders.co.uk

5. ST MARY'S WETLAND AND ISLAND

Location: Wetland at NZ 345 750. Off A193 at N end of Whitley Bay sea front. Island off nearby shore.
Access: Island accessible by causeway at low tide.
Habitat: Coastal, rocks.

Tyne & Wear

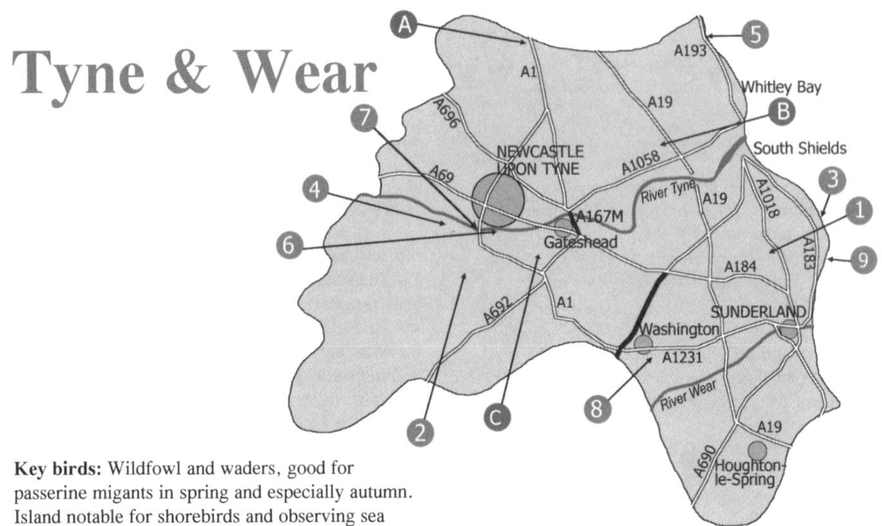

Key birds: Wildfowl and waders, good for passerine migants in spring and especially autumn. Island notable for shorebirds and observing sea passage.
Contact: Tyneside Bird Club Recorder, Ian Fisher, 74 Benton Park Road, Newcastle upon Tyne NE7 7NB.

6. SHIBDON POND

Gateshead Council.
Location: NZ 192 628. E of Blaydon, S of Scotswood Bridge, close to A1. Car park at Blaydon swimming baths. Open access from B6317 (Shibdon Road).
Access: Open at all times. Disabled access to hide. Key for hide available from Thornley Woodlands Centre (£2).
Facilities: Hide in SW corner of pond. Free leaflet available.
Public transport: At least six buses per hour from Newcastle/Gateshead to Blaydon (bus stop Shibdon Road). Information from Nexus Travel Line (0191 232 5325).
Habitat: Pond, marsh, scrub and damp grassland.
Key birds: *Winter*: Wildfowl, Water Rail, white-winged gulls. *Summer*: Reed Warbler, Sedge Warbler, Lesser Whitethroat, Grasshopper Warbler, Water Rail. *Autumn*: Passage waders and wildfowl, Kingfisher.
Contact: Brian Pollinger, Thornley Woodlands Centre, Rowlands Gill, Tyne & Wear NE39 1AU. 1209 545212.
e-mail: countryside@gateshead.gov.uk
www.gatesheadbirders.co.uk

7. TYNE RIVERSIDE COUNTRY PARK AND THE REIGH

Newcastle City Council
Location: NZ 158 658. From Newcastle to Carlisle by-ass on the A69(T) take A6085 into Newburn. The park is signposted along road to Blaydon. 0.25 miles after this junction, turn due W (the Newburn Hotel is on the corner) and after 0.5 miles the parking and information area is signed just beyond the Newburn Leisure Centre.
Access: Open all year.
Facilities: Car park. Leaflets and walk details available.
Public transport: None.
Habitat: River, pond with reed and willow stands, mixed woodland, open grassland.
Key birds: *Spring/summer*: Swift, Swallow, Whitethroat, Lesser Whitethroat. *Winter*: Sparrowhawk, Kingfisher, Little Grebe, finches, Siskin, Fieldfare, Redwing, duck, Goosander. *All year*: Grey Partridge, Green and Great Spotted Woodpecker, Bullfinch, Yellowhammer.
Contact: The Riverside Country Park, Newburn, Newcastle upon Tyne NE15 8BW.

8. WASHINGTON

The Wildfowl & Wetlands Trust.
Location: NZ 331 566. In Washington. On N bank of River Wear, W of Sunderland. Signposted from A195, A19, A1231 and A182.

Access: Open 9.30am-5pm (summer), 9.30am-4pm (winter). Free to WWT members. Admission charge for non-members. No dogs except guide dogs. Good access for people with disabilities.
Facilities: Visitor centre, toilets, parent and baby room, range of hides. Shop and café.
Public transport: Buses to Waterview Park (250 yards walk) from Washington, from Sunderland, Newcastle-upon-Tyne, Durham and South Shields. Tel: 0845 6060260 for details.
Habitat: Wetlands and woodland.
Key birds: *Spring/summer*: Nesting colony of Grey Heron, other breeders include Common Tern, Oystercatcher, Lapwing. *Winter*: Bird-feeding station visited by Great Spotted Woodpecker, Bullfinch, Jay and Sparrowhawk. Goldeneye and other ducks.
Contact: Andrew Donnison, (Grounds Manager), Wildfowl & Wetlands Trust, District 15, Washington NE38 8LE. 0191 4165454 ext 222. e-mail: andrew.donnison@wwt.org.uk

9. WHITBURN BIRD OBSERVATORY

National Trust/Durham Bird Club.
Location: NZ 414 633.
Access: Access details from Recorder.
Facilities: None.
Public transport: None.
Habitat: Cliff top location.
Key birds: Mainly seawatching but also passerine migrants including rarities.
Contact: Tony Armstrong, 39 Western Hill, Durham City, DH1 4RJ. 0191 386 1519; e-mail ope@globalnetcouk.

OTHER SITES

(full details in previous editions)

A Big Waters
Contact: Trust HQ, 0191 284 6884.
C Wallsend Swallow Pond
Contact: Trust HQ, 0191 284 6884.
D Watergate Forest Park/Washingwell Wood
Contact: Thornley Woodlands Centre, 01207 545212.

Warwickshire

1. ALVECOTE POOLS

Warwickshire Wildlife Trust.
Location: SK 253 034. Located alongside River Anker E of Tamworth. Access via Robey's Lane (off B5000) just past Alvecote Priory car park. Also along towpath via Pooley Hall visitor centre, also number of points along towpath.
Access: Some parts of extensive path system is accessible to disabled. Parking Alvecote Priory car park. Nature trail.
Facilities: Nature trail.
Public transport: Within walking distance of the Alvecote village bus stop.
Habitat: Marsh, pools (open and reedbeds) and woodland.
Key birds: *Spring/summer*: Breeding, Common Tern, Oystercatcher and Little Ringed Plover. Common species include Great Crested Grebe, Tufted Duck and Snipe. Important for wintering, passage and breeding wetland birds.
Contact: Reserves Team, Brandon Marsh Nature Centre, Brandon Lane, Brandon, Coventry CV3 3GW. 024 7630 2912.
e-mail: reserves@warkswt.cix.co.uk

2. BRANDON MARSH

Warwickshire Wildlife Trust.
Location: SP 386 762. Three miles SE of Coventry, 200 yards SE of A45/A46 junction (Tollbar End). Turn E off A45 into Brandon Lane. Reserve entrance 1.25 miles on right.
Access: Open weekdays (9am-5pm), weekends (10am-4.30pm). Entrance charge currently £2.50 (free to Wildlife Trust members). Wheelchair access to nature trail and Wright hide. No dogs.
Facilities: Visitor centre, toilets, tea-room (open at above times), nature trail, six hides.
Public transport: Bus service from Coventry to Tollbar End then 1.25 mile walk. Tel. Travel West Midlands 02476 817032 for bus times.
Habitat: Ten pools, together with marsh, reedbeds, willow carr, scrub and small mixed

woodland in 260 acres, designated SSSI in 1972.
Key birds: *Spring/summer*: Garden Warbler, Grasshopper Warbler, Whitethroat, Lesser Whitethroat, Hobby, Little Ringed Plover, Whinchat, Wheatear. *Autumn/winter*: Dunlin, Ruff, Snipe, Greenshank, Green and Common Sandpipers, Wigeon, Shoveler, Pochard, Goldeneye, Siskin, Redpoll. *All year*: Cetti's Warbler, Kingfisher, Water Rail, Gadwall, Little Grebe.
Contact: Ken Bond, Hon. Sec. Brandon Marsh Voluntary Conservation Team, 54 Wiclif Way, Stockingford, Nuneaton, Warwickshire CV10 8NF. 0247 632 8785.

3. KINGSBURY WATER PARK

Warwickshire County Council.
Location: SP 203 960. Signposted 'Water Park' from J9 M42, A4097 NE of Birmingham.
Access: Open all year except Christmas Day.
Facilities: Four hides, two with wheelchair access. Miles of flat surfaced footpaths, free loan scheme for mobility scooters. Cafes, Information Centre with gift shop.
Public transport: Call for advice.
Habitat: Open water; numerous small pools, some with gravel islands; gravel pits; silt beds with reedmace, reed, willow and alder; rough areas and grassland.
Key birds: *Summer*: Breeding warblers (nine species), Little Ringed Plover, Great Crested and Little Grebes. Shoveler, Shelduck and a thriving Common Tern colony. Passage waders (esp. spring). *Winter*: Wildfowl, Short-eared Owl.
Contact: Country Park Manager's Office, Kingsbury Water Park, Bodymoor Heath Lane, Sutton Coldfield, West Midlands B76 0DY. 01827 872660; e-mail parks@warwickshiregovuk www.warwickshiregovuk/countryside.

4. WHITACRE HEATH

Warwickshire Wildlife Trust.
Location: SP 209 931. Three miles N of Coleshill, just W of Whitacre Heath village.
Access: Trust members only.
Facilities: Five hides.
Public transport: Within walking distance of Lea Marston village bus stop.
Habitat: Pools, wet woodland and grassland.

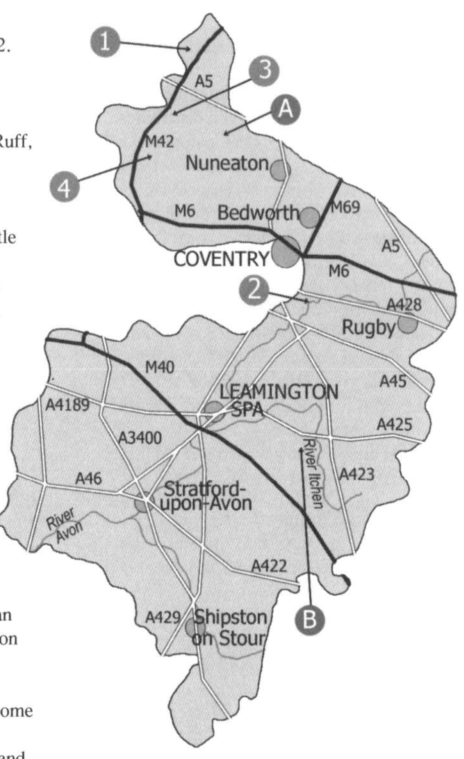

Warwickshire

Key birds: *Summer*: Sedge Warbler, Reed Warbler, Lesser Whitethroat, Whitethroat, Garden Warbler, Willow Warbler and Blackcap. Migrant Curlew, Whinchat. Also Snipe, Water Rail and Kingfisher.
Contact: Reserves Team, Brandon Marsh Nature Centre, (see Brandon Marsh entry).

OTHER SITES
(full details in previous editions)

A. Hartshill Hayes Country Park
Contact: Country Park Manager's Office, 01827 872660.

B. Ufton Fields
Contact: Trust HQ, 024 7630 2912.

West Midlands

1. LICKEY HILLS COUNTRY PARK

Birmingham County Council.
Location: Eleven miles SW of Birmingham City Centre.
Access: Open all year.
Facilities: Car park, visitor centre with wheelchair pathway with viewing gallery, picnic site, toilets, café, shop.
Public transport: Bus: West Midlands 62 Rednal (20 mins walk to visitor centre). Rail: Barnt Green (25 mins walk through woods to the centre).
Habitat: Hills covered with mixed deciduous woodland, conifer plantations and heathland.
Key birds: *Spring/summer*: Warblers, Tree Pipit, Redstart. *Winter*: Redwing, Fieldfare. *All year*: Common woodland species.
Contact: The Visitor Centre, Warren Lane, Rednal, Birmingham, B45 8ER. 0121 4477106. e-mail: visitorcentre@lickeyhills.fsnet.co.uk

2. MARSH LANE NATURE RESERVE

Packington Estate Enterprises Limited.
Location: SP 217 804. Equidistant between Birmingham and Coventry, both approx 7-8 miles away. Off A452 between A45 and Balsall Common, S of B4102/A452 junction. Turn right into Marsh Lane and immediately right onto Old Kenilworth Road (now a public footpath), to locked gate. Key required for access.
Access: Only guide dogs allowed. Site suitable for disabled. Access is by day or year permit only. Membership rates: annual - adult £21, OAP £16, children (under 16) £11 husband/wife £37, OAP husband/wife £28.50. Contact address below (9am-5.15pm). Regular newsletter provided to annual permit holders; day adult £3, OAP £2.75, children (under 16) £2 obtained from Golf Professional Shop, Stonebridge Golf Centre, Somers Road, off Hampton Lane, Meriden, nr Coventry CV7 7PL (tel 01676 522442) only three to four minutes car journey from site. Open Mon-Sun (7am-7pm). Stonebridge Golf Centre open to non-members. Visitors can obtain drinks and meals at Stonebridge Golf Centre. £26.75 deposit required for key. Readily accessible for coaches.
Facilities: No toilets or visitor centre. Four hides and hard tracks between hides. Car park behind locked gates.
Public transport: Hampton-in-Arden railway station within walking distance on footpath loop. Bus no 194 stops at N end of Old Kenilworth Road one mile from reserve gate.
Habitat: Two large pools with islands, three areas of woodland, five acre field set aside for arable growth for finches and buntings as winter feed.
Key birds: 165 species. *Summer*: Breeding birds include Little Ringed Plover, Common Tern, most species of warbler including Grasshopper. Good passage of waders in Apr, May, Aug and Sept. Hobby and Buzzard breed locally.
Contact: Nicholas P Barlow, Packington Hall, Packington Park, Meriden, Nr Coventry CV7 7HF. 01676 522020. www.packingtonestate.net

3. ROUGH WOOD CHASE

Walsall Metropolitan Borough Council
Location: SJ 987 012. NW of Walsall town centre. From J10 of M6 travelling N, turn L on A454 then R on A462. Turn first R onto Bloxwich Road North then R into Hunts Lane. Car park is on R.
Access: Open at all times.
Facilities: Car park, footpaths, nature trail.
Public transport: WMT bus no 341 from Walsall, Park street and Willenhall.
Habitat: Mature oak and mixed woodland, grassland, open water.
Key birds: Common woodland and water species.
Contact: Countryside Services, Dept of Leisure & Community Services, PO box 42, The Civic Centre, Darwall Street, Walsall WS1 1TZ. 01922 650000;(Fax)01922 721862. www.walsall.gov.uk

4. SANDWELL VALLEY 1

Metropolitan Borough Council.
Location: SP 012 918 & SP 028 992.
Access: Access and car park from Dagger Lane or Forge Lane, West Bromwich.
Facilities: Mainly public open space.
Public transport: Call for advice.
Habitat: Nature reserve, lakes, woods and farmland.
Key birds: *Summer*: Breeding Lapwing, Little Ringed Plover, Sparrowhawk. Great Spotted and Green Woodpeckers, Tawny Owl, Reed Warbler. Passage waders.
Contact: Senior Ranger, Sandwell Valley Country

Park, Salters Lane, West Bromwich, W Midlands B71 4BG. 0121 553 0220 or 2147.

5. SANDWELL VALLEY 2

RSPB
Location: SP 035 928. Great Barr, Birmingham. Follow signs S from M6 J7 via A34. Take right at 1st junction onto A4041. Take 4th left onto Hamstead Road (B4167), then right at first mini roundabout onto Tanhouse Avenue.
Access: Half mile of paths accessible to assisted and powered wheelchairs with some gradients (please ring centre for further information), centre fully accessible.
Facilities: Visitor centre and car park (open Tue-Sun 9.30am-5pm) with viewing area, small shop and hot drinks, four viewing screens.
Public transport: Bus: 16 from Corporation Street (Stand CJ), Birmingham City Centre (ask for Tanhouse Avenue). Train: Hamstead Station, then 16 bus for one mile towards West Bromwich from Hamstead (ask for Tanhouse Avenue).
Habitat: Open water, wet grassland, reedbed, dry grassland and scrub.
Key birds: *Summer*: Lapwing, Reed Warbler, Willow Tit. *Passage*: Sandpipers, Yellow Wagtail, chats, Common Tern. *Winter*: Water Rail, Snipe, Jack Snipe, Goosander, Bullfinch, woodpeckers and wildfowl.
Contact: Colin Horne, 20 Tanhouse Avenue, Great Barr, Birmingham B43 5AG. 0121 3577395.

OTHER SITES

(full details in previous editions)

A. Smestow Valley LNR
Contact: Leisure Services, Wolverhampton Council, 01902 556556

B. Swan Pool and The Swag
Contact: Countryside Services, Walsall Metropolitan Borough Council, 01922 650000. www.walsall.gov.uk

Wiltshire

1. FYFIELD DOWNS NNR

English Nature.
Location: On the Marlborough Downs. From the A345 at the N end of Marlborough a minor road signed Broad Hinton, bisects the downs, dripping steeply at Hackpen Hill to the A361 just before Broad Hinton. From Hackpen Hill walk S to Fyfield Down.
Access: Open all year, but avoid the racing gallops. Keep dogs on leads.
Facilities: Car park. **Public transport:** None.
Habitat: Downs.
Key birds: *Spring*: Ring Ouzel possible passage, Wheatear, Cuckoo, Redstart, common warblers. *Summer*: Possible Quail. *Winter*: Occasional Hen Harrier, possible Merlin, Golden Plover, Short-eared Owl, thrushes. *All year*: Sparrowhawk, Buzzard, Kestrel, partridges, Green and Great Spotted Woodpeckers, Goldfinch, Corn Bunting.
Contact: English Nature (Wiltshire team), Prince Maurice Court, Hambleton, Devizes, Wiltshire SN10 2RT. 01380 726344.
e-mail: wiltshire@english-nature.org.uk

2. JONES'S MILL NATURE RESERVE

Wiltshire Wildlife Trust.
Location: SU 170 611. From Pewsey, follow the B3087 for 0.5 miles toward Burbage. Turn L at the crossroads into Dursden Lane. Continue along the lane and over a railway bridge. Parking is limited on the left-hand verge. Walk a short distance along the lane to the reserve entrance, a sunken track just before the 1st house on the L.
Access: Open all year as long as the habitat is not damaged.
Facilities: None.
Public transport: None.
Habitat: River, former water meadows, fen carr, pond.
Key birds: *Spring/summer*: Warblers. *All year*: Kingfisher, Little Grebe, Bullfinch, Snipe, other common species.
Contact: Wiltshire Wildlife Trust, Elm Tree Court, Long Street, Devizes, Wiltshire, SN10 1NJ. 01722 790770.
e-mail: admin@wiltshirewildlife.org
www.wiltshirewildlife.org

3. LANGFORD LAKE

Wiltshire Wildlife Trust.
Location: SU 037 370. Nr Steeple Langford, S of A36, approx eight miles W of Salisbury. In the centre of the village, turn S into Duck Street, signposted Hanging Langford. Langford Lakes is the first turning on the L just after a small bridge across the River Wylye.
Access: Opened to the public in Sept 2002. Main gates opening the during the day - ample parking. Advance notice required for coaches. No dogs allowed on this reserve.
Facilities: Four hides, all accessible to wheelchairs. Cycle stands provided (250m from Wiltshire Cycleway between Great Wishford and Hanging Langford).
Public transport: Nearest bus stop 500m - X4 Service between Salisbury and Warminster.
Habitat: Three former gravel pits, with newly created islands and developing reed fringes. 12 ha (29 acres) of open water; also wet woodland, scrub, chalk river.
Key birds: *Summer*: Breeding Coot, Moorhen, Mallard Tufted Duck, Pochard, Gadwall, Little Grebe, Great Crested Grebe. Also Kingfisher, Common Sandpiper, Grey Wagtail, warblers (eight species). *Winter*: Wildfowl, sometimes also Wigeon, Shoveler, Teal, Water Rail, Little Egret, Bittern. *Passage*: Sand Martin, Green Sandpiper, waders, Black Tern.
Contact: Wiltshire Wildlife Trust, Duck Street, Steeple Langford, Salisbury,Wiltshire SP3 4NH. 01722 790770. www.wiltshirewildlife.org
e-mail: admin@wiltshirewildlife.org

4. SAVERNAKE FOREST

Forest Enterprise.
Location: From Marlborough the A4 Hungerford road runs along the N side of the forest. Two pillars mark the Forest Hill entrance 1.5 miles E of the A346/A4 junction. The Grand Avenue leads straight through the middle of woodland to join a minor road from Stibb Green on A346 N of Burbage to A4 W of Froxfield.
Access: Open all year.
Facilities: Car park, picnic site at NW end by A346. Fenced-off areas should not be entered unless there is a footpath.
Public transport: None.
Habitat: Ancient woodland, with one of the largest collections of veteran trees in Britain.
Key birds: *Spring/summer*: Garden Warbler, Blackcap, Willow Warbler, Chiffchaff, Wood Warbler, Redstart, occasional Nightingale, Tree Pipit, Spotted Flycatcher. *Winter*: Finch flocks possibly inc Siskin Redpoll, Brambling. *All year*: Sparrowhawk, Buzzard, Woodcock, owls, all three woodpeckers, Marsh, Tit, Willow Tit, Jay and other woodland birds.
Contact: Forest Enterprise, Postern Hill, Marlborough, 01672 512520.
e-mail: admin@wiltshirewildlife.org
www.wiltshirewildlife.org

OTHER SITES

(full details in previous editions)

A. Swillbrook Lakes
Contact: Wiltshire Wildlife Trust, 01380 725670.

Worcestershire

1. KNAPP AND PAPERMILL

Worcestershire Wildlife Trust.
Location: SO 749 522. Take A4103 SW from Worcester; R at Bransford roundabout then L towards Suckley and reserve is approx three miles (do not turn off for Alfrick). Park at Bridges Stone layby (SO 751 522), cross road and follow path to the Knapp House.
Access: Open daily exc Christmas Day. Large parties should contact Warden
Facilities: Nature trail, small visitor centre, wildlife garden, Kingfisher viewing screen.
Public transport: None.
Habitat: Broadleaved woodland, unimproved grassland, fast stream, old orchard in Leigh Brook Valley.
Key birds: *Summer*: Breeding Grey Wagtail, Kingfisher, Spotted Flycatcher nests in Warden's garden, all three woodpeckers. Buzzard, Sparrowhawk and Redstart also occur. Also otter.
Contact: The Warden, Knapp and Papermill reserve, The Knapp, Alfrick, Worcester WR6 5HR. 01886 832065.

2. TIDDESLEY WOOD

Worcestershire Wildlife Trust.
Location: SO 929 462. Take A44 from Pershore to Worcester. Turn L near town boundary just before the summit of the hill towards Besford and Croome. The entrance to reserve is on L after about 0.75 miles.
Access: Open all year except Christmas Day. Cycles and horses only allowed on the bridleway. Please keep dogs fully under control. As there is a military firing range at the SW corner of the wood, do not enter the area marked by red flags. The NE plot is private property and visitors should not enter the area. Not suitable for the disabled.
Facilities: Information board. May find numbered posts around the reserve which were described in an old leaflet.
Public transport: None.
Habitat: Ancient woodland, conifers.
Key birds: *Spring*: Chiffchaff, Blackcap, Cuckoo, occasional Nightingale. *All year*: Crossbill, Coal Tit, Goldcrest, Sparrowhawk, Willow Tit, Marsh Tit. *Winter*: Redwing, Fieldfare.
Contact: Worcestershire Wildlife Trust, Lower Smite Farm, Smite Hill, Hindlip, Worcester, WR3 8SZ. 01905 754919. e-mail: worcswt@cix.co.uk www.worcswildlifetrust.co.uk

3. UPTON WARREN

Worcestershire Wildlife Trust.
Location: SO 936 675. Two miles S of Bromsgrove on A38.
Access: Always open except Christmas Day. Trust membership gives access, or day permit from sailing centre. Disabled access to west hide at moors only. Dogs on leads.
Facilities: Seven hides, maps at entrances, can be very muddy.
Public transport: Birmingham/Worcester bus passes reserve entrance.
Habitat: Fresh and saline pools with muddy islands, some woodland and scrub.
Key birds: *Winter*: Wildfowl. *Spring/autumn*: Passage waders, Common Tern, Cetti's Warbler, Oystercatcher and Little Ringed Plover, many breeding warblers.
Contact: A F Jacobs, 3 The Beeches, Upton Warren, Bromsgrove, Worcs B61 7EL. 01527 861370.

4. WYRE FOREST

English Nature/Worcs Wildlife Trust.
Location: SO 750 760. A456 out of Bewdley.
Access: Observe reserve signs and keep to paths. Forestry Commission visitor centre at Callow Hill. Fred Dale Reserve is reached by footpath W of B4194 (parking at SO776763).
Facilities: Facilities for disabled (entry by car) if Warden telephoned in advance.
Public transport: None.
Habitat: Oak forest, conifer areas, birch heath, stream.
Key birds: Buzzard, Pied Flycatcher, Wood Warbler, Redstart, all three woodpeckers, Woodcock, Crossbill, Siskin, Hawfinch, Kingfisher, Dipper, Grey Wagtail, Tree Pipit.
Contact: Tim Dixon, 01531 638500.

OTHER SITES

(full details in previous editions)

A. Monkwood Nature Reserve
Contact: Trust HQ, 01905 754919.
B. Trench Wood
Contact: Trust HQ, 01905 754919.

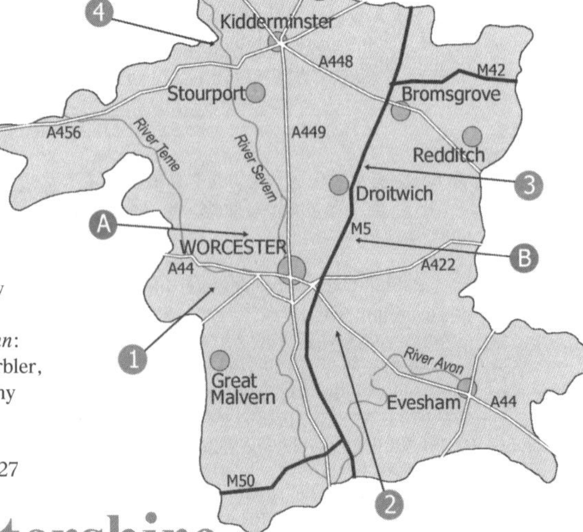

Worcestershire

Yorkshire, East

1. BEMPTON CLIFFS

RSPB (North of England Office).
Location: TA 197 738. Near Bridlington. Take cliff road N from Bempton Village off B1229 to car park and visitor centre
Access: Visitor centre open Mar-Nov and weekends in Dec and Feb. Public footpath along cliff top with observation points. Four miles of chalk cliffs, highest in the county.
Facilities: Visitor centre, toilets. Viewing platforms.Picnic area.
Public transport: Railway 1.5 miles - irregular bus service to village 1.25 miles.
Habitat: Seabird nesting cliffs, farmland, scrub.
Key birds: Best to visit May to mid-July for eg Puffin, Gannet (only colony on English mainland), Fulmar, Kittiwake; also nesting Tree Sparrow, Corn Bunting; good migration watchpoint for skuas, shearwaters and terns.
Contact: Site Manager, RSPB Visitor Centre, Cliff Lane, Bempton, Bridlington, E Yorks YO15 1JF. 01262 851179.

2. BLACKTOFT SANDS

RSPB (North of England Office).
Location: SE 843 232. Eight miles E of Goole on minor road between Ousefleet and Adlingfleet.
Access: Open 9am-9pm or dusk if earlier. RSPB members free, £3 permit for non-members, £2 concessionary, £1 children, £6 family.
Facilities: Car park, toilets, visitor centre, six hides, footpaths suitable for wheelchairs.
Public transport: Goole/Scunthorpe bus (Sweynes' Coaches stops outside reserve entrance).
Habitat: Reedbed, saline lagoons, lowland wet grassland, willow scrub.
Key birds: *Summer*: Breeding Avocet, Marsh Harrier, Bearded Tit, passage waders (exceptional list inc many rarities). *Winter*: Hen Harrier, Merlin, Peregrine, wildfowl.
Contact: Pete Short (Warden) & Simon Wellock (Asst Warden), Hillcrest, Whitgift, Nr Goole, E Yorks DN14 8HL. 01405 704665.
e-mail: simonwellock@rspb.org.uk or peteshort@rspb.org.uk www.rspb.org.uk

3. SPURN NNR

Yorkshire Wildlife Trust.
Location: Entrance Gate TA 417 151. 26 miles from Hull. Take A1033 from Hull to Patrington then B1445 from Patrington to Easington and unclassed roads on to Kilnsea and Spurn Head.
Access: Normally open at all times. Vehicle admission fee (at present £2.50). No charge for pedestrians. No dogs allowed under any circumstances, not even in cars. Coaches by permit only (must be in advance).
Facilities: Chemical portaloos next to information centre. Information centre open weekends, Bank Holidays, school holidays. Three hides. Cafe at point open weekends Apr to Oct 10am to 5pm.
Public transport: Nearest bus service is at Easington (3.5 miles away).
Habitat: Sand dunes with marram and sea buckthorn scrub. Mudflats around Humber Estuary.
Key birds: *Spring*: Many migrants on passage and often rare birds such as Red-backed Shrike, Bluethroat etc. *Autumn*: Passage migrants and rarities like Wryneck, Pallas's Warbler. *Winter*: Waders and Brent Goose.
Contact: Spurn Reserves Officer, Spurn NNR, Blue Bell, Kilnsea, Hull HU12 0UB.
e-mail: spurnywt@ukonline.co.uk

4. TOPHILL LOW NATURE RESERVE

Yorkshire Water.
Location: TA 071 482. Nine miles SE of Driffield and ten miles NE of Beverley. Signposted from village of Watton on A164.
Access: Open Wed-Sun and Bank Holiday Mon. Apr-Oct (9am-6pm). Nov-Mar (9am-4pm). Charges: £2.50 per person. £1 concessions. No dogs allowed. Provision for disabled visitors (paths, ramps, hides, toilet etc).
Facilities: Visitor centre with toilets. 13 hides (five with access for wheelchairs). Nature trails. Coaches are welcome.
Public transport: None.
Habitat: Open water (two reservoirs), marshes, wader scrapes, woodland and thorn scrub.
Key birds: *Winter*: Wildfowl, gulls, Water Rail, Kingfisher. *Spring/early summer*: Passage Wood Sandpiper and Black Tern. Breeding Pochard, Kingfisher and Barn Owl. *Late Summer/autumn:* Up to 20 species of passage wader.
Contact: Peter Izzard, Tophill Low Nature Reserve, Watton Carrs, Driffield, East Yorkshire YO25 9RH. 01377 270690.

Yorkshire, North

1. COATHAM MARSH

Tees Valley Wildlife Trust.
Location: NZ 585 250. Located on W edge of Redcar. Access from minor road to Warrenby from A1085/A1042.
Access: Reserve is open throughout daylight hours. Please keep to permissive footpaths only.
Facilities: Two hides. Key required for one of these - available to Tees Valley Wildlife Trust members for £10 deposit. No toilets or visitor centre.
Public transport: Very frequent bus service between Middlesbrough and Redcar. Nearest stops are in Coatham 0.25 mile from reserve (Arriva tel 0870 6082608). Redcar Central Station one mile from site. Frequent trains from Middlesbrough and Darlington.
Habitat: Freshwater wetlands, lakes, reedbeds.
Key birds: *Spring/autumn*: Wader passage (including Wood Sandpiper and Greenshank). *Summer:* Passerines (including Sedge Warbler, Yellow Wagtail). *Winter:* Ducks (including Smew). Occasional rarities, Water Rail, Great White Egret, Avocet.
Contact: Mark Fishpool, Tees Valley Wildlife Trust, Bellamy Pavilion, Kirkleatham, Redcar, Cleveland TS10 5NW. 01642 759900.
e-mail: teesvalleywt@cix.co.uk
www.wildlifetrust.org.uk/teesvalley

2. FILEY BRIGG ORNITHOLOGICAL GROUP BIRD OBSERVATORY

FBOG and Yorkshire Wildlife Trust (The Dams).
Location: TA 10 68 07. Two access roads into Filey from A165 (Scarborough to Bridlington road). Filey is ten miles N of Bridlington and eight miles S of Scarborough.
Access: Opening times - no restrictions. Dogs only in Parish Wood and The Old Tip (on lead). Coaches welcome. Park in the North Cliff Country Park.
Facilities: No provisions for disabled at present. Two hides at The Dams, one on The Brigg (open most weekends from late Jul-Oct, key can be hired from Country Park café). Toilets in Country Park (Apr-Nov 1) and town centre. Nature trails at The Dams, Parish Wood/Old Tip. Cliff top walk for seabirds along Cleveland Way.
Public transport: All areas within a mile of Filey railway station. Trains into Filey tel. 08457 484950; buses into Filey tel. 01723 503020
Habitat: The Dams - two freshwater lakes, fringed with some tree cover and small reedbeds. Parish Wood - a newly built wood which leads to the Old Tip, the latter has been fenced (for stock and crop strips) though there is a public trail. Carr Naze has a pond and can produce newly arrived migrants.
Key birds: *The Dams*: Breeding and wintering water birds, breeding Sedge Warbler, Reed Warbler and Tree Sparrow. *The Tip*: Important for breeding Sky Lark, Meadow Pipit, common warblers and Grey Partridge. *Winter:* Area for buntings, including Lapland. *Seawatch Hide*: Jul-Oct. All four skuas, shearwaters, terns. *Winter*: Divers and grebes. T*otem Pole Field:* A new project should encourage breeding species and wintering larks, buntings etc. Many sub-rare/rare migrants possible at all sites.
Contact: Lez Gillard, Recorder, 12 Sycamore Avenue, Filey, N Yorks YO14 9NU. 01723 516383. e-mail: lezgillard@tiscali.co.uk
www.fbog.co.uk

3. LOWER DERWENT VALLEY

English Nature (North & East Yorks).
Location: SE 691 447. Six miles SE of York, stretching 12 miles S along the River Derwent from Newton-on-Derwent to Wressle and along the Pocklington Canal. Visitor facilities at Bank Island, Wheldrake Ings YWT (SE 691 444), Thorganby (SE 693 422) and North Duffield Carrs (SE 698 366).
Access: Open all year. No dogs. Disabled access at North Duffield Carrs (two hides and car park). 500m path.
Facilities: North Duffield Carrs - two hides, wheelchair access. Wheldrake Ings (YWT) - five hides. Bank Island - two hides, viewing tower. Thorganby - viewing platform.
Public transport: Bus from York/Selby - contact First (01904 622992). Bicycle stands provided in car parks at Bank Island and North Duffield Carrs.
Habitat: Hay meadow and pasture, swamp, open water and alder carr woodland.
Key birds: *Spring/summer:* Breeding wildfowl and waders including Garganey and Ruff. Barn Owl and warblers. *Winter:* 20,000-plus waterfowl including Whooper Swan, Bewick's Swan, wild geese and Wigeon. Large gull roost including

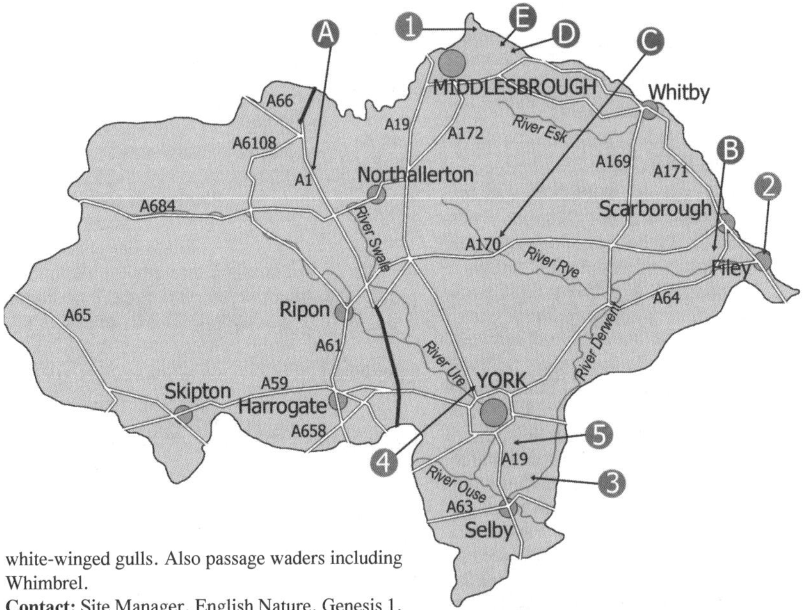

white-winged gulls. Also passage waders including Whimbrel.
Contact: Site Manager, English Nature, Genesis 1, Heslington Road, York YO10 5ZQ. 01904 435500. e-mail: york@english-nature.org.uk Leaflet available SAE please or check website www.english-nature.org.uk

4. MOORLANDS WOOD RESERVE

Yorkshire Wildlife Trust.
Location: From the York ring road, take A19 Thirsk/Northallerton road. After 1.6km turn R at The Blacksmith's Arms pub for Skelton. Go through the village. After 3.2km, look for an open parking area at a wide verge on the L alongside the wood and just before the entrance gate.
Access: Open all year. Entry free except May-Jun when a small charge is made.
Facilities: Car park, woodland paths. Suitable for wheelchairs.
Public transport: None.
Habitat: Mature mixed woodland, ponds, agricultural land.
Key birds: *Spring/summer*: Cuckoo, Curlew, Garden Warbler, Blackcap, Spotted Flycatcher. *Winter*: Thrushes, Siskin. *All year*: Tawny Owl, Great Spotted Woodpecker, tits inc Marsh Tit, Jay, Treecreeper, Redpoll.
Contact: 10 Toft Green, York YO1 6JT. 01904 659570. e-mail: yorkshirewt@cix.co.uk www.yorkshire-wildlife-trust.org.uk

5. WHELDRAKE INGS LOWER DERWENT VALLEY NNR

Yorkshire Wildlife Trust.
Location: Leave the York ring road S onto A19 Selby road. After one mile turn L to Wheldrake, signed Wheldrake 4 and Thorganby 6.5. After 3.5 miles pass through Wheldrake and continue towards Thorganby. After a sharp R bend turn L after 0.5 miles onto an unsigned tarmac track. Look for two old stone gateposts with pointed tops. The car park is about 0.25 miles down the track. To reach the reserve, cross the river bridge and turn R over a stile.
Access: Open all year. Please keep to the riverside path. From Apr-Sep.
Facilities: Car park, four hides.
Public transport: None.
Habitat: Water meadows, river, scrub, open water.
Key birds: *Spring/summer*: Ducks, Grey Partridge, Turtle Dove, some waders, Spotted Flycatcher, warblers. *Winter*: Occasional divers and scarce grebes. wildfowl inc. Pintail, Pochard, Goshawk, Hen Harrier, Water Rail, Short-eared Owl, thrushes, good mix of other birds.
Contact: 10 Toft Green, York, YO1 6JT. 01904 659570. e-mail: yorkshirewt.@cix.co.uk

OTHER SITES
(full details in previous editions)

A. Bolton on Swale Lake
Contact: Yorkshire Wildlife Trust, 01904 659570
B. Burton Riggs LNR
Contact: Yorkshire Wildlife Trust, 01904 659579
C. Duncombe Park NNR
Contact: Duncombe Park Estate, 01439 770213
D. Huntcliff
Contact: Tees Valley Wildlife Trust, 01642 759900
E. Saltburn Gill
Contact: Tees Valley Wildlife Trust, 01642 759900

Yorkshire, South & West

1. BRETTON COUNTRY PARK AND OXLEY BANK WOOD

Yorkshire Wildlife Trust/Wakefield MDC.
Location: SE 295 125. Fifteen miles S of L and N of Sheffield. Leave the motorway at J38. Take A637 Huddersfield road to N. After 0.5 miles entrance to Park is on L. Can also park in Sculpture Park's car park, which is first L off A637 in West Bretton.
Access: Open all year. Permit required for the Yorkshire Wildlife Trust area.
Facilities: Car park, visitor centre, information leaflets.
Public transport: None.
Habitat: Landscaped park, mature woodland, two lakes.
Key birds: *Spring/summer*: Cuckoo, warblers, Spotted Flycatcher, Sand Martin, Swallow. *Winter*: Fieldfare, Redwing, Brambling, Redpoll, Siskin, Hawfinch. *All year*: Kingfisher, all three woodpeckers, Little and Tawny Owls, Linnet, Bullfinch, Yellowhammer, usual woodland birds.
Contact: 10 Toft Green, York, YO1 6JT. 01904 659570. e-mail: yorkshirewt@cix.co.uk www.yorkshire-wildlife-trust.org.uk

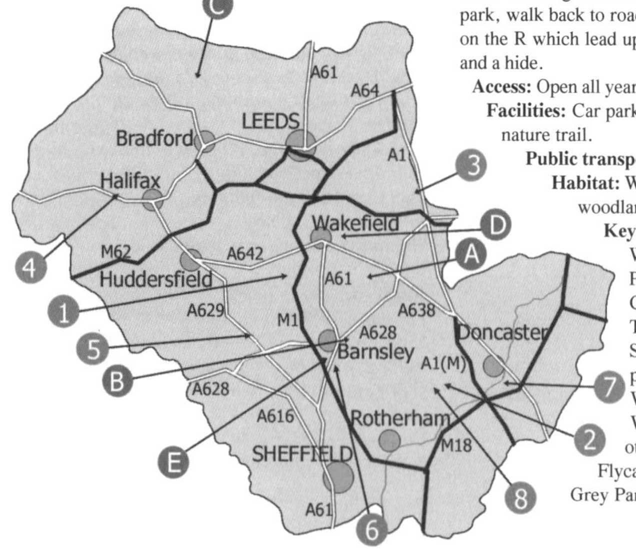

2. DENABY INGS NATURE RESERVE

Yorkshire Wildlife Trust.
Location: The reserve is on A6023 from Mexborough. Look for a L fork signed Denaby Ings Nature Reserve. Proceed along Pastures Road for 0.5 miles and watch for a 2nd sign on the R marking entrance to car park. From car park, walk back to road to a set of concrete steps on the R which lead up to a small visitor centre and a hide.
Access: Open all year.
Facilities: Car park, visitor centre, hide, nature trail.
Public transport: None.
Habitat: Water, deciduous woodland, marsh, willows.
Key birds: *Spring/summer*: Waterfowl, Little Ringed Plover, Turtle Dove, Cuckoo, Little Owl, Tawny Owl, Sand Martin, Swallow, Whinchat, possible Grasshopper Warbler, Lesser Whitethroat, Whitethroat, other warblers, Spotted Flycatcher, Red-legged and Grey Partridges, Kingfisher.

Passage: Waders, Common, Arctic and Black Terns, Redstart, Wheatear. *Winter*: Whooper Swan, wildfowl, Jack Snipe, waders, Grey Wagtail, Short-eared Owl, Stonechat, Fieldfare, Redwing, Brambling, Siskin. *All year*: Corn Bunting, Yellowhammer, all three woodpeckers possible, Willow Tit, common woodland birds.
Contact: 10 Toft Green, York YO1 6JT. 01904 659570. e-mail: yorkshirewt@cix.co.uk

3. FAIRBURN INGS

RSPB (North West England Office).
Location: SE 452 277. 12.5 miles from Leeds, six miles from Pontefract, 3.5 miles from Castleford situated next to A1 at Fairburn turn-off.
Access: Reserve and hides open every day (9am-dusk). Centre with shop open weekdays (11am-4pm) and weekends (10am-5pm) and Bank Holidays. Hot and cold drinks available. Dogs on leads at all times. Boardwalk leading to Pickup Pool and feeding station and paths to centre wheelchair-friendly.
Facilities: Reserve hides include three open at all times with one locked at dusk. Toilets open when centre open or 9am-5pm. Disabled access to toilets. All nature trails follow public paths and are open at all times.
Public transport: Nearest train stations are Castleford or Pontefract. Buses approx every hour from Pontefract and Tadcaster. Infrequent from Castleford and Selby.
Habitat: Open water due to mining subsidence, wet grassland, marsh and willow scrub, reclaimed colliery spoil heaps.
Key birds: *Winter*: A herd of Whooper Swan usually roost. Normally up to five Smew (including male), Wigeon, Gadwall, Goosander, Goldeneye. *Spring*: Osprey, Wheatear, Little Gull and five species of tern pass through. *Summer*: Breeding birds include Reed and Sedge Warblers, Shoveler, Gadwall, Cormorant.
Contact: Chris Drake, Information Warden, Fairburn Ings Visitor Centre, Newton Lane, Fairburn, Castleford WF10 2BH. 01977 603796.

4. HARDCASTLE CRAGS

National Trust.
Location: From Halifax, follow A646 W for five miles to Hebden Bridge and pick up National Trust signs in town centre. These take you to A6033 Kighley Road. Follow this for 0.75 miles. Turn L at National Trust sign to car parks.
Access: Open all year.
Facilities: Two car parks, trails.
Public transport: None.
Habitat: Wooded valley, ravines, streams.
Key birds: *Spring/summer*: Cuckoo, Redstart, Lesser Whitethroat, Garden Warbler, Blackcap, Wood Warbler, Chiffchaff, Spotted Flycatcher, Pied Flycatcher. *All year*: Sparrowhawk, Kestrel, Green and Great Spotted Woodpeckers, Tawny Owl, Jay, Marsh Tit and other woodland species.
Contact: National Trust, 27 Tadcaster Road, Dringhouses, York YO2 2QG.

5. INGBIRCHWORTH RESERVOIR

Yorkshire Water.
Location: Leave M1 at J37 and take A628 to Manchester and Penistone. After five miles you reach a roundabout. Turn R onto A629 Huddersfield road. After 2.5 miles you reach Ingbirchworth. At a sign for The Fountain Inn, turn L. Pass a pub, cross the dam, proceed straight forward onto the track leading to the car park. From the car park, follow the footpath round the reservoir.
Access: Open all year. One of the few reservoirs in the area with access.
Facilities: Car park, picnic tables.
Public transport: None.
Habitat: Reservoir, small strip of deciduous woodland.
Key birds: *Spring/summer*: Whinchat, warblers, woodland birds, House Martin. *Spring/autumn passage*: Little Ringed Plover, Ringed Plover, Dotterel, waders, Common Tern, Arctic Tern, Black Tern, Yellow Wagtail, Wheatear. *Winter*: Wildfowl, Golden Plover, waders, occasional rare gull such as Iceland or Glaucous, Grey Wagtail, Fieldfare, Redwing, Brambling, Redpoll.
Contact: Yorkshire Water, PO Box 52, Bradford BD3 7YD.

6. OLD MOOR WETLAND CENTRE

Barnsley MBC Countryside Unit.
Location: SE 422 011. From M1 J36, then A6195. From A1 J37, then A635 and A6195 – follow brown signs.
Access: Open Apr 1-Oct 31 (Wed-Sun 9am-5pm), Nov 1-Mar 31 (Wed/Thu-Sat/Sun 10am-4pm). Entry fee with Annual Membership available.
Facilities: Toilets (including disabled), large visitor centre and shop, five superb hides. All sites including hides fully accessible for disabled.

Public transport: Buses: information from South Yorkshire Passenger Transport 01709 589200.
Habitat: Lakes and flood meadows, wader scrape and reedbeds.
Key birds: *Winter*: Large numbers of wildfowl. *Summer*: Breeding waders and wildfowl. Rare vagrants recorded annually.
Contact: Debra Bushby, Old Moor Wetland Centre, Off Manvers Way, Broomhill, Wombwell, Barnsley, South Yorkshire S73 0YF. 01226 751593 Fax: 01226 751617.
e-mail: oldmoor@barnsley.gov.uk
www.barnsley.gov.uk

7. POTTERIC CARR

Yorkshire Wildlife Trust.
Location: SE 589 007. From M18 junction 3 take A6182 (Doncaster) and at first roundabout take third exit; entrance and car park are on R after 50m.
Access: Access by permit only. Parties must obtain prior permission.
Facilities: Field Centre (light refreshments, toilet) open (10 a.m.-3 p.m. Sun) all year and Tuesday lunchtimes. Eight hides (three for disabled). During early part of 2005, the Reserve will be being upgraded (still open for visitors with temporary café) and will be relaunched around mid 2005 with revised opening times, refurbished hides, improved café and toilet facilities, extended facilities for disabled; ticketing 7 days/week and Field Centre 4 days per week. Ring answerphone or see website from March 2005 for details.
Public transport: Buses from Doncaster to new B&Q store travel close to entrance.
Habitat: Reed fen, subsidence ponds, artificial pools, grassland, woodland.
Key birds: 95 species have bred. Nesting waterfowl (inc. Shoveler, Gadwall, Pochard), Water Rail, Kingfisher, all three woodpeckers, Lesser Whitethroat, Reed and Sedge Warblers, Willow Tit. *Passage/winter*: Bittern, Marsh Harrier, Black Tern, waders, wildfowl.
Contact: Answerphone (01302 364152) for further contact information, telephone nos. etc. or see www.potteric-carr.org.uk

8. SPROTBOROUGH FLASH RESERVE AND THE DON GORGE

Yorkshire Wildlife Trust.
Location: From the A1, follow A630 to Rotherham 3 miles W of Doncaster. After half a mile, turn R at traffic lights to Sprotborough. After approx one mile the road drops down slopes of the Gorge. Cross a bridge over the river. After crossing another bridge over a canal, turn immediately L. Park in a small roadside parking area on L beside the canal. Walk along the canal bank, past The Boat Inn, to reserve entrance.
Access: Open all year.
Facilities: Three hides, footpaths.
Public transport: None.
Habitat: River, reed, gorge, woodland.
Key birds: *Summer*: Turtle Dove, Cuckoo, hirundines, Lesser Whitethroat, Whitethroat, Garden Warbler, Blackcap, Chiffchaff, Willow Warbler, Spotted Flycatcher. *Spring/autumn passage*: Little Ringed Plover, Dunlin, Greenshank, Green Sandpiper, waders, Yellow Wagtail. *Winter/all year*: Wildfowl, Water Rail, Snipe, Little Owl, Tawny Owl, all three woodpeckers, thrushes, Siskin, possible Corn Bunting.
Contact: 10 Toft Green, York YO1 6JT. 01904 659570.e-mail: yorkshirewt@cix.co.uk
www.yorkshire-wildlife-trust.org.uk

OTHER SITES

(full details in previous editions)

A. Anglers Country Park

Contact: Leisure Services, Wakefield Metropolitan Borough Council, 01924 302600.

B. Carlton Marsh

Contact: Barnsley MBC Countryside unit, 01226 772142.

C. Denso Marston Nature Reserve

Contact: Andrew Clarke, Denso Marston, 01274 582266.

D. Pugneys Country Park

Contact: Wakefield Metropolitan Borough Council, 01924 306090.

E. Worsbrough Country Park

Contact: Cultural Services, Worsbrough Mill, 01226 774527.

SCOTLAND

Border Counties

Borders

1. BEMERSYDE MOSS

Scottish Wildlife Trust.
Location: NT 614 340. Four miles E of Melrose on minor road, between Melrose and Smailholm.
Access: Permit required.
Facilities: Hide with parking nearby.
Public transport: None.
Habitat: Shallow loch and marsh.
Key birds: *Summer*: Large Black-headed Gull colony, Black-necked Grebe, Grasshopper Warbler. *Winter:* Wildfowl, waders on migration, raptors.
Contact: Trust HQ, 0131 312 7765.

2. GUNKNOWE LOCH AND PARK

Borders Council.
Location: NT 523 51. Two miles from Galashiels on the A6091. Park at Gunknowe Loch.
Access: Open all year.
Facilities: Car park, paths.
Public transport: None.
Habitat: River, parkland, scrub, woodland.
Key birds: *Spring/summer*: Grey Wagtail, Kingfisher, Sand Martin, Blackcap, Sedge and Grasshopper Warblers. *Passage*: Yellow Wagtail, Whinchat, Wheatear. *Winter*: Thrushes, Brambling, Wigeon, Tufted Duck, Pochard, Goldeneye. *All year*: Great Spotted and Green Woodpeckers, Redpoll, Goosander, possible Marsh Tit.
Contact: Borders Council, Newton Street, Boswells, Melrose TD6 0SA. 01835 824000; e-mail: enquiries@scotborders.gov.uk

3. THE HIRSEL

The Estate Office, The Hirsel.
Location: NT 827 403. Signed off the A698 Kelso-Coldstream road on the outskirts of Coldstream.
Access: Open all year. Private estate so please stick to the public paths.
Facilities: Car parks, visitor centre, leaflets, trails.
Public transport: Bus: Coldstream, Kelso, Berwick-upon-Tweed, Edinburgh.
Habitat: Freshwater loch, reeds, woods.
Key birds: *Spring/summer*: Redstart, Garden Warbler, Blackcap, flycatchers, possible Water Rail, wildfowl. *Autumn*: Wildfowl, Goosander, possible Green Sandpiper. *Winter*: Whooper Swan, Pink-footed Goose, Wigeon, Goldeneye, Pochard, occasional Smew, Scaup, Slavonian Grebe.
Contact: The Estate Office, The Hirsel, Coldstream TD12 4LF. 01890 882834.

4. PEASE DEAN

Scottish Wildlife Trust.
Location: NT 790 705. W of St Abb's Head. Park at Pease Bay Caravan Park off A1107.
Access: Open all year.
Facilities: Leaflet available from the tourist office in Eyemouth.
Public transport: None.
Habitat: Valley woodland.
Key birds: Valuable landfall, feeding and sheltering site for migrants.
Contact: Trust HQ, 0131 312 7765.

5. ST ABB'S HEAD

National Trust for Scotland.
Location: NT 914 693. Lies five miles N of Eyemouth. Follow A1107 from A1.
Access: Reserve open all year. Keep dogs on lead. Cliff path is not suitable for disabled visitors.
Facilities: Visitor centre and toilets open daily Apr-Oct.
Public transport: Nearest rail station is Berwick-upon-Tweed. Bus service from Berwick, tel 018907 81533.
Habitat: Cliffs, coastal grasslands and freshwater loch.
Key birds: *Apr-Aug*: Seabird colonies with large numbers of Kittiwake, auks, Shag, Fulmar, migrants. *Apr-May and Sept-Oct*: Good autumn seawatching.
Contact: Kevin Rideout, Rangers Cottage, Northfield, St Abbs, Borders TD14 5QF. 018907 71443. e-mail: krideout@nts.org.uk www.nts.org.uk

OTHER SITES
(full details in previous editions)

A. Duns Castle
Contact: Trust HQ, 0131 312 7765
B. Yetholm Loch
Contact: Trust HQ, 0131 312 7765

Dumfries & Galloway

6. BLACK CRAIG WOOD

Scottish Wildlife Trust.
Location: Off the A75 halfway between Bridge of Cree and Newton Stewart. Park on grass verge.
Access: Open all year.
Facilities: None.
Public transport: None.
Habitat: Fossil sea-cliff, oak woodland.
Key birds: Woodland and field species.
Contact: Scottish Wildlife Trust, Cramond House, Kirk Cramond, Gramond Glebe Road, Edinburgh EH4 6NS. 0131 312 7765.
e-mail: scottishwt@cix.co.uk www.swt.org.uk

7. CAERLAVEROCK NNR

Scottish Natural Heritage.
Location: NY 040 645. SE of Dumfries. From B725 and Caerlaverock Castle.
Access: Open all year. Visitors may enter the reserve. Care must be taken in relation to cattle and electric fences being present during summer months. The saltmarsh and mudflats can be dangerous especially during high tides; visitors should consult the reserve manager for advice. No permit, but organised groups should apply to the reserve manager in advance. Research and surveys require approval of the reserve manager.
Facilities: Woodland/saltmarsh walks, visitor room, picnic area, small hide/shelter, cycle racks, on-site information.
Public transport: Buses from Dumfries.
Habitat: Saltmarsh, mudflats, fen.
Key birds: *Winter*: Barnacle and Pink-footed Geese, Whooper Swan, Pintail, Mallard, Teal, Wigeon, Scaup, Goosander, Knot, Oystercatcher, Curlew, Redshank, Lapwing and many more!
Contact: Alan Steel, SNH Reserve Office, Hollands Farm Road, Caerlaverock, Dumfries DG1 4RS. 01387 770275.

8. CAERLAVEROCK

The Wildfowl & Wetlands Trust.
Location: NY 051 656. From Dumfries take B725 towards Bankend.
Access: Open daily except Christmas Day.
Facilities: 20 hides, heated observatory, two towers, sheltered picnic area. Self-catering accommodation and camping facilities. Nature trails in summer.
Public transport: Buses from Dumfries.
Habitat: Saltmarsh, grassland.
Key birds: *Winter*: Wildfowl esp. Barnacle Goose (max 14,000) and Whooper Swan.
Contact: Eastpark Farm, Caerlaverock, Dumfries DG1 4RS. 01387 770200.

9. CAIRNSMORE OF FLEET NNR

Scottish Natural Heritage.
Location: NX 555 635. NW of Gatehouse of Fleet on B796.
Access: Open all year.
Facilities: Car park, visitor centre.
Public transport: None.
Habitat: Upland and moorland.
Key birds: Good variety of moorland birds.
Contact: Visitor Centre, 01557 814435.

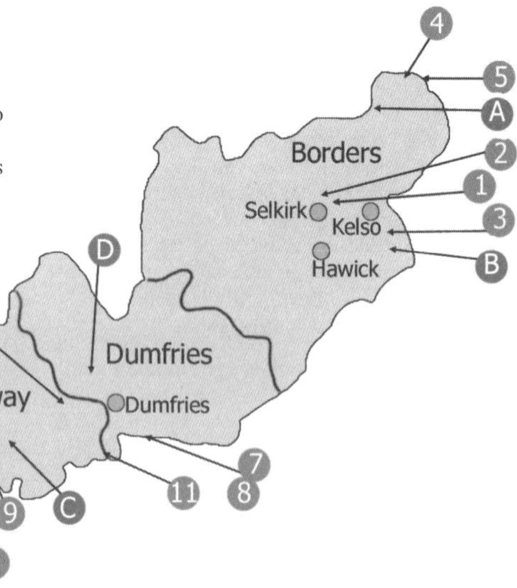

10. KEN/DEE MARSHES

RSPB (South & West Scotland Office).
Location: NX 699 684. Six miles from Castle Douglas - good views from A762 and A713 roads to New Galloway.
Access: From car park at entrance to farm Mains of Duchrae. Open during daylight hours. No dogs.
Facilities: Hides, nature trails. Three miles of trails available, nearer parking for elderly and disabled, but phone warden first. Part of Red Kite trail.
Public transport: None.
Habitat: Marshes, woodlands, open water.
Key birds: *All year:* Mallard, Grey Heron, Buzzard. *Spring/summer*: Pied Flycatcher, Redstart, Tree Pipit, Sedge Warbler. *Winter*: Greenland White-fronted and Greylag Geese, birds of prey (Hen Harrier, Peregrine, Merlin, Red Kite).
Contact: RSPB, 01671 402861.

11. MERSEHEAD

RSPB (South & West Scotland Office).
Location: NX 925 560. From Dalbeattie, take B793 or A710 SE to Caulkerbush.
Access: Open at all times.
Facilities: Hide, nature trails, information centre and toilets. **Public transport:** None.
Habitat: Wet grassland, arable farmland, saltmarsh, inter-tidal mudflats.
Key birds: *Winter*: Up to 9,500 Barnacle Geese, 4,000 Teal, 2,000 Wigeon, 1,000 Pintail, waders (inc. Dunlin, Knot, Oystercatcher). *Summer*: Breeding birds include Lapwing, Redshank, Sky Lark.
Contact: Eric Nielson, Mersehead, Southwick, Mersehead, Dumfries DG2 8AH. 01387 780298.

12. MULL OF GALLOWAY

RSPB (South & West Scotland Office).
Location: NX 156 304. Most southerly tip of Scotland - five miles from village of Drummore, S of Stranraer.
Access: Open at all times. Access suitable for disabled. Disabled parking by centre. Centre open summer only (Apr-Oct).
Facilities: Visitor centre, toilets, nature trails, CCTV on cliffs.
Public transport: None.
Habitat: Sea cliffs, coastal heath.
Key birds: *Spring/summer*: Guillemot, Razorbill, Kittiwake, Black Guillemot, Puffin, Fulmar, Raven, Wheatear, Rock Pipit, Twite. Migrating Manx Shearwater. *All year*: Peregrine.
Contact: Paul Collin, Gairland, Old Edinburgh Road, Minnigaff, Newton Stewart DG8 6PL. 01671 402851.

13. WIGTOWN BAY

Dumfries & Galloway Council.
Location: NX 465 545. Between Wigtown and Creetown. It is the largest LNR in Britain at 2,845 ha. The A75 runs along E side with A714 S to Wigtown and B7004 providing superb views of the LNR.
Access: Open at all times. The hides are disabled friendly. Main accesses: Roadside lay-bys on A75 near Creetown and parking at Martyr's Stake and Wigtown Harbour.
Facilities: Hide at Wigtown Harbour with views over River Bladnoch, saltmarsh and fresh water wetland has disabled access from harbour car park. Also a small hide at Martyr's Stake car park and walks and interpretation in this area. Visitor room in Wigtown County Buildings has interpretation facilities and a commanding view of the bay. CCTV of Ospreys breeding in Galloway during summer and wetland birds in winter. Open Mon-Sat (10am-5pm, later some days). Sun (2pm-5pm).
Public transport: Travel Information Line 08457 090510 (local rate 9am-5pm Mon-Fri). Bus No 415 for Wigtown and west side. Bus No 431 or 500 X75 for Creetown and E side.
Habitat: Estuary with extensive saltmarsh/merse and mudflats with newly developed fresh water wetland at Wigtown Harbour.
Key birds: *Winter*: Internationally important for Pink-footed Goose, nationally important for Curlew, Whooper Swan and Pintail, with major gull roost and other migratory coastal birds. *Summer*: Breeding waders and duck.
Contact: Elizabeth Tindal, County Buildings, Wigtown, DG8 9JH01988 402 401, mobile 07702 212 728. e-mail: Elizabeth.Tindal@dumgal.gov.uk

OTHER SITES

(full details in previous editions)

C. Carstramon Wood
Contact: Trust HQ, 0131 3127765.
D. Stenhouse Wood
Contact: Trust HQ, 0131 3127765.
E. Wood Of Cree
Contact: RSPB, 01671 402861.

Central Scotland

Argyll

1. COLL RSPB RESERVE

RSPB (South & West Scotland Office).
Location: NM 168 561. By ferry from Oban. Take the B8070 W from Arinagour for five miles. Turn R at Arileod. Continue for about one mile. Park at end of the road. Reception point at Totronald.
Access: Open all year. Please avoid walking through fields and crops.
Facilities: Car park, information bothy at Totronald, guided walks in summer. Corn Crake viewing bench.
Public transport: None.
Habitat: Sand dunes, beaches, machair grassland, moorland, farmland.
Key birds: *Spring/summer*: Corn Crake, Redshank, Lapwing, Snipe. *Winter*: Barnacle and Greenland White-fronted Geese.
Contact: RSPB Coll Nature Reserve, Totronald, Isle of Coll, Argyll, PA78 6TB, 01879 230301.

2. LOCH GRUINART, ISLAY

RSPB Scotland (South & West Scotland Office).
Location: Sea loch on N coast, seven miles NW from Bridgend.
Access: Hide open all hours, no dogs, visitor centre open (10am-5pm), disabled access to hide, toilets.
Facilities: Toilets, visitor centre, hide, trail.
Public transport: None.
Habitat: Low wet grasslands, moorland.
Key birds: *Sept-Apr*: Barnacle and Greenland White-fronted Goose. *May-Aug*: Corn Crake. *Sept-Nov*: Migrating wading birds.
Contact: Liz Hathaway, RSPB Scotland, Bushmills Cottage, Gruinart, Isle of Islay PH44 7PP. 01496 850505. e-mail: liz.hathaway@rspb.org.uk www.rspb.org.uk

3. MACHRIHANISH SEABIRD OBSERVATORY

Eddie Maguire and John McGlynn.
Location: NR 628 209. Southwest Kintyre, Argyll. Six miles W of Campbeltown on A83, then B843.
Access: Daily May-Oct. Wheelchair access. Dogs welcome. Parking for three cars.
Facilities: Seawatching hide, toilets in nearby village.
Public transport: Regular buses from Campbeltown (West Coast Motors, tel 01586 552319).
Habitat: Marine, rocky shore and upland habitats.
Key birds: *Summer:* Golden Eagle, Peregrine and Twite. *Autumn:* Passage seabirds and waders. Gales often produce inshore movements of Leach's Petrel and other scarce seabirds including Balearic Shearwater and Grey Phalarope. *Winter:* Great Northern Diver.
Contact: Eddie Maguire, 25B Albyn Avenue, Campbeltown, Argyll PA28 6LX. 07919 660292. www.mso.1c24.net

OTHER SITES

(full details in previous editions)

A. Knapdale Reserve
Contact: Scottish Wildlife Trust (West Region), 0131 312 7765.

Ayrshire

4. AYR GORGE WOODLANDS

Scottish Wildlife Trust.
Location: NS 457 249. From Ayr take A719 NE for about three miles to A77. Go straight over the roundabout onto B473 and continue to Failford. Park in the lay-by in village.
Access: Open all year. Access by well-maintained path along west bank of River Ayr.
Facilities: Footpaths, interpretation boards, leaflets.
Public transport: None.
Habitat: Woodland.
Key birds: Woodland and riverside birds.
Contact: Scottish Wildlife Trust, Cramond House, Kirk Cramond, Cramond Glebe Road, Edinburgh, EH4 6NS, 0131 3127765.
e-mail: scottishwt@cix.co.uk

5. GARNOCK FLOODS

Scottish Wildlife Trust.
Location: NS 305 418. N of Irvine. From A78 N, take the one-way road to Bogside, just beyond A737 interchange. Park on roadside. Best viewed from cycle track along E boundary.
Access: Open all year.
Facilities: None.
Public transport: Bus service on A737, 1-2km distant.
Habitat: River, ponds, fields, wood.
Key birds: *Spring/summer*: Sedge and Willow Warblers, Lesser Whitethroat, Sand Martin. *Winter*: Wildfowl inc Goldeneye, Mute Swan, occasional Garganey, waders inc Ruff, Redshank and Snipe. Winter thrushes. *All year*: Kestrel, Sparrowhawk, Buzzard.
Contact: Wildlife Trust HQ (see Ayr Gorge).

OTHER SITES

(full details in previous editions)

B. Culzean Castle & Country Park
Contact: National Trust, 0131 243 9300.
C. Dalmellington Moss Nature Reserve
Contact: Scottish Wildlife Trust, 0131 312 7765.

Clyde

6. FALLS OF CLYDE

Scottish Wildlife Trust.
Location: NS 88 34 14. Approx one mile S of Lanark. Directions from Glasgow – travel S on M74 until J7 then along A72, following signs for Lanark and New Lanark.
Access: Open daylight hours all year. Partial disabled access.
Facilities: Visitor centre open 11am-5pm all year. Toilets and cafeteria on site. Seasonal viewing facility for Peregrines. Numerous walkways and ranger service offers comprehensive guided walks programme.
Public transport: Scotrail trains run to Lanark (0845 7484950). Local bus service from Lanark to New Lanark.
Habitat: River Clyde gorge, waterfalls, mixed riparian/conifer woodlands, meadow, pond.
Key birds: More than 100 species of bird recorded on the reserve, including unrivalled views of breeding Peregrine. Others include Goshawk, Barn Owl, Kingfisher, Dipper, Lapwing, Pied Flycatcher and Sky Lark.
Contact: Dr Stuart Glen, The Falls of Clyde Reserve, New Lanark, South Lanark ML11 9DB. 01555 665262. e-mail: fallsofclyde@cix.co.uk www.swt.org.uk

7. HOGGANFIELD PARK

Glasgow City Council (LNR).
Location: Free car park at entrance on Cumbernauld Road (A80), three miles NE of Glasgow city centre.
Access: Open all year.
Facilities: None.
Public transport: Call for advice.
Habitat: Loch with island, marsh, woodland, grassland.
Key birds: Wildfowl include Tufted Duck, Goldeneye and Goosander. *Autumn*: Ruddy Duck. *Winter*: Whooper Swan and Smew, Jack Snipe on marsh. Occasional Slavonian Grebe. *Summer*: Breeding Reed Bunting and woodland birds.
Contact: Iain Gibson, 0141 287 5665; e-mail iain.gibson@land.glasgow.gov.uk.

8. KNOCKSHINNOCK LAGOONS

Scottish Wildlife Trust.
Location: NS 776 113. Car park off B741 (New Cumnock to Dalmellington road), or from Kirkbrae in New Cumnock.
Access: Open all year. Access from Church Lane, New Cumnock.
Facilities: None.
Public transport: None.
Habitat: Mining spoil, lagoons, meadows, woodland.
Key birds: *Summer*: Breeding Redshank, Lapwing, Snipe, Curlew, Shoveler, Teal, Pochard and Garganey. *Winter*: Whooper Swans and large number of ducks. *Spring/autumn*: Good for migrating waders.
Contact: Trust HQ, 0131 312 7765

9. LOCHWINNOCH

RSPB (South & West Scotland Office).
Location: NS 358 582. 18 miles SW of Glasgow, adjacent to A760.
Access: Open every day except Christmas and Boxing Day, Jan 1 and Jan 2. (10am-5pm).
Facilities: Special facilities for schools and disabled. Refreshments available. Visitor centre, hides.

Public transport: Rail station adjacent, bus services nearby.
Habitat: Shallow lochs, marsh, mixed woodland.
Key birds: *Winter*: Wildfowl (esp. Whooper Swan, Greylag, Goosander, Goldeneye). Occasional passage migrants inc. Whimbrel, Greenshank. *Summer*: Breeding Great Crested Grebe, Water Rail, Sedge and Grasshopper Warblers.
Contact: RSPB Nature Centre, Largs Road, Lochwinnoch, Renfrewshire PA12 4JF. 01505 842663; fax 01505 843026;
e-mail lochwinnoch@rspb.org.uk

OTHER SITES
(full details in previous editions)

D. Barons Haugh
Contact: RSPB, 0141 331 0993

Fife

10. EDEN ESTUARY

Fife Council.
Location: NO 470 195. The reserve can be accessed from Guardbridge, St Andrews (one mile) on A91, and from Leuchars via Tentsmuir Forest off A919 (four miles).
Access: The Eden Estuary Centre is open (9am-5pm) every day except Christmas Day, New Year's Day and the day of the Leuchars airshow. Reserve is open all year, but a permit (from Ranger service) is required to access the N shore. Limited coach access and coach charge if using Kinshaldy car park.
Facilities: Visitor centre at Guardbridge. Information panels at Outhead. Hide at Balgove Bay (key from Ranger Service).
Public transport: Leuchars train station. Regular buses Cupar-Dundee-St Andrews. Tel: 01334 474238.
Habitat: Saltmarsh, river, tidal flats, sand dunes.
Key birds: *Winter*: Main interest is wildfowl and waders, best place in Scotland to see Black-tailed Godwit. Other species include Grey Plover, Shelduck, Bar-tailed Godwit. Offshore Common and Velvet Scoter occur and Surf Scoter is regularly seen. Peregrine, Merlin and Short-eared Owl occur in winter.
Contact: Les Hatton, Fife Ranger Service, Craigtown Country Park, St Andrews, Fife KY16 8NX. 01334 473047/07985 707593 (mobile).
e-mail: refrs@craigtoun.freserve.co.uk

11. ISLE OF MAY BIRD OBSERVATORY

Facilities: Hostel accommodation in ex-lighthouse (the Low Light) for up to six, Apr-Oct; usual stay is one week. No supplies on island; visitors must take own food and sleeping bag. Five Heligoland traps used for ringing migrants when qualified personnel present. SNH Warden usually resident Apr-Sep.
Key birds: Twelve species of nesting seabirds, including Kittiwake, Guillemot, Razorbill and Fulmar.
Bookings: Mike Martin, 2 Manse Park, Uphall, W Lothian EH52 6NX. 01506 855285;
e-mail: mwa.martin@virgin.net,

12. LOCHORE MEADOWS

Fife Ranger Service.
Location: NT165 958. Exit the M90 at J4. Drive E past Kelty on the A909. Turn L onto the B996 Cowdenbeath-Kinross road after one mile and take the 1st R to a car park.
Access: Open all year.
Facilities: Car park, hide. Suitable for wheelchairs.
Public transport: Bus: from Cowdenbeath/ Dunfermline to Kelty.
Habitat: Loch, meadows and woodland.
Key birds: *Spring/summer*: Little and Great Crested Grebes, Pintail, Pochard, Snipe, Grasshopper, Wood and Sedge Warblers, Whitethroat, Whinchat, Reed Bunting, Common Sandpiper, Redshank, Curlew, hirundines. *Winter*: Whooper Swan, Pintail, Wigeon, Teal, Pochard, Redwing, Fieldfare, Redpoll, Siskin.
Contact: Fife Ranger Service, Lochore Meadows Country Park, Crosshill, Lochgelly, Fife, 01592 414300.

OTHER SITES
(full details in previous editions)

E. Cameron Reservoir
Contact: Sheila Taylor, 23 Huntly Place, St Andrews, Fife, KY16 8XA01334 475541.
F. Cullaloe Nature Reserve
Contact: Trust HQ, 0131 3127765.
G. Isle Of May NNR
Contact: For Observatory accomodation: David Thorne, Craigurd House, Blyth Bridge, West

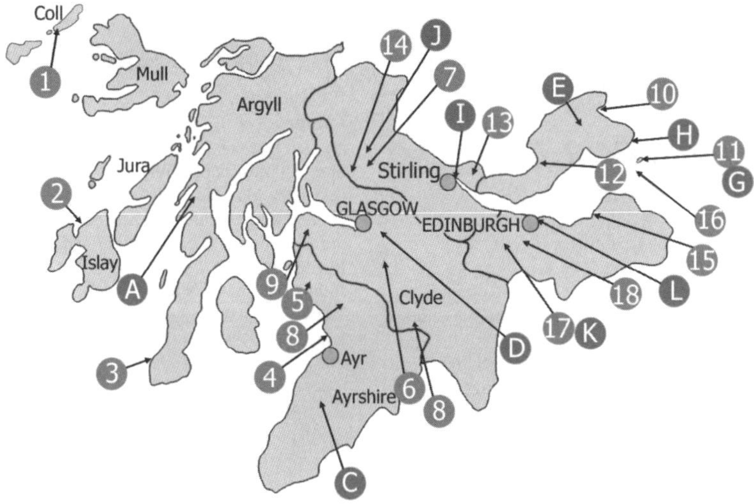

Linton, Peeblesshire EH46 7AH. For all other enquiries: SNH, 46 Crossgate, Cupar, Fife KY15 5HS.

H. Kilminning Coast
Contact: Trust HQ, 0131 3127765.

Forth

13. GARTMORN DAM

Clackmannanshire Council.
Location: NS 912 940. Approx one mile NE of Alloa, signposted from A908 in Sauchie.
Access: Open at all times. No charge. Access road not suitable for large coaches.
Facilities: Visitor centre with toilets. Open 8.30am-8.00pm daily (Apr-Sept inclusive) and 1pm-4pm (weekends only Oct-Mar). One hide, key obtainable from visitor centre. Provision for disabled.
Public transport: Bus service to Sauchie. First Bus, 01324 613777. Stirling Bus Station, 01786 446 474.
Habitat: Open water (with island), woodland – deciduous and coniferous, farmland.
Key birds: *Summer*: Great Crested Grebe, breeding Sedge and Reed Warblers. *Autumn*: Migrant waders. *Winter*: Wildfowl (regionally important site), Kingfisher, Water Rail.
Contact: Clackmannanshire Ranger Service, Lime Tree House, Alloa, Clackmannanshire FK10 1EX. 01259 450000. e-mail: rangers@clacks.gov.uk www.clacksweb.org.uk

14. INVERSNAID

RSPB (South & West Scotland Office).
Location: NN 337 088. On E side of Loch Lomond. Via B829 W from Aberfoyle, then along minor road to car park by Inversnaid Hotel.
Access: Open all year.
Facilities: None.
Public transport: None.
Habitat: Deciduous woodland rises to craggy ridge and moorland.
Key birds: *Summer*: Breeding Buzzard, Blackcock, Grey Wagtail, Dipper, Wood Warbler, Redstart, Pied Flycatcher, Tree Pipit. The loch is on a migration route, especially for wildfowl and waders.
Contact: RSPB South & West Scotland Office, 10 Park Quadrant, Glasgow, G3 6BS. 0141 331 0993.

OTHER SITES
(full details in previous editions)

I. Cambus Pools
Contact: Trust HQ 0131 312 7765.
J. Queen Elizabeth Forest Park
Contact: Forest Enterprise 0131 3340303.

Lothian

15. ABERLADY BAY

East Lothian Council (LNR).
Location: NT 472 806. From Edinburgh take A198 E to Aberlady. Reserve is 1.5 miles E of Aberlady village.
Access: Open at all times. Please stay on footpaths to avoid disturbance. Disabled access from reserve car park. No dogs.
Facilities: Small car park and toilets. Notice board with recent sightings at end of footbridge.
Public transport: Edinburgh to N Berwick bus service stops at reserve (request), service no 124. Railway 4 miles away at Longniddry.
Habitat: Tidal mudflats, saltmarsh, freshwater marsh, dune grassland, scrub, open sea.
Key birds: *Summer*: Breeding birds include Shelduck, Eider, Reed Bunting and up to eight species of warbler. Passage waders inc. Green, Wood and Curlew Sandpipers, Little Stint, Greenshank, Whimbrel, Black-tailed Godwit. *Winter*: Divers (esp. Red-throated), Red-necked and Slavonian Grebes and geese (large numbers of Pink-footed geese roost); sea-ducks, waders.
Contact: Ian Thomson, 4 Craigielaw, Longniddry, East Lothian EH32 0PY. 01875 870588.

16. BASS ROCK

Location: NT602873. Island in Firth of Forth, lying E of North Berwick.
Access: Private property. Regular daily sailings from N Berwick around Rock; local boatman has owner's permission to land individuals or parties by prior arrangement. For details contact Fred Marr, N Berwick on 01620 892838.
Facilities: None.
Public transport: None.
Habitat: Sea cliffs.
Key birds: The spectacular cliffs hold a large Gannet colony, (up to 9,000 pairs), plus auks, Kittiwake, Shag and Fulmer.

17. CALDER WOOD COUNTRY PARK

Local authority
Location: NT 077 670. N of Livingston.
Access: Open all year. Parking available off Bank Street in Mid Calder. Walk down the footpath beside the Masonic Hall or park in the lay-by on the A71 between the two shale bings, then along the roadside to the crash barrier and in.
Facilities: None.
Public transport: None.
Habitat: Woodland, marshland.
Key birds: *Spring/summer*: Woodcock, Tawny Owl, Grasshopper Warbler, Yellowhammer, Blackcap, Garden Warbler. *Winter*: Goldcrest, Redpoll, Willow Tit. *All year*: Dipper, Grey Wagtail, Sparrowhawk.

18. GLADHOUSE RESERVOIR

Scottish Water.
Location: NT 295 535. S of Edinburgh off the A703.
Access: Open all year although there is no access to the reservoir itself. Most viewing can be done from the road (telescope required).
Facilities: Small car park on north side. Not suitable for coaches.
Public transport: None.
Habitat: Reservoir, grassland, farmland.
Key birds: *Spring/summer*: Oystercatcher, Lapwing, Curlew. Possible Black Grouse. *Winter*: Geese, including Pinkfeet, Twite, Brambling, Hen Harrier.
Contact: Scottish Water, PO Box 8855, Edinburgh, EH10 6YQ, 0845 601 8855.
e-mail: customer.service@scottishwater.co.uk
www.scottishwater.co.uk

OTHER SITES

(full details in previous editions)

K. Almondell and Calderwood CP

Contact: Almondell and Calderwood CP 01506 882254.

L. Bawsinch & Duddingston Loch

Contact: Trust HQ, 0131 312 7765.

Eastern Scotland

Angus & Dundee

1. LOCH OF KINNORDY

RSPB (East Scotland).
Location: NO 351 539. Car park on B951 one mile W of Kirriemuir. Perth 45 minutes drive, Dundee 30 minutes drive, Aberdeen one hour drive.
Access: Open dawn-dusk. Disabled access to two hides via short trails.
Facilities: Three birdwatching hides.
Public transport: Nearest centre is Kirriemuir.
Habitat: Freshwater loch, fen, carr, marsh.
Key birds: *Spring/summer*: Osprey, Black-necked Grebe, Blacked-headed Gull. *Winter*: Wildfowl including Goosander, Goldeneye and Whooper Swan.
Contact: Alan Leitch, RSPB, 1 Atholl Crescent, Perth PH1 5NG. 01738 639783.
e-mail: alan.leitch@rspb.org www.rspb.org

2. LOCH OF LINTRATHEN

Scottish Wildlife Trust.
Location: NO 27 54. Seven miles W of Kirriemuir. Take B951 and choose circular route on unclassified roads round loch.
Access: Public hide planned but to date, Scottish Wildlife Trust hide (members' permit system only). Good viewing points from several places along unclassified roads.
Facilities: None.
Public transport: None.
Habitat: Oligatrophic/mesotrophic loch. Surrounded by mainly coniferous woodland.
Key birds: *Summer*: Osprey. *Winter*: Greylag Goose, Goosander, Whooper Swan, Wigeon, Teal.
Contact: Rick Goater, SWT, Annat House, South Anag, Ferryden, Montrose, Angus DD10 9UT. 01674 676555. e-mail: swtnero@cix.co.uk

3. MONTROSE BASIN

Scottish Wildlife Trust on behalf of Angus Council.
Location: NO 690 580 Centre of Basin. NO 702 565 Wildlife SWT Centre on A92. 1.5 miles from centre of Montrose.
Access: Apr 1-Oct 31 (10.30am-5pm). Nov 1-Mar 31, (10.30am-4pm).
Facilities: Visitor centre, shop, vending machine, toilets, disabled access to centre, two hides on western half of reserve.
Public transport: Train 1.5 miles in Montrose. Buses same as above.
Habitat: Estuary, saltmarsh, reedbeds, farmland.
Key birds: Pink-footed Goose - up to 35,000 arrive Oct. Wintering wildfowl and waders. Breeding Eider Ducks.
Contact: Karen van Eeden, Scottish Wildlife Trust, Montrose Basin Wildlife Centre, Rossie Braes, Montrose DD10 9TJ. 01674 676336.
e-mail: montrosebasin@swt.org.uk

4. SEATON CLIFFS

Scottish Wildlife Trust.
Location: NO 667 416. 30 acre cliff reserve, less than a mile from Arbroath town centre. Car parking at N end of promenade at Arbroath.
Access: Open all year.
Facilities: Nature trail with interpretation boards.
Public transport: None.
Habitat: Red sandstone cliffs with nature trail.
Key birds: Seabirds inc. Eider, auks, terns; Rock Dove and House Martin breed.
Contact: Wildlife Trust HQ, 0131 312 7765.

OTHER SITES

(full details in previous editions)

A. Balgavies Loch
Contact: Montrose Basin Centre, 01674 676336.

Moray & Nairn

5. CULBIN SANDS

RSPB (North Scotland Office).
Location: NH 900 580. Approx ½ mile from Nairn. Access to parking at East Beach car park, signed off A96.
Access: Open at all times. Not suitable for wheelchairs.
Facilities: Toilets at car park. Track along dunes and saltmarsh.

Public transport: Buses stop in Nairn, half mile W of site. Train station in Nairn three-quarters mile W of reserve.
Habitat: Saltmarsh, sandflats, dunes.
Key birds: *Winter*: Flocks of Common Scoter, Long-tailed Duck, Knot, Bar-tailed Godwit, Red-breasted Merganser. Rapters like Peregrine, Merlin and Hen Harrier attracted by wader flocks. Roosting geese. *Summer*: Breeding Ringed Plover, Oystercatcher and Common Tern.
Contact: RSPB North Scotland Office, Etive House, Beechwood Park, Inverness IV2 3BW. 01463 715000. e-mail: nsro@rspb.org.uk

6. SPEY BAY LEIN (THE)

Scottish Wildlife Trust.
Location: NJ 325 657. Eight miles NE of Elgin. From Elgin take A96 and B9015 to Kingston. Reserve is immediately E of village. Car parks at Kingston and Tugnet.
Access: Open all year.
Facilities: Wildlife centre.
Public transport: None.
Habitat: Shingle, rivermouth and coastal habitats.
Key birds: *Summer*: Osprey, waders, wildfowl. *Winter*: Seaduck and divers offshore (esp. Long-tailed Duck, Common and Velvet Scoters, Red-throated Diver).
Contact: Trust HQ, 0131 312 7765.

NE Scotland

7. FORVIE NNR

Scottish Natural Heritage.
Location: NK 034 289.
Access: Dogs on leads only. Reserve open at all times but ternery closed Apr 1 to end of Aug annually. Stevenson Forvie Centre open every day (Apr-Sept) and, when staff are available, outside those months.
Facilities: Interpretive display and toilets in Stevenson Forvie Centre. Bird hide, waymarked trail. Space is available for coach parking at the Stevenson Forvie Centre and main car park at the Ythan Estuary.
Public transport: Bluebird No 263 to Cruden Bay. Ask for the Newburgh or Collieston Crossroads stop. Tel: 01224 591381.
Habitat: Estuary, dunes, coastal heath.
Key birds: *Spring/summer*: Eider and terns nesting. *Winter*: Waders and wildfowl on estuary.
Contact: Alison Matheson (Area Officer), Scottish Natural Heritage, Stevenson Forvie Centre, Little Collieston Croft, Collieston, Aberdeenshire AB41 8RU. 01358 751330. www.snh.org.uk

8. FOWLSHEUGH

RSPB (East Scotland).
Location: NO 879 80. Cliff top path N from Crawton, signposted from A92, three miles S of Stonehaven.
Access: Unrestricted. Boat trips (May-Jul) from Stonehaven Harbour. Booking essential. Contact East Scotland regional office. Tel: 01224 624824.
Facilities: New car park (council) with limited number of spaces 200 yards from reserve (replaced following the storm damage of 1999).
Public transport: None.
Habitat: Sea cliffs.
Key birds: Spectacular seabird colony, mainly Kittiwake and auks. Bottle-nosed dolphins seen regularly.
Contact: The Warden, Starnafin, Crimond, Fraserburgh AB43 8QN. 01346 532017. e-mail: strathbeg@rspb.org.uk

9. GLEN TANAR NNR

Glen Tanar Estate.
Location: 47 96. On the A93 Banchory-Braemar road. From Aboyne turn S across the river, then W on the B976. At Bridge o'Ess, turn L to Braeloine to the car park.
Access: Open all year.
Facilities: Car parks, visitor centre (open Apr-Sep), trails. Do not attempt the summits unless you are properly prepared.
Public transport: None.
Habitat: Remnant of old Caledonian forest, heather moorland, mountains.
Key birds: *All year*: Black Grouse, Woodcock, Siskin, Grey Wagtail, Dipper. *Winter*: Possible Golden Eagle.
Contact: Ranger, Glen Tanar Estate, Brooks House, Glen Tanar, Aboyne, Aberdeenshire AB34 5EU. 01339 880047. e-mail: office@glentanar.co.uk

10. LOCH OF STRATHBEG

RSPB (East Scotland).
Location: NK 057 581. Near Crimond on the A90, nine miles S of Fraserburgh.

Access: Due to a change in management at Crimond airfield, public access across the airfield to our Fen, Bay and Bank Hides has been temporarily suspended. We are working to establish an alternative pedestrian access. To confirm the latest details, please ring the reserve before visiting. Starnafin visitor centre and Tower Pool hide open at all times dawn-dusk. (Loch hides, access restricted to between 8.00am and 4.00pm daily.) No dogs except guide dogs please. Visitor centre now fully accessible to wheelchairs and disabled visitors.
Facilities: Visitor centre and observation room at Starnafin, four hides, Tower Pool hide, accessible via 1,000 metre footpath from Starnafin, (three hides overlooking Loch accessed via MOD airfield). Toilets (with disabled access), car parking.
Public transport: Access to whole of reserve is difficult without a vehicle. Bus service runs between Fraserburgh and Peterhead, stopping at Crimond just over one mile from visitor centre.
Habitat: Dune loch with surrounding marshes, reedbeds, grasslands, dunes and agricultural land.
Key birds: *Winter*: Internationally important numbers of Whooper Swan, Pink-footed and Barnacle Geese, large numbers of winter duck including Smew. *Spring/summer*: Waders, Black-headed Gull, Common Tern, Water Rail, farmland birds including Corn Bunting. *Spring/autumn*: Spoonbill, Little Egret, Marsh Harrier, passage waders including Black-tailed Godwit.
Contact: RSPB Warden, RSPB Loch of Strathbeg, Starnafin, Crimond, Fraserburgh, AB43 8QN. 01346 532017. e-mail: strathbeg@rspb.org.uk

11. LONGHAVEN CLIFFS

Scottish Wildlife Trust.
Location: NK 116 394. Two miles S of Peterhead. Take A952 S from Peterhead and then A975 to Bullers of Buchan (gorge).
Access: Access from car park at Blackhills quarry or Bullers of Buchan.
Facilities: Leaflet available from Mark Young, Mechlepark, Oldmeldrum, Inverurie, Aberdeenshire, AB5 0DC.
Public transport: None.
Habitat: Rugged red granite cliffs and cliff-top vegetation.
Key birds: *May-July:* Nine species of breeding seabird inc. Kittiwake, Shag, Guillemot, Razorbill, Puffin.
Contact: Trust HQ, 0131 312 7765.

OTHER SITES
(full details in previous editions)

B. Haddo Country Park
Contact: Aberdeenshire Ranger Service, 01651 851489.
C. St Cyrus
Contact: Scottish Natural Heritage, 01674 830736.

Perth & Kinross

12. BEN LAWYERS

National Trust for Scotland.
Location: Off A827, 1.5 miles NE of Killin, N of Loch Tay.
Access: Open all year.

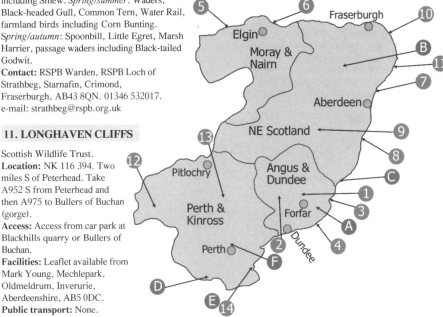

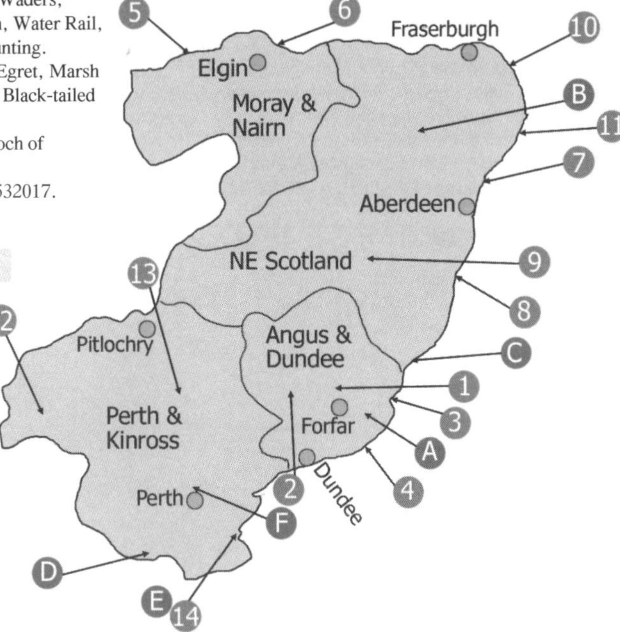

Facilities: Car park, visitor centre daily 10am-5pm (25 Mar-29 Sep) may close for 30 mins for lunch between 1pm-2pm. Toilets (one suitable for disabled), information.
Public transport: None.
Habitat: Perthshire's highest mountain.
Key birds: *Spring/summer*: Ring Ouzel, warblers, Curlew. *All year*: Raven, Red Grouse, Ptarmigan, Dipper.
Contact: Ranger's Office, National Trust for Scotland, Lynedoch, Main Street, Killin FK21 8UW. Visitor Centre (01567) 820397 or office (01567) 820988. www.nts.org.uk

13. LOCH OF THE LOWES

Scottish Wildlife Trust.
Location: NO 042 435. Sixteen miles N of Perth, two miles NE of Dunkeld - just off A923 (signposted).
Access: Visitor centre open Apr-Sept inclusive (10am-5pm), mid-Jul to mid-Aug (10am-6pm). Observation hide open all year - daylight hours. No dogs allowed. Partial access for wheelchairs.
Facilities: Visitor centre with toilets, observation hide.
Public transport: Railway station - Birnam/ Dunkeld - three miles from reserve. Bus from Dunkeld - two miles from reserve.
Habitat: Freshwater loch with fringing woodland.
Key birds: Breeding Ospreys(Apr-end Aug). Nest in view, 200 metres from hide. Wildfowl and woodland birds. Greylag roost (Oct-Mar).
Contact: Mr Stoneman, (Manager), Scottish Wildlife Trust, Loch of the Lowes, Visitor Centre, Dunkeld, Perthshire PH8 0HH. 01350 727337.

14. VANE FARM NNR

RSPB (East Scotland).
Location: NT 160 993. By Loch Leven. Take exit 5 from M90 onto B9097.
Access: Open daily (10am-5pm) except Christmas Day, Boxing Day, Jan 1and Jan 2. Cost £3 adults, £2 concessions, 50p children, £6 family. Free to members. No dogs except guide dogs. Disabled access to shop, coffee shop, observation room and toilets. Coach parking available for up to 2 coaches. Free car parking.
Facilities: Shop, coffee shop and observation room overlooking Loch Leven and the reserve. There is a 1.25 mile hill trail through woodland and moorland. Wetland trail with three observation hides. Toilets, including disabled.
Public transport: Nearest train station Cowdenbeath (nine miles away). Nearest bus station Kinross at Green Hotel (five miles away).
Habitat: Wet grassland and flooded areas by Loch Leven. Arable farmland. Native woodland and heath moorland.
Key birds: *Spring/summer*: Breeding and passage waders (including Lapwing, Redshank, Snipe, Curlew). Farmland birds (including Sky Lark and Yellowhammer). *Winter*: Whooper Swan, Bewick's Swan, Pink-footed Goose.
Contact: Ken Shaw, Senior Site Manager, Vane Farm Nature Centre, Kinross, Tayside KY13 9LX. 01577 862355. e-mail: vanefarm@rspb.co.uk

OTHER SITES

(full details in previous editions)

D. Doune Ponds

Contact: Stirling Council Countryside Ranger Service, Viewforth, Stirling FK8 2ET.

E. Loch Leven

Contact: SNH, Loch Leven Laboratory, 01577 864439.

F. Quarrymill Woodland Park

Contact: Gannochy Trust, Isle Road, Perth, Perthshire, 01738 633 890.

Highlands & Islands

Highland & Caithness

1. ABERNETHY FOREST RESERVE – LOCH GARTEN

RSPB (North Scotland Office).
Location: NH 981 184. 2.5 miles from Boat of Garten, eight miles from Aviemore. Off B970, follow 'RSPB Ospreys' road signs (between Apr - Aug only).
Access: Osprey Centre open daily 10am-6pm (Apr to end Aug). Disabled access. No dogs (guide dogs only). No charge to RSPB members. Non-members: adults £2.50, senior citizens £1.50, children 50p.
Facilities: Osprey Centre overlooking nesting Ospreys, toilets, optics and CCTV live pictures.
Public transport: Bus service to Boat of Garten from Aviemore, 2.5 mile footpath to Osprey Centre. Steam railway to Boat of Garten from Aviemore.
Habitat: Caledonian pine wood.
Key birds: Ospreys nesting from Apr to Aug, Crested Tit, Crossbill, red squirrel. In 2004 hide provided views of lekking Capercaillies Apr to mid-May.
Contact: R W Thaxton, RSPB, Forest Lodge, Nethybridge, Inverness-shire PH25 3EF. 01479 821894.

2. BEINN EIGHE

Scottish Natural Heritage.
Location: NG 990 620. By Kinlochewe, Wester Ross, 50 miles from Inverness and 20 miles from Gairloch on A832.
Access: Reserve open at all times, no charge. Visitor centre open Easter-Oct (10am-5pm).
Facilities: Visitor centre, toilets, woodland trail and mountain trail - self-guided with leaflets from visitor centre. Trails suitable for all abilities.
Public transport: Very limited.
Habitat: Caledonian pine forest, dwarf shrub heath, mountain tops, freshwater loch shore.
Key birds: Golden Eagle, Scottish Crossbill, Ptarmigan, Red Grouse, Siskin. *Summer*: Black-throated Diver, Redwing, Snow Bunting.
Contact: David Miller, Reserve Manager, Anancaun, Kinlochewe, Ross-shire IV22 2PD. 01445 760254. e-mail: david.miller@snh.gov.uk

3. BEN MORE COIGACH

Scottish Wildlife Trust.
Location: NC 075 065. 10 miles N of Ullapool, W of A835.
Access: Access at several points from minor road off A835 to Achiltibuie. Open all year, do not enter croftland without permission.
Facilities: None.
Public transport: None.
Habitat: Loch, bog, mountain and moorland.
Key birds: Upland birds (inc. Ptarmigan, Raven, Ring Ouzel, Golden Plover, Twite). *Winter:* Grazing Barnacle Goose.
Contact: John Smith, North Keanchullish, Ullapool, Wester Ross IV26 2TW. 01854 612531.

4. FORSINARD

RSPB (North Scotland).
Location: NC 89 04 25. 30 miles SW of Thurso on A897. Turn off A9 at Helmsdale from the South (24 miles) or A836 at Melvich from the N coast road (14 miles).
Access: Open at all times, but few birds Nov-Feb. Contact visitor centre during breeding season (mid-Apr to end Jun) and during deerstalking season (Jul 1-Feb 15) for advice. Self-guided trail open all year, no dogs, not suitable for wheelchairs.
Facilities: Visitor centre open Apr 1-Oct (9am-6pm), seven days per week. Static and AV displays, live CCTV and webcam link to Hen Harrier nest in breeding season. Wheelchair access to centre and toilet. Guided walks Tue and Thu, May-Aug. Hotel nearby.
Public transport: Train from Inverness and Thurso (0845 484950) visitor centre in Forsinard Station building.
Habitat: Blanket bog, upland hill farm.
Key birds: Golden Plover, Greenshank, Dunlin, Hen Harrier, Merlin, Short-eared Owl.
Contact: RSPB, Reserve Office, Forsinard, Sutherland KW13 6YT. 01641 571225.
e-mail: forsinard@rspb.org.uk

5. HANDA

Scottish Wildlife Trust.
Location: NC 138 480. Accessible by boat from Tarbet, near Scourie - follow A894 N from Ullapool 40 miles. Continue another three miles, turn left down single track road another three miles to Tarbet.
Access: Open April-Sept. Boats leave 9.30am-2pm (last boat back 5pm). Dogs not allowed. Visitors are asked for a contribution of £2 towards costs. Not suitable for disabled due to uneven terrain.
Facilities: Three mile circular path, shelter (no toilets on island - use those in Tarbet car park). Visitors are given introductory talk and a leaflet with map on arrival.
Public transport: Post bus to Scourie (tel 01549 402357 Lairg Post Office). Train to Lairg (tel 0845 484950 National Train enquiries). No connecting public transport between Scourie and Tarbet.
Habitat: Sea cliffs, blanket bog.
Key birds: *Spring/summer*: Biggest Guillemot and Razorbill colony in Britain and Ireland. Also nationally important for Kittiwake, Arctic and Great Skuas. Puffin, Shag, Fulmar and Common and Arctic Terns also present.
Contact: Mark Foxwell, Conservation Manager Unit 4A, 3 Carsegate Road North, Inverness IV3 8PU. 01463 714746.
e-mail: mfoxwell@swt.org.uk
Charles Thomson (Boatman) 01971 502347

6. INSH MARSHES

RSPB (North Scotland Office).
Location: NN 775 999. In Spey Valley, two miles NE of Kingussie on B970 minor road.
Access: Open at all times. No disabled access. Coach parking available along access road to car park.
Facilities: Information viewpoint, two hides, three nature trails. Not suitable for disabled. No toilets.
Public transport: Nearest rail station Kingussie (two miles).
Habitat: Marshes, woodland, river, open water.
Key birds: *Spring/summer*: Waders (Lapwing, Curlew, Redshank, Snipe), wildfowl (including Goldeneye and Wigeon), Spotted Crake, Wood Warbler, Redstart, Tree Pipit. *Winter*: Hen Harrier, Whooper Swan, other wildfowl.
Contact: Pete Moore, Ivy Cottage, Insh, Kingussie, Inverness-shire PH21 1NT. 01540 661518. e-mail: pete.moore@rspb.org.uk
www.kincraig.com/rspb.htn

7. ISLE OF EIGG

Scottish Wildlife Trust.
Location: NM 38 48. Small island S of Skye, reached by ferry from Maillaig or Arisaig (approx 12 miles).
Access: Ferries seven days per week (weather permitting) during summer. Four days per week (weather permitting) Sept-Apr. Coach parties would need to transfer to ferries for visit to Eigg. Please contact ferry companies prior to trip.
Facilities: Pier centre – shops/Post Office, tea-room, craftshop, toilets.
Public transport: Caledonian MacBrayne Ferries NE from Mallaig (tel: 01687 462403), *MV Sheerwater* from Arisaig (tel: 01678 450 224).
Habitat: Moorland (leading to sgurr pitchstone ridge), wood and scrub, hay fields, shoreline. Marsh and bog.
Key birds: Red-throated Diver, Golden Eagle, Buzzard, Raven. *Summer*: Manx Shearwater, Arctic Tern, various warblers, Twite, etc.
Contact: John Chester, Millers Cottage, Isle of Eigg, Small Isles PH42 4RL. 01687 482477.
www.isleofeigg.org

8. ISLE OF RUM

SNH (North West Region).
Location: NM 370 970. Island lying S of Skye. Passenger ferry from Mallaig, take A830 from Fort William.
Access: Contact Reserve Office for details of special access arrangements relating to breeding birds, deer stalking and deer research.
Facilities: Kinloch Castle Hostel, 01687 462037, Bayview Guest House, 01687 462023. General store and post office, guided walks in summer.
Public transport: Caledonian MacBrayne ferry from Mallaig, 01687 450224, www.arisaig.co.uk
Habitat: Coast, moorland, woodland restoration, montane.
Key birds: *Summer:* Large Manx Shearwater colonies on hill tops; breeding auks (inc. Black Guillemot), Kittiwake, Fulmar, Eider, Golden Plover, Merlin, Red-throated Diver, Golden Eagle.
Contact: SNH Reserve Office, Isle of Rum PH43 4RR, 01687 462026; fax 01687 462805.

9. LOCH FLEET

Scottish Wildlife Trust.
Location: NH 794 965. Site lies two miles S of Golspie on the A9 and five miles N of Dornoch.

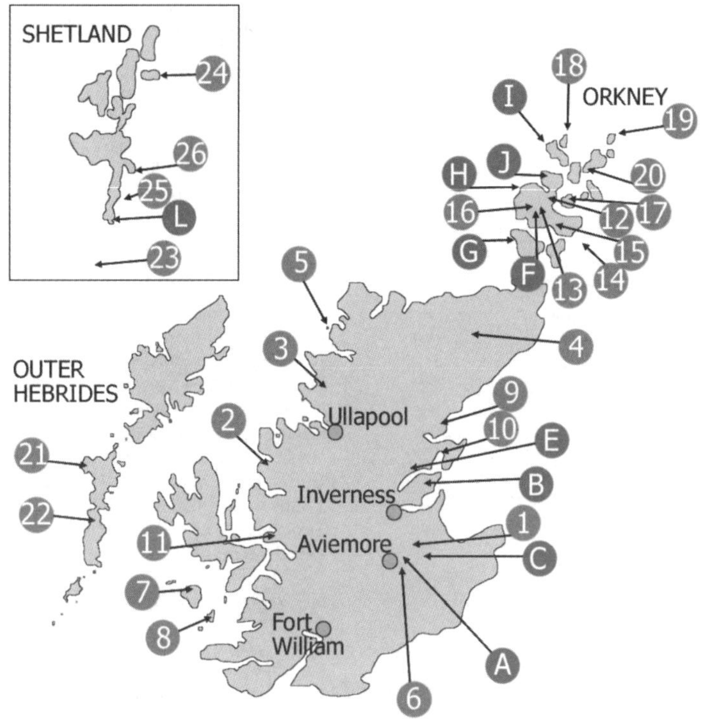

View across tidal basin from A9 or unclassified road to Skelbo.
Access: Park at Little Ferry or in lay-bys around the basin.
Facilities: Guided walks in Summer. Interpretive centre.
Public transport: None.
Habitat: Tidal basin, sand dunes, shingle, woodland, marshes.
Key birds: *Winter*: Important feeding place for ducks and waders. The sea off the mouth of Loch Fleet is a major wintering area for Long-tailed Duck, Common and Velvet Scoters, Eider Duck. Pinewood off minor road S from Golspie to Little Ferry, with Crossbill, occasional Crested Tit.
Contact: Trust HQ, 0131 312 7765.

10. NIGG BAY RSPB RESERVE

RSPB (North Scotland Office).
Location: NH 805 731. One mile (1.6km) N of Nigg village on the B9175.
Access: Open at all times.
Facilities: Hide, car park.
Public transport: Bus: for info call Stagecoach on 01463 239292. Train station at Fearn, four miles.
Habitat: Extensive area of mudflat, saltmarsh and wet grassland.
Key birds: *Winter*: Large flocks of wintering waders, waterfowl and Pink-footed Geese. *Summer*: Breeding Lapwing, Oystercatcher, Redshank. Osprey feeding in the bay.
Contact: RSPB North Scotland Office, Etive House, Beechwood Park, Inverness IV2 3BW. 01463 715000. e-mail: nsro@rspb.org.uk

11. RAHOY HILLS RESERVE

Scottish Wildlife Trust.
Location: NM 690 535. Part of Morvern peninsula, facing Mull. Enter Black Glen from Acharn.
Access: Open all year. Permit required.
Facilities: None.
Public transport: None.
Habitat: Mountain, oak woods, hill lochans.

Key birds: *Spring/summer*: Golden Eagle, Common Sandpiper, Pied Flycatcher, woodland birds. Pine marten and wildcat in the area.
Contact: Cramond House, Kirk Cramond, Cramond Glebe Road, Edinburgh, EH4 6NS, 0131 3127765. e-mail: enquiries@swt.org.uk www.swt.org.uk

OTHER SITES
(full details in previous editions)

A. Cairngorm NNR
Contact: SNH, 01479 810477.
B. Fairy Glen
Contact: RSPB, 01463 715000.
C. Glenborrodale RSPB Reserve
Contact: RSPB ,01463 715000.
D. Loch Ruthven
Contact: RSPB, 1463 715000
E. Udale Bay RSPB Reserve
Contact: RSPB, 01463 715000.

Orkney

12. BIRSAY MOORS

RSPB (East Scotland).
Location: Access to hide at Burgar Hill (HY 344 257), signposted from A966 at Evie. Birsay Moors viewed from layby on B9057 NW of Dounby (HY 347 245).
Access: Open access all year round.
Facilities: One hide at Burgar Hill very good for watching breeding Red-throated Divers Apr to Aug.
Public transport: Orkney Coaches. Service within 0.5 mile of reserve. Tel: 01856 877500.
Habitat: Diverse example of Orkney moorland - wet and dry heath, bog, mire, scrub and some farmland.
Key birds: *Spring/summer*: Nesting Hen Harrier, Merlin, Great and Arctic Skuas, Short-eared Owl, Golden Plover, Curlew, Red-throated Diver. *Winter*: Hen Harrier roost.
Contact: The Warden, 12/14 North End Road, Stromness, Orkney KW16 3HG. 01856 850176. e-mail: orkney@rspb.org.uk

13. BRODGAR

RSPB (East Scotland).
Location: HY 296 134. Reserve surrounds the Ring of Brodgar, part of the Heart of Neolithic Orkney World Heritage Site on the B9055 off the Stromness-Finstown Road.
Access: Open all year.
Facilities: Footpath, circular route approx one mile.
Public transport: Orkney Coaches. Service within 0.5 mile of reserve. Tel: 01856 877500.
Habitat: Farmland including species rich grassland, loch shores.
Key birds: *Spring/summer*: Breeding waterfowl on farmland and nine species of waders breed here. The farmed grassland is suitable for Corn Crake and provides water, food and shelter for finches, larks and buntings. *Winter*: Large numbers of Golden Plover, Curlew and Lapwing.
Contact: The Warden, 12/14 North End Road, Stromness, Orkney KW16 3HG. 01856 850176. e-mail: orkney@rspb.org.uk

14. COPINSAY

RSPB (East Scotland).
Location: HY 610 010. Access by private boat or hire boat from mainland Orkney.
Access: Open all year round.
Facilities: House on island open to visitors, but no facilities. No toilets or hides.
Public transport: None.
Habitat: Sea cliffs, farmland.
Key birds: *Summer*: Stunning seabird-cliffs with breeding Kittiwake, Guillemot, Black Guillemot, Puffin, Razorbill, Shag, Fulmar, Rock Dove, Eider, Twite, Raven and Greater Black-backed Gull. Passage migrants esp. during periods of E winds.
Contact: The Warden, 01856 850176.
S Foubisher (boatman) 01856 741252 - cannot sail if wind is in the east

15. HOBBISTER

RSPB (East Scotland).
Location: HY 396 070 or HY 381 068. Near Kirkwall.
Access: Open access between A964 and the sea. Dogs on leads please.
Facilities: A council maintained footpath to Waulkmill Bay, two car parks, walks along peat-cutters' tracks.

Public transport: Orkney Coaches. Tel: 01856 877500.
Habitat: Orkney moorland, bog, fen, saltmarsh, coastal cliffs, scrub.
Key birds: *Summer*: Breeding Hen Harrier, Merlin, Short-eared Owl, Red Grouse, Red-throated Diver, Eider, Merganser, Black Guillemot. Wildfowl and waders at Waulkmill Bay. *Autumn/winter*: Waulkmill for sea ducks, divers, auks and grebes (Long-tailed Duck, Red, Black and Great Northern Divers, Slavonian Grebe).
Contact: The Warden, 01856 850176.
e-mail: orkney@rspb.org.uk

16. LOONS (THE)

RSPB (East Scotland).
Location: HY 246 242. Access to hide (only) via minor road from A986, three miles N of Dounby.
Access: Hide open all year.
Facilities: One hide with wheelchair access. No nature trail nor toilets.
Public transport: Orkney Coaches (01856 877500).
Habitat: The best remaining wetland in Orkney.
Key birds: *Summer*: Breeding Pintail, Red-breasted Merganser and waders (inc. Snipe, Redshank, Black-tailed Godwit), Common and Black-headed Gulls, Arctic Tern. *Winter*: Regular flock of Greenland White-fronted Goose.
Contact: The Warden, 01856 850176.
e-mail: orkney@rspb.org.uk

17. MILL DAM

RSPB (East Scotland).
Location: HY 483 178.
Access: Hide open all year.
Facilities: Hide with wheelchair access.
Public transport: Vehicular ferry from Kirkwall to Shapinsay, 30 minute walk from ferry. (Orkney Ferries 01856 872044).
Habitat: Wetland. A little gem affording great views from the hide of ducks and waders in Spring, Autumn and Winter.
Key birds: *All year:* Shoveler, Pintail, Gadwall, Ruddy Duck, gulls. *Winter:* Whooper Swans, Wigeon, Teal, Shoveler.
Contact: The Warden, 01856 850176.
e-mail: orkney@rspb.org.uk

18. NORTH HILL, PAPA WESTRAY

RSPB (East Scotland).
Location: HY 496 538. Small island lying NE of Westray, reserve at N end of island's main road.
Access: Access at all times. During breeding season report to summer warden at Rose Cottage, 650 yards S of reserve entrance (Tel 01857 644240.) or use trail guide.
Facilities: Nature trails, hide/info hut.
Public transport: Orkney Ferries (01856 872044), Loganair Ferries (01856 872494).
Habitat: Sea cliffs, maritime heath.
Key birds: *Summer*: Close views of colony of Puffin, Guillemot, Razorbill and Kittiwake. Black Guillemot nest under flagstones around reserve's coastline. One of UK's largest colonies of Arctic Tern, also Arctic Skua.
Contact: Apr-Aug, The Warden at Rose Cottage, Papa Westray DW17 2BU. 01857 644240.
2. RSPB Orkney Office 12/14 North End Road, Stromness, Orkney KW16 3AG. 01856 850176.
e-mail: orkney@rspb.org.uk
www.rspb.co.uk

19. NORTH RONALDSAY BIRD OBSERVATORY

Location: HY 64 52. 35 miles from Kirkwall, Orkney mainland
Access: Open all year except Christmas.
Facilities: Accommodation, display room, meals, snacks etc for non-residents, fully licenced, toilets, croft walk.
Public transport: Twice daily (Mon-Sat) subsidised flights from Kirkwall (Loganair 01856 872494). Sunday flights in Summer. Once weekly ferry from Kirkwall (Fri or Sat), some Sun sailings in summer (Orkney Ferries Ltd 01856 872044).
Habitat: Crofting island with a number of eutrophic and oligotrophic wetlands. Coastline has both sandy bays and rocky shore. Walled gardens concentrate passerines.
Key birds: *Spring/Autumn*: Prime migration site including regular BBRC species. Wide variety of breeding seabirds, wildfowl and waders. *Winter:* Waders and wildfowl include Whooper Swan and hard weather movements occur.
Contact: Alison Duncan, North Ronaldsay Bird Observatory, Twingness, North Ronaldsay, Orkney KW17 2BE. 01857 633200.
e-mail: alison@nrbo.prestel.co.uk
www.nrbo.f2s.com

20. ONZIEBUST, EGILSAY

RSPB (East Scotland).
Location: HY 470 287.
Access: Open al all times, use trail guide.
Facilities: Nature trail, display in pier waiting room. Tours by arrangement with warden.
Public transport: Orkney Ferries to Egilsay (via Rousay and Wyre) from Tingwall Pier. Tel: 01856 751360.
Habitat: Wetland, farmland, sandy and rocky shore.
Key birds: *Summer:* Breeding Corn Crake, Lapwng, Redshank, Snipe, Curlew, Twite, Sky Lark, Reed Bunting, Shoveler, Arctic Tern. Also Otter.
Contact: The Warden, Onziebust, Egilsay, Orkney KW17 2QD. 01856 821395.
e-mail: orkney@rspb.org.uk

OTHER SITES

(full details in previous editions)

F. Cottascarth and Rendall Moss
Contact: The Warden,01856 850176.

G. Hoy
Contact: 1. The Warden, 01856 791298.
2. Ley House, Hoy, Orkney KW16 3NJ.

H. Marwick Head
Contact: The Warden, 01856 850176.

I. Noup Cliffs, Westray
Contact: In Summer - RSPB Warden, 01857 644 240. Other times -RSPB Orkney Office, 01856 850176.

J. Trumland, Rousay
Contact: The Warden,01856 821395.

Outer Hebrides

21. BALRANALD

RSPB (North Scotland Office).
Location: NF 705 707. From Skye take ferry to Lochmaddy, North Uist. Drive W on A867 for 20 miles to reserve. Turn off main road three miles NW of Bayhead at signpost to Houghharry.
Access: Open at all times, no charge. Dogs on leads. Disabled access.
Facilities: Visitor centre and toilets - disabled access. Marked nature trail.
Public transport: Bus service (tel 01876 560244).
Habitat: Freshwater loch, machair, coast and croft lands.
Key birds: *Summer*: Corn Crake, Corn Bunting, Lapwing, Oystercatcher, Dunlin, Ringed Plover, Redshank, Snipe. *Winter*: Twite, Greylag Goose, Wigeon, Teal, Shoveler. *Passage*: Barnacle Goose, Pomarine Skua, Long-tailed Skua.
Contact: Jamie Boyle, 9 Grenitote, Isle of North Uist, H56 5BP. 01876 560287.
e-mail: james.boyle3@btinternet.com

22. LOCH DRUIDIBEG

SNH (North West Region).
Location: NF 782 378. South Uist.
Access: Restricted access during breeding season.
Facilities: None.
Public transport: Regular bus service passes reserve.
Habitat: Loch, machair, coast, moorland.
Key birds: *Summer*: Breeding Greylag, waders, Corn Crake, wildfowl.
Contact: SNH Area Officer, Stilligarry, South Uist, HS8 5RS. 01870 620238; fax 01870 620350.

Shetland

23. FAIR ISLE BIRD OBSERVATORY

Fair Isle Bird Observatory.
Location: HZ 2172.
Access: Open from end Apr-end Oct. Free to roam everywhere except one croft (Lower Leogh).
Facilities: Public toilets at Airstrip and Stackhoull Stores (shop). Accommodation at Fair Isle Bird Observatory (phone/e-mail: for brochure/details). Guests can be involved in observatory work and get to see birds in the hand. Slide shows, guided walks through Ranger Service.
Public transport: Tue, Thurs, Sat - ferry (12 passengers) from Grutness, Shetland. Tel: Jimmy or Florrie Stout 01595 760222. Mon, Wed, Fri, Sat - air (7 seater) from Tingwall, Shetland. Tel: Loganair 01595 840246.
Habitat: Heather moor and lowland pasture/ crofting land. Cliffs.
Key birds: Large breeding seabird colonies (auks, Gannet, Arctic Tern, Kittiwake, Shag, Arctic Skua and Great Skua). Many common and rare migrants Apr/May/early Jun, late Aug-Nov.
Contact: Deryk Shaw (Warden), Hollie Shaw (Administrator), Fair Isle Bird Observatory, Fair

Isle, Shetland ZE2 9JU. 01595 760258.
e-mail: fairisle.birdobs@zetnet.co.uk
www.fairislebirdobs.co.uk

24. FETLAR

RSPB (East Scotland).
Location: HU 603 917. Lies E of Yell. Take car ferry from Gutcher, N Yell. Booking advised. Tel: 01957 722259.
Access: Part of RSPB reserve (Vord Hill) closed mid-May-end Jul. Entry during this period is only by arrangement with warden.
Facilities: Hide at Mires of Funzie. Displays etc at interpretive centre, Houbie. Toilets at ferry terminal, shop and interpretive centre.
Public transport: None.
Habitat: Serpentine heath, rough hill lane, upland mire.
Key birds: *Summer*: Breeding Red-throated Diver, Eider, Shag, Whimbrel, Golden Plover, Dunlin, skuas, Manx Shearwater, Storm Petrel. Red-necked Phalarope on Loch of Funzie (HU 655 899) viewed from road or RSPB hide overlooking Mires of Funzie.
Contact: RSPB North Isles Officer, Bealance, Fetlar, Shetland ZE2 9DJ. Tel/Fax: 01957 733246.
e-mail: malcolm.smith@rspb.org.uk

25. MOUSA

RSPB (Shetland Office).
Location: HU 460240. Small uninhabited island east of Sandwick in South Mainland of Shetland.
Access: By ferry from Leebitton Pier, Sandwick, Shetland - mid-Apr–mid-Sept.
Facilities: The Mousa Broch is the best preserved Iron Age tower in the world (World Heritage Site).
Public transport: Buses run to Sandwick from Lerwick. Details of ferry available from Tom Jamieson (01950 431367) or his web site (www.mousaboattrips.co.uk.).
Habitat: A small uninhabited island with maritime grassland and a small area of shell sand.
Key birds: *Summer*: Storm Petrels can be seen on the special night trips run by Tom Jamieson. Arctic Tern, Arctic and Great Skuas, Black Guillemot and Puffin.
Contact: Tom Jamieson, RSPB Shetland Office, East House, Sumburgh Head Lighthouse, Virkie, Shetland ZE3 9JN. 01950 460800.

26. ISLE OF NOSS NNR

Scottish Natural Heritage (Shetland Office).
Location: HU 531 410. Four miles by car ferry and road to the E of Lerwick. Take ferry to Bressay and follow signs for Noss. Park at end of road and walk to shore (600 yards) where ferry to island will collect you (if red flag is flying, island is closed due to sea conditions). Freephone 0800 107 7818 for daily ferry information.
Access: Access (Tue, Wed, Fri, Sat, Sun) 10am-5pm, May-late Aug. Access by zodiac inflatable so may be unsuitable for disabled. No dogs allowed on ferry.
Facilities: Visitor centre, toilets.
Public transport: None. Post car available, phone Royal Mail on 01595 820200. Cycle hire in Lerwick.
Habitat: Dune grassland, moorland, blanket bog, sea cliffs.
Key birds: *Spring/summer:* Fulmar, Shag, Gannet, Arctic Tern, Kittiwake, Great Black-backed Gull, Great Skua, Arctic Skua, Guillemot, Razorbill, Puffin, Black Guillemot, Eider.
Contact: Simon Smith, Scottish Natural Heritage, Stewart Building, Alexandra Wharf, Lerwick, Shetland ZE1 0LL. 01595 693345.
e-mail: simon.smith@snh.gov.uk

OTHER SITES

(full details in previous editions)

L. Sumburgh Head

Contact: RSPB Shetland Office, 01950 460 800.

East Wales

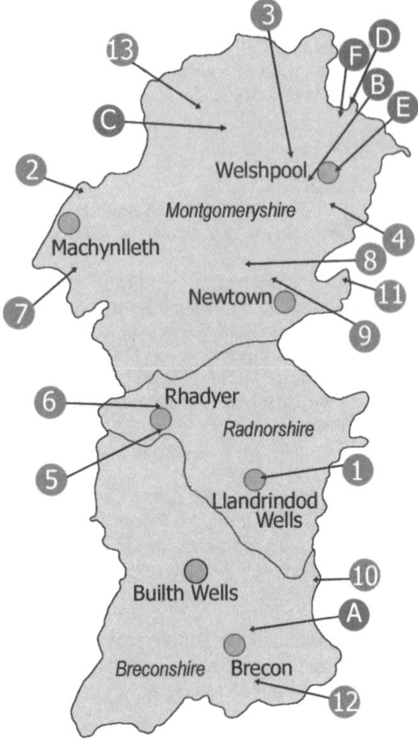

1. BAILEY EINON LNR

Radnorshire Wildlife Trust.
Location: SO 083 613. From Llandrindod Wells, take the Craig Road leading to Cefnllys Lane. At Shaky Bridge there is a car park and picnic site. A kissing-gate downstream from the picnic site marks the reserve entrance. Please do not park in front of the kissing-gate.
Access: Open all year.
Facilities: Car park, picnic site, waymarked trail.
Public transport: None.
Habitat: Woodland, river.
Key birds: *Spring/summer*: Pied Flycatcher, Redstart, Wood Warbler. *All year*: Great Spotted Woodpecker, Buzzard, usual woodland birds.
Contact: Warwick House, High Street, Llandrindod Wells, Powys, LD1 6AG. 01597 823298. www.waleswildlife.co.uk
e-mail: radnorshirewt@cix.co.uk

2. BWLCHCOEDIOG RESERVE

W K and Mrs J Evans.
Location: SH 878 149. From Machynlleth take A489 NE for 14 miles. Half mile east of Mallwyd, turn left into Cwm Cewydd, then 1.25 miles up the valley. Park at Bwlchcoediog House.
Access: Open all year round. No dogs in fenced areas. Please keep to paths.
Facilities: None.
Public transport: None.
Habitat: Farmland, woodland, streams, two ponds, lake.
Key birds: *Summer:* Breeding Tree Pipit, Redstart, Garden and Wood Warblers, Pied and Spotted Flycatchers. *Winter:* Woodcock, Brambling, Raven, Buzzard, Sparrowhawk. *All Year*: Siskin, occasional Peregrine, Red Kite, Dipper.
Contact: W K and Mrs J Evans, Bwlchcoediog Isaf, Cwm Cewydd, Mallwyd, Machynlleth, Powys SY20 9EE. 01650 531243.

3. COED PENDUGWM

Montgomeryshire Wildlife Trust.
Location: SJ 103 142. On a minor road one mile N of Pontrobert towards Llanfihangel. Park on the reserve car park down a short but steep track opposite Pendugwm Farm.
Access: Open all year.
Facilities: Footpaths.
Public transport: None.
Habitat: Broadleaved woodland, stream.
Key birds: *Spring/summer*: Pied Flycatcher, Redstart. *All year*: Buzzard, Sparrowhawk, woodpeckers, usual woodland species. Good for mammals.
Contact: Collot House, 20 Severn Street, Welshpool, Powys, SY21 7AD. 01938 555654.
e-mail: montwt@cix.co.uk
www.wildlifetrust.org.uk/montgomeryshire

4. DOLYDD HAFREN

Montgomeryshire Wildlife Trust.
Location: SJ 208 005. W of B4388. Go through Forden village and on about 1.5 miles. Turn right at sharp left bend at Gaer Farm to car park at end of track.
Access: Open at all times - dogs to be kept on lead at all times.
Facilities: Two bird hides.

Public transport: None.
Habitat: Riverside flood meadow – bare shingle, permanent grassland, ox-bow lakes and new pools.
Key birds: Goosander, Redshank, Lapwing, Snipe, Oystercatcher, Little Ringed Plover. *Winter*: Curlew.
Contact: Al Parrot, c/o Trust HQ, Collot House, 20 Severn Street, Welshpool, Powys SY21 7AD. 01938 555654. www.wildlifetrust.org.uk/montwt e-mail: montwt@cixcompulink.co.uk

5. GILFACH

Radnorshire Wildlife Trust.
Location: SN 952 714. Two miles NW from Rhayader/Rhaeadr-Gwy. Take minor road to St Harmon from A470 at Marteg Bridge.
Access: Centre Easter-Sept 31 (10am-5pm). Apr (every day). May/Jun (Fri-Mon). Jul/Aug (every day). Sept (Fri-Mon). Reserve open every day all year. Dogs on leads only. Disabled access and trail.
Facilities: Visitor centre – open as above. Way-marked trails.
Public transport: None.
Habitat: Upland hill farm, river, oak woods, meadows, hill-land.
Key birds: *Spring/summer*: Pied Flycatcher, Redstart. *All year*: Dipper, Red Kite.
Contact: Tim Thompson, Gilfach, St Harmon, Rhaeadr-Gwy, Powys LD6 5LF. 01597 870 301. e-mail: tim@ratgilfoelfisnet.co.uk http// westwales.co.uk/gilfach.htm

6. GLASLYN, PLYNLIMON

Montgomeryshire Wildlife Trust.
Location: SN 826 941. Nine miles SE of Machynlleth. Off minor road between the B4518 near Staylittle and the A489 at Machynlleth. Go down the track for about a mile.
Access: Open at all times – dogs on a lead at all times.
Facilities: Footpath.
Public transport: None.
Habitat: Heather moorland and upland lake.
Key birds: Red Grouse, Short-eared Owl, Meadow Pipit, Sky Lark, Wheatear and Ring Ouzel, Red Kite, Merlin, Peregrine. Goldeneye – occasional. *Winter*: Greenland White-fronted Goose.
Contact: Montgomeryshire Wildlife Trust, 01938 555654. e-mail: montwt@cix.compulink.co.uk www.wildlifetrust.org.uk/montwt

7. LLANGORSE LAKE

Privately owned.
Location: Head NW on A40 between Brecon and Crickhowell, turn off at Bwlich onto B4560. A minor road from Cathedine leads to the S shore. Access to the N shore is at Llangorse village.
Access: Open all year. A footpath from the parking area near Llangorse only goes along the W and S shore to Llagasty-Talyllyn.
Facilities: None.
Public transport: Train from Cardiff to Merthyr Tydfil then bus to Brecon. Only one post bus per day to Llangorse.
Habitat: The second largest natural lake in Wales.
Key birds: *Winter*: Wildfowl, Cormorants, Snipe, Jack Snipe, occasional Bittern. *Passage*: Dunlin, Oystercatcher, Ringed Plover, Black-tailed Godwit, Whimbrel, Greenshank, Green Sandpiper, Little Gull, terns.
Contact: Trust HQ, 01874 625708.

8. LLYN MAWR

Montgomeryshire Wildlife Trust.
Location: SO 009 971. From Newtown, head NW on A470 and then take minor 'no through' road N of Clatter. Stay close to shore.
Access: Permit required.
Facilities: None.
Public transport: None.
Habitat: Upland lake, wetland, scrub.
Key birds: *Summer*: Breeding Great Crested Grebe, Black-headed Gull, Snipe, Curlew, Whinchat. *Winter*: Occasional Goldeneye, Goosander, Whooper Swan.
Contact: Trust HQ, 01938 555654.

9. PWLL PENARTH

Montgomeryshire Wildlife Trust.
Location: SO 137 926. Take B4568 from Newtown to Llanllwchaiarn, turn down by the church and follow lane for a mile to sewage works gates.
Access: Open at all times. Disabled access via Severn Trent sewage works between 9am-4pm, Mon-Fri only. Dogs to be kept on lead at all times.
Facilities: Two hides.
Public transport: None.
Habitat: Lake, Sand Martin bank, arable crops.
Key birds: *Late spring/summer*: Sand Martin, Lapwing, Sky Lark, Grey Wagtail. *Winter*: Buntings, finches. *All year*: Kingfisher, Mallard, Coot, Canada Goose, Ruddy Duck.

Contact: Mike Green, Collot House, 20 Severn Street, Welshpool, Powys SY21 7AD. 01938 555654. e-mail: montwt@cix.compulink.co.uk www.wildlifetrust.org.uk/montwt

10. PWLL-Y-WRACH

Brecknock Wildlife Trust.
Location: SO 165 327. Between Hay-on-Wye and Brecon at foot of Black Mountains. Half mile SE of Talgarth. At the T-junction in the centre of Talgarth (Tourist Information Centre on your R) turn R and take an almost immediate L round a very sharp ninety degree bend. After 20m turn L opposite the Bell Hotel and follow the minor road for 1.5 miles past The Prya Centre (formerly the Mid Wales Hospital) on the L. The road narrows and the nature reserve car park is a few hundred yards on your R.
Access: A small car park which can take about six cars. A coach could be accommodated provided the car park is not already full.
Facilities: A network of footpaths, including a disabled access path.
Public transport: Bus 39 to Talgarth (Brecon to Hay-on-Wye).
Habitat: Steep valley woodland, stream and waterfall.
Key birds: Dipper, Grey Wagtail, woodland species (inc. Pied Flycatcher, Wood Warbler). Dormouse colony.
Contact: Trust HQ, 01874 625708.

11. ROUNDTON HILL

Montgomeryshire Wildlife Trust.
Location: SO 293 947. SE of Montgomery. From Churchstoke on A489, take minor road to Old Churchstoke, R at phone box, then first R.
Access: Open access. Tracks rough in places.
Facilities: Car park. Waymarked trails.
Public transport: None.
Habitat: Ancient hill grassland, woodland, streamside wet flushes, scree, rock outcrops.
Key birds: Buzzard, Raven, Wheatear, all three woodpeckers, Tawny Owl, Redstart, Linnet, Goldfinch.
Contact: Trust HQ, 01938 555654.

12. TALYBONT RESERVOIR

(Dwr Cymru) Welsh Water.
Location: SO 100 190. Take minor road off B4558 S of Talybont, SE of Brecon.
Access: No access to reservoir area, view from road.
Facilities: Displays at the Glyn Collwm information centre at Aber, between the reservoir and Talybont. Bird hide.
Public transport: None.
Habitat: Reservoir, woodland.
Key birds: *Winter*: Wildfowl (inc. Goldeneye, Goosander, Whooper Swan), Redpoll, Siskin. Migrant waders.

13. VYRNWY (LAKE)

RSPB (North Wales Office).
Location: SJ 020 193. Located WSW of Oswestry. Nearest village is Llanfyllin on A490. Take B4393 to lake.
Access: Reserve open all year. Visitor centre open Apr-Dec (10.30am-4.30pm), Dec-Apr weekends only (10.30am-4.30pm).
Facilities: Toilets, visitor centre, hides, nature trails, coffee shop, RSPB shop, craft workshops.
Public transport: Train and bus Welshpool (25 miles away).
Habitat: Heather moorland, woodland, meadows, rocky streams and large reservoir.
Key birds: Dipper, Kingfisher, Pied Flycatcher, Wood Warbler, Redstart, Peregrine and Buzzard.
Contact: Jo Morris, Centre Manager, RSPB Lake Vyrnwy Reserve, Bryn Awel, Llanwddyn, Oswestry, Salop SY10 0LZ. 01691 870278. e-mail: lake.vyrnwy@rspb.org.uk

OTHER SITES

(full details in previous editions)

A. Brechfa Pool

Contact: Trust HQ, 01874 625708.

B. Cwm-Y-Wydden

Contact: Montgomeryshire Wildlife Trust, 01938 555654.

C. Elan Valley

Contact: Elan Valley Visitor Centre, 01597 810880.

D. Llanymynech Rocks

Contact: Montgomeryshire Wildlife Trust, 01738 555654.

E. Severn Farm Pond

Contact: Montgomeryshire Wildlife Trust, 01938 555654.

F. Ty Brith Meadows

Contact: Montgomeryshire Wildlife Trust, 01938 555654.

North Wales

1. BARDSEY BIRD OBSERVATORY

Bardsey Bird Observatory.
Location: SH 11 21. Private 444 acre island. One hour boat journey from Pwllheli (18 miles SW of Bangor).
Access: Mar-Nov. No dogs. Visitor accommodation in 150-year-old farmhouse (two single, two double, two x four dorms).
To stay at the Observatory contact Alicia Normand (tel 01758 760667, e-mail bob&lis@solfach.freeserve.co.uk). Day visitors by Bardsey Ferries (01758 730326).
Facilities: Public toilets available for day visitors. Three hides, one on small bay, two seawatching.
Public transport: Trains from Birmingham to Pwllheli. Tel: 0345 484950. Arriva bus from Bangor to Pwllheli. Tel: 0870 6082608.
Habitat: Sea-birds cliffs viewable from boat only. Farm and scrubland, Spruce plantation, willow copses and gorse-covered hillside.
Key birds: *All Year*: Chough, Peregrine. *Spring/summer*: Manx Shearwaters (16,000 pairs), other seabirds. Migrant warblers, chats, Redstart, thrushes. *Autumn*: Many rarities including Eye-browed Thrush, Lanceolated Warbler, Iberian Chiffchaff, Collared Flycatcher, etc.
Contact: Steven Stansfield, Cristin, Ynys Enlli (Bardsey), off Aberaron, via Pwllheli, Gwynedd LL53 8DE. 07855 264151. www.bbfo.org.uk
e-mail: warden@bbfo.org.uk

2. CEIRIOG FOREST

Forest Enterprise.
Location: SJ 166 384. From Llangollen, take minor road S to Glyn Ceiriog and on to Nantyr. Turn R at a white cottage called Bryn Awel, through a gate marked Glyndyfrdwy into the forest. Park at the Forest Enterprise picnic site.
Access: Open all year. Long walk on metalled track.
Facilities: None. **Public transport:** None.
Habitat: Heather moor, woodland.
Key birds: *Spring/summer*: Redstart, Pied Flycatcher, Wood Warbler, Whinchat, Tree Pipit, Ring Ouzel, Wheatear. *All year*: Black Grouse, Dipper, Grey Wagtail, Red Grouse, Raven, Chaffinch, Redpoll, Siskin, Crossbill, all three woodpeckers, Sparrowhawk, Buzzard.
Contact: Forest Enterprise Wales, Victoria Terrace, Aberystwyth, Ceredigion, SY23 2DQ. 01970 612367.

3. CEMLYN

North Wales Wildlife Trust.
Location: SH 337 932. Ten miles from Holyhead, Anglesey, minor roads from A5025 at Tregele.
Access: Open all the time. Dogs on leads. Disabled viewing from adjacent road. During summer months walk on seaward side of ridge and follow signs.
Facilities: None. **Public transport:** None.
Habitat: Brackish lagoon, shingle, ridge.
Key birds: *Summer*: Breeding terns. *Winter*: Waders/ducks (including Little Grebe, Goldeneye and Shoveler).
Contact: Chris Wynne,376 High Street, Bangor, Gwynedd LL57 1YE. 01248 351541.
e-mail: nwwt@cix.co.uk
www.wildlifetrust.org.uk/northwales

4. COEDYDD ABER NNR

CCW (North West Area).
Location: SH 660 710. E of Bangor, off A55 towards Penmaenmawr.
Access: From car park at Bont Newydd, N of Aber Falls. Permit required for places away from designated routes.
Facilities: Small visitor centre. Leaflets.
Public transport: Buses from Bangor and Conwy to Abergwyngregyn Village
Habitat: Upland valley, deciduous woodland, river and spectacular waterfall.
Key birds: *All year:* Dipper, Grey Wagtail, Buzzard, Raven, woodland birds. *Summer:* Warblers and Ring Ouzel.
Contact: Duncan Brown (Summer Warden), 01286 672500.

5. CONNAHS QUAY

Deeside Naturalists' Society.
Location: SJ 275 715. NW of Chester. Take B5129 from Queensferry towards Flint, two miles.
Access: Advance permit required.
Facilities: Field studies centre, four hides.
Public transport: None.
Habitat: Saltmarsh, mudflats, grassland scrub,

open water, wetland meadow.
Key birds: High water roosts of waders, inc. Black-tailed Godwit, Oystercatcher, Redshank, Spotted Redshank. Passage waders. *Winter*: Wildfowl (inc. Teal, Pintail, Goldeneye), Merlin, Peregrine.
Contact: R A Roberts, 8 Kelsterton Road, Connahs Quay, Flintshire CH5 4BJ.

6. CONWY

RSPB (North Wales Office).
Location: SH 799 771. On E bank of Conwy Estuary. Access from A55 at exit signed to Conwy and Deganwy.
Access: Open daily (10am-5pm) or dusk if earlier. Closed for Christmas Day.
Facilities: Visitor centre, toilets including disabled. Two hides, all accessible to wheelchairs. Trails firm and level, though a little rough in places. Two further hides accessible to pedestrians.
Public transport: Train service to Llandudno Junction. Bus service to Tesco supermarket, Llandudno Junction. Tel: 08706 082 608.
Habitat: Open water, islands, reedbeds, grassland, estuary.
Key birds: *Spring/summer:* Breeding Reed and Sedge Warblers, Lapwing, Redshank, Little Ringed Plover, Sky Lark, Reed Bunting and rarities. *Autumn:* Passage waders, spectacular Starling roost and rarities. *Winter:* Kingfisher, Goldeneye, Water Rail, Red-breasted Merganser, wildfowl.
Contact: Alan Davies, Conwy RSPB Nature Reserve, Llandudno Junction, Conwy, North Wales LL33 9XZ. 01492 584091.

7. GORS MAEN LLWYD

North Wales Wildlife Trust.
Location: SH 975 580. W of Betws-y-Coed. Follow A5 to Cerrigydrudion (seven miles S of site), then take B4501 and go past the Llyn Brennig Visitor Centre. Approx two miles beyond centre, turn right (still on B4501). First car park on right approx 300 yards after the cattle grid.
Access: Open all the time. Dogs on leads. Keep to the paths. Rare breeding birds on the heather so keep to paths.
Facilities: In second car park by lake shore there are toilets and short walk to bird hide. Paths are waymarked, but can be very wet and muddy in poor weather.
Public transport: None.
Habitat: Heathland. Heather and grass overlooking large lake.
Key birds: *Summer*: Red and Black Grouse, Hen Harrier, Merlin, Sky Lark, Curlew. *Winter*: Wildfowl on lake.
Contact: Neil Griffiths, Reserves Officer, NWWT, 376 High Street, Bangor, Gwynedd LL57 1YE. 01248 351541. e-mail: nwwt@cix.co.uk www.wildlifetrust.org.uk/northwales

8. LLYN ALAW

Welsh Water/United Utilities.
Location: SH 390 865. Large lake five miles from Amlwch in northern part of Anglesey. Signposted from A55/A5/B5112/B5111/B5109.
Access: Open all year. No dogs to hides or sanctuary area but dogs allowed (maximum two per adult) in other areas.
Facilities: Toilets (including disabled), two hides, two nature trails, information centre, car parks, network of mapped walks, picnic sites, information boards.
Public transport: Not to within a mile.
Habitat: Large area of standing water, shallow reedy bays, hedges, scrub, woodland, marsh, grassland.
Key birds: *Summer*: Lesser Whitethroat, Sedge and Grasshopper Warblers, Little and Great Crested Grebes, Tawny Owl, Barn Owl, Buzzard. *Winter*: Whooper Swan, Goldeneye, Hen Harrier, Short-eared Owl, Redwing, Fieldfare, Peregrine, Raven. *All year*: Bullfinch, Siskin, Redpoll, Goldfinch, Stonechat. *Passage waders*: Ruff, Spotted Redshank, Curlew Sandpiper, Green Sandpiper.
Contact: Jim Clark, Llyn Alaw, Llantrisant, Holyhead LL65 4TW. 01407 730762.
e-mail: llynalaw@amserve.net

9. LLYN CEFNI

Welsh Water/United Utilities.
Location: SH 440 775. A reservoir located two miles NW of Llangefni, in central Anglesey. Follow B5111 or B5109 from the village.
Access: Open at all times. Dogs allowed except in sanctuary area.
Facilities: Toilets (near waterworks), picnic site, hide, information boards.
Public transport: Bus 32, 4 (45 Sat only, 52 Tue and Thu only). Tel 0870 6082608 for information.
Habitat: Large area of open water, reedy bays, coniferous woodland, carr, scrub.
Key birds: *Summer*: Whitethroat, Sedge and Grasshopper Warblers, Buzzard, Tawny Owl, Little Grebe, Gadwall, Shoveler. *Winter*:

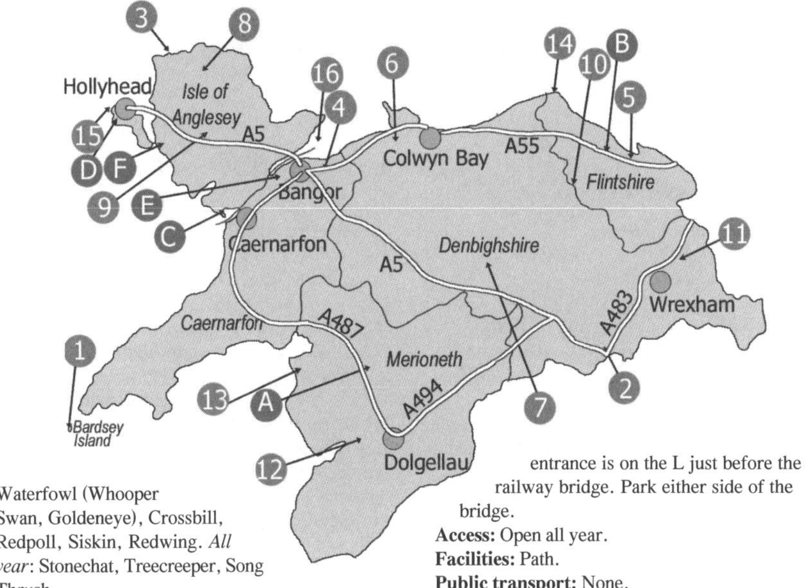

Waterfowl (Whooper Swan, Goldeneye), Crossbill, Redpoll, Siskin, Redwing. *All year*: Stonechat, Treecreeper, Song Thrush.
Contact: Jim Clark, Llyn Alaw, Llantrisant, Holyhead LL65 4TW. 01407 730762. e-mail: llynalaw@amserve.net

10. LOGGERHEADS COUNTRY PARK

Denbighshire County Council.
Location: Four miles from Mold, off A494.
Access: Open all year.
Facilities: Large car park, visitor centre, café, leaflet.
Public transport: Denbighshire Passenger Transport Group, 01824 706968.
Habitat: Limestone woodland, river.
Key birds: *Spring/summer*: Pied and Spotted Flycatchers, Redstart, Garden Warbler, Blackcap, Wood Warbler, Chiffchaff. *All year*: All three woodpeckers, Tawny Owl, Sparrowhawk, Nuthatch, Treecreeper, Goldcrest, Redpoll, Hawfinch. Occasional Crossbill.
Contact: Loggerheads Country Park, Loggerheads, Mold, Denbighshire, CH5 5LH. 01352 810586.

11. MARFORD LNR

North Wales Wildlife Trust.
Location: SJ 357 560. From Wrexham follow signs for the A483 to Chester. Just past a roundabout turn R onto the B5445 to Gresford and Marford. At Marford turn L into Springfield Lane, just past the Trevor Arms Hotel. The reserve entrance is on the L just before the railway bridge. Park either side of the bridge.
Access: Open all year.
Facilities: Path.
Public transport: None.
Habitat: Disused sand and gravel pit, cliff face, grassland, scrub, woodland, pool.
Key birds: *Spring/summer*: Spotted Flycatcher, Wood Warbler, good range of migrant birds. *All year*: Woodpeckers inc. Lesser Spotted, Linnet, Yellowhammer, woodland birds.
Contact: Adrian Lloyd Jones, Loggerheads Country Park, Nr Mold, Denbighshire CH7 5LH. 01248 351541. e-mail: nwwt@cix.co.uk www.wildlifetrust.org.uk/northwales

12. MAWDDACH VALLEY

RSPB (North Wales Office).
Location: SH 696 185 (information centre). Two miles W of Dolgellau on A493. Next to toll bridge at Penmaenpool.
Access: Reserve open at all times. Information centre open daily during Easter week and from Whitsun to first weekend of Sept (11am-5pm). Between Easter week and Whitsun, weekends only (noon-4pm).
Facilities: Toilets and car park at information centre.
Public transport: Buses run along A493. Morfa Mawddach railway halt four miles from information centre.
Habitat: Oak woodlands of Coed Garth Gell and willow/alder scrub at Arthog Bog SSSI.
Key birds: *Spring/summer*: Pied Flycatcher, Redstart and Tree Pipit. *Winter*: Raven, roving

flocks of Siskin, Redpoll with Goosander and Goldeneye on the estuary.
Contact: The Warden, Ynys-Hir Reserve, Eglwys-Fach, Machynlleth, Powys SY20 8TA. 01654 700222. e-mail: mawddach@rspb.org.uk

13. MORFA HARLECH NNR

Countryside Council for Wales.
Location: SH 574 317. N of Harlech, off A496.
Access: Open all year.
Facilities: Car park.
Public transport: Nearest bus stop at Dyffryn Arddudwy Post office, 1 mile S. Bus Gwynedd, 01286 679535. Train to Dyffryn Ardudwy (half mile)
Habitat: Shingle, coast, marsh, estensive dunes.
Key birds: *Spring/summer*: Whitethroat, Spotted Flycatcher, Grasshopper Warbler, migrants. *Passage*: Waders, Manx Shearwater, ducks. *Winter*: Divers, Whooper Swan, Wigeon, Teal, Pintail, Scaup, Common Scoter, Hen Harrier, Merlin, Peregrine, Short-eared Owl, Little Egret, Water Pipit, Snow Bunting, Twite. *All year/ breeding*: Redshank, Lapwing, Ringed Plover, Snipe, Curlew, Shelduck, Oystercatcher, Stonechat, Whinchat, Wheatear, Linnet, Reed Bunting, Sedge Warbler. Red-breasted Merganser, Kestrel, gulls.
Contact: CCW, Maes y Ffynnon, Ffordd, Bangor, Gwynedd, LL57 2DN. 0845 1306229.
e-mail: enquiries@ccw.gov.uk www.ccw.gov.uk

14. POINT OF AIR

RSPB (North Wales Office).
Location: SJ 140 840. At mouth of the Dee Estuary. Three miles E of Prestatyn. Access from A548 coast road to Talacre village. Park at end of Station Road.
Access: Open at all times.
Facilities: Car park, public hide overlooking saltmarsh and mudflats. No visitor centre. Toilets in Talacre village. Group bookings, guided walks and events. Wheelchair access planned end 2004. Track is 10 min walk (1km).
Public transport: Bus - Prestatyn (Arriva 11, 11A/Crossville). Rail - Prestatyn.
Habitat: Intertidal mud/sand, saltmarsh, shingle.
Key birds: *Spring/summer*: Breeding Sky Lark, Meadow Pipit, Reed Bunting. *Late summer*: Pre-migratory roost of Sandwich and Common Terns. *Autumn*: Passage waders. *Winter*: Roosting waterfowl (eg Shelduck, Pintail), Oystercatcher, Curlew, Redshank, Merlin, Peregrine, Short-eared Owl. Rarities have occurred.
Contact: John Harrison, Burton Point Farm, Station Road, Burton, Nr Neston, Cheshire CH64 5SB. 0151 3367681.
e-mail: john.harrison@rspb.org.uk

15. SOUTH STACK CLIFFS

RSPB (North Wales Office).
Location: SH 205 823. W of Holyhead, Anglesey. Take A5 to Holyhead and follow brown tourist signs to South Stack.
Access: No restrictions.
Facilities: Car parks. Information centre (Ellin's Tower) with windows overlooking main auk colony open daily (11am-5pm Easter-Sep), with live TV of the seabirds. Public footpaths.
Public transport: Mainline station Holyhead. Infrequent bus service, Holyhead-South Stack. Tel. 0870 608 2608.
Habitat: Sea cliffs, maritime heath.
Key birds: Peregrine, Chough, Fulmar, Puffin, Guillemot, Razorbill, Kittiwake, Shag, migrant warblers. Seabirds on passage.
Contact: Alastair Moralee, Plas Nico, South Stack, Holyhead, Anglesey LL65 1YH. 01407 764973.

16. TRAETH LAFAN

Gwynedd Council.
Location: NE of Bangor, stretching to Penmaenmawr. 1) Minor road from old A55 near Tal-y-Bont (SH 610 710) to Aber Ogwen car park by coast (SH 614 723). 2) Also access from minor road from Aber village to Morfa Aber LNR (SH 646 731) 3) track to Morfa Madryn LNR (SH 667 743), and 4) Llanfairfechan promenade (SH 679 754).
Access: Open access from 1,2, 3 and 4.
Facilities: Public paths. 2) Car park and hide. 3) Hides. 4) Toilets and cafés.
Public transport: Call council for advice or log on to www.gwynedd.gov.uk
Habitat: Intertidal sands and mudflats, wetlands, streams. SPA, SSSI, cSAC (candidate Special Area of Conservation) and LNR.
Key birds: Third most important area in Wales for wintering waders; of national importance for moulting Great Crested Grebe and Red-breasted Merganser; internationally important for Oystercatcher and Curlew; passage waders; winter concentrations of Goldeneye and Greenshank, and of regional significance for wintering populations of Black-throated, Red-

throated & Great Northern Divers and Black-necked & Slavonian Grebes.
Contact: Countryside Wardens, Gwynedd Council, Council Offices, Caernarfon LL55 1SH. 01286 679381; e-mail: CefnGwlad@gwynedd.gov.uk

OTHER SITES

(full details in previous editions)

A. Cadair Idris
Contact: Cyngor Cefn Gwlad Cymru, 01766 781803.

B. Coed-Y-Felin LNR
Contact: North Wales Wildlife Trust, 01248 351541.

C. Newborough Warren
Contact: CCW North West Area, 01248 716422.

D. Pehnros Coastal Park

E. Spinnies
Contact: North Wales Wildlife Trust, 01248 351541.

F. Valley Wetlands
Contact: RSPB (Welsh Region), 01248 363800.

South Wales

1. ABERTHAW SALTMARSH

The Wildlife Trust of South and West Wales.
Location: ST 037 661. E of Aberthaw Power Station, W of Barry.
Access: Open access. Park in East Aberthaw.
Facilities: None.
Public transport: Call Trust for advice.
Habitat: Lias limestone cliffs, saltmarsh, pebble beach, saline lagoon, coastal scrub.
Key birds: *All year:* Stonechat, Black Redstart is regular. *Spring:* Migrants. *Autumn*: Migrant waders and passerines. *Winter*: Peregrine. Good seawatching.
Contact: Trust HQ, 01656 724100.
e-mail: information@wtsww.cix.co.uk

2. CROES ROBERT RESERVE

Gwent Wildlife Trust.
Location: SO 475 060. Leave Monmouth on the B4293 towards Trellech. Turn R past Trellech School to Cwmcarvan. After 1.25 miles turn R and the reserve and car park will be on the R.
Access: Open all year.
Facilities: None.
Public transport: None.
Habitat: Broadleaved woodland, springs, wet flushes.
Key birds: *Spring/summer*: Warblers, Woodcock. *All year*: Great Spotted Woodpecker, Bullfinch, Long-tailed Tit.
Contact: 16 White Swan Court, Church Street, Monmouth, Gwent, NP25 3NY. 01600 715501.
e-mail: gwentwildlife@cix.co.uk

3. CWM CLYDACH

RSPB (South Wales Office).
Location: SN 584 026. Three miles N of J45 on M4, through the village of Clydach on B4291.
Access: Open at all times along public footpaths and waymarked trails. Coach parking not available.
Facilities: Nature trails, car park, information boards.

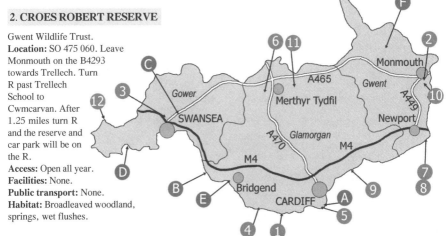

Public transport: Buses from Swansea stop at reserve entrance. Nearest railway station is eight miles away in Swansea.
Habitat: Oak woodland on steep slopes lining the banks of the fast-flowing Lower Clydach River.
Key birds: *Spring/summer*: Nesting Buzzard, Sparrowhawk and Raven. Nestboxes are used by Pied Flycatcher, Redstart and tits while Wood Warbler, all three species of woodpecker, Nuthatch, Treecreeper and Tawny Owl also nest. Dipper and Grey Wagtail frequent the river.
Contact: Martin Humphreys, 2 Tyn y Berllan, Craig Cefn Parc, Clydach, Swansea SA6 5TL. 01792 842927.

4. CWM COL-HUW

The Wildlife Trust of South and West Wales.
Location: SS 957 674. Site includes Iron Age fort, overlooking Bristol Channel. From Bridgend take B4265 S to Llanwit Major. Follow beach road from village.
Access: Park in seafront car park. Climb steps. Open all year.
Facilities: All year toilets and café. Information boards.
Public transport: None.
Habitat: Unimproved grassland, woodland, scrub and Jurassic blue lias cliff.
Key birds: Cliff-nesting House Martin colony, breeding Fulmar, Grasshopper Warbler. Large autumn passerine passage. Peregrine. Seawatching vantage point. Occasional Chough.
Contact: Trust HQ, 01656 724100.
e-mail: information@wtsww.cix.co.uk

5. LAVERNOCK POINT

The Wildlife Trust of South and West Wales.
Location: ST 182 680. Public footpaths S of B4267 between Barry & Penarth.
Access: No restrictions.
Facilities: None.
Public transport: Call Trust for advice.
Habitat: Cliff top, unimproved grassland, dense scrub.
Key birds: Seawatching in late summer; Glamorgan's best migration hotspot in autumn.
Contact: Trust HQ, 01656 724100.
e-mail: information@wtsww.cix.co.uk

6. LLYN FACH

The Wildlife Trust of South and West Wales.
Location: SN 905 038. From Merthyr Tydfil take A465 W to Hirwaun, then head S on A4061 to car park 1.8 miles away.
Access: Open dawn to dusk.
Facilities: None.
Public transport: None.
Habitat: Lake, bog, cliff and scree, surrounded by plantations.
Key birds: Nesting Raven, Ring Ouzel also Buzzard, Sparrowhawk. Chance of Peregrine and Goshawk.
Contact: Trust HQ, 01656 724100.
e-mail: information@wtsww.cix.co.uk

7. MAGOR MARSH

Gwent Wildlife Trust.
Location: ST 427 867. S of Magor. Leave M4 at exit 23, turning R onto B4245. Follow signs for Redwick in Magor village. S of Magor village, look for gate on Whitewall Common on E side of reserve.
Access: Open all year. Keep to path.
Facilities: Hide. Car park, footpaths and boardwalks.
Public transport: Bus service to Magor village. Reserve is approx 10 mins walk along Redwick road.
Habitat: Sedge fen, reedswamp, willow carr, damp hay meadows and open water.
Key birds: Important for wetland birds. *Spring*: Reed, Sedge and Grasshopper Warbler, occasional Garganey and Green Sandpiper on passage. Hobby and Peregrine. *Winter*: Teal, Bittern records in two recent years. *All year*: Snipe, Reed Bunting, Cetti's Warbler and Water Rail.
Contact: 16 Swan Court, Church Street, Monmouth NP25 3NY. 01600 715501.
e-mail: gwentwildlife@cix.co.uk
www.wildlifetrust.org.uk/gwent

8. MAGOR PILL TO COLDHARBOUR PILL

Gwent Wildlife Trust.
Location: ST 437 847. Overlooks River Severn, E of Newport.
Access: Access from Magor Pill Farm track down to sea wall.
Facilities: None.
Public transport: None.
Habitat: Foreshore, intertidal mudflats.
Key birds: Passage and winter waders.
Contact: 16 Swan Court, Monmouth, Gwent NP25 3NY. 01600 715501.
e-mail: gwentwildlife@cix.co.uk

9. PETERSTONE WENTLOOGE

Gwent Wildlife Trust.
Location: ST 269 800. Reserve overlooks Severn Estuary, between Newport and Cardiff. Take B4293 to Peterstone Wentlooge village.
Access: Park in large lay-by opposite the church and take path to the sea wall.
Facilities: None.
Public transport: None.
Habitat: Foreshore, inter-tidal mudflats, grazing.
Key birds: Passage waders and winter wildfowl.
Contact: Trust HQ, 01600 715501.

10. PRIORY WOOD SSSI

Gwent Wildlife Trust.
Location: SO 352 058. N of the Usk near Chain Bridge.
Access: Open all year. Very limited parking.
Facilities: None.
Public transport: None.
Habitat: Varied broadleaved woodland with cherry trees.
Key birds: *Spring/summer*: Pied Flycatcher, warblers. *All year*: Great Spotted Woodpecker, usual woodland species. *Winter*: Hawfinch occasionally seen.
Contact: 16 White Swan Court, Church Street, Monmouth, Gwent, NP25 3NY. 01600 715501. e-mail: gwentwildlife@cix.co.uk www.wildlifetrust.org.uk/gwent

11. SILENT VALLEY RESERVE

Gwent Wildlife Trust.
Location: SO 187 062. Take the A4046 S from Ebbw Vale into village of Cwm. Take L turn soon after entering village, just beyond Bailey's Arms. Park in car park on R about 0.3 miles up Cendl Terrace. Walk N across flat grass playing area and along path to reserve entrance.
Access: Open all year.
Facilities: None.
Public transport: None.
Habitat: One of the most westerly and highest natural beech woods in Britain.
Key birds: *Spring/summer*: Pied Flycatcher, Redstart. *Winter*: Siskin, Redpoll, tits. *All year*: usual woodland species, Great Spotted Woodpecker.
Contact: 16 White Swan Court, Church Street, Monmouth, Gwent, NP25 3NY. 01600 715501. e-mail: gwentwildlife@cix.co.uk www.wildlifetrust.org.uk/gwent

12. WHITEFORD NNR

Location: SS 450 960. Pass through Llanmadoc village, downhill, turn R at church to Cwm Ivy. Lane leads from here downhill to Whiteford Plantation. Follow footpath through Plantation, across Burrows to hide on Berges Island.
Access: Free access. Best to get to hide before a.m. high water for waders and wildfowl.
Facilities: None. Area not recommended for those with restricted mobility but excellent view of Whiteford Marsh from hillside road above Britannia Inn at Cheriton.
Public transport: None.
Habitat: Conifer plantation, marsh, mudflats.
Key birds: *Autumn/winter*: Divers, Red-necked, Slavonian and Black-necked Grebes, Brent Goose, Wigeon, Teal, Pintail and Eider. Common and Jack Snipe occur, with Whimbrel and Spotted Redshank on passage. Turnstone and Purple Sandpiper at Whiteford Point.

OTHER SITES

(full details in previous editions)

A. Cosmeston Lakes Country Park
Contact: Cosmeston Lakes CP, 02920 701678.
B. Kenfig NNR
Contact: David Carrington, Ton Kenfig, Bridgend, CF33 4PT. 01656 743386.
C. Melincwrt Waterfalls
Contact: Wildlife Trust HQ, 01656 724100.
D. Oxwich
Contact: CCW, 01792 763500.
E. Parc Slip Nature Park
Contact: Wildlife Trust HQ, 01656 724100.
F. Strawberry Cottage Wood.
Contact: Jerry Lewis, Y Bwthyn Gwyn, Coldbrook, Abergavenny, Monmouthshire NP7 9TD. (H)01873 855091;(W)01633 644856.

West Wales

1. CORS CARON

CCW (West Wales Area).
Location: SN 697 632 (car park). Reached from B4343 N of Tregaron.
Access: Open access to S of car park along the railway to boardwalk, out to SE bog. Access to rest of the reserve by permit. Dogs on lead. Access for coaches.
Facilities: None at present.
Public transport: None.
Habitat: Raised bog, river, fen, wet grassland, willow woodland, reedbed.
Key birds: *Summer*: Lapwing, Redshank, Curlew, Red Kite, Grasshopper Warbler, Whinchat. *Winter:* Teal, Wigeon, Whooper Swan, Hen Harrier, Red Kite.
Contact: Paul Culyer, CCW, Neuaddlas, Tregaron, Ceredigion. 01974 298480. e-mail: p.culyer@ccw.gov.uk www.ccw.gov.uk

2. DINAS & GWENFFRWD

RSPB (South Wales Office).
Location: SN 788 472. N of Llandovery. Dinas car park off B road to Llyn Brianne Reservoir.
Access: Public nature trail at Dinas open at all times.
Facilities: None
Public transport: Nearest station at Llandovery.
Habitat: Hillside oakwoods, streams, bracken slopes and moorland.
Key birds: Buzzard, Pied Flycatcher, Redstart, Wood Warbler, Tree Pipit, Red Kite and Peregrine in area. Dipper, Goosander, Raven.
Contact: Mr M Humphreys, 2 Tyn y Berllan, Craig Cefn Par, Clydach, Swansea SA6 5TL. 01792 842927. www.rspb.org.uk

3. DYFI

CCW (West Wales Area).
Location: SN 610 942. Large estuary area W of Machynlleth. Public footpaths off A493 E of Aberdyfi, and off B4353 (S of river); minor road from B4353 at Ynyslas to dunes and parking area.
Access: Ynyslas dunes and the estuary have unrestricted access. No access to Cors Fochno (raised bog) for casual birdwatching; permit required for study and research purposes. Good views over the bog and Aberleri marshes from W bank of Afon Leri.
Facilities: Public hide overlooking marshes beside footpath at SN 611 911.
Public transport: None.
Habitat: Sandflats, mudflats, saltmarsh, creeks, dunes, raised bog, grazing marsh.
Key birds: *Winter:* Greenland White-fronted Goose, wildfowl, waders and raptors. *Summer*: Breeding wildfowl and waders (inc. Teal, Shoveler, Merganser, Lapwing, Curlew, Redshank).
Contact: Mike Bailey, CCW Warden, Plas Gogerddan, Aberystwyth, Ceredigion SY23 3EE. 01970 821100.

4. THE NATIONAL WETLANDS CENTRE, WALES

The Wildfowl & Wetlands Trust.
Location: SS 533 984. Leave M4 at junction 48. Signposted from A484, E of Llanelli.
Access: Open daily (9.30am-6.00pm summer, earlier in winter) closed Christmas Eve and Christmas Day.
Facilities: Visitor centre, restaurant, hides, education

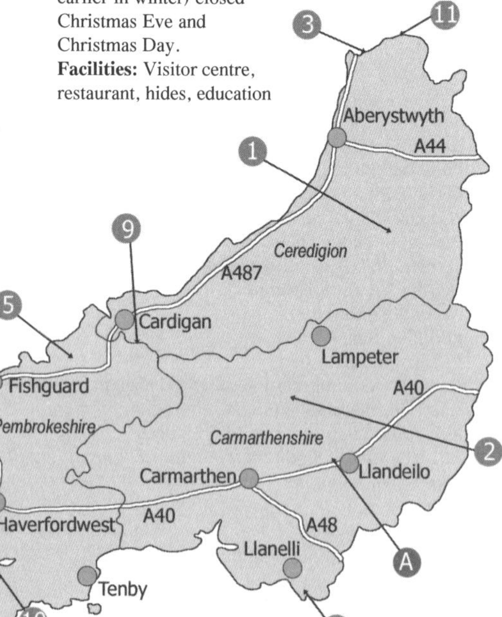

facilities, disabled access. Overlooks Burry Inlet.
Public transport: None.
Habitat: Inter-tidal mudflats, reedbeds, pools, marsh, waterfowl collection.
Key birds: Large flocks of Curlew, Oystercatcher, Redshank on saltmarsh. *Winter*: Pintail, Wigeon, Teal. Also Little Egret, Short-eared Owl, Peregrine
Contact: Nigel Williams, Centre Manager, Llwynhendy, Llanelli SA14 9SH. 01554 741087; (Fax)01554 744101. www.wwt.org.uk
e-mail: info.llanelli@wwt.org.uk

5. PENGELLI FOREST

The Wildlife Trust of South and West Wales.
Location: SN 123 396. Between Fishguard and Cardigan. Take minor road off A487 from Felindre Farchog/Eglwyswrw.
Access: Open all year. No permit required, but keep to trails.
Facilities: Trails. **Public transport:** None.
Habitat: 40 acre sessile oak wood, 120 acre mixed oak/ash wood (inc. scrub, rides).
Key birds: *Summer*: Pied Flycatcher, Redstart, Wood Warbler. *All year*: Buzzard, Raven, woodpeckers.
Contact: Welsh Wildlife Centre, Cilgerran, Cardigan SA43 2TB. 01239 621212.

6. RAMSEY ISLAND

RSPB (South Wales Office).
Location: SM 706237. One mile offshore St Justinians slipway, two miles W of St Davids.
Access: Open every day, Apr 1-Oct 31.
Facilities: Toilets, small RSPB shop, tuck shop, hot drinks and snacks, self-guiding trail.
Public transport: Trains to Haverfordwest Station. Hourly buses to St Davids, bus to St Justinians.
Habitat: Acid grassland, maritime heath, seacliffs.
Key birds: *Spring/summer*: Cliff-nesting auks (Guillemot, Razorbill). Kittiwake, Lesser, Great Black-backed, Herring Gulls, Shag, Peregrine, Raven, Chough, Lapwing, Wheatear, Stonechat.
Contact: RSPB Wales Headquarters, Sutherland House, Castle Bridge, Cowbridge Rd East, Cardiff CF11 9AB. 02920 353000.

7. SKOKHOLM ISLAND

The Wildlife Trust of South and West Wales.
Location: SM 738 037. Island lying S of Skomer.
Access: Day visits, Mon only Jun-Aug from Martinshaven. Weekly accomm. Apr-Sep, tel 01239 621212 for details and booking.
Facilities: Call for details.
Public transport: None.
Habitat: Cliffs, bays and inlets.
Key birds: *Summer*: Large colonies of Razorbill, Puffin, Guillemot, Manx Shearwater, Storm Petrel, Lesser Black-backed Gull. Migrants inc. rare species.
Contact: Trust HQ, 01239 621212.

8. SKOMER ISLAND

The Wildlife Trust of South and West Wales.
Location: SM 725 095. Fifteen miles from Haverfordwest. Take B4327 turn-off for Marloes, embarkation point at Martin's Haven, two miles past village.
Access: Apr 1-Oct 31. Boats sail at 10am, 11am and noon every day except Mon (Bank Holidays excluded). Closed four days beginning of Jun for seabird counts. Not suitable for infirm (steep landing steps and rough ground).
Facilities: Information centre, toilets, two hides, wardens, booklets, guides, nature trails.
Public transport: None.
Habitat: Maritime cliff, bracken, bluebells and red campion, heathland, freshwater ponds.
Key birds: Largest colony of Manx Shearwater in the world (overnight). Puffin, Guillemot, Razorbill (Apr-end Jul). Kittiwake (until end Aug), Fulmar (absent Oct), Short-eared Owl (during day Jun and Jul), Chough, Peregrine, Buzzard (all year), migrants.
Contact: Juan Brown, Skomer Island, Marloes, Pembs SA62 2BJ. 07971 114302.
e-mail: skomer@wtww.co.uk

9. WELSH WILDLIFE CENTRE

The Wildlife Trust of South and West Wales.
Location: SN 188 451. Two miles SE of Cardigan. River Teifi is N boundary. Signposted from Cardigan to Fishguard Road.
Access: Open 10am-5pm all year. Free parking for WTSWW members, £5 non-members. Dogs welcome - on a lead. Disabled access to visitor centre, paths, four hides.
Facilities: Visitor centre, restaurant, network of paths and seven hides.
Public transport: Train station, Haverfordwest (23 miles). Bus station in Cardigan. Access on foot from Cardigan centre, ten mins.
Habitat: Wetlands, marsh, swamp, reedbed, open water, creek (tidal), river, saltmarsh, woodland.
Key birds: Cetti's Warbler, Kingfisher, Water

Rail, Greater Spotted Woodpecker, Dipper, gulls, Marsh Harrier, Sand Martin, Hobby, Redstart, occasional Bittern and Red Kite.
Contact: The Welsh Wildlife Centre, Cilgerran, Cardigan SA43 2TB. 01239 621212.
e-mail: information@wtsww.cix.co.uk

10. WESTFIELD PILL

The Wildlife Trust of South and West Wales.
Location: SM 958 073.
Access: Open all year.
Facilities: Car park, cycle track.
Public transport: None.
Habitat: Freshwater lagoons, disused railway embankment, scrub, woodland margins.
Key birds: *Spring/summer*: Hirundines, Whitethroat, Blackcap, Spotted Flycatcher. *Passage*: waders. *Winter*: Little Grebe, Peregrine, Water Rail, Woodcock, Fieldfare, Redwing, Siskin, Redpoll. *All year*: Sparrowhawk, Kingfisher, Tawny Owl, Grey Wagtail, Dunnock, Raven, Bullfinch.
Contact: Trust HQ, 01239 621212.

11. YNYS-HIR

RSPB (CYMRU).
Location: SN 68 29 63. Off A487 Aberystwyth - Machynlleth road in Eglwys-fach village. Six miles SW of Machynlleth.
Access: Open every day (9am-9pm or dusk if earlier). Visitor centre open daily Apr-Oct (10am-5pm), Wed-Sun Nov-Mar (10am-4pm). Coaches welcome but please call for parking information.
Facilities: Visitor centre and toilets, both with disabled access. Numerous trails, seven hides, drinks machine.
Public transport: Bus service to Eglwys-fach from either Machynlleth or Aberystwyth, tel. 01970 617951. Rail service to Machynlleth.
Habitat: Estuary, freshwater pools, woodland and wet grassland.
Key birds: *Winter*: Greenland White-fronted Goose, Wigeon, Hen Harrier, Barnacle Goose. *Spring/summer*: Wood Warbler, Redstart, Pied Flycatcher. *All year*: Peregrine, Red Kite, Buzzard, Goshawk
Contact: Frances Hazell, Eglwys-fach, Machynlleth, Powys SY20 8TA. 01654 700222.
e-mail: ynyshir@rspb.org.uk

OTHER SITES

(full details in previous editions)

A. Castle Woods
Contact: Wildlife Trust HQ, 01239 621212.

Northern Ireland

Co Antrim

BOG MEADOWS

Ulster Wildlife Trust.
Location: J 315 726. Two miles SW of Belfast city centre. Signposted from the Falls Road. (OS map 15).
Access: Open at all times. Coach parties welcome.
Facilities: Car park, bird hide, disabled access, high quality paths.
Public transport: City bus from city centre or taxi.
Habitat: Wet grassland, scrub, ponds, reedbed.
Key birds: *Summer*: Breeding Sedge Warbler, Grasshopper Warbler, Stonechat, Grey Wagtail, Blackcap, Reed Bunting. *Winter*: Water Rail, Snipe, Teal, occasional Long-eared Owl.
Contact: Annie O'Kane, Ulster Wildlife Trust, 163 Stewartstown Road, Dunmurry, Belfast BT17 0HW. 028 9062 8647.
e-mail: ulster@bogmeadows.fsnet.co.uk

BREEN OAKWOOD

Department of the Environment NI.
Location: D 125 338. Off the Armoy-Glenshesk-Ballycastle road.
Access: No restrictions.
Facilities: None.
Public transport: None.
Habitat: Oak and birch woodland, a rare habitat in N Ireland.

Key birds: Wood Warbler.
Contact: Dept of the Environment NI, Portrush Countryside Centre, 8 Bath Road, Portrush, Co Antrim BT56 8AP. 028 7082 3600.

ECOS NATURE RESERVE

Ulster Wildlife Trust.
Location: D 118 036. 0.5 miles NE of Ballymena town centre. OS map 9.
Access: Open at all times. Coaches welcome.
Facilities: Environmental centre, car park, toilets, disabled access, bird hide, high-quality paths.
Pulbic transport: Bus from Ballymena town centre or within easy walking distance.
Habitat: Lake, wet meadows, willow coppice.
Key birds: *Summer*: Breeding Snipe, Sedge Warbler, Grasshopper Warbler, Reed Bunting. *Winter*: Teal, Goldeneye, Lapwing, Curlew. Rarities have included, White-winged Black Tern and Hoopoe in recent years.
Contact: Andrew Upton, 3 New Line, Crossgar, Co Down BT30 9EP. 028 4483 0282. e-mail: andrew.upton@ulsterwildifetrust.org

GLENARM

Ulster Wildlife Trust.
Location: D 301 132. Gate by B97 0.5 mile SW Glenarm, 15 miles from Ballymena. OS 1:50 000 sheet 9.
Access: Wildlife Trust members. Not suitable for coaches.
Facilities: None.
Public transport: Ulsterbus - from Ballymena.
Habitat: Species rich grassland, oak woodland.
Key birds: *Summer*: Breeding Blackcap, Garden Warbler, Wood Warbler, Redpoll, Buzzard, Dipper, Common Crossbill, Grey Wagtail, Raven.
Contact: See Ecos Nature Reserve.

ISLE OF MUCK

Ulster Wildlife Trust.
Location: D 464 024. Situated off NR tip of Island Magee, Co Antrim (OS Map 9).
Access: Permit required to land on island from UWT. Island only accessible by boat.
Facilities: None. **Public transport:** None.
Habitat: Offshore island with cliffs and stack
Key birds: *Summer*: Fulmar, Manx Shearwater, Peregrine, Kittiwake, terns, Guillemot, Razorbill, Black Guillemot, Puffin. *Winter*: Red-throated Diver.
Contact: See Ecos Nature Reserve.

JOHN McSPARRAN MEMORIAL FARM

Ulster Wildlife Trust.
Location: D 201 317. Situated off A2 one mile up Glendun, Co Antrim (OS Map 5).
Access: Open Mon-Fri (9am-5pm) except Bank Hols. Not suitable for coaches.
Facilities: Organic farm with rare breeds, native tree nursery and waymarked trails.
Public transport: Bus passes Glendun Viaduct twice a day.
Habitat: Upland hill farm, river, heather moorland and bog.
Key birds: *Summer*: Hen Harrier, Red Grouse, Golden Plover, Whinchat, Dipper, Spotted Flycatcher.
Contact: Farm Manager, Glendun, Cushendun, Co Antrm BT44 0PZ. 028 2176 1403. www.ulsterwildlifetrust.org

KEBBLE

Department of the Environment NI.
Location: D 095 515. W end of Rathlin Island, off coast from Ballycastle.
Access: Scheduled ferry service from Ballycastle.
Facilities: None.
Public transport: None.
Habitat: Sea cliffs, grass, heath, lake, marsh.
Key birds: Major cliff-nesting colonies of auks (inc. Puffin), Fulmar and Kittiwake; also Buzzard and Peregrine. Manx Shearwater and other seabirds on passage.
Contact: See Breen Oakwood.

LAGAN MEADOWS

Ulster Wildlife Trust.
Location: J 335 703. Within Lagan Valley Regional Park, two miles from Belfast city centre, off Malone Road - signposted at Bladon Drive.
Access: Open at all times. Coaches welcome.
Facilities: Main paths suitable for disabled access - from Lagan towpath.
Public transport: No 71 bus from Belfast city centre.
Habitat: Ponds, wet unimproved grassland, marsh, tussock sedge, scrub.
Key birds: *Summer*: Breeding Reed Bunting, Sedge Warbler, Blackcap. *Winter*: Redpoll, Snipe.
Contact: See Ecos Nature Reserve.

LOUGH NEAGH ISLANDS

c/o Department of the Environment NI.
Location: The largest body of water in Ireland, due W of Belfast.
Access: Landing is only by arrangement with Warden.
Facilities: None. **Public transport:** None.
Habitat: Islands.
Key birds: On most of the 80 islands within the reserve there are breeding wildfowl (inc. Gadwall, Shelduck), gulls, terns.
Contact: EHS Central Region Office, Peatlands Country Park, 33 Derryhubbert Road, Dungannon, Co Tyrone BT71 6NW. 028 3885 1102.

PORTMORE LOUGH

RSPB (Northern Ireland Office).
Location: J 107 685. Eight miles from Lurgan. Signposted from Aghalee village.
Access: Open every day, unmanned. No access to meadows during winter. Limited disabled facilities.
Facilities: Car park, toilets, information shelter and one hide.
Public transport: None.
Habitat: Lowland wet grassland, scrub and reedbed.
Key birds: *Spring/summer*: Breeding Curlew, Snipe, Lapwing. *Winter*: Greylag Goose, Whooper Swan and a variety of wildfowl.
Contact: John Scovell, 02897 510097; mobile 07736 792516. e-mail: john.scovell@rspb.org.uk

RANDALSTOWN FOREST

c/o Department of the Environment NI.
Location: 088 872. Two miles S of Randalstown, lying alongside N edge of Lough Neagh.
Access: Open all year. No permit required, but keep to trails.
Facilities: Public hide.
Public transport: None.
Habitat: Mixed woodland and scrub.
Key birds: *Summer*: Breeding Great Crested Grebe, Sedge Warbler, Blackcap. *Winter*: Teal, Gadwall, Goldeneye. Also Kingfisher.
Contact: See Lough Neagh Islands.

RATHLIN ISLAND

RSPB (Northern Ireland Office).
Location: Of NE coast of County Antrim. Five mile ferry journey from Ballycastle.
Access: Apr-Aug by appointment with warden only. Four miles from harbour, approx 100 steps. No toilets. Small shelter.
Facilities: RSPB viewpoint at the West Lighthouse.
Public transport: Caledonian MacBrayne ferry service from Ballycastle to Rathlin, tel 028 207 69299. Minibus from harbour to West Lighthouse, tel 028 207 63909.
Habitat: Sea cliffs and offshore stacks.
Key birds: *Spring/summer*: Puffin, Guillemot, Razorbill, Fulmar, Kittiwake.
Contact: RSPB Northern Ireland Office, South Cleggan, Rathlin Island, Ballycastle, Co Antrim, 028 207 63948.

REA'S WOOD

c/o Department of the Environment NI.
Location: J 142 855. One mile S of Antrim.
Access: Open all year. No permit, but keep to trails.
Facilities: None.
Public transport: None.
Habitat: Lough Neagh shore, wet alder woodland and scrub.
Key birds: Wildfowl and woodland species (inc. Blackcap, Jay).
Contact: See Lough Neagh Islands.

SLIEVENACLOY

Ulster Wildlife Trust.
Location: J 255 712. Situated in the Belfast Hills, take Ballycolin Road off A01 (OS Map 15).
Access: Permit currently required from project officer. Not suitable for coaches.
Facilities: None at present, currently being developed.
Public transport: Bus service from Belfast to Glenavy.
Habitat: Unimproved grassland, scrub.
Key birds: *Summer*: Snipe, Curlew, Sky Lark, Grey Wagtail, Wheatear, Grasshopper Warbler, Reed Bunting. *Winter*: Hen Harrier, Merlin, Fieldfare, Snow Bunting.
Contact: Mark Edgar, Slievenacloy Project Officer, c/o Colin Glen Forest Park Centre,163 Stewartstown Road, Dunmurry, Belfast BT17 0HW. 028 9062 8647.
e-mail: slievenacloy@btopenworld.com

Co Armagh

OXFORD ISLAND

Craigavon Borough Council.
Location: J 061 608. On shores of Lough Neagh, 2.5 miles from Lurgan, Co Armagh. Signposted from J10 of M1.
Access: Site open at all times. Car parks are locked at varying times depending on seasons (see signs). Coach parking available. Lough Neagh Discovery Centre open every day Apr-Sept (10am-6pm Mon-Sat, 10am-7pm Sun), Oct-Mar (10am-5pm Wed-Sun). Dogs on leads please. Most of site and all of Centre accessible for wheelchairs. Wheelchairs and mobility scooters available for visitors.
Facilities: Public toilets, Lough Neagh Discovery Centre with exhibitions, loop system for hard-of-hearing, shop and café. Four miles of footpaths, five birdwatching hides, children's play area, picnic tables, public jetties. Guided walks available (pre-booking essential). Varied programme of events.
Public transport: Ulsterbus Park'n Ride at Lough Road, Lurgan is 0.5 miles from reserve entrance. Tel 028 9033 3000. Lurgan Railway Station, 3 miles from reserve entrance.
Habitat: Freshwater lake, ponds, wet grassland, reedbed, woodland.
Key birds: *Winter*: Large flocks of wildfowl, especially Pochard, Tufted Duck, Goldeneye and Scaup (mainly Dec/Jan). Whooper and Bewick's Swans (Oct-Apr). *Summer*: Sedge Warbler, Grasshopper Warbler and Great Crested Grebe.
Contact: Rosemary Mulholland, Conservation Officer, Lough Neagh Discovery Centre, Oxford Island NNR, Lurgan, Co Armagh, N Ireland BT66 6NJ. 028 383 322205. www.oxfordisland.com
e-mail: oxford.island@craigavon.gov.uk

Co Down

BELFAST LOUGH RESERVE

RSPB (Northern Ireland Office).
Location: Take A2 N from Belfast and follow signs to Belfast Harbour Estate. Both entrances to reserve have checkpoints. From Dee Street 2 miles to reserve, from Tillysburn entrance 1 mile.
Access: Dawn to dusk.
Facilities: Lagoon overlooked by observation room (check for opening hours), two view points.
Public transport: None.
Habitat: Mudflats, wet grassland, freshwater lagoon.
Key birds: Noted for Black-tailed Godwit numbers and excellent variety of waterfowl in spring, autumn and winter, with close views. Rarities have included Buff-breasted, Pectoral, White-rumped and Semi-palmated Sandpipers, Spotted Crake, Amerian Wigeon, Laughing Gull.
Contact: Anthony McGeehan, 028 9147 9009.

CASTLE ESPIE

The Wildfowl & Wetlands Trust.
Location: J 474 672. On Strangford Lough 10 miles E of Belfast, signposted from A22 in the Comber area.
Access: Open daily except Christmas Day (10.30am Mon-Sat, 11.30am Sun).
Facilities: Visitor centre, educational facilities, views over lough, three hides, woodland walk.
Public transport: Call for advice.
Habitat: Reedbed filtration system with viewing facilities.
Key birds: *Winter*: Wildfowl esp. pale-bellied Brent Goose, Scaup. *Summer:* Warblers. Wader scrape has attracted Little Egret, Ruff, Long-billed Dowitcher, Killdeer.
Contact: James Orr, Centre Manager, Castle Espie, Ballydrain Road, Comber, Co Down BT23 6EA. 028 9187 4146.

COPELAND BIRD OBSERVATORY

Location: Situated on a 40-acre island on outer edge of Belfast Lough, four miles N of Donaghadee.
Access: Access is by chartered boat from Donaghadee.
Facilities: Observatory open Apr-Oct most weekends and some whole weeks. Hostel-type accommodation for up to 20. Daily ringing, bird census, sea passage recording. General bookings: Neville McKee, 67 Temple Rise, Templepatrick, Co. Antrim BT39 0AG (tel 028 9443 3068).
Habitat: Grassy areas, rock foreshore.
Key birds: Large colony of Manx Shearwaters; Black Guillemot, Eider, Water Rail also nest. *Summer*: Visiting Storm Petrels. Moderate passage of passerine migrants.
Contact: Dr Peter Munro, Talisker Lodge, 54B Templepatrick Road, Ballyclare, Co Antrim BT39 9TX. 028 9332 3421.

CRAWFORDSBURN COUNTRY PARK

Department of the Environment NI.
Location: J 467 826. Signposted off A2 Belfast-Bangor road.
Access: Open at all times.
Facilities: Car parks.
Public transport: None.
Habitat: Sea, shore (rocky and sandy), woodland, glen, open fields.
Key birds: Woodland and grassland species; Dipper; Eider, gulls, divers, terns, shearwaters can all be seen offshore, esp. in autumn.
Contact: Ciaran McLarnon, Crawfordsburn Country Park, Bridge Road South, Helen's Bay, Co Down BT19 1LD. 028 9185 3621.

DORN

c/o Department of the Environment NI.
Location: J 593 568. On the Ards Peninsula, E of Strangford Loch, near Ardkeen on Kircubbin to Portaferry coastal route.
Access: Access only by arrangement with warden.
Facilities: None. **Public transport:** None.
Habitat: Marine foreshore, mudflats and seabed.
Key birds: Waders; wildfowl (inc. pale-bellied Brent Goose). Common seal.
Contact: Quoile Countryside Centre, 5 Quay Road, Downpatrick, Co Down BT30 7JB. 028 4461 5520.

KILLARD

c/o Department of the Environment NI.
Location: J 610 433. Access from Millquarter Bay on coastal road four miles S of Strangford village.
Access: Open all year. No permit, but keep to trails.
Facilities: None. **Public transport:** None.
Habitat: Varied rocky and sandy shoreline.
Key birds: Waders (inc. Purple Sandpiper in winter). Good seawatching (esp. shearwaters, skuas). *Summer*: Breeding Fulmar, Shelduck, Stonechat and Sand Martin. Rare orchids.
Contact: See Dorn.

MURLOUGH

National Trust.
Location: J 394 338. Ireland's first nature reserve, between Dundrum and Newcastle, close to Mourne Mountains.
Access: Permit needed except on marked paths.
Facilities: Visitor centre.
Public transport: Local bus service from Belfast-Newcastle passes reserve entrances.
Habitat: Sand dunes, heathland.
Key birds: Waders and wildfowl occur in Inner Dundrum Bay adjacent to the reserve; divers and large numbers of Scoter (inc. regular Surf Scoter) and Merganser in Dundrum Bay.
Contact: Head Warden, Murlough NNR, The Stable Yard, Keel Point, Dundrum, Newcastle, Co Down BT33 0NQ. Tel/fax 028 437 51467;
e-mail umnnrw@smtpntrustorguk.

NORTH STRANGFORD LOUGH

National Trust.
Location: J 510 700. View from adjacent roads and car parks; also from hide at Castle Espie (J 492 675).
Access: Call for advice.
Facilities: Hide.
Public transport: None.
Habitat: Extensive tidal mudflats, limited saltmarsh.
Key birds: Major feeding area for pale-bellied Brent Goose, also Pintail, Wigeon, Whooper Swan. Waders (inc. Dunlin, Knot, Oystercatcher, Bar-tailed Godwit).
Contact: Head Warden, National Trust, Strangford Lough Wildlife Scheme, Strangford Lough Wildlife Centre, Castle Ward, Strangford, Co Down BT30 7LS. Tel/fax 028 4488 1411;
e-mail uslwcw@smtpntrustorguk.

QUOILE PONDAGE

c/o Department of the Environment NI.
Location: J 500 478. One mile N of Downpatrick on road to Strangford, at S end of Strangord Lough.
Access: Open all year. No permit, but keep to trails.
Facilities: Large modern hide, visitor centre. Nature trail.
Public transport: None.
Habitat: Freshwater pondage to control flooding, with many vegetation types on shores.
Key birds: Many wildfowl species, woodland birds; migrant and wintering waders including Spotted Redshank, Ruff and Black-tailed Godwit.
Contact: Warden, Quoile Countryside Centre, 5 Quay Road, Downpatrick, Co Down BT30 7JB. 028 4461 5520.

Co Londonderry

LOUGH FOYLE

RSPB (Northern Ireland Office).
Location: C 545 237. Large sea lough NE of Londonderry. Take minor roads off Limavady-Londonderry road to view-points (choose high tide) at Longfield Point, Ballykelly, Faughanvale.
Access: Open all year. No permit, but keep to trails.
Facilities: None.
Public transport: None.
Habitat: Beds of eel-grass, mudflats, surrounding agricultural land.
Key birds: Staging-post for migrating wildfowl (eg. 15,000 Wigeon, 4,000 pale-bellied Brent Geese in Oct/Nov). *Winter*: Slavonian Grebe, divers, Bewick's and Whooper Swans, Bar-tailed Godwit, Golden Plover, Snow Bunting. *Autumn*: Waders (inc. Ruff, Little Stint, Curlew Sandpiper, Spotted Redshank).
Contact: RSPB N Ireland HQ (01232 491547),

ROE ESTUARY

c/o Department of the Environment NI.
Location: C 640 295. Access off A2 coast road between Castlerock and Limavady. E of Londonderry.
Access: Open all year. No permit, but keep to trails.
Facilities: None.
Public transport: None.
Habitat: Mudflats and saltings (beware soft mud), sand dunes.
Key birds: Pale-bellied Brent Goose, many wildfowl and wader species.
Contact: Warden, NW Nature Reserves Office, The Cornstore, Dogleap Road, Limavady, Co Londonderry BT49 9NN. 028 7776 3982.

ROE VALLEY COUNTRY PARK

c/o Department of the Environment NI.
Location: C 678 203. Signposted off Belfast-Londonderry and Limavady-Dungiven roads.
Access: Open at all times.
Facilities: Car parks, visitor centre, nature trail, pathways.
Public transport: None.
Habitat: Mixed woodland and gorge.
Key birds: Typical woodland and river species, inc. Wood Warbler, Dipper, Grey Wagtail.
Contact: See Roe Estuary.

UMBRA

Ulster Wildlife Trust.
Location: C 725 355. Ten miles W of Coleraine on A2 – entrance beside automatic railway crossing about 1.5 miles W of Downhill. OS 1:50 000 sheet 4.
Access: Wildlife Trust members. Not suitable for coaches.
Facilities: None.
Public transport: Ulsterbus service to Downhill from Coleraine.
Habitat: Sand dunes.
Key birds: *Summer*: Breeding Sky Lark. *Winter*: Woodcock, Peregrine, plus Great Northern Diver offshore.
Contact: See Ecos Nature Reserve.

Isle of Man

BALLALOUGH REEDBEDS RESERVE

Manx Wildlife Trust.
Location: SC 258 682. Accessible from the Castletown by-pass on the A5, which forms part of the S boundary of the reserve.
Access: Open all year. **Facilities:** Car park.
Public transport: None.
Habitat: Meadow, reedbed.
Key birds: *Spring/summer*: Willow Warbler, Sedge Bunting, Reed Bunting.
Contact: Tricia Sayle, Reserves Officer, Manx Wildlife Trust, Tynwald Mills, St John's, Isle of Man IM4 3AE. 01624 801985.
e-mail: manxwt@cix.co.uk
www.wildlifetrust.org.uk/manxwt

BREAGLE GLEN

Manx Wildlife Trust/Castletown Town Commissioners Habitats.
Location: SC 196 688. In Port Erin from St Georges Crescent, which forms the whole N and W boundary.
Access: Open all year. **Facilities:** None.

Public transport: Regular bus service from Douglas to Port Erin and then short walk.
Habitat: Small woodland area, shrubs.
Key birds: *Passage*: Yellow-browed Warbler, Barred Warbler, Firecrest, Red-breasted Flycatcher have been recorded.
Contact: See Ballalough Reedbeds Reserve.

CALF OF MAN BIRD OBSERVATORY

Administration Department, Manx National Heritage.
Location: SC 15 65. Small island off the SW tip of the Isle of Man. Local boat from Port Erin or Port St Mary.
Access: Apr-Oct. No dogs, fires or camping.
Facilities: Accommodation for eight people in three bedrooms at Observatory Apr-Oct. Bookings: Administration Department (address below).
Public transport: Local boat from Port Erin or Port St Mary.
Habitat: Heather/bracken moor and seabird cliffs.
Key birds: *All year*: Hen Harrier, Peregrine and Chough. *Summer*: Breeding seabirds (nine species including Storm Petrel, Manx Shearwater). Excellent spring and autumn migration, seabird migration best in autumn.
Contact: Tim Bagworth, (Warden), Manx National Heritage, Manx Museum, Douglas, Isle of Man IM1 3LY.

CLOSE SARTFIELD

Manx Wildlife Trust.
Location: SC 361 956. From Ramsey drive W on A3. Turn on to B9, take third right and follow this road for nearly a mile. Reserve entrance on R.
Access: Open all year. No dogs. Boardwalk and Path suitable for wheelchairs from car park through wildflower meadow and willow scrub to hide.
Facilities: Car park, hide, reserve leaflet (50p, available from office) outlines circular walk.
Public transport: None.
Habitat: Wildflower-rich hay meadow, marshy grassland, willow scrub/developing birch woodland, bog.
Key birds: *Winter*: Large roost of Hen Harrier. *Summer*: Corn Crake (breeding 1999 and 2000 after 11 years' absence), Curlew, warblers.
Contact: See Ballalough Reedbeds Reserve.

COOILDARRY

Manx Wildlife Trust.
Location: SC 319 896. Entrance approximately one mile S of Kirk Michael village, left of A3.
Access: Open all year round. Not suitable for disabled. Dogs to be kept on a lead.
Facilities: Well-maintained paths throughout. Leaflet (50p) available from office. Nearest toilets in Kirk Michael village.
Public transport: Buses run regularly past the lower entrance off A4.
Habitat: Woodland.
Key birds: Raven, Sparrowhawk.
Contact: See Ballalough Reedbeds Reserve.

CURRAGH KIONDROGHAD

Manx Wildlife Trust.
Location: Turn into Church Road from the A2 near Onchan. Park on the L as the road dips. To reach the reserve cross a piece of land on the L owned by Onchan Commissioners.
Access: Open all year. **Facilities:** None.
Public transport: Regular bus service from Douglas to Onchan and then short walk.
Habitat: Wetland, trees, neutral grassland, swamp.
Key birds: *Spring/summer*: Woodcock, Grey Wagtail, Chiffchaff. *Winter*: Hen Harrier.
Contact: See Ballalough Reedbeds Reserve.

CRONK Y BING

Manx Wildlife Trust.
Location: NX 381 017. Take A10 coast road N from Jurby. Approx two miles along there is a sharp right hand turn over a bridge. Before the bridge there is a track to the left. A parking area is available at the end of the track.
Access: Open all year round. Dogs to be kept on a lead. Not suitable for the disabled.
Facilities: None. **Public transport:** None.
Habitat: Open dune and dune grassland.
Key birds: *Summer*: Terns. *Winter*: Divers, grebes, skuas, gulls.
Contact: See Ballalough Reedbeds Reserve.

DALBY MOUNTAIN

Manx Wildlife Trust.
Location: SC 233769. Approx two miles S of Dalby village, lying adjacent to the A27.
Access: Open all year round. Dogs to be kept on a lead. Not suitable for wheelchairs.
Facilities: None.
Public transport: None.
Habitat: Heathland.
Key birds: Hen Harrier, Red Grouse.
Contact: See Ballalough Reedbeds Reserve.

COUNTY DIRECTORY

Nuthatch by Keith Offord

ENGLAND

THE INFORMATION in the directory has been obtained either from the persons listed or from the appropriate national or other bodies. In some cases, where it has not proved possible to verify the details directly, alternative responsible sources have been relied upon. When no satisfactory record was available, previously included entries have sometimes had to be deleted. Readers are requested to advise the editor of any errors or omissions.

AVON

See Somerset.

BEDFORDSHIRE

Bird Atlas/Avifauna
An Atlas of the Breeding Birds of Bedfordshire 1988-92 by R A Dazley and P Trodd (Bedfordshire Natural History Society, 1994).

Bird Recorder
Dave Odell, The Hobby, 74 The Links, Kempston, Bedford, MK42 7LT. 01234 857149; e-mail: davehobby@onetel.net.uk

Bird Report
BEDFORDSHIRE BIRD REPORT (1946-), from Mary Sheridan, 28 Chestnut Hill, Linslade, Leighton Buzzard, Beds LU7 2TR. 01525 378245.

BTO Regional Representative & Regional Development Officer
RR. Phil Cannings, 30 Graham Gardens, Luton, Beds, LU3 1NQ. H:01582 400394; W:01234 842220; e-mail: philcannings@btopenworld.com

RDO. Judith Knight, 381 Bideford Green, Linslade, Leighton Buzzard, Beds, LU7 2TY. Home 01525 378161; e-mail: judy.knight@tinyonline.co.uk

Club
BEDFORDSHIRE BIRD CLUB. (1992; 247). Miss Sheila Alliez, Flat 61 Adamson Court, Adamson Walk, Kempston, Bedford, MK42 8QZ.
e-mail: alliezsec@peewit.freeserve.co.uk
www.bedsbirdcub.org.uk
Meetings: 8.00pm, last Tuesday of the month (Sep-Mar), Maulden Village Hall, Maulden, Beds.

Ringing Groups
IVEL RG. Errol Newman, 29 Norse Road, Goldington, Bedford, MK41 0NR. 01234 343119; e-mail: lew.n@virgin.net

RSPB. Dr A D Evans, 6 Jennings Close, Potton, Sandy, Beds, SG19 2SE.

RSPB Local Groups
BEDFORD. (1970; 80). Barrie Mason, 6 Landseer Walk, Bedford, MK41 7LZ. 01234 262280.
Meetings: 7.30pm, 3rd Thursday of the month, A.R.A. Manton Lane, Bedford.

EAST BEDFORDSHIRE. (1973; 75). Terence C Park, 8 Back Street, Biggleswade, Beds, SG18 8JA. 01767 221363.

LUTON AND SOUTH BEDFORDSHIRE. (1973; 120). Mick Price, 120 Common Road, Kensworth, BedsLU6 3RG. 01582 873268.
Meetings: 7.45pm, 2nd Wednesday of the month, Houghton Regis Social Centre, Parkside Drive, Houghton Regis, Dunstable.

Wildlife Trust
See Cambridgeshire,

BERKSHIRE

BirdAtlas/Avifauna
The Birds of Berkshire by P E Standley et al (Berkshire Atlas Group/Reading Ornithological Club, 1996).

Bird Recorder
RECORDER (Records Committee and rarity records). Chris DR Heard, 3 Waterside Lodge, Ray Mead Road, Maidenhead, Berkshire SL6 8NP. 01628 633828; e-mail: chris.heard@virgin.net

ASSISTANT RECORDER (Rare breeding records, bird survey data). Derek J Barker, 40 Haywood Gardens, Woodlands Park, Maidenhead, Berkshire SL6 3LZ. 01628 820125.

Bird Reports
BERKSHIRE BIRD BULLETIN (Monthly, 1986-), from Brian Clews, 118 Broomhill, Cookham, Berks SL6 9LQ. 01628 525314;
e-mail: brian.clews@btconnect.com

BIRDS OF BERKSHIRE (1974-), from Secretary of the Reading Ornithological Club.

BIRDS OF THE THEALE AREA (1988-), from Secretary, Theale Area Bird Conservation Group.

NEWBURY DISTRICT BIRD REPORT (1959-), from Secretary, Newbury District Ornithological Club.

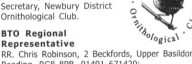

BTO Regional Representative
RR. Chris Robinson, 2 Beckfords, Upper Basildon, Reading, RG8 8PB. 01491 671420;
e-mail: berks_bto_rep@btinternet.com

Clubs

BERKSHIRE BIRD BULLETIN GROUP. (1986; 100). Berkshire Bird Bulletin Group, PO Box 680, Maidenhead, Berks SL6 9ST. 01628 525314; e-mail: brian.clews@btconnect.com

NEWBURY DISTRICT ORNITHOLOGICAL CLUB. (1959; 110). Trevor Maynard, 15 Kempton Close, Newbury, Berks RG14 7RS. 01635 36752; e-mail: info@ndoc.org.uk
www.ndoc.org.uk.

READING ORNITHOLOGICAL CLUB. (1945; 200). Renton Righelato, 63 Hamilton Road, Reading RG1 5RA. 0787 981 2564;
e-mail: renton@righelato.net
www.theroc.org.uk
Meetings: 8pm, alternate Wednesdays (Oct-Mar). University of Reading.

THEALE AREA BIRD CONSERVATION GROUP. (1988; 75). Brian Uttley, 65 Omers Rise, Burghfield Common, Reading RG7 3HH. 0118 9832894.
Meetings: 8pm, 1st Tuesday of the month, Englefield Social Club.

Ringing Groups

NEWBURY RG. J Legg, 1 Malvern Court, Old Newtown Road, Newbury, Berks, RG14 7DR.
e-mail: janlegg@btinternet.com

RUNNYMEDE RG. D G Harris, 22 Blossom Way, Hounslow, TW5 9HD.
e-mail: daveharris@tinyonline.co.uk

RSPB Local Groups

EAST BERKSHIRE. (1974; 200). Ken Panchen, 7 Knottocks End, Beaconsfield, Bucks, HP9 2AN. 01494 675779; e-mail: ken.panchen@care4free.net

READING. (1986; 80). Carl Feltham, 39 Moriston Close, Reading, RG30 2PW. 0118 941 1713.

WOKINGHAM & BRACKNELL. (1979; 200). Patrick Crowley, 56 Ellis Road, Crowthorne, Berks RG45 6PT. 01344 776473;
e-mail: patrick.crowley@btinternet.com
www.wbrspb.btinternet.co.uk
Meetings: 8.00pm, 2nd Thursday of the month (Sep-Jun), Finchampstead Memorial Hall, Wokingham.

Wildlife Hospitals

KESTREL LODGE. D J Chandler, 101 Sheridan Avenue, Caversham, Reading, RG4 7QB. 01189 477107. Birds of prey, ground-feeding birds, waterbirds, seabirds. Temporary homes for all except large birds of prey. Veterinary support. Small charge.

SWAN LIFELINE. Wendy Hermon, Treatment Centre Co-ordinator, Swan Treatment Centre, Cuckoo Weir Island, South Meadow Lane, Eton, Windsor, Berks, SL4 6SS. 01753 859397; fax 01753 622709; www.swanlifeline.org.uk
Registered charity. Thames Valley 24-hour swan rescue and treatment service. Veterinary support and hospital unit. Operates membership scheme.

Wildlife Trust

Director, See Oxfordshire,

BUCKINGHAMSHIRE

BirdAtlas/Avifauna

The Birds of Buckinghamshire ed by P Lack and D Ferguson (Buckinghamshire Bird Club, 1993).

Bird Recorder

Andy Harding, 15 Jubilee Terrace, Stony Stratford, Milton Keynes, MK11 1DU. H:01908 565896; W:01908 653328; e-mail: a.v.harding@open.ac.uk

Bird Reports

AMERSHAM BIRDWATCHING CLUB ANNUAL REPORT (1975-), from Secretary,

BUCKINGHAMSHIRE BIRD REPORT (1980-), from Rosie Hamilton, 56 Church Hill, Cheddington, Leighton Buzzard, Beds, LU7 0SY.

NORTH BUCKS BIRD REPORT (10 pa), from Recorder.

BTO Regional Representative & Regional Development Officer

RR. Mick A'Court, 6 Chalkshire Cottages, Chalkshire Road, Butlers Cross, Bucks, HP17 0TW. H:01296 623610; W:01494 462246;
e-mail: a.arundinaceous@virgin.net
mick@focusrite.com

RDO. Peter Hearn, 160 High Street, Aylesbury, Bucks HP20 1RE. Home & fax 01296 581520; Work 01296 424145.

Clubs

BUCKINGHAMSHIRE BIRD CLUB. (1981; 340). Roger S Warren, 11 Westwood Road, Marlow, Bucks SL7 2AT. 01628 484807.
www.hawfinches.freeserve.co.uk

NORTH BUCKS BIRDERS. (1977; 50). Andy Harding, 15 Jubilee Terrace, Stony Stratford, Milton Keynes, MK11 1DU. H:01908 565896; W:01908 653328.
Meetings: Last Tuesday of the month (Nov, Jan, Feb, Mar), The Cock, High Street, Stony Stratford.

Ringing Groups

HUGHENDEN RG. Peter Edwards, 8 The Brackens, Warren Wood, High Wycombe, Bucks, HP11 1EB. 01494 535125.

RSPB Local Groups

See also Herts: Chorleywood,

AYLESBURY. (1981; 220). Barry Oxley, 3 Swan

Close, Station Road, Blackthorn, Bicester, Oxon, OX25 1TU. 01869 247780.

NORTH BUCKINGHAMSHIRE. (1976; 430). Jim Parsons, 8 The Mount, Aspley Guise, Milton Keynes, MK17 8EA. 01908 582450.
Meetings: 8.00pm, 2nd Tuesday of the month, Jennie Lee Theatre, Bletchley Leisure Centre.

Wildlife Hospitals
MILTON KEYNES WILDLIFE HOSPITAL. Mr & Mrs V Seaton, 150 Bradwell Common Boulevard, Milton Keynes, MK13 8BE. 01908 604198; www-tec.open,ac.uk/staff/robert/robert.html
Registered charity. All species of British birds and mammals. Veterinary support.

WILDLIFE HOSPITAL TRUST. St Tiggywinkles, Aston Road, Haddenham, Aylesbury, Bucks HP17 8AF. 01844 292292; fax 01844 292640;
e-mail: mail@sttiggywinkles.org.uk
www.sttiggywinkles.org.uk
Registered charity. All species. Veterinary referrals and helpline for vets and others on wild bird treatments. Full veterinary unit and staff. Pub: Bright Eyes (free to members - sae).

Wildlife Trust
Director, See Oxfordshire,

CAMBRIDGESHIRE

BirdAtlas/Avifauna
An Atlas of the Breeding Birds of Cambridgeshire (VC 29) P M M Bircham et al (Cambridge Bird Club, 1994).
The Birds of Cambridgeshire: checklist 2000 (Cambridge Bird Club)

Bird Recorders
CAMBRIDGESHIRE. John Oates, 7 Fassage Close, Lode, Cambridge CB5 9EH. 01223 812546, (M) 07860 132708. e-mail: joates9151@aol.com

HUNTINGDON & PETERBOROUGH. John Clark, 7 West Brook, Hilton, Huntingdon, Cambs, PE28 9NW. 01480 830472.

Bird Reports
CAMBRIDGESHIRE BIRD REPORT (1925-), from Secretary, Cambridge Bird Club.

PAXTON PITS BIRD REPORT (1994-)
£3 inc postage, from Trevor Gunton, 15 St James Road, Little Paxton, Cambs PE19 6QW. (Tel/fax) 01480 473562.

PETERBOROUGH BIRD CLUB REPORT (1999-), from Secretary, Peterborough Bird Club.

BTO Regional Representatives
CAMBRIDGESHIRE. John Le Gassick, 17 Acacia Avenue, St Ives, Cambs PE27 6TN. 01480 391991; e-mail: john.legassick@ntlworld.com

HUNTINGDON & PETERBOROUGH. Phillip Todd, 01733 810832;
e-mail: huntspbororr@yahoo.co.uk

Clubs
CAMBRIDGESHIRE BIRD CLUB. (1925; 290). Bruce Martin, 178 Nuns Way, Cambridge, CB4 2NS. 01223 700656;
e-mail: bruce.s.martin@ntlworld.com
www.cambridgeshirebirdclub.org.uk
Meetings: 2nd Friday of the month, St John's Church Hall, Hills Road, Cambridge/ Milton CP Visitors Centre, Milton, Cambridge.

GREATER PETERBOROUGH ORNITHOLOGICAL GROUP (1983; 20). Martin Coates, 63 Primrose Way, Stamford, PE9 4BU. 01780 755016; e-mail: martin.shelagh@virgin.net

PETERBOROUGH BIRD CLUB. (1999; 210) Janet Darke (acting secretary), 34 High Street, Stilton, Peterborough PE3 6LJ. 01733 243556;
e-mail: janet@jdarke.freeserve.co.uk
www.peterboroughbirdclub.org.uk

ST NEOTS BIRD & WILDLIFE CLUB. (1993; 150). Stuart Elsom, 117 Andrew Road, Eynesbury, St Neots, Cambridgeshire PE19 2PP.
e-mail: stuart.elsom@tringa.co.uk
www.paxton-pits.org.uk
Meetings: 7.30pm, various Tuesdays, St Neots Bowling Club, St Anselm Place, check website for details.

Ringing Group
WICKEN FEN RG. Dr C J R Thorne, 17 The Footpath, Coton, Cambs, CB3 7PX. 01954 210566; e-mail: cjrt@cam.ac.uk

RSPB Local Groups
CAMBRIDGE. (1977; 150). Colin Kirtland, 22 Montgomery Road, Cambridge, CB4 2EQ. 01223 363092.
Meetings: 8pm, 3rd Wednesday of the month (Sep-May), Chemistry Lab, Lemsfield Road, Cambridge.

HUNTINGDONSHIRE. (1982; 200). Pam Peacock, Old Post Office, Warboys Road, Pidley, Huntingdon, Cambs, PE28 3DA. 01487 840615;
e-mail: pam.peacock@care4free.net
www.huntsrspb.co.uk
Meetings: 7.30pm, last Wednesday of the month (Sep-Apr), Free Church, St Ives.

Wetland Bird Survey Organisers
CAMBRIDGESHIRE OLD COUNTY. Bruce Martin, 178 Nuns Way, Cambridge, CB4 2NS. (H) 01223 363656; (W) 01223 246644;
e-mail: bruce.s.martin@ntlworld.com

NENE WASHES. Charlie Kitchin, RSPB Nene Washes, 21a East Delph, Whittlesey, Cambs PE7 1RH. 01733 205140.

Wildlife Trust
WILDLIFE TRUST OF BEDS, CAMBS, NORTHANTS & PETERBOROUGH. (1990; 12,000). The Manor House, Broad Street, Great Cambourne, Cambridgeshire CB3 6DH. 01954 713500; fax 01954 710051;
e-mail: cambridgeshire@wildlifebcnp.org
www.wildlifebcnp.org

CHESHIRE

BirdAtlas/Avifauna
The Birds of Sandbach Flashes 1935-1999 by Andrew Goodwin and Colin Lythgoe (The Printing House, Crewe, 2000).

Bird Recorder (inc Wirral)
Tony Broome, 4 Larchwood Drive, Wilmslow, Cheshire, SK9 2NU. 01625 540434;
e-mail: tonybroome@cawos.org

Bird Report
CHESHIRE & WIRRAL BIRD REPORT (1969-), from David Cogger, 113 Nantwich Road, Middlewich, Cheshire, CW10 9HD. 01606 832517;
e-mail:memsec@cawos.org
www.cawos.org

SOUTH EAST CHESHIRE ORNITHOLOGICAL SOCIETY BIRD REPORT (1985-), from Secretary, South East Cheshire Ornithol Soc. 01270 582642.

BTO Regional Representatives & Regional Development Officer
MID RR. Paul Miller, 01928 787535;
e-mail: huntershill@worldline.co.uk

NORTH & EAST RR. Charles Hull, Edleston Cottage, Edleston Hall Lane, Nantwich, Cheshire, CW5 8PL. 01270 628194;
e-mail: edleston@yahoo.co.uk

SOUTH RR & RDO. Charles Hull, Edleston Cottage, Edleston Hall Lane, Nantwich, Cheshire, CW5 8PL. 01270 628194;
e-mail: edleston@yahoo.co.uk

Clubs

CHESHIRE & WIRRAL ORNITHOLOGICAL SOCIETY. (1988; 375). David Cogger, 113 Nantwich Road, Middlewich, Cheshire, CW10 9HD. 01606 832517; www.cawos.org
e-mail: memsec@cawos.org
Meetings: 7.45pm, 1st Friday of the month, Knutsford Civic Centre.

CHESTER & DISTRICT ORNITHOLOGICAL SOCIETY. (1967; 50). David King, 13 Bennett Close, Willaston, South Wirral, CH64 2XF. 0151 327 7212.

KNUTSFORD ORNITHOLOGICAL SOCIETY. (1974; 45). Roy Bircumshaw, 267 Longridge, Knutsford, Cheshire, WA16 8PH. 01565 634193.
www.10x50.com
Meetings: 7.30pm, 4th Friday of the month (not Dec), Jubilee Hall, Knutsford.

LANCASHIRE & CHESHIRE FAUNA SOCIETY. (1914; 140). Dave Bickerton, 64 Petre Crescent, Rishton, Lancs, BB1 4RB. 01254 886257;
e-mail: bickertond@aol.com
www.lacfs.org.uk

LYMM ORNITHOLOGY GROUP. (1975; 65). Mrs Ann Ledden, 4 Hill View, Widnes, WA8 9AL. 0151 424 0441; e-mail: secretary-log@tiscali.co.uk
Meetings: 8.00pm, last Friday of the month (Aug-May), Lymm Village Hall.

MID-CHESHIRE ORNITHOLOGICAL SOCIETY. (1963; 80). Les Goulding, 7 Summerville Gardens, Stockton Heath, Warrington WA4 2EG. 01925 265578; e-mail: les@goulding7.fsnet.co.uk
http://myweb.tiscali.co.uk/barnowl
Meetings: 7.30pm, 2nd Friday of the month (Oct-Mar), Hartford Village Hall.

NANTWICH NATURAL HISTORY SOCIETY. (1979; 40). Mike Holmes, 4 Tenchers Field, Stapeley, Nantwich, Cheshire CW5 7GR.01270 611577; e-mail: mike@mimprove.com
www.nantnats.fsnet.co.uk

SOUTH EAST CHESHIRE ORNITHOLOGICAL SOCIETY. (1964; 120). Colin Lythgoe, 11 Waterloo Road, Haslington, Crewe, CW1 5TF. 01270 582642.
www.secos.freeuk.com
Meetings: 7.30pm, 2nd Friday (Sept-Apr), St Mathews Church Hall, Elworth.

WILMSLOW GUILD BIRDWATCHING GROUP. (1965; 67). Tom Gibbons, Chestnut Cottage, 37 Strawberry Lane, Wilmslow, Cheshire, SK9 6AQ. 01625 520317.
Meetings: 7.30pm last Friday of the month, Wilmslow Guild, Bourne St, Wilmslow.

Ringing Groups
MERSEYSIDE RG. P Slater, 45 Greenway Road, Speke, Liverpool, L24 7RY.

SOUTH MANCHESTER RG. C M Richards, Fairhaven, 13 The Green, Handforth, Wilmslow, Cheshire, SK9 3AG. 01625 524527; e-mail: cliveandkay.richards@care4free.net

RSPB Local Groups
CHESTER. (1987; 350). Bernard Wright, Carden Smithy, Clutton, Chester, CH3 9EP. 01829 782243; e-mail: knoydart@globalnet.co.uk

MACCLESFIELD. (1979; 394). Ray Evans, 01625 432635; e-mail: chair@macclesfieldrspb.org.uk
www.macclesfieldrspb.org.uk

NORTH CHESHIRE. (1976; 100) Please contact RSPB for further details.

Wildlife Hospitals
RSPCA STAPELEY GRANGE WILDLIFE HOSPITAL. London Road, Stapeley, Nantwich, Cheshire, CW5 7JW. 0870 442 7102. All wild birds. Oiled bird wash facilities and pools. Veterinary support.

SWAN SANCTUARY. Mrs C Clements, 24 St David's Drive, Callands, Warrington, WA5 5SB. 01925 636245. Veterinary support.

Wildlife Trust
CHESHIRE WILDLIFE TRUST. (1962; 3600). Grebe House, Reaseheath, Nantwich, Cheshire CW5 6DG. 01270 610180; fax 01270 610430; e-mail: cheshirewt@cix.co.uk www.wildlifetrust.org.uk/cheshire

CORNWALL

Bird Recorders
CORNWALL. K Wilson, No.1 Tol-pedn House, School Hill Road, St Levan, Penzance, Cornwall, TR19 6LP. 01736 871800; e-mail: kesteraw@yahoo.co.uk

ISLES OF SCILLY. John Higginson, 30 Sallyport, St Mary's, Isles of Scilly, TR21 0JE.

Bird Reports
BIRDS IN CORNWALL (1931-), from Colin Boyd, 4 Henliston Drive, Helston, Cornwall, TR13 8BW.

ISLES OF SCILLY BIRD REPORT and NATURAL HISTORY REVIEW 2000 (1969-), from Club secretary, Isles of Scilly Bird Group.

ISLES of SCILLY BIRD GROUP

BTO Regional Representatives & Regional Development Officer
CORNWALL RR. Position vacant.

ISLES OF SCILLY RR & RDO. Will Wagstaff, 42 Sally Port, St Mary's, Isles of Scilly, TR21 0JE. 01720 422212; e-mail: william.wagstaff@virgin.net

Clubs
CORNWALL BIRDWATCHING & PRESERVATION SOCIETY. (1931; 990). Darrell Clegg, 55 Lower Fore Street, Saltash, Cornwall PL12 6JQ. www.cbwps.org.uk

CORNWALL WILDLIFE TRUST PHOTOGRAPHIC GROUP. (40). David Chapman, 41 Bosence Road, Townshend, Nr Hayle, Cornwall TR27 6AL. 01736 850287; e-mail: david@ruralimages.freeserve.co.uk www.ruralimages.freeserve.co.uk

ISLES OF SCILLY BIRD GROUP. (2000; 510). Nigel Hudson, Post Office Flat, Hugh Street, St Mary's, Isles of Scilly TR21 0LL01720 422267; e-mail: nig-hudson@tiscali.co.uk www.scillybirding.co.uk

Ringing Group
SCILLONIA SEABIRD GROUP. Peter Robinson, 19 Pine Park Road, Honiton, Devon, EX14 2HR. (Tel/fax) 01404 549873; e-mail: pjrobinson2@compuserve.com

RSPB Local Group
CORNWALL. (1972; 600). Gordon Mills, 11 Commercial Square, Camborne, Cornwall TR14 8JZ. 01209 713144 (eve).
Meetings: Indoor meetings (Oct-Apr), outdoor throughout the year.

Wildlife Hospital
MOUSEHOLE WILD BIRD HOSPITAL & SANCTUARY ASSOCIATION LTD. Raginnis Hill, Mousehole, Penzance, Cornwall, TR19 6SR. 01736 731386. All species. No ringing.

Wetland Bird Survey Organisers
CORNWALL (Excl. Tamar Complex) Graham Hobin, Lower Drift Farmhouse, Drift, Buryas Bridge, Penzance TR19 6AA; e-mail: graham@birdbrain.freeserve.co.uk

TAMAR COMPLEX. Gladys Grant, 18 Orchard Crescent, Oreston, Plymouth, PL9 7NF. 01752 406287

Wildlife Trust
CORNWALL WILDLIFE TRUST. (1962; 6,000). Five Acres, Allet, Truro, Cornwall, TR4 9DJ. 01872 273939; fax 01872 225476; e-mail: cornwt@cix.co.uk www.cornwallwildlifetrust.org.uk

THE ISLES OF SCILLY WILDLIFE TRUST. Carn Thomas, Hugh Town, St Marys, Isles of Scilly TR21 0PT. 01720 422153; fax 01720 422153; e-mailenquiries@ios-wildlifetrust.org.uk www.ioswildlifetrust.org.uk

CUMBRIA

BirdAtlas/Avifauna
The Breeding Birds of Cumbria by Stott, Callion, Kinley, Raven and Roberts (Cumbria Bird Club, 2002).

Bird Recorders
COUNTY. Colin Raven, 18 Seathwaite Road, Barrow-in-Furness, Cumbria, LA14 4LX; e-mail: colin@walneyobs.fsnet.co.uk

NORTH EAST (Carlisle & Eden). Michael F Carrier, Lismore Cottage, 1 Front Street, Armathwaite, Cumbria, CA4 9PB. 01697 472218.

NORTH WEST (Allerdale & Copeland). J K Manson, Fell Beck, East Road, Egremont, Cumbria, CA22 2ED. 01946 822947;
e-mail: jake@jakemanson.freeserve.co.uk

SOUTH (South Lakeland & Furness). Ronnie Irving, 24 Birchwood Close, Kendal, Cumbria, LA9 5BJ. 01539 727523;
e-mail:ronnie@fenella.fslife.co.uk

Bird Reports
BIRDS AND WILDLIFE IN CUMBRIA (1970-), from D Clarke, Tullie House Museum, Castle Street, Carlisle, Cumbria, CA3 8TP;
e-mail: DavidC@carlisle-city.gov.uk

WALNEY BIRD OBSERVATORY REPORT, from Warden, see Reserves.

BTO Regional Representatives
NORTH RR. Clive Hartley, Marsh Cottage, Burgh-by-Sands, Carlisle CA5 6AX. 01228 576349;
e-mail: clivehartley@marshcott.freeserve.co.uk

SOUTH RR. Stephen Dunstan, 29 Greenfinch Court, Herons Reach, Blackpool, FY3 8FG. 01253 301009; e-mail: stephen@greenfinch.fslife.co.uk

Clubs
ARNSIDE & DISTRICT NATURAL HISTORY SOCIETY. (1967; 221). Mrs GM Smith, West Wind, Orchard Road, Arnside, via Carnforth, Cumbria, LA5 0DP. 01524 762522.
Meetings: 7.30pm, 2nd Thursday of the month (Sept-Apr). WI Hall, Arnside. (Also summer walks).

CUMBRIA BIRD CLUB. (1989; 230). Clive Hartley, Marsh Cottage, Burgh-by-Sands, Carlisle CA5 6AX. 01228 576349.
www.cumbriabirdclub.freeserve.co.uk
Meetings: Various evenings and venues (Oct-Mar) check on website for further details. £2 for non-members.

CUMBRIA RAPTOR STUDY GROUP

CUMBRIA RAPTOR STUDY GROUP. (1992). P N Davies, Snowhill Cottage, Caldbeck, Wigton, Cumbria, CA7 8HL. 016973 71249; e-mail: pete.caldbeck@virgin.net

Ringing Groups
EDEN RG. G Longrigg, Mere Bank, Bleatarn, Warcop, Appleby, Cumbria, CA16 6PX.

MORECAMBE BAY WADER RG. J Sheldon, 415 West Shore Park, Barrow-in-Furness, Cumbria, LA14 3XZ. 01229 473102.

WALNEY BIRD OBSERVATORY. K Parkes, 176 Harrogate Street, Barrow-in-Furness, Cumbria, LA14 5NA. 01229 824219.

RSPB Local Groups
CARLISLE. (1974; 400). Bob Jones, 130 Greenacres, Wetherall, Carlisle.
Meetings: 7.30pm, Wednesday monthly, Tithe Barn, Carlisle.

SOUTH LAKELAND. (1973; 340). Ms Kathleen Atkinson, 2 Langdale Crescent, Windermere, Cumbria, LA23 2HE. 01539 444254.

WEST CUMBRIA. (1986; 230). Neil Hutchin, Meadows Edge, 3 Camerton Road, Great Broughton, Cockermouth, Cumbria, CA13 0YR. 01900 825231; e-mail: neil@hutchin50.fsnet.co.uk

Wetland Bird Survey Organiser
DUDDON ESTUARY. Bob Treen, 5 Rydal Close, Dalton-in-Furness, Cumbria LA15 8QU. 01229 464789.

Wildlife Trust
CUMBRIA WILDLIFE TRUST. (1962; 5,000). Plumgarths, Crook Road, Kendal, Cumbria LA8 8LX. 01539 816300; fax 01539 816301;
e-mail: mail@cumbriawildlifetrust.org.uk
www.wildlifetrust.org.uk/cumbria

DERBYSHIRE

Bird Recorders
1. Rare breeding records. Roy A Frost, 66 St Lawrence Road, North Wingfield, Chesterfield, Derbyshire, S42 5LL. 01246 850037.

2. Records committee & rarity records. Rodney W Key, 3 Farningham Close, Spondon, Derby, DE21 7DZ. 01332 678571; e-mail: r.key3@ntlworld.com

3. JOINT RECORDER and Annual Report editor. Richard M R James, 10 Eastbrae Road, Littleover, Derby, DE23 1WA. 01332 771787;
e-mail: rmrjames@yahoo.com

Bird Reports
BENNERLEY MARSH WILDLIFE GROUP ANNUAL REPORT, from Secretary.

CARSINGTON BIRD CLUB ANNUAL REPORT, from Secretary.

DERBYSHIRE BIRD REPORT (1954-), from Bryan Barnacle, Mays, Malthouse Lane, Froggatt, Hope Valley, Derbyshire S32 3ZA. 01433 630726;
e-mail: barney@mays1.demon.co.uk

OGSTON BIRD CLUB REPORT (1970-), from Secretary.

BTO Regional Representatives
NORTH RR. Dave Budworth, 121 Wood Lane, Newhall, Swadlincote, Derbys, DE11 0LX. 01283 215188; e-mail: dbud01@aol.com

SOUTH RR. Dave Budworth, 121 Wood Lane, Newhall, Swadlincote, Derbys, DE11 0LX. 01283 215188; e-mail: dbud01@aol.com

Clubs

BENNERLEY MARSH WILDLIFE GROUP. (1995; 135). Richard Rogers, 19 Arundel Drive, Beeston, Nottingham, NG9 3LN; email: rtnr@breathe.com

BAKEWELL & DISTRICT BIRD STUDY GROUP. (1987; 70). Bill Millward, Dale House, The Dale, Hope Valley, Derbys S32 1AQ.

BUXTON FIELD CLUB. (1946; 71). B Aries, 1 Horsefair Avenue, Chapel-en-le-Frith, High Peak, Derbys, SK23 9SQ. 01298 815291;
e-mail: brian.aries@horsefair.ndo.co.uk
Meetings: 7.30pm, Saturdays fortnightly (Oct-Mar), Methodist Church Hall, Buxton.

CARSINGTON BIRD CLUB. (1992; 257). Mrs Dorothy Evans, 0775 992 4259;
e-mail: dmevans41@lineone.net
www.carsingtonbirdclub.co.uk
Meetings: 7.30pm, 3rd Tuesday of the month (Sep-Mar), Hognaston Village Hall, Nr Ashbourne, Derbyshire.

DERBYSHIRE ORNITHOLOGICAL SOCIETY. (1954; 550). Steve Shaw, 84 Moorland View Road, Walton, Chesterfield, Derbys, S40 3DF. 01246 236090;
e-mail: steveshaw@ornsoc.freeserve.co.uk
www.derbyshireOS.org.uk
Meetings: 7.30pm, last Friday of the winter months, various venues.

OGSTON BIRD CLUB. (1969; 1126). Mrs Ann Hunt, 2 Sycamore Avenue, Glapwell, Chesterfield, S44 5LH. 01623 812159
www.ogstonbirdclub.co.uk

SOUTH PEAK RAPTOR STUDY GROUP. (1998; 12). M E Taylor, 76 Hawksley Avenue, Newbold, Chesterfield, Derbys, S40 4TL. 01246 277749.

Ringing Groups

DARK PEAK RG. W M Underwood, Ivy Cottage, 15 Broadbottom Road, Mottram-in-Longdendale, Hyde, Cheshire SK14 6JB.
e-mail: w.m.underwood@talk21.com

SORBY-BRECK RG. Geoff P Mawson, Moonpenny Farm, Farwater Lane, Dronfield, Sheffield, S18 1RA. 01246 415097;
e-mail: gpmawson@hotmail.com

SOUDER RG. Dave Budworth, 121 Wood Lane, Newhall, Swadlincote, Derbys, DE11 0LX. 0121 6953384.

RSPB Local Groups

CHESTERFIELD. (1987; 274). Tony Atkinson, 01246 233840; e-mail: TAA@care4free.net

DERBY. (1973; 520). Brian Myring, 74 The Bancroft, Etwall, Derby, DE65 6NF. 01283 734851.
Meetings: 7.30pm, 1st Wednesday of the month (Sep-Apr), Lund Pavilion, Derbyshire County Cricket Ground.

HIGH PEAK. (1974; 200). Peter Griffiths, 17 Clifton Drive, Marple, Stockport SK6 6PP. 0161 427 5325.
Meetings: 7.30pm, 3rd Tuesday of the month (Sep-May), Marple Senior Citizens Hall.

Wildlife Trust

DERBYSHIRE WILDLIFE TRUST. (1962; 5,000). East Mill, Bridgefoot, Belper, Derbyshire DE56 1XH. 01773 881188; fax 01773 821826;
e-mail: derbywt@cix.co.uk
www.derbyshirewildlifetrust.org.uk

DEVON

BirdAtlas/Avifauna

Tetrad Atlas of Breeding Birds of Devon by H P Sitters (Devon Birdwatching & Preservation Society, 1988).

Bird Recorder

Mike Tyler, The Acorn, Shute Road, Kilmington, Axminster, Devon EX13 7ST. 01297 34958;
e-mail: mike@mwtyler.freeserve.co.uk

Bird Reports

DEVON BIRD REPORT (1928-), from H Kendall, 33 Victoria Road, Bude, Cornwall, EX23 8RJ. 01288 353818;
e-mail: harvey.kendall@btopenworld.com

LUNDY FIELD SOCIETY ANNUAL REPORT (1946-), from Secretary. Index to Report is on Society's website.

BTO Regional Representative & Regional Development Officer

John Woodland, Glebe Cottage, Dunsford, Exeter, EX6 7AA. Tel/fax 01647 252494;
e-mail: jwoodland@btodv.fsnet.co.uk

Clubs

DEVON BIRDWATCHING & PRESERVATION SOCIETY. (1928; 1,200). Mrs Joy Vaughan, 28 Fern Meadow, Okehampton, Devon, EX20 1PB. 01837 53360;
e-mail: joy@vaughan411.freeserve.co.uk

KINGSBRIDGE & DISTRICT NATURAL HISTORY SOCIETY. (1989; 130). Martin Catt, Migrants Rest, East Prawle, Kingsbridge, Devon, TQ7 2DB. 01548 511443;
e-mail: martin.catt@btinternet.com

LUNDY FIELD SOCIETY. (1946; 450). Frances Stuart, 3 Lower Linden Road, Clevedon, North Somerset BS21 7SU. 01275 871434;
e-mail: fs@ifrc.co.uk
www.lundy.org.uk

TOPSHAM BIRDWATCHING & NATURALISTS' SOCIETY. (1969; 100). Mrs Janice Vining, 2 The Maltings, Fore Street, Topsham, Exeter, EX3 0HF. 01392 873514; e-mail: tbnsociety@hotmail.com www.members.tripod.co.uk/tbns
Meetings: 7.30pm, 2nd Friday of the month (Sep-May), Matthews Hall, Topsham.

Ringing Groups
DEVON & CORNWALL WADER RG. R C Swinfen, 72 Dunraven Drive, Derriford, Plymouth, PL6 6AT. 01752 704184.

LUNDY FIELD SOCIETY. A M Taylor, 26 High Street, Spetisbury, Blandford, Dorset, DT11 9DJ. 01258 857336; e-mail: ammataylor@yahoo.co.uk

SLAPTON BIRD OBSERVATORY. Peter Ellicott, 10 Chapel Road, Alphington, Exeter, EX2 8TB. 01392 277387.

RSPB Local Groups
EXETER & DISTRICT. (1974; 466). John Allan, 01626 821344;
e-mail: john-allan@coxland.fsnet.co.uk

NORTH DEVON. (1976; 68). David Gayton, 29 Merrythorne Road, Fremington, Barnstaple, Devon, EX31 3AL. 01271 371092.
e-mail: hevdav@aol.com
Meetings: 7 for 7.30pm, last Friday of the month, The Civic Centre, Barnstaple

PLYMOUTH. (1974; 600). Mrs Eileen Willey, 11 Beverstone Way, Roborough, Plymouth, PL6 7DY. 01752 208996.

Wildlife Hospitals
BIRD OF PREY CASUALTY CENTRE. Mrs J E L Vinson, Crooked Meadow, Stidston Lane, South Brent, Devon, TQ10 9JS. 01364 72174.
Birds of prey, with emergency advice on other species. Aviaries, releasing pen. Veterinary support.

BONDLEIGH BIRD HOSPITAL. Manager, Samantha Hart, North Tawton, Devon, EX20 2AJ. 01837 82328.
All species. 14 aviaries, 2 aquapens. Veterinary support available, if requested, with payment of full charges.

CATT, Martin. Migrants Rest, East Prawle, Kingsbridge, Devon, TQ7 2DB. 01548 511443; e-mail: martin.catt@btinternet.com. Collects and records oiled birds and gives initial treatment before forwarding to cleaning station.

HURRELL, Dr LH, 201 Outland Road, Peverell, Plymouth, PL2 3PF. 01752 771838.
Birds of prey only. Veterinary support.

TORBAY WILDLIFE RESCUE CENTRE. Malcolm Higgs, 6A Gerston Place, Paignton, S Devon, TQ3 3DX. 01803 557624. www.twrs.fsnet.co.uk
All wild birds, inc. oiled. Pools, aviaries, intensive care, washing facilities. Open at all times. 24-hr veterinary support. Holding areas off limits to public as all wildlife must be returned to the wild.

Wetland Bird Survey Organiser
TAMAR COMPLEX. Gladys Grant, 18 Orchard Crescent, Oreston, Plymouth, PL9 7NF. 01752 406287.

Wildlife Trust
DEVON WILDLIFE TRUST. (1962; 10,600). Shirehampton House, 35-37 St David's Hill, Exeter, EX4 4DA. 01392 279244; fax 01392 433221;
e-mail: contactus@devonwt.cix.co.uk
www.devonwildlifetrust.org.uk

DORSET

BirdAtlas/Avifauna
Dorset Breeding Bird Atlas (working title). In preparation.

Bird Recorder
James Lidster, 35 Napier Road, Poole, Dorset BH15 4LX. 01202 672406;
e-mail: dorsetbirds@btopenworld.com

Bird Reports
DORSET BIRDS (1987-), from Miss J W Adams, 16 Sherford Drive, Wareham, Dorset, BH20 4EN. 01929 552299.

THE BIRDS OF CHRISTCHURCH HARBOUR (1959-), from Ian Southworth, 1 Bodowen Road, Burton, Christchurch, Dorset BH23 7JL.
e-mail: ianbirder@aol.com

PORTLAND BIRD OBSERVATORY REPORT, from Warden, see Reserves,

BTO Regional Representatives
Catherine and Graham Whitby, 2 Helston Close, Portesham, Weymouth, Dorset, DT3 4EY. 01305 871301; e-mail:
catherineandgraham@portisham2.fsnet.co.uk

Clubs
CHRISTCHURCH HARBOUR ORNITHOLOGICAL GROUP. (1956; 150). John Hall, 15 Kingsbere Gardens, Haslemere Avenue, Highcliffe, Dorset, BH23 5BQ. 01425 275610.

DORSET BIRD CLUB. (1987; 530). Mrs Eileen Bowman, 53 Lonnen Road, Colehill, Wimborne, Dorset, BH21 7AT. 01202 884788.
www.dorsetbirdclub.org.uk
Meetings: Usually 7.30pm, no set day or venue.

DORSET NATURAL HISTORY & ARCHAEOLOGICAL SOCIETY. (1845; 2188). Dorset County Museum, High West Street,

Dorchester, Dorset, DT1 1XA. 01305 262735; e-mail: dorsetcountymuseum@dor-mus.demon.co.uk www.dor-mus.demon.co.uk

Ringing Groups
CHRISTCHURCH HARBOUR RS. E C Brett, 3 Whitfield Park, St Ives, Ringwood, Hants, BH24 2DX. e-mail: ed_brett@lineone.net

PORTLAND BIRD OBSERVATORY. Martin Cade, Old Lower Light, Portland Bill, Dorset, DT5 2JT. 01305 820553; e-mail: obs@btinternet.com www.portlandbirdobs.btinternet.co.uk

STOUR RG. R Gifford, 62 Beacon Park Road, Upton, Poole, Dorset, BH16 5PE.

RSPB Local Groups
BLACKMOOR VALE. (1981; 106). Mrs Margaret Marris, 15 Burges Close, Marnhull, Sturminster Newton, Dorset, DT10 1QQ. 01258 820091. **Meetings:** 7.30pm, 3rd Friday in the month, Gillingham Primary School.

EAST DORSET. (1974; 435). Tony Long (Group Leader: S.Cresswell), 93 Wimborne Road, Corfe Mullen, Wimborne, BH21 3DS. 01202 880508; e-mail: tony@joan1206.fsnet.co.uk
Meetings: 7.30pm, 2nd Wednesday of the month, St Mark's church hall, Talbot Village.

POOLE. (1982; 305). John Derricott, 51 Dacombe Drive, Upton, Poole, Dorset, BH16 5JJ. 01202 776312.

SOUTH DORSET. (1976; 400). Marion Perriss, Old Barn Cottage, Affpuddle, Dorchester, Dorset, DT2 7HH. 01305 848268;
e-mail: affpuddle@btinternet.com.

Wildlife Hospital
SWAN RESCUE SANCTUARY. Ken and Judy Merriman, The Wigeon, Crooked Withies, Holt, Wimborne, Dorset, BH21 7LB. 01202 828166; mobile 0385 917457;
e-mail: ken@swan-rescue.fsnet.co.uk
www.swan-rescue.co.uk
Swans. Hospital unit with indoor ponds and recovery pens. Outdoors: 35 ponds and lakes, and recovery pens. 24-hr veterinary support. Viewing by appointment only.

Wetland Bird Survey Organisers
THE FLEET & PORTLAND HARBOUR. Steve Groves, Abbotsbury Swannery, New Barn Road, Abbotsbury, Dorset, DT3 4JG. (W) 01305 871684; e-mail: abbotsbury.swannery@btinternet.com

RADIPOLE & LODMOOR. Keith Ballard, RSPB Visitor Centre, Swannery Carpark, Weymouth, Dorset, DT4 7TZ. 01305 778313.

Wildlife Trust
DORSET WILDLIFE TRUST. (1961; 8,000). Brooklands Farm, Forston, Dorchester, Dorset, DT2 7AA. 01305 264620; fax 01305 251120; e-mail: dorsetwt@cix.co.uk; http://www.wildlifetrust.org.uk/dorset/

DURHAM

BirdAtlas/Avifauna
A Summer Atlas of Breeding Birds of County Durham by Stephen Westerberg/Keith Bowey. (Durham Bird Club, 2000)

Bird Recorders
Tony Armstrong, 39 Western Hill, Durham City, DH1 4RJ. 0191 386 1519;
e-mail: ope@globalnet.co.uk

CLEVELAND. Rob Little, 5 Belgrave Court, Seaton Carew, Hartlepool TS25 1BF. 01429 428940.

Bird Reports
BIRDS IN DURHAM (1971-), from D Sowerbutts, 9 Prebends Fields, Gilesgate, Durham, DH1 1HH.

CLEVELAND BIRD REPORT (1974-), from Mr J Sharp, 10 Glendale, Pinehills, Guisborough, TS14 8JF. 01287 633976.

BTO Regional Representatives
David L Sowerbutts, 9 Prebends Field, Gilesgate Moor, Durham, DH1 1HH. H:0191 386 7201; W:0191 374 3011;
e-mail: d.l.sowerbutts@durham.ac.uk

CLEVELAND RR. Russell McAndrew, 5 Thornhill Gardens, Hartlepool, TS26 0HX. 01429 277291.

Clubs
DURHAM BIRD CLUB. (1975; 263). Kevin Spindloe, 31 Comrie Road, Hartlepool, TS25 4JQ. 01429 867550; e-mail: kevinspindloe@hotmail.com

SUMMERHILL (HARTLEPOOL) BIRD CLUB. (2000; 75). Kevin Spindloe, 31 Comrie Road, Hartlepool, TS25 4JQ1430 867550.

TEESMOUTH BIRD CLUB. (1960; 260). Chris Sharp, 20 Auckland Way, Hartlepool, TS26 0AN. 01429 865163. www.teesmouthbc.freeserve.co.uk
Meetings: 7.30pm, 1st Wednesday of the month (Sep-Apr), Billingham Arms Hotel, Billingham.

Ringing Groups
DURHAM RG. S Westerberg, 32 Manor Road, Medomsley, Consett, Co Durham, DH8 6QW. 01207 563862.

DURHAM DALES RG. J R Hawes, Fairways, 5 Raby Terrace, Willington, Crook, Durham, DL15 0HR.

RSPB Local Group
DURHAM. (1974; 125). Lo Brown, 4 Ann's Place, Langley Moor, Durham, DH7 8JY. 0191 378 2433. **Meetings:** 7.30pm, 2nd Tuesday of the month

(Oct-Mar), Room CG83, adjacent to Scarborough Lecture Theatre, University Science Site, Stockton Road entrance.

Wetland Bird Survey Organisers
TEES ESTUARY. Mike Leakey, c/o Energy Information Centre, Nuclear Electric, Tees Road, Hartlepool, TS25 2BZ. (W) 01912 816316; e-mail: mike.leakey@english-nature.org.uk

Wildlife Trust
DURHAM WILDLIFE TRUST. (1971; 3,500). Rainton Meadows, Chilton Moor, Houghton-le-Spring, Tyne & Wear, DH4 6PU. 0191 5843112; fax 0191 584 3934; e-mail: durhamwt@cix.co.uk www.wildlifetrust.org.uk/durham

ESSEX

Bird Atlas/Avifauna
Birds of Essex (provisional title) by Simon Woods (Essex Birdwatching Society, date to be announced).

The Breeding Birds of Essex by M K Dennis (Essex Birdwatching Society, 1996). New county avifauna, edited by Simon Wood.

Bird Recorder
SENIOR RECORDER. Howard Vaughan, 103 Darnley Road, Strood, Rochester, Kent ME2 2EY. 01634 325864;
e-mail: howardebs@blueyonder.co.uk

JOINT RECORDER. Roy Ledgerton (joint), 25 Bunyan Road, Braintree, Essex CM7 2PL. 01376 326103; e-mail: r.ledgerton@virgin.net

JOINT RECORDER. Paul Levey (joint), 5 Hedingham Place, Rectory Road, Rochford, Essex SS4 1UP. 01702 549070;
e-mail: essex.birds@btopenworld.com

JOINT RECORDER. Bob Flindall, 60 Lady Lane, Chelmsford, Essex CM2 0TH. 01245 344206;
e-mail: robert.flindall@btinternet.com

Bird Report
ESSEX BIRD REPORT (inc Bradwell Bird Obs records) (1950-), from Peter Dwyer, Sales Officer, 48 Churchill Avenue, Halstead, Essex, CO9 2BE. Tel/fax 01787 476524;
e-mail: petedwyer@petedwyer.plus.com or pete@northessex.co.uk

BTO Regional Representatives & Regional Development Officer
NORTH-EAST RR & RDO. Peter Dwyer, 48 Churchill Avenue, Halstead, Essex, CO9 2BE. Tel/fax 01787 476524;
e-mail: petedwyer@petedwyer.plus.com or pete@northessex.co.uk

NORTH-WEST RR. Roy Ledgerton, 25 Bunyan Road, Braintree, Essex, CM7 2PL. 01376 326103; e-mail: r.ledgerton@virgin.net

SOUTH RR. Position vacant.

Club
ESSEX BIRDWATCHING SOCIETY. (1949; 700). Roy Ledgerton, 25 Bunyan Road, Braintree, Essex, CM7 2PL. 01376 326103;
e-mail: r.ledgerton@virgin.net
www.essexbirdwatchsoc.co.uk

The ESSEX BIRDWATCHING SOCIETY

Meetings: 1st Friday of the month (Oct-Mar), Friends' Meeting House, Rainsford Road, Chelmsford.

Ringing Groups
ABBERTON RG. C P Harris, Wylandotte, Seamer Road, Southminster, Essex, CM0 7BX.

BASILDON RG. B J Manton, 72 Leighcliff Road, Leigh-on-Sea, Essex, SS9 1DN. 01702 475183;
e-mail: bjmanton@lineone.net

BRADWELL BIRD OBSERVATORY. C P Harris, Wyandotte, Seamer Road, Southminster, Essex, CM0 7BX.

RSPB Local Groups
CHELMSFORD AND CENTRAL ESSEX. (1976; 5,500). Mike Logan Wood, Highwood, Ishams Chase, Wickham Bishops, Essex, CM8 3LG. 01621 892045;
e-mail: mike.lw@tiscali.co.uk
Meetings: 8pm, Thursdays, eight times a year. The Cramphorn Theatre, Chelmsford.

COLCHESTER. (1981; 220). Mrs V Owen, Tawnies, Hall Lane, Langenhoe, Colchester, CO5 7NA.
Meetings: 7.45pm, 2nd Thursday of the month (Sep-Apr), Shrub End Community Hall, Shrub End Road, Colchester.

SOUTHEND. (1983; 200). Graham Mee, 24 Sunbury Court, North Shoebury, Essex SS3 8TB. 01702 297554; www.southendrspb.co.uk
e-mail: grahamm@southendrspb.co.uk
Meetings: 8pm, usually 1st Monday of the month (Sep-May), Maybrook, 303 Southchurch Road, Southend on Sea.

Wetland Bird Survey Organisers
STOUR ESTUARY. Rick Vonk, RSPB, Unit 3 Court Farm, 3 Stutton Road, Brantham, Suffolk CO11 1PW. (Day) 01473 328006.

LEE VALLEY. Ian Kendall, 18 North Barn, Broxbourne, Herts EN10 6RR;
e-mail ikendall@leevalleypark.org.uk

ESSEX (Other Sites). Howard Vaughan, 103 Darnley Road, Strood, Rochester, Kent ME2 2EY. 01634 325864 (after 7pm);
e-mail; howardebs@blueyonder.co.uk

Wildlife Trust
ESSEX WILDLIFE TRUST. (1959; 15,500). Abbots Hall Farm, Great Wigborough, Colchester, CO5 7RZ. 01621 862960; fax 01621 862990; e-mail: admin@essexwt.org.uk www.essexwt.org.uk

GLOUCESTERSHIRE

Bird Atlas/Avifauna
Atlas of Breeding Birds of the North Cotswolds. (North Cotswold Ornithological Society, 1990)

Bird Recorder
GLOUCESTERSHIRE EXCLUDING S.GLOS (AVON). Richard Baatsen, e-mail: baatsen@surfbirder.com

Bird Reports
CHELTENHAM BIRD CLUB BIRD REPORT (1998-), from Secretary.

GLOUCESTERSHIRE BIRD REPORT (1953-), from David Cramp, 2 Ellenor, Alderton, Tewkesbury, GL20 8NZ. 01242 620281.

NORTH COTSWOLD ORNITHOLOGICAL SOCIETY ANNUAL REPORT (1983-), from Secretary.

BTO Regional Representative
Mike Smart, 143 Cheltenham Road, Gloucester, GL2 0JH. Home/work 01452 421131; e-mail: smartmike@smartmike.fsnet.co.uk

Clubs
CHELTENHAM BIRD CLUB. (1976; 85). Mrs Frances Meredith, 14 Greatfield Drive, Charlton Kings, Cheltenham, GL53 9BU. 01242 516393; e-mail: chelt.birds@virgin.net www.beehive.thisisgloucestershire.co.uk/cheltbirdclub
Meetings: 7.15pm, Mondays (Oct-Mar), Bournside School, Warden Hill Road, Cheltenham.

DURSLEY BIRDWATCHING & PRESERVATION SOCIETY. (1953; 500). Paul Walkden, 32 Oakfield Way, Sharpness, Berkeley, Glos, GL13 9UU. 01453 811029. email: paul_walkden@hotmail.com http://beehive.thisisgloucestershire.co.uk
Meetings: 7.45pm, 2nd and 4th Monday (Sept-Mar), Dursley Community Centre.

GLOUCESTERSHIRE NATURALISTS' SOCIETY. (1948; 600). Mike Smart, Gloucestershire Naturalists' Society, Greystones, Church Lane, Bridgend, Stonehouse, GL10 2BG; e-mail: enquiries@glosnats.org.uk www.glosnats.org.uk

NORTH COTSWOLD ORNITHOLOGICAL SOCIETY. (1982; 70). T Hutton, 15 Green Close, Childswickham, Broadway, Worcs, WR12 7JJ. 01386 858511.
Meetings: Monthly field meetings, usually Sunday 9.30.

Ringing Groups
COTSWOLD WATER PARK RG. R Hearn, Wildfowl & Wetlands Trust, Slimbridge, Glos, GL2 7BT. 01453 891900 ext 185; e-mail: richard.hearn@wwt.org.uk

SEVERN ESTUARY GULL GROUP. M E Durham, 6 Glebe Close, Frampton-on-Severn, Glos, GL2 7EL. 01452 741312.

SEVERN VALE RG. R Hearn, Wildfowl & Wetlands Trust, Slimbridge, Glos, GL2 7BT. 01453 891900 ext 185; e-mail: richard.hearn@wwt.org.uk

WILDFOWL & WETLANDS TRUST. R Hearn, Wildfowl & Wetlands Trust, Slimbridge, Glos, GL2 7BT. 01453 891900 ext 185; e-mail: richard.hearn@wwt.org.uk

RSPB Local Group
GLOUCESTERSHIRE. (1972; 740). David Cramp, 2 Ellenor, Alderton, Tewkesbury, GL20 8NZ. 01242 620281.
Meetings: 7.30pm, 3rd Tuesday of the month, Sir Thomas Rich's School, Gloucester.

Wildlife Hospital
GLOUCESTER WILDLIFE RESCUE CENTRE. Alan and Louise Brockbank, 1 Moorend Lodge, Moorend, Hartpury, Glos GL19 3DG. 01452 700038; e-mail: info@gloswildliferescue.fsnet.co.uk www.gloswildliferescue.fsnet.co.uk
Intensive care, treatment and rehabilitation facilities. Vetinary support. No restrictions or conditions.

VALE WILDLIFE RESCUE - WILDLIFE HOSPITAL + REHABILITATION CENTRE. Ms Caroline Gould, Station Road, Beckford, Tewkesbury, Glos, GL20 7AN. 01386 882288; (Fax) 01386 882299; e-mail: info@vwr.org.uk www.vwr.org.uk
All wild birds. Intensive care. Registered charity. Veterinary support.

Wetland Bird Survey Organisers
SEVERN ESTUARY – GLOUCESTERSHIRE. Colette Hall, Slimbridge, Gloucester, GL2 7BT. 01453 890333.

GLOUCESTERSHIRE (Inland). Les Jones, Chestnut House, Water Lane, Somerford Keynes, Cirencester, Glos GL7 6DS; e-mail: leslie@somerfordk.freeserve.co.uk

Wildlife Trust
GLOUCESTERSHIRE WILDLIFE TRUST. (1961; 6,200). Dulverton Building, Robinswood Hill Country Park, Reservoir Road, Gloucester, GL4 6SX. 01452 383333; fax 01452 383334;

e-mail: info@gloucestershirewildlifetrusts.co.uk
www.gloucesterwildlife.co.uk

HAMPSHIRE

Bird Atlas/Avifauna
Birds of Hampshire by J M Clark and J A Eyre (Hampshire Ornithological Society, 1993).

Bird Recorder
John Clark, 4 Cygnet Court, Old Cove Road, Fleet, Hants, GU51 2RL. Tel/fax 01252 623397; e-mail: johnclark@cygnetcourt.demon.co.uk

Bird Reports
HAMPSHIRE BIRD REPORT (1955-), from Mrs Margaret Boswell, 5 Clarence Road, Lyndhurst, Hants, SO43 7AL. 023 8028 2105; e-mail: mag.bos@btinternet.com
2002 edition £9 including p&p.

BTO Regional Representative & Regional Development Officer
Glynne C Evans, Waverley, Station Road, Chilbolton, Stockbridge, Hants, SO20 6AL. H:01264 860697; e-mail: hantsbto@hotmail.com

Clubs
HAMPSHIRE ORNITHOLOGICAL SOCIETY. (1979; 955). Peter Dudley, 3 Copsewood Road, Hythe, Southampton, SO45 5DX. 02380 847149; e-mail: peterf.dudley@tiscali.co.uk

SOUTHAMPTON & DISTRICT BIRD GROUP. (1994; 68). Vic Short, 20 Westbroke Gardens, Romsey, SO51 7RQ. 01794 511843; e-mail: vicshort@btopenworld.com
Meetings: Programme available.

Ringing Groups
FARLINGTON RG. D A Bell, 38 Holly Grove, Fareham, Hants, PO16 7UP.

ITCHEN RG. W F Simcox, 10 Holdaway Close, Kingsworthy, Winchester, SO23 7QH. e-mail: wsimcox@sparsholt.ac.uk

LOWER TEST RG. J Pain, Owlery Holt, Nations Hill, Kingsworthy, Winchester, SO23 7QY. 023 8066 7919; e-mail: jessp@hwt.org.uk

RSPB Local Groups
BASINGSTOKE. (1979; 90). Peter Hutchins, 35 Woodlands, Overton, Whitchurch, RG25 3HN. 01256 770831;
e-mail: fieldfare@jaybry.gotadsl.co.uk
Meetings: 7.30pm, 3rd Tuesday of the month (Sept-May), Church Cottage, St Michael's Church, Church Square, Basingstoke.

NORTH EAST HAMPSHIRE. (1976; 220). Graham Dumbleton, 28 Castle Street, Fleet, Hants, GU52 7ST. 01252 622699.
www.northeasthantsrspb.org.uk

PORTSMOUTH. (1974; 205). Gordon Humby, 19 Charlesworth Gardens, Waterlooville, Hants, PO7 6AU. 02392 353949.
Meetings: 4th Saturday of the month, programme for members, St Colmans Church Hall, Cosham.

WINCHESTER & DISTRICT. (1974; 162). Maurice Walker, Jesmond, 1 Compton Way, Olivers Battery, Winchester, SO22 4EY. 01962 854033.
Meetings: 7.30pm, 1st Tuesday of the month (not Jul or Aug), Cromwell Suite, The Stanmore, Winchester.

Wetland Bird Survey Organisers
HAMPSHIRE (Estuaries/Coastal). Dave Unsworth, 5 Nelson Road, Bishopstoke, Eastleigh, Hampshire, SO59 7BR. 01703 329191;
e-mail: David_Unsworth@mcga.gov.uk

HAMPSHIRE (Inland - excluding Avon Valley). Keith Wills, 51 Peabody Road, Farnborough, GU14 6EB. (H) 01252 548408;
e-mail: keithb.wills@ukgateway.net

AVON VALLEY. John Clark, 4 Cygnet Court, Old Cove Road, Fleet, Hants. 01252 623397;
e-mail: johnclark@cygnetcourt.demon.co.uk

Wildlife Hospital
NEW FOREST OWL SANCTUARY. Bruce Berry, New Forest Owl Sanctuary, Crow Lane, Crow, Ringwood, Hants, BH24 1EA. 01425 476487;
e-mail: nfosowls@aol.com
www.owlsanctuary.co.uk
A selection of owls, hawks and falcons from around the world with flying demonstrations at set times throughout the day. An opportunity to observe birds of prey at close range, an enjoyable day for the whole family. Open daily from Feb to Nov.

Wildlife Trust
HAMPSHIRE & ISLE OF WIGHT WILDLIFE TRUST. (1960; 11,295). Beechcroft House, Vicarage Lane, Curdridge, Hampshire SO32 2DP. 01489 774 400; fax 023 8068 8900;
e-mail: feedback@hwt.org.uk
www.hwt.org.uk

WIGHT TRUST. 2 High Street, Newport, Isle of Wight PO30 1SS. 01983 533 180;
e-mail: feedback@hwt.org.uk

HEREFORDSHIRE

Bird Recorder
Steve Coney, 5 Springfield Road, Withington, Hereford, HR1 3RU. 01432 850068;
e-mail: coney@bluecarrots.com

Bird Report
THE YELLOWHAMMER - Herefordshire Ornithological Club annual report, (1951-), from Mr I Evans, 12 Brockington Drive, Tupsley, Hereford, HR1 1TA. 01432 265509;
e-mail: iforelaine@care4free.net

BTO Regional Representative
Steve Coney, 5 Springfield Road, Withington, Hereford, HR1 3RU. 01432 850068; e-mail: coney@bluecarrots.com

Club
HEREFORDSHIRE ORNITHOLOGICAL CLUB. (1950; 409). TM Weale, Foxholes, Bringsty Common, Worcester, WR6 5UN. 01886 821368;
e-mail: weale@tinyworld.co.uk
www.herefordshirebirding.net
Meetings: 7.30pm, 2nd and 5th Thursday of the month in autumn/winter, Holmer Parish Centre, Holmer, Hereford.

Ringing Group
LLANCILLO RG. Dr G R Geen, 6 The Copse, Bannister Green, Felsted, Dunmow, Essex, CM6 3NP. 01371 820189; e-mail: thegeens@aol.com

Wildlife Hospital
ATHENE BIRD SANCTUARY. B N Bayliss, 61 Chartwell Road, Hereford, HR1 2TU. 01432 273259.
Birds of prey, ducks and waders, seabirds, pigeons and doves. Heated cages, small pond. Veterinary support.

Wildlife Trust
HEREFORDSHIRE NATURE TRUST. (1962; 1450). Lower House Farm, Ledbury Road, Tupsley, Hereford, HR1 1UT. 01432 356872; fax 01432 275489; e-mail: herefordwt@cix.co.uk
www.wildlifetrust.org.uk/hereford

HERTFORDSHIRE

Bird Atlas/Avifauna
Birds at Tring Reservoirs by R Young et al (Hertfordshire Natural History Society, 1996).

Mammals, Amphibians and Reptiles of Hertfordshire by Hertfordshire NHS in association with Training Publications Ltd, 3 Finway Court, Whippendell Road, Watford WD18 7EN, (2001).

The Breeding Birds of Hertfordshire by K W Smith et al (Herts NHS, 1993).

Bird Recorder
Mike Ilett, 14 Cowper Crescent, Bengeo, Hertford, Herts, SG14 3DY.
e-mail: michael.ilett@uk.tesco.com

Bird Report
HERTFORDSHIRE BIRD REPORT (1908-1998), from Hon Secretary, Herts Bird Club, 46 Manor Way, Boreham Wood, Herts, WD6 1QY.

BTO Regional Representative & Regional Development Officer
Chris Dee, 26 Broadleaf Avenue, Thorley Park, Bishop's Stortford, Herts, CM23 4JY. H:01279 755637; e-mail: chris_w_dee@hotmail.com

Clubs
FRIENDS OF TRING RESERVOIRS. (1993; 350). Judith Knight, 381 Bideford Green, Linslade, Leighton Buzzard, Beds, LU7 2TY. 01525 378161.
www.fotr.org.uk

HERTFORDSHIRE BIRD CLUB. (1971; 290) Part of Hertfordshire NHS. Jim Terry, 46 Manor Way, Borehamwood, HertsWD6 1QY. 020 8905 1461;
e-mail: jim@jayjoy.fsnet.co.uk
http://fly.to/hertsbirdclub

HERTFORDSHIRE NATURAL HISTORY SOCIETY. Christine Shepperson, 63 Station Road, Smallford, Herts. AL4 0HB; www.hnhs.org
e-mail: shepperson@waitrose.com

Ringing Groups
AYLESBURY VALE RG (main activity at Marsworth). S M Downhill, 12 Millfield, Berkhamsted, Herts, HP4 2PB. 01442 865821;
e-mail: smdjbd@waitrose.com

MAPLE CROSS RG. P Delaloye,
e-mail: pdelaloye@tiscali.co.uk

RYE MEADS RG. Chris Dee, 26 Broadleaf Avenue, Thorley Park, Bishop's Stortford, Herts, CM23 4JY. H:01279 755637;
e-mail: chris_w_dee@hotmail.com

TRING RG. Mick A'Court, 6 Chalkshire Cottages, Chalkshire road, Butlers Cross, Bucks, HP17 0TW. H:01296 623610; W:01494 462246;
e-mail: mick@focusrite.com
a.arundinaceous@virgin.net

RSPB Local Groups
CHORLEYWOOD & DISTRICT. (1977; 142). Sam Thomas, 36 Field Way, Rickmansworth, Herts WD3 2EJ. 01923 449917.
Meetings: 8pm, last Thursday of the month (Sept-May).

HARPENDEN. (1974; 1,000). Geoff Horn, 41 Ridgewood Drive, Harpenden, AL5 3LJ. 01582 765443; e-mail: geoffrhorn@yahoo.co.uk
Meetings: Check with group contact for details.

HEMEL HEMPSTEAD. (1973; 150). Paul Green, 207 Northridge Way, Hemel Hempstead, Herts, HP1 2AU. 01442 266637;
e-mail: paul@310nrwhh.freeserve.co.uk
www.hemelrspb.org.uk
Meetings: 8pm, 1st Monday of the month (Sep-Jun), The Cavendish School.

HITCHIN & LETCHWORTH. (1973; 106). Ms Jean Crystal, Amadeus House, Charlton, Hitchin, Herts, SG4 7TE. 01462 433912;
e-mail: jeanlcrystal@aol.com
http://uk.geocities.com/hitchin_letchworth_rspb
Meetings: 7.30pm, 1st Friday of the month, The Settlement, Nevells Road, Letchworth.

POTTERS BAR & BARNET. (1977; 1800). Stan Bailey, 23 Bowmans Close, Potters Bar, Herts, EN6 5NN. 01707 646073.
Meetings: 2.00pm, 2nd Tuesday of the month, St Johns URC Hall, Mowbray Road, Barnet, 8.00pm, changeable Mondays, Wyllyotts Centre, Potters Bar.

ST ALBANS. (1979; 1550 in catchment area). John Maxfield, 46 Gladeside, Jersey Farm, St Albans, Herts, AL4 9JA. 01727 832688;
e-mail: peterantram@antram.demon.co.uk
www.antram.demon.co.uk/
Meetings: 8.00pm, 2nd Tuesday of the month (Sep-May), St Saviours Church Hall, Sandpit Lane, St Albans.

SOUTH EAST HERTS. (1971; 150). Phil Blatcher, 3 Churchfields, Broxbourne, Herts, EN10 7JU. 01992 441024;
e-mail: SE_Herts_RSPB@hotmail.com
http://uk.geocities.com/seherts_rspb
Meetings: 8.00pm, last Tuesday of the month, URC Church Hall, Mill Lane, Broxbourne.

STEVENAGE. (1982; 1,300 in the catchment area). Mrs Ann Collis, 16 Stevenage Road, Walkern, Herts, 01483 861547.
Meetings: 7.30pm, 3rd Tuesday of the month, Friends Meeting House, Cuttys Lane, Stevenage.

WATFORD. (1974; 590). Philip and Marilyn McGovern, 65 Harford Drive, Watford WD17 3DQ. 01923 243761. www.members.lycos.co.uk/watford_RSPB
Meetings: 7.30pm, 2nd Wednesday of the month (Sep-Jun), St Andrews Church Hall, Langley Road, Watford.

Wildlife Hospital
SWAN CARE. Secretary, Swan Care, 14 Moorland Road, Boxmoor, Hemel Hempstead, Herts, HP1 1NH. 01442 251961.
Swans. Sanctuary and treatment centre. Veterinary support.

Wildlife Trust
HERTS & MIDDLESEX WILDLIFE TRUST. (1964; 8500). Grebe House, St Michael's Street, St Albans, Herts, AL3 4SN. 01727 858901; fax 01727 854542; e-mail: info@hmwt.org
www.wildlifetrust.org.uk/herts/

ISLE OF WIGHT

Bird Recorder
G Sparshott, Leopards Farm, Main Road, Havenstreet, Isle of Wight, PO33 4DR. 01983 882549; e-mail: grahamspa@aol.com

Bird Reports
ISLE OF WIGHT BIRD REPORT (1986-) (Pre-1986 not available), from Mr DJ Hunnybun, 40 Churchill Road, Cowes, Isle of Wight, PO31 8HH. 01983 292880.

BTO Regional Representative
James C Gloyn, 3 School Close, Newchurch, Isle of Wight, PO36 0NL. 01983 865567;
e-mail: gloynjc@yahoo.com

Clubs
ISLE OF WIGHT NATURAL HISTORY & ARCHAEOLOGICAL SOCIETY. (1919; 500). Dr Margaret Jackson, The Fruitery, Brook Hill, Brook, Newport, Isle of Wight, PO30 6EP. 01983 740015.

ISLE OF WIGHT ORNITHOLOGICAL GROUP. (1986; 135). Mr DJ Hunnybun, 40 Churchill Road, Cowes, Isle of Wight, PO31 8HH. 01983 292880.

RSPB Local Group
ISLE OF WIGHT. (1979; 206). Please contact RSPB for further details.

Wildlife Trust
Director, See Hampshire,

KENT

Bird Atlas/Avifauna
Birding in Kent by D W Taylor et al (Kent Ornithological Society, 1981). Pica Press
Kent Ornithological Society Winter Bird Survey by N Tardivel (KOS, 1984).

Bird Recorder
Don Taylor, 1 Rose Cottages, Old Loose Hill, Loose, Maidstone, Kent, ME15 0BN. 01622 745641; e-mail: don@collared.free-online.co.uk

Bird Reports
DUNGENESS BIRD OBSERVATORY REPORT (1989-), from Warden, see Reserves.

KENT BIRD REPORT (1952-), from Dave Sutton, 61 Alpha Road, Birchington, Kent, CT7 9ED. 01843 842541; e-mail: dave@suttond8.freeserve.co.uk

SANDWICH BAY BIRD OBSERVATORY REPORT, from Warden, see Reserves,

BTO Regional Representative
RR. Martin Coath, 77 Oakhill Road, Sevenoaks, Kent, TN13 1NU. 01732 460710;
e-mail: mcoath@onetel.com

Club
KENT ORNITHOLOGICAL SOCIETY. (1952; 720). Mrs Ann Abrams, 4 Laxton Way, Faversham, Kent ME13 8LJ. www.kentos.org.uk
e-mail: annie@chrisabrams.plus.com
Meetings: 7.45pm monthly on a Friday, St Paul's Church Hall, Boxley Road, Maidstone.

Ringing Groups
DARTFORD RG. R Taylor, 21 Dallin Road, Plumstead, London SE18 3NY.

DUNGENESS BIRD OBSERVATORY. David Walker, Dungeness Bird Observatory, Dungeness, Romney Marsh, Kent, TN29 9NA. 01797 321309;
e-mail: dungeness.obs@tinyonline.co.uk
www.dungenessbirdobs.org.uk

RECULVER RG. Chris Hindle, 42 Glenbervie Drive, Herne Bay, Kent, CT6 6QL. 01227 373070;
e-mail: christopherhindle@hotmail.com

SANDWICH BAY BIRD OBSERVATORY. K Thornton, Sandwich Bay Bird Observatory, Guilford Road, Sandwich, Kent, CT13 9PF. 01304 617341; e-mail: sbbot@talk21.com

SWALE WADER GROUP. Rod Smith, 67 York Avenue, Chatham, Kent, ME5 9ES. 01634 865863; e-mail: rodandmarg@tiscali.co.uk

RSPB Local Groups
CANTERBURY. (1973; 216). Jean Bomber, St Heliers, 30a Castle Road, Tankerton, Whitstable, Kent, CT5 2DY. 01227 277725.
http://cantrspb.members.easyspace.com/
Meetings: 8.00pm, 2nd Wednesday of the month (Sept-Apr), Chaucer Technology School, Spring Lane, Canterbury.

GRAVESEND & DISTRICT. (1977; 260). Malcolm Jennings, 206 Lower Higham Road, Gravesend, Kent DA12 2NN. 01474 322171.
Meetings: 7.45pm, 2nd Wednesday of the month (Sep-May), St Botolph's Hall, North Fleet, Gravesend.

MAIDSTONE. (1973; 250). Dick Marchese, 11 Bathurst Road, Staplehurst, Tonbridge, Kent, TN12 0LG. 01580 892458
www.vidler23.freeserve.co.uk/
Meetings: 7.30pm, 3rd Thursday of the month, Grove Green Community Hall, Penhurst Close, Grove Green, opposite Tesco's.

MEDWAY. (1974; 230). Sue Carter, 31 Ufton Lane, Sittingbourne, ME10 1JB. 01795 427854
www.medway-rspb.pwp.blueyonder.co.uk
Meetings: 7.45pm, 3rd Tuesday of the month (except Aug), Strood Library, Bryant Road, Strood.

SEVENOAKS. (1974; 300). Bernard Morris, New House, Kilkhampton, Bude, Cornwall, EX23 9RZ. 01288 321727; or 07967 564699; (Fax) 01288 321838;
e-mail: bernard@amorris32.freeserve.co.uk
Meetings: 7.45pm, 2nd Thursday of the month, Plaza Suite, Stag Theatre.

SOUTH EAST KENT. (1981; 200). Pauline McKenzie-Lloyd, Hillside, Old Park Avenue, Dover, Kent CT16 2DY. 01304 826529.
Meetings: 7.30pm, 3rd Tuesday of the month (Sep-May), United Reform Church, Folkestone.

THANET. (1976; 170). Paul Hale, 2 Shutler Road, Broadstairs, Kent, CT10 1HD. 01843 601482;
e-mail: paulhale@btopenworld.com
Meetings: 7.30pm, last Tuesday of the month, Holy Trinity Church Hall.

TONBRIDGE. (1975; 120 reg attendees/1700 in catchment). Ms Gabrielle Sutcliffe, 1 Postern Heath Cottages, Postern Lane, Tonbridge, Kent, TN11 0QU. 01732 365583.
Meetings: 7.45pm 3rd Wednesday of the month (Sept-Apr), St Phillips Church, Salisbury Road.

Wetland Bird Survey Organisers
EAST KENT. Ken Lodge, 14 Gallwey Avenue, Birchington, Kent CT7 9PA. 01843 843105;
e-mail: kenlodge@minnisbay15.freeserve.co.uk

MEDWAY ESTUARY & NORTH KENT MARSHES. Alan Johnson, RSPB, Bromhay Farm, Cooling, Rochester, Kent ME3 8DS. 01634 222480.

SWALE ESTUARY. Alan Johnson, RSPB, Bromhay Farm, Cooling, Rochester, Kent ME3 8DS. 01634 222480.

Wildlife Hospital
RAPTOR CENTRE. Eddie Hare, Ivy Cottage, Groombridge Place, Groombridge, Tunbridge Wells, Kent, TN3 9QG. 01892 861175; (fax) 01892 863761. www.raptorcentre.co.uk
Birds of prey. Veterinary support.

Wildlife Trust
KENT WILDLIFE TRUST. (1958; 10,500). Tyland Barn, Sandling, Maidstone, Kent, ME14 3BD. 01622 662012; fax 01622 671390;
e-mail: kentwildlife@cix.co.uk
www.kentwildlifetrust.org.uk

LANCASHIRE

Bird Atlas/Avifauna
An Atlas of Breeding Birds of Lancaster and District by Ken Harrison (Lancaster & District Birdwatching Society, 1995).

Breeding Birds of Lancashire and North Merseyside (2001), sponsored by North West Water. Contact: Bob Pyefinch, 12 Bannistre Court, Tarleton, Preston PR4 6HA.

ENGLAND

Bird Recorder
(See also Manchester).

Inc North Merseyside. Steve White, 102 Minster Court, Crown Street, Liverpool, L7 3QD. 0151 707 2744; e-mail: stephen.white2@tesco.net

Bird Reports
BIRDS OF LANCASTER & DISTRICT (1959-), from Secretary, Lancaster & District BWS, 01524 734462.

EAST LANCASHIRE ORNITHOLOGISTS' CLUB BIRD REPORT (1982-), from Secretary, 01282 617401; e-mail: doug.windle@care4free.net

BLACKBURN & DISTRICT BIRD CLUB ANNUAL REPORT (1992-), from Doreen Bonner, 6 Winston Road, Blackburn, BB1 8BJ. Tel/fax; 01254 261480; www.blackburnbirds.freeuk.com

FYLDE BIRD REPORT (1983-), from Secretary, Fylde Bird Club,

LANCASHIRE BIRD REPORT (1914-), from Secretary, Lancs & Cheshire Fauna Soc,

ROSSENDALE ORNITHOLOGISTS' CLUB BIRD REPORT (1977-) from Secretary, Rossendale Ornithologists Club.

BTO Regional Representatives & Regional Development Officer
EAST RR. Tony Cooper, 28 Peel Park Avenue, Clitheroe, Lancs, BB7 1ET. 01200 424577; e-mail: tonycooper@beeb.net

NORTH & WEST RR. Keith Woods, 2 Oak Drive, Halton, Lancaster, LA2 6QL. 01524 811478; e-mail: woods.keith@btopenworld.com

SOUTH RR. Philip Shearwood, Netherside, Green Lane, Whitestake, Preston, PR4 4AH. 01772 745488; e-mail: phil.shearwood@virgin.net

Clubs
BLACKBURN & DISTRICT BIRD CLUB. (1991; 134). Jim Bonner, 6 Winston Road, Blackburn, BB1 8BJ. Tel/fax; 01254 261480. www.blackburnbirds.freeuk.com
Meetings: Normally 7.30pm, 1st Monday of the month, (Sept-Apr), St Silas' Church Hall, Preston New Road.

CHORLEY & DISTRICT NATURAL HISTORY SOCIETY. (1979; 170). Phil Kirk, Millend, Dawbers Lane, Euxton, Chorley, Lancs, PR7 6EB. 01257 266783; e-mail: philipdkirk@clara.co uk www.philkirk.clara.net/cdnhs/
Meetings: 7.30pm, 3rd Thursday of the month (Sept-Apr), St Mary's Parish Centre, Chorley

EAST LANCASHIRE ORNITHOLOGISTS' CLUB. (1955; 45). Doug Windle, 39 Stone Edge Road, Barrowford, Nelson, Lancs, BB9 6BB. 01282 617401; e-mail: doug.windle@care4free.net
Meetings: 7.30pm, 1st Monday of the month, St Anne's Church Hall, Feuce, Nr Burnley.

FYLDE BIRD CLUB. (1982; 60). Paul Ellis, 18 Staining Rise, Blackpool, FY3 0BU. 01253 891281; e-mail: paul.ellis24@btopenworld.com or kinta.beaver@man.ac.uk www.fyldebirdclub.org
Meetings: 7.45pm, 4th Tuesday of the month, Blackpool Cricket Club, Stanley Park, Blackpool (room above bar).

FYLDE NATURALISTS' SOCIETY. (1946; 140). Gerry Stephen, 10 Birch Way, Poulton-le-Fylde, Blackpool, FY6 7SF. 01253 895195.

LANCASHIRE & CHESHIRE FAUNA SOCIETY. (1914; 140). Dave Bickerton, 64 Petre Crescent, Rishton, Lancs, BB1 4RB. 01254 886257; e-mail: bickertond@aol.com www.lacfs.org.uk

LANCASHIRE BIRD CLUB. (1996). Dave Bickerton, 64 Petre Crescent, Rishton, Lancs, BB1 4RB. 01254 886257; e-mail: bickertond@aol.com www.lacfs.org.uk

LANCASTER & DISTRICT BIRD WATCHING SOCIETY. (1959; 200). Andrew Cadman, 57 Greenways, Over Kellet, Carnforth, Lancs, LA6 1DE. 01524 734462; e-mail: ldbws@yahoo.co.uk http://libweb.lancs.ac.uk/ldbws.htm
Meetings: 7.30pm, last Monday of the month (Sep-Apr, not Dec), Unitarian Church, Scotforth, Lancaster.

ROSSENDALE ORNITHOLOGISTS' CLUB. (1976; 35). Ian Brady, 25 Church St, Newchurch, Rossendale, Lancs, BB4 9EX. 01706 222120.
Meetings: 7.30pm, 3rd Monday of the month, Weavers Cottage, Bacup Road, Rawtenstall.

Ringing Groups
FYLDE RG. G Barnes, 17 Lomond Avenue, Marton, Blackpool, FY3 9QL.

MORECAMBE BAY WADER RG. J Sheldon, 415 West Shore Park, Barrow-in-Furness, Cumbria, LA14 3XZ. 01229 473102.

NORTH LANCS RG. John Wilson BEM, 40 Church Hill Avenue, Warton, Carnforth, Lancs, LA5 9NU.

SOUTH WEST LANCASHIRE RG. J D Fletcher, 4 Hawksworth Drive, Freshfield, Formby, Merseyside, L37 7EZ. 01704 877837.

RSPB Local Groups
BLACKPOOL. (1983; 170). Alan Stamford, 6 Kensington Road, Cleveleys, FY5 1EP. 01253 859662.
Meetings: 7.30pm, 2nd Friday of the month (Sept-June), Frank Townend Centre, Beach Road, Cleveleys.

LANCASTER. (1972; 176). John Wilson BEM, 40 Church Hill Avenue, Warton, Carnforth, Lancs, LA5 9NU.

Wetland Bird Survey Organisers
RIBBLE ESTUARY. Mr Mike Gee, Ribble Estuary National Nature Reserve, Reserve Office, Old Hollow, Marsh Road, Banks PR9 8DU. 01704 225624; e-mail: english-nature@ribble-nnr.freeserve.co.uk

NORTH LANCASHIRE (Inland). Pete Marsh, Leck View Cottage, Ashle's farm, High Tatham, Lancaster, LA2 8PH. 01524 264944; e-mail: pbmarsh@btopenworld.com

Wildlife Trust
THE WILDLIFE TRUST FOR LANCASHIRE, MANCHESTER AND NORTH MERSEYSIDE. (1962; 3,500). The Barn, Berkeley Drive, Bamber Bridge, Preston, PR5 6BY. 01772 324129; fax: 01772 628849; e-mail: lancswt@cix.co.uk www.wildlifetrust.org.uk/lancashire

LEICESTERSHIRE & RUTLAND

Bird Recorder
Rob Fray, 5 New Park Road, Aylestone, Leicester, LE2 8AW. 0116 223 8491; e-mail: robfray@fray-r.freeserve.co.uk

Bird Reports
LEICESTERSHIRE & RUTLAND BIRD REPORT (1941-), from Mrs S Graham, 5 Brading Road, Leicester, LE3 9BG. 0116 262 5505; e-mail: jsgraham83@aol.com

RUTLAND NAT HIST SOC ANNUAL REPORT (1965-), from Secretary, 01572 747302.

BTO Regional Representative
LEICESTER & RUTLAND. Tim Grove, 35 Clumber Street, Melton Mowbray, Leicestershire LE13 0ND. 01664 850766; e-mail: k.grove1@ntlworld.com

Clubs
BIRSTALL BIRDWATCHING CLUB. (1976; 50). Ken J Goodrich, 6 Riversdale Close, Birstall, Leicester, LE4 4EH. 0116 267 4813.
Meetings: 7.30pm, 2nd Tuesday of the month (Oct-Apr), Longslade Community College, Martin Luther Building.

LEICESTERSHIRE & RUTLAND ORNITHOLOGICAL SOCIETY. (1941; 520). Mrs Marion Vincent, 48 Templar Way, Rothley, Leicester, LE7 7RB. 0116 230 3405 www.lros.org.uk
Meetings: 7.30pm, 1st Friday of the month, Leicester Adult Education College, Wellington St, Leicester. Additional meeting at Rutland Water Birdwatching Centre, Nov 26th 2004.

MARKET HARBOROUGH & DISTRICT NATURAL HISTORY SOCIETY. (1971; 40). Mrs Marion Mills, 36 Nelson Street, Market Harborough, Leics LE16 9AY. 01858 462346.
Meetings: 7.30pm, 2nd Monday in the month, Welland Park College

RUTLAND NATURAL HISTORY SOCIETY. (1964; 256). Mrs L Worrall, 6 Redland Close, Barrowden, Oakham, Rutland, LE15 8ES. 01572 747302. www.rnhs.org.uk
Meetings: 7.30pm, 1st Tuesday of the month (Oct-Apr), Oakham C of E School, Burley Road, Oakham.

Ringing Groups
RUTLAND WATER RG. D Roizer, 38 Kestrel Road, Oakham, Rutland, LE15 6BU.

STANFORD RG. M J Townsend, 87 Dunton Road, Broughton Astley, Leics, LE9 6NA.

RSPB Local Groups
LEICESTER. (1969; 1,600 in catchment area). Chris Woolass, 136 Braunstone Lane, Leicester, LE3 2RW. 0116 2990078; e-mail: chris@jclwoolass.freeserve.co.uk
Meetings: 7.30pm, 1st Friday of the month (Sep-May), Adult Education Centre.

LOUGHBOROUGH. (1970; 300). Robert Orton, 12 Avon Road, Barrow-on-Soar, Leics, LE12 8LE. 15094 13936.
Meetings: Monthly Friday nights, Loughborough University.

Wetland Bird Survey Organisers
LEICESTERSHIRE & RUTLAND (excl Rutland Water). Mr Andrew Harrop, 30 Dean Street, Oakham, LE15 6AF. (H) 01572 757134; e-mail: andrew.harrop@virgin.net

RUTLAND WATER. Tim Appleton, Fishponds Cottage, Stamford Road, Oakham, LE15 8AB. (Day) 01572 770651; e-mail: awbc@rutlandwater.org.uk

Wildlife Trust
LEICESTERSHIRE & RUTLAND WILDLIFE TRUST. (1956; 3,000). Brocks Hill Environment Centre, Washbrook Lane, Oadby, Leicestershire LE2 5JJ. 0116 272 0444; fax 0116 272 0404; e-mail: info@lrwt.org.uk www.lrwt.org.uk

LINCOLNSHIRE

Bird Recorders
NORTH. Covered temporarily by South Lincs Recorder.

SOUTH. Steve Keightley, Redclyffe, Swineshead

Road, Frampton Fen, Boston PE20 1SG. 01205 290333; e-mail: s.keightley@tesco.net

Bird Reports
LINCOLNSHIRE BIRD REPORT inc Gibraltar Point Bird Obs (1979-), from R K Watson, 8 High Street, Skegness, Lincs, PE25 3NW. 01754 763481.

SCUNTHORPE & NORTH WEST LINCOLNSHIRE BIRD REPORT (1973-), from Secretary, Scunthorpe Museum Society, Ornithological Section.

BTO Regional Representatives & Regional Development Officer
EAST RR. Position vacant.

NORTH RR. John Turner, 01652 650119; e-mail: johnturner17@onetel.com

SOUTH RR. Richard & Kay Heath, 56 Pennytoft Lane, Pinchbeck, Spalding, Lincs, PE11 3PQ. 01775 767055; e-mail: heathsrk@ukonline.co.uk

WEST RR. Peter Overton, Hilltop Farm, Welbourn, Lincoln, LN5 0QH. Work 01400 273323; e-mail: nyika@biosearch.org.uk

RDO. Nicholas Watts, Vine House Farm, Deeping St Nicholas, Spalding, Lincs, PE11 3DG. 01775 630208.

Club
LINCOLNSHIRE BIRD CLUB. (1979; 220). Janet Eastmead, 3 Oxeney Drive, Langworth, Lincoln LN3 5DD. 01522 754522; e-mail: jee@freeuk.com
Meetings: Local groups hold winter evening meetings (contact Secretary for details).

SCUNTHORPE MUSEUM SOCIETY (Ornithological Section). (1973; 50). Keith Parker, 7 Ryedale Avenue, Winterton, Scunthorpe, Lincs DN15 9BJ.
Meetings: 7.15pm, 3rd Monday of the month (Sep-Apr), Scunthorpe Museum, Oswald Road.

Ringing Groups
GIBRALTAR POINT BIRD OBSERVATORY. Mark Grantham, 12 Sybill Wheeler Close, Thetford, Norfolk, IP24 1TG. 01842 750050; (M) 07818 497470.

MID LINCOLNSHIRE RG. J Mawer, 2 The Chestnuts, Cwmby Road, Searby, Lincolnshire DN38 6EH. 01652 628583.

WASH WADER RG. P L Ireland, 27 Hainfield Drive, Solihull, W Midlands, B91 2PL. 0121 704 1168; e-mail: enquiries@wwrg.org.uk

RSPB Local Groups
GRIMSBY AND CLEETHORPES. (1986; 2200). Andy Downes, Meadowcroft, 17 Bulwick Avenue, Scartho, Grimsby, DN33 3BH. 01472 319257; e-mail: andrewandlynndownes@ntlworld.com
Meetings: 7.30pm, 1st Monday of the month (Sept-May), Cromwell Banqueting Suite, Cromwell Road, Cleethorpes.

LINCOLN. (1974; 250). Peter Skelson, 26 Parksgate Avenue, Lincoln, LN6 7HP. 01522 695747; e-mail: peterskelson@lincolnrspb.org.uk www.lincolnrspb.org.uk
Meetings: 7.30pm, 2nd Tuesday of the month (not Jun, Jul, Aug, Dec), The Lawn, Union Road, Lincoln.

SOUTH LINCOLNSHIRE. (1987; 350). Barry Hancock, The Limes, Meer Booth Road, Antons Gowt, Boston, Lincs, PE22 7BG. 01205 280057; e-mail: info@southlincsrspb.org.uk www.southlincsrspb.org.uk

Wetland Bird Survey Organisers
HUMBER ESTUARY - MID SOUTH. Ian Shepherd, 38 Lindsey Road, Cleethorpes, Lincolnshire DN35 8TN. (H) 01472 697142.

WASH – LINCOLNSHIRE. Lewis James, RSPB Snettisham, 13 Beach Road, Snettisham, King's Lynn, Norfolk PE31 7RA. 01485 542689.

Wildlife Hospital
FEATHERED FRIENDS WILD BIRD RESCUE. Colin Riches, 5 Blacksmith Lane, Thorpe-on-the-Hill, Lincoln, LN6 9BQ. 01522 684874.
All species. Purpose-built hospital unit. Heated cages, etc. Membership and adoption scheme available. Quarterly newsletter. Veterinary support.

Wildlife Trust
LINCOLNSHIRE WILDLIFE TRUST. (1948; 10,800). Banovallum House, Manor House Street, Horncastle, Lincs, LN9 5HF. 01507 526667; fax 01507 525732; e-mail: lincstrust@cix.co.uk www.lincstrust.co.uk

LONDON, GREATER

Bird Atlas/Avifauna
The Breeding Birds Illustrated magazine of the London Area, 2002. ISBN 0901009 121 ed Jan Hewlett (London Natural History Society).

Bird Recorder see also Surrey
Andrew Self, 16 Harp Island Close, Neasden, London, NW10 0DF.
e-mail: andrewself@lineone.net
www.lnhs.org.uk

Bird Report
CROYDON BIRD SURVEY (1995), from Secretary, Croydon RSPB Group, 020 8777 9370.

LONDON BIRD REPORT (20-mile radius of St Paul's Cath) (1936-), from Catherine Schmitt, 4 Falkland Avenue, London, N3 1QR.

BTO Regional Representative & Regional Development Officer
LONDON & MIDDLESEX RR. Derek Coleman, 23c Park Hill, Carshalton, Surrey, SM5 3SA. 020 8669 7421.

Clubs

LONDON NATURAL HISTORY SOCIETY (Ornithology Section). (1858; 1,000). Ms N Duckworth, 9 Abbey Court, Cerne Abbas, Dorchester, Dorset, DT2 7JH. 01300 341 195.
www.lnhs.org.uk
Meetings: Regular and varied, see programme on website.

MARYLEBONE BIRDWATCHING SOCIETY. (1981; 88). Judy Powell, 7 Rochester Terrace, London, NW1 9JN. 020 7485 0863;
e-mail: birdsmbs@yahoo.com
www.geocities.com/birdsmbs

Ringing Groups
LONDON GULL STUDY GROUP - (SE including Hampshire, Surrey, Susex, Berkshire and Oxfordshire). (Also includes Hampshire, Surrey, Sussex, Berkshire and Oxfordshire). No longer in operation but able to give information on gulls in the SE area. Mark Fletcher, 24 The Gowans, Sutton-on-the-Forest, York, YO61 1DJ.
e-mail: m.fletcher@csl.gov.uk

RUNNYMEDE RG. D G Harris, 22 Blossom Waye, Hounslow, TW5 9HD.
e-mail: daveharris@tinyonline.co.uk

RSPB Local Groups
BEXLEY. (1979; 180). David James, 78 Colney Road, Dartford, DA1 1UH. 01322 274791;
e-mail: dartdiva56@hotmail.com
Meetings: 7.30pm, 3rd Friday of the month, Hurstmere School Hall, Hurst Road, Sidcup.

BROMLEY. (1972; 285). Bob Francis, 2 Perry Rise, Forest Hill, London, SE23 2QL. 020 8669 9325
www.bromleyrspb.org.uk
Meetings: 2nd Wednesday of the month (Sep-Jun), Large Hall, Bromley Central Library Building, Bromley High Street.

CENTRAL LONDON. (1974; 350). Miss Annette Warrick, 12 Tredegar Sq, London, E3 5AD. 020 8981 9624;
e-mail: annette@warricka.freeserve.co.uk
www.janja@dircon.co.uk/rspb
Meetings: 2nd Thursday of the month (Sep-May), St Columba's church Hall, Pont St, London SW1.

CROYDON. (1973; 4,000 in catchment area). Sheila Mason, 5 Freshfields, Shirley, Croydon, CR0 7QS. 020 8777 9370
www.croydon-rspb.org.uk

ENFIELD. (1971; 2,700). Norman G Hudson, 125 Morley Hill, Enfield, Middx, EN2 0BQ. 020 8363 1431.

HAVERING. (1972; 270). David Coe, 8 The Fairway, Upminster, Essex, RM14 1BS. 01708 220710.
Meetings: 8.00pm, 2nd Friday of the month, Hornchurch Library, North Street, Hornchurch.

NORTH LONDON. (1974; 3,000). John Parsons, 65 Rutland Gardens, Harringay, London, N4 1JW. 020 8802 9537.

NORTH WEST LONDON RSPB GROUP. (1983; 2,000 in catchment area). Bob Husband, The Firs, 49 Carson Road, Cockfosters, Barnet, Herts, EN4 9EN. 020 8441 8742.
Meetings: 8.00pm, last Tuesday of the month (Sept-Apr), Union Church Hall, Eversfield Gardens, Mill Hill, NW7 (new for 2005).

PINNER & DISTRICT. (1972; 300). Dennis Bristow, 118 Crofts Road, Harrow, Middx, HA1 2PJ. 020 8863 5026.
Meetings: 8pm, 2nd Thursday of the month, Church Hall, St John The Baptist parish church, Pinner.

RICHMOND & TWICKENHAM. (1979; 375). Steve Harrington, 93 Shaftesbury Way, Twickenham, TW2 5RW. 020 8898 4539.
Meetings: 8.00pm, 1st Wednesday of the month, York House, Twickenham.

WEST LONDON. (1973; 400). Alan Bender, 020 8841 1952.

Wildlife Hospitals
WILDLIFE RESCUE & AMBULANCE SERVICE. Barry and June Smitherman, 19 Chesterfield Road, Enfield, Middx, EN3 6BE. 020 8292 5377.
All categories of wild birds. Emergency ambulance with full rescue equipment, boats, ladders etc. Own treatment centre and aviaries. Veterinary support. Essential to telephone first.

Wildlife Trust
LONDON WILDLIFE TRUST. (1981; 7,500). Harling House, 47-51 Great Suffolk Street, London, SE1 0BS. 0207 261 0447; fax 0207 261 0538;
e-mail: enquiries@wildlondon.org.uk
www.wildlifetrust.org.uk/london

MANCHESTER, GREATER

Bird Atlas/Avifauna
Breeding Birds in Greater Manchester by Philip Holland et al (1984).

Bird Recorder
RECORDER AND REPORT EDITOR. Mrs A Judith Smith, 12 Edge Green Street, Ashton-in-Makerfield, Wigan, WN4 8SL. 01942 712615; e-mail: judith@gmbirds.freeserve.co.uk www.gmbirds.freeserve.co.uk

ASSISTANT RECORDER. Ian McKerchar, 42 Green Ave, Astley, Manchester, M29 7EH. 01942 701758; e-mail: ian@mckerchar1.freeserve.co.uk

ASSISTANT RECORDER. Antony Wainwright, 17 Hobart St, Halliwell, Bolton BL1 3PY. 01204 456415; e-mail: AtnWain@aol.com

Bird Reports
BIRDS IN GREATER MANCHESTER (1976-), from Mrs M McCormick, 91 Sinderland Road, Altrincham WA14 5JJ (only editions up to year 2000. Year 2001 onwards from County Recorder).

LEIGH ORNITHOLOGICAL SOCIETY BIRD REPORT (1971-), from J Critchley, 2 Albany Grove, Tyldesley, Manchester, M29 7NE. 01942 884644.

BTO Regional Representative & Regional Development Officer
RR. Steve Sutthill, 01457 836 360; e-mail: steve@marctheprinters.org

RDO. Jim Jeffery, 20 Church Lane, Romiley, Stockport, Cheshire, SK6 4AA. H:0161 494 5367; W:01625 522107 ext 112; e-mail: jim_jeffrey1943@yahoo.co.uk

Clubs
GREATER MANCHESTER BIRD CLUB. (1954; 70). Dr R Sandling, Maths Dept, The University, Manchester M13 9PL. e-mail: rsandling@man.ac.uk

GREATER MANCHESTER BIRD RECORDING GROUP. (2002: 40) Restricted to contributors of the county bird report. Mrs A Judith Smith, 01942 712615; e-mail: judith@gmbirds.freeserve.co.uk www.gmbirds.freeserve.co.uk

HALE ORNITHOLOGISTS. (1968; 67). Ms Diana Grellier, 8 Apsley Grove, Bowdon, Altrincham, Cheshire, WA14 3AH. 0161 928 9165.
Meetings: 7.45pm, 2nd Wednesday of the month (Sept-July), St Peters Assembly Rooms, Hale.

LEIGH ORNITHOLOGICAL SOCIETY. (1971; 150). Mr D Shallcross, 10 Holden Brook Close, Leigh, Lancs, WN7 2HL. 01942 260161; e-mail: chairman@leighos.org.uk www.leighos.org.uk
Meetings: 7.15pm, Fridays, Leigh Library (check website for details).

ROCHDALE FIELD NATURALISTS' SOCIETY. (1970; 90). Mrs J P Wood, 196 Castleton Road, Thornham, Royton, Oldham, OL2 6UP. 0161 345 2012; www.rochdaleonline.org (listed under societies and events)

STOCKPORT BIRDWATCHING SOCIETY. (1972; 80). Dave Evans, 36 Tatton Road South, Stockport, Cheshire, SK4 4LU. 0161 432 9513; e-mail: dave.36tatton@ntlworld.com
Meetings: 7.30pm, last Wednesday of the month, Tiviot Dale Church.

Ringing Groups
LEIGH RG. A J Gramauskas, 21 Elliot Avenue, Golborne, Warrington, WA3 3DU. 0151 929215.

SOUTH MANCHESTER RG. C M Richards, Fairhaven, 13 The Green, Handforth, Wilmslow, Cheshire, SK9 3AG. 01625 524527; e-mail: cliveandray.richards@care4free.net

RSPB Local Groups
BOLTON. (1978; 320). Mrs Alma Schofield, 29 Redcar Road, Little Lever, Bolton, BL3 1EW. 01204 791745.
Meetings: 7.30pm, Thursdays (dates vary), Main Hall, Smithills School, Smithills Dean Road, Bolton.

MANCHESTER. (1972; 3,600 in catchment area). Peter Wolstenholme, 31 South Park Road, Gatley, Cheshire, SK8 4AL. 0161 428 2175.

STOCKPORT. (1979; 250). Brian Hallworth, 69 Talbot Street, Hazel Grove, Stockport, SK7 4BJ. 0161 456 5328; e-mail: brian.hallworth@ntlworld.com
Meetings: 7.30pm, 2nd Monday of the month (Sep-Apr), Stockport College of Technology, Lecture Theatre B.

WIGAN. (1973; 80). Mr A Rimmer, 01942 241402.

Wildlife Hospital
THREE OWLS BIRD SANCTUARY AND RESERVE. Trustee, Nigel Fowler/Sam Harper, Wolstenholme Fold, Norden, Rochdale, OL11 5UD. 01706 642162; 24-hr helpline 07973 819389; e-mail: info@threeowls.co.uk www.threeowls.co.uk
Registered charity. All species of wild bird. Rehabilitation and release on Sanctuary Reserve. Open every Sunday 1200-1700, otherwise visitors welcome by appointment. Bi-monthly newsletter. Veterinary support.

Wildlife Trust
Director, See Lancashire,

MERSEYSIDE & WIRRAL

Bird Atlas see Cheshire

Bird Recorders see Cheshire; Lancashire

Bird Reports see also Cheshire
HILBRE BIRD OBSERVATORY REPORT, from Warden, see Reserves,

NORTHWESTERN BIRD REPORT (1938-irregular), from Secretaries, Merseyside Naturalists' Assoc,

BTO Regional Representatives
MERSEYSIDE RR and RDO. Bob Harris, 2 Dulas Road, Wavertree Green, Liverpool, L15 6UA. Work 0151 706 4311; e-mail: harris@liv.ac.uk

WIRRAL RR. Paul Miller, 01928 787535; e-mail: huntershill@worldline.co.uk

Clubs
MERSEYSIDE NATURALISTS' ASSOCIATION. (1938; 260). Steven Cross, 0151 920 5718.

WIRRAL BIRD CLUB. (1977; 150). Mrs Hilda Truesdale, Cader, 8 Park Road, Meols, Wirral, CH47 7BG. 0151 632 2705; www.wirralbirdclub.com

Ringing Groups
MERSEYSIDE RG. P Slater, 45 Greenway Road, Speke, Liverpool, L24 7RY.

SOUTH WEST LANCASHIRE RG. J D Fletcher, 4 Hawksworth Drive, Freshfield, Formby, Merseyside, L37 7EZ. 01704 877837.

RSPB Local Groups
LIVERPOOL. (1966; 162). Chris Tynan, 10 Barker Close, Huyton, Liverpool, L36 0XU. 0151 480 7938; e-mail: christtynan@aol.com
www.livbird.pwp.blueyonder.co.uk
Meetings: 7 for 7.30pm, 3rd Monday of the month (Sep-Apr), Mossley Hill Parish Church, Junc. Rose Lane and Elmswood Rd.

SEFTON COAST. (1980; 150). Peter Taylor, 26 Tilston Road, Walton, Liverpool, L9 6AJ. 0151 524 1905; e-mail: ptaylor@liv.ac.uk
www.scmg.freeserve.co.uk
Meetings: 7.30pm, 2nd Tuesday of the month, St Lukes Church Hall, Liverpool Road, Crosby.

SOUTHPORT. (1974; 250). Group Leader, 01704 872421.

WIRRAL. (1982; 120). Martyn Jamieson, 9 Banks Road, Heswall, Wirral, Merseyside CH60 9JS. 0151 342 7813;
email: martynjamieson@merseymail.com
Meetings: 7.30pm, 1st Thursday of the month (Sep-Jun), Bromborough Civic Hall.

Wetland Bird Survey Organiser
DEE ESTUARY. Colin Wells, Burton Farm Point, Station Road, Nr Neston, South Wirral CH64 5SB.

Wildlife Trust
Director, See Lancashire,

NORFOLK

Bird Atlas/Avifauna
The Birds of Norfolk by Moss Taylor, Michael Seago, Peter Allard & Don Dorling (Pica Press, 1999).

Bird Recorder
Giles Dunmore, 49 Nelson Road, Sheringham, Norfolk, NR26 8DA. 01263 822550;
e-mail:jdunmore@ukgateway.net

Bird Reports
CLEY BIRD CLUB 10-KM SQUARE BIRD REPORT (1987-), from Secretary.

NAR VALLEY ORNITHOLOGICAL SOCIETY ANNUAL REPORT (1976-), from Secretary.

NORFOLK BIRD & MAMMAL REPORT (1953-), from Secretary, Norfolk and Norwich Naturalists Society, Castle Museum, Norwich, NR1 3JU.

NORFOLK ORNITHOLOGISTS' ASSOCN ANNUAL REPORT (1961-), from Secretary.

BTO Regional Representatives
NORTH-EAST RR. Chris Hudson, Cornerstones, Ringland Road, Taverham, Norwich, NR8 6TG. 01603 868805; e-mail: chris.hudson@osb.uk.net

NORTH-WEST RR. Position vacant

SOUTH-EAST RR. Chris Day, 01493 664115; e-mail: chris.day@rspb.org.uk

SOUTH-WEST RR. Vince Matthews, Rose's Cottage, The Green, Merton, Thetford, Norfolk, IP25 6QU. 01953 884125;
e-mail: vamatthews@tiscali.co.uk

Clubs
CLEY BIRD CLUB. (1986; 400). Peter Gooden, 45 Charles Road, Holt, Norfolk, NR25 6DA. 01263 712368.
Meetings: 8.00pm, Wednesdays, monthly (Dec-Feb), George Hotel, Cley.

GREAT YARMOUTH BIRD (1989; 60). Keith R Dye, 104 Wolseley Road, Great Yarmouth, Norfolk, NR31 0EJ. 01493 600705.
Meetings: 7.45pm, 4th Monday of the month, Rumbold Arms, Southtown Road.

NAR VALLEY ORNITHOLOGICAL SOCIETY. (1976; 125). Ian Black, Three Chimneys, Tumbler Hill, Swaffham, Norfolk, PE37 7JG. 01760 724092; e-mail: ian_a_black@hotmail.com

NORFOLK & NORWICH NATURALISTS' SOCIETY. (1869; 490). The Secretary, Norfolk and Norwich Naturalist's Society, c/o The Castle Museum, Norwich, Norfolk NR1 3JU. 01263 712282; e-mail: leecha@dialstart.net

NORFOLK BIRD CLUB. (1992; 350). Vernon Eve, Pebble House, The Street, Syderstone, King's Lynn, Norfolk, PE31 8SD. 01485 578121.

NORFOLK ORNITHOLOGISTS' ASSOCIATION. (1962; 1,100). Jed Andrews, Broadwater Road, Holme-next-Sea, Hunstanton, Norfolk, PE36 6LQ. 01485 525406.

WENSUM VALLEY BIRDWATCHING SOCIETY. (2003; 93). David Pelling, Farthings, 2 Pound Lane, North Tuddenham, Dereham, Norfolk NR20 3DA. 01362 692424;
e-mail: alwyn.jackson@tesco.net

Ringing Groups

BTO NUNNERY RG. Dawn Balmer, c/o BTO, The Nunnery, Thetford, Norfolk IP24 2PU.
e-mail: dawn.balmer@bto.org
www.nunnery-ringing.org.uk

HOLME BIRD OBSERVATORY. J M Reed, 21 Hardings, Panshanger, Welwyn Garden City, Herts, AL7 2EQ. 01707 336351.

NORTH WEST NORFOLK RG. J M Reed, 21 Hardings, Panshanger, Welwyn Garden City, Herts, AL7 2EQ. 01707 336351.

SHERINGHAM RG. D Sadler, Denver House, 25 Holt Road, Sheringham, Norfolk, NR26 8NB. 01263 821904; e-mail: dhsadler@onetel.net.uk

UEA RG. D Thomas, 15 Grant Street, Norwich, NR2 4HA.

WASH WADER RG. P L Ireland, 27 Hainfield Drive, Solihull, W Midlands, B91 2PL. 0121 704 1168; e-mail: enquiries@wwrg.org.uk

WISSEY RG. Dr S J Browne, End Cottage, 24 Westgate Street, Hilborough, Norfolk, IP26 5BN. e-mail: sjbathome@aol.com

RSPB Local Groups

NORWICH. (1972; 360). Charles Seagrave, 2 Riverside Cottages, Barford, Norwich, NR9 4BE. 01603 759752;
e-mail: seagrave@connectfree.co.uk
www.NorwichRSPB.org.uk
Meetings: 7.30pm, 2nd Monday of the month (except Aug), Hellesdon Community Centre, Middletons Lane, Hellesdon, Norwich (entrance of Woodview Road).

WEST NORFOLK. (1977; 247). Mr R Gordon, 3 Rectory Close, King's Lynn, Norfolk, PE32 1AS. 01485 600937;
e-mail: robanngordon@btopenworld.com
Meetings: 7.30pm, 3rd Wednesday of the month (Sep-Apr), South Wootton Village Hall, Church Lane, South Wootton, King's Lynn.

Wetland Bird Survey Organisers

BREYDON WATER. Peter Allard, 39 Mallard Way, Bradwell, Great Yarmouth, Norfolk NR3 8JY. 01493 657798.

NORTH NORFOLK COAST. Michael Rooney, English Nature, Hill Farm Offices, Main Road, Wells-next-the–Sea, Norfolk NR23 1AB. 01328 711866.

INLAND. Tim Strudwick, RSPB Strumpshaw Fen, Staithe Cottage, Low Road, Strumpshaw, Norfolk NR13 4HS. 01603 715191.

Wildlife Trust

NORFOLK WILDLIFE TRUST. (1926; 17,500). Bewick House, 22 Thorpe Road, Norwich, Norfolk NR1 1RY. 01603 625540; fax 01603 598300;
e-mail: admin@norfolkwildlifetrust.org.uk
www.wildlifetrust.org.uk/norfolk/

NORTHAMPTONSHIRE

Bird Recorder

Paul Gosling, 23 Newtown Road, Little Irchester, Northants, NN8 2DX. 01933 227709;
e-mail: paul_gosling@lineone.net

Bird Report

NORTHAMPTONSHIRE BIRD REPORT (1969-), from Alan Coles, 99 Rickyard Road, The Abours, Northants NN3 3RR.

BTO Regional Representative & Regional Development Officer

RR. Bill Metcalfe, Blendon, Rockingham Hills, Oundle, Peterborough, PE8 4QA. 01832 274797.

RDO. Bill Metcalfe, Blendon, Rockingham Hills, Oundle, Peterborough, PE8 4QA. 01832 274797.

Clubs

DAVENTRY NATURAL HISTORY SOCIETY. (1970; 18). Leslie G Tooby, The Elms, Leamington Road, Long Itchington, Southam, Warks, CV47 9PL. 0192 681 2269.
Meetings: 7.30pm, last Wednesday of the month, United Reformed Church Rooms, Foundry Place, Daventry.

NORTHAMPTONSHIRE BIRD CLUB. (1973; 100). Mrs Eleanor McMahon, Oriole House, 5 The Croft, Hanging Houghton, Northants, NN6 9HW. 01604 880009.
Meetings: 7.30pm, 1st Thursday of the month. Village Hall, Pound Lane, Moulton, Northants.

Ringing Group

NORTHANTS RG. D M Francis, 2 Brittons Drive, Billing Lane, Northampton, NN3 5DP.

RSPB Local Groups
MID NENE. (1975; 350). Michael Ridout, Melrose, 140 Northampton Road, Rushden, Northants, NN10 6AN. 01933 355544.
Meetings: 7.30pm, 2nd or 3rd Thursday of the month (Sep-Apr), The Saxon Hall, Thorpe Street/ Brook Street, Raunds.

NORTHAMPTON. (1978; 3,000). Liz Wicks, 6 Waypost Court, Lings, Northampton, NN3 8LN. 01604 513991; e-mail: lizydrip@ntlworld.com
Meetings: 7.30pm, 2nd Thursday of the month, Kingsthorpe Methodist Church Hall, Kingsthorpe, Northampton.

Wetland Bird Survey Organiser
Robert Ratcliffe, 173 Montague Road, Bilton, Rugby, Warks CV22 6LG. 01788 336983.

Wildlife Trust
Director, See Cambridgeshire,

NORTHUMBERLAND

Bird Atlas/Avifauna
The Atlas of Breeding Birds in Northumbria edited by J C Day et al (Northumberland and Tyneside Bird Club, 1995).

Bird Recorder
Ian Fisher, 74 Benton Park Road, Newcastle upon Tyne, NE7 7NB. 0191 266 7900;
e-mail: ian@hauxley.freeserve.co.uk
www.ntbc.org.uk

Bird Reports
BIRDS IN NORTHUMBRIA (1970-), from Muriel Cadwallender, 22 South View, Lesbury, NE66 3PZ. 01665 830884;
e-mail: tomandmurielcadwallender@hotmail.com

BIRDS ON THE FARNE ISLANDS (1971-), from Secretary, Natural History Society of Northumbria, 0191 2326386; e-mail: NHSN@ncl.ac.uk

BTO Regional Representative & Regional Development Officer
RR. Tom Cadwallender, 22 South View, Lesbury, Alnwick, Northumberland, NE66 3PZ. H:01665 830884; W:01670 533039;
e-mail: tomandmurielcadwallender@hotmail.com

RDO. Muriel Cadwallender, 22 South View, Lesbury, Alnwick, Northumberland, NE66 3PZ. 01665 830884;
e-mail: tomandmurielcadwallender@hotmail.com

Clubs
NATURAL HISTORY SOCIETY OF NORTHUMBRIA. (1829; 850). David C Noble-Rollin, Hancock Museum, Barras Bridge, Newcastle upon Tyne, NE2 4PT. 0191 232 6386;
e-mail: nhsn@ncl.ac.uk
www.NHSN.ncl.ac.uk
Meetings: 7.00pm, every Friday in the winter, The Hancock Museum.

NORTH NORTHUMBERLAND BIRD CLUB. (1984; 210). Brian Slater, 54 The Dunterns, Alnwick, Northumberland, NE66 1AW. 01665 602126.
Meetings: 7.30pm, 2nd Firday of the month (Sep-Jun), Bamburgh Pavillion (below castle).

NORTHUMBERLAND & TYNESIDE BIRD CLUB. (1958; 270). Sarah Barratt, 18 Frances Ville, Scotland Gate, Northumberland, NE62 5ST. 01670 827465: e-mail: sarah.barratt@btopenworld.com

Ringing Groups
BAMBURGH RS. Mike S Hodgson, 31 Uplands, Monkseaton, Whitley Bay, Tyne & Wear, NE25 9AG. 0191 252 0511.

NATURAL HISTORY SOCIETY OF NORTHUMBRIA. Dr C P F Redfern, Westfield House, Acomb, Hexham, Northumberland, NE46 4RJ.

NORTHUMBRIA RG. Secretary. B Galloway, 34 West Meadows, Stamfordham Road, Westerhope, Newcastle upon Tyne, NE5 1LS. 0191 286 4850.

Wetland Bird Survey Organisers
NORTHUMBERLAND COAST. Roger Norman, 1 Prestwick Gardens, Kenton, Newcastle-upon-Tyne, NE3 3DN. 01912 858314;
e-mail: r.norman@clara.net

NORTHUMBERLAND (Inland). Steve Holliday, 2 Larriston Place, Cramlington, Northumberland NE23 8ER. 01670 731063;
e-mail: steve@sjjholliday.freeserve.co.uk

Wildlife Hospitals
BERWICK SWAN & WILDLIFE TRUST. The Honourable Secretary, North Road Industrial Estate, Berwick upon Tweed, TD15 1UN. 01289 302882; e-mail: mail@swan-trust.org.uk
www.swan-trust.org.uk
Registered charity. All categories of birds. Pools for swans and other waterfowl. Veterinary support.

BERWICK SWAN
and Wildlife Trust

Wildlife Trust
NORTHUMBERLAND WILDLIFE TRUST. (1962; 5,000). The Garden House, St Nicholas Park, Jubilee Road, Newcastle upon Tyne, NE3 3XT. 0191 284 6884; fax 0191 284 6794;
e-mail: northwildlife@cix.co.uk
www.wildlifetrust.org.uk/northumberland

NOTTINGHAMSHIRE

Bird Recorders
Andy Hall, 10 Staverton Road, Bilborough, Nottingham NG8 4ET. 0115 916 9763; e-mail: andy.h11@ntlworld.com

Bird Reports
LOUND BIRD REPORT (1990-), from Mr G Hobson, 11 Sherwood Road, Harworth, Doncaster, DN11 8HY. 01302 743654

BIRDS OF NOTTINGHAMSHIRE (1943-), from Mr Davis, 3 Windrush Close, Bramcote View, Nottingham, NG9 3LN. 0115 922 8547; e-mail: prlg@talk21.com

BTO Regional Representative & Regional Development Officer
RR. Mrs Lynda Milner, 6 Kirton Park, Kirton, Newark, Notts, NG22 9LR. 01623 862025; e-mail: lyndamilner@hotmail.com

Clubs
COLWICK PARK WILDLIFE GROUP. (1994; 150). Michael Walker, 14 Ramblers Close, Colwick, Nottingham, NG4 2DN. 0115 961 5494; www.colwick2000.freeserve.co.uk

LOUND BIRD CLUB. (1991; 50). Gary Hobson, 11 Sherwood Road, Harworth, Doncaster, South Yorkshire DN11 8HY. 01302 743654; (m) 0771 2244469; e-mail: loundbirdclub:tiscali.co.uk

NETHERFIELD WILDLIFE GROUP. (1999; 130). Philip Burnham, 57 Tilford Road, Newstead Village, Nottingham, NG15 0BU. 01623 401980.

NOTTINGHAMSHIRE BIRDWATCHERS. (1935; 420). Ms Jenny Swindels, 21 Chaworth Road, West Bridgeford, Nottingham NG2 7AE. 0115 9812432; e-mail: j.swindells@btinternet.com www.nottmbirds.org.uk

WOLLATON NATURAL HISTORY SOCIETY. (1976; 99). Mrs P Price, 33 Coatsby Road, Hollycroft, Kimberley, Nottingham, NG16 2TH. 0115 938 4965.
Meetings: 7.30pm, 3rd Monday of the month, St mary's Church Hall, Wollaton.

Ringing Groups
BIRKLANDS RG. A D Lowe, 12 Midhurst Way, Clifton Estate, Nottingham, NG11 8DY. e-mail: alowe@mansfield.gov.uk

NORTH NOTTS RG. Adrian Blackburn, Suleska, 1 Richmond Road, Retford, Notts, DN22 6SJ. 01777 706516; (M) 07718 766873: e-mail: blackburns@suleska.freeserve.co.uk

SOUTH NOTTINGHAMSHIRE RG. K J Hemsley, 8 Grange Farm Close, Toton, Beeston, Notts, NG9 6EB. e-mail: k.hemsley@ntlworld.com

TRESWELL WOOD INTEGRATED POPULATION MONITORING GROUP. Chris du Feu, 66 High Street, Beckingham, Notts, DN10 4PF. e-mail: chris@beckingham0.demon.co.uk

RSPB Local Groups
MANSFIELD AND DISTRICT. (1986; 200). John Barlow, 240 Southwell Road West, Mansfield, Notts NG18 4LB. 01623 626647.
Meetings: 7.30pm, 1st Thursday of the month, Kay Hall, Ladybrook Lane.

NOTTINGHAM. (1974; 514). Andrew Griffin, Hawthorn Cottage, Thoroton, Notts, NG13 9DS. 01949 851426; e-mail: andrew@thoroton.f.sworld.co.uk www.notts-rspb.org.uk
Meetings: 7.30pm, 1st Wednesday of the month, Nottingham Mechanics, North Sherwood Street, Nottingham.

Wetland Bird Survey Organiser
Gary Hobson, 11 Sherwood Road, Harworth, Doncaster, DN11 8HY. 01302 743654.

Wildlife Trust
NOTTINGHAMSHIRE WILDLIFE TRUST. (1963; 4,300). The Old Ragged School, Brook Street, Nottingham, NG1 1EA. 0115 958 8242; fax 0115 924 3175; e-mail: nottswt@cix.co.uk www.wildlifetrust.org.uk/nottinghamshire

OXFORDSHIRE

Bird Atlas/Avifauna
Birds of Oxfordshire by J W Brucker et al (Oxford, Pisces, 1992).
The New Birds of the Banbury Area by T G Easterbrook (Banbury Ornithological Society, 1995).

Bird Recorder
Ian Lewington, 119 Brasenose Road, Didcot, Oxon, OX11 7BP. 01235 819792; e-mail: ian@recorder.fsnet.co.uk

Bird Reports
BIRDS OF OXFORDSHIRE (1921-), from Roy Overall, 30 Hunsdon Road, Iffley, Oxford, OX4 4JE. 01865 775632.

BANBURY ORNITHOLOGICAL SOCIETY ANNUAL REPORT (1952-), from A Turner, 33 Newcombe Close, Milcombe, Nr Banbury, Oxon, OX15 4RN. 01295 720938.

BTO Regional Representatives & Regional Development Officer
NORTH. Frances Marks, 15 Insall Road, Chipping Norton, Oxon, OX7 5LF. 01608 644425.

SOUTH RR. Mr John Melling, 17 Lime Grove, Southmoor, Nr Abingdon, Oxon OX13 5DN; e-mail: bto-rep@oos.org.uk

Clubs
BANBURY ORNITHOLOGICAL SOCIETY. (1952; 100). 6 Cranleigh Close, Banbury, Oxon, OX16 9NJ. 01608 644425. www.banburyornithologicalsociety.org.uk

OXFORD ORNITHOLOGICAL SOCIETY. (1921; 320). David Hawkins, The Long House, Park Lane, Long Hanborough, Oxon, OX29 8RD. 01993 880027; e-mail: dhawkins@dircon.co.uk www.oos.org.uk
Meetings: Various dates, Stratford Brake, Kidlington.

Ringing Group
EDWARD GREY INSTITUTE. Dr A G Gosler, c/o Edward Grey Institute, Department of Zoology, South Parks Road, Oxford, OX1 3PS. 01865 271158.

RSPB Local Groups
OXFORD. (1977; 100). Ian Kilshaw, 6 Queens Court, Bicester, Oxon, OX26 6JX. Tel 01869 601901; (fax) 01869 600565;
e-mail: ian.kilshaw@ntlworld.com
www.rspb-oxford.org.uk
Meetings: Normally 1st Thursday of the month, Methodist Church Hall, Newhigh Street, Headington.

VALE OF WHITE HORSE. (1977; 275). David Lovegrove, 17 Chiltern Crescent, Wallingford, Oxon, OX10 0PE. 01491 835692.
Meetings: 7.30pm, 3rd Monday of the month (Sep-May).

Wetland Bird Survey Organiser
OXFORDSHIRE (South). Catherine Ross, Duck End Cottage, 40 Sutton Lane, Witney, Oxfordshire, OX29 5RU. (H) 01865 881552;
e-mail: catherine@duckend6332.freeserve.co.uk

Wildlife Trust
BBOWT. (1959; 11,000). The Lodge, 1 Armstrong Road, Littlemore, Oxford, OX4 4XT. 01865 775476; fax 01865 711301; e-mail: bbowt@cix.co.uk
www.wildlifetrust.org.uk/berksbucksoxon/

SHROPSHIRE

Bird Atlas/Avifauna
Atlas of the Breeding Birds of Shropshire (Shropshire Ornithological Society, 1995).

Bird Recorder
Geoff Holmes, 22 Tenbury Drive, Telford Estate, Shrewsbury, SY2 5YF. 01743 364621;
e-mail: geoff.holmes4@btopenworld.com

Bird Report
SHROPSHIRE BIRD REPORT (1956-) Annual, from Helen Griffiths (Hon Secretary), 104 Noel Hill Road, Cross Houses, Shrewsbury SY5 6LD. 01743 761507; www.shropshirebirds.com
e-mail: helen.griffiths@english-nature.org.uk

BTO Regional Representative
Allan Dawes, Rosedale, Chapel Lane, Trefonen, Oswestry, Shrops, SY10 9DX. 01691 654245;
e-mail: allandawes@btinternet.com

Club
SHROPSHIRE ORNITHOLOGICAL SOCIETY. (1955; 800). Helen Griffiths (Hon Secretary), 104 Noel Hill Road, Cross Houses, Shrewsbury SY5 6LD. 01743 761507;
e-mail: helen.griffiths@english-nature.org.uk
www.shropshirebirds.com
Meetings: 7.15pm, 1st Thursday of month (Oct-Apr), Shirehall, Shrewsbury.

RSPB Local Group
SHROPSHIRE. (1992; 240). Roger M Evans, 31 The Wheatlands, Bridgnorth, WV16 5BD.
Meetings: 3rd Thursday of the month (Sep-Apr), Council Chamber, Shirehall, Shrewsbury. Also field trips year round.

Wetland Bird Survey Organiser
Bill Edwards, Hopton Villa, Maesbury Marsh, Oswestry, SY10 8JA. (H) 01691 656679.

Wildlife Trust
SHROPSHIRE WILDLIFE TRUST. (1962; 2,000). 193 Abbey Foregate, Shrewsbury, Shropshire SY2 6AH. 01743 284280; fax 01743 284281;
e-mail: shropshirewt@cix.co.uk
www.shropshirewildlifetrust.org.uk

SOMERSET & BRISTOL

Bird Atlas/Avifauna
The Birds of Exmoor and the Quantocks by DK Ballance and BD Gibbs. (Isabelline Books, 2 Highbury House, 8 Woodland Crescent, Falmouth TR11 4QS. 2003).

Atlas of Breeding Birds in Avon 1988-91 by R L Bland and John Tully (John Tully, 6 Falcondale Walk, Westbury-on-Trym, Bristol BS9 3JG, 1992).

Bird Recorders
Brian D Gibbs, 23 Lyngford Road, Taunton, Somerset, TA2 7EE. 01823 274887;
e-mail: brian.gibbs@virgin.net
www.somornithosoc.freeserve.co.uk

BATH, NE SOMERSET, BRISTOL, S GLOS. Harvey Rose, 12 Birbeck Road, Bristol, BS9 1BD.

H:0117 968 1638; W:0117 331 1666;
e-mail: h.e.rose@bris.ac.uk

Bird Reports

AVON BIRD REPORT (1977-), from Richard L Bland, 11 Percival Road, Bristol, BS8 3LN. Home/W:01179 734828;
e-mail: richardbland@blueyonder.co.uk

EXMOOR NATURALIST (1974-), from Secretary, Exmoor Natural History Society.

SOMERSET BIRDS (1913-), from David Ballance, Flat 2, Dunboyne, Bratton Lane, Minehead, Somerset, TA24 8SQ. 01643 706820.

BTO Regional Representatives & Secretary

AVON RR. Richard L Bland, 11 Percival Road, Bristol, BS8 3LN. Home/W:01179 734828;
e-mail: richardbland@blueyonder.co.uk

AVON REGIONAL SECRETARY. John Tully, 6 Falcondale Walk, Westbury-on-Trym, Bristol, BS9 3JG. 0117 950 0992; e-mail: johntully4@aol.com

SOMERSET RR. Eve Tigwell, Hawthorne Cottage, 3 Friggle Street, Frome, Somerset, BA11 5LP. 01373 451630; e-mail: evetigwell@aol.com

Clubs

BRISTOL NATURALISTS' SOCIETY (Ornithological Section). (1862; 550). Dr Mary Hill, 15 Montrose Avenue, Redland, Bristol, BS6 6EH. 0117 942 2193; e-mail: terry@jhill15.fsnet.co.uk
www.bristolnats.org.uk
Meetings: 7.00pm, Wednesday or Friday (check for dates), Westmorland Hall, Westmorland Road, Bristol.

BRISTOL ORNITHOLOGICAL CLUB. (1966; 660). Mrs Judy Copeland, 19 St George's Hill, Easton-in-Gordano, North Somerset, BS20 0PS. Tel/fax 01275 373554;
www.boc-bristol.org.uk
e-mail: judy.copeland@ukgateway.net
Meetings: 7.30pm, 3rd Thursday of the month, Newman Hall, Grange Court Road, Westbury-on-Trym.

CAM VALLEY WILDLIFE GROUP. (1994: 295). Helena Crouch, Bronwen, Farrington Road, Paulton, Bristol, BS39 7LP. 01761 410731.
e-mail: jim-helena@supanet.com
www.camvalleywildlifegroup.org.uk

EXMOOR NATURAL HISTORY SOCIETY. (1974; 450). Miss Caroline Giddens, 12 King George Road, Minehead, Somerset, TA24 5JD. 01643 707624; e-mail: carol.enhs@virgin.net
Meetings: 7.30pm, 1st Wednesday of the month (Oct-Mar), Methodist Church Hall, The Avenue, Minehead.

MID-SOMERSET NATURALISTS' SOCIETY. (1949; 20). Roy Brearly, 2 Quayside, Bridgwater, Somerset, TA6 3TA. 01278 427100.

SOMERSET ORNITHOLOGICAL SOCIETY. (1923; 350). Miss Sarah Beavis, The Old Surgery, 4 The Barton, Hatch Beauchamp, Taunton, Somerset, TA3 6SG. 01823 480948.
www.somornithosoc.freeserve.co.uk

Ringing Groups

CHEW VALLEY RS. W R White, Church View Cottage, Mead Lane, Blagdon, N Somerset, BS40 7UA. 01761 463157 (evgs);
e-mail: warwickw@architen.com

GORDANO VALLEY RG. Lyndon Roberts, 20 Glebe Road, Long Ashton, Bristol, BS41 9LH. 01275 392722; e-mail: mail@lyndonroberts.com

RSPCA. S Powell, 1 Rosemill Cottage, Rosemill Lane, Ilminster, Somerset, TA19 5PR.

STEEP HOLM RS. A J Parsons, Barnfield, Tower Hill Road, Crewkerne, Somerset, TA18 8BJ. 01460 73640.

RSPB Local Groups

BATH AND DISTRICT. (1989; 220). Anne Workman, 6 Englishcombe Way, Bath, BA2 2EU. 01225 428091.
Meetings: 7.30pm, 3rd Wednesday of the month (Sep-Mar), Bath Society Meeting Room, Green Park Station, Bath.

CREWKERNE & DISTRICT. (1979; 335). Denise Chamings, Daniels Farm, Lower Stratton, South Petherton, Somerset, TA13 5LP. 01460 240740;
e-mail: rspb@crewkerne.fslife.co.uk
www.crewkerne.fslife.co.uk
Meetings: 7.30pm, 3rd Thursday of the month (Sep-Apr), The Day Centre, Crewkerne.

TAUNTON. (1975; 148). Eric Luxton, 33 Hoveland Lane, Taunton, Somerset, TA1 2EY. 01823 283033; e-mail: eric.luxton@btinternet.com

WESTON-SUPER-MARE (N SOMERSET). (1976; 215). Don Hurrell, Freeways, Star, Winscombe, BS25 1PS. 01934 842717.
Meetings: 7.30pm, 1st Thursday of the month (Sep-Apr), St Pauls Church Hall.

Wetland Bird Survey Organisers

SEVERN ESTUARY - SOMERSET & BRISTOL. Harvey Rose, 12 Birbek Road, Stoke Bishop, Bristol, BS9 1BD. (H) 0117 9681638; (W) 0117 9287992.

SOMERSET LEVELS. Steve Meen, RSPB West Sedgemoor, Dewlands Farm, Redhill, Curry Rivel, Langport, Somerset TA10 0PH. 01458 252805;
e-mail: steve.meen@rspb.org.uk

Wildlife Trusts

AVON WILDLIFE TRUST. (1980; 4,500). Wildlife Centre, 32 Jacobs Wells Road, Bristol, BS8 1DR.

0117 917 7270; fax 0117 929 7273;
e-mail: mail@avonwildlifetrust.org.uk
www.avonwildlifetrust.org.uk

SOMERSET WILDLIFE TRUST. (1964; 8,000). Fyne Court, Broomfield, Bridgwater, Somerset, TA5 2EQ. 01823 451587; fax 01823 451671;
e-mail: somwt@cix.co.uk
www.wildlifetrust.org.uk/somerset

STAFFORDSHIRE

Bird Recorder
Mrs Gilly Jones, 4 The Poplars, Lichfield Road, Abbots Bromley, Rugeley, Staffs, WS15 3AA;
e-mail: staffs-recorder@westmidlandbirdclub.com
www.westmidlandbirdclub.com

Bird Report See West Midlands

BTO Regional Representatives
NORTH EAST. John Cameron, 01889 564568.

SOUTH & CENTRAL. Martin Godfrey, 01785 229 713; e-mail: MartinandRosie@aol.com

WEST. Martin Godfrey, 01785 229 713;
e-mail: MartinandRosie@aol.com

Clubs
SOUTH PEAK RAPTOR STUDY GROUP. (1998; 12). M E Taylor, 76 Hawksley Avenue, Newbold, Chesterfield, Derbys, S40 4TL. 01246 277749.

WEST MIDLAND BIRD CLUB (STAFFORD BRANCH). Gerald Ford, 01630 673409;
e-mail: stafford@westmidlandbirdclub
www.westmidlandbirdclub.com/stafford
Meetings: 7.15pm, 2nd Friday of the month (Oct-Mar), The Centre for The Blind, in North Walls, Stafford.

WEST MIDLAND BIRD CLUB (TAMWORTH BRANCH). (1992). Barbara Stubbs, 19 Alfred Street, Tamworth, Staffs, B79 7RL. 01827 57865;
e-mail: tamworth@westmidlandbirdclub
www.westmidlandbirdclub.com/tamworth
Meetings: 7.30pm, last Friday of the month (Sep-Apr), Phil Dix Center.

RSPB Local Groups
BURTON-ON-TRENT. (1973; 50). Dave Lummis, 121 Wilmot Road, Swadlincote, Derbys, DE11 9EN. 01283 219902. www.basd-rspb.co.uk
Meetings: 7.30pm 1st Wednesday of the month, All Saint's Church, Bronston Road, Burton.

LICHFIELD & DISTRICT. (1977; 1,150). Ray Jennett, 12 St Margarets Road, Lichfield, Staffs, WS13 7RA. 01543 255195.
Meetings: 7.30pm, 2nd Tuesday of the month (Jan-May, Sept-Dec), St Mary's Centre.

NORTH STAFFORDSHIRE. (1982; 187). John Booth, 32 St Margaret Drive, Sneyd Green, Stoke-on-Trent, ST1 6EW. 01782 262082;
www.geocities.com/nsrspb
Meetings: 7.30pm, 3rd Wednesday of the month, Medical Institute, Hartshill (no correspondence here please).

SOUTH WEST STAFFORDSHIRE. (1972; 190). Mrs Theresa Dorrance, 39 Wilkes Road, Codsall, Wolverhampton, WV8 1RZ. 01902 847041;
e-mail: sqt@dorrances.freeserve.co.uk
Meetings: 8.00pm, 2nd Tuesday of the month, Codsall Village Hall.

Wetland Bird Survey Organisers
Gilly Jones, 4 The Poplars, Lichfield Road, Abbots Bromley, Rugeley, Staffordshire WS15 3AA.

Wildlife Hospitals
BRITISH WILDLIFE RESCUE CENTRE. Alfred Hardy, Amerton Working Farm, Stowe-by-Chartley, Stafford, ST18 0LA. 01889 271308.
On A518 Stafford/Uttoxeter road. All species, including imprints and permanently injured. Hospital, large aviaries and caging. Open to the public every day. Veterinary support.

GENTLESHAW BIRD OF PREY HOSPITAL. Jenny Smith, 5 Chestall Road, Cannock Wood, Rugeley, Staffs, WS15 4RB. 01785 850379
www.gentleshawwildlife.co.uk
Registered charity. All birds of prey (inc. owls). Hospital cages and aviaries; release sites. Veterinary support. Also GENTLESHAW BIRD OF PREY AND WILDLIFE CENTRE, Fletchers Country Garden Centre, Stone Road, Eccleshall, Stafford. 01785 850379 (1000-1700).

RAPTOR RESCUE, BIRD OF PREY REHABILITATION. J M Cunningham, 8 Harvey Road, Handsacre, Rugeley, Staffs, WS15 4HF. 01543 491712; (Nat. advice line) 0870 241 0609;
e-mail: mickcunningham@btinternet.com
www.raptorrescue.org.uk
Birds of prey only. Heated hospital units. Indoor flights, secluded aviaries, hacking sites, rehabilitation aviaries/flights. Falconry rehabilitation techniques, foster birds for rearing young to avoid imprinting. Veterinary support. Reg charity no. 283733.

Wildlife Trust
STAFFORDSHIRE WILDLIFE TRUST. (1969; 4,000). The Wolseley Centre, Wolseley Bridge, Stafford, ST17 0YT. 01889 880100; fax 01889 880101; e-mail: staffswt@cix.co.uk
www.staffs-wildlife.org.uk

SUFFOLK

Bird Atlas/Avifauna
Birds of Suffolk by S H Piotrowski (February 2003).

Bird Recorders
NORTH EAST. Dave Thurlow,
e-mail: dave.thurlow@rspb.org.uk

SOUTH EAST (inc. coastal region from Slaughden Quay southwards). Lee Woods,
e-mail: leejanwoods@ntlworld.com

WEST (whole of Suffolk W of Stowmarket, inc. Breckland). Colin Jakes, 7 Maltward Avenue, Bury St Edmunds, Suffolk, IP33 3XN. 01284 702215;
e-mail: cjjakes@supanet.com

Bird Report
SUFFOLK BIRDS (inc Landguard Bird Observatory Report) (1950-), from Ipswich Museum, High Street, Ipswich, Suffolk.

BTO Regional Representative
Mick T Wright, 15 Avondale Road, Ipswich, IP3 9JT. 01473 710032;
e-mail: micktwright@btinternet.com

Clubs
LAVENHAM BIRD CLUB. (1972; 54). Mike Lewis, 6 Grammar School Place, Sudbury, Suffolk CO10 2GE. 01787 324488.

SUFFOLK ORNITHOLOGISTS' GROUP. (1973; 650). Andrew M Gregory, 1 Holly Road, Ipswich, IP1 3QN. 01473 253816.
Meetings: Last Thursday of the month (Jan-Mar, Oct-Nov), Holiday Inn, Ipswich.

Ringing Groups
DINGLE BIRD CLUB. Dr D Pearson, 4 Lupin Close, Reydon, Southwold, Suffolk, IP18 6NW. 01502 722348.

LACKFORD RG. Dr Peter Lack, 11 Holden Road, Lackford, Bury St Edmunds, Suffolk, IP28 6HZ.
e-mail: peter.diane@tinyworld.co.uk

LANDGUARD RG. Mr SH Piotrowski, 29 Churchfields Road, Long Stratton, Norfolk, NR15 2WH. 01508 531115.

MARKET WESTON RG. Dr R H W Langston, Walnut Tree Farm, Thorpe Street, Hinderclay, Diss, Norfolk, IP22 1HT.
e-mail: rlangston@wntfarm.demon.co.uk

RSPB Local Groups
BURY ST EDMUNDS. (1982; 150). Trevor Hart, 7 Westgart Gardens, Bury St Edmunds, Suffolk, IP33 3LB. 01284 705165.

IPSWICH. (1975; 200). BJ Cooper, Ipswich Group Leader, 115 Bucklesham Road, Ipswich, Suffolk IP3 8TX. 01473 431752;
e-mail: b.cooper9@ntlworld.com
Meetings: 7.30pm, 2nd Thursday of the month (Sep-Apr), Sidegate Primary School, Sidegate Lane, Ipswich.

LOWESTOFT & DISTRICT. (1976; 130). Mr E Beaumont, 52 Squires Walk, Lowestoft, Suffolk, NR32 4LA. 01502 560126;
e-mail: groupleader@lowestoft-rspb-group.org.uk
www.lowestoft-rspb-group.org.uk

WOODBRIDGE. (1986; 350). Colin Coates, 42A Bredfield Road, Woodbridge, Suffolk, IP12 1JE. 01394 385209.

Wetland Bird Survey Organisers
ALDE COMPLEX. Rodney West, Flint Cottage, Stone Common, Blaxhall, Woodbridge, IP12 2DP. (H) 01728 689171;
e-mail: Rodney@justecology.co.uk

DEBEN ESTUARY. Nick Mason, Evening Hall, Hollesley, Nr Woodbridge, Ipswich, IP12 3QU. (H) 01359 411150; e-mail: nick.mason@talk21.com

STOUR ESTUARY. Rick Vonk, RSPB, Unit 3 Court Farm, 3 Stutton Road, Brantham, Suffolk CO11 1PW. (D) 01473 328006;
e-mail: rick.vonk@rspb.org.uk

SUFFOLK (other sites). Alan Miller, Suffolk Wildlife Trust, 9 Valley Terrace, Valley Road, Leiston, IP16 4AP. (Day) 01728 833405;
e-mail: alanm@suffolkwildlife.cix.co.uk

Wildlife Trust
SUFFOLK WILDLIFE TRUST. (1961; 15,000). Brooke House, The Green, Ashbocking, Ipswich, IP6 9JY. 01473 890089; fax 01473 890165;
e-mail: suffolkwildlife@cix.co.uk
www.wildlifetrust.org.uk/suffolk

SURREY

Bird Atlas/Avifauna
Birds of Surrey (avifauna). Due 2005.

Bird Recorder (inc London S of Thames & E to Surrey Docks)
VICE COUNTY OF SURREY (includes Greater London south of the Thames and east to the Surrey Docks, excludes Spellhorne). Jeffery Wheatley, 9 Copse Edge, Elstead, Godalming, Surrey, GU8 6DJ. 01252 702450; (Fax) 01252 703650.

Bird Report
SURBITON AND DISTRICT BIRD WATCHING SOCIETY (1972-), from Thelma Caine, 21 More Lane, Esher, Surrey KT10 8AJ.

SURREY BIRD REPORT (1952-), from J Gates, 90 The Street, Wrecclesham, Farnham, Surrey, GU10 4QR. 01252 727683.

BTO Regional Representative
Hugh Evans, 31 Crescent Road, Shepperton, Middx, TW17 8BL. 01932 227781;
e-mail: hugh_w_evans@lineone.net

Clubs
SURBITON & DISTRICT BIRDWATCHING SOCIETY. (1954; 200). Gary Caine, 21 More Lane, Esher, Surrey KT10 8AJ. 01372 468432; e-mail: hockley@sdbws.ndo.co.uk www.sdbws.ndo.co.uk
Meetings: 7.30pm, 3rd Tuesday of the month, Surbiton Library Annex.

SURREY BIRD CLUB. (1957; 420). Mrs Jill Cook, Moorings, Vale Wood Drive, Lower Bourne, Farnham, Surrey, GU10 3HW. 01252 792876; e-mail: jilck@aol.com www.surreybirdclub.org.uk

Ringing Groups
HERSHAM RG. A J Beasley, 29 Selbourne Avenue, New Haw, Weybridge, Surrey, KT15 3RB. e-mail: abeasley00@hotmail.com

RUNNYMEDE RG. D G Harris, 22 Blossom Waye, Hounslow, TW5 9HD.
e-mail: daveharris@tinyonline.co.uk

RSPB Local Groups
DORKING & DISTRICT. (1982; 310). Alan Clark, 11 Maplehurst, Fetcham, Surrey, KT22 9NB. 01372 450607; e-mail: alanclark@tinyonline.co.uk
Meetings: Friday Night and Wednesday afternoons, Christian Centre, next to St Martin's Church, Dorking.

EAST SURREY. (1984; 150-200). Brian Hobley, 26 Alexandra Road, Warlingham, Surrey, CR6 9DU. 01883 625404.
Meetings: 8.00pm, 2nd Wednesday of the month (Sep-Jul), Whitehart Barn, Godstone.

EPSOM & EWELL. (1974; 168). Janet Gilbert, 78 Fairfax Avenue, Ewell, Epsom, Surrey, KT17 2QQ. 0208 394 0405.
Meetings: 7.45pm, 2nd Tuesday of the month, Bourne Hall, Ewell.

GUILDFORD AND DISTRICT. (1974; 550). Alan Bowen, Newlands, 13 Mountside, Guildford, Surrey, GU2 4JD. 01483 567041;
e-mail: alan.and.monica.bower@care4free.net
Meetings: 2.15pm, 2nd Tuesday and 7.45pm, 4th Wednesday, Onslow Village Hall, Guildford.

NORTH WEST SURREY. (1973; 140). Ms Mary Braddock, 20 Meadway Drive, New Haw, Surrey, KT15 2DT. 01932 858692;
e-mail: mary.braddock@virgin.net
www.nwsurreyrspb.org.uk
Meetings: 7.45pm, 4th Wednesday of the month (not Dec, Jul, Aug), Sir William Perkins School, Chertsey.

Wetland Bird Survey Organiser
Jeffery Wheatley, 9 Copse Edge, Elstead, Godalming, Surrey, GU8 6DJ. 01252 702540;
e-mail: j.j.wheatley@btinternet.com

Wildlife Hospitals
THE SWAN SANCTUARY. See National Directory

WILDLIFE AID. Simon Cowell, Randalls Farm House, Randalls Road, Leatherhead, Surrey, KT22 0AL. 01372 377332; 24-hr emergline 09061 800 132 (50p/min); fax 01372 375183;
e-mail: wildlife@pncl.co.uk
www.wildlife-aid.org.uk/wildlife
Registered charity. Wildlife hospital and rehabilitation centre helping all native British species. Special housing for birds of prey. Membership scheme and fund raising activities. Veterinary support.

Wildlife Trust
SURREY WILDLIFE TRUST. (1959; 7500). School Lane, Pirbright, Woking, Surrey, GU24 0JN. 01483 795440; fax 01483 486505;
e-mail: surreywt@cix.co.uk
www.surreywildlifetrust.co.uk

SUSSEX

Bird Atlas/Avifauna
The Birds of Selsey Bill and the Selsey Peninsula (a checklist to year 2000) From: Mr O Mitchell, 21 Trundle View Close, Barnham, Bognor Regis, PO22 0JZ.

Birds of Sussex ed by Paul James (Sussex Ornithological Society, 1996).

Fifty Years of Birdwatching, a celebration of the acheivements of the Shoreham District OS from 1953 onwards. from Shoreham District Ornithological Society, 7 Berberis Court, Shoreham by Sea, West Sussex BN43 6JA. £15 plus £2.50 p&p.

Bird Recorder
John A Hobson, 23 Hillside Road, Storrington, W Sussex, RH20 3 LZ. 01903 740155;
e-mail: jahobson23@tiscali.co.uk

Bird Reports
BIRDS OF RYE HARBOUR NR ANNUAL REPORT (1977- published every 5 years), from Dr Barry Yates, see Clubs.

PAGHAM HARBOUR LOCAL NATURE RESERVE ANNUAL REPORT, from Warden, see Reserves,

SHOREHAM DISTRICT ORNITHOLOGICAL SOCIETY ANNUAL REPORT (1952-) - back issues available, from The Secretary, 01273 452 497.

SUSSEX BIRD REPORT (1963-), from J E Trowell, Lorrimer, Main Road, Icklesham, Winchelsea, E Sussex, TN36 4BS.
e-mail: membership@susos.org.uk
www.susos.org.uk

BTO Regional Representative
Dr A Barrie Watson, 83 Buckingham Road,

Shoreham-by-Sea, W Sussex, BN43 5UD. 01273 452472; e-mail: abwatson@mistral.co.uk

Clubs

FRIENDS OF RYE HARBOUR NATURE RESERVE. (1973; 1,600). Dr Barry Yates, 2 Watch Cottages, Nook Beach, Winchelsea, E Sussex, TN36 4LU. 01797 223862; e-mail: yates@clara.net www.naturereserve.ryeharbour.org
Meetings: Monthly talks in winter, monthly walks all year.

HENFIELD BIRDWATCH. (1999; 110). Mike Russell, 31 Downsview, Small Dole, Henfield, West Sussex, BN5 9YB. 01273 494311; e-mail: mikerussell@sussexwt.org.uk

SHOREHAM DISTRICT ORNITHOLOGICAL SOCIETY. (1953; 120). Mrs B Reeve, The Old Rectory, Coombes, Lancing, W Sussex, BN15 0RS. 01273 452497.
Meetings: 7.30pm, 1st Tuesday of the month, St Peter's Church Hall, Shoreham-by-Sea.

SUSSEX ORNITHOLOGICAL SOCIETY. (1962; 1,500). Mr Richard Cowser, Beavers Brook, The Thatchway, Angmering, BN16 4HJ. 01903 770259; www.susos.org.uk e-mail:secretary@susos.org.uk

Ringing Groups

BEACHY HEAD RS. R D M Edgar, 32 Hartfield Road, Seaford, E Sussex BN25 4PW.

CUCKMERE RG. Tim Parmenter, 22 The Kiln, Burgess Hill, W Sussex, RH15 0LU. 01444 236526.

RYE BAY RG. P Jones, Elms Farm, Pett Lane, Icklesham, Winchelsea, E Sussex, TN36 4AH. 01797 226374; e-mail: phil@wetlandtrust.org

STEYNING RINGING GROUP. B R Clay, 30 The Drive, Worthing, W Sussex, BN11 5LL. e-mail: brian.clay@ntlworld.com

RSPB Local Groups

BATTLE. (1973; 100). Miss Lynn Jenkins, 61 Austen Way, Guestling, Hastings, E Sussex, TN35 4JH. 01424 432076; e-mail: battlerspb@freewire.co.uk www.battlerspb.freewire.co.uk
Meetings: 7.45pm, last Tuesday of the month, St Mary's Church Hall, Battle.

BRIGHTON & DISTRICT. (1974; 450). Marion Couldery, 81 Hove Park Road, Hove, East Sussex BN3 6LN. 01273 555750; www.rspb.port5.com e-mail: MarionCouldery@aol.com
Meetings: 7.30pm, 4th Thursday of the month, All Saints Church Hall, Eaton Road, Hove.

CHICHESTER & SW SUSSEX. (1979; 245). Mr R Storkey, 216 Goring Road, Goring by Sea, Worthing, W Sussex BN12 2PQ.

CRAWLEY & HORSHAM. (1978; 148). Andrea Saxton, 104 Heath Way, Horsham, W Sussex, RH12 5XS. 01403 242218.
Meetings: 8.00pm, 3rd Wednesday of the month (Sept-Apr), The Friary Hall, Crawley.

EAST GRINSTEAD. (1998; 218). Nick Walker, 14 York Avenue, East Grinstead, W Sussex, RH19 4TL. 01342 315825.
Meetings: 8.00pm, last Wednesday of the month, Larec Parish Hall, De La Ware Road, East Grinstead.

EASTBOURNE & DISTRICT. (1993; 520). David Jode, 01323 422368

HASTINGS & ST LEONARDS. (1983; 145). Richard Prebble, 1 Wayside, 490 Sedlescombe Road North, St Leonards-on-Sea, E Sussex, TN37 7PH. 01424 751790.
Meetings: 7.30pm, 3rd Friday of the month, Taplin Centre, Upper Maze Hill.

Wildlife Hospital

BRENT LODGE BIRD & WILDLIFE TRUST. Penny Cooper, Brent Lodge, Cow Lane, Sidlesham, Chichester, West Sussex, PO20 7LN. 01243 641672.
All species of wild birds and small mammals. Full surgical and medical facilities (inc. X-ray). Purpose-built oiled bird washing unit. Veterinary support.

Wildlife Trust

SUSSEX WILDLIFE TRUST. (1961; 11,000). Woods Mill, Shoreham Road, Henfield, W Sussex, BN5 9SD. 01273 492630; fax 01273 494500; e-mail: enquiries@sussexwt.org.uk www.sussexwt.org.uk

TYNE & WEAR

Bird Recorders

See Durham; Northumberland.

Bird Report See Durham; Northumberland.

Clubs

NATURAL HISTORY SOCIETY OF NORTHUMBRIA. (1829; 900). David C Noble-Rollin, Hancock Museum, Barras Bridge, Newcastle upon Tyne, NE2 4PT. 0191 232 6386; e-mail: nhsn@ncl.ac.uk

NORTHUMBERLAND & TYNESIDE BIRD CLUB. (1958; 270). Sarah Barratt, 3 Haydon Close, Red House Farm, Gosforth, Newcastle upon Tyne, NE3 2BY. 0191 213 6665.

RSPB Local Groups

NEWCASTLE UPON TYNE. (1969; 250). No new leader at time of going to press, please contact RSPB North East Regional Office, 0191 212 6100.
Meetings: Meetings held at Newcastle Civic Centre, Barras Bridge, Newcastle Upon Tyne.

SUNDERLAND & SOUTH TYNESIDE. (1982; 25). Paul Metters, Almonte, 1 Bloomfield Drive, Elemore View, East Rainton, Houghton-le-Spring, Tyne & Wear, DH5 9SF. 0191 5120083.

Wetland Bird Survey Organiser
NORTHUMBERLAND COAST. Roger Norman, 1 Prestwick Gardens, Kenton, Newcastle-upon-Tyne, NE3 3DN. (H) 01912 858314;
e-mail: r.norman@clara.net

WARWICKSHIRE

Bird Recorder
Jonathan Bowley, 17 Meadow Way, Fenny Compton, Southam, Warks, CV47 2WD. 01295 770069;
e-mail: warwks-recorder@westmidlandbirdclub.com

Bird Report See West Midlands.

BTO Regional Representatives
WARWICKSHIRE. Mark Smith, 01926 735398;
e-mail: marksmith36@ntlworld.com

RUGBY. Barrington Jackson, 5 Harris Drive, Rugby, Warks, CV22 6DX. 01788 814466;
e-mail: jacksonbj2@aol.com

Clubs
NUNEATON & DISTRICT BIRDWATCHERS' CLUB. (1950; 88). Alvin K Burton, 23 Redruth Close, Horeston Grange, Nuneaton, Warwicks, CV11 6FG. 024 7664 1591.
Meetings: 7.30pm, 3rd Thursday of the month (Sep-May), Hatters Space Community Centre, Upper Abbey Street, Nuneaton.

Ringing Groups
ARDEN RG. Roger J Juckes, 24 Croft Lane, Temple Grafton, Alcester, Warks B49 6PA. 01789 778748.

BRANDON RG. David Stone, Overbury, Wolverton, Stratford-on-Avon, Warks, CV37 0HG. 01789 731488.

RSPB Local Group
See West Midlands.

Wildlife Trust
WARWICKSHIRE WILDLIFE TRUST. (1970; 7,000). Brandon Marsh Nature Centre, Brandon Lane, Coventry, CV3 3GW. 024 7630 2912; fax 024 7663 9556; e-mail: admin@warkswt.cix.co.uk
www.warwickshire-wildlife-trust.org.uk

WEST MIDLANDS

Bird Atlas/Avifauna
The Birds of the West Midlands edited by Graham Harrison et al (West Midland Bird Club, 1982). Revised edition due.

Bird Recorder
Tim Hextell, 39 Windermere Road, Handsworth, Birmingham, B21 9RQ. 0121 551 9997;
www.westmidlandbirdclub.com

Bird Reports
THE BIRDS OF SMESTOW VALLEY AND DUNSTALL PARK (1988-), from Secretary, Smestow Valley Bird Group.

WEST MIDLAND BIRD REPORT (inc Staffs, Warks, Worcs and W Midlands) (1934-), from Mr J Reeves, 9 Hintons Coppice, Knowle, Solihull, B93 9RF.

BTO Regional Representative
BIRMINGHAM & WEST MIDLANDS. Position vacant.

Clubs
SMESTOW VALLEY BIRD GROUP. (1988; 56). Frank Dickson, 11 Bow Street, Bilston, Wolverhampton, WV14 7NB. 01902 493733.

WMBC

WEST MIDLAND BIRD CLUB. (1929; 2,000). Mr MJ West, 6 Woodend Road, Walsall, WS5 3BG. 01922 639931; e-mail: secretary@westmidlandbirdclub.com
www.westmidlandbirdclub.com

WEST MIDLAND BIRD CLUB (BIRMINGHAM BRANCH). (1995; 800). Martin Kendrick, c/o PO Box 1, Studley, Warwickshire B80 7JG;
e-mail: birmingham@westmidlandbirdclub.com
www.westmidlandbirdclub.com/birmingham

WEST MIDLAND BIRD CLUB (SOLIHULL BRANCH). Jim Winsper, 32 Links Road, Hollywood, Birmingham, B14 4TP.
e-mail: solihull@westmidlandbirdclub
www.westmidlandbirdclub.com/solihull

Ringing Groups
MERCIAN RG (Sutton Coldfield). R L Castle, 91 Maney Hill Road, Sutton Coldfield, West Midlands, B72 1JT. 0121 686 7568.

RSPB Local Groups
BIRMINGHAM. (1975; 100). John Bailey, 52 Gresham Road, Hall Green, Birmingham, B28 0HY. 0121 777 4389
www.rspb-birmingham.org.uk
Meetings: 7.30pm, 3rd Thursday of the month (Sep-Jun), Salvation Army Citadel, St Chads, Queensway, Birmingham.

COVENTRY & WARWICKSHIRE. (1969; 130). Alan King, 69 Westmorland Road, Coventry, CV2 5BO. 024 7672 7348.

SOLIHULL. (1983; 2600). John Roberts, 115 Dovehouse Lane, Solihull, West Midlands, B91 2EQ. 0121 707 3101.

Meetings: 7.30pm, usually 2nd Tuesday of the month, Oliver Bird Hall, Church Hill Road, Solihull.

STOURBRIDGE. (1978; 150). Paul Banks, 4 Sandpiper Close, Wollescote, Stourbridge, DY9 8TD. 01384 898948;
e-mail: picapica@tinyworld.co.uk
Meetings: 7.30pm, 2nd Wednesday of the month (Sep-May), Stourbridge Town Hall, Crown Centre, Stourbridge.

SUTTON COLDFIELD. (1986; 250). Joanna Bazen, 66 Station Road, Wylde Green, Sutton Coldfield, B73 5LA. 0121 354 5626.
Meetings: 7.30pm, 1st Monday of the month, Bishop Vesey's Grammer School.

WALSALL. (1970). Mike Pittaway, 2 Kedleston Close, Bloxwich, Walsall WS3 3TW. 01922 710568;
e-mail: chair@rspb-walsall.org.uk
www.rspb-walsall.org.uk
Meetings: 7.30pm, 3rd Wednesday of the month, St Marys School, Jesson Road, Walsall.

WOLVERHAMPTON. (1974; 110). Ian Wiltshire, 25 Oakridge Drive, Willenhall, WV12 4EN. 01902 630418.
Meetings: 7.30pm, 2nd Wednesday of the month (Sept-Apr), The Newman Centre, Haywood Drive, Tettenhall, Wolverhampton.

Wildlife Hospitals

KIDD, D J. 20 Parry Road, Ashmore Park, Wednesfield, Wolverhampton, WV11 2PS. 01902 863971.
All birds of prey, esp. owls. Aviaries, isolation pens. Veterinary support.

WEDNESFIELD ANIMAL SANCTUARY. Jimmy Wick, 92 Vicarage Road, Nordley, Wednesfield, Wolverhampton, WV11 1SF. 01902 823064.
Birds of prey, softbills, seed-eaters. Brooders, incubators, outdoor aviaries, heated accommodation. Telephone first. Veterinary support.

Wildlife Trust

THE BIRMINGHAM AND BLACK COUNTRY WILDLIFE TRUST. (1980; 900). 28 Harborne Road, Edgbaston, Birmingham, B15 3AA. 0121 454 1199; fax 0121 454 6556;
e-mail: info@bbcwildlife.org.uk

WILTSHIRE

Bird Atlas/Avifauna

Birds of Wiltshire. Due early 2005.

Bird Recorder

Rob Turner, 14 Ethendun, Bratton, Westbury, Wilts, BA13 4RX. 01380 830862;
e-mail: robt14@btopenworld.com

Bird Report

Published in Hobby (journal of the Wiltshire OS) *(1975-),* from John Osborne, 4 Fairdown Avenue, Westbury, Wiltshire BA13 3HS. 01373 864598;
e-mail: jobo@care4free.net

BTO Regional Representatives

NORTH. Position vacant.

SOUTH. Andrew Carter, Standlynch Farm, Downton, Salisbury, SP5 3QR. 01722 710382;
e-mail: standlynch@aol.com

Clubs

SALISBURY & DISTRICT NATURAL HISTORY SOCIETY. (1952; 181). J Pitman, 10 The Hardings, Devizes Road, Salisbury, SP2 9LZ. 01722 327395.
Meetings: 7.30pm, 3rd Thursday of the month (Sept-Apr), Lecture Hall, Salisbury Museum, Kings House, The Close, Salisbury.

WILTSHIRE ORNITHOLOGICAL SOCIETY. (1974; 480). Phil Deacon, 12 Rawston Close, Nythe, Swindon, Wilts SN3 3PW. 01793 528930;
e-mail: phil.deacon@tinyworld.co.uk

Ringing Group

COTSWOLD WATER PARK RG. R Hearn, Wildfowl & Wetlands Trust, Slimbridge, Glos, GL2 7BT. 01453 891900 ext 185;
e-mail: richard.hearn@wwt.org.uk

WEST WILTSHIRE RG. Mr M.J. Hamzij, 13 Halfway Close, Trowbridge, Wilts, BA14 7HQ.
e-mail: mikehamzij@halfway11.freeserve.co.uk

RSPB Local Groups

NORTH WILTSHIRE. (1973; 104). Derek Lyford, 9 Devon Road, Swindon, SN2 1PQ. 01793 520997;
e-mail: derek.lyford@virgin.net
www.communigate.co.uk/wilts/nwiltsrspb
Meetings: 7.30pm, 1st Tuesday of the month (Sep-Jun), Swindon Community Centre, Jennings St, Swindon.

SOUTH WILTSHIRE. (1986; 820). Tony Goddard, Clovelly, Lower Road, Charlton All Saints, Salisbury, SP5 4HQ. 01725 510309.
Meetings: 7.30pm, Tuesday evenings (monthly), City Hall, Salisbury.

Wildlife Hospital

CALNE WILD BIRD AND ANIMAL RESCUE CENTRE. Tom and Caroline Baker, 2 North Cote, Calne, Wilts, SN11 9DL. 01249 817893.
All species of birds. Large natural aviaries (all with ponds), release areas, incubators, heated cages. Day and night collection. Veterinary support.

Wildlife Trust

WILTSHIRE WILDLIFE TRUST. (1962; 10,000). Elm Tree Court, Long Street, Devizes, Wilts, SN10 1NJ. 01380 725670; fax 01380 729017;
e-mail: admin@wiltshirewildlife.org
www.wiltshirewildlife.org

WORCESTERSHIRE

Bird Recorder
Andy Warr, 14 Bromsgrove Street, Worcester WR3 8AR. 01905 28281;
e-mail: worcs-recorder@westmidlandbirdclub.com

Bird Report See West Midlands.

BTO Regional Representative
G Harry Green MBE, Windy Ridge, Pershore Road, Little Comberton, Pershore, Worcs, WR10 3EW. 01386 710377;
e-mail: harrygreen@britishlibrary.net

Ringing Group
WYCHAVON RG. J R Hodson, 15 High Green, Severn Stoke, Worcester, WR8 9JS. 01905 754919(day), 01905 371333(eve);
e-mail: john.hodson@tesco.net

Club
WEST MIDLAND BIRD CLUB (KIDDERMINSTER BRANCH). Celia Barton, 28A Albert Street, Wall Heath, Kingswinford DY6 0NA. 01384 839838;
e-mail: kidderminster@westmidlandbirdclub.com
Meetings: 7.30pm, 4th Wednesday of the month (Sep-May), St Oswalds Church Centre, Broadwaters, Kidderminster.

RSPB Local Group
WORCESTER & MALVERN. (1980; 300). Garth Lowe, Sunnymead, Old Storridge, Alfrick, Worcester, WR6 5HT. 01886 833362.
Meetings: 7.30pm, 2nd Wednesday in month (Sept-May), Powick Village Hall.

Wildlife Trust
WORCESTERSHIRE WILDLIFE TRUST. (1968; 8,000). Lower Smite Farm, Smite Hill, Hindlip, Worcester, WR3 8SZ. 01905 754919; fax 01905 755868; e-mail: worcswt@cix.co.uk
www.worcswildlifetrust.co.uk

YORKSHIRE

Bird Atlas/Avifauna
Atlas of Breeding Birds in the Leeds Area 1987-1991 by Richard Fuller et al (Leeds Birdwatchers' Club, 1994).

The Birds of Halifax by Nick Dawtrey (only 20 left), 14 Moorend Gardens, Pellon, Halifax, W Yorks, HX2 0SD.

The Birds of Yorkshire by John Mather (Croom Helm, 1986).

An Atlas of the Breeding Birds of the Huddersfield Area, 1987-1992. by Brian Armitage et al (2000) - very few copies left.

Birds of Barnsley by Nick Addey (Pub by author, 114 Everill Gate Lane, Broomhill, Barnsley S73 0YJ, 1998).

Bird Recorders
CHAIRMAN OF REPORTS COMMITTEE. Geoff Dobbs, 12 Park Avenue, Hull, HU5 3ER. 01482 341524; e-mail: geoffdobbs@aol.com

VC61 (East Yorkshire), Dale Middleton, The Siskins, 34 Hull Road, Hornsea East Yorkshire. 01964 536848.

VC62 (North Yorkshire East). Russell Slack, 64 Sundew Gardens, High Green, Sheffield, S35 4DU. 01142 845300; e-mail: russ@birdguides.com

VC63 (South & West Yorkshire). Covering the following groups - Barnsley Bird Study, Blacktoft Sands RSPB, Doncaster and District OS, Rotherham and District OS, Sheffield Bird Study and SK58 Birders. John Wint, 9 Yew Tree Park, Whitley, Goole, DN14 0NZ. 01977 662826;
e-mail: john.wint@tesco.net

VC63 (South & West Yorkshire). Covering the following groups - Fairburn Ings RSPB, Halifax Birdwatchers, Huddersfield Birdwatchers, Castleford NS, Ardsley Reservoir Birdwatchers, Leeds Birdwatching Club, Sorby NHS, Wakefield NS, Five Towns Bird Group. Mike Barnett, 12 Woodlands Close, Derby Dale, Huddersfield HD8 7RH. 01484 865961.

VC64 (West Yorkshire) /Harrogate & Craven. Jim Pewtress, 31 Piercy End, Kirbymoorside, York, YO62 6DQ. 01751 431001;
e-mail: jim.pewtress@btopenworld.com

VC65 (North Yorkshire West). Steve Worwood, 18 Coltsgate Hill, Ripon HG4 2AB. 01765 602518;
e-mail: s.worwood@bronco.com

Bird Reports
BARNSLEY & DISTRICT BIRD STUDY GROUP REPORT (1971-), from Secretary.

BRADFORD NATURALISTS' SOCIETY ANNUAL REPORT, from Mr I Hogg, 23 St Matthews Road, Bankfoot, Bradford, BD5 9AB. 01274 727902.

BRADFORD ORNITHOLOGICAL GROUP REPORT (1987-), from Jenny Barker, 4 Chapel Fold, Slack Lane, Oakworth, Keighley, BD22 0RQ.

DONCASTER BIRD REPORT (1955-), from Mr M Roberts, 30 St Cecilia's Road, Belle Vue, Doncaster, DN4 5EG. 01302 361731.

FILEY BRIGG BIRD REPORT (1976-), from Mr C Court, 12 Pinewood Avenue, Filey, YO14 9NS.

FIVE TOWNS BIRD REPORT (1995-), from Secretary, Five Towns Bird Group.

HALIFAX BIRDWATCHERS' CLUB ANNUAL REPORT (1991-), from Nick C Dawtrey, 14

Moorend Gardens, Pellon, Halifax, W Yorks, HX2 0SD. 01422 364228.

HARROGATE & DISTRICT NATURALISTS' ORNITHOLOGY REPORT (1996-), from Secretary.

HULL VALLEY WILDLIFE GROUP REPORT (2000-) incorporating Tophill Low recording area). from Geoff Dobbs, 12 Park Avenue, Hull, HU5 3ER. 01482 341524; e-mail: geoffdobbs@aol.com

BIRDS IN HUDDERSFIELD (1966-), from Mr Brian Armitage, 106 Forest Road, Dalton, Huddersfield HD5 8ET. 01484 305054; e-mail: brian.armitage@ntlworld.com

LEEDS BIRDWATCHERS' CLUB ANNUAL REPORT (1949-), from Secretary.

BIRDS OF ROTHERHAM (1975-), from Secretary, Rotherham Orn Soc, www.rotherhambirds.co.uk (check website for current publication details).

BIRDS IN THE SHEFFIELD AREA (1973-), from Tony Morris, 4A Raven Road, Sheffield, S7 1SB. e-mail: tonyjmorris@blueyonder.co.uk www.sbsg.org

THE BIRDS OF SK58 (1993-), from Secretary, SK58 Birders.

SPURN BIRD OBSERVATORY ANNUAL REPORT, from Warden, see Reserves.

WINTERSETT AREA ANNUAL REPORT (1988-), from Steve Denny, 13 Rutland Drive, Crofton, Wakefield, WF4 1SA.01924 864487.

YORK ORNITHOLOGICAL CLUB ANNUAL REPORT (1970-), from Peter Watson, 1 Oak Villa, Hodgson Lane, Upper Poppleton, York YO26 6EA. 01904 795063.

YORKSHIRE NATURALISTS' UNION: BIRD REPORT (1940-), from John A Newbould, Stonecroft, 3 Brookmead Close, Sutton Poyntz, Wemouth, Dorset, DT3 6RS.

BTO Regional Representatives & Regional Development Officers

NORTH-EAST RR. Michael Carroll, 01751 476550.

NORTH-WEST RR. Gerald Light, 01756 753720.

SOUTH-EAST AND SOUTH-WEST RR. Chris Falshaw, 6 Den Bank Crescent, Sheffield, S10 5PD. 0114 230 3857; e-mail: chris@falshaw.f9.co.uk

EAST RR. Cliff Carter, 01964 535038; e-mail: clifford.carter@ntlworld.com.

BRADFORD RR & RDO. Mike L Denton, 77 Hawthorne Terrace, Crosland Moor, Huddersfield, HD4 5RP. 01484 646990.

HARROGATE RR. Mike Brown, 48 Pannal Ash Drive, Harrogate, N Yorks, HG2 0HU. H:01423 567382; W:01423 507237; e-mail: mike@ppcmail.co.uk

LEEDS & WAKEFIELD RR & RDO. Peter Smale, 2A Hillcrest Rise, Leeds, LS16 7DL. 0113 226 9526; e-mail: petersmale@ntlworld.com

RICHMOND RR. John Edwards, 7 Church Garth, Great Smeaton, Northallerton, N Yorks, DL6 2HW. H:01609 881476; W:01609 780780 extn 2452; e-mail: john@garthwards.fsnet.co.uk

YORK RR. Rob Chapman, 12 Moorland Road, York, YO10 4HF. 01904 633558; e-mail: robert.chapman@tinyworld.co.uk

Clubs

BARNSLEY BIRD STUDY GROUP. (1970; 35). Graham Speight, 58 Locke Avenue, Kingstone, Barnsley, South Yorkshire S70 1QH. 01226 321300.
Meetings: 7.15pm, 1st Thursday in the month (Nov-Mar), Old Moor Wetland Centre, Wombwell.

BRADFORD NATURALISTS' SOCIETY. (1875; 30). D R Grant, 19 The Wheatings, Ossett, W Yorks, WF5 0QQ. 01924 273628.
Meetings: 7.30pm, Mondays, Richmond Building, University of Bradford.

BRADFORD ORNITHOLOGICAL GROUP. (1987; 200). Shaun Radcliffe, 8 Longwood Avenue, Bingley, W Yorks, BD16 2RX. 01274 770960; www.bradfordbirders.co.uk

CASTLEFORD & DISTRICT NATURALISTS' SOCIETY. (1956; 25). Michael J Warrington, 31 Mount Avenue, Hemsworth, Pontefract, W Yorks, WF9 4QE. 01977 614954; michael@warrington31mount.freeserve.co.uk.
Meetings: 7.30pm, Tuesdays monthly (Sep-Mar), Whitwood College, Castleford (check with secretary for dates).

DONCASTER & DISTRICT ORNITHOLOGICAL SOCIETY. (1955; 40). D Hazard, 01302 788044; e-mail: davehazard@btopenworld.com

FILEY BRIGG ORNITHOLOGICAL GROUP. (1977; 70). Jack Whitehead, 15 The Beach, Filey, N Yorkshire, YO14 9LA. 01723 514565.

FIVE TOWNS BIRD GROUP. (1994; 20). Robert Knight, 2 Milnes Grove, Airedale, Castleford, W Yorkshire, WF10 3EZ. 01977 510761; e-mail: f.t.b.g@lineone.net

HALIFAX BIRDWATCHERS' CLUB. (1992). Nick C Dawtrey, 14 Moorend Gardens, Pellon, Halifax, W Yorks, HX2 0SD. 01422 364228.

HARROGATE & DISTRICT NATURALISTS' SOCIETY. (1947; 400). Mrs J McClean, 6 Rossett Park Road, Harrogate, N Yorks, HG2 9NP. 01423 879095; e-mail: joan_mcclean@hotmail.com
Meetings: 7.45pm, Wednesday, fortnightly from 13/10/04, St Robert's Centre, Harrogate.

HORNSEA BIRD CLUB. (1967; 35). John Eldret, 44 Rolston Road, Hornsea, HU18 1UH. 01964 532854.
Meetings: 7.30pm, 3rd Friday of the month (Sep-Mar), Hornsea Library.

HUDDERSFIELD BIRDWATCHERS' CLUB. (1966; 80). David Butterfield, 15 Dene Road, Skelmanthorpe, Huddersfield, HD8 9BU. 01484 862006; e-mail: dbutt52@hotmail.com
www.HuddersfieldBirdwatchersClub@groups.msn.com
Meetings: 7.30pm, Tuesdays, fortnightly, Children's Library (section), Huddersfield Library and Art Gallery, Princess Alexandra Walk, Huddersfield.

HULL VALLEY WILDLIFE GROUP. (1997; 175). The Secretary, Roy Lyon, 650 Hotham Road South, Hull HU5 5LE.
www.hvwg.co.uk

LEEDS BIRDWATCHERS' CLUB. (1949; 60). Mrs Shirley Carson, 2 Woodhall Park Gardens, Stanningley, Pudsey, W Yorks, LS28 7XQ. 0113 255 2145; e-mail: shirley.carson@care4free.net
Meetings: 7.15pm Monday fortnightly, Quaker Meeting House, Wordhouse Lane, Leeds.

NEW SWILLINGTON INGS BIRD GROUP. (1989; 30). Nick Smith, 40 Holmsley Lane, Woodlesford, Leeds, LS26 8RN. 0113 282 6154.
Meetings: 7.30pm, 1st Thursday of even months, Two Pointers Inn, Woodlesford, Leeds.

PUDSEY ORNITHOLOGY CLUB. (1989; 23). Alan Patchett, 102 Half Mile Lane, Leeds, LS13 1DB. 0113 2299038.

ROTHERHAM & DISTRICT ORNITHOLOGICAL SOCIETY. (1974; 90). Malcolm Taylor, 18 Maple Place, Chapeltown, Sheffield, S35 1QW. 0114 246 1848. http://members.lycos.co.uk/RDOS
www.rotherhambirds.co.uk
Meetings: 7.30pm, 2nd Friday of the month.

SCALBY NABS ORNITHOLOGICAL GROUP. (1993; 15). R.N.Hopper (Membership Secretary), 10A Ramshill Road, Scarborough, N Yorkshire, YO11 2QE. 01723 369537.
www.scarborough-birding.org.uk

SHEFFIELD BIRD STUDY GROUP. (1972; 160). Matthew Capper, 1 Birchinlee Cottage, Bamford Mill, The Hollow, Bamford, Hope Valley, S33 0AU. 01433 650815;
e-mail: matthew-capper@capper.freeserve.co.uk
Meetings: 7.15pm, 2nd Wednesday of the month (Sep-Jun), Lecture Theatre 5, Sheffield University Arts Tower.

SK58 BIRDERS. (1993; 60). Andy Hirst, 15 Hunters Drive, Dinnington, Sheffield, S25 2TG. 01909 560310;
e-mail: sk58birders@sk58.freeserve.co.uk
www.sk58.freeserve.co.uk
Chair: Mick Clay, 2 High St, S.Anston, Sheffield. 01909 566000.
Meetings: 7.30pm, last Wednesday of the month (except Aug), Upstairs Room, Loyal Trooper pub, South Anston.

SORBY NHS (ORNITHOLOGICAL SECTION). (1918; 40). Mr R Butterfield, General Secretary, 159 Bell Hagg Road, Sheffield S6 5DA.
e-mail: secretary@sorby.org.uk
www.sorby.org.uk

SOUTH PEAK RAPTOR STUDY GROUP. (1998; 12). M E Taylor, 76 Hawksley Avenue, Newbold, Chesterfield, Derbys, S40 4TL. 01246 277749.

WAKEFIELD NATURALISTS' SOCIETY. (1851; 40). Philip Harrison, 392 Dewsbury Road, Wakefield, W Yorks, WF2 9DS. 01924 373604.
Meetings: 7.30pm, 2nd Tuesday of the month (Sep-Apr), Friends Meeting House, Thornhill Street, Wakefield.

YORK ORNITHOLOGICAL CLUB. (1967; 80). Ian Traynor, The Owl House, 137 Osbaldwick Lane, York, YO10 3AY. e-mail: info@yorkbirding.org.uk
www.yorkbirding.org.uk
Meetings: 7.30pm, 1st Tuesday of the month, Friends' Meeting House, Friargate, York (see website).

YORKSHIRE NATURALISTS' UNION (Ornithological Section). (1940; 500). W F Curtis, Farm Cottage, Atwick, Driffield, YO25 8DH. 01964 532477. www.ynu.org.uk

Ringing Groups

BARNSLEY RG. M C Wells, 715 Manchester Road, Stocksbridge, Sheffield, S36 1DQ. 0114 288 4211.

DONCASTER RG. D Hazard, 41 Jossey Lane, Scawthorpe, Doncaster, S Yorks, DN5 9DB. 01302 788044; e-mail: davehazard@btopenworld.com

EAST DALES RG. S P Worwood, 18 Coltsgate Hill, Ripon, N Yorks, HG4 2AB.

EAST YORKS RG. Peter J Dunn, 43 West Garth Gardens, Cayton, Scarborough, N Yorks, YO11

3SF. 01723 583149; e-mail: pjd@fbog.co.uk

SORBY-BRECK RG. Geoff P Mawson, Moonpenny Farm, Farwater Lane, Dronfield, Sheffield, S18 1RA. 01246 415097; e-mail: gpmawson@hotmail.com

SOUTH CLEVELAND RG. W Norman, 2 Station Cottages, Grosmont, Whitby, N Yorks, YO22 5PB. 01947 895226; e-mail: wilfgros@lineone.net

SPURN BIRD OBSERVATORY. I D Walker, 31 Walton Park, Pannal, Harrogate, N Yorks, HG3 1EJ. 01423 879408.

TEES RG. E Wood, Southfields, 16 Marton Moor Road, Nunthorpe, Middlesbrough, Cleveland, TS7 0BH. 01642 323563; e-mail; redshank@ntlworld.co.uk

WINTERSETT RG. P Smith, 16 Templar Street, Wakefield, W Yorks, WF1 5HB. 01924 375082.

RSPB Local Groups
AIREDALE AND BRADFORD. (1972; 3,500 in catchement area). RSPB North West Regional Office, Westleigh Mews, Wakefield Road, Denby Dale HD8 8QD. 01484 861148.
www.communigate.co.uk/brad/rspbairedalebradfordlocalgroup/index.phtml
Meetings: 7.30pm, monthly on Fridays, Room 3, Shipley Library.

CLEVELAND. (1974; 200). Mark Stokeld, 38 Ash Grove, Kirklevington, Cleveland, TS15 9NQ. 01642 783819; e-mail: mark@stokeld.demon.co.uk www.stokeld.demon.co.uk

CRAVEN & PENDLE. (1986; 250). Ian Cresswell, Dove House, Skyreholme, Skipton, N Yorks, BD23 6DE. 01756 720355; e-mail: ian@cravenandpendlerspb.org www.cravenandpendlerspb.org

DONCASTER. (1984; 100). Sue Clifton, West Lodge, Wadworth Hall Lane, Wadworth, Doncaster, DN11 9BH. Tel/fax 01302 854956; e-mail: sue@westlodge53.freeserve.co.uk
Meetings: 7.30pm 2nd Wednesday of the month (Sept-Apr), contact Sue Clifton for venue.

EAST YORKSHIRE. (1986;110). Trevor Malkin, 49 Taylors Field, Driffield, E Yorks, YO25 6FQ. 01377 257325.
www.eymg.freeserve.co.uk

HUDDERSFIELD & HALIFAX. (1981; 200). David Hemingway, 267 Long Lane, Dalton, Huddersfield, HD5 9SH. 01484 301920; e-mail: d.hemingway@ntlworld.com

HULL & DISTRICT. (1983; 334). Derek Spencer, The Old Brewhouse, Main Road, Burton Pidsea, Hull, HU12 9AX. 01964 670024.

LEEDS. (1974; 450). Linda Jenkinson, 112 Eden Crescent, Burley, Leeds, LS4 2TR. 0113 230 4595 www.rspb-leeds.ndo.co.uk
Meetings: 7.30pm, 3rd Wednesday of the month (Sep-Apr), Lecture Theatre B, School of Mechanical Engineering, University of Leeds.

SHEFFIELD. (1981; 500). John Badger, 24 Athersley Gardens, Owlthorpe, Sheffield, S20 6RW. 0114 247 6622; www.rspb-sheffield.org.uk
Meetings: 7.30pm 1st Thursday of the month (Sept-May), Central United Reformed Church, Norfolk St, Sheffield.

WAKEFIELD. (1987; 150). Paul Disken, 6 Northfield Road, Dewsbury, W Yorks, WF13 2JX. 01924 456352.
Meetings: 7.30pm, 4th Thursday of the month (Sep-Apr), Ossett War Memorial community Centre, Prospect Road, Ossett.

WHITBY. (1977; 120). Fred Payne, 16 Hermitage Way, Sleights, Whitby, N Yorks, YO22 5HG. 01947 810022.

YORK. (1973; 600). Chris Lloyd, 7 School Lane, Upper Poppleton, York, YO26 6JS. 01904 794865; e-mail: chris.a.lloyd@care4free.net
www.yorkrspb.org.uk
Meetings: 7.30pm, Tues, Wed or Thurs, Temple Hall, York St John College, Lord Mayors Walk, York.

Wildlife Hospital
ANIMAL HOUSE WILDLIFE WELFARE. Mrs C Buckroyd, 14 Victoria Street, Scarborough, YO12 7SS. 01723 371256; shop 01723 375162.
All species of wild birds. Oiled birds given treatment before forwarding to cleaning stations. Incubators, hospital cages, heat pads, release sites. Birds ringed before release. Prior telephone call requested. Collection if required. Veterinary support. Charity shop at 127 Victoria Road.

Wildlife Trusts
TEES VALLEY WILDLIFE TRUST. (1979; 4,000). Bellamy Pavilion, Kirkleatham Old Hall, Kirkleatham, Redcar, Cleveland, TS10 5NW. 01642 759900; fax 01642 480401; e-mail: teesvalleywt@cix.co.uk
www.wildlifetrust.org.uk/teesvalley

SHEFFIELD WILDLIFE TRUST. (1985; 250). 37 Stafford Road, Sheffield, S2 2SF. 0114 263 4335; fax 0114 263 4345; e-mail: sheffieldwt@cix.co.uk

YORKSHIRE WILDLIFE TRUST. (1946; 8,000). 10 Toft Green, York, YO1 6JT. 01904 659570; fax 01904 613467; e-mail: yorkshirewt@cix.co.uk
www.yorkshire-wildlife-trust.org.uk

SCOTLAND

For this section we are following the arrangement of the Scottish recording areas as set out by the Scottish Ornithologists' Club.

Bird Report
See Scottish Ornithologists' Club in National Directory

Club
See Scottish Ornithologists' Club in National Directory.

ANGUS & DUNDEE

Bird Recorder
ANGUS & DUNDEE. Dan A Carmichael, 2a Reres Road, Broughty Ferry, Dundee, DD5 2QA. 01382 779981; e-mail: dan@carmichael2a.fsworld.co.uk

Bird Report
ANGUS & DUNDEE BIRD REPORT (1974-), from Secretary, SOC Tayside Branch.

BTO Regional Representatives & Regional Development Officer
ANGUS RR & RDO. Ken Slater, Braedownie Farmhouse, Glen Clova, Kirriemuir, Angus, DD8 4RD. 01575 550233.

Clubs
ANGUS & DUNDEE BIRD CLUB. (1997; 183). Bob McCurley, 22 Kinnordy Terrace, Dundee,DD4 7NW. 01382 462944; e-mail: redcastle@onetel.com
www.angusbirding.homestead.com
Meetings: 7.30pm, Tuesdays, Montrose Basin Wildlife Centre.

SOC TAYSIDE BRANCH. (145). James Whitelaw, 36 Burn Street, Dundee, DD3 0LB. 01382 819391

Ringing Group
TAY RG. Ms S Millar, Edenvale Cottage, 1 Lydox Cottages, Dairsie, Fife, KY15 4RN.

RSPB Members' Groups
DUNDEE. (1972;110). Ron Downing, 3 Lynnewood Place, Dundee, DD4 7HB. 01382 451987.

Wetland Bird Survey Organisers
ANGUS INLAND (Excluding Montrose Basin). Graham Christer, The Ivy, 8 West Hemming Street, Letham, Forfar, Angus DD8 2PU.

MONTROSE BASIN. The Warden, SWT, Montrose Basin Wildlife Centre, Rossie Braes, Montrose, DD10 9JT. 01674 676336;
e-mail montrosebasin@swt.org.uk

ARGYLL

Bird Recorder
ARGYLL. Paul Daw, Tigh-na-Tulloch, Tullochgorm, Minard, Argyll, PA32 8YQ. 01546 886260;
e-mail: monedula@globalnet.co.uk

Bird Reports
ARGYLL BIRD REPORT (1984-), from Dr Bob Furness, The Cnoc, Tarbet, Dunbartonshire G83 7DG. 01301 702603;
e-mail: r.furness@bio.gla.ac.uk

MACHRIHANISH SEABIRD OBSERVATORY REPORT (1992-), from Observatory, see Reserves & Observatories.

SANDA ISLAND BIRD REPORT (2002-), from Iain Livingstone, 57 Strathview Road, Bellshill, Lanarkshire ML4 2UY.

BTO Regional Representatives
ARGYLL (MULL, COLL, TIREE AND MORVERN). Sue Dewar, 01680 812594;
e-mail: sue@wingsovermull.fsnet.co.uk

ARGYLL MAINLAND, BUTE, GIGHA AND ARRAN. Position vacant.

ISLAY, JURA, COLONSAY RR. Dr Malcolm Ogilvie, Glencairn, Bruichladdich, Isle of Islay, PA49 7UN. 01496 850218;
e-mail: maogilvie@indaal.demon.co.uk

Club
ARGYLL BIRD CLUB. (1983; 152). Sue Furness, The Cnoc, Tarbet, Argyll, G83 7OG. 01301 702603;
www.argyllbirdclub.org

ISLE OF MULL BIRD CLUB. (2001;142), Len White, Ard Dochas, Lochdon, Isle of Mull, Argyll PA64 6AP.01680 812335;
e-mail: arddochas@aol.com
www.mullbirds.com
Meetings: 7.30pm, Craignure Village Hall.

Ringing Group
TRESHNISH AUK RG. S W Walker, Snipe Cottage, Hamsterley, Bishop Auckland, Co Durham, DL13 3NX.
e-mail: snipe@snipe.screaming.net

HELENSBURGH. (1975; 62). Steve Chadwin, 01436 831241.

SCOTLAND

AYRSHIRE

Bird Recorder
AYRSHIRE. Angus Hogg, 11 Kirkmichael Road, Crosshill, Maybole, Ayrshire, KA19 7RJ.
e-mail: recorder@ayrshire-birding.org.uk

Bird Reports
AYRSHIRE BIRD REPORT (1976-), from Recorder or Dr RG Vernon, 29 Knoll Park, Ayr KA7 4RH.

BTO Regional Representatives
AYRSHIRE RR. Brian Broadley, 01290 424241;
e-mail: maggie_broadley@hotmail.com

Club
SOC AYRSHIRE. (1962; 145). Henry Martin, 9 Shawfield Avenue, Ayr, KA7 4RE. 01292 442086; www.ayrshire-birding.org.uk
Meetings: 7.30pm, 2nd Wednesday of most months, in the Refectory, SAC Auchincruive by Ayr.

RSPB Members' Groups
CENTRAL AYRSHIRE. (1978; 50). James Thomson, Sundrum Smithy, Ayr, KA6 6LR. 01292 570351.
Meeting: 7.30pm, last Wednesday of the month (Sep-May), Carnegie Library in Ayr.

NORTH AYRSHIRE. (1976; 180). Duncan Watt, 28 Greenbank, Dalry, Ayrshire, KA24 5AY. www.narspb.org.uk
Meetings: 7.30pm, various Fridays (Aug-Apr), Ardrossan Civic Centre, open to all. Full list available.

Wetland Bird Survey Organiser
Mr David Grant, 16 Thorn Avenue, Coylton, Ayr KA6 6NL. (H) 01292 570491;
e-mail: d.grant@au.sac.as.uk

Wildlife Hospital
HESSILHEAD WILDLIFE RESCUE CENTRE. Gay & Andy Christie, Gateside, Beith, Ayrshire, KA15 1HT. 01505 502415;
e-mail: info@hessilhead.org.uk
www.hessilhead.org.uk
All species. Releasing aviaries. Veterinary support. Visits only on open days please.

BORDERS

Bird Atlas/Avifauna
The Breeding Birds of South-east Scotland, a tetrad atlas 1988-1994 by R D Murray et al. (Scottish Ornithologists' Club, 1998).

Bird Recorder
Ray Murray, 4 Bellfield Crescent, Eddleston, Peebles, EH45 8RQ. 01721 730677;
e-mail: ray.d.murray@ukgateway.net

Bird Report
BORDERS BIRD REPORT (1979-), from Malcolm Ross, The Tubs, Dingleton Road, Melrose, Borders TD6 9QP.

BTO Regional Representative & Regional Development Officer
RR. Alex Copland, 01353 509 51676 (work);
e-mail: crex@eircom.net

Club
SOC BORDERS BRANCH. (90). Vicky McLellan, 18 Glen Crescent, Peebles, EH45 9BS. 01721 724580.

Ringing Group
BORDERS RG. (1991; 10) Dr T W Dougall, 38 Leamington Terrace, Edinburgh, EH10 4JL. Office tel 0131 469 5557; Office fax 0131 469 5599.

RSPB Members' Group
BORDERS. (1995; 94). Jim Stillie, 01750 20660.

CAITHNESS

Bird Recorder
CAITHNESS. Stan Laybourne, Old Schoolhouse, Harpsdale, Halkirk, Caithness, KW12 6UN. 01847 841244; e-mail:stanlaybourne@talk21.com

Bird Reports
CAITHNESS BIRD REPORT (1983-97), from Julian Smith, St John's, Brough, Dunnet, Caithness; e-mail: designsmith@madasafish.com

BTO Regional Representative
CAITHNESS. Hugh Clark, Bellfield, 3 Lindsay Place, Wick, Caithness, KW1 4PF. 01955 605372;
e-mail: hugh@lindsayplace.fsnet.co.uk

Clubs
SOC CAITHNESS BRANCH. (51). Stan Laybourne, Old Schoolhouse, Harpsdale, Halkirk, Caithness, KW12 6UN. 01847 841244;
e-mail:stanlaybourne@talk21.com

CLYDE

Bird Atlas/Avifauna
A Guide to Birdwatching in the Clyde Area (2001) by Cliff Baister and Marin Osler (Scottish Ornithologists' Club, Clyde branch).

Clyde Breeding Bird Atlas. In preparation.

Bird Recorders
CLYDE ISLANDS. Bernard Zonfrillo, 28 Brodie Road, Glasgow, G21 3SB. 0141 557 079i;
e-mail: b.zonfrillo@bio.gla.ac.uk

CLYDE. Iain P Gibson, 8 Kenmure View, Howwood, Johnstone, Renfrewshire, PA9 1DR. 01505 705874;
e-mail: iain.gibson@land.glasgow.gov.uk

Bird Reports
CLYDE BIRDS (1973-), from Jim & Valerie Wilson, 76 Laigh Road, Newton Mearns, Glasgow, G77 5EQ. e-mail: jim.val@btinternet.com

BTO Regional Representatives
ARRAN, BUTE, CUMBRAES. Position vacant.

LANARK, RENFREW, DUMBARTON. Position vacant.

Club
SOC CLYDE BRANCH. (300). Alison Robertson, Flat2/3, 3 Priorwood Court, Glasgow, G13 1GE. 0141 9581747;
e-mail: alison@bogcotton.freeserve.co.uk

Ringing Groups
CLYDE RG. (1979; 18) I Livingstone, 57 Strathview Road, Bellshill, Lanarkshire, ML4 2UY. 01698 749844; e-mail: iainlivcrg@aol.com

RSPB Members' Groups
GLASGOW. (1972; 149). Jim Coyle, 6 Westerlands, Anniesland, Glasgow, G12 0FB. 0141 579 7565; e-mail: j.coyle13@ntlworld.com
Meetings: 7.30pm, 1st Wednesday of the month (Sep-Apr), Woodside Halls or Fotheringay Centre.

HAMILTON. (1976;90). Mr Niall Whyte, Secretary, 12 Balmoral Place, West Mains, East Kilbride G74 1EP. 01355 900099;
e-mail: niall.whyte@blueyonder.co.uk
www.baronshaugh.co.uk
Meetings: 7.30pm, 3rd Thursday of the month, Strathclyde Water Centre, Strathclyde Country Park, Motherwell.

RENFREWSHIRE. (1986; 200). Jim Sutherland, 0141 6397028.

Wetland Bird Survey Organisers
ARGYLL & ISLANDS. Malcolm Ogilvie, Glencairn, Bruichladdich, Isle of Islay, PA49 7UN. 01496 850218; e-mail: maogilvie@indaal.demon.co.uk

ARRAN. Audrey Walters, Sula, Margnaheglish Road, Lamlash, Isle of Arran KA27 8LE.

CLYDE ESTUARY. Jim & Valerie Wilson, 76 Laigh Road, Newton Mearns, Glasgow G77 5EQ. (H) 0141 639 2516; e-mail: Jim.Val@btinternet.com

GLASGOW/RENFREWSHIRE/LANARKSHIRE. Jim & Valerie Wilson, 76 Laigh Road, Newton Mearns, Glasgow G77 5EQ. (H) 0141 639 2516; e-mail: Jim.Val@btinternet.com

DUMFRIES & GALLOWAY

Bird Recorders
Paul N Collin, Gairland, Old Edinburgh Road, Minnigaff, Newton Stewart, Wigtownshire, DG8 6PL. 01671 402861; e-mail: paul.collin@rspb.org.uk

Bird Report
DUMFRIES & GALLOWAY REGION BIRD REPORT (1985-), from Peter Norman, Low Boreland, Tongland Road, Kirkcudbright, DG6 4UU. 01557 331429.

BTO Regional Representatives
DUMFRIES RR. Duncan Irving, 12 Great Eastern Drive, Glencaple, Dumfries DG1 4QZ. 01387 770265; e-mail: DJ.Irving@care4free.net

KIRKCUDBRIGHT RR. Andrew Bielinski, 41 Main Street, St Johns Town of Dalry, Castle Douglas, Kirkcudbright, DG7 3UP. 01644 430418;
e-mail: andrewb@bielinski.fsnet.co.uk

WIGTOWN RR. Geoff Sheppard, The Roddens, Leswalt, Stranraer, Wigtownshire, DG9 0QR. 01776 870 685; e-mail: geoff.sheppard@tesco.net

Clubs
SOC DUMFRIES BRANCH. (1961; 105). Brian Smith, Rockiemount, Colvend, Dalbeattie, Dumfries, DG5 4QW. 01556 620617.
Meetings: 7.30pm, 2nd Wednesday of the month (Sept-Apr), Cumberland St Day Centre.

SOC STEWARTRY BRANCH. (1976; 77). Miss Joan Howie, 60 Main Street, St Johns Town of Dalry, Castle Douglas, Kirkcudbrightshire, DG7 3UW. 01644 430226.
Meetings: 7.30pm, usually 2nd Thursday of the month (Sep-Apr), Kells School, New Galloway.

SOC WEST GALLOWAY BRANCH. (1975; 50). Geoff Sheppard, The Roddens, Leswalt, Stranraer, Wigtownshire, DG9 0QR.
e-mail: geoff.sheppard@tesco.net
Meetings: 7.30pm, 2nd Tuesday of the month (Oct-Mar), Stranraer Library.

Ringing Group
NORTH SOLWAY RG. Geoff Sheppard, The Roddens, Leswalt, Stranraer, Wigtownshire, DG9 0QR. e-mail: geoff.sheppard@tesco.net

RSPB Members' Group
GALLOWAY. (1985; 170). Robert M Greenshields, Nether Linkins, Gelston, Castle Douglas, DG7 1SU. 01556 680217.
Meetings: 7.30pm 3rd Tuesday in the month, Castle Douglas High School.

Wetland Bird Survey Organisers
AUCHENCAIRN. Euan MacAlpine, Auchenshore, Auchencairn, Castle Douglas, Galloway DG7 1QZ.

DUMFRIES & GALLOWAY (OTHER SITES). Steve Cooper, Wildfowl & Wetlands Trust, Eastpark Farm, Caerlaverock, Dumfries DG1 4RS. 01387 770200; e-mail: steve.cooper@wwt.org.uk

LOCH RYAN. Geoff Shepherd, The Roddens, Leswalt, Stranraer, Wigtonshire DG9 0QR.
e-mail: geoff.sheppard@tesco.net

ROUGH FIRTH. Judy Baxter, Saltflats Cottage, Rockcliffe, Dalbeattie, DG5 4QQ. 01556 630262; e-mail: Jbaxter@nts.org.uk

SOLWAY ESTUARY (NORTH). Steve Cooper, Wildfowl & Wetlands Trust, Eastpark Farm, Caerlaverock, Dumfries DG1 4RS. 01387 770200; e-mail: steve.cooper@wwt.org.uk

WIGTOWN. Paul Collin, Gairland, Old Edinburgh Road, Minnigaff, Newton Stewart, DG8 6PL. 01671 402861.

FIFE

Bird Atlas/Avifauna
The Fife Bird Atlas 2003 by Norman Elkins, Jim Reid, Allan Brown, Derek Robertson & Anne-Marie Smout. Available from Allan W. Brown (FOAG), 61 Watts Gardens, Cupar, Fife KY15 4UG, Tel. 01334 656804, email: swans@allanwbrown.co.uk

Bird Recorders
FIFE REGION INC OFFSHORE ISLANDS (NORTH FORTH). David Ogilvie, 25 Fillons Road, Kirkcaldy, Fife KY2 6LT.
e-mail: davidogilvie8@aol.com

ISLE OF MAY BIRD OBSERVATORY. Iain English, 19 Nethan Gate, Hamilton, S Lanarks, ML3 8NH. e-mail: i.english@talk21.com

Bird Reports
FIFE BIRD REPORT (1988-) (FIFE & KINROSS BR 1980-87), from Willie McBay, 41 Shamrock Street, Dunfermline, Fife, KY12 0JQ. 01383 723464; e-mail: wmcbay@aol.com

ISLE OF MAY BIRD OBSERVATORY REPORT (1985-), from David Thorne, Craigurd House, Blyth Bridge, West Linton, Peeblesshire, EH46 7AH.

BTO Regional Representative
FIFE & KINROSS RR. Norman Elkins, 18 Scotstarvit View, Cupar, Fife, KY15 5DX. 01334 654348; e-mail: jandnelkins@rapidial.co.uk

Clubs
FIFE BIRD CLUB. (1985; 250). Willie McBay, 41 Shamrock Street, Dunfermline, Fife, KY12 0JQ. 01383 723464.
Meetings: 7.30pm, (various evenings), Dean Park Hotel, Chapel Level, Kirkcaldy.

LOTHIANS AND FIFE MUTE SWAN STUDY GROUP. (1978) Allan & Lyndesay Brown, 61 Watts Gardens, Cupar, Fife, KY15 4UG.
e-mail: swans@allanwbrown.co.uk
www.swanscot.org.uk

SOC FIFE BRANCH. (1956;170). Fiona Butler, 7 Marionfield Place, Cupar, Fife, KY15 5JN. 01334 654895.

Ringing Groups
ISLE OF MAY BIRD OBSERVATORY. Margaret Thorne, Craigurd House, West Linton, Peebles EH46 7AH. 01721 752612.

TAY RG. Ms S Millar, Edenvale Cottage, 1 Lydox Cottages, Dairsie, Fife, KY15 4RN.

Wetland Bird Survey Organisers
FIFE (excluding estuaries). Allan Brown, 61 Watts Gardens, Cupar, Fife KY15 4UG;
e-mail: swans@allanwbrown.co.uk

EDEN ESTUARY. Les Hatton, Fife Ranger Service, Silverdaleburn House, Largo Road, By Leven, KY8 5PU. (Day) 01333 429785.

TAY ESTUARY. Norman Elkins, 18 Scotstarvit View, Cupar, Fife KY15 5DX. 01334 654348;
e-mail: jandnelkins@rapidial.co.uk

Wildlife Hospital
SCOTTISH SPCA WILD LIFE REHABILITATION CENTRE. Middlebank Farm, Masterton Road, Dunfermline, Fife, KY11 8QN. 01383 412520
All species. Open to visitors, groups and school parties. Illustrated talk on oiled bird cleaning and other aspects of wildlife rehabilitation available. Veterinary support.

FORTH

Bird Recorder
UPPER FORTH (Does not include parts of Stirling in Loch Lomondside/Clyde Basin). Dr C J Henty, Edgehill East, 7b Coneyhill Road, Bridge of Allan, Stirling, FK9 4EL. 01786 832166

Bird Report
FORTH AREA BIRD REPORT (1975-) - enlarged report published annually in *The Forth Naturalist and Historian*, University of Stirling, from Dr Henty (see recorder) or Hon Sec. Lindsay Corbett, University of Stirling, Stirling FK9 4LA. 01259 215091.

BTO Regional Representative
CENTRAL. Neil Bielby, 56 Ochiltree, Dunblane, Perthshire, FK15 0DF. 01786 823830;
e-mail: neil.bielby@tiscali.co.uk

Club
SOC CENTRAL SCOTLAND BRANCH. (1968; 101). Ian Wilson, 100 Causewayhead Road, Stirling, FK9 5HJ. 01786 473877.
Meetings: 7.30pm, 1st Thursday of the month (Sep-Apr), The Smith Art Gallery and Museum, Dumbarton Road, Stirling.

RSPB Members' Group
FORTH VALLEY. (1996; 150). David Redwood, 8 Strathmore Avenue, Dunblane, Perthshire FK15 9HX. 01786 825493; e-mail: d.redwood@tesco.net http://forthrspb.p5.org.uk
Meetings: 7.30pm, 3rd Thursday of the month (Sept-Apr), Cowane Centre, Stirling.

Wetland Bird Survey Organiser
CENTRAL (excl Forth Estuary. Neil Bielby, 56 Ochiltree, Dunblane, Perthshire FK15 0DF. (H) 01786 823830; e-mail: neil.bielby@tiscali.co.uk

HIGHLAND

Bird Atlas/Avifauna
The Birds of Sutherland by Alan Vittery (Colin Baxter Photography Ltd, 1997).
Birds of Skye by Andrew Currie. In preparation.

Bird Recorders
ROSS-SHIRE, INVERNESS-SHIRE, SUTHERLAND. Alastair McNee, Liathach, 4 Balnafettack Place, Inverness IV3 8TQ. 01463 220493; (M) 07763 927814;
e-mail: aj.mcnee@care4free.net

Bird Reports
HIGHLAND BIRD REPORT (1991-), from Recorder. 2003 edition £7.50 including p&p.

BTO Regional Representatives & Regional Development Officers
INVERNESS & SPEYSIDE RR & RDO. Hugh Insley, 1 Drummond Place, Inverness, IV2 4JT. 01463 230652; e-mail: hugh.insley@freeuk.com

RUM, EIGG, CANNA & MUCK RR & RDO. Bob Swann, 14 St Vincent Road, Tain, Ross-shire, IV19 1JR. 01862 894329;
e-mail: bob.swann@freeuk.com

ROSS-SHIRE RR. Simon Cohen (not confirmed at time of going to press)

SUTHERLAND. David Devonport, 01408 641 295; e-mail: d.devonport@btinternet.com

SKYE. Robert McMillan, 01471 866305;
e-mail: Bob@Skye-birds.com

Clubs
EAST SUTHERLAND BIRD GROUP. (1976; 80). Tony Maimwood, 13 Ben Bhraggie Drive, Golspie, Sutherland KW10 6SX. 01408 633247;
e-mail: tony.maimwood@which.net
Meetings: 7.30pm, Last Monday of the month (Oct, Nov, Jan, Feb, Mar), Golspie Community Centre.

SOC HIGHLAND BRANCH. (1955; 151). Janet Crummy, Coalhaugh, Tomatin, Inverness, IV13 7YS. 01808 511261.
Meetings: 7.45pm, 1st Tuesday of the month, Inverness Marriott Hotel.

Ringing Groups
HIGHLAND RG. Bob Swann, 14 St Vincent Road, Tain, Ross-shire, IV19 1JR.
e-mail: bob.swann@freeuk.com

RSPB Members' Group
HIGHLAND. (1987; 198). Richard Prentice, Lingay, Lewiston, Drumnadrochit, Inverness, IV63 6UW. 01456 450526

Wetland Bird Survey Organisers
MORAY BASIN COAST. Bob Swann, 14 St Vincent Road, Tain, Ross-shire IV19 1JR. 01862 894329; e-mail: bob.swann@hcs.uhi.ac.uk

MORAY & NAIRN (Inland). Martin Cook, Rowanbrae, Clochan, Buckie, Banffshire AB56 5EQ. (H) 01542 850296.

SKYE & LOCHALSH. Bob McMillan, 10/11 Elgol, Nr Broadford, Isle of Skye IV49 9BL. 01471 866305; e-mail: bob@skye-birds.com

LOTHIAN

Bird Atlas/Avifauna
The Breeding Birds of South-east Scotland, a tetrad atlas 1988-1994 by R D Murray et al. (Scottish Ornithologists' Club, 1998).

Bird Recorder
David J Kelly, 20 Market View, Tranent, East Lothian, EH32 9AX.
e-mail: dj_kelly@btinternet.com

Bird Reports
LOTHIAN BIRD REPORT (1979-), from Lothian SOC Branch Secretary.

WEST LOTHIAN BIRD CLUB REPORT (1991-), from Secretary, West Lothian Bird Club.

BTO Regional Representative
Alan Heavisides, 9 Addiston Crescent, Balerno, Edinburgh, EH14 7DB. 0131 449 3816;
e-mail: a.heavisides@napier.ac.uk

Clubs
EDINBURGH NATURAL HISTORY SOCIETY. (1869; 200). Miss Joan Fairlie, 14 Regulas Road, Edinburgh EH9 2ND. 0131 6691470.

FOULSHIELS BIRD GROUP. (1991; 5). Frazer Henderson, 2 Elizabeth Gardens, Stoneyburn, W Lothian, EH47 8BP. 01501 762972

LOTHIANS AND FIFE MUTE SWAN STUDY GROUP. (1978; 12) Allan & Lyndesay Brown, 61 Watts Gardens, Cupar, Fife, KY15 4UG.
e-mail: swans@allanwbrown.co.uk

LOTHIAN SOC. (1936; 370). John Hamilton, 30 Swanston Gardens, Edinburgh, EH10 7DL. 0131 445 5317;
e-mail: john.r.hamilton31@btopenworld.com

www.lsoc.btinternet.co.uk
Meetings: 7.30pm, 2nd Tuesday (Sep-Apr, not Dec), Lounge 2, Meadowbank Sports Stadium.

WEST LOTHIAN BIRD CLUB. (1990; 20). Alan Paterson, 17 Main Street, Winchburgh, Broxburn, W Lothian.

Ringing Group
LOTHIAN RG. Mr M Cubitt, 12 Burgh Mills Lane, Linlithgow,West Lothian EH49 7TA.

RSPB Members' Group
EDINBURGH. (1974;480). Hugh Conner, 22 Tippet Knowes Court, Winchburgh,West Lothian, EH52 6UW. e-mail: h.m.conner@blueyonder.co.uk
http://rspb-edin.pwp.blueyonder.co.uk
Meetings: 7.30pm, 3rd Tuesday or Wednesday of the month (Sep-Apr), Napier University, Merchiston Campus, Colinton Road, Edinburgh.

Wetland Bird Survey Organisers
FORTH ESTUARY (North). Alastair Inglis, 5 Crowhill Road, Dalgety Bay, Fife KY11 5LJ.

FORTH ESTUARY (Outer South). Duncan Priddle, c/o City of Edinburgh Countryside Ranger Service, Hermitage House, 69a Braid Road, Edinburgh EH10 6JF. (Day) 0131 4477145;
e-mail: duncan@cecrangerservice.demon.uk

LOTHIAN (excl estuaries). Joan Wilcox, 18 Howdenhall Gardens, Edinburgh, Midlothian EH16 6UN. (H) 0131 6648893

TYNINGHAME ESTUARY. John Muir Country Park, Town House, Dunbar, East Lothian EH42 1ER. (W) 01368 863886;
e-mail: randerson@eastlothian.gov.uk

MORAY & NAIRN

Bird Atlas/Avifauna *The Birds of Moray and Nairn* by Martin Cook (Mercat Press, 1992).

Bird Recorder
NAIRN. Martin J H Cook, Rowanbrae, Clochan, Buckie, Banffshire, AB56 5EQ. 01542 850296;
e-mail: martin.cook9@virgin.net

MORAY. Martin J H Cook, Rowanbrae, Clochan, Buckie, Banffshire, AB56 5EQ. 01542 850296;
e-mail: martin.cook9@virgin.net

Bird Reports
BIRDS IN MORAY AND NAIRN (1999-), from Moray Recorder, 01542 850296;
e-mail: martin.cook9@virgin.net

MORAY & NAIRN BIRD REPORT (1985-1998), from Moray Recorder, 01542 850296;
e-mail: martin.cook9@virgin.net

BTO Regional Representatives
NAIRN RR. Bob Proctor, 78 Marleon Field, Elgin, Moray, IV30 4GE. 01343 548395;
e-mail: bob.proctor@rspb.org.uk

MORAY RR. Bob Proctor, 78 Marleon Field, Elgin, Moray, IV30 4GE. 01343 548395;
e-mail: bob.proctor@rspb.org.uk

Wetland Bird Survey Organisers
LOSSIE ESTUARY. Bob Proctor, 78 Marleon Field, Silvercrest, Bishopmill, Elgin, IV30 4GE;
e-mail: bob.proctor@rspb.org.uk

MORAY & NAIRN (Inland). Martin Cook, Rowanbrae, Clochan, Buckie, Banffshire, AB56 5EQ. 01542 850296.

NORTH EAST SCOTLAND

Bird Atlas/Avifauna
The Birds of North East Scotland by S T Buckland, M V Bell & N Picozzi (North East Scotland Bird Club, 1990).

Bird Recorder
NORTH-EAST SCOTLAND. Andrew Thorpe, 30 Monearn Gardens, Milltimber, Aberdeen, AB13 0EA. e-mail: andrewthorpe4@aol.com

Bird Reports
NORTH-EAST SCOTLAND BIRD REPORT (1974-), from Dave Gill, Drakemyre Croft, Cairnorrie, Methlick, Aberdeenshire, AB41 7JN. 01651 806252;
e-mail: dave@drakemyre.freeserve.co.uk

BTO Regional Representatives & Regional Development Officer
ABERDEEN RDO, Kath Hamper, 9 Mid Street, Inverallochy, Fraserburgh, Aberdeenshire, AB43 8YA. 01346 583015.

ABERDEEN. John Littlejohn,
e-mail: j.w.littlejohn@talk21.com

KINCARDINE & DEESIDE. Graham Cooper, Westbank, Beltie Road, Torphins, Banchory, Aberdeen, AB31 4JT. H:01339 882706

Clubs
SOC GRAMPIAN BRANCH. (1956; 110). John Wills, Bilbo, Monymusk, Inverurie, Aberdeenshire, AB51 7HA. 01467 651296;
e-mail: bilbo@monymusk.freeserve.co.uk
Meetings: 7.30pm, 1st or 2nd Monday of the month (Sep-Apr), Sportsman's Club, 11 Queens Road, Aberdeen.

Ringing Groups
ABERDEEN UNIVERSITY RG. Andrew Thorpe, Ocean Laboratory and Centre for Ecology, Aberdeen University, Newburgh, Ellon, Aberdeenshire, AB41 6AA.
e-mail: a.thorpe@abdn.ac.uk

GRAMPIAN RG. R Duncan, 86 Broadfold Drive, Bridge of Don, Aberdeen, AB23 8PP. e-mail: Raymond@waxwing.fsnet.co.uk

RSPB Members' Group
ABERDEEN. (1975; 190). Dr MJ Williams, 48 Oakhill Road, Aberdeen, AB15 5ES. 01224 208046.
Meetings: 7.30pm, 2nd Tuesday of the month, Lecture Theatre, Zoology Dept, Tillydrone Av, Aberdeen.

Wildlife Hospital
GRAMPIAN WILDLIFE REHABILITATION TRUST. 40 High Street, New Deer, Turriff, Aberdeenshire, AB53 6SX. 01771 644489 Veterinary surgeon. Access to full practice facilities. Will care for all species of birds.

ORKNEY

Bird Atlas/Avifauna
The Birds of Orkney by CJ Booth et al (The Orkney Press, 1984).

Bird Recorder
Mr EJ Williams, Fairholm, Finstown, Orkney, KW17 2EQ. 01856 761317; e-mail: jim@geniefea.freeserve.co.uk

Bird Report
ORKNEY BIRD REPORT (inc North Ronaldsay Bird Report) (1974-), from Mr EJ Williams, Fairholm, Finstown, Orkney, KW17 2EQ. e-mail: jim@geniefea.freeserve.co.uk

BTO Regional Representative & Regional Development Officer
Colin Corse, Garrisdale, Lynn Park, Kirkwall, Orkney, KW15 1SL. H:01856 874484; W:01856 884156; e-mail: ccorse@garrisdale1.fstnet.co.uk

Club
SOC ORKNEY BRANCH. (1993; 15). Stuart Williams, Crafty, Firth, Orkney, KW17 2ES. e-mail: stuart@gavia.freeserve.co.uk

Ringing Groups
NORTH RONALDSAY BIRD OBSERVATORY. Ms A E Duncan, Twingness, North Ronaldsay, Orkney, KW17 2BE.
e-mail: alison@nrbo.prestel.co.uk
www.nrbo.f2s.com

ORKNEY RG. Colin J Corse, Garrisdale, Lynn Park, Kirkwall, Orkney, KW15 1SL. H:01856 874484; W:01856 884156;
e-mail: ccorse@garrisdale1.fstnet.co.uk

SULE SKERRY RG. Dave Budworth, 121 Wood Lane, Newhall, Swadlincote, Derbys, DE11 0LX. 0121 6953384.

RSPB Members' Group
ORKNEY. (1985; 300 in catchment area). Neil McCance, West End, Burray, Orkney. 01856 731260.
Meetings: Meetings advertised in newsletter and local press, held at Kirkwall Community Centre.

Wetland Bird Survey Organiser
ORKNEY (other sites). Eric Meek, RSPB, 12/14 North End Road, Stromness, Orkney KW16 3AG. 01856 850176.

OUTER HEBRIDES

Bird Recorder
OUTER HEBRIDES AND WESTERN ISLES. Andrew Stevenson, andrew@bornish.fsnet.co.uk

Bird Report
OUTER HEBRIDES BIRD REPORT (1989-), from Recorder.

BTO Regional Representatives & Regional Development Officer
BENBECULA & THE UISTS RR & RDO. 01876 580328; e-mail: brian.rabbitts@virgin.net

LEWIS & HARRIS RR. 1. Tony Pendle, 3 Linsiadar, Isle of Lewis, HS2 9DR. 01851 621311;
e-mail: ellerpendle@madasafish.com

LEWIS & HARRIS RR. 2. Chris Reynolds, 11 Reef, Isle of Lewis, HS2 9HU. 01851 672376;
e-mail: juliareynolds@btinternet.com

Ringing Group
SHIANTS AUK RG. David Steventon, Welland House, 207 Hurdsfield Road, Macclesfield, Cheshire, SK10 2PX. 01625 421936

UISTS AND BENBECULA. Brian Rabbitts, 01876 580328; e-mail: brian.rabbits@virgin.net

PERTH & KINROSS

Bird Recorder
PERTH & KINROSS. Ron Youngman, Blairchroisk Cottage, Ballinluig, Pitlochry, Perthshire, PH9 0NE. 01796 482324; e-mail: blairchroisk@aol.com

Bird Report
PERTH & KINROSS BIRD REPORT (1974-), from Recorder.

BTO Regional Representatives & Regional Development Officer
PERTHSHIRE RR. Position vacant.

Clubs
PERTHSHIRE SOCIETY OF NATURAL SCIENCE (Ornithological Section). (1964; 52). Miss Esther Taylor, 23 Verena Terrace, Perth,PH2 0BZ. 01738 621986.

Meetings: 7.30pm, Wednesdays (Oct-Mar), Perth Museum.

RSPB Members' Groups
TAYSIDE. (1988; 160). Alan Davis, 6 Grey Street, Perth, PH2 0JJ. 01738 622480

Wetland Bird Survey Organiser
TAY ESTUARY. Norman Elkins, 18 Scotstarvit View, Cupar, Fife KY15 5DX. 01334 654348; e-mail: jandnelkins@rapidial.co.uk

SHETLAND

Bird Recorders
FAIR ISLE. Deryk Shaw, Bird Observatory, Fair Isle, Shetland, ZE2 9JU.
e-mail: fairisle.birdobs@zetnet.co.uk

SHETLAND. Micky Maher, Hamarsgarth, Haroldswick, Shetland, ZE2 9ED. (01595) 711677 or 711528; e-mail:recorder@birdclub.shetland.co.uk

Bird Reports
FAIR ISLE BIRD OBSERVATORY REPORT (1949-), from Scottish Ornithologists' Club, Harbour Point, Newhailes Road, Musselburgh EH21 6SJ. 0131 653 0653.

SHETLAND BIRD REPORT (1969-) no pre-1973 available, from Martin Heubeck, East House, Sumburgh Lighthouse, Virkie, Shetland, ZE3 9JN; e-mail: martinheubeck@btinternet.com

BTO Regional Representative
RR and RDO. Dave Okill, Heilinabretta, Cauldhame, Trondra, Shetland, ZE1 0XL. 01595 880450.

Club
SHETLAND BIRD CLUB. (1973; 200). Reinoud Norde, Lindale, Ireland, Bigton, Shetland, ZE2 9JA. 01950 422467:
e-mail: reinoud.norde@lineone.net

Ringing Groups
FAIR ISLE BIRD OBSERVATORY. Deryk Shaw, Bird Observatory, Fair Isle, Shetland, ZE2 9JU.
e-mail: fairisle.birdobs@zetnet.co.uk

SHETLAND RG. Dave Okill, Heilinabretta, Cauldhame, Trondra, Shetland, ZE1 0XL. H:01595 880450; W:01595 696926

Wetland Bird Survey Organiser
Paul Harvey, Shetland Biological Records Centre, Shetland Amenity Trust, 22-24 North Road, Lerwick, Shetland, ZE1 3NG. (Day) 01595 694688; e-mail: sbrc@zetnet.co.uk

WALES

Bird Report
See Welsh Ornithological Society in National Directory

BTO Honorary Wales Officer
BTO WALES OFFICER. John Lloyd, Cynghordy, Llandovery, SA20 0LN.
e-mail: thelloyds@dial.pipex.com

Club
See Welsh Ornithological Society in National Directory.

EAST WALES

Bird Atlas/Avifauna
Birds of Radnorshire. In preparation, due spring 2005.

The Gwent Atlas of Breeding Birds by Tyler, Lewis, Venables & Walton (Gwent Ornithological Society, 1987).

Bird Recorders
BRECONSHIRE. Martin F Peers, Cyffylog, 2 Aberyscir Road, Cradoc, Brecon, Powys, LD3 9PB. 01874 623774.

GWENT. Chris Jones, 22 Walnut Drive, Caerleon, Newport, Gwent, NP6 1SB. 01633 423439;
e-mail: countyrecorder@gwentbirds.org.uk

MONTGOMERYSHIRE. Brayton Holt, Scops Cottage, Pentrebeirdd, Welshpool, Powys, SY21 9DL. 01938 500266.

RADNORSHIRE. Pete Jennings, Penbont House, Elan Valley, Rhayader, Powys, LD6 5HS. H:01597 811522; W:01597 810880;
e-mail: petejelanvalley@hotmail.com

Bird Reports
BRECONSHIRE BIRDS (1962-), from Brecknock Wildlife Trust.

GWENT BIRD REPORT (1964-), from Jerry Lewis, Y Bwthyn Gwyn, Coldbrook, Abergavenny, Monmouthshire, NP7 9TD. (H) 01873 855091; (W) 01633 644856

MONTGOMERYSHIRE BIRD REPORT (1981-82), from Montgomeryshire Wildlife Trust.

RADNOR BIRDS (1987/92-), from Radnorshire Recorder.

BTO Regional Representatives
BRECKNOCK RR. John Lloyd, Cynghordy, Llandovery, Carms, SA20 0LN.
e-mail; thelloyds@dial.pipex.com

GWENT RR. Jerry Lewis, Y Bwthyn Gwyn, Coldbrook, Abergavenny, Monmouthshire, NP7 9TD. (H) 01873 855091; (W) 01633 644856

MONTGOMERY RR. Jane Kelsall, Holly Bank, Moel-y-Garth, Welshpool, Powys SY21 9JA. 01938 556438; e-mail: jane@melodeons.com

RADNORSHIRE RR. Position vacant.

Clubs
GWENT ORNITHOLOGICAL SOCIETY. (1964; 350). T J Russell, The Pines, Highfield Road, Monmouth, Gwent, NP25 3HR. 01600 716266.
Meetings: 7.30pm, alternate Saturdays (Sept-Apr), Goytre Village Hall.

MONTGOMERYSHIRE FIELD SOCIETY. (1946; 190). Maureen Preen, Ivy House, Deep Cutting, Pool Quay, Welshpool, Powys, SY21 9LJ. Tel: Mary Oliver, 01686 413518.
Meetings: 3rd Saturday of the month (Nov, Jan, Feb, Mar), Methodist Church Hall, Welshpool. Field trips (Apr-Oct).

MONTGOMERYSHIRE WILDLIFE TRUST BIRD GROUP. (1997; 110). A M Puzey, Four Seasons, Arddleen, Llanymynech, Powys, SY22 6RU. 01938 590578.

RADNOR BIRD GROUP. (1986; 60). Pete Jennings, Penbont House, Elan Valley, Rhayader, Powys, LD6 5HS. 01597 811522;
e-mail: petejelanvalley@hotmail.com

Ringing Groups
GOLDCLIFF RG. Vaughan Thomas, Gilgal Cottage, Gilfach, Llanvaches, S Wales, NP26 3AZ. 01633 817161.

LLANGORSE RG. Jerry Lewis, Y Bwthyn Gwyn, Coldbrook, Abergavenny, Monmouthshire, NP7 9TD. H:01873 855091; W:01633 644856

Wetland Bird Survey Organisers
RADNORSHIRE. Peter Jennings, Pentbont House, Elan Valley, Rhayader, Powys, LD6 5HS. (H) 01597 811522; (Day) 01597 810880.

BRECONSHIRE. Andrew King, Heddfan, Pennorth, Brecon LD3 7EX;
e-mail: heddfan25@hotmail.com

Wildlife Trusts
BRECKNOCK WILDLIFE TRUST. (1963; 893). Lion House, Bethel Square, Brecon, Powys, LD3 7AY. 01874 625 708; fax 01874 625 708;
e-mail: brecknockwt@cix.co.uk
www.wildlifetrust.org.uk/brecknock

GWENT WILDLIFE TRUST. (1963; 1,200). 16 White Swan Court, Church Street, Monmouth, Gwent, NP25 3NY. 01600 715501; fax 01600 715832;
e-mail: gwentwildlife@cix.co.uk
www.wildlifetrust.org.uk/gwent

MONTGOMERYSHIRE WILDLIFE TRUST. (1982; 1000). Collot House, 20 Severn Street, Welshpool, Powys, SY21 7AD. 01938 555654; fax 01938 556161; e-mail: montwt@cix.co.uk
www.wildlifetrust.org.uk/montgomeryshire

RADNORSHIRE WILDLIFE TRUST. (1987; 789). Warwick House, High Street, Llandrindod Wells, Powys, LD1 6AG. 01597 823298; fax 01597 823274; e-mail: radnorshirewt@cix.co.uk
www.waleswildlife.co.uk

NORTH WALES

Bird Atlas/Avifauna
The Birds of Caernarfonshire by John Barnes (1998, from Lionel Pilling, 51 Brighton Close, Rhyl LL18 3HL).

Bird Recorders
ANGLESEY. Stephen Culley, Millhouse, Penmynydd Road, Menai Bridge, Anglesey, LL59 5RT; e-mail: SteCul10@aol.com

CAERNARFON. John Barnes, Fach Goch, Waunfawr, Caernarfon, LL55 4YS. 01286 650362.

DENBIGHSHIRE & FLINTSHIRE. Norman Hallas, 63 Park Avenue, Wrexham,LL12 7AW. Tel/fax 01978 290522; e-mail: normanhallas@aol.com

MEIRIONNYDD. D L Smith, 3 Smithfield Lane, Dolgellau, Gwynedd, LL40 1BU. 01341 421064;
e-mail: d.smith@ccw.gov.uk

Bird Reports
BARDSEY BIRD OBSERVATORY ANNUAL REPORT, from Warden, see Reserves.

CAMBRIAN BIRD REPORT (sometime Gwynedd Bird Report) (1953-), from Mr Rhion Pritchard, Pant Afonig, Hafod Lane, Bangor, Gwynedd, LL57 4BU; e-mail: rhion@pritchardr.freeserve.co.uk

CLWYD BIRD REPORT (2002-), from Dr Anne Brenchley, Ty'r Fawnog, 43 Black Brook, Sychdyn, Mold, Flints, CH7 6LT. 01352 750118.

MEIRIONNYDD BIRD REPORT Published in Cambrian Bird Report (above).

WREXHAM BIRDWATCHERS' SOCIETY ANNUAL REPORT (1982-), from Secretary, Wrexham Birdwatchers' Society.

BTO Regional Representatives & Regional Development Officer
ANGLESEY RR. Tony White, 01407 710137; e-mail: wylfor@greg5360.freeserve.co.uk

CAERNARFON RR. John Barnes, Fach Goch, Waunfawr, Caernarfon, LL55 4YS. 01286 650362.

CLWYD EAST RR. Anne Brenchley, Ty'r Fawnog, 43 Black Brook, Sychdyn, Mold, CH7 6LT. e-mail: anne.brenchley@cbrg1.idps.co.uk

CLWYD WEST RR. Mel ab Owain, 31 Coed Bedw, Abergele, Conwy, LL22 7EH. 01745 826528; e-mail: melabowain@cix.co.uk

MEIRIONNYDD RR. Peter Haveland, Ty Manceinion, Penmachno, Betws-y-Coed, Sir Gonwy, LL24 0UD. e-mail: peter.haveland@tesco.net

Clubs
BANGOR BIRD GROUP. (1947; 100). Secretary, Bangor Bird Group, 12 St Helens Street, Caernarfon, Gwynedd LL55 2HU. e-mail: n.brown@bangor.ac.uk

CAMBRIAN ORNITHOLOGICAL SOCIETY. (1952; 190). Mr Rhion Pritchard, Pant Afonig, Hafod Lane, Bangor, Gwynedd, LL57 4BU. 01248 671301; http://mysite.freeserve.com/cambrianos **Meetings:** 7.30pm, 1st Friday of the month, Pensychnant Centre, Sychnant Pass.

CLWYD BIRD RECORDING GROUP. Anne Brenchley, Ty'r Fawnog, 43 Black Brook, Sychdyn, Mold, CH7 6LT. e-mail: anne.brenchley@cbrg1.idps.co.uk

CLWYD ORNITHOLOGICAL SOCIETY. (1956; 45). EE Jones, Sandiway, Llanasa, Holywell, Flintshire, CH8 9NE. 01745 852984.

DEE ESTUARY CONSERVATION GROUP. (1973; 25 grps). N J Friswell, 8 Oaklands Crescent, Tattenhall, Chester, CH3 9QT. 01829 770463.

DEESIDE NATURALISTS' SOCIETY. (1973; 500). Secretary, 38 Kelsterton Road, Connah's Quay, Flintshire CH5 4BJ; e-mail: richard@deeestuary.co.uk www.deeestuary.co.uk/dns/index.htm

WREXHAM BIRDWATCHERS' SOCIETY. (1974; 90). Miss Marian Williams, 10 Lake View, Gresford, Wrexham, Clwyd, LL12 8PU. 01978 854633. **Meetings:** 7.30pm, 1st Friday of the month (Sep-Apr), Gresford Memorial Hall, Gresford.

Ringing Groups
BARDSEY BIRD OBSERVATORY. Steven Stansfield, Bardsey Island, off Aberdaron, Pwllheli, Gwynedd, LL53 8DE. 07855 204151; e-mail: warden@bbfo.org.uk

MERSEYSIDE RG. P Slater, 45 Greenway Road, Speke, Liverpool, L24 7RY.

SCAN RG. D J Stanyard, Court Farm, Groeslon, Caernarfon, Gwynedd, LL54 7UE. 01286 881 669.

RSPB Local Group
NORTH WALES. (1986; 130). Paul Braid, 01492 516260; e-mail: p.braid@virgin.net

Wetland Bird Survey Organisers
CONWY ESTUARY. Alan Davies, RSPB Conwy Reserve, Llandudno Junction, LL31 9XZ. 01492 584091: e-mail: alan.davies@rspb.org.uk

ANGLESEY (other sites). Ian Sims, Plas Nico, South Stack, Holyhead, LL65 1TH.

CAERNARFONSHIRE (excl Traeth Lafan). Rhion Pritchard, Pant Afonig, Hafod Lane, Bangor, Gwynedd LL57 4BU. (H) 01248 671301; e-mail: RhionPritchard@gwynedd.gov.uk

CLWYD (Coastal). Mr Peter Wellington, 4 Cheltenham Avenue, Rhyl, Clwyd LL18 4DN. (H) 01745 354232.

MERIONETH (other sites). Mr Trefor Owen, Crochendy Twrog, Maentwrog, Blaenau Ffestiniog, LL41 3YU. (H) 01766 590302.

TRAETH LAFAN. Mr Rhion Pritchard, Pant Afonig, Hafod Lane, Bangor, Gwynedd LL57 4BU. (Day) 01286 679462; e-mail: RhionPritchard@gwynedd.gov.uk

Wildlife Trust
NORTH WALES WILDLIFE TRUST. (1963; 2,400). 376 High Street, Bangor, Gwynedd, LL57 1YE. 01248 35154; fax 01248 353192; e-mail: nwwt@cix.co.uk www.wildlifetrust.org.uk/northwales

SOUTH WALES

Bird Atlas/Avifauna
An Atlas of Breeding Birds in West Glamorgan by David M Hanford et al (Gower Ornithological Society, 1992).

Birds of Glamorgan by Clive Hurford and Peter Lansdown (Published by the authors, c/o National Museum of Wales, Cardiff, 1995)

Bird Recorders
GLAMORGAN (EAST). Steve Moon, 36 Rest Bay Close, Porthcawl, Bridgend, CF36 3UN. e-mail: moonsj@bridgend.gov.uk

GOWER (WEST GLAMORGAN). Robert Taylor, 285 Llangyfelach Road, Brynhyfryd, Swansea, SA5 9LB. 01792 464780; (mobile) 07970 567007.

Bird Reports
EAST GLAMORGAN BIRD REPORT (title varies 1963-95) 1996-2003, from Richard G Smith, 35 Manor Chase, Gwaun Miskin, Pontypridd, Rhondda Cynon Taff, S Wales CF38 2JD. e-mail: rgsmith@birdpix.freeserve.co.uk

GOWER BIRDS (1965-), from Audrey Jones, 24 Hazel Road, Uplands, Swansea, SA2 0LX. 01792 298859.

BTO Regional Representatives & Regional Development Officer
EAST GLAMORGAN (former Mid & South Glam) RR. Rob Nottage, 32 Village Farm, Bonvilston, Cardiff, CF5 6TY.
e-mail: rob@nottages.freeserve.co.uk

WEST RR. Bob Howells, Ynys Enlli, 14 Dolgoy Close, West Cross, Swansea, SA3 5LT.
e-mail: bobhowells31@hotmail.com

Clubs
CARDIFF NATURALISTS' SOCIETY. (1867; 225). Stephen R Howe, Department of Geology, National Museum of Wales, Cardiff, CF10 3NP.
e-mail: steve.howe@nmgw.ac.uk
Meetings: 7.30pm, various evenings, Lecture Theatre EO.02, Llandaff Campus Unic, Western Avenue, Cardiff.

GLAMORGAN BIRD CLUB. (1990; 300+). Steve Moon, Kenfig National Nature Reserve, Ton Kenfig, Pyle, Bridgend, CF33 4PT.
e-mail: moonsj@bridgend.gov.uk
Meetings: 8pm, winter months, Kenfig Reserve Centre.

GOWER ORNITHOLOGICAL SOCIETY. (1956; 120). Audrey Jones, 24 Hazel Road, Uplands, Swansea, SA2 0LX. 01792 298859.
www.glamorganbirds.org.uk
Meetings: 7.15pm, 4th Friday of the month (Sep-Mar), Enviroment Centre, Swansea.

Ringing Groups
FLAT HOLM RG. Brian Bailey, Tamarisk House, Wards Court, Frampton-on-Severn, Glos, GL2 7DY. e-mail: brian@sandbservices.fsnet.co.uk

KENFIG RG. Mr D.G. Carrington, 25 Bryneglwys Gardens, Porthcawl, Bridgend, Mid Glamorgan, CF36 5PR.

RSPB Local Groups
CARDIFF & DISTRICT. (1973). Joy Lyman, 5 Dros-Y-Morfa, Rumney, Cardiff, CF3 3BL. 029 2077 0031.
Meetings: 7.30pm, various Fridays (Sept-May), UWIC, Cynoed Road, Cardiff.

WEST GLAMORGAN. (1985; 346). Maggie Cornelius, 01792 229244.
www.westglam-rspb.org.uk

Wetland Bird Survey Organisers
WEST GLAMORGAN. Bob Howells, Ynys Enlli, 14 Dolgoy Close, West Cross, Swansea, SA3 5LT. (H) 01792 405363;
e-mail: bobhowells31@hotmail.com

EAST GLAMORGAN. Rob Nottage, 32 Village Farm, Bonvilston, Cardiff, CF5 6TY;
e-mail: rob@nottages.freeserve.co.uk

SEVERN ESTUARY. Niall Burton, c/o The BTO, The Nunnery, Thetford, Norfolk IP27 2PU. 01842 750050; e-mail: niall.burton@bto.org

Wildlife Hospitals
GOWER BIRD HOSPITAL. Karen Kingsnorth and Simon Allen, Valetta, Sandy Lane, Pennard, Swansea, SA3 2EW. 01792 371630;
e-mail: info@gowerbirdhospital.org.uk
All species of wild birds, also hedgehogs and small mammals. Prior phone call essential. Gower Bird Hospital cares for sick, injured and orphaned wild birds and animals with the sole intention of returning them to the wild. Post release radio tracking projects, ringing scheme. Contact us for more information.

LLEWELLYN, Paul. 104 Manselfield Road, Murton, Swansea, SA3 3AG.
e-mail: p.j.llewellyn@swansea.ac.uk
All species of birds but specialist knowledge of raptors. Veterinary support.

Wildlife Trust
WILDLIFE TRUST OF SOUTH AND WEST WALES. (1961; 1300). Fountain Road, Tondu, Bridgend, CF32 0EH. 01656 724100; fax 01656 729880; e-mail: glamorganwt@cix.co.uk

WEST WALES

Bird Atlas/Avifauna
Birds of Pembrokeshire by Jack Donovan and Graham Rees (Dyfed Wildlife Trust, 1994).

Bird Recorders
CARMARTHENSHIRE. Tony Forster, Ffosddu, Salem, Llandeilo, Carmarthenshire, SA19 7NS. 01558 824237; e-mail: tony-forster@supanet.com

CEREDIGION. Hywel Roderick, 32 Prospect Street, Aberystwyth, Ceredigion, SY23 1JJ.
e-mail: hywel@adar.freeserve.co.uk

PEMBROKESHIRE. 1. Jack Donovan MBE, The Burren, 5 Dingle Lane, Crundale, Haverfordwest, Pembrokeshire, SA62 4DJ. 01437 762673.

2. Graham Rees, 22 Priory Avenue, Haverfordwest, Pembrokeshire, SA61 1SQ. 01437 762877.

Bird Reports
CARMARTHENSHIRE BIRD REPORT (1982-), from Carmarthenshire Recorder.

CEREDIGION BIRD REPORT (biennial 1982-87; annual 1988-), from Wildlife Trust West Wales.

PEMBROKESHIRE BIRD REPORT (1981-), from TJ Price, 2 Wordsworth Ave, Haverfordwest, Pembrokeshire, SA61 1SN.

BTO Regional Representatives & Regional Development Officer
CARDIGAN RR. Moira Convery, 41 Danycoed, Aberystwyth, SY23 2HD.
e-mail: moira@mconvery.freeserve.co.uk

CARMARTHEN RR. Colin Jones, 01554 821632;
e-mail: trosserch2:aol.com

PEMBROKE RR. Annie and Bob Haycock, 1 Rushmoor, Martletwy, Pembrokeshire, SA67 8BB.

Clubs
CARMARTHENSHIRE BIRD CLUB.(2003; 69). Ian Hainsworth, 23 Rhyd y Defaid Drive, Swansea, SA2 8AJ. 01792 205693;
e-mail: ian.hains@ntlworld.com
www.carmarthenshirebirds.co.uk

LLANELLI NATURALISTS. (1971; 100). Richard Pryce, Trevethin, School Road, Pwll, Llanelli, Carmarthenshire, SA15 4AL.
e-mail: pryceeco@aol.com
Meetings: 1st Thursday of the month, YWCA Llanelli (see programme in local libraries).

PEMBROKESHIRE BIRD GROUP. (1993; 60). T J Price, 2 Wordsworth Ave, Haverfordwest, Pembs, SA61 1SN. 01437 779667.
Meetings: 7.30pm, 2nd Monday of the month (Oct-Apr), The Patch, Furzy Park, Haverfordwest.

Ringing Group
PEMBROKESHIRE RG. J Hayes, 3 Wades Close, Holyland Road, Pembroke, SA71 4BN. 01646 687036.

Wetland Bird Survey Organiser
BURRY INLET (North). Graham Rutt, 13 St James Gardens, Uplands, Swansea, A1 6DY. (Day) 01792 325603.

DYFI/DYSYNNI ESTUARIES. Dick Squires, Cae'r Berllan, Eglwys-Fach, Machynlleth, SY20 8TA. 01654 781265;
e-mail: dick.squires@rspb.org.uk

CARDIGAN (excl Dyfi Estuary). Dick Squires, Cae'r Berllan, Eglwys-Fach, Machynlleth, SY20 8TA. 01654 781265;
e-mail: dick.squires@rspb.org.uk

Wildlife Hospitals
NEW QUAY BIRD HOSPITAL. Jean Bryant, Penfoel, Cross Inn, Llandysul, Ceredigion, SA44 6NR. 01545 560462.
All species of birds. Fully equipped for cleansing oiled seabirds. Veterinary support.

WEST WILLIAMSTON OILED BIRD CENTRE. Mrs J Hains, Lower House Farm, West Williamston, Kilgetty, Pembs, SA68 0TL. 01646 651236. Facilities for holding up to 200 Guillemots, etc. for short periods. Initial treatment is given prior to despatch to other washing centres during very large oil spills; otherwise birds are washed at the Centre with intensive care and rehabilitation facilities. Also other species. Veterinary support.

Wildlife Trust
WILDLIFE TRUST OF SOUTH AND WEST WALES. (1938; 3100). Welsh Wildlife Centre, Cilgerran, Cardigan, SA43 2TB.
e-mail: june@wildlife-wales.org.uk
www.wildlife-wales.org.uk

CHANNEL ISLANDS

Ringing Group
The Channel Islands ringing scheme is run by the Société Jersiaise.

ALDERNEY

Bird Recorder
Mark Atkinson, No 4, Ferndale Estate, Newtown, Alderney, BY9 3YR. 01481 823286.

Bird Report
ALDERNEY SOCIETY ORNITHOLOGY REPORT (1992-), from Recorder.

BTO Regional Representative
Jamie Hooper, 1 Trinity Cottages, Torteval, Guernsey, GY8 0QD. Tel/fax 01481 266924;
e-mail: jamie.hooper@cwgsy.net

Wildlife Trust
ALDERNEY WILDLIFE TRUST
Wildlife Tourism Information Centre, Victoria Street, St Anne, Alderney GY9 3AA. 01481 822935; (Fax) 01481 822935;
e-mail: info@alderneywildlife.org
www.alderneywildlife.org

GUERNSEY

Bird Atlas/Avifauna
Birds of the Bailiwick of Guernsey (working title). In preparation.

Bird Recorder
Mark Lawlor, Pentland, 15 Clos des Pecqueries, La Passee, St Sampson's, Guernsey, GY2 4TU. 01481 258168. e-mail: mplawlor@cwgsy.net

Bird Report
REPORT & TRANSACTIONS OF LA SOCIETE GUERNESIAISE (1882-), from Recorder.

BTO Regional Representative
Jamie Hooper, 1 Trinity Cottages, Torteval, Guernsey, GY8 0QD. Tel/fax 01481 266924; e-mail: jamie.hooper@cwgsy.net

Clubs
LA SOCIÉTIÉ GUERNESIAISE (Ornithological Section). (1882; 30). Vic Froome, La Cloture, Coutil de Bas Lane, St Sampsons, Guernsey, GY2 4XJ. 01481 254841. www.societe.org.gg

RSPB Local Group
GUERNSEY. (1975; 350+). Michael Bairds, Les Quatre Vents, La Passee, St Sampsons, Guernsey, GY2 4TS. 01481 255524;
e-mail: mikebairds@cwgsy.net
www.rspbguernsey.co.uk

Wetland Bird Survey Organiser
GUERNSEY COAST. Wayne Turner, Rooster's View, Rue de La Boullerie, St Andrews, Guernsey, GY6 8XQ. 01481 239832;
e-mail: roosters@cwgsy.net

Wildlife Hospital
GUERNSEY. GSPCA ANIMAL SHELTER. Mrs Jayne Le Cras, Rue des Truchots, Les Fiers Moutons, St Andrews, Guernsey, Channel Islands, GY6 8UD. 01481 257261;
e-mail: jaynelecras@gspca.org.gg. All species. Modern cleansing unit for oiled seabirds. 24-hour emergency service. Veterinary support.

JERSEY

Bird Recorder
Tony Paintin, 16 Quennevais Gardens, St Brelade, Jersey, Channel Islands, JE3 8FQ. 01534 741928; e-mail: cavokjersey@hotmail.com

Bird Report
JERSEY BIRD REPORT, from Secretary (Publications), Société Jersiaise.

BTO Regional Representative
Tony Paintin, 16 Quennevais Gardens, St Brelade, Jersey, Channel Islands, JE3 8FQ. 01534 741928; e-mail: cavokjersey@hotmail.com

Club
SOCIÉTIÉ JERSIAISE (Ornithological Section). (1948; 40). Roger Noel, 7 Pier Road, St Helier, Jersey, JE2 4XW. 01534 758314.
www.societe-jersiaise.org
Meetings: 8.00pm, alternate Thursdays throughout the year, Museum in St.Helier.

Wildlife Hospital
JERSEY. JSPCA ANIMALS' SHELTER. Pru Bannier, 89 St Saviour's Road, St Helier, Jersey, JE2 4GJ. 01534 724331; fax 01534 871797; e-mail: info@jspca.org.je. All species. Expert outside support for owls and raptors. Oiled seabird unit. Veterinary surgeon on site. Educational Centre.

ISLE OF MAN

Bird Atlas/Avifauna
Manx Bird Atlas. Five-year BBS and Winter Atlas research completed. Publication in preparation. Contact: Chris Sharpe (see below, BTO)

Bird Recorder
Dr Pat Cullen, Troutbeck, Cronkbourne, Braddan, Isle of Man, IM4 4QA. Home: 01624 623308; Work 01624 676774; e-mail: bridgeen@mcb.net

Bird Reports
MANX BIRD REPORT (1947-), published in *Peregrine*. From G D Craine, 8 Kissack Road, Castletown, Isle of Man, IM9 1NP;
e-mail: g.craine@advsys.co.uk

CALF OF MAN BIRD OBSERVATORY ANNUAL REPORT, from Secretary, Manx National Heritage, Manx Museum, Douglas, Isle of Man, IM1 3LY.

BTO Regional Representative & Regional Development Officer
RR. Dr Pat Cullen, as above, 01624 623308

RDO. Chris Sharpe, 33 Mines Road, Laxey, Isle of Man, IM4 7NH. 01624 861130;
e-mail: chris@manxbirdatlas.org.uk

Club
MANX ORNITHOLOGICAL SOCIETY. (1967; 150). Mrs A C Kaye, Cronk Ny Ollee, Glen Chass, Port St Mary, Isle of Man, IM9 5PL. 01624 834015

Ringing Group
CALF OF MAN BIRD OBSERVATORY. Tim Bagworth, Calf of Man, c/o Kionsleau, Plantation Road, Port St Mary, Isle of Man, IM9 5AY. Mobile 07624 462858

MANX RINGING GROUP. Chris Sharpe, 33 Mines Road, Laxey, Isle of Man, IM4 7NH. 01624 861130; e-mail: chris@manxbirdatlas.org.uk

Wetland Bird Survey Organiser
Pat Cullen, Troutbeck, Cronkbourne, Braddan, Isle of Man, IM4 4QA. (H) 01624 623308; (W) 01624 676774; e-mail: bridgeen@mcb.net

Wildlife Trust
MANX WILDLIFE TRUST. (1973; 900). The Courtyard, Tynwald Mills, St Johns, Isle of Man IM4 3AE. 01624 801985; (fax) 01624 801022; e-mail: manxwt@cix.co.uk
www.wildlifetrust.org.uk/manxwt/

NORTHERN IRELAND

Bird Recorder
George Gordon, 2 Brooklyn Avenue, Bangor, Co Down, BT20 5RB. 028 9145 5763; e-mail: gordon@ballyholme2.freeserve.co.uk

Bird Reports
NORTHERN IRELAND BIRD REPORT, from Secretary, Northern Ireland, Birdwatchers' Association (see National Directory).

IRISH BIRD REPORT, Included in Irish Birds, BirdWatch Ireland in National Directory.

COPELAND BIRD OBSERVATORY REPORT, from see Reserves.

BTO Regional Representatives
ANTRIM & BELFAST. Position vacant.

ARMAGH. David W A Knight, 20 Mandeville Drive, Tandragee, Craigavon, Co Armagh, BT62 2DQ. 01762 840658 or 028 38 840658; e-mail: david.knight@waterni.gov.uk

DOWN. Position vacant.

LONDONDERRY. Charles Stewart, Bravallen, 18 Duncrun Road, Bellarena, Limavady, Co Londonderry, BT49 0JD. 028 77 750468.

TYRONE SOUTH & FERMANAGH. Position vacant.

TYRONE NORTH. Mary Mooney, 20 Leckpatrick Road, Ballymagorry, Strabane, Co Tyrone, BT82 0AL. 028 7188 2442; e-mail: memooney@foxlodge.healthnet.co.uk

Clubs
NORTHERN IRELAND BIRDWATCHERS' ASSOCIATION See National Directory.

NORTHERN IRELAND ORNITHOLOGISTS' CLUB See National Directory.

CASTLE ESPIE BIRDWATCHING CLUB. (1995; 60). Dot Blakely, 8 Rosemary Park, Bangor, Co Down, BT20 3EX. 028 9145 0784

Ringing Groups
ANTRIM & ARDS RG. M McNeely, 35 Balleyvalley Heights, Banbridge, Co Down, BT32 4AQ.028 406 29823

COPELAND BIRD OBSERVATORY. C W Acheson, 28 Church Avenue, Dunmurry, Belfast, BT17 9RS.

NORTH DOWN RINGING GROUP. Hugh Thurgate, 16 Inishmore, Killyleagh, Downpatrick, Co Down, BT30 9TP.

RSPB Local Groups
ANTRIM. (1977; 23). Brenda Campbell, 028 9332 3657.

BANGOR. (1973; 25). Northern Ireland RSPB Headquarters, Belvoir Park Forest, Belfast, BT8 4QT. 028 9049 1547.

BELFAST. (1970; 130). Northern Ireland RSPB Headquarters, Belvoir Park Forest, Belfast, BT8 4QT. 028 9049 1547.

COLERAINE. (1978; 45). Peter Robinson, 34 Blackthorn Court, Coleraine, Co Londonderry, BT52 2EX. 028 7034 4361; (mob)0780 3529472; e-mail: peter-g@pgrobinson.freeserve.co.uk
Meetings: 7.30pm, third Monday of the month (Sept-Apr), Alliance Youth Works, Atillery Road, Coleraine.

FERMANAGH. (1977; 28). Doreen Morrison, 91 Derrin Road, Cornagrade, Enniskillen, Co Fermanagh, BT74 6BA. 028 6632 6654
Meetings: 7.30pm, 4th Tuesday of the month, St Macartans Church Hall.

LARNE. (1974; 35). Jimmy Christie, 314 Coast Road, Ballygally, Co Antrim, BT40 2QZ. 028 2858 3223.
Meetings: 7.30pm, 1st Wednesday of the month, Larne Library Members Room.

LISBURN. (1978; 30). David McCreedy, 10 Downside Avenue, Banbridge, Co Down, BT32 4BP. 028 4062 6125.

Wetland Bird Survey Organisers
ANTRIM, BELFAST LOUGH. John O'Boyle, Environment & Heritage Service, Commonwealth House, 35 Castle Street, Belfast BT1 1GU. 028 9054 6521; e-mail: john.oboyle@doeni.gov.uk

ANTRIM, LOUGHS NEAGH & BEG. Steve Foster, Peatlands Park, 33 Derryhubbert Road, Verner's Bridge, Dungannon BT71 6NW. (W)028 3832 2398; e-mail: Stephen.foster@doeni.gov.uk

ARMAGH, LOUGHS NEAGH & BEG. Steve Foster, Peatlands Park, 33 Derryhubbert Road, Verner's Bridge, Dungannon, BT71 6NW. (W)028 3832 2398; e-mail: Stephen.foster@doeni.gov.uk

DOWN, BELFAST LOUGH. John O'Boyle, Environment & Heritage Service, Commonwealth House, 35 Castle Street, Belfast BT1 1GU. 028 9054 6521; e-mail: john.oboyle@doeni.gov.uk

DOWN, CARLINGFORD LOUGH. Frank Carroll, 292 Barcroft Park, Newry, Co. Down BT35 8ET. (H) 01693 68015

DOWN, LOUGHS NEAGH & BEG. Steve Foster, Peatlands Park, 33 Derryhubbert Road, Verner's Bridge, Dungannon, BT71 6NW. (W)028 3832 2398; e-mail: Stephen.foster@doeni.gov.uk

DOWN, OUTER ARDS. Neil McCulloch, Environment & Heritage Service, Commonwealth House, 35 Castle Street, Belfast BT1 1GU. 01232 251477; e-mail: neil.mcCulloch@doeni.gov.uk

DOWN, STRANGFORD LOUGH. Paddy Mackie, Mahee island, Comber, Newtonards, Co. Down, BT23 6EP. (Tel/fax)028 9754 1420.

FERMANAGH. Neil McCulloch, Environment & Heritage Service, Commonwealth House, 35 Castle Street, Belfast BT1 1GU. 01232 251477; e-mail: neil.mcCulloch@doeni.gov.uk

LONDONDERRY, BANN ESTUARY. Hill Dick, 33 Hopefield Avenue, Portrush, Co. Antrim BT56 8HB.

LONDONDERRY, LOUGHS NEAGH & BEG. Steve Foster, Peatlands Park, 33 Derryhubbert Road, Verner's Bridge, Dungannon, BT71 6NW. (W)028 3832 2398; e-mail: Stephen.foster@doeni.gov.uk

TYRONE, LOUGHS NEAGH & BEG. Steve Foster, Peatlands Park, 33 Derryhubbert Road, Verner's Bridge, Dungannon, BT71 6NW. (W) 028 3832 2398; e-mail: Stephen.foster@doeni.gov.uk

Wildlife Hospital

TACT WILDLIFE CENTRE. Mrs Patricia Nevines, 2 Crumlin Road, Crumlin, Co Antrim, BT29 4AD. Tel/fax 028 944 22900; e-mail: t.a.c.t@care4free.net. All categories of birds treated and rehabilitated; released where practicable, otherwise given a home. Visitors (inc. school groups and organisations) welcome by prior arrangement. Veterinary support.

Wildlife Trust

ULSTER WILDLIFE TRUST. (1978; 2,100). 3 New Line, Crossgar, Co Down, BT30 9EP. 028 4483 0282; fax 028 4483 0888; e-mail: info@ulsterwildlifetrust.org www.ulsterwildlifetrust.org

REPUBLIC OF IRELAND

Bird Recorders

1. Oran O'Sullivan, BirdWatch Ireland, Ruttledge House, 8 Longford Place, Monkstown, Co Dublin. +353 (0) 1 2804322; fax +353 (0) 1 2844407; e-mail: bird@indigo.ie

2. Rarities. Paul Milne, 100 Dublin Road, Sutton, Dublin 13, +353 (0)1 8325653; e-mail: paul.milne@oceanfree.net

Bird Reports

IRISH BIRD REPORT, Warden, BirdWatch Ireland (see National Directory).

CAPE CLEAR BIRD OBSERVATORY ANNUAL REPORT,

CORK BIRD REPORT (1963-71; 1976-), Included in Irish Birds.

EAST COAST BIRD REPORT (1980-), Contact BirdWatch Ireland.

BirdWatch Ireland Branches

Branches may be contacted in writing via BirdWatch Ireland HQ.

Ringing Groups

CAPE CLEAR BIRD OBSERVATORY. S Wing, 30 Irsher Street, Appledore, Devon, EX39 1RZ.

GREAT SALTEE RS. O J Merne, 20 Cuala Road, Bray, Co Wicklow,

MUNSTER RG. K P Collins, Ballygambon, Lisronagh, Clonmel, Co Tipperary. e-mail: kevcoll@indigo.ie

SHANNON WADER RG. P A Brennan, The Crag, Stonehall, Newmarket-on-Fergus, Co Clare,

ARTICLES IN BIRD REPORTS

Angus and Dundee Bird Report 2003
Garden ringing success by Allen Hall
Swifts in Forfar since 1978 by Lawson Grant
Visible migration at Barry by Clive Mackay
Laughing Gull - Angus and Dundee 2nd record by Alan J Leitch

Argyll Bird Report Vol 18 (for 2001)
Snowy Egret a Balvicar; The first British record by Bill Jackson
Arctic Redpoll *carduelis hornemanni* on Islay, 22 September 2001 - the first Argyll record by Tristan ap Rheinallt
Breeding of Red-throated Divers *Gavia Stellata* on Islay in 2002 by Aubrey and Edith Collin
Increasing numbers of Greylag and Canada Geese breeding in mainland sea lochs by JCA Craik

Avon Bird Report
Kumlien's Gulls in Avon by KE Vinicombe
Caspian Gull at Harnhill tip, Elberton by JP Martin
The very earliest local bird recorders by RL Bland
Avon Breeding Birds Survey 2002 by J Tully
Avon Ringing Report 2002 by LF Roberts
A century ago by HE Rose

Ayrshire Birds and Butterflies 2003
Lady Isle by Dave Grant
Kestrel in Ayrshire 2003 by Gordon Riddle
Sparrowhawk breeding details 2003 by Ian Todd
Recent rarities in Ayrshire by Angus Hogg
Ayrshire butterfly report 2003 by Nicola Macintyre

Borders Bird Report no 21 2001-2
SOC bird records spreadsheet
Ringing in Scottish Borders 2001 and 2002
The first successful breeding of Red-necked Grebe for Britain

Breconshire Birds 2003
The decline of the Lapwing in Breconshire by Martin Peers
Llangorse Lake ringing report by Jerry Lewis and Bob Haycock

Buckinghamshire Bird Report 2002
The Red-rumped Swallow at Furzton Lake - a first for Buckinghamshire by Simon Nichols
The Cattle Egret at Hughenden - a first for Buckinghamshire by Warren Claydon

Cambrian Bird Report 2003
The Black Lark at South Stack

Cambridgeshire Bird Report 2002
Arable to wetland - restoring habitat for birds in the Cambridgeshire Fens by James Cadbury
Yellow Wagtail survey in Cambridgeshire in 2002 by Bill Jordan
The Hanson-RSPB wetland project - an update by Jon Haw and Andy Roberts
The status of breeding birds in Cambridgeshire from the Breeding Bird Survey 1994-2002 by Louise Bacon

Carmarthenshire Bird Report 2002
Ravens in Carmarthenshire by Andrew Dixon
The birds of the Cynnant Valley 1982-2002 by John Lloyd

Ceredigion Bird Report 2002
Passage of the Leach's Petrel and Little Gull off Aberaeron on 6th February 2002 by Arfon Williams
Dyfi Lapwing research by Roy Bamford

Cheshire and Wirral Bird Report 2002
Black Grouse release scheme in Eastern Cheshire by S Blamire
Avocets breeding - a first for Cheshire by D Platt
Breeding Water Rail survey of the Dee Estuary by CE Wells
An estimate of the number of Red Grouse in Cheshire by JV Oxenham
The Witton limebeds by P Hill
Database statistics by S Blamire

Clwyd Bird Report 2002
All Wales Common Scoter survey by Dr S Whitehead CCW
Ring Ouzels at World's End by Paul Kenyon
Our bit of the River Clwyd by Louise and Elvet Jones
An expanding Tree Sparrow colony by John Hickerton
Weather report for 2002 by Len Walks
Yellowhammer report for Clwyd by Dr Anne Brenchley

Devon Bird Report
Little Egret - first reported Devon breeding record by Barrie Whitehall
Bird movements in the Exe Estuary and marshes Feb 2002 by Donald Campbell
Shearwater feeding frenzy off north-west Devon 2002 by Mark Darleston
What ever happened to the Elegant Tern? By John Forty and Bob Normand
Little Ringed Plover - first Devon breeding record by Sara McMahon
Looking back on the 1952 and 1977 reports by Peter Goodfellow
The BTO Breeding Bird Survey (BBS) Devon results 2002 by John Woodland

Essex Bird Report 2002
Seasonal summary of 2002 records by Andy Goodey
County records 2002 by Andy Goodey and Howard Vaughan
Earliest and latest dates of summer and winter visitors by Howard Vaughan
Wildfowl count tables by Howard Vaughan
Rarity descriptions by various authors
Rainham Marshes RSPB reserve 2002 by Dominic Funnell
Old Hall Marshes RSPB reserve 2002 by Chris Tyas
Bradwell Bird Observatory 2002 by Nick Green

Fair Isle Bird Observatory Report 2003
Investigations into disease states and causes of death of birds on Fair Isle by Jason Weine
Dispersal and arrival of Arctic Skuas by Sarah Davis
Variations in Bonxie ecology across Shetland by Steve Votier
Has anyone seen 100 species in a day in Fair Isle? by Roy Dennis
Weather statistics by Dave Wheeler
Earliest and latest migrants by Alan Bull
Rarity descriptions by Deryk Shaw
Changes to the Fair Isle list by Deryk Shaw

Glamorgan Bird Report no 41, 2002
Weather summary by Alan Rosney
Observations on Swallow migration 2002
Kenfig ringing report by David G Carrington
Glamorgan ringing report by Peter M Howlett
Flat Holm gull counts by Brian Bailey
Action plans for birds (and for people) by Rob Nottage
The identification of the 'Kenfig Skua' by Paul Bristow
Butterfly and moth summaries by Barry Stewart and David Gilmore

ARTICLES IN BIRD REPORTS

Gower Birds 2003
The distribution of Little Egret in the Burry Inlet by Barry Stewart
Ivory Gull in Swansea Bay, 29th November-5th December 2002 by RJ Howells
A brown Skua in Glamorgan (*Catharacta Antarctica)* by Steve Moon and David Carrington

Hampshire Bird Report 2002
Hampshire ringing report 2001 by DA Bell
Current bird surveys in Hampshire by GC Evans
Solent waterbird population changes 1986/87 - 2000/1 by DJ Unsworth
Survey of breeding birds along the Hampshire section of the Basingstoke Canal 2002 by GJS Rowland
Stilt Sandpiper - a new species for Hampshire by Dr RB Wynn
Avocet - first breeding record for Hampshire in 2002 by T Carpenter
Savi's Warblers breeding in Hampshire - a historical perspective by B Duffin
Breeding Goshawk in Hampshire - a first? By W Percy, A Page and A Lucas

Highland Bird Report 2003
The status of Magpies in Highland by Dave Butterfield
Highland ringing group report by Bob Swann
The Storm Petrel colonies at Eilean Hoan and Priest Island by Hugh Insley, Steph Elliot and Kenny L Graham

The Isle of Wight Bird Report 2002
The wetland bird survey 2001/2 by JM Cheverton
Seeing 200 species in a year in the Isle of Wight by DJ Hunnybun
Local rarity - Red-backed Shrike at Culver Down by KB Gillamm
Status of Nuthatch in the Isle of Wight by DJ Hunnybun

Jersey Bird Report 2003
The Stonechat in Jersey by M Handschuh

Kent Bird Report 2001
Canvasback in Kent - new to Britain and Ireland by Paul Larkin and Dave Mercer
Rock Pipit survey 2001 by Ian Hodgson
Firecrest survey 2001 by Andrew Henderson

Lancashire Bird Report 2002
Lapwing survey of Lancashire 2002-3 by SJ White
Distribution and population size of urban House Sparrows in North Merseyside 2001-2 by SJ White

Leicestershire and Rutland Bird Report 2003
Red-rumped Swallow - new to the county list by Andy Mackay
Little Egrets in Leicestershire and Rutland by Rob Fray
Great Grey Shrikes in Leicestershire and Rutland by Rob Fray
Leicestershire and Rutland records review by Rob Fray
Leicestershire and Rutland ringing report by Nigel Judson

London Bird Report 2000
Honey Buzzard influx autumn 2000 by Andrew Self
Status of various geese in London 2000 by Helen Baker
Bird counts in Kensington gardens by R Sanderson
Birds of Rainham Marsh Part IV by Mike Dennis
Breeding bird survey in London 2000 by DA Coleman
Ringing report by 2000 by R Taylor

Birds in Moray and Nairn 2002
Mute Swan breeding in Moray and Nairn in 2002 by Bob Proctor
Changes in summer migrant arrival dates by Martin Cook

Montgomershire Bird Report 1998-1999
Montgomery Canal Mute Swan survey by Roger Matthews
Fluctuations in bird populations by Brayton Holt
Lapwing and Curlew breeding actively in Montgomery by Alwyn Hughes
Windows over a salt marsh by J Marshall

Norfolk Bird Report 2002
Wetland bird surveys
Norfolk bird atlas
Systematic list
Introductions, escapes, ferals and hybrids
Earliest and latest dates for summer migrants
Latest and earliest dates for winter migrants
Non-accepted and non-submitted records
Ringing report
A history and celebration of 50 years of the Norfolk Bird Report
The Marsh Harrier in Norfolk
The History and development of Sheringham Bird Observatory
Pallid Harrier at Cockthorpe/Stiff key - first for Norfolk

NE Scotland Bird Report 2002
Northern Goshawk in NE Scotland by M Marguss and G Legge
A new breeding bird atlas for NE Scotland by I Francis
Recording 'Scottish Crossbills' M Collinson
The Stone-curlew at Blackdog by SL Rivers
The occurrence of Great Grey Shrike in NE Scotland 1970-2000 by RH Minshull
St Cyrus - a birding paradise? by HI Scott

Pembrokeshire Bird Report 2003
Special 'BAP' breeding bird survey RJ Haycock

The Shropshire Bird Report 2002
An estimate of the breeding population of Barn Owls in Shropshire by Glenn Bishton and John Lightfoot
The Stiperstones breeding bird survey 2002 by Loo Smith
BTO breeding bird survey 2002 Allan Dawes
BTO breeding waders and wet meadow survey 2002 by Allan Dawes
Venus Pool 2002
Rose-coloured Starling and Minsterley by Dawn Balmer

Wiltshire Bird Report 2002 (*Hobby*)
Specied new to Wiltshire:
Whiskered Tern at the Cotswold Water Park, by GL Webber and KJ Bent
Bluewinged Teal at the Cotswold Water Park by N Adams
Wiltshire Farming and Wildlife Advisory Group by S Smart

Yorkshire Rare and Scarce Bird Report 2001
Proposed review of Yorkshire Bean Goose records
Review of Yorshire Caspian Gull record

NATIONAL DIRECTORY

Purple Sandpiper by Keith Offord

ARMY ORNITHOLOGICAL SOCIETY (1960; 250).
Open to MOD employees and civilians who have an interest in their local MOD estate. Activities include field meetings, expeditions, the preparation of checklists of birds on Ministry of Defence property, conservation advice and an annual bird count. Annual journal *The Osprey*, published with the RNBWS and RAFOS from easter 2001. Bulletins/newsletters twice a year.
Contact: Secretary AOS, Headquarters Defence Logistics Organisation, Room 7261, MOD Main Building, Whitehall, London, SW1A 2HB; e-mail: tim.hallchurch@oxfordstrategic.com http://armyos.tripod.com

ASSOCIATION FOR THE PROTECTION OF RURAL SCOTLAND (1926).
Works to protect Scotland's countryside from unnecessary or inappropriate development, recognising the needs of those who live and work there and the necessity of reconciling these with the sometimes competing requirements of recreational use.
Contact: Gladstone's Land, 3rd Floor, 483 Lawnmarket, Edinburgh EH1 2NT. 0131 225 7012/3; (Fax)0131 225 6592; www.aprs.org.uk
e-mail: info@ruralscotland.org

ASSOCIATION OF COUNTY RECORDERS AND EDITORS (1993; 120).
The basic aim of ACRE is to promote best practice in the business of producing county bird reports, in the work of Recorders and in problems arising in managing record systems and archives. Organises periodic conferences and publishes *newsACRE.*
Contact: Secretary, M J Rogers, 2 Churchtown Cottages, Towednack, St Ives, Cornwall TR26 3AZ. 01736 796223;
e-mail: judith@gmbirds.freeserve.co.uk

BARN OWL TRUST (1988).
Registered charity. Aims to conserve the Barn Owl and its environment through conservation, education, research and information. Free leaflets on all aspects of Barn Owl conservation. Educational material inc. video and resource pack. Book *Barn Owls on Site*, a guide for planners and developers (priced). Works with and advises landowners, farmers, planners, countryside bodies and others to promote a brighter future for Britain's Barn Owls. Currently pursuing proactive conservation schemes in SW England to secure breeding sites and form a stable basis for population expansion. Open to phone calls Mon-Fri (9.30-5.30). Send SAE for information.
Contact: Secretary, Barn Owl Trust, Waterleat, Ashburton, Devon TQ13 7HU. 01364 653026;
e-mail: info@barnowltrust.org.uk
www.barnowltrust.org.uk

BIRD OBSERVATORIES COUNCIL (1970).
Objectives are to provide a forum for establishing closer links and co-operation between individual autonomous observatories and to help co-ordinate the work carried out by them. All accredited bird observatories affiliated to the Council undertake a ringing programme and provide ringing experience to those interested, most also provide accommodation for visiting birdwatchers.
Contact: Secretary, Peter Howlett, c/o Dept of Biodiversity, National Museums & Galleries, Cardiff CF10 3NP. 0292 057 3233; (Fax) 0292 023 9009;
e-mail: peter.howlett@nmgw.ac.uk
www.birdobscouncil.org.uk

BIRD STAMP SOCIETY (1986; 250).
Quarterly journal *Flight* contains philatelic and ornithological articles. Lists all new issues and identifies species. Runs a quarterly Postal Auction; number of lots range from 400 to 800 per auction.
Contact: Secretary, Graham Horsman, 9 Cowley Drive, Worthy Down, Winchester, Hants SO21 2QW. 01962 889381; (Fax) 01962 887423.

BIRDWATCH IRELAND (1968; 10,000+).
The trading name of the Irish Wildbird Conservancy, a voluntary body founded in 1968 by the amalgamation of the Irish Society for the Protection of Birds, the Irish Wildfowl Conservancy and the Irish Ornithologists' Club. Now the BirdLife International partner in Ireland with 21 voluntary branches. Conservation policy is based on formal research and surveys of birds and their habitats. Owns or manages an increasing number of reserves to protect threatened species and habitats. Publishes *Wings* quarterly and *Irish Birds* annually, in addition to annual project reports and survey results.
Contact: Rockingham House, Newcastle, Co. Wicklow, Ireland. +353 (0)1 2819878; (Fax) +353 (0)1 2819763; e-mail: info@birdwatchireland.org
www.birdwatchireland.ie

BRITISH BIRDS RARITIES COMMITTEE (1959).
The Committee adjudicates records of species of rare occurrence in Britain (marked 'R' in the Log Charts). Its annual report, which is published in *British Birds*. The BBRC also assesses records from the Channel Islands. In the case of rarities trapped for ringing, records should be sent to the Ringing Office of the British Trust for Ornithology, who will in turn forward them to the BBRC.
Contact: Hon Secretary, M J Rogers, 2

Figures appearing in brackets following the names of organisations indicate the date of formation and, if relevant, the current membership.

Churchtown Cottages, Towednack, St Ives, Cornwall TR26 3AZ. 01736 796223.
e-mail: secretary@bbrc.org.uk
www.bbrc.org.uk

BRITISH DRAGONFLY SOCIETY.
The BDS aims to promote the conservation and study of dragonflies. Members receive two issues of *Dragonfly News* and *BDS Journal* each year in spring and autumn. There are countrywide field trips, an annual members day and training is available on aspects of dragonfly ecology.
Contact: Hon Secretary, Dr WH Wain, The Haywain, Hollywater Road, Bordon, Hants GU35 0AD. www.dragonflysoc.org.uk

BRITISH FALCONERS' CLUB (1927; 1,200).
Largest falconry club in Europe, with regional branches. Its aim is to encourage responsible falconers and conserve birds of prey by breeding, holding educational meetings and providing facilities, guidance and advice to those wishing to take up the sport. Publishes *The Falconer* annually and newsletter twice yearly.
Contact: Director, Home Farm, Hints, Tamworth, Staffs B78 2DW. Tel/(Fax)01543 481737;
e-mail: admin@britishfalconersclub.co.uk
www.britishfalconersclub.co.uk

BRITISH MUSEUM (NAT HIST) see Walter Rothschild Zoological Museum

BRITISH ORNITHOLOGISTS' CLUB (1892; 600).
Membership open only to members of the British Ornithologists' Union. A registered charity, the Club's objects are 'the promotion of scientific discussion between members of the BOU, and others interested in ornithology, and to facilitate the publication of scientific information in connection with ornithology'. The Club maintains a special interest in avian systematics, taxonomy and distribution. About eight dinner meetings are held each year. Publishes the *Bulletin of the British Ornithologists' Club* quarterly, also (since 1992) a continuing series of occasional publications.
Contact: Hon Secretary, Cdr M B Casement OBE RN, Dene Cottage, West Harting, Petersfield, Hants GU31 5PA. 01730 825280;
e-mail: mbcasement@aol.com.uk

BRITISH ORNITHOLOGISTS' UNION (1858; 1,500).
Founded by Professor Alfred Newton FRS and one of the world's oldest and most respected ornithological societies. It aims to promote ornithology within the scientific and birdwatching communities, both in Britain and around the world. This is largely achieved by the publication of its quarterly international journal, *Ibis* (1859-),

featuring work at the cutting edge of our understanding of the world's birdlife. An active programme of meetings, seminars and conferences inform ornithologists and birdwatchers about ornithological studies being undertaken around the world. This often includes research projects that have received financial assistance from the BOU's ongoing programme of Ornithological Research Grants, which includes student sponsorship. Part of the BOU Library is housed at the Linnean Society, whilst copies of exchange journals, books reviewed in *Ibis* and offprints are held as part of the Alexander Library in the Zoology Department of the University of Oxford (see Edward Grey Institute). The BOU Records Committee maintains the official British List (see below).
Contact: Administrator, Steve Dudley, BOU, Dept. of Zoology, University of oxford, South Parks Road, Oxford OX1 3PS. 01865 281842; (Fax) 01865 281842; e-mail: bou@bou.org.uk
www.bou.org.uk www.ibis.ac.uk

BRITISH ORNITHOLOGISTS' UNION RECORDS COMMITTEE
The BOURC is a standing committee of the British Ornithologists' Union. Its function is to maintain the British List, the official list of birds recorded in Great Britain. The up-to-date list can be viewed on the BOU website. Where vagrants are involved it is concerned only with those which relate to potential additions to the British List (ie first records). In this it differs from the British Birds Rarities Committee (qv). In maintaining the British List, it also differs from the BBRC in that it examines, where necessary, important pre-1950 records, monitors introduced species for possible admission to or deletion from the List, and reviews taxonomy and nomenclature generally. BOURC reports are published in *Ibis.* Decisions contained in these reports which affect the List are also announced via the popular birdwatching press.
Contact: Secretary, Dr Tim Melling, BOU, Dept. of Zoology, University of oxford, South Parks Road, Oxford OX1 3PS. 01865 281842; (Fax) 01865 281842; e-mail: bourc.sec@bou.org.uk
www.bou.org.uk

BRITISH TRUST FOR ORNITHOLOGY (1933; 12,500).
A registered charity governed by an elected Council, it has a rapidly growing membership and enjoys the support of a large number of county

and local birdwatching clubs and societies through the BTO/Bird Clubs Partnership. Its aims are: To promote and encourage the wider understanding, appreciation and conservation of birds through scientific studies using the combined skills and enthusiasm of its members, other birdwatchers and staff. Through the fieldwork of its members and other birdwatchers, the BTO is responsible for the majority of the monitoring of British birds, British bird population and their habitats. BTO surveys include the National Ringing Scheme, the Nest Record Scheme, the Breeding Bird Survey (in collaboration with JNCC and RSPB), and the Waterways Breeding Bird Survey - all contributing to an integrated programme of population monitoring. The BTO also runs projects on the birds of farmland and woodland, also (in collaboration with WWT, RSPB and JNCC) the Wetland Bird Survey, in particular Low Tide Counts. Garden BirdWatch, which started in 1995, now has more than 14,000 participants. The Trust has 140 voluntary regional representatives (see County Directory) who organise fieldworkers for the BTO's programme of national surveys in which members participate. The results of these co-operative efforts are communicated to government departments, local authorities, industry and conservation bodies for effective action. For details of current activities see National Projects. Members receive *BTO News* six times a year and have the option of subscribing to the thrice-yearly journal, *Bird Study* and twice yearly *Ringing & Migration*. Local meetings are held in conjunction with bird clubs and societies; there are regional and national birdwatchers' conferences, and specialist courses in bird identification and modern censusing techniques. Grants are made for research, and members have the use of a lending and reference library at Thetford and the Alexander Library at the Edward Grey Institute of Field Ornithology (qv).
Contact: Director, Professor Jeremy J D Greenwood, British Trust for Ornithology, The Nunnery, Thetford, Norfolk, IP24 2PU, 01842 750050; (fax) 01842 750030; www.bto.org e-mail: btostaff@bto.org

BRITISH WATERFOWL ASSOCIATION
The BWA is an association of enthusiasts interested in keeping, breeding and conserving all types of waterfowl, including wildfowl and domestic ducks and geese. It is a registered charity, without trade affiliations, dedicated to educating the public about waterfowl and the need for conservation as well as to raising the standards of keeping and breeding ducks, geese and swans in captivity.
Contact: Mrs Sue Schubert, PO Box 163, Oxted RH8 0WP. 01892 740212;
e-mail: info@waterfowl.org.uk
www.waterfowl.org.uk

BRITISH WILDLIFE REHABILITATION COUNCIL (1987).
Its aim is to promote the care and rehabilitation of wildlife casualties through the exchange of information between people such as rehabilitators, zoologists and veterinary surgeons who are active in this field. Organises an annual symposium or workshop. Publishes a regular newsletter. Supported by many national bodies including the Zoological Society of London, the British Veterinary Zoological Society, the RSPCA, the SSPCA, and the Vincent Wildlife Trust.
Contact: Secretary, Wildlife Department, RSPCA, Wilberforce Way, Southwater, Horsham, W Sussex RH13 9RS. www.bwrc.org.uk

BTCV (1959).
Involves people of all ages in practical conservation work, much of which directly affects bird habitats. There are more than 2,500 local conservation groups affiliated to BTCV, which also provides a service to many other bodies including the JNCC, RSPB, WWT and county wildlife trusts, national parks, water authorities, local authorities and private landowners. More than 750 training courses are run annually on the theory of management and practical techniques, for example woodland and wetland management, hedging, etc. Runs working holidays in UK and overseas. Publishes a quarterly newsletter, *The Conserver*, a series of practical handbooks and a wide range of other publications. Further information and a list of local offices is available from the above address.
Contact: Conservation Centre, 163 Balby Road, Doncaster, South Yorkshire DN4 0RH. 01302 572 244; (Fax) 01302 310 167: www.btcv.org.uk
e-mail: Information@btcv.org.uk

BTCV SCOTLAND
Runs 7-14 day 'Action Breaks' in Scotland during which participants undertake conservation projects; weekend training courses in environmental skills; midweek projects in Edinburgh, Glasgow, Aberdeen, Stirling and Inverness.
Contact: Balallan House, 24 Allan Park, Stirling FK8 2QG. 01786 479697; (Fax) 01786 465359;
e-mail: stirling@btcv.org.uk www.btcv.org.uk

CAMPAIGN FOR THE PROTECTION OF RURAL WALES (1928; 3,500)
Its aims are to help the conservation and enhancement of the landscape, environment and

amenities of the countryside, towns and villages of rural Wales and to form and educate opinion to ensure the promotion of its objectives. It recognises the importance of the indigenous cultures of rural Wales and gives advice and information upon matters affecting protection, conservation and improvement of the visual environment.

YDCW CPRW

Contact: Director, Peter Ogden, Ty Gwyn, 31 High Street, Welshpool, Powys SY21 7YD. 01938 552525/556212; (Fax)552741; e-mail: info@cprw.org.uk www.cprw.org.uk

CENTRE FOR ECOLOGY & HYDROLOGY (CEH)
The work of the CEH, a component body of the Natural Environment Research Council, includes a range of ornithological research, covering population studies, habitat management and work on the effects of pollution. The CEH has a long-term programme to monitor pesticide and pollutant residues in the corpses of predatory birds sent in by birdwatchers, and carries out detailed studies on affected species. The Biological Records Centre (BRC), which is part of the CEH, is responsible for the national biological data bank on plant and animal distributions (except birds).
Contact: Director, Monks Wood, Abbots Ripton, Huntingdon PE28 2LS. 01487 772400; (Fax) 01487 773467; e-mail: monkswood@ceh.ac.uk www.ceh.ac.uk

COUNTRY LAND AND BUSINESS ASSOCIATION (50,000).
The CLA is at the heart of rural life and is the voice of the countryside for England and Wales, campaigning on issues which directly affect those who live and work in rural communities. Its members together manage 60% of the countryside. CLA members range from some of the largest landowners, with interests in forest, moorland, water and agriculture, to some of the smallest with little more than a paddock or garden.
Contact: Secretary, 16 Belgrave Square, London, SW1X 8PQ. 020 7235 0511; (Fax) 020 7235 4696; e-mail: mail@cla.org.uk www.cla.org.uk

COUNTRYSIDE AGENCY (1999)
Is the statutory body working to make life better for people in the countryside and improve the quality of the countryside for everyone. The Countryside Agency will help to achieve the following; empowered, active and inclusive communities, high standards of rural services, vibrant local economies, all countryside managed sustainably, recreation opportunities for all, realising the potential of the urban fringe. The Countryside Agency is funded by Defra who is a major customer for their work.
Offices:
North East Region. Cross House, Westgate Road, Newcastle upon Tyne NE1 4XX, 0191 269 1600; (Fax) 0191 269 1601
North West Region. 7th Floor, Bridgewater House, Whitworth Street, Manchester M1 6LT. 0161 237 1061; (fax) 0161 237 1062
Haweswater Road, Penrith, Cumbria CA11 7EH. 01768 865752; (fax) 01768 890414.
South West Region. Bridge House, Sion Place, Clifton Down, Bristol BS8 4AS. 0117 973 9966; (fax) 0117 923 8086.
Second Floor, 11-15 Dix's Field, Exeter EX1 1QA. 01392 477150; (fax) 01392 477151.
Yorkshire & The Humber Region. 4th Floor Victoria Wharf, No 4 The Embankment, Sovereign Street, Leeds LS1 4BA. 0113 246 9222; (fax) 0113 246 0353
East Midlands Region. 18, Market Place, Bingham, Nottingham NG13 9AP. 01949 876200; (fax) 01949 876222
West Midlands Region. 1st Floor, Vincent House, Tindal Bridge, 92-93 Edward Street, Birmingham B1 2RA. 0121 233 9399:(fax) 0121 233 9286
Eastern Region. 2nd Floor, City House, 126-128 Hills Road, Cambridge CB2 1PT. 01223 354462; (fax) 01223 273550.
South East Region. Dacre House, Dacre Street, London SW1H 0DH, 020 7340 2900; (fax) 020 7340 2911.
Sterling House, 7 Ashford Road, Maidstone ME14 5BJ. 01622 765222; (fax) 01622 662102.
Contact: Chief Executive, Richard Wakeford, John Dower House, Crescent Place, Cheltenham, Glos GL50 3RA. 01242 521381; (Fax) 01242 584270.

COUNTRYSIDE COUNCIL FOR WALES
The Government's statutory adviser on wildlife, countryside and maritime conservation matters in Wales. It is the executive authority for the conservation of habitats and wildlife. Through partners, CCW promotes protection of landscape, opportunities for enjoyment, and support of those who live, work in, and manage the countryside. It enables these partners, including local authorities, voluntary organisations and interested individuals, to pursue countryside management projects through grant aid. CCW is accountable to the National Assembly for Wales which appoints its Council members and provides its annual grant-in-aid.

Area Offices:
West Area. Plas Gogerddan, Aberystwyth, Ceredigian, SY23 3EE. 01970 821100; e-mail: westarea@ccw.gov.uk
North West Area. Llys y bont, Ffordd y Parc, Parc Menai, Bangor, Gwynedd, LL57 4BH. 01248 672500; e-mail: northwestarea@ccw.gov.uk
South and East Area. Unit 7, Castleton Court, Fortran Road, St Mellons, Cardiff CF3 0LT. 02920 772400.
South and East Area. Eden House, Ithon Road, Llandrindod, Powys, LD1 6AS, 01597 827400; email: llandrindod@ccw.gov.uk
North East Area. Victoria House, Grosvenor Street, Mold CH7 1EJ. 01352 706600.
Contact: Maes-y-Ffynnon, Penrhosgarnedd, Bangor, Gwynedd. 01248 385500; (Fax) 01248 355782; (Enquiry unit) 0845 1306229. www.ccw.gov.uk

CPRE (formerly Council for the Protection of Rural England) (1926; 59,000).
Patron HM The Queen. CPRE now has 43 county branches and 200 local groups. We are people who care passionately about our countryside and campaign for it to be protected and enhanced for the benefit of everyone. Membership open to all.
Contact: CPRE National Office, 128 Southwark Street, London SE1 0SW. 020 7981 2800; (fax) 020 7981 2899; e-mail: info@cpre.org.uk www.cpre.org.uk

DEPARTMENT OF THE ENVIRONMENT FOR NORTHERN IRELAND
Responsible for the declaration and management of National Nature Reserves, the declaration of Areas of Special Scientific Interest, the administration of Wildlife Refuges, the classification of Special Protection Areas under the EC Birds Directive, the designation of Special Areas of Conservation under the EC Habitats Directive and the designation of Ramsar sites under the Ramsar Convention. It administers the Nature Conservation and Amenity Lands (Northern Ireland) Order 1985, the Wildlife (Northern Ireland) Order 1985, the Game Acts and the Conservation (Natural Habitats, etc) Regulations (NI) 1995 and the Environment (Northern Ireland) Order 2002.
Contact: Bob Bleakley, Environment and Heritage Service, Commonwealth House, 35 Castle Street, Belfast BT1 1GU. 028 9054 6521; e-mail: bob.bleakley@doeni.gov.uk www.ehsni.gov.uk

DISABLED BIRDER'S ASSOCIATION (2000; 250).
The DBA is a registered charity and international movement, which aims to promote access to reserves and other birding places and to a range of services, so that people with different needs can follow the birding obsession as freely as able-bodied people. Membership is currently free and open to all, either disabled or able-bodied. We are keen for new members to help give a strong voice to get our message across to those who own and manage nature reserves to ensure that they think about access when they are planning and improving their facilities. We are also seeking to influence those who provide birdwatching services and equipment. The DBA runs an annual overseas trip.
Contact: DBA, 18 St Mildreds Road, Cliftonville, Margate, Kent CT9 2LT. e-mail: bo@fatbirder.com www.disabledbirdersassociation.org.uk

EDWARD GREY INSTITUTE OF FIELD ORNITHOLOGY (1938).
The EGI takes its name from Edward Grey, first Viscount Grey of Fallodon, a life-long lover of birds and former Chancellor of the University of Oxford, who gave his support to an appeal for its foundation capital. The Institute now has a permanent research staff; it usually houses some 12-15 research students, two or three senior visitors and post-doctoral research workers. The EGI also houses Prof Sir John Krebs's Ecology & Behaviour Group, which studies the ecology, demography and conservation of declining farmland birds. Field research is carried out mainly in Wytham Woods near Oxford and on the island of Skomer in West Wales. In addition there are laboratory facilities and aviary space for experimental work. The Institute houses the Alexander Library, one of the largest collections of 20th Century material on birds in the world. The library is supported by the British Ornithologists Union who provides much of the material. Included in its manuscript collections are diaries, notebooks and papers of ornithologists. It also houses the British Falconers Club library. The Library is open to members of the BOU and the Oxford Ornithological Society; other bona fide ornithologists may use the library by prior arrangement.
Contact: Head, Dr BC Sheldon, Department of Zoology, South Parks Road, Oxford OX1 3PS. 01865 271274, Alexander Library 01865 271143; e-mail: lynne.bradley@zoology.oxford.ac.uk; e-mail: lnda.birch@zoo.ox.ac.ukweb-site, EGI: http://egiwcruzool.zoo.ox.ac.uk/EGI/egihome.htm web-site library http://users.ox.ac.uk/~zoolib/

ENGLISH NATURE (1991)
Advises Government on nature conservation in

England. It promotes, directly and through others, the conservation of England's wildlife and geology within the wider setting of the UK and its international responsibilities. It selects, establishes and manages National Nature Reserves (many of which are described in the Reserves and Observatories section), and identifies and notifies Sites of Special Scientific Interest. It provides advice and information about nature conservation and supports and conducts research relevant to these functions. Through the Joint Nature Conservation Committee (qv), English Nature works with sister organisations in Scotland and Wales on UK and international nature conservation issues.

Local Teams:

Bedfordshire and Cambridgeshire. Ham Lane House, Ham Lane, Nene Park, Orton Waterville, Peterborough PE2 5UR, 01733 405850; fax 01733 394093; e-mail: beds.cambs.nhants@english-nature.org.uk.

Cheshire and Lancashire. Pier House, 1st Floor, Wallgate, Wigan WN3 4AL. 01942 820342; fax 01942 820364; e-mail: northwest@english-nature.org.uk.

Cornwall & Isles of Scilly. Trevint House, Strangways Villas, Truro TR1 2PA. 01872 265710; fax 01872 262551;
e-mail: cornwall@english-nature.org.uk.

Cumbria. Juniper House, Murley Moss, Oxenholme Road, Kendal LA9 7RL. 01539 792800; fax 01539 792830; e-mail; cumbria@english-nature.org.uk.

Devon. Level 2, Rensdale House, Bonhay Rd, Exeter, EX4 3AW, 01392 889770; fax 01392 437999; e-mail: devon@english-nature.org.uk.

Dorset. Slepe Farm, Arne, Wareham, Dorset BH20 5BN. 01929 557450; fax 01929 554752;
e-mail: dorset@english-nature.org.uk.

Eastern Area. The Maltings, Wharf Road, Grantham, Lincs NG31 6BH. 01476 584800; fax 01476 570927;
e-mail: eastmidlands@english-nature.org.uk

Essex, London and Hertfordshire. Harbour House, Hythe Quay, Colchester CO2 8JF. 01206 796666; fax 01206 794466;
e-mail; essex.herts@english-nature.org.uk.

Hampshire and Isle of Wight. 1 Southampton Road, Lyndhurst, Hants SO43 7BU. 02380 283944; fax 02380 283834;
e-mail; hants.iwight@english-nature.org.uk.

Hereford and Worcester. Bronsil House, Eastnor, Nr Ledbury HR8 1EP. 01531 638500; fax 01531 638501; e-mail: Hereford and Worcester @english-nature.org.uk.

Humber to Pennines. Bull Ring House, Northgate, Wakefield, W Yorks WF1 1HD. 01924 334500; fax 01924 201507;
e-mail; humber.pennines@english-nature.org.uk.

Kent. The Countryside Management Centre, Coldharbour Farm, Wye, Ashford, Kent TN25 5DB. 01233 812525; fax 01233 812520;
e-mail; kent@english-nature.org.uk.

Norfolk. 60 Bracondale, Norwich NR1 2BE. 01603 598400; fax 01603 762552;
e-mail: norfolk@english-nature.org.uk.

North and East Yorkshire. Genesis 1, University Road, Heslington, York YO10 5ZQ. 01904 435500; fax 01904 435520;
e-mail: york@english-nature.org.uk.

North Mercia (Shrops, Staffs, Warks, W Mid). Attingham Park, Shrewsbury SY4 4TW. 01743 709611; fax 01743 709303;
e-mail: North Mercia @english-nature.org.uk.

Northumbria. Stocksfield Hall, Stocksfield, Northumberland NE4 7TN. 01661 845500; fax 01661 845501;
e-mail: northumbria@english-nature.org.uk.

Peak District and Derbyshire. Endcliffe, Deepdale Business Park, Ashford Road, Bakewell DE45 1GT. 01629 816640; fax 01629 816679. e-mail: peak.derbys@english-nature.org.uk.

Somerset and Gloucester. Roughmoor, Bishop's Hull, Taunton, Somerset TA1 5AA. 01823 283211; fax 01823 272978;
e-mail: somerset@english-nature.org.uk.

Suffolk. Regent House, 110 Northgate Street, Bury St Edmunds, Suffolk IP33 1HP. 01284 762218; fax 01284 764318;
e-mail: suffolk@english-nature.org.uk.

Sussex and Surrey. Phoenix House, 32-33 North Street, Lewes, E Sussex BN7 2PH. 01273 476595; fax 01273 483063;
e-mail: sussex.surrey@english-nature.org.uk.

Thames and Chilterns. Foxhold House, Thornford Road, Crookham Common, Thatcham, Berks RG19 8EL. 01635 268881; fax 01635 267027;
e-mail: thames.chilterns@english-nature.org.uk.

Wiltshire. Prince Maurice Court, Hambleton Avenue, Devizes, Wilts SN10 2RT. 01380 726344; fax 01380 721411;
e-mail: wiltshire@english-nature.org.uk.

ENGLISH NATURE

Head Office: Northminster House, Peterborough, PE1 1UA. 01733 455100; (Fax) 01733 455103;
e-mail: enquiries@english-nature.org.uk
www.english-nature.org.uk

ENVIRONMENT AGENCY (THE) (1996)
A non-departmental body that aims to protect and improve the environment and to contribute towards the delivery of sustainable development

NATIONAL DIRECTORY

through the integrated management of air, land and water. Functions include pollution prevention and control, waste minimisation, management of water resources, flood defence, improvement of salmon and freshwater fisheries, conservation of aquatic species, navigation and use of inland and coastal waters for recreation. Sponsored by the Department of the Environment, Transport and the Regions, MAFF and the Welsh Office.
Regional Offices
Anglian. Kingfisher House, Goldhay Way, Orton Goldhay, Peterborough PE2 5ZR. 01733 371811; fax 01733 231840.
North East. Rivers House, 21 Park Square South, Leeds LS1 2QG. 0113 244 0191; fax 0113 246 1889.
North West. Richard Fairclough House, Knutsford Road, Warrington WA4 1HG. 01925 653999; (fax) 01925 415961.
Midlands. Sapphire East, 550 Streetsbrook Road, Solihull B91 1QT. 0121 711 2324; fax 0121 711 5824.
Southern. Guildbourne House, Chatsworth Road, Worthing, W Sussex BN11 1LD. 01903 832000; fax 01903 821832.
South West. Manley House, Kestrel Way, Exeter EX2 7LQ. 01392 444000; fax 01392 444238.
Thames. Kings Meadow House, Kings Meadow Road, Reading RG1 8DQ. 0118 953 5000; fax 0118 950 0388.
Wales. Rivers House, St Mellons Business Park, St Mellons, Cardiff CF3 0EY. 029 2077 0088; fax 029 2079 8555.
Contact: Rio House, Waterside Drive, Aztec West, Almondsbury, Bristol BS32 4UD. 01454 624400; (Fax)01454 624409; (Enquiry line) 08708 506 506. www.environment-agency.gov.uk

FARMING AND WILDLIFE ADVISORY GROUP (FWAG) (1969).
An independent UK-registered charity led by farmers and supported by government and leading countryside organisations. Its aim is to unite farming and forestry with wildlife and landscape conservation. Active in most UK counties. There are 110 Farm Conservation Advisers who give practical advice to farmers and landowners to help them integrate environmental objectives with commercial farming practices.

Contact:
English Head Office, FWAG, National Agricultural Centre, Stoneleigh, Kenilworth, Warwickshire CV8 2RX. 02476 696 699;(Fax) 02476 696 699;
e-mail: info@fwag.org.uk
www.fwag.org.uk
Northern Ireland, FWAG, National Agricultural Centre, Stoneleigh, Kenilworth, Warwickshire CV8 2RX. 0771 3333152;
e-mail: sean.convery@fwag.org.uk
Scottish Head Office, FWAG Scotland, Algo Business Centre, Glenearn Road, Perth PH2 0NJ. 01738 450500; (Fax) 01738 450495;
e-mail steven.hunt@fwag.org.uk
Wales Head Office. FWAG Cymru, Ffordd Arran, Dolgellau, Gwynedd LL40 1LW. 01341 421456; (Fax) 01341 422757; e-mail: cymru@fwag.org.uk

FIELD STUDIES COUNCIL (1943).
Manages Centres where students from schools, universities and colleges of education, as well as individuals of all ages, stay and study various aspects of the environment under expert guidance. The courses include many for birdwatchers, providing opportunities to study birdlife on coasts, estuaries, mountains and islands. There are some courses demonstrating bird ringing and others for members of the Wildlife Explorers. The length of the courses varies: from a weekend up to seven days' duration. Research workers and naturalists wishing to use the records and resources are welcome. FSC Overseas includes birdwatching in its programme of overseas courses.
Centres:
Blencathra Field Centre, Threlkeld, Keswick, Cumbria CA12 4SG, 017687 79601;
e-mail: enquiries.bl@field-studies-council.org
Castle Head Field Centre, Grange-over-Sands, Cumbria LA11 6QT, 015395 38120,
e-mail: enquiries.ch@field-studies-council.org
Dale Fort Field Centre, Haverfordwest, Pembs SA62 3RD, 01646 636205,
e-mail: enquiries.df@field-studies-council.org
Epping Forest Field Centre, High Beach, Loughton, Essex, IG10 4AF, 020 8502 8500,
e-mail: enquiries.ef@field-studies-council.org
Flatford Mill Field Centre, East Bergholt, Suffolk, CO7 6UL, 01206 297110,
e-mail: enquiries.fm@field-studies-council.org
Derrygonnelly Field Centre, Tir Navar, Creamery St, Derrygonnelly, Co Fermanagh, BT93 6HW. 028 686 41673,
e-mail: enquiries.dg.@field-studies-council.org
Juniper Hall Field Centre, Dorking, Surrey, RH5 6DA, 0845 458 3507,
e-mail: enquiries.jh@field-studies-council.org
Kindragan Field Centre, Enochdhu, Blairgowrie, Perthshire PH10 7PG. 01250 870150, e-mail: kindrogan@btinternet.com
Margam Park Field Centre, Port Talbot SA13 2TJ.

01639 895636,
e-mail: margam_sustainable_centre@hotmail.com
Malham Tarn Field Centre, Settle, N Yorks, BD24 9PU, 01729 830331,
e-mail: fsc.malham@ukonline.co.uk
Nettlecombe Court, The Leonard Wills Field Centre, Williton, Taunton, Somerset, TA4 4HT, 01984 640320,
e-mail: enquiries.nc@field-studies-council.org
Orielton Field Centre, Pembroke, Pembs, SA71 5EZ, 01646 623920,
e-mail: enquiries.or@field-studies-council.org
Preston Montford Field Centre, Montford Bridge, Shrewsbury, SY4 1DX, 01743 852040,
e-mail: enquiries.pm@field-studies-council.org
Rhyd-y-creuau, the Drapers' Field Centre Betws-y-coed, Conwy, LL24 0HB, 01690 710494,
e-mail: enquiries.rc@field-studies-council.org
Slapton Ley Field Centre, Slapton, Kingsbridge, Devon, TQ7 2QP, 01548 580466,
e-mail: enquiries.sl@field-studies-council.org
Contact:
Head Office, Preston Montford, Montford Bridge, Shrewsbury, SY4 1HW, 01743 852100; (Fax) 01743 852101; www.field-studies-council.org
e-mail: fsc.headoffice@ field-studies-council.org
FSC Overseas, Preston Montford, Montford Bridge, Shrewsbury SY4 1HW. 01743 852150; (Fax) 01743 852101;
e-mail: fsc.overseas@field-studies-council.org

FLIGHTLINE
Northern Ireland's daily bird news service. Run under the auspices of the Northern Ireland Birdwatchers' Association (qv).
Contact: George Gordon, 2 Brooklyn Avenue, Bangor, Co Down BT20 5RB. 028 9146 7408;
e-mail: gordon@ballyholm2.freeserve.co.uk

FORESTRY COMMISSION
The Forestry Commission of Great Britain is the government department responsible for the protection and expansion of Britain's forests and woodlands. The organisation is run from national offices in England, Wales and Scotland, working to targets set by Commissioners and Ministers in each of the three countries. Its objectives are to protect Britain's forests and resources, conserve and improve the biodiversity, landscape and cultural heritage of forests and woodlands, develop opportunities for woodland recreation and increase public understanding and community participation in forestry.
Head Office:
Forestry Commission, Silvan House, 231 Corstorphine Road, Edinburgh, EH12 7AT; 0131 334 0303; (Fax) 0131 334 3047; Media enquiries: 0131 314 6550. Public enquiries: 0845 367 3787.
e-mail: enquiries@forestry.gsi.gov.uk
www.forestry.gov.uk
Details of wildlife viewing sites aross the country can be found on www.forestry.gov.uk/forestry/wildwoods
Forestry Commission National Offices:
England: Great Eastern House, Tenison Road, Cambridge CB1 2DU. 01223 314546; (Fax) 01223 460699, e-mail: fc.nat.off.eng@forestry.gsi.gov.uk
Scotland: Address as contact above, 0131 334 0303, (Fax) 0131 314 615,
e-mail: fcscotland@forestry.gsi.gov.uk
Wales: Victoria Terrace, Aberystwyth, Ceredigion SY23 2DQ. 01970 625866; (Fax) 01970 626177.

(1971; 100,000). The largest international network of environmental groups in the world, represented in 68 countries. It is one of the leading environmental pressure groups in the UK. It has a unique network of campaigning local groups, working in 200 communities in England, Wales and Northern Ireland. It is largely funded by supporters with more than 90% of income coming from individual donations, the rest from special fundraising events, grants and trading.
Contact: 26/28 Underwood Street, London, N1 7JQ. 020 7490 1555; (Fax) 020 7490 0881;
e-mail: info@foe.co.uk www.foe.co.uk

GAME CONSERVANCY TRUST (1933; 24,000).
A registered charity which researches the conservation of game and other wildlife in the British countryside. More than 60 scientists are engaged in detailed work on insects, pesticides, birds (30 species inc. raptors) mammals (inc. foxes), and habitats. The results are used to advise government, landowners, farmers and conservationists on practical management techniques which will benefit game species, their habitats, and wildlife. Each June an *Annual Review* of 100 pages lists about 60 papers published in the peer-reviewed scientific press.
Contact: Director General, Dr G R Potts, Fordingbridge, Hampshire, SP6 1EF. 01425 652381; (Fax) 01425 651026;
e-mail: info@gct.org.uk www.gct.org.uk

GAY BIRDERS CLUB (1995; 300+).
A voluntary society for lesbian, gay and bisexual birdwatchers, their friends and supporters, over the age of consent, in the UK and worldwide. The club has up to 400 members and a network of regional contacts. It organises day trips, weekends and longer events at notable birding locations in the UK and abroad; about 200+ events in a year. Members receive a quarterly newletter with details

of all events. There is a Grand Get Together every 18 months. Membership £12 waged and £5 unwaged.
Contact: GeeBeeCee, BCM-Mono, London, WC1N 3XX. e-mail: enquiries@gbc-online.org.uk www.gbc-online.org.uk

GOLDEN ORIOLE GROUP (1987).
Organises censuses of breeding Golden Orioles in parts of Cambridgeshire, Norfolk and Suffolk. Maintains contact with a network of individuals in other parts of the country where Orioles may or do breed. Studies breeding biology, habitat and food requirements of the species.
Contact: Jake Allsop, 5 Bury Lane, Haddenham, Ely, Cambs CB6 3PR. 01353 740540; e-mail: jakeallsop@aol.com www.goldenoriolegroup.org.uk

HAWK AND OWL TRUST (1969).
Registered charity dedicated to the conservation and appreciation of all birds of prey including owls. Publishes a newsletter *Peregrine* and educational materials for all ages. The Trust achieves its major aim of creating and enhancing wild habitats for birds of prey through projects which involve practical research, creative conservation and education. Projects are often conducted in close partnership with landowners, farmers and others. Members are invited to take part in population studies, field surveys, etc. Studies of Barn and Little Owls, Hen Harrier, and Goshawk are in progress. The Trust's National Conservation and Education Centre at Newland Park, Gorelands Lane, Chalfont St Giles, Bucks, is now open to the public and offers schools and other groups cross-curricular environmental activities.
Contact: Membership administration: 11 St Mary's Close, Abbotskerswell, Newton Abbot, Devon, TQ12 5QF.

Contact: Director, Colin Shawyer, c/o Zoological Society of London, Regents Park, London NW1 4RY. Tel/(Fax)01582 832182; e-mail: hawkandowltrust@aol.com www.hawkandowl.org

IRISH RARE BIRDS COMMITTEE (1985).
Assesses records of species of rare occurrence in the Republic of Ireland. Details of records accepted and rejected are incorporated in the Irish Bird Report, published annually in *Irish Birds*. In the case of rarities trapped for ringing, ringers in the Republic of Ireland are required to send their schedules initially to the National Parks and Wildlife Service, 51 St Stephen's Green, Dublin 2. A copy is taken before the schedules are sent to the British Trust for Ornithology.
Contact: Hon Secretary, Paul Milne, 100 Dublin Road, Sutton, Dublin 13. +353 (0)1 8325653; e-mail: paul.milne@oceanfree.net

JOINT NATURE CONSERVATION COMMITTEE (1990).
A committee of the three country agencies (English Nature, Scottish Natural Heritage, and the Countryside Council for Wales), together with independent members and representatives from Northern Ireland and the Countryside Agency. It is supported by specialist staff. Its statutory responsibilities include the establishment of common standards for monitoring, the analysis of information and research; advising Ministers on the development and implementation of policies for or affecting nature conservation; the provision of advice and the dissemination of knowledge to any persons about nature conservation; and the undertaking and commissioning of research relevant to these functions. JNCC additionally has the UK responsibility for relevant European and wider international matters. The Species Team, located at the HQ address above, is responsible for terrestrial bird conservation.
Contact: Monkstone House, City Road, Peterborough PE1 1JY. 01733 562626; (Fax) 01733 555948; e-mail: feedback@jncc.gov.uk www.jncc.gov.uk

LINNEAN SOCIETY OF LONDON (1788).
Named after Carl Linnaeus, the 18th century Swedish biologist, who created the modern system of scientific biological nomenclature, the Society promotes all aspects of pure and applied biology. It houses Linnaeus's collection of plants, insects and fishes, library and correspondence. The Society has a major reference library of some 100,000 volumes. Publishes the *Biological, Botanical and Zoological Journals*, and the *Synopses of the British Fauna*.
Contact: Executive Secretary, Adrian Thomas, Burlington House, Piccadilly, London W1J 0BF. 020 7434 4479; (Fax) 020 7287 9364; e-mail: adrian@linnean.org www.linnean.org

LITTLE OWL STUDY GROUP (2002; 37).
Formed to promote the study and conservation of Little Owls (*Athene noctua*) in Britain and to develop a population monitoring network for Little Owls. The LOSG is part of the International Little Owl Working Group, a Europe-wide organisation networking Little Owl Research and Conservation. The Little Owl is declining at an alarming rate across Europe and is endangered in at least three

Western European countries. To combat this, a European Species Action Plan is being developed, to put in place the necessary monitors, conservation, and education measures for its long term survival. Project *Athene* is the British leg of this SAP. (See National Projects).
Contact: Roy Leigh, c/o Biota, The Old Barn, Moseley Hall Farm, Chilford Road, Knutsford, Cheshire WA16 8RB. 0871 734 0111; (Fax) 0871 734 0555; e-mail: rsl@biota.co.uk

MANX ORNITHOLOGICAL SOCIETY see County Directory

MANX WILDLIFE TRUST see County Directory

NATIONAL BIRDS OF PREY CENTRE (1967).
Concerned with the conservation and captive breeding of all raptors. Approx 85 species on site. Birds flown daily. Open Feb-Nov.
Contact: Mrs J Parry-Jones MBE, Newent, Glos, GL18 1JJ. 0870 9901992; e-mail: jpj@icbp.org www.nbpc.co.uk

NATIONAL TRUST (1895; 3.1million).
Charity depending on voluntary support of its members and the public. Largest private landowner with over 603,862 acres of land and nearly 600 miles of coast. Works for the preservation of places of historic interest or natural beauty, in England, Wales and N Ireland. The Trust's coast and countryside properties are open to the public at all times, subject only to the needs of farming, forestry and the protection of wildlife. More than a quarter of the Trust's land holding is designated SSSI or ASSI (N Ireland) and about 10% of SSSIs in England and Wales are wholly or partially owned by the Trust, as are 31 NNRs (eg Blakeney Point, Farne Islands, Wicken Fen and large parts of Strangford Lough, N Ireland). Fifteen per cent of Ramsar Sites include Trust land, as do 27% of SPAs. 71 of the 117 bird species listed in the UK Red Data Book are found on Trust land.
Contact:
Conservation Directorate, 33 Sheep Street, Cirencester, Glos GL7 1RQ. 01285 651818.
Northern Ireland Office: Rowallane House, Saintfield, Ballynahinch, Co. Down BT24 7LH. 028 975 10721.
London Central Office, 36 Queen Anne's Gate, London, SW1H 9AS. 020 7222 9251.
www.nationaltrust.org.uk

NATIONAL TRUST FOR SCOTLAND (1931; 230,000).
An independent charity, its 90 properties open to the public are described in its annual guide.
Contact: Marketing Department, Wemyss House, 28 Charlotte Square, Edinburgh, EH2 4ET. 0131 243 9300; e-mail: information@nts.org.uk www.nts.org.uk

NATURE PHOTOGRAPHERS' PORTFOLIO (1944).
A society for photographers of wildlife, especially birds. Circulates postal portfolios of prints and transparencies.
Contact: Hon Secretary, A Winspear-Cundall, 8 Gig Bridge Lane, Pershore, Worcs WR10 1NH. 01386 552103.
www.nature-photographers-portfolio.co.uk

NORTH SEA BIRD CLUB(1979; 200).
The stated aims of the Club are to: provide a recreational pursuit for people employed offshore; obtain, collate and analyse observations of all birds seen offshore; produce reports of observations, including an annual report; promote the collection of data on other wildlife offshore. Currently we hold in excess of 100,000 records of birds, cetaceans and insects reported since 1979.
Contact: Andrew Thorpe, (Recorder), Ocean Laboratory and Centre for Ecology, Aberdeen University, Newburgh, Ellon, Aberdeenshire AB41 6AA. www.abdn.ac.uk/nsbc
e-mail: a.thorpe@abdn.ac.uk or nsbc@abdn.ac.uk

NORTHERN IRELAND BIRDWATCHERS' ASSOCIATION (1991; 90).
The NIBA Records Committee, established in 1997, has full responsibility for the assessment of records in N Ireland. NIBA also publishes the *Northern Ireland Bird Report*.
Contact: Hon Secretary, William McDowell, 4 Gairloch Park, Holywood, Co Down BT18 0LZ. 028 9059 4390; e-mail: williamm.mcdowell@ntlworld.com

NORTHERN IRELAND ORNITHOLOGISTS' CLUB (1965; 150).
Operates a Tree Sparrow nestbox scheme and a winter feeding programme for Yellowhammers. Has a regular programme of lectures and field trips for members. Publishes *The Harrier* quarterly.
Contact: Gary Wilkinson, The Roost, 139 Windmill Road, Hillsborough, Co Down BT26 6NP 028 9263 9254; e-mail: garrywilkinson@roost139.fsnet.co.uk
www.nioc.fsnet.co.uk

PEOPLE'S DISPENSARY FOR SICK ANIMALS (1917).
Registered charity. Provides free veterinary treatment for sick and injured animals whose owners qualify for this charitable service.
Contact: Director General, Mrs Marilyn Rydstrom, Whitechapel Way, Priorslee, Telford, Shrops TF2 9PQ. 01952 290999; e-mail: pr@pdsa.org.uk
www.pdsa.org.uk

RARE BREEDING BIRDS PANEL (1973).
An independent body funded by the JNCC and RSPB. Both bodies are represented on the panel as are BTO and ACRE. It collects all information on rare breeding birds in the United Kingdom, so that changes in status can be monitored as an aid to present-day conservation and stored for posterity. Special forms are used (obtainable free from the secretary and the website) and records should if possible be submitted via the county and regional recorders. Since 1996 the Panel also monitors breeding by scarcer non-native species and seeks records of these in the same way. Annual report is published in *British Birds*. For details of species covered by the Panel see Log Charts and the websites.
Contact: Secretary, Dr Malcolm Ogilvie, Glencairn, Bruichladdich, Isle of Islay PA49 7UN. 01496 850218; e-mail: rbbp@indaal.demon.co.uk
www.rbbp.org.uk

ROYAL AIR FORCE ORNITHOLOGICAL SOCIETY (1965; 295).
RAFOS organises regular field meetings for members, carries out ornithological census work on MOD properties and mounts major expeditions annually to various UK and overseas locations. Publishes a Newsletter twice a year, a Journal annually, and reports on its expeditions and surveys.
Contact: General Secretary, RAFOS, MOD DE(C) Conservation, Blandford House, Farnborough Road, Aldershot, Hants GU11 2HA. 01225 468416.

ROYAL NAVAL BIRDWATCHING SOCIETY (1946; 167 full and 93 associate members and library).
Covering all main ocean routes, the Society has developed a system for reporting the positions and identity of seabirds and landbirds at sea by means of standard sea report forms. Maintains an extensive world-wide sea-bird database. Members are encouraged to photograph birds while at sea and a library of photographs and slides is maintained. Publishes a Bulletin and an annual report entitled *The Sea Swallow*.

Contact: Hon Secretary, FS Ward Esq., 16 Cutlers Lane, Stubbington, Fareham, Hants PO14 2JN. +44 1329 665931; e-mail: infor@rnbws.co.uk
www.rnbws.co.uk

ROYAL PIGEON RACING ASSOCIATION (1897; 39,000).
Exists to promote the sport of pigeon racing and controls pigeon racing within the Association. Organises liberation sites, issues rings, calculates distances between liberation sites and home lofts, and assists in the return of strays. May be able to assist in identifying owners of ringed birds caught or found.
Contact: General Manager, RPRA, The Reddings, Cheltenham, GL51 6RN. 01452 713529; e-mail: gm@rpra.org or strays@rpra.org
www.rpra.org

ROYAL SOCIETY FOR THE PREVENTION OF CRUELTY TO ANIMALS (1824; 43,690).
In addition to its animal homes, the Society also runs a woodland study centre and nature reserve at Mallydams Wood in East Sussex and specialist wildlife rehabilitation centres at West Hatch, Taunton, Somerset TA3 5RT (01823 480156), at Station Road, East Winch, King's Lynn, Norfolk PE32 1NR (01553 842336), and London Road, Stapeley, Nantwich, Cheshire CW5 7JW (0870 4427102). Inspectors are contacted through their Regional Communications Centres, which can be reached via the Society's 24-hour national cruelty and advice line: 08705 555 999.
Contact: RSPCA Headquarters, Willberforce Way, Horsham, West Sussex RH13 9RS. 0870 0101181; (Fax)0870 7530048.
www.rspca.org.uk

RSPB (1889; 1,036,000).
UK Partner of BirdLife International, and Europe's largest voluntary wildlife conservation body. The RSPB, a registered charity, is governed by an elected body (see also RSPB Phoenix and RSPB Wildlife Explorers). Its work in the conservation of wild birds and habitats covers the acquisition and management of nature reserves; research and surveys; monitoring and responding to development proposals, land use practices and pollution which threaten wild birds and biodiversity; and the provision of an advisory service on wildlife law enforcement.
Work in the education and information field includes formal education in schools and colleges, and informal activities for children through Wildlife Explorers; publications (including *Birds*, a quarterly magazine for members, *Bird Life*, a bi-monthly

magazine for RSPB Wildlife Explorers, *Wild Times* for under-8s); displays and exhibitions; the distribution of moving images about birds; and the development of membership activities through Members' Groups.

The RSPB currently manages 182 nature reserves in the UK, covering more than 313,000 acres; more than 50% of this area is owned. Sites are carefully selected, mostly as being of national or international importance to wildlife conservation. The aim is to conserve a countrywide network of reserves with all examples of the main bird communities and with due regard to the conservation of plants and other animals. Visitors are generally welcome to most reserves, subject to any restrictions necessary to protect the wildlife or habitats.

Current national projects include extensive work on agriculture, and conservation and campaigning for the conservation of the marine environment and to halt the illegal persecution of birds of prey. Increasingly, there is involvement with broader environmental concerns such as climate change and transport.

The RSPB's International Dept works closely with Birdlife International and its partners in other countries and is involved with numerous projects overseas, especially in Europe and Asia.

Regional Offices

RSPB North England, 4 Benton Terrace, Sandyford Road, Newcastle upon Tyne NE2 1QU. 0191 212 0353.

RSPB North West, Westleigh Mews, Wakefield Road, Denby Dale, Huddersfield HD8 8QD. 01484 861148.

RSPB Central England, 46 The Green, South Bar, Banbury, Oxon OX16 9AB. 01295 253330.

RSPB East Anglia, Stalham House, 65 Thorpe Road, Norwich NR1 1UD. 01603 661662.

RSPB South East, 2nd Floor, Frederick House, 42 Frederick Place, Brighton BN1 4EA. 01273 775333.

RSPB South West, Keble House, Southernhay Gardens, Exeter EX1 1NT. 01392 432691.

RSPB Scotland HQ, Dunedin House, 25 Ravelston Terrace, Edinburgh EH4 3TP. 0131 311 6500.

RSPB North Scotland, Etive House, Beechwood Park, Inverness IV2 3BW. 01463 715000.

RSPB East Scotland, 10 Albyn Terrace, Aberdeen AB1 1YP. 01224 624824.

RSPB South & West Scotland, 10 Park Quadrant, Glasgow G3 6BS. 0141 331 0993.

RSPB North Wales, Maes y Ffynnon, Penrhosgarnedd, Bangor, Gwynedd LL57 2DW. 01248 363800.

RSPB South Wales, Sutherland House, Castlebridge, Cowbridge Road East, Cardiff CF11 9AB. 029 2035 3000.

RSPB Northern Ireland, Belvoir Park Forest, Belfast BT8 7QT. 028 9049 1547.

Contact: Chief Executive, Graham Wynne, The Lodge, Sandy, Beds SG19 2DL. 01767 680551; (Fax) 01767 692365;
e-mail: (firstname.name)@rspb.org.uk
www.rspb.org.uk

RSPB WILDLIFE EXPLORERS and RSPB PHOENIX (formerly YOC) (1965; 140,000).
Junior section of the RSPB. There are more than 300 groups run by 700 volunteers. Activities include projects, holidays, roadshows, competitions, and local events for children, families and teenagers. Publishes 2 bi-monthly magazines, *Bird Life* (aimed at 8-12 year olds) and *Wild Times* (aimed at under 8s) and 1 quarterly magazine *Wingbeat* (aimed at teenagers).
Contact: Principal Youth Officer, David Chandler, RSPB Youth Unit, The Lodge, Sandy, Beds SG19 2DL. 01767 680551; e-mail: explorers@rspb.org.uk and phoenix@rspb.org.uk
www.rspb.org.uk/youth

SCOTTISH BIRDS RECORDS COMMITTEE (1984).
Set up by the Scottish Ornithologists' Club to ensure that records of species not deemed rare enough to be considered by the British Birds Rarities Committee, but which are rare in Scotland, are fully assessed; also maintains the official list of Scottish birds.
Contact: Secretary, R W Forrester, The Gables, Eastlands Road, Rothesay, Isle of Bute PA20 9JZ.
www.the-soc.org.uk

SCOTTISH NATURAL HERITAGE (1991).
Statutory body established by the Natural Heritage (Scotland) Act 1991 and responsible to Scottish Ministers. Its aim is to promote Scotland's natural heritage, its care and improvement, its responsible enjoyment, its greater understanding and appreciation and its sustainable use.
Contact: Chief Executive, SNH, Ian Jardine, 12 Hope Terrace, Edinburgh, EH9 2AS. 0131 447 4784; (Fax)0131 446 2277; www.snh.org.uk
e-mail: enquiries@snh.org.uk

SCOTTISH ORNITHOLOGISTS' CLUB (1936; 2,250).
The Club has 14 branches (see County Directory). Each with a programme of winter meetings and field trips throughout the year. The SOC organises an annual weekend conference in the autumn anda joint

SOC/BTO one-day birdwatchers' conference in spring. Publishes quarterly newsletter *Scottish Bird News*, the bi-annual *Scottish Birds*, the annual *Scottish Bird Report* and the *Raptor Round Up*. The SOC is developing a new resource centre in Scotland, details of which can be found on the website.
Contact: Development Manager, Bill Gardner MBE, Harbour Point, Newhailes Road, Musselburgh EH21 6SJ. 0131 653 0653; (Fax)0131 6530654; e-mail: mail@the-soc.org.uk www.the-soc.fsnet.co.uk

SCOTTISH SOCIETY FOR THE PREVENTION OF CRUELTY TO ANIMALS (1839).
Represents animal welfare interests to Government, local authorities and others. Educates young people to realise their responsibilities. Maintains an inspectorate to patrol and investigate and to advise owners about the welfare of animals and birds in their care. Maintains 13 welfare centres, two of which include oiled bird cleaning centres. Bird species, including birds of prey, are rehabilitated and where possible released back into the wild.
Contact: Braehead Mains, 603 Queensferry Road, Edinburgh EH4 6EA. 0131 339 0222; (Fax) 0131 339 4777; e-mail: enquiries@scottishspca.org www.scottishspca.org

SCOTTISH WILDLIFE TRUST (1964; 22,000).
Has members' groups throughout Scotland. Aims to conserve all forms of wildlife and has over 125 reserves, many of great birdwatching interest, covering some 50,000 acres. Member of The Wildlife Trusts partnership and organises Scottish Wildlife Watch. Publishes *Scottish Wildlife* three times a year.
Contact: Cramond House, Off Cramond Glebe Road, Edinburgh EH4 6NS. 0131 312 7765; (Fax)0131 312 8705; e-mail: enquiries@swt.org.uk www.swt.org.uk

SEABIRD GROUP (1966; 350).
Concerned with conservation issues affecting seabirds. Co-ordinates census and monitoring work on breeding seabirds; has established and maintains the Seabird Colony Register in collaboration with the JNCC; organises triennial conferences on seabird biology and conservation topics. Small grants available to assist with research and survey work on seabirds. Publishes the *Seabird Group Newsletter* every four months and the journal, *Atlantic Seabirds,* quarterly in association with the Dutch Seabird Group.
Contact: Bob Swann, 14 St Vincent Road, Tain, Ross-shire IV19 1JR. 01862 894329; e-mail: bob.swann@freeuk.com

SOCIETY OF WILDLIFE ARTISTS (1964; 70 Members, 10 Associates).
Registered charity. Annual exhibitions held in Sept/Oct at the Mall Galleries, London.
Contact: President, Bruce Pearson (retires end 2004), Federation of British Artists, 17 Carlton House Terrace, London SW1Y 5BD. 020 7930 6844. www.swla.co.uk

SWAN SANCTUARY (THE)
Founded by Dorothy Beeson BEM. A registered charity which operates nationally, with 6 rescue centres in the UK and 1 in Ireland. Has a fully equipped swan hospital with an operating theatre, 2 treatment rooms, x-ray facilities and a veterinary surgeon. Present site has 3 lakes and 10 rehabilitation ponds where some 3,000 swans a year are treated. 24-hour service operated, with volunteer rescuers on hand to recover victims of oil spills, vandalism etc. A planned new site will allow visitors. Provides education and training. Reg. charity number 1002582.
Contact: Secretary, Field View, Pooley Green, Egham, Surrey TW20 8AT. 01784 431667; (Fax)01784 430122; e-mail: swans@swanuk.org.uk www.swanuk.org.uk

SWAN STUDY GROUP (80).
An association of both amateur and professionals, from around the UK. Most are concerned with Mute Swans, but Bewick's and Whooper Swan biologists are also active members. The aim of the Group is to provide a forum for communication and discussion, and to help co-ordinate co-operative studies. Annual meetings are held at various locations in the UK at which speakers give presentations on their own fieldwork.
Contact: Helen Chisholm, 14 Buckstone Howe, Edinburgh, EH10 6XF. 0131 445 2351; e-mail: h.chisholm@aol.ac.uk

THE BRITISH LIBRARY SOUND ARCHIVE WILDLIFE SECTION (1969).
(Formerly BLOWS - British Library of Wildlife Sounds). The most comprehensive collection of bird sound recordings in existence: over 130,000 recordings of more than 8,000 species of birds worldwide, available for free listening. Copies or sonograms of most recordings can be supplied for private study or research and, subject to copyright clearance, for commercial uses. Contribution of new material and enquiries on all aspects of wildlife sounds and recording techniques are welcome. Publishes *Bioacoustics* journal, CD and

cassette guides to bird songs. Comprehensive catalogue available on-line at http:\\cadensa.bl.uk
Contact: Curator, Richard Ranft, British Library, National Sound Archive, 96 Euston Road, London NW1 2DB. 020 7412 7402/3; e-mail: nsa-wildsound@bl.uk
www.bl.uk/sound-archive

THE MAMMAL SOCIETY (1954; 2,500).
The Mammal Society is the voice for British mammals and the only organisation solely dedicated to the study and conservation of all British mammals. It seeks to raise awareness of mammals, their ecology and their conservation needs, to survey British mammals and their habitats to identify the threats they face, to promote mammal studies in the UK and overseas, to advocate conservation plans based on sound science, to provide current information on mammals through its publications, to involve people of all ages in its efforts to protect mammals, to educate people about British mammals and to monitor mammal population changes.
Contact: Enquiries, 2B Inworth Street, London SW11 3EP. 020 7350 2200; (Fax) 020 7350 2211; e-mail: enquiries@mammal.org.uk
www.mammal.org.uk

UK400 CLUB (1981).
Serves to monitor the nation's leading twitchers and their life lists, and to keep under review contentious species occurrences. Publishes a bi-monthly magazine Rare Birds and operates a website; www.uk400clubonline.co.uk. Membership open to all.
Contact: L G R Evans, 8 Sandycroft Road, Little Chalfont, Amersham, Bucks HP6 6QL. 01494 763010; e-mail: LGREUK400@aol.com
www.uk400clubonline.co.uk

ULSTER WILDLIFE TRUST **see County Directory**

WADER STUDY GROUP (1970; 600).
An association of wader enthusiasts, both amateur and professional, from all parts of the world. The Group aims to maintain contact between them, to help in the organisation of co-operative studies, and to provide a vehicle for the exchange of information. Publishes the Wader Study Group Bulletin three times a year and holds annual meetings throughout Europe.
Contact: Membership Secretary, Wader Study Group, Rod West, c/o BTO, The Nunnery, Thetford, Norfolk IP24 2PU.
e-mail: rodwest@ndirect.co.uk
www.waderstudygroup.org

WALTER ROTHSCHILD ZOOLOGICAL MUSEUM
Founded by Lionel Walter (later Lord) Rothschild, the Museum displays British and exotic birds (1500 species) including many rarities and extinct species. Galleries open all year except Dec 24-26. Adjacent to the Bird Group of the Natural History Museum - with over a million specimens and an extensive ornithological library, an internationally important centre for bird research.
Contact: Akeman Street, Tring, Herts HP23 6AP. 020 7942 6171.
www.nhm.ns.uk/museum/tring

WELSH KITE TRUST (1996).
A registered charity that undertakes the conservation and annual monitoring of Red Kites in Wales. It attempts to locate all the breeding birds, to compile data on population growth, productivity, range expansion etc. The Trust liaises with landowners, acts as consultant on planning issues and with regard to filming and photography, and represents Welsh interests on the UK Kite Steering Group. Provides a limited rescue service for injured kites and eggs or chicks at risk of desertion or starvation. Publishes a newsletter Boda Wennol twice a year, sent free to members of Friends of the Welsh Kite and to all landowners with nesting Kites.
Contact: Tony Cross, Samaria, Nantmel, Llandrindod Wells, Powys LD1 6EN. 01597 825981; e-mail: tony.cross@welshkitetrust.org
www.welshkitetrust.org

WELSH ORNITHOLOGICAL SOCIETY (1988; 250).
Promotes the study, conservation and enjoyment of birds throughout Wales. Runs the Welsh Records Panel which adjudicates records of scarce species in Wales. Publishes the journal Welsh Birds twice a year, along with newsletters, and organises an annual conference.
Contact: Paul Kenyon, 196 Chester Road, Hartford, Northwich CW8 1LG. 01606 77960; e-mail: pkenyon196@aol.com
www.members.aol.com/welshos/cac

WETLAND TRUST
Set up to encourage conservation of wetlands and develop study of migratory birds, and to foster international relations in these fields. Destinations for recent expeditions inc. Brazil, Senegal, The Gambia, Guinea-Bissau, Nigeria, Kuwait, Thailand, Greece and Jordan. Large numbers of birds are ringed each year in Sussex and applications are

invited from individuals to train in bird ringing or extend their experience.
Contact: AJ Martin, Elms Farm, Pett Lane, Icklesham, Winchelsea, E Sussex TN36 4AH. 01797 226374; e-mail: alan@wetlandtrust.org

WILDFOWL & WETLANDS TRUST (THE)
(1946; 106,000 members and 4,700 bird adopters). Registered charity founded by the late Sir Peter Scott, its mission - to conserve wetlands and their biodiversity. WWT has nine centres with reserves (see Arundel, Caerlaverock, Castle Espie, Llanelli, Martin Mere, Slimbridge, Washington, Welney, and The London Wetland Centre in Reserves and Observatories section). The centres are nationally or internationally important for wintering wildfowl; they also aim to raise awareness of and appreciation for wetland species, the problems they face and the conservation action needed to help them. Programmes of walks and talks are available for visitors with varied interests - resources and programmes are provided for school groups. Centres, except Caerlaverock and Welney, have wildfowl from around the world, inc. endangered species. Research Department works on population dynamics, species management plans and wetland ecology. The Wetland Advisory Service (WAS) undertakes contracts, and Wetland Link International promotes the role of wetland centres for education and public awarenes
Contact: Chief Executive, Martin Spray, Slimbridge, Glos, GL2 7BT. 01453 891900; (Fax) 01453 890827; e-mail: info.slimbridge@wwt.org.uk www.wwt.org.uk

WILDLIFE SOUND RECORDING SOCIETY
(1968; 327).
Works closely with the Wildlife Section of the National Sound Archive. Members carry out recording work for scientific purposes as well as for pleasure. A field weekend is held each spring, and members organise meetings locally. Four CD sound magazines of members' recordings are produced for members each year, and a journal, Wildlife Sound, is published twice a year.
Contact: Hon Membership Secretary, WSRS, Mike Iannantuoni, 36 Wenton Close, Cottesmore, Oakham, Rutland LE15 7DR. 01572 812447; www.scbm.fsnet.co.uk/usrs.htm

WILDLIFE TRUSTS (THE)
A nationwide network of 47 local Wildlife Trusts and 100 urban Wildlife Groups which work to protect wildlife in town and country. The Wildlife Trusts manage more than 2,300 nature reserves, undertake a wide range of other conservation and education activities, and are dedicated to the achievement of a UK richer in wildlife. Members magazine Natural World is published three times a year by Emap Active. See also Wildlife Watch.

Contact: Chief Executive, Stephanie Hilborne, The Kiln, Waterside, Mather Road, Newark NG24 1WT. 01636 677711; (Fax) 01636 670001; e-mail: info@wildlife-trusts.cix.co.uk www.wildlifetrusts.org

WILDLIFE WATCH (1971; 24,000+).
The junior branch of The Wildlife Trusts (see previous entry). It supports 1,500 registered volunteer leaders running Watch groups across the UK. Publishes Watchword and Wildlife Extra.
Contact: Development Officer, Avril Rawson, The Wildlife Trusts, The Kiln, Waterside, Mather Road, Newark NG24 1WT. 0870 0367711; (Fax) 00870 0360101;
e-mail: watch@wildlife-trusts.cix.co.uk
www. www.wildlifewatch.org.uk

WWF-UK (1961).
WWF is the world's largest independent conservation organisation, comprising 27 national organisations. It works to conserve endangered species, protect endangered spaces, and address global threats to nature by seeking long-term solutions with people in government and industry, education and civil society. Publishes WWF News (quarterly magazine).
Contact: Chief Executive, Robert Napier, Panda House, Weyside Park, Catteshall Lane, Godalming, Surrey GU7 1XR. 01483 426444; (Fax) 01483 426409; www.wwf-uk.org

ZOOLOGICAL PHOTOGRAPHIC CLUB
(1899).
Circulates black and white and colour prints of zoological interest via a series of postal portfolios.
Contact: Hon Secretary, Martin B Withers, 93 Cross Lane, Mountsorrel, Loughborough, Leics LE12 7BX. 0116 229 6080.

ZOOLOGICAL SOCIETY OF LONDON
(1826).
Carries out research, organises symposia and holds scientific meetings. Manages the Zoological Gardens in Regent's Park (first opened in 1828) and Whipsnade Wild Animal Park near Dunstable, Beds, each with extensive collections of birds. The Society's library has a large collection of ornithological books and journals. Publications include the Journal of Zoology, Animal Conservation, Conservation Biology book series, The Symposia and The International Zoo Yearbook.
Contact: Director General, Regent's Park, London, NW1 4RY. 020 7722 3333.
www.zsl.org

INTERNATIONAL DIRECTORY

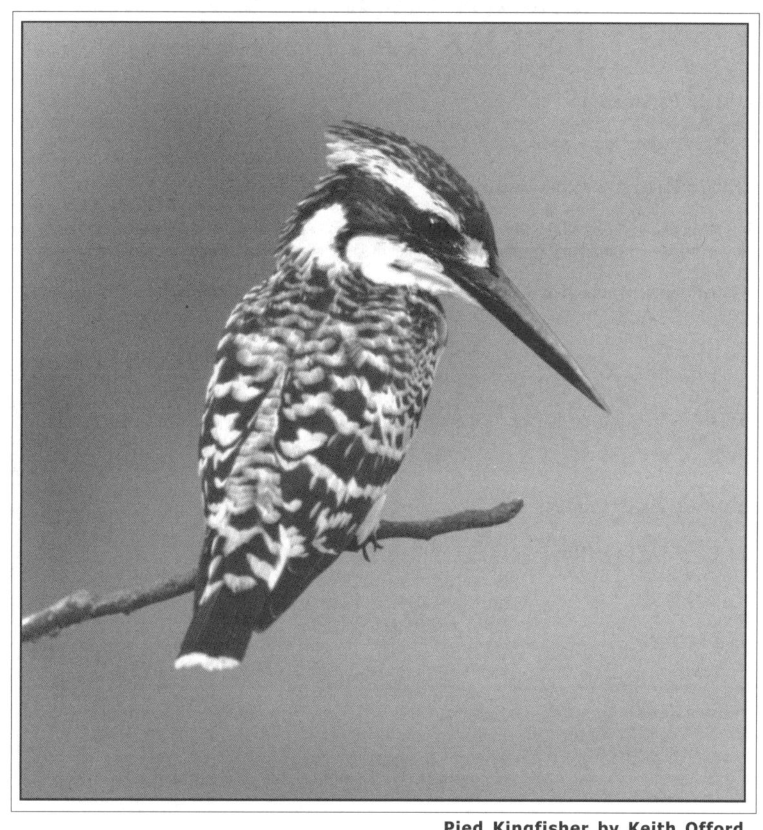

Pied Kingfisher by Keith Offord

The BirdLife Partnership

BirdLife is a Partnership of non-governmental organisations (NGOs) with a special focus on conservation and birds. Each NGO Partner represents a unique geographic territory/country.

The BirdLife Network explained

Partners: Membership-based NGOs who represent BirdLife in their own territory. Vote holders and key implementing bodies for BirdLife's Strategy and Regional Programmes in their own territories.

Partners Designate: Membership-based NGOs who represent BirdLife in their own territory, in a transition stage to becoming full Partners. Non-vote holders.

Affiliates: Usually NGOs, but also individuals, foundations or governmental institutions when appropriate. Act as a BirdLife contact with the aim of developing into, or recruiting, a BirdLife Partner in their territory.

Secretariat: The co-ordinating and servicing body of BirdLife International.

Secretariat Addresses

BirdLife Cambridge Office
BirdLife International
Wellbrook Court
Girton Road
Cambridge CB3 0NA
United Kingdom
Tel. +44 1 223 277 318
Fax +44 1 223 277200
E-mail: birdlife@birdlife.org.uk
http://www.birdlife.net

BirdLife Americas Regional Office
Birdlife International
Vicente Cárdenas 120 y Japon, 3rd Floor
Quito
Ecuador
Postal address
BirdLife International
Casilla 17-17-717
Quito
Ecuador
Tel. +593 2 453 645
Fax +593 2 459 627
E-mail: birdlife@birdlife.org.ec
http://www.geocities.com/RainForest/Wetlands/6203

BirdLife Asia Regional Office
Jl. Jend. Ahmad Yani No. 11
Bogor 16161
Indonesia
Postal address
PO Box 310/Boo
Bogor 16003
Indonesia
Tel. +62 251 333 234/+62 251 371 394
Fax +62 251 357 961
E-mail: birdlife@indo.net.id
http://www.kt.rim.or.jp/~birdinfo/indonesia

BirdLife European Regional Office
Droevendaalsesteeg 3a PO Box 127, NL- 6700 AC, Wageningen
The Netherlands
Tel. +31 317 478831
Fax +31 317 478844
E-mail: birdlife@birdlife.agro.nl

European Community Office (ECO)
BirdLife International
22 rue de Toulouse
B-1040 Brussels
Belgium
Tel. +32 2280 08 30
Fax +32 2230 38 02
E-mail: bleco@ibm.net

BirdLife Middle East Regional Office
BirdLife International
c/o Royal Society for the Conservation of Nature (RSCN)
PO Box 6354
Amman 11183
Jordan
Tel: +962 6 535-5446
Fax: +962 6 534-7411
E-mail: birdlife@nol.com.jo

AFRICA

PARTNERS

Burkina Faso
Fondation des Amis de la Nature (NATURAMA), 01 B.P. 6133, Ouagadougou 01.
e-mail: naturama@fasonet.bf

Ethiopia
Ethiopian Wildlife and Natural History Society, PO Box 13303, Addis Ababa, Pub: *Agazen; Ethiopian Wildl. and Nat. Hist. Newsl. (& Annual Report); Ethiopian Wildl. and Nat. Hist. Soc. Quarterly News (WATCH); Walia (WATCH) (Ethiopia).*
e-mail: ewnhs@telecom.net.et
http://ewnhs@telecom.net.et

Ghana
Ghana Wildlife Society, PO Box 13252, Accra, Pub: *Bongo News; NKO (The Parrots).*
e-mail: wildsoc@ighmail.com

Kenya
Nature Kenya, PO Box 44486, 00100 GPO. Nairobi. Pub: *Bulletin of the EANHS; Journal of East African Natural; Kenya Birds.*
e-mail: eanhs@africaonline.co.ke
www.naturekenya.org

Nigeria
Nigerian Conservation Foundation, PO Box 74638, Victoria Island, Lagos. Pub: *NCF Matters/ News/Newsletter; Nigerian Conservation Foundation Annual Report.*
e-mail: ncf@hyperia.com
http://ncf@hyperia.com

Seychelles
Nature Seychelles, BirdLife Seychelles, P O Box 1310, Suite 202, Aarti Chambers, Mont Fleuri, Mahe. Pub: *Zwazo - a BirdLife Seychelles Newsletter.*
e-mail: birdlife@seychelles.net

Sierra Leone
Conservation Society of Sierra Leone, PO BOX 1292, Freetown. Pub: *Rockfowl Link, The.*
e-mail: cssl@sierratel.sl

South Africa
BirdLife South Africa, PO Box 515, Randburg 2125, Pub: *Newsletter of BirdLife South Africa; Ostrich.*
e-mail: info@birdlife.org.za
www.birdlife.org.za

Tanzania
Wildlife Conservation Society of Tanzania, PO Box 70919, Dar es Salaam, Pub: *Miombo.*
e-mail: wcst@africaonline.co.tz

Uganda
Nature Uganda, PO Box 27034, Kampala. Pub: *Naturalist - A Newsletter of the East Africa Nat. His. Soc.*
e-mail: eanhs@infocom.co.ug

PARTNERS DESIGNATE

Tunisia
Association "Les Amis des Oiseaux", Avenue 18 Janvier 1952, Ariana Centre, App. C209, 2080 Ariana, Tunis. Pub: *Feuille de Liaison de l'AAO; Houbara, l'.*
e-mail: aao.bird@planet.tn
http://aao.bird@planet.tn

Zimbabwe
BirdLife Zimbabwe, PO Box CY 161, Causeway, Harare. Pub: *Babbler (WATCH) (Zimbabwe); Honeyguide.*
e-mail: birds@zol.co.zw

AFFILIATES

Botswana
Botswana Bird Club, IUCN Private Bag 00300, Gaborone, Pub: *Babbler (WATCH) (Botswana).*

Burundi
Association Burundaise pour la Protection des Oiseaux, P O Box 7069, Bujumbura
e-mail: aboburundi@yahoo.fr

Cameroon
Cameroon Ornithological Club,
PO Box 3055, Messa, Yaoundé.
e-mail: coc@iccnet.cm

Egypt
Sherif Baha El Din, 3 Abdala El Katib St, Dokki, Cairo.
e-mail: baha@internetegypt.com

Rwanda
Association pour la Conservation de la Nature au Rwanda, P O Box 4290, Kigali,
e-mail: acnr_@hotmail.com

Zambia
Zambian Ornithological Society, Box 33944, Lusaka 10101, Pub: *Zambian Ornithological Society Newsletter.*
e-mail: zos@zamnet.zm
www.fisheagle.org

AMERICAS

PARTNERS

Argentina
Aves Argentina / AOP, 25 de Mayo 749, 2 piso, oficina 6, 1002 Buenos Aires. Pub: *Hornero; Naturaleza & Conservacion; Nuestras Aves; Vuelo de Pajaro.*
e-mail: info@avesargentinas.org.ar
http://members.tripod.com/~HARPIA/aop.html

Belize
The Belize Audubon Society, 12 Fort Street, PO Box 1001, Belize City. Pub: *Belize Audubon Society Newsletter.*
e-mail: base@btl.net
www.belizeaudubon.org

Bolivia
Asociacion Armonia, Calle Mexico 110, esquina Ecuador, Casilla 3081, Santa Cruz de la Sierra. Pub: *Aves en Bolivia.*
e-mail: armonia@scbbs-bo.com
http://armonia@scbbs-bo.com

Brown Pelican by Keith Offord

Canada
Bird Studies Canada, PO Box/160, Port Rowan, Ontario N0E 1M0. Pub: *Bird Studies Canada - Annual Report; Birdwatch Canada.*
e-mail: mbradstreet@bsc-eoc.org
www.bsc-eoc.org

Canada
Canadian Nature Federation (CNF), 1 Nicholas Street, Suite 606, Ottawa, Ontario, K1N 7B7. Pub: *Grass 'n Roots; IBA News Canada; Nature Canada; Nature Matters; Nature Watch News (CNF).*
e-mail: cnf@cnf.ca www.cnf.ca

Ecuador
Fundación Ornithológica del Ecuador, La Tierra 203 y Av. de los Shyris, Casilla 17-17-906, Quito.
e-mail: cecia@uio.satnet.net
www.geocities.com/RainForest/Jungle/7633/ingles.html

Jamaica
BirdLife Jamaica, 2 Starlight Avenue, Kingston 6, Pub: *Broadsheet: BirdLife Jamaica; Important Bird Areas Programme Newsletter.*
e-mail: birdlifeja@yahoo.com
www.birdelifejamaica.com

Panama
Panama Audubon Society, Apartado 2026, Ancón, Balboa. Pub: *Toucan.*
e-mail: audupan@psi.net.pa
www.pananet.com/audubon

Venezuela
Sociedad Conservacionista Audubon de, Apartado 80.450, Caracas 1080-A, Venezuela. Pub: *Audubon (Venezuela) (formerly Boletin Audubon).*
e-mail: audubondevenezuela
@audubondevenezuela.org

PARTNERS DESIGNATE

Mexico
CIPAMEX, Apartado Postal 22-012, D.F. 14091, Mexico. Pub: *AICA's; Cuauhtli Boletin de Cipa Mex.*
e-mail: cipamex@campus.iztacala.unam.mx
http://coro@servidor.unam.mx

Paraguay
Guyra Paraguay,, Coronel Rafael Franco 381 c/ Leandro Prieto, Casilla de Correo 1132, Asunción. Pub: *Boletin Jara Kuera.*
e-mail: guyra@highway.com.py
www.mbertoni.org.py

United States
National Audubon Society, 700 Broadway, New York, NY, 10003. Pub: *American Birds; Audubon (USA); Audubon Field Notes; Audubon Bird Conservation Newsletter.*
e-mail: jwells@audobon.org
www.audubon.org

Chile
Union de Ornitologis de Chile (UNORCH), Casilla 13.183, Santiago 21. Pub: *Boletin Chileno de Ornitologia; Boletin Informativo (WATCH) (Chile).*
e-mail: unorch@entelchile.net
www.geocities.com/RainForest/4372

AFFILIATES

Bahamas
Bahamas National Trust, PO Box N-4105, Nassau. Pub: *Bahamas Naturalist; Currents; Grand Bahama Update.*
e-mail: bnt@bahamas.net.bs
http://bnt@bahamas.net.bs
www.bahamas.net.bs/environment

Cuba
Dr Martín Acosta, Museo Historia Natural, Facultad de Biologia, U.H., 25 e/J e I Vedado, La Habana.
e-mail: poey@comuh.uh.cu

El Salvador
SalvaNATURA, 33 Avenida Sur #640, Colonia Flor Blanca, San Salvador.
e-mail: salvanatura@saltel.net

Falkland Islands
Falklands Conservation, PO Box 26, Stanley,. or Falklands Conservation, 1 Princes Avenue, Finchley, London N3 2DA, UK. Pub: *Falklands Conservation.*
e-mail: conservation@horizon.co.fk
www.falklands-nature.demon.co.uk

Honduras
Sherry Thorne, c/o Cooperación Técnica, Apdo 30289 Toncontín, Tegucigalpa.
e-mail: pilar_birds@yahoo.com

Suriname
Foundation for Nature Preservation in Suriname, Cornelis Jongbawstraat 14, PO BOX 12252, Paramaribo
e-mail: stinasu@sr.net

Uruguay
GUPECA, Casilla de Correo 6955, Correo Central, Montevideo. Pub: *Achara.*
e-mail: gupeca@adinet.com.uy
www.uruguayos.nu/gupeca/achara.htm

ASIA

PARTNERS

Japan
Wild Bird Society of Japan (WBSJ), International Centre-WING, 2-35-2 Minamidaira, Hino City, Tokyo, 191-0041, Japan. Pub: *Strix; Wild Birds; Wing.*
e-mail: int.center@wing-wbsj.or.jp

Malaysia
Malaysian Nature Society, PO Box 10750, 50724 Kuala Lumpur. Pub: *Enggang; Suara Enggang; Malayan Nature Journal; Malaysian Naturalist.*
www.mns.org.my
e-mail: natsoc@po.jaring.my

Philippines
Haribon Foundation, Suites 401-404 Fil-Garcia Bldg, 140 Kalayaan Avenue cor. Mayaman St, Diliman, Quezon CIty 1101. Pub: *Haribon Foundation Annual Report; Haring Ibon; Philippine Biodiversity.*
e-mail: birdlife@haribon.org.ph
www.haribon.org.ph

Singapore
Nature Society (Singapore), The Sunflower, 510 Geylang Road, 02-05, The Sunflower, 398466. Pub: *Nature News; Nature Watch (Singapore).*
e-mail: natsoc@singnet.com.sg
www.post1.com/home/naturesingapore

Taiwan
Wild Bird Society of Taiwan, 1F, No. 3, Lane 36 Chinglung St., 116 Taipei, Taiwan. Pub: *Yuhina Post.*
e-mail: wbst@ms12.hinet.net
http://wildbird.hinet.net/taipei

Thailand
Bird Conservation Society of Thailand, 69/12 Soi Ramindra, 24 Jarakheebua Lardprao, Bangkok, 10230. Pub: *Bird Conservation Society of Thailand.*
e-mail: bcst@box1.a-net.net.th

PARTNER DESIGNATE

India
Bombay Natural History Society, Hornbill House,

Shaheed Bhagat Singh Road, Mumbai-400 023. Pub: *Buceros; Hornbill; Journal of the Bombay Natural History Society.*
e-mail: bnhs@bom4.vsnl.net.in
www.museums.or.ke/eanhs/eanhs.html

AFFILIATES

Hong Kong
The Hong Kong Birdwatching Society, GPO BOX 12460. Pub: *Hong Kong Bird Report.*
e-mail: hkbws@hkbws.org.uk
http://hkbws@hkbws.org.uk
www.hkbws.org.hk

Nepal
Bird Conservation Nepal, GPO 12465, Kathmandu. Pub: *Bird Conservation Nepal (Danphe); Ibisbill.*
e-mail: birdlife@mos.com.np
http://birdlife@mos.com.np

Pakistan
Ornithological Society of Pakistan, PO Box 73, 109D Dera Ghazi Khan, 32200. Pub: *Pakistan Journal of Ornithology.*
e-mail: osp@mul.paknet.com.pk

Sri Lanka
Field Ornithology Group of Sri Lanka, Dept of Zoology, University of Colombo, Colombo 03. Pub: *Malkoha - Newsletter of the Field Ornithology Group of Sri Lanka.*
e-mail: fogsl@slt.lk
http://fogsl@slt.lk

EUROPE

PARTNERS

Austria
BirdLife Austria, Museumplatz 1/10/8, AT-1070 Wien. Pub: *Egretta; Vogelschutz in Osterreich.*
e-mail: birdlife@blackbox.at

Belgium
BirdLife Belgium (BNVR-RNOB-BNVS), Kardinaal, Mercierplein 1, 2800 Mechelen, Belgium.
e-mail: wim.vandenbossche@natuurpunt.be
www.natuurreservaten.be

Bulgaria
Eesti Ornitiliigiaühing (EOÜ), PO Box 50, BG-1111, Sofia. Pub: *Neophron (& UK).*
e-mail: bspb_hq@bspb.org

Czech Republic
Czech Society for Ornithology (CSO), Hornomecholupska 34, CZ-102 00 Praha 10. Pub: *Ptaci Svet; Sylvia; Zpravy Ceske Spolecnosti Ornitologicke.*
e-mail: cso@birdlife.cz

Denmark
Dansk Ornitologisk Forening (DOF), Vesterbrogade 138-140, 1620 Kobenhavn V. Pub: *DAFIF - Dafifs Nyhedsbrev; Dansk Ornitologisk Forenings Tidsskrift; Fugle og Natur.*
e-mail: dof@dof.dk
www.dof.dk

Estonia
Estonian Ornithological Society (EOU), PO Box 227, Vesti Str. 4, EE-50002 Tartu, Estonia. Pub: *Hirundo Eesti Ornitoogiauhing.*
e-mail: jaanus.elts@eoy.ee
www.loodus.ee/hirundo

Finland
BirdLife SUOMI Finland, Annankatu 29 A, PO Box 1285, FI 00101, Helsinki. Pub: *Linnuston-Suojelu; Linnut; Tiira.*
e-mail: office@birdlife.fi
www.birdlife.fi

France
Ligue pour la Protection des Oiseaux (LPO), La Corderie Royale, BP 263, FR-17305, Rochefort Cedex. Pub: *Lettre Internationale; Ligue Francaise Pour La Protection des Oiseaux; Oiseau, L' (LPO); Outarde infos.*
e-mail: lpo@lpo-birdlife.asso.fr
http://lpo@lpo-birdlife.a

Germany
Naturschutzbund Deutschland, Herbert-Rabius-Str. 26, D-53225 Bonn, Germany. Pub: *Naturschutz Heute (NABU) Naturschutzbund Deutschland.*
e-mail: Naturschutz.heute@NABU.de
NABU@NABU.de

Gibraltar
Gibraltar Ornithological and Nat. History Society, Jew's Gate, Upper Rock Nature Reserve, PO Box 843, GI. Pub: *Alectoris; Gibraltar Nature News.*
e-mail: gohns@gibnet.gi
www.gibraltar.gi/gonhs

Greece
Hellenic Ornithological Society (HOS), Vas. Irakleiou 24, GR-10682 Athens, Greece, GR-10681, Athens. Pub: *HOS Newsletter.*
e-mail: birdlife-gr@ath.forthnet.gr
www.ornithologiki.gr

Hungary
Hungarian Orn. and Nature Cons. Society (MME), Kolto u. 21, Pf. 391, HU-1536, Budapest. Pub: *Madartani Tajekoztato; Madartavlat; Ornis Hungarica; Tuzok.*
e-mail: mme@mme.hu
www.mme.hu

Iceland
Icelandic Society for the Protection of Birds, Fuglaverndarfélag Islands, PO Box 5069, IS-125 Reykjavik, Iceland.
e-mail: fuglavernd@fuglavernd.is

Ireland
BirdWatch Ireland, Ruttledge House, 8 Longford Place, Monkstown, Co. Dublin. Pub: *Irish Birds; Wings (IWC Birdwatch Ireland).*
e-mail: bird@indigo.ie
www.birdwatchireland.ie

Israel
Society for the Protection of Nature in Israel, Hashsela 4,
Tel-Aviv 66183. Pub: *SPNI News.*
e-mail: ioc@netvision.net.il
http://ioc@netvision.net.il

Italy
Lega Italiana Protezione Uccelli (LIPU), Via Trento 49, IT-43100, Parma. Pub: *Ali Giovani; Ali Notizie.*
e-mail: lipusede@box1.tin.it
www.lipu.it

Latvia
Latvijas Ornitologijas Biedriba (LOB), Ak 1010 Riga-50, LV 1050. Pub: *Putni Daba.*
e-mail: putni@parks.lv

Luxembourg
Letzebuerger Natur-a Vulleschutzliga (LNVL), Kraizhaff, route de Luxembourg.L-1899 Kockelscheuer. Pub: *Regulus (WATCH); Regulus Info (& Annual Report) (WATCH); Regulus Wissenschaftliche Berichte (WATCH).*
e-mail: secretary@luxnatur.lu
www.luxnatur.lu

Malta
BirdLife Malta, 57 Marina Court, Flat 28, Triq Abate Rigord, MT-Ta' Xbiex, MSD 12, MALTA. Pub: *Bird Talk (WATCH) (Malta); Bird's Eye View (WATCH) (Malta); Il-Merill.*
e-mail: info@birdlifemalta.org
www.birdlifemalta.org

Netherlands
Vogelbescherming Nederland, PO Box 925, NL-3700 AX Zeist. Pub: *Vogelniews; Vogels.*
e-mail: birdlife@vogelbescherming.nl

Norway
Norsk Ornitologisk Forening, Sandgata 30 B, N-7012 Trondheim, Norway. Pub: *Fuglearet; Fuglefauna; Var; Ringmerkaren.*
e-mail: nof@birdlife.no
www.birdlife.no

Poland
Polish Society for the Protection of Birds (OTOP), PO Box 335, PL-80-958, Gdansk 50. Pub: *Ptaki; Ptasie Ostoje.*
e-mail: office@otop.most.org.pl

Portugal
Sociedade Portuguesa para o Estuda das, Aves (SPEA), Rua da Vitoria, 53-2 Dto, 1100-618, Lisboa. Pub: *Pardela.*
e-mail: spea@ip.pt
www.spea.pt

Romania
Romanian Ornithological Society (SOR), Str. Gheorghe Dima 49/2, RO-3400 Cluj. Pub: *Alcedo; Buletin AIA; Buletin de Informare Societatea Ornitologica Romana; Milvus (Romania).*
e-mail: sorcj@codec.ro
http://sorcj@codec.ro

Slovakia
Soc. for the Prot. of Birds in Slovakia (SOVS), PO Box 71, 093 01 Vranov nad Topl'ou. Pub: *Spravodaj SOVS; Vtacie Spravy.*
e-mail: sovs@changenet.sk
www.sovs.miesto.sk

Slovenia
BirdLife Slovenia (DOPPS), Drustvo Za Opazovanje in Proucevanje Ptic Slovenije. Pub: *Acrocephalus; Svet Ptic.*
e-mail: dopps@dopps-drustvo.si

Spain
Sociedad Espanola de Ornitologia (SEO), C/ Melquiades Biencinto 34, E-28053, Madrid. Pub: *Ardeola; Areas Importantes para las Aves.*
e-mail: seo@seo.org
www.seo.org

Sweden
Sveriges Ornitologiska Forening (SOF), Ekhagsvagen 3, SE 104-05, Stockholm. Pub:

Fagelvarld; var; Ornis Svecica.
e-mail: birdlife@sofnet.org
www.sofnet.org

Switzerland
Schweizer Vogelschutz (SVS), BirdLife Schweiz, Postfach, 8036 Zurich. Pub: *Oiwvos Ornis; Ornis Junior; Ornithologische Beobachter; Der Ornithos; Steinadler.*
e-mail: svs@birdlife.ch
www.birdlife.ch

Turkey
Dogal Hayati Koruna Dernegi (DHKD), Buyuk Postane Caddesi No.: 43-45, Kat: 5-6 Bahcekapi 34420, Istanbul. Pub: *Kelaynak; Kuscu Bulteni.*
e-mail: kelaynak@dhkd.org
www.dhkd.org

United Kingdom
Royal Society for the Protection of Birds, The Lodge, Sandy, Bedfordshire, SG19 2DL.
e-mail: info@RSPB.org.UK

PARTNERS DESIGNATE

Albania
Albanian Society for the Protection of Birds, Museum of Natural Science, Rr. E. Kavajes 132, Tirana
e-mail: mns@albmail.com

Nightingale by Keith Offord

Belarus
Bird Conservation Belarus (APB), PO Box 306, BY 220050. Pub: *Subbuteo - The Belarusian Ornithological Bulletin.*
e-mail: APB-Minsk@mail.ru

Iceland
Icelandic Institute of Natural History, PO Box 5320, IS-125 Reykjavik. Pub: *Bliki.*
e-mail: bliki@ni.is
http://ni.is/bliki.htm

Lithuania
Lietuvos Ornitologu Draugija (LOD), Naugarduko St. 47-3, LT-2006, Vilnius, Lithuania. Pub: *Baltasis Gandras.*
e-mail: lod@birdlife.lt
www.birdlife.lt

Russian Federation
Russian Bird Conservation Union (RBCU), Building 1, Shosse Entuziastov 60, 111123, RU-Moscow. Pub: *Newsletter of the Russian Bird Conservation Union.*
e-mail: rbcu@online.ru
http://rbcu@online.ru

Ukraine
Ukrainian Union for Bird Conservation (UTOP), PO Box 33, Kiev, 1103, UA. Pub: *Life of Birds.*
e-mail: utop@iptelecom.net.ua
http://utop@iptelecom.net.ua

AFFILIATES

Liechtenstein
Botanish-Zoologische Gesellschaft, Im Bretscha 22, FL-9494 Schaan, Liechtenstein.
e-mail: broggi@pingnet.li or renat@pingnet.li

Andorra
Associacio per a la Defensa de la Natura, Apartado de Correus Espanyols No 96, Andora La Vella, Principat d'Andorra. Pub: *Aiguerola.*
e-mail: and@andorra.ad

Croatia
Croatian Society for Bird and Nature Protection, Iirski Trg 9, HR-10000 Zagreb, Croatia. Pub: *Troglodytes.*
e-mail: jasmina@mahazu.hazu.hr
http://jasmina@mahazu.hazu.

Cyprus
Cyprus Ornithological Society, PO Box 28076, CY-Nicosia 2090, Cyprus.
e-mail: melis@cytanet.com.cy

Georgia
Georgian Centre for the Conservation of Wildlife, 1 Mosashvili Str, 99 Tbilisi GE-380073, Georgia.
e-mail: Ramaz_Gokhelashvili@dai.com

Switzerland
UNEP/Global Resource Information Database, International Environment House (IEH), 11 Chemin des Anemones, 1219 Chatelaine, Geneva. Pub: *GRID - Geneva Quarterly Bulletin.*
e-mail: info@grid.unep.ch
www.grid.unep.ch/

MIDDLE EAST

PARTNERS

Jordan
Royal Society of the Conservation of Nature, PO Box 6354, Jubeiha-Abu-Nusseir Circle, Amman 11183. Pub: *Al Reem.*
e-mail: adminrscn@rscn.org.jo
www.rscn.org.jo

Lebanon
Society for the Protection of Nature and Natural Resources in Lebanon, PO Box 11-8281, Beirut, Lebanon.
e-mail: r-jaradi@cyberia.net.lb

PARTNER DESIGNATE

Palestine
Wildlife Palestine Association, PO BOX 89, Beit Sahour. Pub: *Palestine Wildlife Society - Annual Report.* www.wildlife-pal.org
e-mail: wildlife@palnet.com

AFFILIATES

Bahrain
Dr Saeed A. Mohamed, PO Box 40266, Bahrain.
e-mail: sam53@batelco.com.bh

Iran, Islamic Republic of
Dr Jamshid Mansoori, Head, Ornithology Unit, Department of the Environment, PO Box: 5181, Tehran 15875, Iran.
e-mail: birdlifeiran@hotmail.com

Saudi Arabia
National Commission for Wildlife Cons & Dev, NCWDC, PO Box 61681, Riyadh 11575. Pub: *Phoenix; The.*
e-mail: ncwcd@zajil.net

PACIFIC

PARTNER

Australia
Birds Australia, 415 Riversdale Road, Hawthorn East, VIC 3123, Australia. Pub: *Australia Garcilla; Birds Australia Annual Report; Eclectus; Emu; Wingspan (WATCH) (Australia); from wingspan@birdsaustralia.com.au.*
e-mail: mail@birdsaustralia.com.au
www.birdsaustralia.com.au

AFFILIATES

Fiji
Dr Dick Watling, c/o Environment Consultants Fiji, P O Box 2041, Government Buildings, Suva, Fiji.
e-mail: watling@is.com.fj

French Polynesia
Société d'Ornithologie de Polynésie "Manu", B.P. 21 098, Papeete, Tahiti.
e-mail: sop.manu@mail.pf

Palau
Palau Conservation Society, PO BOX 1811, Koror, PW96940. Pub: *Ngerel a Biib.*
e-mail: pcs@palaunet.com

Samoa
O le Si'osi'omaga Society Incorporated, O le Si'osi'omaga Society Inc., P O Box 2282, Apia, Western Samoa.
e-mail: ngo_siosiomaga@samoa.ws

New Zealand
Royal Forest & Bird Protection Society of, PO Box 631, Wellington. Pub: *Forest & Bird; Forest & Bird Annual Report; Forest & Bird Conservation News.*
e-mail: l.bates@wn.forest-bird.org.nz
www.forest-bird.org.nz

INTERNATIONAL ORGANISATIONS

AFRICAN BIRD CLUB.
c/o Birdlife International as below.
e-mail (general): keithbetton@hotmail.com
(membership and sales):
e-mail: membership@africanbirdclub.org
www.africanbirdclub.org
Pub: *Bulletin of the African Bird Club.*

BIRDLIFE INTERNATIONAL.
Wellbrook Court, Girton Road, Cambridge, CB3 ONA, +44 (0)1223 277318; fax +44 (0)1223 277200,
Pub: *World Birdwatch.* www.birdlife.net

EAST AFRICA NATURAL HISTORY SOCIETY see Kenya in preceding list.

EURING (European Union for Bird Ringing).
Euring Data Bank, Institute of Ecological Research, PO Box 40, NL-6666 ZG Heteren, Netherlands.
www.euring.org/index.html

EUROPEAN WILDLIFE REHABILITATION ASSOCIATION (EWRA).
Les Stocker MBE, c/o Wildlife Hospital Trust, Aston Road, Haddenham, Aylesbury, Bucks, HP17 8AF, +44 (0)1844 292292; fax +44 (0)1844 292640, www.sttiggywinkles.org.uk

FAUNA AND FLORA INTERNATIONAL.
Great Eastern House, Tenison Road, Cambridge, CB1 2TT, +44 (0)1223 571000; fax +44 (0)1223 461481, www.fauna-flora.org
e-mail: info@flora.org
Pub: *Fauna & Flora News; Oryx.* www.ffi.org.uk

LIPU-UK
(the Italian League for the Protection of Birds).
David Lingard, Fernwood, Doddington Road, Whisby, Lincs, LN6 9BX, +44 (0)1522 689030,
e-mail: david@lipu-uk.org www.lipu-uk.org
Pub: *The Hoopoe*, annually, *Ali Notizie,* quarterley.

NEOTROPICAL BIRD CLUB.
As OSME below. Pub: *Cotinga.*
www.neotropicalbirdclub.org

ORIENTAL BIRD CLUB.
As OSME below. Pub: *The Forktail; Bull OBC.*
www.orientalbirdclub.org

ORNITHOLOGICAL SOCIETY OF THE MIDDLE EAST (OSME).
c/o The Lodge, Sandy, Beds, SG19 2DL.
Pub: *Sandgrouse.*
www.osme.org

TRAFFIC International (formerly Wildlife Trade Monitoring Unit).
219 Huntingdon Road, Cambridge, CB3 ODL, +44 (0)1223 277427; fax +44 (0)1223 277237.
Pub: *TRAFFIC Bulletin.*
e-mail: traffic@trafficint.org
www.traffic.org

WEST AFRICAN ORNITHOLOGICAL SOCIETY.
R E Sharland, 1 Fisher's Heron, East Mills, Hants, SP6 2JR. Pub: *Malimbus.*

WETLANDS INTERNATIONAL.
PO Box 471, 6700 AL Wageningen, Netherlands, +31 317 478854; fax +31 317 478850,
Pub: *Wetlands.*
e-mail: post@wetlands.org
www.wetlands.org

WORLD OWL TRUST.
The World Owl Centre, Muncaster Castle, Ravenglass, Cumbria, CA18 1RQ, +44 (0)1229 717393; fax +44 (0)1229 717107,
www.owls.org

WORLD PHEASANT ASSOCIATION.
7-9 Shaftesbury St, Fordingbridge, Hants SP6 1JF. 01425 657 129; (Fax) 01425 658 053.
Pub: *WPA News.*
www.pheasant.org.uk

WORLD WIDE FUND FOR NATURE.
Avenue du Mont Blanc, CH-1196 Gland, Switzerland, +41 22 364 9111; fax +41 22 364 5358,
www.panda.org

QUICK REFERENCE SECTION

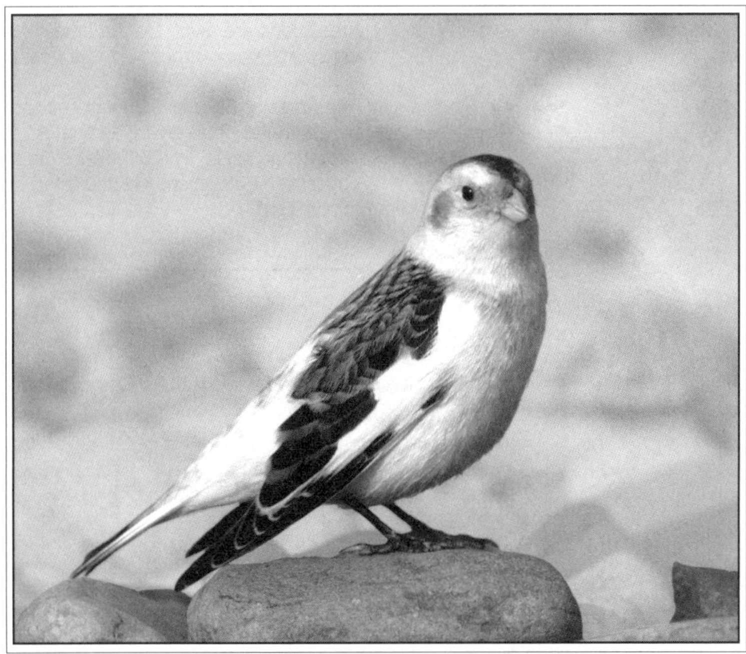

Snow Bunting by Keith Offord

TIDE TABLES: USEFUL INFORMATION

BRITISH SUMMER TIME
In 2005 BST applies from 0100 on 27 March to 0100 on 30 October.

Note that all the times in the following tables are GMT.
During British Summer Time one hour should be added.

Predictions are given for the times of high water at Dover throughout the year.

The times of tides at the locations shown here may be obtained by adding or subtracting their 'tidal difference' as shown opposite (subtractions are indicated by a minus sign).

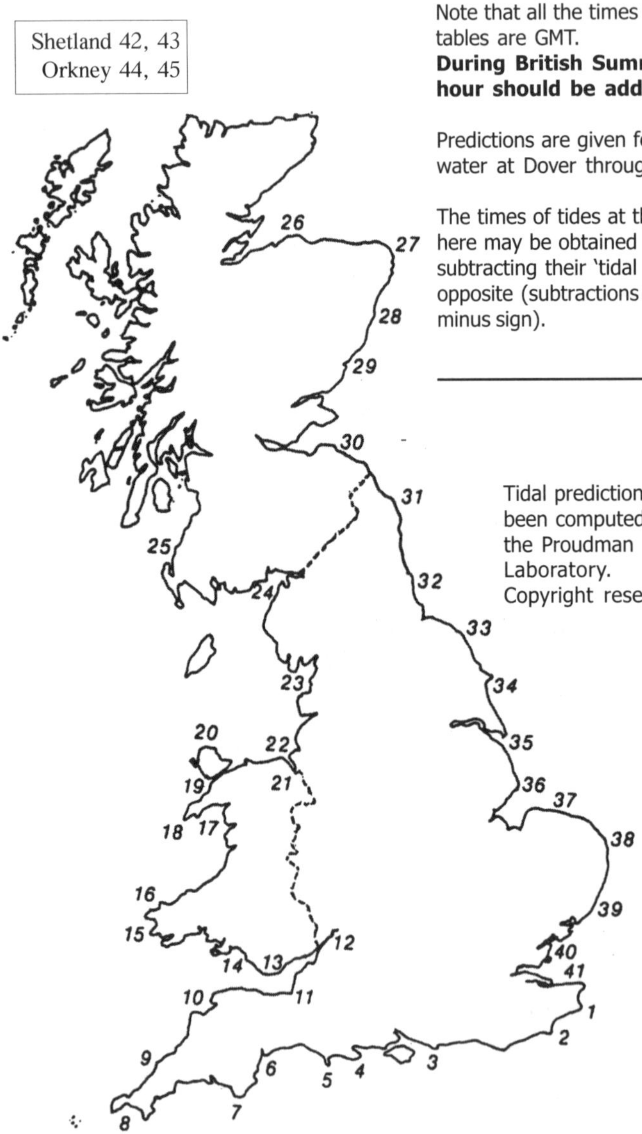

Tidal predictions for Dover have been computed by the Proudman Oceanographic Laboratory.

Shetland 42, 43
Orkney 44, 45

Map showing locations for which tidal differences are given on facing page.

TIDE TABLES 2005

Example 1
To calculate the time of first high water at Girvan on February 20
1. Look up the time at Dover (08 54)* = 08:54 am
2. Add the tidal difference for Girvan = 0.54
3. Therefore the time of high water at Girvan = 09:48 am

Example 2
To calculate the time of second high water at Blakeney on June 19
1. Look up the time at Dover (20 37) = 8:37 pm
2. Add 1 hour for British Summer Time (21 37) = 9:37 pm
3. Subtract the tidal difference for Blakeney = - 4.07
4. Therefore the time of high water at Blakeney = 5:30 pm

*All Dover times are shown on the 24-hour clock.
Thus, 08 14 = 08.14 am; 14 58 = 2.58
Following the time of each high water the height of the tide is given, in metres.

(Tables beyond April 2006 are not available at the time of going to press.)

TIDAL DIFFERENCES

1	Dover	See pp 338-341
2	Dungeness	-0 12
3	Selsey Bill	0 09
4	Swanage (lst H.W.Springs)	-2 36
5	Portland	-4 23
6	Exmouth (Approaches)	-4 48
7	Salcombe	-5 23
8	Newlyn (Penzance)	5 59
9	Padstow	-5 47
10	Bideford	-5 17
11	Bridgwater	-4 23
12	Sharpness Dock	-3 19
13	Cardiff (Penarth)	-4 16
14	Swansea	-4 52
15	Skomer Island	-5 00
16	Fishguard	-3 48
17	Barmouth	-2 45
18	Bardsey Island	-3 07
19	Caernarvon	-1 07
20	Amlwch	-0 22
21	Connahs Quay	0 20
22	Hilbre Island (Hoylake/West Kirby)	-0 05
23	Morecambe	0 20
24	Silloth	0 51
25	Girvan	0 54
26	Lossiemouth	0 48
27	Fraserburgh	1 20
28	Aberdeen	2 30
29	Montrose	3 30
30	Dunbar	3 42
31	Holy Island	3 58
32	Sunderland	4 38
33	Whitby	5 12
34	Bridlington	5 53
35	Grimsby	-5 20
36	Skegness	-5 00
37	Blakeney	-4 07
38	Gorleston	-2 08
39	Aldeburgh	-0 13
40	Bradwell Waterside	1 11
41	Herne Bay	1 28
42	Sullom Voe	-1 34
43	Lerwick	0 01
44	Kirkwall	-0 26
45	Widewall Bay	-1 30

NB. Care should be taken when making calculations at the beginning and end of British Summer Time. See worked examples above.

Time Zone **GMT** Tidal Predictions : **HIGH WATERS 2005** Units **METRES**

Datum of Predictions = **Chart Datum : 3.67 metres below Ordnance Datum (Newlyn)**

British Summer Time : **27th March to 30th October**

DOVER

January

DATE	DAY		Morning hr min	m	Afternoon hr min	m
1	Sa		02 07	6·1	14 19	5·8
2	Su		02 44	6·0	15 01	5·7
3	M	☾	03 27	5·9	15 51	5·6
4	Tu		04 19	5·7	16 52	5·5
5	W		05 21	5·7	17 58	5·5
6	Th		06 26	5·7	19 04	5·6
7	F		07 32	5·9	20 09	5·8
8	Sa		08 34	6·1	21 12	6·1
9	Su		09 33	6·3	22 10	6·4
10	M	●	10 31	6·5	23 03	6·6
11	Tu		11 26	6·7	23 55	6·7
12	W		** **	* *	12 19	6·7
13	Th		00 43	6·8	13 10	6·6
14	F		01 29	6·8	13 59	6·5
15	Sa		02 13	6·7	14 44	6·3
16	Su		02 58	6·5	15 32	6·0
17	M	☽	03 46	6·2	16 24	5·7
18	Tu		04 41	5·9	17 24	5·5
19	W		05 44	5·6	18 34	5·3
20	Th		06 57	5·5	19 46	5·3
21	F		08 09	5·5	20 49	5·5
22	Sa		09 09	5·6	21 40	5·7
23	Su		09 58	5·8	22 24	6·0
24	M		10 41	6·0	23 00	6·2
25	Tu	○	11 16	6·1	23 35	6·3
26	W		11 48	6·2	** **	* *
27	Th		00 08	6·4	12 20	6·2
28	F		00 40	6·4	12 51	6·2
29	Sa		01 12	6·4	13 21	6·2
30	Su		01 42	6·4	13 52	6·1
31	M		02 11	6·3	14 26	6·0

DOVER

February

DATE	DAY		Morning hr min	m	Afternoon hr min	m
1	Tu		02 47	6·2	15 06	5·9
2	W	☾	03 32	6·0	16 00	5·7
3	Th		04 31	5·8	17 07	5·5
4	F		05 42	5·7	18 25	5·4
5	Sa		07 03	5·6	19 52	5·5
6	Su		08 26	5·8	21 11	5·9
7	M		09 34	6·1	22 10	6·3
8	Tu	●	10 31	6·4	22 59	6·6
9	W		11 21	6·6	23 44	6·8
10	Th		** **	* *	12 09	6·7
11	F		00 27	6·9	12 54	6·7
12	Sa		01 08	6·9	13 34	6·6
13	Su		01 46	6·8	14 11	6·4
14	M		02 26	6·6	14 51	6·1
15	Tu		03 06	6·3	15 36	5·8
16	W	☽	03 54	5·9	16 29	5·4
17	Th		04 55	5·5	17 41	5·1
18	F		06 15	5·1	19 10	5·0
19	Sa		07 43	5·1	20 26	5·2
20	Su		08 54	5·3	21 22	5·5
21	M		09 46	5·6	22 05	5·9
22	Tu		10 25	5·9	22 41	6·1
23	W		10 57	6·0	23 13	6·3
24	Th	○	11 26	6·2	23 44	6·5
25	F		11 55	6·3	** **	* *
26	Sa		00 15	6·5	12 23	6·4
27	Su		00 44	6·6	12 53	6·4
28	M		01 12	6·6	13 22	6·3

DOVER

March

DATE	DAY		Morning hr min	m	Afternoon hr min	m
1	Tu		01 41	6·5	13 55	6·3
2	W		02 13	6·4	14 34	6·1
3	Th	☾	02 56	6·2	15 26	5·8
4	F		03 57	5·8	16 35	5·5
5	Sa		05 17	5·5	18 08	5·2
6	Su		06 58	5·4	19 55	5·4
7	M		08 33	5·7	21 09	5·8
8	Tu		09 36	6·1	22 01	6·3
9	W		10 26	6·4	22 45	6·6
10	Th	●	11 10	6·6	23 26	6·9
11	F		11 51	6·7	** **	* *
12	Sa		00 05	7·0	12 29	6·7
13	Su		00 41	7·0	13 04	6·6
14	M		01 17	6·8	13 39	6·4
15	Tu		01 52	6·6	14 14	6·2
16	W		02 28	6·3	14 54	5·9
17	Th	☽	03 11	5·8	15 43	5·5
18	F		04 08	5·3	16 52	5·0
19	Sa		05 35	4·9	18 27	4·8
20	Su		07 17	4·9	19 55	5·0
21	M		08 33	5·1	20 54	5·4
22	Tu		09 23	5·5	21 37	5·8
23	W		10 00	5·8	22 12	6·1
24	Th		10 28	6·0	22 43	6·3
25	F	○	10 55	6·2	23 13	6·5
26	Sa		11 23	6·4	23 42	6·6
27	Su		11 52	6·5	** **	* *
28	M		00 12	6·6	12 25	6·5
29	Tu		00 41	6·6	12 57	6·5
30	W		01 14	6·6	13 32	6·4
31	Th		01 50	6·4	14 16	6·1

DOVER

April

DATE	DAY		Morning hr min	m	Afternoon hr min	m
1	F		02 38	6·1	15 11	5·8
2	Sa	☾	03 46	5·6	16 29	5·4
3	Su		05 21	5·3	18 12	5·2
4	M		07 12	5·4	19 50	5·5
5	Tu		08 30	5·8	20 54	5·9
6	W		09 26	6·1	21 41	6·3
7	Th		10 10	6·4	22 22	6·6
8	F	●	10 49	6·6	23 00	6·8
9	Sa		11 26	6·6	23 38	6·9
10	Su		** **	* *	12 01	6·6
11	M		00 13	6·8	12 36	6·5
12	Tu		00 49	6·7	13 10	6·4
13	W		01 22	6·4	13 43	6·2
14	Th		01 56	6·1	14 21	5·9
15	F		02 37	5·7	15 06	5·5
16	Sa	☽	03 32	5·2	16 10	5·1
17	Su		04 55	4·9	17 35	4·9
18	M		06 33	4·8	19 05	5·0
19	Tu		07 50	5·1	20 10	5·3
20	W		08 41	5·4	20 55	5·7
21	Th		09 18	5·7	21 32	6·0
22	F		09 49	6·0	22 04	6·2
23	Sa		10 17	6·2	22 35	6·4
24	Su	○	10 49	6·4	23 07	6·6
25	M		11 23	6·5	23 41	6·7
26	Tu		11 59	6·6	** **	* *
27	W		00 18	6·6	12 40	6·5
28	Th		00 57	6·5	13 24	6·4
29	F		01 43	6·3	14 16	6·1
30	Sa		02 44	5·9	15 19	5·8

TIDE TABLES 2005

Time Zone **GMT** | Tidal Predictions : **HIGH WATERS 2005** | Units **METRES**

Datum of Predictions = **Chart Datum : 3.67 metres below Ordnance Datum (Newlyn)**

British Summer Time : **27th March to 30th October**

DOVER — May

DATE	DAY		Morning hr min	m	Afternoon hr min	m
1	Su	☾	04 01	5·6	16 35	5·5
2	M		05 34	5·4	18 06	5·5
3	Tu		07 04	5·6	19 28	5·7
4	W		08 10	5·8	20 26	6·0
5	Th		09 01	6·1	21 13	6·3
6	F		09 44	6·3	21 54	6·5
7	Sa		10 22	6·4	22 34	6·6
8	Su	●	10 59	6·4	23 11	6·6
9	M		11 37	6·5	23 49	6·6
10	Tu		** **	* *	12 13	6·4
11	W		00 26	6·4	12 50	6·3
12	Th		01 01	6·2	13 25	6·1
13	F		01 38	5·9	14 03	5·9
14	Sa		02 17	5·6	14 45	5·7
15	Su		03 08	5·3	15 39	5·4
16	M	☽	04 14	5·1	16 43	5·2
17	Tu		05 31	5·0	17 58	5·1
18	W		06 44	5·1	19 05	5·3
19	Th		07 41	5·3	19 59	5·6
20	F		08 24	5·6	20 41	5·9
21	Sa		09 02	5·9	21 19	6·2
22	Su		09 39	6·2	21 57	6·4
23	M	○	10 18	6·4	22 36	6·5
24	Tu		10 59	6·5	23 19	6·6
25	W		11 45	6·5	** **	* *
26	Th		00 05	6·6	12 34	6·5
27	F		00 56	6·5	13 28	6·4
28	Sa		01 55	6·3	14 24	6·2
29	Su		02 58	6·0	15 22	6·0
30	M	☾	04 07	5·8	16 26	5·9
31	Tu		05 20	5·7	17 38	5·8

DOVER — June

DATE	DAY		Morning hr min	m	Afternoon hr min	m
1	W		06 32	5·7	18 49	5·9
2	Th		07 35	5·8	19 48	6·0
3	F		08 27	5·9	20 40	6·1
4	Sa		09 13	6·0	21 25	6·2
5	Su		09 57	6·1	22 08	6·3
6	M	●	10 38	6·2	22 52	6·3
7	Tu		11 19	6·3	23 33	6·3
8	W		11 56	6·3	** **	* *
9	Th		00 12	6·2	12 34	6·3
10	F		00 49	6·1	13 11	6·2
11	Sa		01 25	5·9	13 48	6·1
12	Su		02 03	5·7	14 26	5·9
13	M		02 44	5·6	15 08	5·7
14	Tu		03 32	5·4	15 57	5·6
15	W	☽	04 29	5·3	16 55	5·5
16	Th		05 30	5·2	17 55	5·5
17	F		06 29	5·3	18 53	5·6
18	Sa		07 25	5·5	19 48	5·8
19	Su		08 17	5·8	20 37	6·0
20	M		09 06	6·0	21 26	6·3
21	Tu		09 57	6·2	22 15	6·4
22	W	○	10 48	6·4	23 07	6·5
23	Th		11 40	6·6	** **	* *
24	F		00 02	6·6	12 33	6·6
25	Sa		00 58	6·5	13 25	6·6
26	Su		01 56	6·4	14 17	6·5
27	M		02 52	6·3	15 08	6·4
28	Tu	☾	03 47	6·1	16 00	6·2
29	W		04 45	5·9	16 57	6·0
30	Th		05 45	5·7	17 59	5·9

DOVER — July

DATE	DAY		Morning hr min	m	Afternoon hr min	m
1	F		06 47	5·6	19 04	5·8
2	Sa		07 49	5·6	20 06	5·8
3	Su		08 47	5·7	21 02	5·9
4	M		09 37	5·9	21 53	6·0
5	Tu		10 21	6·0	22 38	6·0
6	W	●	11 02	6·2	23 19	6·1
7	Th		11 41	6·3	23 56	6·1
8	F		** **	* *	12 18	6·3
9	Sa		00 33	6·1	12 53	6·3
10	Su		01 07	6·0	13 26	6·3
11	M		01 41	6·0	14 00	6·2
12	Tu		02 13	5·8	14 34	6·1
13	W		02 49	5·7	15 12	5·9
14	Th	☽	03 32	5·6	15 56	5·8
15	F		04 24	5·5	16 50	5·7
16	Sa		05 24	5·4	17 54	5·6
17	Su		06 30	5·5	19 00	5·7
18	M		07 41	5·6	20 07	5·9
19	Tu		08 48	5·9	21 11	6·1
20	W		09 49	6·2	22 10	6·4
21	Th	○	10 43	6·4	23 03	6·6
22	F		11 34	6·7	23 58	6·7
23	Sa		** **	* *	12 23	6·8
24	Su		00 50	6·7	13 11	6·8
25	M		01 42	6·6	13 56	6·8
26	Tu		02 28	6·4	14 40	6·7
27	W		03 13	6·2	15 25	6·4
28	Th	☾	04 00	5·9	16 14	6·2
29	F		04 53	5·7	17 13	5·8
30	Sa		05 59	5·4	18 23	5·5
31	Su		07 14	5·3	19 41	5·5

DOVER — August

DATE	DAY		Morning hr min	m	Afternoon hr min	m
1	M		08 24	5·5	20 48	5·6
2	Tu		09 22	5·7	21 43	5·7
3	W		10 07	5·9	22 26	5·9
4	Th		10 46	6·1	23 04	6·1
5	F	●	11 21	6·3	23 38	6·1
6	Sa		11 55	6·4	** **	* *
7	Su		00 11	6·2	12 29	6·5
8	M		00 41	6·2	13 00	6·5
9	Tu		01 10	6·2	13 29	6·4
10	W		01 38	6·1	13 56	6·3
11	Th		02 07	6·0	14 26	6·2
12	F		02 42	5·9	15 04	6·0
13	Sa	☽	03 29	5·7	15 56	5·8
14	Su		04 32	5·5	17 06	5·6
15	M		05 49	5·4	18 29	5·5
16	Tu		07 21	5·4	19 57	5·7
17	W		08 45	5·8	21 11	6·0
18	Th		09 46	6·2	22 07	6·4
19	F	○	10 35	6·6	22 57	6·7
20	Sa		11 20	6·8	23 44	6·8
21	Su		** **	* *	12 04	7·0
22	M		00 30	6·8	12 47	7·0
23	Tu		01 14	6·7	13 26	7·0
24	W		01 53	6·5	14 06	6·8
25	Th		02 31	6·3	14 45	6·5
26	F	☾	03 15	6·0	15 32	6·1
27	Sa		04 05	5·6	16 29	5·6
28	Su		05 13	5·3	17 48	5·2
29	M		06 41	5·1	19 22	5·1
30	Tu		08 04	5·3	20 38	5·4
31	W		09 05	5·6	21 33	5·6

Time Zone **GMT**

Tidal Predictions : **HIGH WATERS 2005**

Units **METRES**

Datum of Predictions = **Chart Datum : 3.67 metres below Ordnance Datum (Newlyn)**

British Summer Time : **27th March to 30th October**

DOVER

September

DATE	DAY		Morning hr min	m	Afternoon hr min	m
1	Th		09 50	5·9	22 12	5·9
2	F		10 25	6·2	22 45	6·1
3	Sa	●	10 57	6·4	23 14	6·2
4	Su		11 28	6·5	23 41	6·3
5	M		11 59	6·6	** **	* *
6	Tu		00 09	6·4	12 27	6·6
7	W		00 36	6·4	12 53	6·5
8	Th		01 03	6·3	13 18	6·5
9	F		01 32	6·3	13 48	6·4
10	Sa		02 07	6·1	14 26	6·2
11	Su	☽	02 52	5·9	15 18	5·8
12	M		03 57	5·5	16 38	5·4
13	Tu		05 30	5·2	18 25	5·3
14	W		07 24	5·4	20 06	5·6
15	Th		08 41	5·8	21 11	6·1
16	F		09 34	6·3	22 00	6·5
17	Sa		10 19	6·7	22 43	6·7
18	Su	○	11 00	7·0	23 24	6·9
19	M		11 40	7·1	** **	* *
20	Tu		00 04	6·9	12 18	7·1
21	W		00 41	6·8	12 54	7·0
22	Th		01 17	6·6	13 29	6·7
23	F		01 53	6·3	14 07	6·4
24	Sa		02 34	6·0	14 51	6·0
25	Su	☾	03 23	5·6	15 50	5·4
26	M		04 31	5·2	17 14	5·0
27	Tu		06 04	5·0	19 01	4·9
28	W		07 36	5·1	20 20	5·2
29	Th		08 38	5·5	21 12	5·6
30	F		09 23	5·9	21 49	5·9

DOVER

October

DATE	DAY		Morning hr min	m	Afternoon hr min	m
1	Sa		09 58	6·2	22 18	6·1
2	Su		10 28	6·4	22 43	6·3
3	M	●	10 57	6·5	23 09	6·4
4	Tu		11 24	6·6	23 35	6·5
5	W		11 51	6·7	** **	* *
6	Th		00 04	6·5	12 19	6·6
7	F		00 34	6·5	12 49	6·6
8	Sa		01 07	6·4	13 22	6·4
9	Su		01 46	6·2	14 04	6·1
10	M	☽	02 35	5·9	15 04	5·7
11	Tu		03 49	5·5	16 39	5·3
12	W		05 30	5·3	18 36	5·4
13	Th		07 17	5·5	20 00	5·7
14	F		08 24	6·0	20 58	6·2
15	Sa		09 13	6·4	21 43	6·5
16	Su		09 56	6·7	22 21	6·7
17	M	○	10 34	6·9	22 59	6·8
18	Tu		11 11	7·0	23 35	6·8
19	W		11 48	7·0	** **	* *
20	Th		00 12	6·7	12 25	6·8
21	F		00 49	6·5	13 01	6·6
22	Sa		01 25	6·3	13 38	6·2
23	Su		02 04	6·0	14 21	5·8
24	M		02 51	5·7	15 16	5·4
25	Tu	☾	03 51	5·3	16 35	5·0
26	W		05 11	5·0	18 16	4·9
27	Th		06 46	5·1	19 38	5·1
28	F		07 55	5·4	20 31	5·5
29	Sa		08 41	5·8	21 09	5·8
30	Su		09 19	6·1	21 39	6·0
31	M		09 50	6·3	22 05	6·2

DOVER

November

DATE	DAY		Morning hr min	m	Afternoon hr min	m
1	Tu		10 19	6·5	22 34	6·4
2	W	●	10 49	6·6	23 04	6·5
3	Th		11 20	6·6	23 38	6·6
4	F		11 54	6·6	** **	* *
5	Sa		00 15	6·6	12 30	6·5
6	Su		00 57	6·4	13 14	6·3
7	M		01 43	6·2	14 06	6·0
8	Tu		02 42	5·9	15 18	5·7
9	W	☽	03 56	5·7	16 49	5·5
10	Th		05 21	5·6	18 23	5·5
11	F		06 47	5·7	19 35	5·8
12	Sa		07 52	6·0	20 31	6·1
13	Su		08 42	6·3	21 16	6·3
14	M		09 26	6·6	21 56	6·5
15	Tu		10 07	6·7	22 35	6·6
16	W	○	10 46	6·8	23 13	6·6
17	Th		11 26	6·7	23 52	6·6
18	F		** **	* *	12 05	6·6
19	Sa		00 30	6·5	12 43	6·4
20	Su		01 08	6·3	13 21	6·1
21	M		01 46	6·1	14 03	5·8
22	Tu		02 28	5·8	14 51	5·5
23	W	☾	03 19	5·6	15 51	5·2
24	Th		04 19	5·3	17 06	5·0
25	F		05 31	5·2	18 25	5·1
26	Sa		06 44	5·3	19 26	5·3
27	Su		07 42	5·6	20 13	5·5
28	M		08 27	5·8	20 51	5·8
29	Tu		09 05	6·1	21 26	6·1
30	W		09 40	6·3	22 03	6·3

DOVER

December

DATE	DAY		Morning hr min	m	Afternoon hr min	m
1	Th	●	10 18	6·5	22 41	6·4
2	F		10 57	6·6	23 24	6·6
3	Sa		11 41	6·6	** **	* *
4	Su		00 09	6·6	12 27	6·5
5	M		01 00	6·5	13 21	6·4
6	Tu		01 52	6·4	14 20	6·2
7	W		02 47	6·2	15 25	5·9
8	Th	☽	03 47	6·0	16 34	5·8
9	F		04 53	5·9	17 45	5·7
10	Sa		06 02	5·9	18 53	5·7
11	Su		07 08	6·0	19 52	5·8
12	M		08 06	6·1	20 45	6·0
13	Tu		08 58	6·2	21 33	6·1
14	W		09 46	6·3	22 17	6·3
15	Th	○	10 31	6·4	22 59	6·4
16	F		11 13	6·4	23 38	6·4
17	Sa		11 54	6·3	** **	* *
18	Su		00 18	6·4	12 32	6·2
19	M		00 54	6·3	13 10	6·1
20	Tu		01 31	6·2	13 46	5·9
21	W		02 07	6·1	14 24	5·7
22	Th		02 47	5·9	15 08	5·5
23	F	☾	03 32	5·7	15 58	5·3
24	Sa		04 22	5·5	16 56	5·2
25	Su		05 21	5·4	17 59	5·2
26	M		06 23	5·4	19 00	5·3
27	Tu		07 24	5·6	19 57	5·5
28	W		08 17	5·8	20 49	5·8
29	Th		09 09	6·0	21 40	6·1
30	F		09 57	6·3	22 29	6·3
31	Sa	●	10 46	6·5	23 17	6·5

Time Zone **GMT**

Tidal Predictions : **HIGH WATERS 2006**

Units **METRES**

Datum of Predictions = **Chart Datum : 3.67 metres below Ordnance Datum (Newlyn)**

British Summer Time : **26th March to 29th October**

DOVER

January

DATE	DAY		Morning hr min	m	Afternoon hr min	m
1	Su		11 37	6·6	** **	* *
2	M		00 06	6·7	12 27	6·6
3	Tu		00 56	6·7	13 21	6·6
4	W		01 45	6·7	14 14	6·4
5	Th		02 34	6·6	15 06	6·2
6	F	☽	03 23	6·4	16 00	6·0
7	Sa		04 15	6·2	16 56	5·8
8	Su		05 14	6·0	17 59	5·6
9	M		06 20	5·8	19 08	5·5
10	Tu		07 29	5·7	20 17	5·6
11	W		08 37	5·8	21 16	5·8
12	Th		09 34	5·9	22 05	6·0
13	F		10 22	6·0	22 48	6·2
14	Sa	○	11 04	6·1	23 26	6·3
15	Su		11 42	6·2	** **	* *
16	M		00 02	6·4	12 18	6·2
17	Tu		00 37	6·4	12 51	6·2
18	W		01 11	6·4	13 24	6·1
19	Th		01 43	6·3	13 55	6·0
20	F		02 14	6·2	14 26	5·8
21	Sa		02 45	6·0	15 02	5·7
22	Su	☾	03 23	5·9	15 46	5·5
23	M		04 11	5·6	16 42	5·3
24	Tu		05 13	5·5	17 52	5·2
25	W		06 25	5·4	19 08	5·3
26	Th		07 41	5·5	20 26	5·5
27	F		08 49	5·8	21 29	5·9
28	Sa		09 49	6·1	22 22	6·3
29	Su	●	10 41	6·4	23 10	6·6
30	M		11 30	6·7	23 56	6·8
31	Tu		** **	* *	12 19	6·8

DOVER

February

DATE	DAY		Morning hr min	m	Afternoon hr min	m
1	W		00 43	7·0	13 08	6·8
2	Th		01 26	7·0	13 53	6·6
3	F		02 09	6·9	14 37	6·4
4	Sa		02 52	6·7	15 22	6·2
5	Su	☽	03 39	6·4	16 11	5·8
6	M		04 32	6·0	17 11	5·5
7	Tu		05 40	5·6	18 29	5·2
8	W		07 03	5·3	19 55	5·3
9	Th		08 26	5·4	21 02	5·5
10	F		09 29	5·6	21 53	5·8
11	Sa		10 17	5·8	22 34	6·1
12	Su		10 55	6·0	23 09	6·3
13	M	○	11 27	6·1	23 42	6·4
14	Tu		11 59	6·2	** **	* *
15	W		00 15	6·5	12 29	6·3
16	Th		00 46	6·5	12 56	6·2
17	F		01 14	6·5	13 22	6·2
18	Sa		01 38	6·4	13 48	6·1
19	Su		02 03	6·2	14 17	6·0
20	M		02 34	6·1	14 55	5·8
21	Tu	☾	03 18	5·8	15 47	5·5
22	W		04 19	5·5	17 02	5·2
23	Th		05 44	5·3	18 37	5·1
24	F		07 22	5·3	20 14	5·4
25	Sa		08 44	5·7	21 20	5·9
26	Su		09 43	6·1	22 10	6·3
27	M		10 31	6·5	22 55	6·7
28	Tu	●	11 17	6·8	23 38	7·0

DOVER

March

DATE	DAY		Morning hr min	m	Afternoon hr min	m
1	W		** **	* *	12 01	6·9
2	Th		00 20	7·1	12 46	6·9
3	F		01 01	7·1	13 26	6·7
4	Sa		01 41	7·0	14 04	6·5
5	Su		02 20	6·7	14 45	6·2
6	M	☽	03 04	6·3	15 33	5·8
7	Tu		03 57	5·8	16 34	5·4
8	W		05 07	5·3	17 55	5·0
9	Th		06 43	5·0	19 32	5·1
10	F		08 16	5·2	20 44	5·4
11	Sa		09 19	5·5	21 34	5·7
12	Su		10 03	5·8	22 12	6·0
13	M		10 36	6·0	22 46	6·2
14	Tu	○	11 04	6·1	23 19	6·4
15	W		11 33	6·3	23 48	6·5
16	Th		11 59	6·3	** **	* *
17	F		00 16	6·5	12 25	6·3
18	Sa		00 40	6·5	12 49	6·3
19	Su		01 03	6·4	13 14	6·2
20	M		01 28	6·3	13 45	6·1
21	Tu		02 00	6·2	14 24	5·9
22	W	☾	02 44	5·9	15 16	5·6
23	Th		03 50	5·5	16 36	5·2
24	F		05 31	5·2	18 27	5·1
25	Sa		07 21	5·3	20 02	5·5
26	Su		08 35	5·8	21 02	6·0
27	M		09 29	6·2	21 50	6·4
28	Tu		10 14	6·6	22 32	6·8
29	W	●	10 56	6·8	23 13	7·0
30	Th		11 37	6·8	23 54	7·1
31	F		** **	* *	12 19	6·8

DOVER

April

DATE	DAY		Morning hr min	m	Afternoon hr min	m
1	Sa		00 33	7·0	12 57	6·7
2	Su		01 12	6·8	13 36	6·5
3	M		01 52	6·5	14 17	6·2
4	Tu		02 35	6·1	15 04	5·8
5	W	☽	03 29	5·6	16 03	5·4
6	Th		04 42	5·1	17 23	5·0
7	F		06 20	4·9	18 58	5·0
8	Sa		07 50	5·1	20 11	5·3
9	Su		08 49	5·4	21 02	5·7
10	M		09 33	5·7	21 41	6·0
11	Tu		10 05	5·9	22 15	6·2
12	W		10 34	6·1	22 46	6·3
13	Th	○	11 00	6·2	23 14	6·4
14	F		11 26	6·3	23 41	6·4
15	Sa		11 52	6·3	** **	* *
16	Su		00 06	6·4	12 20	6·3
17	M		00 33	6·4	12 51	6·3
18	Tu		01 05	6·3	13 28	6·2
19	W		01 43	6·1	14 11	5·9
20	Th		02 35	5·8	15 13	5·6
21	F	☾	03 53	5·4	16 39	5·3
22	Sa		05 37	5·3	18 18	5·4
23	Su		07 08	5·5	19 38	5·7
24	M		08 14	5·9	20 35	6·1
25	Tu		09 05	6·2	21 23	6·5
26	W		09 50	6·5	22 05	6·7
27	Th	●	10 31	6·6	22 46	6·9
28	F		11 13	6·7	23 28	6·9
29	Sa		11 54	6·7	** **	* *
30	Su		00 09	6·8	12 36	6·6

SUNRISE AND SUNSET TIMES

Predictions are given for the times of sunrise and sunset on every Sunday throughout the year. For places on the same latitude as the following, add 4 minutes for each degree of longitude west (subtract if east).

These times are in GMT, except between 01 00 on Mar 27 and 01 00 on Oct 30, when the times are in BST (1 hour in advance of GMT).

		London		Manchester		Edinburgh	
		Rise	Set	Rise	Set	Rise	Set
Jan	2	08 06	16 04	08 25	16 02	08 43	15 51
	9	08 04	16 12	08 22	16 11	08 40	16 10
	16	07 59	16 23	08 16	16 22	08 33	16 13
	23	07 51	16 34	08 08	16 35	08 23	16 27
	30	07 42	16 47	07 57	16 48	08 11	16 42
Feb	6	07 31	16 59	07 45	17 02	07 57	16 57
	13	07 18	17 12	07 32	17 16	07 42	17 13
	20	07 05	17 25	07 17	17 29	07 26	17 28
	27	06 50	17 38	07 01	17 43	07 90	17 43
Mar	6	06 35	17 50	06 45	17 56	06 51	17 58
	13	06 19	18 02	06 28	18 10	06 33	18 12
	20	06 03	18 14	06 11	18 22	06 15	18 27
	27	06 47	19 26	06 54	19 35	06 57	19 41
Apr	3	06 31	19 37	06 38	19 48	06 38	19 55
	10	06 16	19 49	06 21	20 01	06 20	20 09
	17	06 01	20 01	06 05	20 14	06 02	20 24
	24	05 46	20 12	05 49	20 26	05 45	20 38
May	1	05 33	20 24	05 34	20 39	05 29	20 52
	8	05 20	20 35	05 21	20 51	05 14	21 06
	15	05 09	20 46	05 08	21 03	05 00	21 19
	22	04 59	20 56	04 58	21 14	04 48	21 32
	29	04 46	21 22	04 43	21 42	04 30	22 02

SUNRISE AND SUNSET TIMES

		London		Manchester		Edinburgh	
		Rise	**Set**	**Rise**	**Set**	**Rise**	**Set**
Jun	5	04 46	21 12	04 43	21 32	04 31	21 52
	12	04 43	21 18	04 40	21 38	04 27	21 59
	19	04 43	21 21	04 39	21 41	04 26	22 02
	26	04 45	21 22	04 41	21 42	04 28	22 03
July	3	04 49	21 20	04 46	21 40	04 33	22 00
	10	04 56	21 16	04 53	21 35	04 41	21 55
	17	05 03	21 09	05 02	21 28	04 51	21 46
	24	05 13	21 01	05 12	21 18	05 03	21 35
	31	05 23	20 50	05 23	21 07	05 15	21 22
Aug	7	05 34	20 38	05 35	20 54	05 26	21 10
	14	05 45	20 25	05 47	20 39	05 40	20 54
	21	05 56	20 11	05 59	20 24	05 54	20 37
	28	06 07	19 56	06 11	20 08	06 07	20 20
Sep	4	06 18	19 40	06 23	19 51	06 23	19 59
	11	06 29	19 24	06 36	19 34	06 37	19 41
	18	06 40	19 08	06 48	19 17	06 50	19 22
	25	06 52	18 52	07 00	19 00	07 04	19 04
Oct	2	07 03	18 36	07 12	18 43	07 18	18 45
	9	07 15	18 20	07 25	18 26	07 32	18 27
	16	07 26	18 05	07 38	18 10	07 46	18 10
	23	07 38	17 51	07 51	17 55	08 01	17 53
	30	06 51	16 37	07 04	16 40	07 16	16 37
Nov	6	07 03	16 25	07 18	16 27	07 30	16 22
	13	07 15	16 14	07 31	16 15	07 45	16 9
	20	07 27	16 05	07 44	16 05	07 59	15 57
	27	07 38	15 58	07 56	15 57	08 13	15 48
Dec	4	07 48	15 53	08 06	15 52	08 24	15 42
	11	07 56	15 52	08 15	15 49	08 34	15 38
	18	08 02	15 52	08 21	15 50	08 40	15 39
	25	08 06	15 56	08 25	15 54	08 44	15 42

GRID REFERENCES

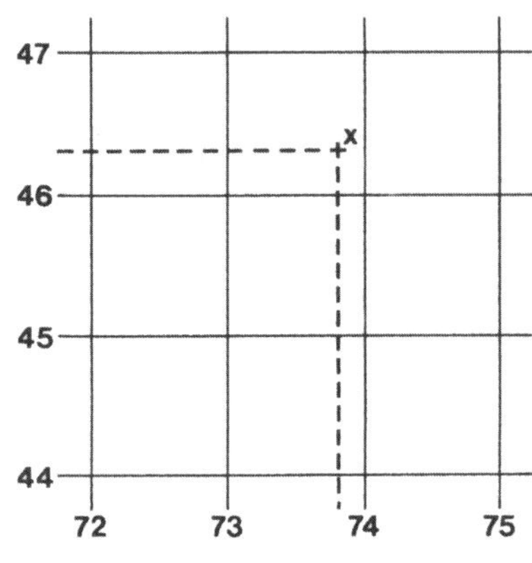

A grid reference is made up of letters and numbers. Two-letter codes are used for 100km squares on the National Grid (opposite) and single-letter codes on the Irish Grid (below).

The squares may be further subdivided into squares of 10km, 1km or 100m, allowing for increasingly specific references. On a given map the lines forming the squares are numbered in the margins, those along the top and bottom being known as 'eastings' and those along the sides as 'northings'. A reference number is made up of the relevant letter code plus two sets of figures, those representing the easting followed by the northing. According to the scale of the map they can either be read off directly or calculated by visually dividing the intervals into tenths. For most purposes three-figure eastings plus three-figure northings are adequate.

The example above, from an Ordnance Survey 'Landranger' map, illustrates how to specify a location on a map divided into lkm squares: the reference for point X is 738463. If that location lies in square SP (see map opposite), the full reference is SP738463.

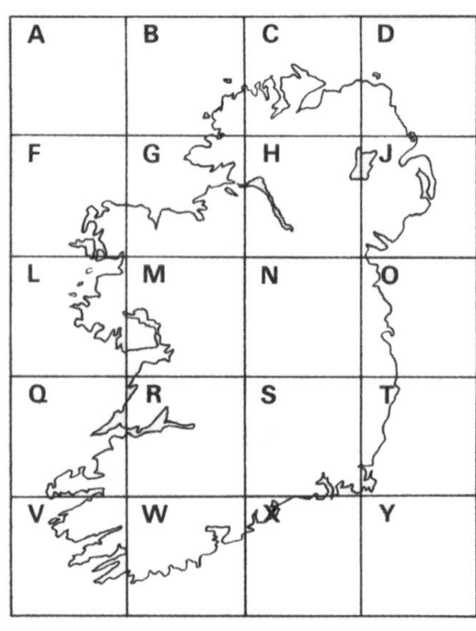

LETTER CODES FOR IRISH GRID 10km SQUARES

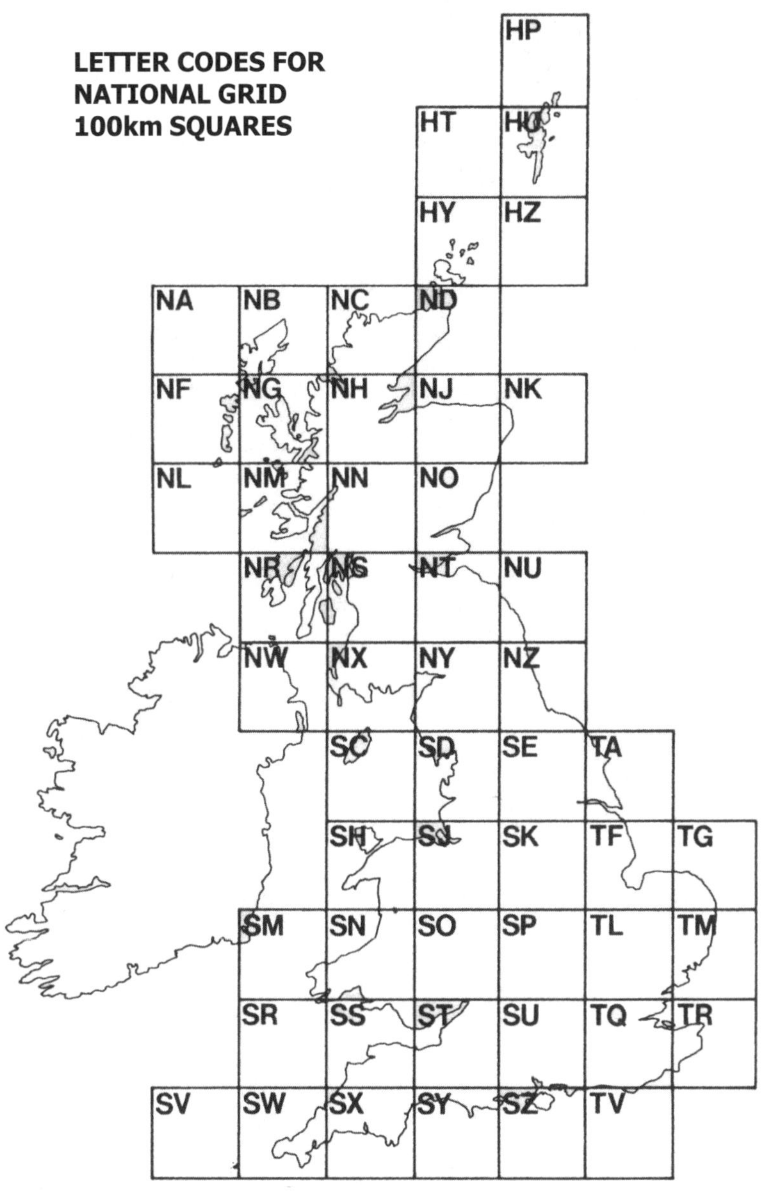
LETTER CODES FOR
NATIONAL GRID
100km SQUARES
HP
HT
HU
HY
HZ
NA
NB
NC
ND
NF
NG
NH
NJ
NK
NL
NM
NN
NO
NR
NS
NT
NU
NW
NX
NY
NZ
SC
SD
SE
TA
SH
SJ
SK
TF
TG
SM
SN
SO
SP
TL
TM
SR
SS
ST
SU
TQ
TR
SV
SW
SX
SY
SZ
TV

SEA AREAS

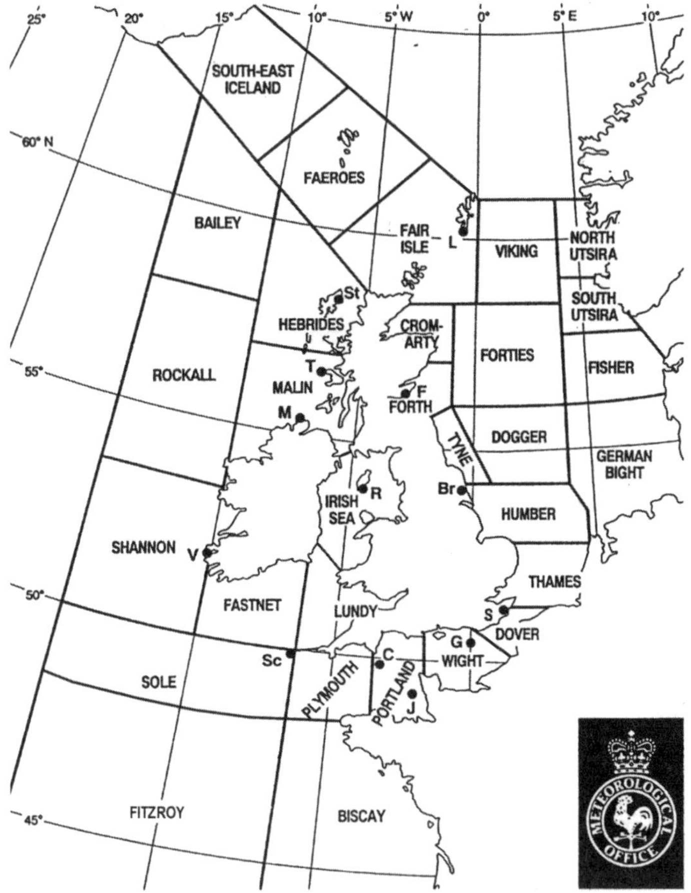

STATIONS WHOSE LATEST REPORTS ARE BROADCAST IN THE 5-MINUTE FORECASTS

Br Bridlington; C Channel Light-Vessel Automatic; F Fife Ness; G Greenwich Light-Vessel Automatic; J Jersey; L Lerwick; M Malin Head; R Ronaldsway; S Sandettie Light-Vessel Automatic; Sc Scilly Automatic; St Stornoway; T Tiree; V Valentia

From information kindly supplied by the Meteorological Office

REVISION OF SEA AREAS

On 4 February 2002, the southern boundary of areas Plymouth and Sole, and the northern boundary of areas Biscay and Finisterre were realigned along the Metarea I/II boundary at 48°27' North. At the same time, sea area Finisterre was renamed FitzRoy.

Did you know that the new FitzRoy shipping area is named after the founder of the Met Office?

SCHEDULE 1 SPECIES

Under the provisions of the Wildlife and Countryside Act 1981 the following bird species (listed in Schedule 1 - Part I of the Act) are protected by special penalties at all times.

Avocet,
Bee-eater
Bittem
Bittern, Little
Bluethroat
Brambling
Bunting, Cirl
Bunting, Lapland
Bunting, Snow
Buzzard, Honey
Chough
Corncrake
Crake, Spotted
Crossbills (all species)
Curlew, Stone
Divers (all species)
Dotterel
Duck, Long-tailed
Eagle, Golden
Eagle, White-tailed
Falcon, Gyr
Fieldfare
Firecrest
Garganey
Godwit, Black-tailed
Goshawk
Grebe, Black-necked
Grebe, Slavonian
Greenshank
Gull, Little
Gull, Mediterranean
Harriers (all species)
Heron, Purple
Hobby
Hoopoe
Kingfisher
Kite, Red
Merlin
Oriole, Golden
Osprey
Owl, Barn
Owl, Snowy
Peregrine
Petrel, Leach's
Phalarope, Red-necked
Plover, Kentish
Plover, Little Ringed
Quail, Common
Redstart, Black
Redwing
Rosefinch, Scarlet
Ruff
Sandpiper, Green
Sandpiper, Purple
Sandpiper, Wood
Scaup
Scoter, Common
Scoter, Velvet
Serin
Shorelark
Shrike, Red-backed
Spoonbill
Stilt, Black-winged
Stint, Temminck's
Swan, Bewick's
Stone-curlew
Swan, Whooper
Tern, Black
Tern, Little
Tern, Roseate
Tit, Bearded
Tit, Crested
Treecreeper, Short-toed
Warbler, Cetti's
Warbler, Dartford
Warbler, Marsh
Warbler, Savi's
Whimbrel
Woodlark
Wryneck

The following birds and their eggs (listed in Schedule 1 - Part II of the Act) are protected by special penalties during the close season, which is Feb 1 to Aug 31 (Feb 21 to Aug 31 below high water mark), but may be killed outside this period - Goldeneye, Greylag Goose (in Outer Hebrides, Caithness, Sutherland, and Wester Ross only), Pintail.

THE BIRDWATCHER'S CODE OF CONDUCT

1. Welfare of birds must come first
Whether your particular interest is photography, ringing, sound recording, scientific study or just birdwatching, remember that the welfare of birds must always come first.

2. Habitat protection
A birds's habitat is vital to its survival and therefore we must ensure that our activities do not cause damage.

3. Keep disturbance to a minimum
Birds' tolerance of disturbance varies between species and seasons. Therefore, it is safer to keep all disturbance to a minimum. No birds should be disturbed from the nest in case the opportunities for predators to take eggs or young are increased. In very cold weather, disturbance to birds may cause them to use vital energy at a time when food is difficult to find. Wildfowlers impose bans during cold weather: birdwatchers should exercise similar discretion.

4. Rare breeding birds
If you discover a rare breeding bird and feel that protection is necessary, inform the appropriate RSPB Regional Officer, or the Species Protection Department at the RSPB, The Lodge, Sandy, Beds SG19 2DL. Otherwise, it is best in almost all circumstances to keep the record strictly secret to avoid disturbance by other birdwatchers and attacks by egg-collectors. Never visit known sites of rare breeding birds unless they are adequately protected. Even your presence may give away the site to others and cause so many other visitors that the birds may fail to breed successfully. Disturbance at or near the nest of species listed on the First Schedule of the Wildlife and Countryside Act 1981 is a criminal offence.

5. Rare migrants
Rare migrants or vagrants must not be harassed. If you discover one, consider the circumstances carefully before telling anyone. Will an influx of birdwatchers disturb the bird or others in the area? Will the habitat be damaged? Will problems be caused with the landowner?

6. The law
The bird protection laws, as now embodied in the Wildlife and Countryside Act 1981, are the result of hard campaigning by previous generations of birdwatchers. As birdwatchers, we must abide by them at all times and not allow them to fall into disrepute.

7. Respect the rights of landowners
The wishes of landowners and occupiers of land must be respected. Do not enter land without permission. Comply with permit schemes. If you are leading a group, do give advance notice of the visit, even if a formal permit scheme is not in operation. Always obey the Country Code.

8. Keeping records
Much of today's knowledge about birds is the result of meticulous record keeping by our predecessors. Make sure you help to add to tomorrow's knowledge by sending records to your county bird recorder.

9. Birdwatching abroad
Behave abroad as you would at home. This code should be firmly adhered to when abroad (whatever the local laws). Well behaved birdwatchers can be important ambassadors for bird protection.

(*Reprinted with permisson from the RSPB)*

THE COUNTRYSIDE CODE

The new Countryside Code, launched in July 2004, followed extensive consultation with the public and stakeholders carried out through the summer of 2003. The new Code is designed to reassure land managers as new public rights of access begin, and to make the public aware of their new rights and responsibilities across the whole countryside.

Be safe – plan ahead and follow any signs
Even when going out locally, it's best to get the latest information about where and when you can go; for example, your rights to go onto some areas of open land may be restricted while work is carried out, for safety reasons or during breeding seasons. Follow advice and local signs, and be prepared for the unexpected.

Leave gates and property as you find them
Please respect the working life of the countryside, as our actions can affect people's livelihoods, our heritage, and the safety and welfare of animals and ourselves.

Protect plants and animals, and take your litter home
We have a responsibility to protect our countryside now and for future generations, so make sure you don't harm animals, birds, plants, or trees.

Keep dogs under close control
The countryside is a great place to exercise dogs, but it's every owner's duty to make sure their dog is not a danger or nuisance to farm animals, wildlife or other people.

Consider other people
Showing consideration and respect for other people makes the countryside a pleasant Environment for everyone – at home, at work and at leisure.

BIRDLINE NUMBERS

NATIONAL AND REGIONAL

Birdline name	To obtain information	To report sightings (hotlines)
National		
Bird Information Service	09068 700222	01263 741140
www.birdingworld.co.uk		
Flightline (Northern Ireland)	028 9146 7408	
Regional		
Northern Ireland	028 9146 7408	
Scotland*	09068 700 234	01292 611 994
Wales *	09068 700 248	01492 544 588
East Anglia	09068 700 245	01603 763 388
www.birdnews.co.uk		or 08000 830 803
Midlands *	09068 700 247	01905 754 154
North East*	09068 700 246	07626 983 963
North West *	09068 700 249	01492 544 588
South East	09068 700 240	07626 966 966
www.southeastbirdnews.co.uk		or 08000 377 240
South West	09068 700 241	07626 923 923

* www.uk-birding.co.uk

Charges
At the time of compilation, calls to premium line numbers cost 60p per minute.

INDEX TO BIRD RESERVES AND OBSERVATORIES

INDEX TO RESERVES

INDEX TO RESERVES

INDEX TO RESERVES

INDEX TO RESERVES